Jonathan Cohen

D0915717

PSYCHODYNAMIC TREATMENT RESEARCH

PSYCHODYNAMIC TREATMENT RESEARCH

A Handbook for Clinical Practice

NANCY E. MILLER, Ph.D.,

LESTER LUBORSKY, Ph.D.,

JACQUES P. BARBER, Ph.D.,

JOHN P. DOCHERTY, M.D.

EDITORS

BasicBooks
A Division of HarperCollins*Publishers*

The opinions expressed herein are those of the individual authors only and do not necessarily reflect the official position of the NIMH, NIDA, or NIH.

Designed by Ellen Levine

Library of Congress Cataloging-in-Publication Data
Psychodynamic treatment research : a handbook for clinical
    practice / Nancy E. Miller . . . [et al.].
        p.   cm.
    Includes bibliographical references and index.
    ISBN 0-465-02877-2
        1. Psychodynamic psychotherapy—Research. 2. Psychoanalysis—Research.
I. Miller, Nancy E.
        [DNLM: 1. Psychoanalytic Therapy.   WM 460.6 P9745]
    RC489.P72P8 1993
    616.89′14—dc20
    DNLM/DLC
    for Library of Congress   92–57904
                                                                    CIP

93 94 95 96 CC/HC 9 8 7 6 5 4 3 2 1

Contents

PART V

MEASURING OUTCOMES

PART VI
WHAT'S NEW AND WHAT'S NEXT

Contributors

Kathryn Baranackie, B.A.,
   Department of Psychiatry, University of Pennsylvania, Philadelphia, Pennsylvania

Jacques P. Barber, Ph.D.,
   Assistant Professor, Center for Psychotherapy Research, Department of Psychiatry, University of Pennsylvania, Philadelphia, Pennsylvania

Katherine Beebe, M.A.,
   Department of Psychology, George Mason University, Fairfax, Virginia

Jeffrey Binder, Ph.D.,
   Psychologist, Georgia School of Professional Psychology, Atlanta, Georgia

James A. Bond, Ph.D.,
   Clinical Psychologist, Private Practice, Ann Arbor, Michigan

Wilma Bucci, Ph.D.,
   Professor, Department of Psychology, Adelphi University, Derner Institute, Garden City, New York

Stephen F. Butler, Ph.D.,
   Director of Psychology, Brookside Hospital, Nashua, New Hampshire

John F. Clarkin, Ph.D.,
  Professor, Department of Psychiatry, Cornell University Medical College, White Plains, New York

Mary Beth Connolly, M.A.,
  Department of Psychology, Vanderbilt University, Nashville, Tennessee

Andrew Cooper, Ph.D.,
  Senior Project Director, VanderVeer Group, Inc., Fort Washington, Pennsylvania

Arnold M. Cooper, M.D.,
  Professor, Department of Psychiatry, Cornell University Medical Center, White Plains, New York

Paul Crits-Christoph, Ph.D.,
  Associate Professor, Director, Center for Psychotherapy Research, Department of Psychiatry, University of Pennsylvania, Philadelphia, Pennsylvania

Janice D. Cumming, Ph.D.,
  Department of Psychology, University of California at Berkeley, Berkeley, California

John Curtis, Ph.D.,
  Assistant Clinical Professor, Department of Psychology, Mount Sinai Hospital/University of California Medical Center, San Francisco, California

Hartvig Dahl, M.D.,
  Professor, Department of Psychiatry, State University of New York, Downstate Medical Center, Brooklyn, New York

David Dickter, B.A.,
  Department of Psychology, Ohio State University, Columbus, Ohio

Louis Diguer, Ph.D.,
  Instructor, Psychology, University of Laval, Quebec, Canada

John P. Docherty, M.D.,
  Clinical Professor, Department of Psychiatry, University of California at Los Angeles, Los Angeles, California; formerly Chief, Psychosocial Treatments Research, National Institute of Mental Health

Lydia V. Flasher, M.D.,
Staff Psychologist, Department of Psychology, Montreal Children's Hospital, Quebec, Canada

Peter Fonagy, Ph.D.,
Freud Memorial Professor, Department of Psychoanalysis; Research Coordinator, Anna Freud Centre, University College, London, England

Louise Gaston, Ph.D.,
Department of Psychiatry, McGill University, Montreal, Quebec, Canada

Jesse D. Geller, Ph.D.,
Director, Yale Psychological Services Clinic, Department of Psychology, Yale University, New Haven, Connecticut

Dianna Hartley, Ph.D.,
Adjunct Assistant Professor, Clinical Psychology, University of Kentucky, Lexington, Kentucky

Leonard M. Horowitz, Ph.D.,
Professor, Department of Psychology, Stanford University, Palo Alto, California

Mardi Horowitz, M.D.,
Professor, Langley Porter Psychiatric Institute, University of California at San Francisco, San Francisco, California; Director, Program on Conscious and Unconscious Mental Processes, John D. and Catherine T. MacArthur Foundation

Adam Horvath, Ph.D.,
Associate Professor, Department of Education, Simon Frazer University, Vancouver, British Columbia, Canada

Wendy Jacobson, M.D.,
Clinical Assistant Professor, Department of Psychiatry, Cornell University Medical College, White Plains, New York

Enrico E. Jones, Ph.D.,
Professor, Department of Psychology, University of California at Berkeley, Berkeley, California

Horst Kächele, M.D.,
Professor, Director, Department of Psychotherapy, Ulm University, Ulm, Germany

Otto F. Kernberg, M.D.,
   Associate Chairman and Medical Director, The New York Hospital,
   Cornell Medical Center, Westchester Division, White Plains, New York

Ellen Luborsky, Ph.D.,
   Psychologist, Director, Children's Treatment Unit, Riverside Mental Health
   Center, Riverdale, New York

Lester Luborsky, Ph.D.,
   Professor, Center for Psychotherapy Research, Department of Psychiatry,
   University of Pennsylvania, Philadelphia, Pennsylvania

Leigh McCullough, Ph.D.,
   Clinical Associate Professor, Department of Psychiatry, Harvard Medical
   School, Cambridge, Massachusetts

Erhard Mergenthaler, Ph.D.,
   Director of Information Section in Psychotherapy, Department of
   Psychotherapy, Ulm University, Ulm, Germany

Nancy E. Miller, Ph.D.,
   Chief, Clinical Research Program, Mental Disorders of the Aging Research
   Branch, Division of Clinical and Treatment Research, National Institute of
   Mental Health, Bethesda, Maryland; Clinical Professor, Department of
   Psychiatry, Uniformed Services University of the Health Sciences

George Moran, Ph.D.,
   Department of Psychology, University College, London, England

David E. Orlinsky, Ph.D.,
   Professor, Committee on Human Development, University of Chicago,
   Chicago, Illinois

J. Christopher Perry, M.D.,
   Research Director, Montreal Jewish Hospital, Montreal, Quebec, Canada

Steven M. Pulos, Ph.D.,
   Associate Professor, Research Evaluation and Development, University of
   Northern Colorado, Longmont, Colorado

Thomas Schacht, Ph.D.,
   Department of Psychiatry, James H. Quillen-Dishner College of Medicine,
   Johnson City, Tennessee

Kelly A. Schmidt, B.A.,
Center for Psychotherapy Research, Department of Psychiatry, University of Pennsylvania, Philadelphia, Pennsylvania

Howard Shevrin, Ph.D.,
Professor of Psychology, Department of Psychiatry, University of Michigan, Ann Arbor, Michigan

George Silberschatz, Ph.D.,
Assistant Clinical Professor, Department of Psychology, Mount Sinai Hospital/University of California Medical Center, San Francisco, California

Barton Singer, Ph.D.,
Adjunct Assistant Professor, Department of Psychiatry, Robert Wood Johnson School of Medicine, Piscataway, New Jersey

Donald P. Spence, Ph.D.,
Professor, Department of Psychiatry, Robert Wood Johnson Medical School, Piscataway, New Jersey

Hans H. Strupp, Ph.D.,
Distinguished Professor, Department of Psychology, Vanderbilt University, Nashville, Tennessee

Virginia Teller, Ph.D.,
Professor, Department of Psychology, Queens College, New York

Stephen P. Tobin, Ph.D.,
Professor, Department of Psychiatry, Cornell University Medical Center, White Plains, New York

Robert S. Wallerstein, M.D.,
Professor, Department of Psychiatry, University of California at San Francisco, San Francisco, California

Acknowledgments

To Our Readers

This book would not have been possible without benefit of the generativity of Sigmund Freud and the contributions of many analysts who followed him; their insights into the human psyche stimulated a revolution in twentieth-century thought and markedly influenced the understanding, treatment, and care of the mentally ill. Although some scientists expressed doubt that key psychodynamic variables could be studied empirically, given the subtlety, richness, and complexity of the clinical situation, a review of the past two decades reveals a record of impressive research achievement.

This volume documents the manner in which Freud's treatment concepts have been ingeniously operationalized and validated. The translation of rich, multifaceted clinical phenomena into definable variables amenable to precise and reliable measurement constitutes a critical milestone in the scientific evolution of our field, an achievement we invite you to share in and to develop further.

Dedications

For Merton Gill, Morton Reiser, George Vaillant, and Robert Wallerstein, each explorers of systematic psychoanalytic truth, whether studied in the realm of the transference, the depths of the limbic system, the domains of defense, or in the unfolding of lives through time; their work has helped the development of a new generation of analytic investigators.

We owe much to the National Institute of Mental Health and the National Institute on Drug Abuse of the National Institutes of Health, whose generous support and guidance significantly advanced our field; to the Fund for Psychoanalytic Research of the American Psychoanalytic Association, which provided long-standing research support for many of the contributors included here; and to the Society for Psychotherapy Research, at whose meetings many of the innovative research methods, models, and measures described in this volume were initially presented.

We are indebted to the authors who had contributed full-length papers to the section on transference-related measures but ultimately were only included in brief form in this handbook (chapter 17); fortunately, their complete versions are to be published in *Psychotherapy Research* (Luborsky, Popp, Barber, Shapiro, and Miller, in press). These authors are Hartvig Dahl, Leonard Horowitz, Mardi Horowitz, Lester Luborsky, J. Christopher Perry, George Silbershatz, Thomas Schacht, William P. Henry, Saul Rosenberg, Virginia Teller, Jacques Barber, Carol Popp, and John Curtis.

We feel warm appreciation to Jo Ann Miller, Basic Books' editor for Professional Books, for her superb editorial advice and supportive management; to Nola Healy Lynch for her prodigious editorial know-how and flair for the best forms of expression; and to Basic Books' reliable and helpful staff, notably, Jane Judge as project editor for this handbook and Stephen Francoeur, skillful troubleshooter.

We thank Yvonne Burnett for her rapid turnaround of computer printouts and for keeping track of the many versions of the many chapters; and Margaret Morris, Kelly Schmidt, Joyce Bell, and Suzanne Johnson for their initiative in helping to bring the book to completion.

—The Editors

With Appreciation

To my cherished colleagues at the Washington Psychoanalytic Institute and Society; and with love to Walter, Jacob, and Jennifer, lights of my heart.

—Nancy E. Miller

For the University of Pennsylvania Center for Psychotherapy Research for its supportive and stimulating atmosphere and facilities; NIDA Grant No. DA 07085 to Paul Crits-Christoph.

—Lester Luborsky and Jacques P. Barber

For the National Institute on Drug Abuse (Research Scientist Award No. MH40710-22), which provided the time to devote to this task; and to various verbally gifted Luborskys for clarifying consultations, most often Ruth, but also Ellen, Lise, and Ellen's children, Miranda and Alexander Outman.

—Lester Luborsky

For Lucienne, Leon, Smadar, Natalie, and Adam for providing me with love, support, time, security, and peace that enabled me to conduct research and scholarly work.

—Jacques P. Barber

For my mentors and colleagues and to National Medical Enterprises for the trust and support to continue this work; and especially to Betty, Jennifer, and Christine, for their love, encouragement, and inspiration.

—John P. Docherty

How This Basic Handbook Helps the Partnership of Clinicians and Clinical Researchers: Preface

LESTER LUBORSKY, JOHN P. DOCHERTY, JACQUES P. BARBER, AND NANCY E. MILLER

CERTAIN NEW IDEAS BURST UPON A FIELD of study as if they will resolve all of its problems. While many react as if the ideas will explain everything, others react as if the ideas can explain nothing (according to the philosopher Suzanne Langer [1942]). After the field has become familiar with the ideas, a second phase begins in which the ideas become part of the main concepts of the field; they are no longer seen as explaining everything, just as another sometimes useful principle. That sequence, overacceptance → overrejection → appropriate acceptance, fits the history of such potent new ideas as Darwin's principle of natural selection and Freud's principle of unconscious motivation of behavior.

It was Freud's principle that made the originating "big bang" in our field of dynamic psychotherapy. Our handbook is part of the phase of appropriate acceptance of the ideas of dynamic psychotherapy, including the principle of unconscious motivation (chapter 16). What we see in our handbook is an evolving sense of where, when, and how the ideas of dynamic therapy do and do not apply.

The phase of appropriate acceptance could be entered only through the clinical-quantitative evaluation of the main ideas of dynamic psychotherapy. In 1984 John Docherty, who was then director of the Psychosocial Treatments Branch of the National Institute of Mental Health, recognized the importance of evaluating the state of knowledge in clinical-quantitative psychodynamic research on psychotherapy. For that purpose an informal group of researchers and clinicians began to exchange ideas on the topic, including Nancy Miller, Dianna Hartley, Paul Crits-Christoph, John T. Curtis, Edward Joseph, Lester Luborsky, Charles Marmar, Robert Michels, Morton

Reiser, Herbert Schlesinger, George Silberschatz, William Sledge, Hans Strupp, and Barry Wolfe.

To continue the work of the group Docherty, Miller, and Luborsky in 1987 launched the plan for a handbook. We decided to ask a larger and even more representative group of clinical researchers to submit chapters on what had been learned through dynamic psychotherapy, both for research and for practice. As we proceeded we saw the enormity of the task, so we enlarged our editorial group to include Jacques Barber, a knowledgeable and energetic psychotherapy researcher.

At the time our handbook was being shaped, the only similar coverage of dynamic psychotherapy's research and practice was in Luborsky and Spence (1971, 1978). But these broad reviews were much sketchier than the presentations planned for our handbook.

The handbook focuses on two main types of psychotherapies: psychoanalysis and psychoanalytic psychotherapy. Psychoanalytic psychotherapy is often called psychodynamic psychotherapy or just dynamic psychotherapy. The central characteristic that defines both psychoanalysis and dynamic psychotherapy is that they foster the understanding of conscious and unconscious motivation from the point of view of the patient (Klein 1970). Both in psychoanalysis and in dynamic psychotherapy the therapist aims to set up conditions that will increase the patient's self-understanding and resolve the patient's main conflicts by means of working on transference and resistance. There are differences between psychoanalysis and dynamic psychotherapy in the frequency of sessions. In dynamic psychotherapy the frequency is usually one or two sessions per week; in psychoanalysis it is three to five per week. Dynamic psychotherapy may have one of two main kinds of time structures: the usual open-ended version and the time-limited, focused version that is becoming somewhat more usual. The short-term versions tend to take twenty-five or fewer sessions.

Of the available studies, we selected those that were both clinical and quantitative. The clinical-quantitative combination appears to us to have the best future for redeveloping the field of dynamic psychotherapy and for establishing where its basic ideas apply and where they do not.

Sources of Revitalization

Our handbook serves two purposes for our field: (1) to decide where we are now and (2) to figure out where we should go from here. The verdict about where we are is mixed: for several decades the field was faltering in its research but now is revitalizing. Sources of vitality include a cadre of productive researchers, methods of coping with a fragile money supply, formation of data banks, new instruments and methods, and renewed confidence in the validity of sessions as a source of data for research.

RESEARCHERS AND THEIR PROGRAMS

Forty of the forty-one psychotherapy research programs worldwide are reviewed in Beutler and Crago (1991); we added one prominent program. Of the forty-one, eighteen are by researchers who are mainly dynamic in background, ten are eclectic in orientation, four are behavioral, four are cognitive-behavioral, three are experiential, one is interpersonal, and one is structural family therapy. The conclusion is obvious: a dynamic orientation is the most common orientation in psychotherapy research programs.

Yet despite the announced theoretical predilections of any orientation, there is a strong and expanding eclecticism throughout. As Beutler and Crago (1991) emphasized, diversity is shown within all theoretical orientations—in the types of psychotherapies studied, the methods used, and the topics investigated. Each type of psychotherapy has become more empirical, clinical, and pragmatic, and at the same time less theoretical (as has been carefully documented by Omer and Dar [1992]). It follows that many of these diverse programs have members who belong to an organization that believes in the integration of diversity, the Society for Exploration of Psychotherapy Integration.

Most researchers in the major programs belong to the multidiscipline Society for Psychotherapy Research, which has grown in the past twenty-five years to 1,200 members in twenty-nine countries. The society serves as a support group and as a sounding board for its members, both through its annual meetings and through its new journal, *Psychotherapy Research,* under the editorship of Hans Strupp (U.S.A.), David Shapiro (England), and Klaus Grawe (Switzerland).

THE FRAGILE MONEY SUPPLY

The earlier faltering in dynamic psychotherapy research may have reflected a significant deficiency in its money supply. Among the sources of support, the most often substantial has been the National Institute of Mental Health (NIMH), particularly the Affective and Anxiety Disorders Branch. Before that the Psychosocial Treatment Branch provided major support; but in the mid-1980s the NIMH director abolished that branch in favor of a disorder-focused structure. The field was hurt by that loss, but many kinds of funding were maintained (Barry Wolfe, personal communication, 1991). The experience underscores the view of Docherty et al. (1993) that the practice of psychotherapy depends on such funding, unlike psychopharmacological treatments, where industry support is also available.

The outlook is not entirely rosy. There has been a marked decrease in the number of grants and the amount of money for two types of grants: psychotherapy process studies and psychodynamic studies of psychotherapy. As of 1992, the treatment branch structure has been restored; treatment grants come through a new combined psychosocial-psychopharmacology branch, the Clinical Treatment Research Branch, within the Division of Clinical and Treatment Research. As of the middle of 1992, both NIMH and the National Institute for Drug Abuse (NIDA) have returned to NIH, with consequences that are too early to evaluate.

Meanwhile, in the last decade NIDA has been farsighted and has increased its research in psychosocial treatments, especially psychotherapies (with Jack Blaine, Lisa Onken, and John Boren as some of its leaders). One sign of this increased research is the Collaborative Study of Psychosocial Treatments for Cocaine Abuse (which includes Paul Crits-Christoph, Lester Luborsky, Aaron T. Beck, George Woody, Charles O'Brien, Michael Thase, Arlene Frank, Roger Weiss, and David Gastfriend).

Over the past twenty years another steady source of support, although more modest in amount, has been the Fund for Psychoanalytic Research (FPR) of the American Psychoanalytic Association. Another potential future energizer and coordinator of research is the Collaborative Multi-Site Program of Psychoanalytic Therapy Research, assembled under the leadership of Robert Wallerstein, which comprises fourteen psychoanalytic research groups. These three agencies—NIMH, NIDA, and FPR— are the most common sources of funds for psychodynamic treatment research.

THE DATA BANKS OF PSYCHOTHERAPY AND PSYCHOANALYTIC SESSIONS

Because it takes so long to acquire a data set suitable for research on long-term psychotherapy, the development of the field has been slow. But in the last decade the grand-scale Ulm text bank has been assembled (chapter 4). Other data banks for psychoanalytic sessions have gradually been assembled, one headed by Lester Luborsky and Sydney Pulver (mostly inherited from the Analytic Research Group of the Institute of the Pennsylvania Hospital) and another led by Sherwood Waldron and associates in the Psychoanalytic Research Consortium, which is housed at the Menninger Foundation.

OPERATIONAL MEASURES AND OTHER USER-FRIENDLY METHODS

Instruments that are reasonable operational measures of key concepts have been developed in the last decade and are sampled in chapters of this book, mostly in part IV. In addition, in chapters 1, 2, 3, and 5, we describe user-friendly methods for clinician-researchers who do not have access to large research teams or budgets.

PHILOSOPHICAL FOUNDATIONS FOR THE RESEARCH USE OF THERAPY SESSIONS

A controversy has long continued about what kinds of inferences can safely be made from therapy sessions. The philosophical challenge was best stated by Grünbaum (1984), who claimed that psychotherapy sessions cannot be used "probatively," meaning that data for sessions cannot be used to *prove* any hypothesis but only to suggest hypotheses. In the style of a logician, Grünbaum has decided that because the data of psychotherapy sessions can be influenced by the therapist, then nothing can be proved from psychotherapy sessions; what is found in sessions *may* be entirely a product of the therapist's suggestions.

The weight of the findings from the studies in our handbook and the arguments by Wallerstein (chapter 6) imply that Grünbaum's (1984) thinking has not been sufficiently influenced by the probability theory that forms the basis of most current statistics. How often is anything in psychology proven in an all-or-none way? Although he is well versed in philosophy, Grünbaum appears to be unfamiliar with empirically based psychotherapy research of the kind reported in this book. The findings in our chapters on theory-based operational measures involved significant degrees of association between the content of the psychotherapy sessions and the outcomes of the therapy. There is a significant probability that these are not entirely based on suggestion by the therapist. Another likely finding that would imply the same conclusion is this: if the central relationship pattern is characteristic of the patient rather than a function of the therapist's suggestions, then the pattern should be evident before the therapist has been met and it should remain recognizably similar after the therapy has been launched (Luborsky 1986).

Who Practices Dynamic Psychotherapies?

Dynamic psychotherapies continue to flourish. They appear to be the most popular orientation of the different forms of psychotherapy nationally and perhaps internationally. A national survey of psychotherapists in the American Psychological Association's Division of Clinical Psychology (Norcross, Prochaska, and Gallager 1989) found that 21 percent of that sample preferred the "psychodynamic orientation." Eclecticism is most popular among these clinical psychologists, although a dynamic orientation is increasing. Among practicing clinical psychologists, the proportion claiming a dynamic orientation increased from 16 percent to 30 percent in the eight years preceding the survey. As would be expected, the preference for dynamic psychotherapies was even larger among clinical practitioners than among academic researchers.

For a sample of 481 clinical psychologists in the American Psychological Association's Division of Psychotherapy who were engaged in psychotherapy, 40 percent endorsed Sullivanian, psychodynamic, or psychoanalytic perspectives as their primary theoretical orientation (Norcross, Prochaska, and Farber, in press). Taken together, as primary or secondary orientations a whopping 70 percent of the total sample endorsed some form of psychodynamic or psychoanalytic orientation! These psychologists also show high career satisfaction.

Another study (Norcross and Prochaska 1988) showed that the large group of professionals who describe themselves as eclectic have frequently integrated psychoanalytic theory into their mixture. Fully 44 percent of the eclectics were trained in a psychodynamic or neo-Freudian viewpoint.

The focus in another study (Norcross et al. 1988) was on the orientation of the therapists' therapists. The results are based on questionnaires to 509 psychologists, psychiatrists, and social workers about their personal treatment experiences. The majority undertook personal treatment with psychoanalytic (41 percent) or psychodynamic (18 percent) psychotherapists.

For of psychiatrists, Marmor (1975) showed that individual psychotherapy was the most widely used form of private treatment for psychiatric patients. If one combines all patients receiving psychotherapy with or without medication, over two-thirds of psychiatric outpatients are found to receive some form of psychosocial treatment.

The Organization of the Handbook

The chapters of this book are arranged generally in the sequential steps that a clinician or researcher would have to take in planning and carrying out a study and applying the results clinically. The book therefore begins with the planning of single case studies. Later chapters deal in turn with evaluating patients, evaluating the therapist, and measuring the treatment process.

A special explanation is needed for the set of chapters in part IV: "Measuring Key Processes," to point out why all of them are about theories and measures of the curative factors in dynamic psychotherapies. These key factors include the establishment of the therapeutic alliance, the making of an accurate clinical formulation by the therapist, the development of self-understanding by the patient, and the incorporation of the gains so that they persist after the termination of the treatment. Each of these curative factors has been translated from a clinical concept into an operational measure that guides the clinician to recognize the forms of the concept as they appear in psychotherapy sessions. Such a translation is called an operational measure because it specifies the operations of the concept in a session and through these specifications allows the development of a reliable measure of the concept. The availability of such measures has also allowed the successful testing of the concept as a predictive factor for the eventual outcome of the treatment.

The closing section of the book tells how to select outcome measures and how to apply the curative factors to maximize the patient's gains in therapy. The book ends with an appraisal of where we stand in this kind of research on psychoanalysis and the other dynamic psychotherapies.

Who Will Find This Book of Special Value?

You may read this book because you are a clinician who is interested in what research has to offer for the practice of psychotherapy; or you are a teaching clinician who should know about such research; or you have a research idea and want to shape it into a study; or you are thinking about doing a research project and you want to get guidance. For all of you, our handbook can be of help. In addition, you can find examples of how to use the research findings to maximize the benefits of the psychotherapy you do (chapter 25).

The book reflects a blending of clinical knowledge and clinical-quantitative research, transmitted and transmuted through three generations: Freud was a first-generation innovator whose clinical ideas and clinical methods were passed on to a second generation, who taught others about his discoveries. We are now into a third generation, which adds to the clinical research style a clinical-quantitative style to test, refine, modify, and apply the knowledge assembled by the first and second generations. The early stirrings of that third generation style go back to the forties and the fifties, but as our handbook shows, the work has flourished in the past few decades. Both the clinical and the clinical-quantitative research style make special contributions, so each chapter in our handbook reflects their partnership and value for practitioners, students, and investigators as well as for makers of public policy.

References

BEUTLER, L., & CRAGO, M. (EDS.). (1991). *Psychotherapy research: An international review of programmatic studies.* Washington, DC: American Psychological Association.

DOCHERTY, J. P., HERZ, M., GUNDERSON, J., PINCUS, H., & FERRIS, S. (1993). *Psychosocial treatment research in psychiatry: A task force report of the American Psychiatric Association.* Washington, DC: American Psychiatric Association.

GRÜNBAUM, A. (1984). *The foundations of psychoanalysis: A philosophical critique.* Berkeley: University of California Press.

KLEIN, G. (1970). *Perception, motives and personality.* New York: Knopf.

LANGER, S. (1942). *Philosophy in a new key.* Cambridge: Harvard University Press.

LUBORSKY, L. (1986). Evidence to lessen Professor Grünbaum's concern about Freud's clinical inference methods. *Behavioral and Brain Sciences 9,* 247–249.

LUBORSKY, L., & SPENCE, D. (1971). Quantitative research on psychoanalytic therapy. In A. E. Bergin & S. L. Garfield (Eds.), *Handbook of psychotherapy and behavior change* (pp. 408–437). New York: Wiley.

LUBORSKY, L., & SPENCE, D. (1978). Quantitative research on psychoanalytic therapy. In S. L. Garfield & A. E. Bergin (Eds.), *Handbook of psychotherapy and behavior change* (rev. ed., pp. 331–368). New York: Wiley.

MARMOR, J. (1975). *Psychiatrists and their patients: A national study of private office practice.* Washington, DC: Joint Information Service at the American Psychiatric Association of the National Association for Mental Health.

NORCROSS, J., & PROCHASKA, J. (1988). A study of eclectic (and interpretive) views revisited. *Professional psychology: Research and practice, 19,* 170–174.

NORCROSS, J., PROCHASKA, J., & FARBER, J. (IN PRESS). Psychologists conducting psychotherapy: New findings and historical comparisons on the Psychotherapy Division membership. *Psychotherapy.*

NORCROSS, J., PROCHASKA, J., & GALLAGHER, K. (1989). Clinical psychologists in the 1980's: Theory, research and practice. *Clinical Psychologist, 42,* 45–53.

NORCROSS, J., STRAUSSER, D., & FALTUS, F. (1988). The therapist's therapist. *American Journal of Psychotherapy, 42,* 53–66.

OMER, H., & DAR, R. (1992). Changing trends in three decades of psychotherapy research: The flight from theory into pragmatics. *Journal of Consulting and Clinical Psychology, 60,* 88–93.

PART I

PLANNING TO STUDY
CLINICAL DATA

CHAPTER 1

Documenting Symptom Formation during Psychotherapy

LESTER LUBORSKY

WHILE LISTENING TO MS. APFEL, a patient in psychotherapy, I noticed that she suddenly stopped talking, then explained her silence: "I just had a thought, but now I've lost it." After about sixteen seconds she recovered the lost thought and said in a relieved tone, "Oh, yes, now I have it." And then she explained the context of her thoughts, ending with the lost thought: "It struck me you weren't really listening." The entire sequence of her words and pauses from the onset of forgetting to the recovery of the lost thought follows:

SESSION 36. . . . the business about, uh, "I present myself to you in such a way that I can't like you," whatever reasoning, uh, is behind that [2 sec.] that, uh, nonsensical statement, uh [*onset of forgetting*] [9 sec.]. Now I've lost the other thing that I was going to say [7 sec.]. [*Point of recovery of the lost thought*] Oh [giggles] [sigh]. Now it's, it's so s—I mean it's silly, but I suppose [clears throat] it needs to be said, because it came to my mind, that, uh, [4 sec.] that, uh, either on Monday or Tuesday, I think—on Monday, probably, I-hah [snort] I became conscious, eh, uh, of these, I mean I hear—a sound that I heard suggested that, uh, that you were, uh, brushing a spot off your, eh, off your trousers or something like, like your, uh, jacket sleeve, uh [3 sec.] and that I recall that while I was talking I had, I mean the fee—it-it *struck me that you, uh, that you weren't really listening.*

I had heard that typical form of momentary forgetting many times before. But at this moment in 1964 as I listened to Ms. Apfel's forgetting, an intention formed that I have never forgotten: to collect examples of momentary forgettings during psychotherapy. I hoped to identify the conditions associated with this type of memory lapse and to develop a method for reliably assessing the meanings of the forgotten thoughts and their temporally associated thoughts.

Since then I have assembled a collection of momentary forgettings and perfected a method for examining their contexts (Luborsky 1967). I tried many ways to analyze the words preceding the patient's forgettings. The analyses usually revealed four preconditions for this kind of forgetting (Luborsky 1988): (1) an increase in cognitive disturbances, such as uncertainty about one's thoughts (Luborsky 1966); (2) an activation of an aspect of the patient's central relationship pattern, such as is revealed in the Core Conflictual Relationship Theme (chapter 17 and Luborsky and Crits-Christoph 1990); (3) a deepening of the involvement in the relationship with the therapist around the time of the forgetting (Luborsky 1967); and (4) a heightened state of anticipated helplessness—which was a central part of Freud's ([1926] 1959) theory of symptom formation.

That early study on momentary forgetting was part of a broad examination of other kinds of recurrent symptoms in psychotherapy. The diverse symptoms studied have included stomach pains in an ulcer patient (Luborsky 1953); precipitous shifts in depression (Luborsky et al. 1984); petit mal attacks (Luborsky et al. 1975); and migraine attacks in a cluster headache patient (Luborsky and Auerbach 1969). When the context was examined for the appearance of these different recurrent symptoms, the same four conditions were found as had been found for momentary forgetting. These four conditions therefore may well be generic for many kinds of recurrent symptoms that appear in the course of psychotherapy.

The Symptom-Context Method

What has been sketched here so far introduces the main topic of this chapter: the procedures of the symptom-context method and what can be learned through it. When a therapist notices the reappearance of certain symptoms, such as depression and anxiety, it can be clinically useful to trace the conditions under which these symptoms appear, and most clinicians try to do so. The symptom-context method is built upon this usual clinical style, but it is more exact and reliable. In this chapter I offer a guide to the method, either for clinical practice or for research.

SELECTING PATIENTS FOR SYMPTOM-CONTEXT STUDIES

Some patients in psychotherapy are especially suitable for symptom-context studies because they show *delimited* and *recurrent* psychological symptoms. A psychological symptom can be defined most simply (Freud [1926] 1959) as an impairment of a usually intact psychological function, such as an ability to remember what one has just intended to say. A delimited symptom has a relatively clear onset and termination within the session. The appearance of such symptoms provides the most suitable data for the symptom-context method.

USING THE METHOD

Identifying the preconditions associated with the appearance of symptoms in psychotherapy sessions requires careful data collection and organization. The following steps provide the necessary controls for the method.

1. Make routine audio or video recordings of the psychotherapy sessions to facilitate the scoring of the contexts of the symptoms that appear in the sessions. Transcribe the sessions.

2. Locate each appearance of each symptom in the sessions and mark the onset point and the endpoint of the symptom. Then divide the context surrounding the symptom into units before and after the symptom. The units can be word units, thought units, or time units.

3. Apply scoring systems that sample the four types of conditions that might foster the symptom's appearance as well as other possible conditions that appear worthy of investigation based on other symptom-context studies.

4. Locate and mark off control units, that is, segments in which no symptom appeared (following exactly the same procedure as in steps 2 and 3). A good system for selecting the locations is to pick control (nonsymptom) units that start at a point that is as far into the session as the onset point of the symptom. These control units allow for comparisons of the symptom context with the nonsymptom context. Such comparisons are vital for interpreting the results; for example, the level of helplessness in the symptom segments needs to be compared with the usual level in the nonsymptom segments.

CASE STUDY

As an example, consider the essence of the method as shown by the case study of Ms. Apfel, who was a patient in psychoanalysis. About 450 tape-recorded sessions covered the duration of the analysis. A small sample of her results will be enough to illustrate the steps in the symptom-context method. More detail about the patient and the study can be found in Luborsky and Mintz (1974) and Luborsky and Crits-Christoph (1990).

Ms. Apfel came for therapy at the age of thirty-one. She was a professional woman who suffered from a recurrent pattern of difficulty maintaining relationships with men; this prevented her from marrying. In each relationship she felt unfairly treated and broke off. After 103 sessions her male analyst (Analyst A) became ill and she was seen then by a female analyst (Analyst B) for about 350 more sessions.

Thirteen instances of momentary forgetting were found in her first 103 sessions. These forgettings fit the essential four criteria for defining a momentary forgetting symptom: (1) the thought was in the patient's mind at one point; (2) it abruptly vanished; (3) the patient reported the loss almost at the moment it occurred; and (4) the point of the onset of the forgetting could be located.

Another verbatim example will illustrate these four criteria. Just as in the first transcript example, the text indicates the point of onset as well as the point of recovery of the lost thought. The recovered thought itself is italicized. However, the recovery of the lost thought is not a required criterion for the inclusion of a forgetting; it is not uniformly evident among momentary forgettings.

SESSION 91. I said I seemed very nicely to have picked on men—[therapist clears throat] who, either intentionally or unintentionally, uh, and then I meant to say, "don't treat me well," and I [2 sec.] then a phrase fla-flashed through my mind [hesitates] "get in my way." [onset of forgetting] [exhales] [12 sec.] Now I don't know what else I was going to say. [4 sec.] [Therapist: You mean you forgot for a moment?] Yes. [2 sec.] I mean that was just preparatory to saying that—that thing—for the phrase, "get in my way," uh, flashed across my mind as I was [2 sec.] trying to get to the sentence I intended to say. [7 sec.] [Point of recovery of lost thought] [exhales] Oh [snort], huh, I just was—I mean *I-I was going—I was saying that the feeling is* [6 sec.] *is, uh, to a degree, justified, except that I do the choosing of the men.* . . .

We marked off on the transcript eleven 50-word units of the patient's speech before and after the forgetting. The same was done for the control (nonsymptom) points. To make the comparison of symptom and nonsymptom segments more objective, all references to momentary forgetting were deleted from the text. The units of speech were then rated by two independent clinicians on 5-point scales for each of thirteen categories. Agreement on most of the categories was moderately good.

Most of the categories we chose had been found to be associated with the appearance of symptoms in other symptom-context studies; a few of them seemed especially pertinent to this patient. They were rejection, reference to therapist (explicit), high involvement with therapist, helplessness, hopelessness, separation concern, anxiety, hostility to therapist (inferred), hostility to therapist (direct), hostility to others, sex and affection, and guilt and shame. The helplessness versus control ratings are presented in figure 1.1.

Rejection was the central symptom-associated category for this patient, based on a clinical review of her sessions. The rejection scale ranges from "none" to "very much." Rejection in this scale is defined as a negative response by another person, especially dislike, lack of interest, withholding, evaluating the patient as inadequate, or revealing an intention to break off with the patient.

The two judges' ratings on the variables were summed for all units. A two-factor repeated measurements analysis of variance (Winer 1962, 302) was calculated for each variable (the eight rated variables with highest agreement between judges plus the two scored measures). Table 1.1 shows

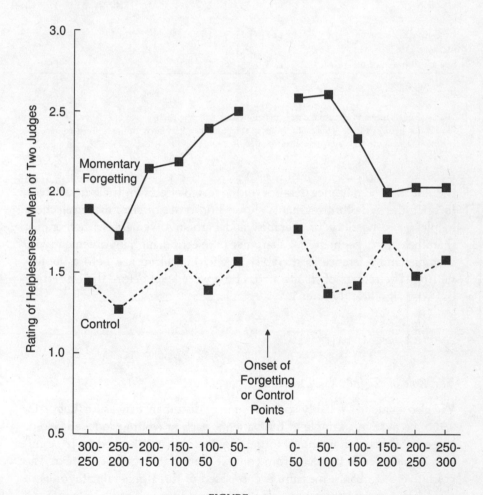

FIGURE 1.1
Helplessness for six 50-word units of patient's speech around the momentary
forgetting (mean of two judges).

TABLE 1.1 *F Ratios from Analyses of Variance on Context Variables*

Ratings and Measures	Among-Control Units	Symptom Mean versus Control Mean	Among-Symptom Units	Unit Preceding Symptom
Rejection	< 1	17.85**[a]	1.74	29.01**
High involvement with therapist	< 1	4.30*	2.84**	22.64**
Reference to therapist (explicit)	< 1	1.72	1.06	7.51*
Helplessness	< 1	17.22**	< 1[b]	12.99*
Hostility to therapist (inferred)	< 1	7.28**	< 1[b]	6.26*
Separation concern	< 1	2.78[a]	1.10[b]	2.15
Shame	< 1	< 1	2.40**[b]	< 1
Guilt	< 1	< 1	1.18	< 1
Cognitive disturbance measure	1.68	< 1	1.02	< 1
Speech disturbance measure	1.63	< 1	1.30	1.99

*$p < .05$
**$p < .01$
[a]Variance of segments in symptom data significantly larger than in control data.
[b]Interaction (error) variance significantly larger in symptom data than in control data. Tests for among-symptom units used within-symptom error term $(df = 130)$.

the statistical significance (F ratios) of the tested effects for the ten variables. In brief, the symptom segments showed (in order of size) more rejection, helplessness, hostility to therapist and high involvement with therapist than the control segments. A sharp rise in rejection, high involvement with therapist and reference to therapist (explicit) occurred just before the forgetting. The ratings of shame across time were level before the forgetting but rose significantly after it.

FINDINGS FOR MS. APFEL

The Role of Cognitive Disturbance.

We also included a reliably coded cognitive disturbance measure (Luborsky 1966) because in a sample of ten patients, each of whom produced two or three instances of momentary forgetting, the measure showed more cognitive disturbance in the symptom context than in the control context. The cognitive disturbance measure is composed of three general categories of disturbance: memory dysfunction, uncertainty about one's knowledge, and unclarity of expression. But when we tried the cognitive disturbance measure on Ms. Apfel's thirteen symptom segments versus thirteen control segments, no significant differences were found. One possible explanation for the finding is that Ms. Apfel, more than any other patient, had a consistent, extremely high cognitive disturbance rate throughout both symptom and nonsymptom segments.

Correspondence with the CCRT.

Another condition for symptom formation might be the arousal of the pattern of conflictual thoughts that are assessed by the Core Conflictual Relationship Theme (CCRT) method. To find Ms. Apfel's pattern the CCRT was analyzed for a sample session (no. 36) by two independent judges. A brief way of explaining the CCRT for Ms. Apfel is provided by figure 1.2, which gives the relationship episodes in session 36 in clockwise order, as they were told. The peripheral circles contain abbreviated versions of the relationship episodes. The core circle contains the CCRT, which is composed of the most often repeated wishes, responses from others, and responses of self in the five episodes in the session. The CCRT was derived from session 36, but it is similar to those in other sessions. It is as follows:

Wish: I wish to be loved and positively responded to and to avoid the recurrent experiences of rejection.
Response from other: Rejects and dominates me.
Response of self: I am self-critical, self-destructive, helpless, and sometimes oppositional (for example, I'm inclined to cancel the session in order to get back at the analyst).

A comparison of the CCRT with the rated context categories shows a correspondence that is especially evident in the identical words used in the response from other: "rejects me." It is also evident in the response of self in which the patient becomes helpless and shows hostility to the therapist (in the form of being oppositional). Other patients also show a correspondence of their forgetting context with their CCRT, as was shown in Luborsky (1988). But why should there be such a correspondence between the momentary forgetting context and the CCRT? It is to be expected in theory because many of the content categories preceding the momentary forgetting are likely to be part of the main conflictual theme, and that theme is assessed through the CCRT. The similarity may also be partly a product of the tendency for forgetting to occur during the relationship episodes with the therapist. As Freud ([1912] 1958) observed, the relationship with the therapist is the hardest one for the patient to deal with openly because it entails expressing thoughts about which the patient is uncomfortable to the very person to whom the thoughts relate.

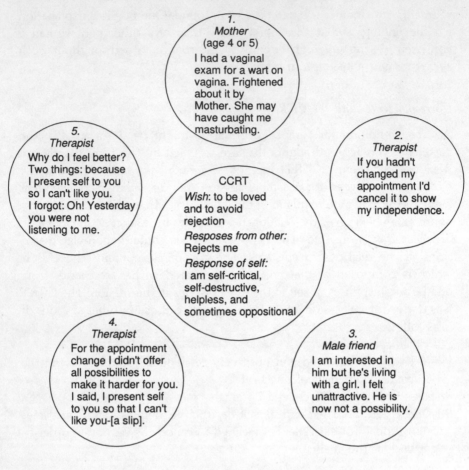

FIGURE 1.2
CCRT and relationship episodes from Ms. Apfel, session 36.

The Role of Involvement with the Therapist.

A mark of the activation of the CCRT is heightened involvement with the therapist. Many signs of this are typically present: among the most obvious and easily counted are direct references to the therapist.

The Role of Helplessness.

When the patient feels helpless to cope with the conflicts, more intense affects or other symptomatic developments are more likely to occur. This statement exactly corresponds with helplessness as the central state in Freud's theory of conditions leading to symptom formation ([1926] 1959).

Summary of Preconditions.

The findings in the case of Ms. Apfel reveal three of the four conditions associated with symptom formation that were listed earlier: the activation of an aspect of the patient's central relationship pattern, which also shows up in the CCRT; the involvement with the therapist, which shows up in the frequency of explicit references to the therapist; and the state of helplessness, which can be rated by clinical judges. For this patient other conditions were also revealed, including expectation of rejection and hostility to the therapist.

Applications of the Symptom-Context Method

INSIGHTS INTO THE PRECONDITIONS OF SYMPTOMS

Through the symptom-context method the therapist can derive reliable information about the meaning of a patient's recurrent symptoms, as illustrated by Ms. Apfel's momentary forgetting. To achieve such benefits, the clinician who is informed about the symptom-context method need only give special attention to understanding the pregnant presymptom moments. The presymptom state reveals the workings of major systems of central psychological conflicts; such systems tend to be more fully exposed to view during shifts than during stasis.

As illustrated in this case study, one of the method's most appealing virtues is its usefulness in the process of assessment of the context in which a symptom appears. The process involves the usual way a clinician makes that assessment: by noticing the repeated temporal association of the symptom with certain types of conflictual themes. The method supplements and strengthens such clinical assessments by providing a controlled way to observe consistencies from one appearance of the symptom to the next. Then it provides an individually appropriate baseline for the findings by a comparison of the consistencies across symptom appearances with the consistencies across nonsymptom occasions.

INSIGHT INTO DIFFERENT TYPES OF SYMPTOMS

Momentary forgetting is not one of the most convenient symptoms for clinical purposes, because its rare and fleeting nature limits its use. A more common and more accessible recurrent symptom is shifts in level of depression in depressed patients. The use of this symptom for study is illustrated in the manual for supportive-expressive psychotherapy (Luborsky 1984, 100–107) by a clinical analysis of a series of shifts in level of depression for one patient. For that patient some of the preconditions were general; for example, shifts toward increased depression were associated with the helplessness that was generated by unfavorable comparisons with others, resulting in a loss of self-esteem.

BENEFITS AND LIMITATIONS

Beyond its main purpose of informing us about the conditions for the formation of neurotic and psychosomatic symptoms, the method has a number of virtues. For one, it enables psychotherapy data to be used not only for finding but also for testing hypotheses. In the present study, for example, we found evidence that is consistent with Freud's ([1926] 1959) theory that helplessness is associated with the antecedents of the forgetting, although other factors are also involved.

The method entails no distortion of the treatment process. The therapeutic process continues as it would ordinarily, and only after the session or after the treatment is completed is an analysis of the data undertaken. In this respect the method is naturalistic: it is based on the systematic collection and analysis of experiments in nature. The method could be applied in any situation in which a continuous record can be made of the context in which a symptom has appeared.

Several other advantages can be listed. The method is economical: selected small samples can be used rather than time-consuming complete sessions, and selected sessions can be used rather than the entire therapy. The method permits a precise description of the actual context—immediate and background, verbal and physiological—in which a symptom develops. It does not rely on retrospective data. Both the onset conditions and postsymptom conditions can be inspected.

Finally, the method can be applied not only to symptoms but also to a variety of recurrent behaviors—such as recurrent laughs or recurrent lip licking, or a dozen other such behaviors that are seen during psychotherapy. We would learn through that comparison the degree to which what we have called the preconditions to symptom formation are really general for many kinds of recurrent behaviors in psychotherapy.

As the method is used it has several other limitations. It has been used so far only to catch consistencies across the occasions of the recurrent behavior. It may, therefore, miss certain cyclical changes, as Fonagy and Moran (chapter 5) point out. Also, it has not been used to identify the varying conditions in a symptom context that instigate a symptom. On one occasion, for example, a combination of conditions may produce a symptom because of a special degree of helplessness; on another occasion the extreme state of cognitive disturbance may cause the symptom to appear. After more studies the analyses will be extended to extract the unique combination of conditions that trigger each symptom occasion.

References

FREUD, S. (1912/1958). The dynamics of transference. In J. Strachey (Ed.), *The standard edition of the complete psychological works of Sigmund Freud* (Vol. 12, pp. 99–108). London: Hogarth Press.

FREUD, S. (1926/1959). Inhibitions, symptoms, and anxiety. In J. Strachey (Ed.), *The standard edition of the complete psychological works of Sigmund Freud* (Vol. 20, pp. 87–174). London: Hogarth Press.

LUBORSKY, L. (1953). Intraindividual repetitive measurements (P-technique) in understanding symptom structure and psychotherapeutic change. In O. H. Mowrer (Ed.), *Psychotherapy: Theory and research.* New York: Ronald Press.

LUBORSKY, L. (1966). *The cognitive disturbance scale.* Unpublished manuscript.

LUBORSKY, L. (1967). Momentary forgetting during psychotherapy and psychoanalysis: A theory and research method. *Motives and thought: Psychoanalytic essays in honor of David Rapaport. Psychological Issues* (Monograph 18/19), pp. 177–217.

LUBORSKY, L. (1984). *Principles of psychoanalytic psychotherapy: A manual for supportive-expressive (SE) treatment.* New York: Basic Books.

LUBORSKY, L. (1988). Recurrent momentary forgetting: Its content and context. In M. Horowitz (Ed.), *Psychodynamics and cognition* (pp. 223–251). Chicago: University of Chicago Press.

LUBORSKY, L., & AUERBACH, A. H. (1969). The symptom-context method: Quantitative studies of symptom formation in psychotherapy. *Journal of the American Psychoanalytic Association, 17,* 68–99.

LUBORSKY, L., & CRITS-CHRISTOPH, P. (1990). *Understanding transference: The CCRT method.* New York: Basic Books.

LUBORSKY, L., DOCHERTY, J., TODD, T., KNAPP, P., MIRSKY, A., & GOTTSCHALK, L. (1975). A context analysis of psychological states prior to petit-mal seizures. *Journal of Nervous and Mental Disease, 160,* 282–298.

LUBORSKY, L., & MINTZ, J. (1974). What sets off momentary forgetting during a psychoanalysis? Methods of investigating symptom-onset conditions. In L. Goldberger & V. Rosen (Eds.), *Psychoanalysis and contemporary science* (Vol. 3, pp. 233–268). New York: International Universities Press.

LUBORSKY, L., SINGER, B., HARTKE, J., CRITS-CHRISTOPH, P., & COHEN, M. (1984). Shifts in depressive state during psychotherapy: Which concepts of depression fit the context of Mr. Q's shifts? In L. N. Rice & L. S. Greenberg (Eds.), *Patterns of change* (pp. 157–193). New York: Guilford Press.

WINER, J. (1962). *Statistical principles in experimental design.* New York: McGraw-Hill.

CHAPTER 2

Tracing Clinical Themes across Phases of Treatment by a Q-Set

ENRICO E. JONES, JANICE D. CUMMING, AND
STEVEN M. PULOS

FORMAL RESEARCH ON THE PSYCHOTHERAPY process has generally been peripheral to the theory of psychoanalytic therapy and has had
little influence on thinking or practice in the field (Strupp and Bergin 1969).
One reason for this is that empiricists often operationalize constructs in
ways that are remote from how clinical problems are conceptualized and
described. Another reason is that psychotherapy research is usually cast in
conventional, large-sample, group comparison designs. The strengths of
group comparison designs are external validity and generalizability. Statements about the psychotherapy process derived from group data, however,
rarely have direct relevance to the clinical problems that confront the
psychotherapist.

Clinical investigation, in contrast, has been traditionally conducted
according to the naturalistic-observational model, relying on the case
study. The primary means of clinical inquiry, teaching, and learning in
psychoanalysis remains the case study method, a fact that is perhaps most
responsible for the lack of relevance of psychotherapy research for clinical
theory and practice.

Empirical researchers regard the case study as unsuitable for formal
scientific inquiry. Although it is acknowledged that the case study method
may be useful in hypothesis generation (Kazdin 1981), the method is
usually considered unsuitable for the establishment of general laws or
principles; these can be achieved, it is argued, only by experimental or
statistical inquiry (Grünbaum 1984; Holt 1978). Some are skeptical even of
the case study's contribution to the process of discovery, much less verification, citing a long list of shortcomings: the problem of assessing the

reliability of data, that is, the manner in which observations are selected and recorded; the lack of controls, potentially allowing numerous sources of variation (Campbell and Stanley 1966); the difficulty in replicating case studies as a consequence of the insufficient description of variables (Kratch-owill 1978); the difficulty in choosing among alternative explanations of the same observations (Spence 1982; Runyan 1984); and the problem of comparing one case study with another (Mendelsohn 1979).

The intensive study of an individual case can, however, provide for the systematic exploration of a range of plausible interpretations, thereby yielding more complete information than formal methods that examine a narrow range of hypotheses. Investigators are beginning to call for a formalization of the case study method in ways that are consonant with the requirements of empirical science (Kazdin 1982; Wallerstein 1986). Criticisms of the case study method can in many instances be addressed by introducing various methodological refinements, including the use of archival data incorporating corroborative evidence from other sources, the selection of cases with controls for extraneous sources of variance, and the standardized application of objective assessments.

Nevertheless, data derived from the intensive investigation of a single case of psychotherapy or psychoanalysis are difficult to study in ways that are relevant both clinically and scientifically. If case studies are to be used in more formal research, what is required are methods of analysis of individual case material that (1) allow the wealth of observation typical of case studies to be reduced to objective, quantifiable dimensions; (2) capture the uniqueness of the individual case; and (3) permit comparisons among observers of the same case, as well as comparisons between and across cases. The Berkeley Psychotherapy Research Group has begun to apply the Q-technique, a methodology long known in psychological research, to these problems with promising effect (Jones, Hall, and Parke 1991).

Q-Methodology in Psychotherapy Research

The Q-sort method was originated by Stephenson (1953) and more thoroughly developed and tested by Block (Block 1961; Block and Haan 1971). It is a method of measurement with a broad range of potential applications, and it is particularly well suited for the description of qualitative psychodynamic data. Though the Q-technique can be used as a method for obtaining self-reports, it is more commonly used by observers. A Q-set consists of a set of items, each of which describes a significant psychological or behavioral feature of an individual or a situation. The specific content of items depends upon the particular objectives of the research. There is no standard Q-set; rather, the goal is to provide a set of items that can capture as comprehensively as possible the critical dimensions of variation among cases under study. After studying the relevant material (such as transcripts of therapy hours) a judge orders the items. Conventionally, the Q-items are printed separately on cards, a convenience that permits the easy arrangement and rearrangement of the items until the desired ordering is obtained. The Q-items are ranked according to the degree to which they characterize the material under study, as will be demonstrated.

The Q-sort is an *ipsative* method; that is, the items are ordered within a unique case, from those most characteristic of the person or situation being described to those least characteristic. This differs from the more conventional *normative* mode of scaling, where comparisons are made between individuals on some dimension of variation. On an ipsative scale the question is posed: "Is Mr. A more anxious or resistant than he is insightful?" On a normative scale, the question would be, "Is Mr. A more anxious or insightful than Mr. B is?" The Q-method provides a way of capturing the uniqueness of each case, as well as permitting the assessment of the similarities or dissimilarities between cases (see Block 1961).

In psychotherapy research the Q-technique was initially used to evaluate treatment outcomes (Rogers and Dymond 1954), though its use for studying psychotherapy process also has a long history (for example, Fiedler 1951; Rawn 1958). Although some of this early research was promising, Q-methodology has not been applied systematically in psychotherapy research despite gaining wide acceptance in other areas of psychology, such as in personality and developmental studies. This relative lack of interest may stem in part from the difficulties involved in constructing adequate Q-sets. Even within the psychodynamic frame there is no exhaustive and fully accepted theory of how patients change, and hence there is no system that includes the complete array of therapist and patient behaviors that might be considered important in the description of a psychotherapy. The means by which a universe of events is made descriptively concrete gives no guarantee that the resulting set of items will provide adequate coverage. It is perhaps partially for this reason that early investigators tended to construct Q-sets aimed at describing quite limited aspects of the treatment process. The relative neglect of the Q-technique stems in part, too, from some troublesome psychometric features of early approaches to the Q-method, particularly the uneven variance of items across subjects and the influence of social desirability on self Q-sorts. Modern approaches to Q-set construction have addressed the problem of content domain and item variance, and the influence of social desirability is not an issue in observer Q-sorts (see Block [1961] for a full technical discussion of the potentials and limitations of Q-methodology).

The Psychotherapy Process Q-Set

The Psychotherapy Process Q-set (PQS) (Jones 1985) has been used to describe psychoanalytic therapy process, to assess the relation of process to outcome, and to analyze the nature of change in process over time. As a method for systematic inquiry, the instrument addresses a number of problems confronted by all process researchers, including decisions regarding the size of the unit of analysis, temporal range, content domain, level of inference, and role and operationalization of theory.

Level or unit of analysis refers to the degree of generality or specificity of the material to be examined. The unit chosen—verbal utterance, problem area, or phase of treatment—depends on the construct or the particular research question being investigated. Some studies have selected units at the micro level, such as patient vocal quality, while others have investigated macro-level units, such as the therapeutic alliance, which refers to a wide range of therapist and patient behaviors. The items of the PQS provide a standard format of clinically meaningful units that observers can use to classify and describe the process material under study.

A related question concerns *temporal range.* Most process rating scales use four- to twenty-minute segments of therapy hours, and judges are asked to rate a dimension of presumed relevance on the basis of relatively brief impressions. These data typically are aggregated without consideration of meaningful factors of timing and context. It has become increasingly clear that aggregate data analyses that use rates, frequencies, or ratios of units across time segments cannot capture change processes. With the Q-technique, an entire treatment hour, not just a small segment, is rated. The therapy hour might be termed a natural time frame; it is a segment of time that has practical utility for researchers as well as inherent meaning for clinicians and patients.

The *content domain* covered by a process measure is crucial. Some filter is needed to select units from the vast number of attributes that can be used to describe the therapy process. The items included in the PQS represent an empirical selection from a pool of several hundred items garnered from existing process measures as well as new items constructed by a panel of clinical judges. Pilot ratings were conducted on video- and audiotapes of psychotherapies representing a wide range of theoretical orientations. The final version of the Q-set describes a broad range of therapeutic phenomena capturing relevant and salient events in the domain of psychotherapy process.

Closely related to choices concerning content domain is the question of *level of interference.* As research moves from micro to macro levels of analysis, there is typically a greater need to rely on inferential judgment;

problems arise when such judgments are informal, implicit, or intuitive. A process Q-set manual (Jones 1985) addresses this difficulty with explicit rules governing raters' use of inference. The Q-items themselves, as defined in the manual, are anchored to behavioral and linguistic cues that can be identified in recordings of hours.

A persistent dilemma in psychotherapy process research concerns the extent to which investigations should be *theory* driven, or at least tied to theoretical constructs. Psychotherapists who accept different paradigms, even within the psychodynamic perspective, broadly defined, often differ importantly in the concepts they use and in their descriptive language. Indeed, they may not even consider the same dimensions. The psychotherapy process Q-items were written, as far as possible, so that formulations could be derived from the Q-items that are compatible with different theoretical viewpoints (see Jones, Hall, and Parke [1991] for a more complete discussion of these topics).

Studies using the PQS have investigated the effects on psychotherapy outcome of therapist actions and techniques and of patient behaviors and attitudes (Jones, Cumming, and Horowitz 1988; Jones, Parke, and Pulos 1992). One such study comparing the process in relatively large samples of psychodynamic and cognitive therapies discovered the importance of psychodynamically oriented techniques for patient improvement in both treatment modalities (Jones and Pulos 1993). The Q-technique permits unusual flexibility in terms of research design and data analytic strategies. It can be applied both in the usual group comparisons or nomothetic designs, in which Q-ratings of groups of hours are compared, and in idiographic, $N = 1$ designs (Jones, Ghannam, Nigg, and Dyer 1993).

An intensive investigation of a single psychoanalytic case (Jones and Windholz 1990) has served as a prototype for the study of single-case and longer-term treatments. Blocks of ten sessions of a six-year analysis were selected at regular intervals over the course of the treatment, and transcripts of these hours were rated in random fashion with the process Q-set. Over time, the patient's discourse became increasingly less intellectualized and dominated by rational thought, became more reflective, and showed a greater access to emotional life and a developing capacity for free association. With time, too, the analyst became increasingly active in challenging the patient's understanding of an experience or an event, in identifying recurrent patterns in her life experience or behavior, in interpreting defenses, and in emphasizing feelings the patient considered wrong, dangerous, or unacceptable. The psychotherapy process Q-set has been applied in process investigations with considerable success and shows particular promise as a method for systematic inquiry of the single analytic case.

DEVELOPMENT OF THE PQS, ITS APPLICATION, AND TRAINING IN ITS USE

The Psychotherapy Process Q-set furnishes a language and rating procedure for the comprehensive description, in clinically relevant terms, of the therapist—patient interaction in a form suitable for quantitative comparison and analysis. Again, the instrument is designed to be applied to an audio- or videotaped record or transcript of a single treatment hour as the unit of observation. An obvious problem is managing the voluminous material produced in a manner that retains the subtlety and complexity of clinical phenomena, while at the same time capturing salience and relevance. Using the psychotherapy hour in its entirety has the advantage of allowing clinical judges to study the material for confirmation of alternative conceptualizations and to assess the gradual unfolding meaning of events. A coding manual (Jones 1985) details instructions for Q-sorting and provides the items and their definitions, along with operational examples, in order to minimize potentially varying interpretations of the items.

After studying the transcript of a therapy hour, clinical judges order the 100 items, which are printed separately on cards to permit easy arrangement and rearrangement. The items are sorted into nine piles ranging on a continuum from least characteristic (category 1) to most characteristic (category 9); the middle pile (category 5) is used for items deemed either neutral or irrelevant for the particular hour being rated. The number of cards sorted into each pile (ranging from five at the extremes to eighteen in the middle, or neutral, category) conforms to a normal distribution. This requires that judges make multiple evaluations among items, thereby avoiding either negative or positive "halo" effects and attenuating the influence of response sets. Although other distributions can be used, this distribution takes into account that conventional statistical indices used to express the similarity between Q-sorts pay less attention to discriminations made in the midrange of a continuum (see Block [1961] for a full discussion of these psychometric issues).

Q-items are anchored to behavioral and linguistic cues that can be identified in recordings. For example, clinical judges are not asked to identify the presence or absence of a defense mechanism in the patient; defense mechanism is a relatively abstract notion. Instead, they are asked to notice whether or not the therapist *makes* a defense interpretation; items are tied to identifiable behaviors. Some minimal clinical experience (one year of supervised psychotherapy) allows judges to become reliable raters after a relatively short period of training with the instrument. A fruitful training technique is to have several observers describe the same therapy transcript. Such calibration sessions are very important in providing the opportunity, after the psychotherapy Q-set has been applied, for discussion among the observers. The observers can discern the bases of disagreement and can begin to separate genuine differences in evaluation from the unwanted differences in the interpretation of items.

RELIABILITY

If the instrument is to be effective, raters must construct similar Q-sorts for a given therapy hour. The interrater reliability for the process Q-set has been consistently satisfactory across a variety of studies and treatment samples, with correlations ranging from .83 to .89 for two raters, and ranging from .89 to .92 using three to ten raters (Jones, Cumming, and Horowitz 1988; Jones and Windholz 1990; Pulos and Jones 1987). Inter-rater reliability is calculated using the Pearson product-moment correlation. The overall levels of profile reliability attained by the Q-set are, then, excellent.

The reliability of the specific items that compose the Q-deck are also an important feature of the instrument. Considerable effort was made to eliminate individual items that could not be rated reliably. Still, item reliability levels are influenced by the range of responses. An item may not demonstrate much variance within a given sample; reliability will, however, be strong when sufficient variation does occur. Average item reliability is quite acceptable, with mean item reliability across several samples of treatment hours achieving .82 (Jones, Parke, and Pulos, 1992).

VALIDITY

Q-sets contain many independent items that function as a descriptive language. A Q-sort of a therapy hour describes many constructs and their interrelations. As a consequence, Q-sorts do not yield scores that can simply be correlated with measures of a single construct. Validation of Q-sets must therefore rest on how fully they describe the phenomena they were designed to investigate.

In a test of discriminant validity in single cases, a videotape of three therapy sessions, conducted with the same patient by well-known proponents of their respective treatment forms (Albert Ellis, Fritz Perls, and Carl Rogers), were rated by ten therapists who represented a variety of theoretical orientations and a range of experience. Results demonstrated that fifty-two Q-items differentiated Rational-Emotive from Gestalt therapy, forty-seven items differentiated Rational-Emotive from Client-centered therapy, and thirty-eight items differentiated Client-centered therapy from Gestalt therapy. The ten items designated most and least characteristic for each form of therapy were then presented to another group of five therapists familiar with these treatment modalities; they successfully matched ($p < .001$) the sets of Q-items with the type of therapy from which they had been derived (Pulos and Jones 1987). This "back translation" of the Q-set indicates that the instrument differentiated types of therapy not only in terms of a large number of significant differences, but also in a manner that accurately captured the nature of the various theoretical orientations. A series of studies has been conducted that clearly demonstrates the instrument's capacity to identify process correlates of outcome in different patient populations and with different indices of patient improvement (Jones and Pulos 1993; Jones, Cumming, and Horowitz 1988).

When an instrument is composed of multiple items, the reflexive advice often given is to do a factor analysis of the measure as a way of reducing the data generated. The Q-set was constructed to minimize the emergence of general factors. Indeed, in a factor-analytic study based on two data sets, which included 70 treatments, 130 separate treatment hours, and 380 Q-sorts, no clear factor structure was found. The absence of factor structure is highly desirable from the standpoint of Q-methodology, since it demonstrates that the PQS is operating as a descriptive language rather than as a set of subscales.

SOME LIMITATIONS AND DATA-ANALYTIC ISSUES

The PQS may be used purely descriptively by, for example, examining the placement of individual items (see the case studies that follow). Correlational techniques may also be used with little difficulty, especially for a descriptive purpose (see Stephenson 1953). When the goal is to make inferences from a sample to a larger population, Q-data can be analyzed using most of the commonly applied data-analytic techniques. However, in using inference statistics the relatively large number of items that constitute the psychotherapy Q-set increase the possibility of a type I error (finding a relationship in a sample that is not true in the population). While techniques exist for minimizing type I errors (see Davis and Gaito 1984), such procedures increase the probability of a type II error (dismissing a relationship observed in a sample as the result of chance when a real relationship does exist in the population). The danger of making type II errors in the early stages of research is that results judged to be nonsignificant may not be investigated further; in contrast, type I errors are not likely to be replicated in subsequent studies.

We are, then, not inclined to impose stringent controls for type I errors across the entire set of Q-items. However, especially in $N = 1$ studies, particular attention is paid to moderate to large effects at the item level which are likely to be robust and clinically meaningful. This can be achieved either by estimating the magnitude of relationships or by visual inspection of trends, a method commonly used to evaluate single case data (Kazdin 1984). Baer (1977) has argued that visual inspection of single case data is more likely than statistical analysis to lead to the identification of potent or marked effects, and is therefore less likely than statistical proce- dures to identify as significant small or subtle changes that may be clinically insignificant (Jacobson and Truax 1991). The case studies presented here apply an informal statistic (Q-item mean relative to size of standard devia- tion) as well as visual inspection to determine trends beyond the normal range of fluctuation. Although this is only one possible mode of analyzing Q-data, it is a robust technique that any clinician can easily apply with a minimum knowledge of statistics and without access to a computer.

Applications: The Intensive Study of the Single Case

The two case studies that follow are from an archive of brief therapy cases collected at the Department of Psychiatry, University of California, San Francisco. Patients whose treatment records were contained in the archive had experienced some traumatic life event, usually involving a loss, within the preceding two or three years and were diagnosed as suffering from a posttraumatic stress disorder (PTSD). Cases for the present intensive case studies were selected from a larger sample of forty female patients from the center's archive who were subjects in a previous study (Jones, Cumming, and Horowitz 1988). Patients and therapists completed an extensive bat- tery of assessment instruments pre- and posttherapy, and all sessions were audiotaped.

Treatment consisted of a twelve-session therapy based on a brief psychodynamic psychotherapy model (Malan 1976). Patients were seen in follow-up interviews four months past termination by the same evaluator who initially interviewed them. The therapy was specifically tailored to focus on the experience of loss and its meaning, thus facilitating a normal grieving process (Horowitz et al. 1986). Outcome was assessed by patient ratings on a variety of measures, including the Brief Symptom Inventory (Derogatis and Melisaratos 1983), the Impact of Events Scale (Horowitz, Wilner, and Alvarez 1979), and the Experience of Stress Scale (Weiss, Wilner, and Horowitz 1984). Therapist and independent clinical evaluator ratings of outcome included the Stress Response Rating Scale, the Experi- ence of Stress Scale, and a modified version of the Brief Psychiatric Rating Scale (Overall and Gorham 1962).

Two cases, one successful and one unsuccessful, were selected for intensive study from the sample of forty patients. A residual gain index for therapy outcome was derived by combining one measure completed by the therapist, one by the patient, and one by the independent clinical evaluator;

a rank ordering of patient outcome scores was then determined. The case identified as successful fell within the upper quartile of the rank order; the less successful case was selected from the bottom quartile of the rank orderings. Transcriptions of therapy hours 1, 5, 8, and 12 were then presented in a random order to a panel of clinical judges for Q-sorting, and each hour was rated independently by three judges. Q-ratings for each hour were combined, yielding a Q-sort composite for each rated hour, in order to ensure reliable ratings. Interrater reliability, calculated by Pearson product-moment correlation coefficients, ranged from .68 to .90, with a mean reliability of .86.

SOME GUIDING HYPOTHESES

Results derived from a large-sample study (Jones, Cumming, and Horowitz 1988) from which the two cases presented here were drawn suggested that important differences in the therapy process between the successful and unsuccessful cases could be expected. In the larger-sample (N = 40) study, patient pretreatment disturbance level proved to be a key moderator variable. Successful therapy with more severely disturbed patients had an external focus, one aimed away from emotional conflicts and personal meanings of experience and toward a more reality oriented construction of the patient's problems. The therapist assumed an actively supportive role by taking over some of the patient's decision-making functions for a time, offering advice and encouraging the patient to take specific action. Successful therapy with less disturbed patients clearly reflected key elements of a brief dynamic treatment model that had as a primary focus the affective responses and personal meanings associated with the patient's traumatic experience. Therapists more often stressed the emotional content in the patient's speech in order to encourage the experience of affect; longstanding focal conflicts were addressed by linking the patient's current and past experiences or perceptions of events; and a relatively common therapist action was transference interpretation, the drawing of connections between interpersonal aspects of therapy and experiences in other relationships. These data guided our hypotheses about the nature of the therapy process in the two cases selected for intensive study.

Q-descriptors that most strongly characterized each treatment were identified by calculating means for the 100 Q-items for the hours rated: sessions 1, 5, 8, and 12. The resulting means were rank ordered, and the ten most and ten least characteristic Q-items were selected. These Q-items means ranged from a high of 8.2 to a low of 1.3 on the 9-point Q-distribution. These most and least characteristic Q-items for the two cases are listed in tables 2.1 and 2.2 later in the chapter.

In order to study the evolution or change in the therapy process in these two cases, items that were increasingly characteristic or increasingly uncharacteristic of the process from the beginning to the end of treatment were identified by evaluating changes in Q-item means relative to size of standard deviation across the four sessions. Only when an item showed a dramatic shift across the sampled hours was fluctuation in item placement reliable and meaningful. Representative Q-items are plotted to show graphically their movement over treatment hours, and to permit visual inspection of patterns of change (as will be demonstrated in figures 2.1 through 2.4).

A SUCCESSFUL TREATMENT: MS. A

Patient A was a twenty-three-year-old woman who came for treatment about nine months after her father died. At the time of evaluation, she was troubled by intrusive thoughts and feelings related to her father's death, and she was quite anxious, guilt-ridden, and fearful. Ms. A complained of numerous physical symptoms and was worried that something was wrong with her body and with her mental health. She believed that she had not adjusted well to the loss of her father. The independent clinical evaluator described her personality as hysterical with schizoid features. Her therapist described her after the first hour as a hysterical personality with narcissistic and obsessional features.

Ms. A's scores on the Global Severity Index (GSI) of the Brief Symptom Inventory showed a 61 percent decline at termination, and she generally maintained these gains at follow-up, reporting a 45 percent decline from pretherapy. On the Experience of Stress Scale (based on operationalized item definitions) the patient rated herself as 60 percent improved at termination; the therapist rated her as 55 percent improved at termination; and the clinical evaluator judged her as 45 percent improved at follow-up. In addition, therapist and evaluator ratings on the Stress Response Rating Scale (range: 1 to 5) indicated that the patient experienced a significant reduction of symptoms, with the therapist's ratings showing a decline from 2.45 at hour 1 to 0.54 at termination, and the interviewer assigning a score of 2.00 at pretherapy and 0.31 at follow-up. Ms. A herself reported feeling very well satisfied with her therapy, giving a scale-high rating of 4 on the Client Satisfaction Scale. Four months after therapy, at follow-up, Ms. A reported that distressing feelings and thoughts about her father's death still came up and that she felt somewhat depressed and irritable. However, she reported that she was continuing to adjust well to the loss, and the independent evaluator agreed with her assessment.

The most and least descriptive Q-items (table 2.1) provide a portrait of the therapy process with Ms. A. The Q-item numbers on the description refer to the items in the table; the word *reversed* (or r) in connection with a Q-item number follows the convention established by Block and Haan (1971) to indicate that the variable required a reversal of meaning in order to be oriented comparably in the narrative. The therapist maintained a supportive, approving, encouraging stance (Q 45), was responsive and affectively involved (Q 9, r), and her comments were judged by our raters as very tactful and kind (Q 77, r). The therapist exerted a good deal of active direction (Q 17) during therapy sessions, and her primary techniques were clarifying and reflecting (Q 65) as well as stressing the emotional content of her patient's speech in order to encourage the experience of affect (Q 81). The therapist also made interpretive remarks fairly often about the patient's relations to particular people in her life (Q 40) and encouraged her to take the actions she thought best (Q 48).

Ms. A spontaneously initiated topics for discussion and brought up problems (Q 15, r), and there were few silences during the hours (Q 12, r). Intense feelings emerged (Q 56, r) as the patient talked about her sadness and her anger over her father's death (Q 94, Q 26). There was an exploration of Ms. A's interpersonal relationships (Q 63) and current life situation (Q 69). She was quite hesitant to make any demands of the therapist (Q 83, r) but felt trusting toward the therapist (Q 44, r) and understood by her (Q 14, r). She also readily understood (Q 5, r) and accepted (Q 42, r) the therapist's comments and observations.

An examination of the movement of Q-items over time helps to elaborate the description of this therapy more completely. In order for a Q-item to be considered to have shifted importantly in the Q-distribution, it must have moved more than two standard deviations in mean value between adjacent hours. Figure 2.1, which represents an "in motion" view of therapy process with Ms. A, charts the mean ratings across judges for representative Q-items for therapy hours 1, 5, 8, and 12. Inspection of mean item ratings for the entire Q-set suggests that therapy process was relatively invariant or stable (only items showing dramatic shifts are displayed in the figures), with perturbations particularly in the early middle phase of the treatment (around hour 5). Those items that do shift seem to be related to aspects of the patient's emotional reactions to the therapist. As Ms. A became more able to express anger (Q 84), probably about her father's death, she also expressed more ambivalence about the therapist (Q 49), and she appeared more wary and less trustful (Q 44). During the later middle phase of therapy (hour 8), Ms. A began to signal her need for the therapist's approval and sympathy (Q 78). In what is probably an in-process indicator of outcome, Ms. A was significantly less troubled by feelings of inadequacy and ineffectiveness (Q 59) at termination.

TABLE 2.1 *Least and Most Descriptive Q-Items for Patient A*

Least Descriptive Q-Items		Most Descriptive Q-Items	
Item	Mean	Item	Mean
9 Therapist is distant, aloof (vs. responsive and affectively involved).	1.3	63 Patient's interpersonal relationships are a major theme.	8.2
14 Patient does not feel understood by therapist.	1.6	65 Therapist clarifies restates, or rephrases patient's communication.	7.8
56 Patient discusses experiences as if distant from his or her feelings.	1.9	94 Patient feels sad or depressed (vs. joyous, cheerful).	7.8
5 Patient has difficulty understanding the therapist's comments.	2.3	45 Therapist adopts supportive stance.	7.7
77 Therapist is tactless.	2.3	81 Therapist emphasizes patient feelings in order to help him or her experience them more deeply.	7.6
15 Patient does not initiate topics; is passive.	2.5	26 Patient experiences discomforting or troublesome (painful) affect.	7.3
44 Patient feels wary or suspicious (vs. trusting and secure).	2.6	17 Therapist actively exerts control over the interaction.	7.3
42 Patient rejects (vs. accepts) therapist's comments and observations.	2.7	69 Patient's current or recent life situation is emphasized in the discussion.	7.3
83 Patient is demanding.	2.7	40 Therapist makes interpretations referring to actual people in the patient's life.	7.2
12 Silences occur during hour.	2.8	48 Therapist encourages independence of action and opinion in the patient.	7.2

AN UNSUCCESSFUL TREATMENT: MRS. D

Mrs. D was a forty-two-year-old woman who entered treatment less than four months after her husband's death. At pretreatment evaluation Mrs. D reported a variety of physical symptoms; she complained of nervousness, restlessness, and problems in her thinking; and she felt plagued by severely intrusive thoughts and feelings about the loss of her husband. The clinical evaluator described her as depressed and hostile; her therapist rated her as anxious and guilty. Both described her personality style as obsessional and attributed to her hysterical and narcissistic traits. A com-

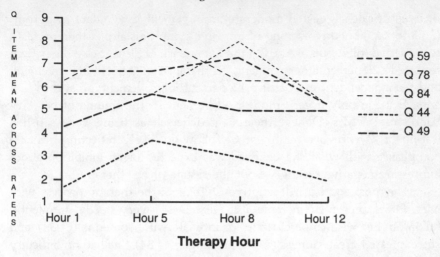

Therapy Hour

Q 49 Patient experiences ambivalent or conflicted feelings about the therapist.
Hour 1 = 4.3   Hour 5 = 5.7   Hour 8 = 5.0   Hour 12 = 5.0
S.D. = 0.54

Q 44 Patient feels wary or suspicious (vs. trusting and secure).
Hour 1 = 1.7   Hour 5 = 3.7   Hour 8 = 3.0   Hour 12 = 2.0
S.D. = 0.92

Q 84 Patient expresses angry or aggressive feelings.
Hour 1 = 6.3   Hour 5 = 8.3   Hour 8 = 6.3   Hour 12 = 6.3
S.D. = 1.00

Q 78 Patient seeks therapist's approval, affection, or sympathy.
Hour 1 = 5.7   Hour 5 = 5.7   Hour 8 = 8.0   Hour 12 = 5.3
S.D. = 1.23

Q 59 Patient feels inadequate and inferior (vs. effective and superior).
Hour 1 = 6.7   Hour 5 = 6.7   Hour 8 = 7.3   Hour 12 = 5.3
S.D. = 0.84

FIGURE 2.1
Process over time with Ms. A: Some transference reactions.

parison of her scores at the pretreatment assessment with those of other patients in the sample of forty showed her to be one of the most psychologically distressed. Mrs. D's scores on the Brief Symptom Inventory showed no change at termination (from 1.17 to 1.28) and perhaps a slight deterioration at follow-up (1.34); therapist and evaluator ratings on the Stress Response Rating Scale also showed little or no change. The Impact

of Events Scale suggested moderate improvement in avoidant symptoms
(3.25 to 2.25) but a worsening of intrusive symptoms at posttherapy (3.14
to 3.71) and follow-up (4.14). On the Experience of Stress Scale the patient
reported a 20 percent improvement, the therapist a 5 percent improvement,
and the independent evaluator a 15 percent improvement; all agreed that
Mrs. D made only a very modest adjustment to the trauma of her husband's death. Mrs. D nevertheless rated herself as being very satisfied
(rating of 4) with her treatment at follow-up, likely reflecting either a
compliance with what she believed was expected or an inhibition about
expressing negative feelings about the results of her therapy.

The most and least descriptive Q-items of the therapy process with
Mrs. D are presented in table 2.2. Mrs. D felt very needy, frequently
talking of her wish to be close to, or intimate with, someone (Q 33), and
she expressed great sadness (Q 94) and anger (Q 84). She had no difficulty
beginning the hours (Q 25, r), was able to assume responsibility for what
was talked about (Q 15, r), understood the therapist (Q 5, r), felt understood by her in return (Q 14, r), and was close to her affective experience,
often expressing deeply felt emotion (Q 56, r). The therapist was neither
condescending nor patronizing (Q 51, r), and judges found little evidence
that her own emotional conflicts intruded inappropriately (Q 24, r); the
absence of silences (Q 12, r) suggests a fluid dialogue. The therapist
emphasized the patient's feelings (Q 81), and was herself emotionally
responsive (Q 9, r). Her interventions were primarily directed at promoting
insight (Q 89, r) through pointing out Mrs. D's defensive maneuvers (Q
36), interpreting warded-off ideas and feelings (Q 67), and identifying
recurrent patterns in the patient's experience or behavior (Q 62). The
therapist was also rated as having a very accurate perception of the
patient's experience in the therapy relationship (Q 28). Consistent with the
hypotheses we derived from the results of larger sample from which Mrs.
D's case was selected, this approach was evidently of little help to Mrs. D.
It seems that as a consequence of her initial high level of disturbance, Mrs.
D was not able to benefit from an approach that had as its primary focus
the affective responses and personal meanings associated with her traumatic loss; indeed, the intervention strategy pursued by the therapist may
actually have contributed to the high degree of troublesome affect that the
patient experienced during treatment hours (Q 26).

The treatment process is further illustrated by those Q-items that
demonstrated the greatest degree of movement across time. Figures 2.2
through 2.4 display graphs for Q-items that demonstrated large shifts over
the course of Mrs. D's treatment. Although many Q-items in this case met
the criteria of shifting more than two standard deviations in mean ratings
across adjacent hours (that is, hours 1 and 5, 5 and 8, or 8 and 12), for
reasons of space only representative items are displayed. At the beginning

TABLE 2.2 *Least and Most Descriptive Q-Items for Patient D*

Least Descriptive Q-Items		Most Descriptive Q-Items	
Item	Mean	Item	Mean
9 Therapist is distant, aloof (vs. responsive and affectively involved).	1.8	81 Therapist emphasizes patient feelings in order to help him or her experience them more deeply.	8.0
15 Patient does not initiate topics; is passive.	1.8	33 Patient talks of feelings about being close to or needing someone.	7.7
5 Patient has difficulty understanding the therapist's comments.	2.1	94 Patient feels sad or depressed.	7.7
12 Silences occur during the hour.	2.4	67 Therapist interprets warded-off or unconscious wishes, feelings, or ideas.	7.5
89 Therapist acts to strengthen defenses (vs. stimulate insight).	2.4	36 Therapist points out the patient's use of defensive maneuvers.	7.3
51 Therapist condescends to or patronizes the patient.	2.7	26 Patient experiences discomforting or troublesome affect.	7.2
25 Patient has difficulty beginning the hour.	2.8	62 Therapist identifies a recurrent theme in the patient's experience or conduct.	7.2
14 Patient does not feel understood by therapist.	2.9	75 Termination of therapy is discussed.	6.9
24 Therapist's own emotional conflicts intrude into the relationship.	3.3	28 Therapist accurately perceives the therapeutic process.	6.8
56 Patient discusses experiences as if distant from his or her feelings.	2.8	84 Patient expresses angry or aggressive feelings.	6.8

of treatment, the therapist assumed a nonjudgmental, supportive stance (figure 2.2, Q 18 and Q 45), and in this early phase of the therapy, Mrs. D felt understood by her therapist (figure 2.3, Q 14). In the middle sessions, however, the therapist increasingly made interpretations about the therapy relationship, the transference, and termination (figure 2.3, Q 98, Q 100, and Q 75). Mrs. D's reaction to this was to feel less understood (figure 2.3, Q 14), and to withdraw emotionally (figure 2.4, Q 26). The termination seems to have provoked a rejecting and intensely ambivalent response from Mrs. D (figure 2.4, Q 39, Q 49, and Q 42) and led to a difficult exchange in the final session (Q 47).

During the termination session, the therapist was rated by our judges as much less accurate in her perception of the patient's emotional state and the nature of her interaction with the patient than earlier in the treatment (figure 2.2, Q 28). Even though the therapist, perhaps hoping to salvage a problematic termination, once again attempted to be more approving and supportive of the patient (figure 2.2, Q 45), the patient was entrenched in a defensive position and was not receptive. The therapist, at the last moment, was unable to help Mrs. D seal over the conflicts and affective reactions that likely were heightened in the treatment, resulting in a slight worsening of her symptoms from pre- to posttherapy. It is possible that Mrs. D, who suffered from a high degree of disturbance relative to the larger study sample, might have benefited from an approach that emphasized less the interpretation of defenses, warded-off feelings, and transference reactions, and more an intervention pointed away from conflicts and toward a reality-oriented construction of her problems (Jones, Cumming, and Horowitz 1988). She might also have fared better in an extended treatment; but in the brief therapy format, conflicts and disturbing emotions were apparently intensified without sufficient time to achieve resolution.

Concluding Notes

Correlational studies of single cases, such as those of Ms. A and Mrs. D conducted by means of the Psychotherapy Process Q-set cannot, in principle, determine causal relationships on the effects of treatments (Barlow and Hersen 1984). It always remains possible that an undetected variable has had a confounding influence. Practically speaking, however, the Q-set provides such a broad range of coverage of variables in the therapy process that it is unlikely that the influence of in-treatment variables will go undetected. The primary goal of the application of the Q-technique to the single case is descriptive. Still, as Chassan (1979) has pointed out, inference about an effect of an intervention is an aspect of every case study. If the data are too meagre to permit a reasonably definitive inference concerning the existence of a treatment effect, they remain at a descriptive level until the accumulation of more data. In the cases of Ms. A and Mrs. D, inferences about the relation between certain qualities of the therapy process and treatment outcome were made in the context of group data which revealed corresponding effects (see Jones, Cumming, and Horowitz 1988). In a sense, these case studies are illustrative, at the level of the individual patient, of treatment effects discovered through the more usual group designs and statistical procedures. It is this kind of two-pronged strategy—that is, identifying treatment effects in group data and then observing them at the level of the individual case—that will further enrich our understanding of the therapy process.

Although the psychotherapy cases presented here are brief treat-

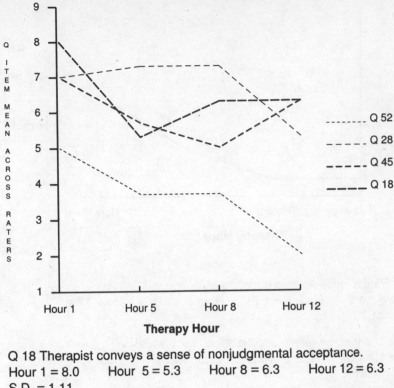

Q 18 Therapist conveys a sense of nonjudgmental acceptance.
Hour 1 = 8.0   Hour 5 = 5.3   Hour 8 = 6.3   Hour 12 = 6.3
S.D. = 1.11

Q 45 Therapist adopts supportive stance.
Hour 1 = 7.0   Hour 5 = 5.7   Hour 8 = 5.0   Hour 12 = 6.3
S.D. = 0.87

Q 28 Therapist accurately perceives the therapeutic process.
Hour 1 = 7.0   Hour 5 = 7.3   Hour 8 = 7.3   Hour 12 = 5.3
S.D. = 0.96

Q 52 Patient relies upon therapist to solve his or her problems.
Hour 1 = 5.0   Hour 5 = 3.7   Hour 8 = 3.7   Hour 12 = 2.0
S.D. = 1.23

FIGURE 2.2
Mrs. D: Changes in process over time.

ments, the method they illustrate is particularly suitable for the intensive investigation of longer-term psychoanalytic treatments. Recognition by trained clinical observers, in a relatively open-ended inquiry, of patterns, consistencies, and covariations using a broad set of elements, such as those represented by the Psychotherapy Process Q-set, allows for the discovery of important phenomena and the relations between them (Greenberg

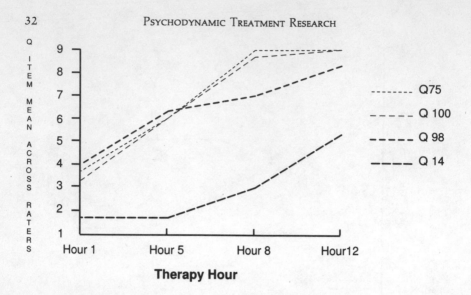

Therapy Hour

Q14 Patient does not feel understood by therapist.
Hour 1 = 1.7   Hour 5 = 1.7   Hour 8 = 3.0   Hour 12 = 5.3
S.D. = 1.73

Q 98 The therapy relationship is a focus of discussion.
Hour 1 = 4.0   Hour 5 = 6.3   Hour 8 = 7.0   Hour 12 = 8.3
S.D. = 1.81

Q 100 Therapist draws connections between therapeutic relationship and other relationships.
Hour 1 = 3.3   Hour 5 = 6.0   Hour 8 = 8.7   Hour 12 = 9.0
S.D. = 2.64

Q 75 Termination of therapy is discussed.
Hour 1 = 3.7   Hour 5 = 6.0   Hour 8 = 9.0   Hour 12 = 9.0
S.D. = 2.59

FIGURE 2.3
Mrs. D: Focus on transference.

1986). Since the Q-items are closely bound not to theoretical concepts but rather to thinking about the nature of the therapy process, the influence of observers' theoretical predilections on their descriptions of process is subdued within the flexible but stabilizing framework provided by the Q-set. The PQS allows the richness of clinical observation to be transformed into objective, quantifiable dimensions. It can capture the uniqueness of the individual case and permit comparisons among observers of the same case, as well as comparisons across cases. As a research method, it has special usefulness in the study of the individual case. Only through the systematic

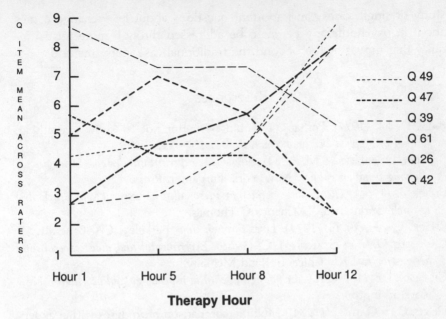

Therapy Hour

Q 42 Patient rejects (vs. accepts) therapist's comments and observations.
Hour 1 = 2.7   Hour 5 = 4.7   Hour 8 = 5.7   Hour 12 = 8.0
S.D. = 2.22

Q 26 Patient experiences discomforting or troublesome (painful) affect.
Hour 1 = 8.7   Hour 5 = 7.3   Hour 8 = 7.3   Hour 12 = 5.3
S.D. = 1.37

Q 61 Patient feels shy and embarrassed (vs. unselfconscious and assured).
Hour 1 = 5.0   Hour 5 = 7.0   Hour 8 = 5.7   Hour 12 = 2.3
S.D. = 1.96

Q 39 There is a competitive quality to the relationship.
Hour 1 = 2.7   Hour 5 = 3.0   Hour 8 = 4.7   Hour 12 = 8.0
S.D. = 2.44

Q 47 When the interaction with the patient is difficult, the therapist
accommodates in an effort to improve relations.
Hour 1 = 5.7   Hour 5 = 4.3   Hour 8 = 4.3   Hour 12 = 2.3
S.D. = 1.37

Q 49 The patient experiences ambivalent or conflicted feelings about the
therapist.
Hour 1 = 4.3   Hour 5 = 4.7   Hour 8 = 4.7   Hour 12 = 8.7
S.D. = 2.06

FIGURE 2.4
Mrs. D: Some features of termination.

study of single cases can important questions about how change comes about in psychotherapy begin to be addressed through more formal inquiry that moves a step beyond the traditional case study method.

References

BAER, D. M. (1977). Perhaps it would be better not to know everything. *Journal of Applied Behavior Analysis, 10,* 167–172.

BARLOW, D., & HERSEN, M. (1984). *Single case experimental designs: Strategies for studying behavior change.* New York: Pergamon Press.

BLOCK, J. (1961). *The Q-sort method in personality assessment and psychiatric research.* Springfield, IL: Charles C Thomas.

BLOCK, J., & HAAN, N. (1971). *Lives through time.* Berkeley, CA: Bancroft.

CAMPBELL, D. T., & STANLEY, J. C. (1966). *Experimental and quasi-experimental designs for research.* Chicago: Rand McNally.

CHASSAN, J. B. (1979). *Research design in clinical psychology and psychiatry.* New York: Irvington.

DAVIS, C., & GAITO, J. (1984). Multiple comparison procedures within experimental research. *Canadian Psychologist, 25*(1), 1–13.

DEROGATIS, L., & MELISARATOS, N. (1983). The Brief Symptom Inventory: An introductory report. *Psychological Medicine, 13,* 595–605.

FIEDLER, F. E. (1951). A method of objective quantification of certain countertransference attitudes. *Journal of Clinical Psychology, 7,* 101–107.

GREENBERG, L. S. (1986). Research strategies. In L. S. Greenberg & W. M. Pinsof (Eds.), *The psychotherapeutic process: A research handbook* (pp. 707–734). New York: Guilford Press.

GRÜNBAUM, A. (1984). *The foundations of psychoanalysis.* Berkeley: University of California Press.

HOLT, R. (1978). *Methods in clinical psychology:* Vol. 2. *Prediction and research.* New York: Plenum Press.

HOROWITZ, M. J., MARMAR, C., KRUPNICK, J., WILNER, N., KALTREIDER, N., & WALLERSTEIN, R. (1984). *Personality styles and brief psychotherapy.* New York: Basic Books.

HOROWITZ, M. J., WILNER, N., & ALVAREZ, W. (1979). Impact of Events Scale: A measure of subjective stress. *Psychosomatic Medicine, 41*(3), 209–218.

JACOBSON, N., & TRUAX, P. (1991). Clinical significance: A statistical approach to defining meaningful change in psychotherapy research. *Journal of Consulting and Clinical Psychology, 59,* 12–19.

JONES, E. E. (1985). *Manual for the Psychotherapy Process Q-Set.* Unpublished manuscript, University of California, Berkeley.

JONES, E. E., CUMMING, J. D., & HOROWITZ, M. J. (1988). Another look at the nonspecific hypothesis of therapeutic effectiveness. *Journal of Consulting and Clinical Psychology, 56*(1), 48–55.

JONES, E. E., GHANNAM, J., NIGG, J. T., & DYER, J. P. (1993). A paradigm for single case research: The time-series study of a long-term psychotherapy for depression. *Journal of Consulting and Clinical Psychology, 31*(3), 381–394.

JONES, E. E., HALL, S., & PARKE, L. (1991). The process of change: The Berkeley Psychotherapy Research Group. In L. E. Beutler & M. Crago (Eds.), *Psychotherapy research: An international review of programmatic studies* (pp. 98–106). Washington, DC: American Psychological Association.

JONES, E. E., PARKE, L. A., & PULOS, S. M. (1992). How therapy is conducted in the private consulting room: A multivariate description of brief dynamic treatments. *Psychotherapy Research, 2*, 16–30.

JONES, E. E., & PULOS, S. M. (1993). Comparing the process in psychodynamic and cognitive-behavioral therapies. *Journal of Consulting and Clinical Psychology, 61*(2), 306–316.

JONES, E. E., & WINDHOLZ, M. (1990). The psychoanalytic case study: Toward a method for systematic inquiry. *Journal of the American Psychoanalytic Association, 38*, 985–1009.

KAZDIN, A. E. (1981). Drawing valid inferences from case studies. *Journal of Consulting and Clinical Psychology, 49*, 183–192.

KAZDIN, A. E. (1982). *Single case research designs.* New York: Oxford University Press.

KAZDIN, A. E. (1984). Statistical analyses for single-case experimental designs. In D. Barlow & M. Hersen (Eds.), *Single case experimental designs* (pp. 285–324). New York: Pergamon Press.

KRATCHOWILL, T. R. (ED.). (1978). *Single subject research.* New York: Academic Press.

MALAN, D. H. (1976). *The frontier of brief psychotherapy.* New York: Plenum Press.

MENDELSOHN, G. (1979). The psychological consequences of cancer: A study of adaptation to somatic illness. *Cahiers d'anthropologie, 4*, 53–92.

OVERALL, J., & GORHAM, D. (1962). The Brief Psychiatric Rating Scale. *Psychological Reports, 10*, 799–812.

PULOS, S., & JONES, E. E. (1987). *A study of the differential validity of the Psychotherapy Process Q-Sort.* Paper presented at the annual meeting of the Western Psychological Association, San Diego, CA.

RAWN, M. L. (1958). An experimental study of transference and resistance phenomena in psychoanalytically oriented psychotherapy. *Journal of Clinical Psychology, 14*, 418–425.

ROGERS, C., & DYMOND, L. (EDS.). (1954). *Psychotherapy and personality change.* Chicago: University of Chicago Press.

RUNYAN, W. M. (1984). *Life histories and psychobiography: Explorations in theory and method.* New York: Oxford University Press.

SPENCE, D. P. (1982). *Narrative truth and historical truth: Meaning and interpretation in psychoanalysis.* New York: Norton.

STEPHENSON, W. (1953). *The study of behavior: Q-technique and its methodology.* Chicago: University of Chicago Press.

STRUPP, H., & BERGIN, A. (1969). Some empirical and conceptual bases for coordinated research in psychotherapy. *International Journal of Psychiatry, 7,* 18–90.

WALLERSTEIN, R. (1986). Psychoanalysis as a science: A response to new challenges. *Psychoanalytic Quarterly, 55,* 414–451.

WEISS, D., WILNER, N., & HOROWITZ, M. (1984). The Stress Response Rating Scale: A clinician's measure for rating the response to serious life events. *British Journal of Clinical Psychology, 23,* 202–215.

CHAPTER 3

Traditional Case Studies and Prescriptions for Improving Them

DONALD P. SPENCE

WHEN FREUD ENDED HIS WORK WITH DORA, he told a friend that he had just finished writing an account so exciting that coming out from under its spell, he felt "short of a drug" (that is, was suffering from withdrawal symptoms; see Klein and Tribich 1982, 14). To this day, the traditional case report remains our most compelling means of communicating clinical findings, and the excitement attached to both reading and writing case histories has lost none of its appeal. Freud's early clinical discussions continue to be studied and restudied, and the form that he developed so well—the classical narrative report—continues to influence the way we present our clinical discoveries. But as this tradition is looked at from a more detached perspective, we begin to find flaws in the method and can identify significant changes in the way it has been practiced over time.

The case method has been described as the "only possible way of obtaining the granite blocks of data on which to build a science of human nature" (Murray 1955); Freud's cases, in particular, have been praised as "rare works of art and a record of the human mind in one of its most unparalleled works of scientific discovery" (Kanzer and Glenn 1980; both citations appear in Runyan 1982). But somewhat more negative views of the case study genre have appeared from time to time and are beginning to attract more attention. In this chapter, we will identify the more telling weaknesses of the genre and discuss how these faults interfere with its evidential role and with the development of viable theory. We will conclude with a summary of possible improvements.[1]

---

[1]This critique is leveled at the clinical case reports that comprise so much of the psychoanalytic literature. It does not apply to the systematic approaches to recording clinical data that are included in the other chapters of this book.

Undesirable Features of the
Traditional Method

When we examine the typical case study in a psychoanalytic journal, we are impressed, first of all, by what might be called its closed texture. Barring a handful of well-publicized exceptions (such as the two analyses of Mr. Z in Kohut 1979), the typical case report tells a single story with heavy reliance on anecdote and narrative persuasion, and with a preference for what might be called singular explanation. The anecdotal nature of the typical case report reveals only the highlights of the clinical encounter, with few details; as a result, anyone who wants to assess whether a particular interpretation might have been formed differently or to decide whether a particular formulation could have been improved will have to look elsewhere. But there is nowhere else to look. The story being told tends to have only one ending and no loose ends. Whereas the average archival report is open to many interpretations (see White 1978), with some building on one set of facts and some building on another, a narrative (and its cousin, the average case study) functions best when all the evidence has been accounted for and no other explanation is possible. When studying a historical archive, we usually come away with more questions than answers; when studying a case report, we come away with our minds made up. In the more successful cases, the facts, patiently gathered and persuasively (artfully?) arranged, build up a pattern that is compelling and necessary; the facts lead directly to a solution, and no other resolution seems likely.

Second, it should be noted that the facts within the typical case report are almost always seen within a positivistic frame. The observer/therapist is separated from the object/patient being studied; facts are as concrete and unambiguous as the patient's height and weight, and a good deal less ambiguous than the patient's heartsounds or the quality of his resting pulse. Facts in the case study are knowable pieces of reality "out there," distinct in size and shape, guiding us inevitably in one direction or the other. While the effect of countertransference on our judgments of the clinical situation is coming to be more widely recognized, that consideration has not, to date, materially affected the nature of the case report. The clinical reality is ambiguous and multiply determined; yet the facts in the usual clinical account are considered signposts or barometer readings which lead us unerringly to the solution. We are gradually coming to learn that many of these "facts" are created by us; that they never exist until we choose to see or hear the clinical encounter in a particular way; and that without the perspective of the treating therapist, they can easily be interpreted differently, or might even disappear.

A third feature of the case study genre which deserves critical attention is the tradition of argument by authority. The evidence is never so complete that we, as readers, can draw our own conclusions about the clinical happenings; therefore, we must defer to the views of the author. But this tradition seriously interferes with the possibility for friendly disagreement; it tends to support the tradition of privileged withholding (about which we will have more to say in a moment) and takes a position that differs in significant ways from the prevailing scientific zeitgeist. Argument by authority stands in the way of open disagreement and denies us the benefits, zealously guarded since the Renaissance, of an adversarial, critical, and dialectical tradition of investigation. We now see that the closed texture of the case report effectively cuts off disagreement because only the author has access to all the facts; thus the author's report is always privileged. But we also know that the first reading of a clinical happening is rarely the last and that certain kinds of understanding emerge only from extended discussion, open disagreement, and spirited challenges to this or that assumption. Thus the nature of the case study, in its usual form, stands in the way of understanding through dialogue and violates our clinical experience, which has sensitized us to the ways in which understanding changes over time.

The problem of privileged withholding has two faces. First, we are sensitive to the need to protect the private life of the patient and we disguise pertinent details in an effort to carry out this aim. Second, and somewhat less in our awareness as authors, is a need to protect ourselves. In carrying out both kinds of disguise, we would seem to be breaking a central clinical rule and going against years of acquired clinical experience. Freud taught us the lesson early in his practice: "I once treated a high official who was bound by his oath of office not to communicate certain things because they were state secrets, and the analysis came to grief as a consequence of this restriction." The reason is clear. "It is very remarkable how the whole task becomes impossible if a reservation is allowed at any single place. But we have only to reflect what would happen if the right of asylum existed at any one point in a town; how long would it be before all the riffraff of the town had collected there?" (Freud [1913] 1958, 136 *n*).

The permission to tell less than the full story (which Freud granted once and, we assume, never again) is extended all the time to authors of clinical cases—that is, to all publishing analysts. By giving the author of a case report the right to tell less than the complete story, we break rules for ourselves which we would never break for our patients. What is more, we exclude from the case report the very details we need to examine in depth and from which we have the most to learn.

Implications of the Traditional
Method for Theory

Because the case study is our primary means of reporting clinical happenings, the defects of the case study genre have important implications for the progress of psychoanalysis as a science. If the case study tends to be anecdotal, selective, consciously and unconsciously self-serving, and biased toward a singular solution, it can be seen that our literature is seriously incomplete. Not only are we being continuously deprived of salient facts, but the facts reported and the interpretations placed on these facts tend to conform to the prevailing zeitgeist because the case study genre tends to inflate the status of prevailing theory. This state of affairs comes about because of the tendency for the case report to highlight the clinical happenings that seem to mesh with received theory and to underplay, or exclude entirely, happenings that cannot be explained, that go against theoretical understanding, or that result in bad therapeutic outcomes. It is well known that reports of suddenly terminated or unsuccessful analyses are significantly hard to find.

The propaganda value of what might be called the average expectable case—the case that tends to confirm received theory—is bolstered by what Campbell and Stanley have called the "error of misplaced precision" (1966, 6). The sheer accumulation of detail—the verbatim report of a critical dream or the precise wording of an interpretation—would seem to enhance significantly the scientific status of the case report. But verbatim details do not necessarily outweigh crucial deletions; the reader may know that the whole truth is not being told, but there is no way of knowing where verbatim reporting stops and selective or disguised reporting begins.

In similar fashion, a series of apparent confirmations may seem to support a particular piece of theory. In actuality, however, the number of reports means very little. In the first place, it is always possible for the diligent researcher to find positive findings. In a discussion of the "corrupting effects of the hypothesis-testing method," McGuire makes the following observation:

> It can be taken for granted that some set of circumstances can be found to confirm *any* expressible relationship, provided that the researcher has sufficient stubbornness, stage management skills, resources, and stamina sooner or later to find or construct a situational context in which the prediced relationship reliably emerges. (McGuire 1983, 15–16; italics added)

To guard against this danger, Greenwald et al. (1986) have argued for an approach that concentrates on the *conditions* under which the phenomena of interest will appear. To avoid the danger of collecting further examples and corrupting positive findings by mere perseverance, they encourage the researcher to study the *pattern* of significant behavior and to understand how a particular happening may emerge in the context of observation.

In the second place, the number of apparent confirmations conveys no useful information if we have no knowledge of the number of failures of confirmation or of the number of case studies not accepted for publication. If, for the sake of argument, we assume that three thousand analysts are currently practicing in the United States and that each is treating an average of five cases, then it follows that a series of five, ten, or even twenty reports that all confirm, for example, the relation between early child abuse and later dissociation would not seem very telling; these numbers represent only .03, .06, and .12 percent of the 15,000 possible cases (3,000 × 5).

In the third place, the significance of the single case tends to be inflated because we read it with a mixture of clinical and aesthetic interest; if the story is well told and the details persuasively presented, we score it high for narrative appeal—a judgment that may be mistaken for clinical importance. But a moment's reflection will show that the latter quality has no relation to the former.

Memory as the Primary Archive

From the very beginning, clinical findings have been stored primarily as memories in the minds of practicing analysts. Michels describes our current knowledge as "almost totally based on the personal experiences and impressions of talented practitioners" (1988, 175). Arlow, in a similar vein, calls attention to the fact that "we are approaching a postapostolic era in psychoanalytic history. . . . Our confidence in our work will have to rely not on the memories of bygone heroes," but on more systematically gathered observational data (1982, 18).

Coded as memories of varying degrees of recency and freshness in a heterogeneous set of minds, our common store of knowledge is anything but a shared source of information. On the contrary, it constitutes a shifting and unreliable data base which is not open to public inspection or consensual validation. Because it is largely hidden, it is not available for the confirmation or disconfirmation of theoretical propositions. And by virtue of its largely memorial nature, the evidence is particularly vulnerable to the influence of theory.

Because there is no public data base, there has taken place over time, a gradual decoupling of theory from evidence. Deprived of a common set of facts that might represent the gist of our collective wisdom, theory is free to tell whatever story it chooses. Deprived of the normal checks and balances of the average field of investigation with its agreed-upon corpus of findings, psychoanalytic theory is free to fill the role of shared fantasy. Under the guise of theory, any number of scenarios can be imagined, published, and circulated, and the fate of these constructions will depend more on the zeitgeist than on the (unseen) data.

Because of the absence of a public record, the shared experience of practicing analysts is vulnerable to two kinds of influence: (1) the tendency to misremember clinical experience in a way that supports received theory and (2) the tendency to associate memories in a way that agrees with received theory (that is, to derive an illusory correlation).

For a controlled demonstration of the way in which popular theory can influence memory, we can go back to a landmark experiment by Robbins (1963) which concerned the way in which early child-rearing practices are misremembered by parents only a few years after the fact. Retrospective reports of standard child-rearing events were compared with clinic records, and significant distortions were found in the recall of such items as (a) when the infant stopped using the bottle; (b) when bowel training was begun; (c) when bladder training was begun; and (d) when the 2 A.M. feeding was stopped. The errors, particularly those made by the mothers, tended to follow the advice of Benjamin Spock as presented in his best-selling book on child rearing *(Baby and Child Care).* The parallel between the expert's advice and the prevailing direction of distortion strongly suggests that the mothers' memories were influenced by a highly visible theory.

The phenomenon of illusory correlation was first described by Chapman and Chapman (1969). They presented a group of naive judges with a set of figure drawings, each accompanied by several diagnostic statements. The set was carefully designed so that there was no relation between the content of the drawing and the accompanying statements. A face with shifty eyes, for example, might carry the statement, "He is concerned about making mistakes," and a face with an open mouth might be accompanied by the sentence, "He suspects that his enemies are out to trick him." Despite the lack of expected correlation, the judges markedly overestimated the co-occurrence of drawings and related statements; in the example just given, they would remember the face with shifty eyes as being accompanied by the sentence describing suspicion of enemies. It will also be noticed that the tendency to "discover" a connection that was not present in fact made it impossible for the judges to form a clear picture of the actual data set.

Recommendations for Improvement

Can the case study be improved? Or should we throw it out and start over? Runyan makes the useful observation that "the case study is not a particular method of collecting information . . . but is rather a form for organizing and presenting information about a specific person and his or her circumstances, which may draw upon a variety of specific techniques of data collection" (1982, 443—44). In other words, perhaps we can fill the old bottles with new wine. He suggests the following criterion: "Tell the story in such a way that the omitted information makes little or no difference in understanding the main structure of the events and arguments in question." More generally, he argues that the case study "offers a theory about a person's behavior in a particular circumstance [or set of circumstances], and this theory needs to be tested by collecting evidence and formulating relevant arguments" (p. 444).

This argument suggests criteria for both inclusion and exclusion. Arguments must be supported by evidence; the more significant the argument, the greater the needed weight of the evidence. And although not everything about the case need be included (a condition true of all branches of science), keep in mind what might be called the principle of no-fault exclusion: what is omitted should make "little or no difference in understanding."

With respect to what should be included, it seems clear that context matters more than instantiation. We have seen that repeated mention of positive instances does nothing to strengthen support of the relevant theory; the examples only take up space. Much more important would be a clear account of the conditions under which a positive instance comes into being; these conditions include not only the pertinent facts of the case, but also the state of the transference and all of the other surrounding factors that allowed this clinical happening to appear at a particular moment, and that allowed the therapist to become aware of its existence. In other words, any positive instance should be accompanied by an account of the interpersonal climate that surrounded the happening.

An awareness of what might be called the Robbins effect—the tendency to remember what seems to fit with established theory—and an awareness of the phenomenon of illusory correlations should make clinicians question any account that agrees with standard theory but is supported by neither verbatim recording nor near-verbatim process notes. Case studies that are lacking this kind of evidential support are little better than hearsay because of the tendency for memory to conform to authority and to correlate observations in a way that is predicted by theory. Even with the best intentions, the clinician who relies on memory alone to supply the data for a case report is almost certainly going to remember the case in a way that supports received theory, and will tend to forget the clinical happening that violates expectation. It is more than a little ironic that the one profession that knows in such detail the ways in which memory can be deceived should be the one that relies so heavily on unaided recall in its clinical reports.

We begin to see that the principle of no-fault exclusion—omitting nothing that makes a difference—can now be enlarged to include evidence that some form of the Robbins effect is not taking place. Presented with an observation that appears to confirm established theory, the reader should be in a position to evaluate the grounds for this happy finding. If no veridical evidence is available, there is every reason to suspect the conclusion.

The principle of no-fault exclusion also relates to the general issue of disguising clinical material for the purpose of protecting confidentiality. It goes without saying that a minimum of disguise is desirable; any alteration, no matter how small, will inevitably carry a price. Early in his practice, Freud warned, in the following words, of the danger of making *any* change: "I consider it a wrong practice, however excellent the motive may be, to alter any detail in the presentation of a case. One can never tell what aspect of a case may be picked out by a reader of independent judgment, and one runs the risk of leading him astray" (Freud [1915] 1957, 263).

If disguise is thought necessary, its boundaries must be clearly specified in an appropriate cautionary statement that makes it clear at what points the data have been changed. As authors become aware of the dangers of undocumented omission and alteration, they may become challenged to find other ways to protect the patient's identity. For example, as interest turns to the more technical questions of psychoanalytic process and interpretive cause and effect, then questions of who and where and when often disappear. As issues of strategy and tactics become more clearly defined, and as our vocabulary becomes more precise, we may find ways to present complicated clinical happenings in a way that reveals nothing about the identity of the patient. (Consider, in this connection, the way in which open-heart surgery can be described without revealing the age, sex, or race of the patient.)

Finally, the principle of no-fault exclusion has a bearing on the precise presentation of the therapeutic dialogue. In arriving at an opinion about the meaning of a particular interchange, we rarely ask detailed questions about exactly what was said by either patient or analyst; instead we rely on a secondhand description of the happening.

We view ourselves as participant-observer, yet rarely is clinical material reported in which we are told what the analyst does or does not say—that is, which conveys how indeed the analyst participates. And rarely are we offered the data of the patient's shifting affective states by which we can ascertain the moment-to-moment response. In thus failing to attune . . . to the contribution of the analyst, *as it is perceived,* and to the verbal and nonverbal cues which may convey its ensuing impact, a major component of the patient's psychic reality— and thereby of his or her history—goes unattended. (Schwaber 1986, 912)

A Suggested Format for Clinical Examples

Detailed discussions of the problem of clinical reporting have been the focus of repeated meetings of the Committee on Scientific Activities of the American Psychoanalytic Association, and the committee's final report (Klumpner and Frank 1991) presents a number of recommendations which deserve careful consideration by all prospective authors.

The committee describes an especially feasible model for improving the scientific status of clinical reports. In one convention of the suggested format, the consistent use of two speakers—patient and analyst—is proposed; the analyst's statements are always presented in capital letters. The speakers are not otherwise named (by *T* and *P*, for example). This typographic convention not only highlights the contrast between speakers, but also facilitates a computer search of the transcripts if that ever becomes necessary or desirable.

A second convention suggests that each utterance be classified in one of three categories: (1) *noncommunicated* thoughts, nonverbal behavior, and adventitious events, to be marked by parentheses; (2) *approximate* wording of spoken discourse, to be presented without quotation marks; and (3) *exact* wording of spoken discourse, marked by quotation marks. Time is indicated on the vertical axis, with the speakers appearing in sequence.

A third convention suggests the use of multiple columns to allow the analyst or outside observer to enter comments on the original material. By means of such a format, the comments themselves become part of the permanent record. If the analyst, for example, had later second thoughts about a section of comments made at the time, he or she could add these in the second column (in parenthesis, to indicate that the thoughts were not spoken). If the analyst had thoughts about an utterance at the time, he or she would write them in the first column (again in parenthesis). The second column could also be used by outside readers who wished to add their observations to the record. The third column could be used by the treating analyst to respond to the comments of others in the second column. He or she might wish to add further unspoken thoughts to clarify an interchange, to supply the background for an interpretation, or otherwise to explain the original clinical happening.

It can be seen that vigorously contested specimens might acquire a family of commentaries over time, just as landmark cases in the law are repeatedly cited in relevant decisions. A review of these reactions would help to deepen our understanding of the original incident. As it becomes clear that outside observers can frequently see the central issues more clearly than the treating analyst, an increasing number of clinicians may be tempted to publish their detailed specimens in the hope of benefiting from this kind of multiple supervision. As new voices join the conversation, new themes emerge from the clinical records, and through the interplay between interpretations, we gain an ever-widening understanding of the original incident.

Two examples of this new format are offered here. The first contains original dialogue and subsequent commentary by the analyst; the second contains original dialogue and reflections by two outside commentators. Capitalization, quotation marks, and parentheses follow the guidelines. In both examples, the patient speaks first. Data for the first specimen are taken from Schwaber 1986; where her original paper first presented the clinical happening and then added her reflections, we have rearranged and integrated the two sets of material to conform to the suggested format and to bring out the way in which utterance corresponds to reflection (table 3.1).

The second example is taken from Dewald (1972) and two subsequent commentaries (table 3.2). After this specimen has appeared in print, the analyst (Paul Dewald)—and possibly the patient—might choose to respond to particular parts of the specimen, clarifying what was meant and thus further deepening our understanding of the incident. Each of these commentaries would be placed in its own column. One can easily understand how a target specimen can quickly generate a family of commentaries, each providing a particular context for interpretation. (The interested reader can find an additional illustration of the committee guidelines, together with the guiding rationale, in Klumpner and Frank 1991, 548–50.)

A careful reading of table 3.2 makes clear the importance of no-fault exclusion. If the target interchange is incomplete, we have lost forever the chance to use what Isakower (1957) has called our "analyzing instrument" as a way of learning the most from the clinical material. If the interchange is incomplete, we have given its author the right to decide what is important and what is not, and as Freud has taught us, "It is very remarkable how the whole task becomes impossible if a reservation is allowed at any single place" ([1915] 1957, 263). But if the target interchange can be presented verbatim, we have not only the best opportunity to understand the clinical happening but are in a position to stimulate outside commentaries which can only add to our cumulative understanding.

Paying serious attention to the details of the particular case makes psychoanalysis a close cousin of the law, and we might extend the usefulness of the case study format by studying the history and process of legal reasoning. Both psychoanalysis and the law depend on procedures that are rule-governed but not rule-bound (see Spence 1987), and both are influenced as much by particular circumstances as by an abstract set of principles. We have much to learn from the law's overarching respect for the public record and the principle that no refuge is taken in private testimony, privileged evidence, or argument by authority. The law could

TABLE 3.1 *Dialogue and Analyst's Commentary*

Patient and Analyst (Schwaber)	Commentary (Schwaber)
Asking repeated questions, rather forcefully demanding to know what I thought about certain life decisions.	
THERE SEEMS A REAL PRESSURE TO GET AN ANSWER?	(Calling the affect to his attention.)
"I felt more isolated this weekend, so I have to recontact with you."	(He makes this connection because he stops to reflect on his affective state. *Now* he sees why he is seeking dialogue with me.)
"I'm sure it doesn't relate to your leaving. . . . Don't get your hopes up."	
"HOPES? WHAT DO YOU MEAN, 'HOPES'?"	(I raised this question because it reflected a view of me that I was seeking to clarify, *not to challenge*.)
"So you'd be able to give me an explanation to be satisfied . . . so you'd have an explanation . . ."	(Was he just fending me off with a kind of sarcasm or warding off his own feelings with an interruption? Maybe so, but still he was saying something about how he was "seeing" me. I had, on other occasions, noted connections between his affective state and separations—perhaps he perceived something in my manner of making these links which he felt as coming more from me than from him.)
"YOU MEAN IT SEEMS THAT MY MOTIVES FOR FINDING AN EXPLANATION MIGHT, IN SOME WAY, TO MEET MY OWN NEEDS . . ."	(His tone shifted after that, seeming to be less pressured. The change in his tone was a response to my intervention. It seemed that something felt familiar about the view of me which has just been elucidated. This recognition brought to mind other occasions—as with a former therapist and with his mother—in which he noted his argumentative tendency in the context of such a perception: namely, that the person's unacknowledged motives toward him have a self-interested base. So he must be wary.)

SOURCE: Adapted from Schwaber 1986, 925–26.

also teach us a respect for the specifics; the best opinions and the most commanding interpretations are always tempered by the relevant detail.

Once we decide to look seriously at our clinical experience, we will find ways of preserving and cataloging our case material as a form of original data (and not a series of illustrative examples). Once we understand the wisdom contained in the unexpected surprise, we will see the virtue of reporting a verbatim extract. Once we see the archival value of

TABLE 3.2 *Dialogue and Two Commentaries*

Patient and Analyst (Dewald)	Commentary (Levenson)	Commentary (Spence)
In the dream, we were in the playpen and it was in Evanston and all of us girls were there. We were dressed up kind of frilly and there were people looking in on us, and the men were in tuxedos. I was lying on the floor and I had no pants on and I kept wondering what the men would think. Before this, when I used to dream that I'm naked, I'd feel embarrassed because I was missing a penis, and I would want to run and hide away. I wasn't last night, although I was unsure, but I thought I wanted to take the chance.		
WHAT COMES TO MIND ABOUT THIS FEELING THAT I MIGHT ACCEPT YOU AS FEMININE AND SOFT AND LOVING?	(Now, in anybody's book, that is a directing query! She is clearly told which part of the dream to pick up.)	
That's just the way you are. You are capable of loving me and of not caring what I look like, and for you it wouldn't make any difference about the—(60-second silence).		
YOU CUT SOMETHING SHORT THERE.		
The surface things.		(Was that what the patient meant? Other possibilities come to mind—frilly clothes or the fact that she was wearing no pants—but Dewald seems bent on one reading of the material, and the thrust of his standard interpretation is anticipated by his comment, "You cut something short there.")
I THINK YOU MEAN THE PRESENCE OR ABSENCE OF A PENIS.		
I'm suddenly getting very nervous and hostile. I had a wonderful feeling until I came but now you are making me feel that I had a penis.	(She gets upset, of course—that's resistance, so he must be right. Why not wonder why the women are little girls in the playpen and the men are grown-up and in tuxedos? Why are the little girls exposed and embarrassed?)	

SOURCES: Dewald 1972, 175; Levenson 1983, 95; Spence 1987, 55.

a cumulative data base, we will find ways of cross-indexing our cases and making our clinical material more available to the interested scholar. Once we see that protecting the patient need not entail distortion, disguise, and anecdotal reporting, we will find ways of making a distinction between material that cannot be published and material (from the same patient) that can be published in full.

From the standpoint of psychoanalytic theory, the usual narrative case report can be seen as a form of resistance which includes an intolerance for ambiguity, a need to get on with the story, and a readiness to leave certain questions unanswered. The closed-textured case report parallels the initial attempt by the patient to tell about his or her life. Both are equally unfaithful to what is being described, and both need further expansion, unpacking, and informed revision to become fully clear.

Telling a Causal Story Systematically

As clinical data are more completely recorded and the principle of no-fault exclusion becomes more widely accepted, it would seem possible to move beyond mere description to the next step: presenting the case study as a causal story. Edelson (1986) reminds us that "Freud links particular causes to particular effects" (p. 92), and it can be seen that the explanation will depend directly on the nature of the evidence. Edelson lists four criteria for telling a causal story: (1) identify the possible cause of an event; (2) specify the temporal relation between cause and effect; (3) give a full description of the theoretical structure and properties of the presumed cause; and (4) give an account of one or more rival explanations, with the aim of showing that the presumed cause better accounts for the data than the other, rival possibilities (see pp. 92–98). Each of these criteria presupposes a near-complete account; one must know as much as the treating analyst to be able to evaluate the explanation.

Each of Edelson's criteria would appear to be enhanced by the principle of no-fault exclusion and by supplemental commentaries. Multiple points of view (as provided in the added commentaries) are particularly useful in suggesting possible causes (criterion 1) and in providing alternative explanations of a clinical happening (criterion 4). Both the near-verbatim specimen and its commentaries deepen our theoretical understanding of the happening (criterion 3). A near-verbatim account, with virtually no omissions, helps us to reconstruct the temporal relation between cause and effect (criterion 2).[2]

[2]In keeping with the principle of no-fault exclusion, it should be obvious that knowledge of the unspoken aspects of the interchange—such as speed, volume, and pressure of

Telling a well-documented causal story can have a permanent impact on theory. As arguments are improved and supported by confirming evidence, conclusions will necessarily carry more weight. Conversely, theory that is not supported by new evidence will tend to fall away. As evidence becomes more detailed and argument more persuasive, case reports will begin to acquire the authority they deserve. By giving readers the chance to evaluate the relevant data, we turn the case report into a replicable experiment by giving each scientist the chance to "inspect the apparatus and try out the shared recipe" (Campbell 1986, 122).

A diverse array of additional empirical formats and systematic approaches for recording and analyzing clinical data in the individual case will be presented in the chapters that follow. As clinicians and researchers become more comfortable with, and more proficient in, their use, and as readers become more enlightened and more actively seize the opportunity to participate in the evaluation of relevant data, traditional (unreliable) case reports can be transformed into a cumulative and public data base. As a permanent archive, they will take the place of fragmentary anecdote and aging memory (and will not be eroded by the loss of the practitioner). As a permanent archive, they will support the systematic study of how ideas and concepts change and how the same words may take on different meanings depending on the surrounding zeitgeist. As a permanent archive, they will—most important of all—bring psychoanalysis closer to the standing of the other sciences.

Summary

Almost a hundred years ago, Abraham Flexner reminded the medical community that their discipline "distrusts general propositions, a priori explanations, grandiose and comforting generalizations. . . . Scientific medicine . . . brushes aside all historic dogma. It gets down to details immediately. . . . To plead in advance a principle couched in pseudo-scientific language . . . is to violate scientific quality" (1910, 157). Somewhat earlier in the report, Flexner observed that the "way to be unscientific is to be partial."

Preservation of detail in the service of impartial reporting—we have kept returning to this principle. Traditional case reports have many of the attractions of a good story, as well as many of the drawbacks. Exciting, evocative, often persuasive, they belong to an ancient (storytelling) tradition that has lost none of its appeal. But as we become more knowledgeable

---

speech; affective resonance; tone of voice; gesticulations; and body movements—by either analyst or patient—can significantly enhance our understanding.

about the functions of narrative, rhetoric, and selective reporting, we begin to find flaws in the method and begin to recognize the growing gap between anecdotal accounts based on largely private evidence and a public data base that is accessible to any interested researcher. As data become more visible and available, they tend to provide a useful check on the unbridled growth of theory; as theory is governed more by evidence, it is no longer free to tell whatever story it chooses.

The alternative method of recording clinical happenings presented here includes fragments of the original patient-analyst dialogue along with comments by the analyst and by outside observers. Each utterance in the fragment is coded separately for exact wording, approximate wording, and uncommunicated thoughts. By making the two sets of comments part of the permanent record, it is possible to multiply perspectives on the meaning of a specific happening and add to our understanding of the original event. As new voices join the debate, new meanings emerge; as these become part of the archive, the development of concepts can be studied more systematically and with an increasing awareness of their historical context.

References

ARLOW, J. A. (1982). Psychoanalytic education: A psychoanalytic perspective. *Annals of Psychoanalysis, 10,* 5–20.

CAMPBELL, D. T. (1986). Science's social system of validity-enhancing collective belief change and the problems of social sciences. In D. W. Fiske & R. A. Shweder (Eds.), *Metatheory in social science.* Chicago: University of Chicago Press.

CAMPBELL, D. T., & STANLEY, J. C. (1966). *Experimental and quasiexperimental designs for research.* New York: Rand McNally.

CHAPMAN, L. J., & CHAPMAN, J. P. (1969). Illusory correlation as an obstacle to the use of valid psychodiagnostic signs. *Journal of Abnormal Psychology, 74,* 271–280.

DEWALD, P. A. (1972). *The psychoanalytic process.* New York: Basic Books.

EDELSON, M. (1986). Causal explanation in science and in psychoanalysis. *Psychoanalytic Study of the Child, 41,* 89–127.

FLEXNER, A. (1910). *Medical education in the United States and Canada.* New York: Carnegie Foundation for the Advancement of Teaching.

FREUD, S. (1913/1958). On beginning the treatment. In J. Strachey (Ed.), *The Standard edition of the complete psychological works of Sigmund Freud* (Vol. 12, pp. 123–144). London: Hogarth Press.

FREUD, S. (1915/1957). A case of paranoia running counter to the psychoanalytic theory of the disease. In J. Strachey (Ed.), *The Standard edition of the complete psychological works of Sigmund Freud* (Vol. 14, pp. 261–272). London: Hogarth Press.

Greenwald, A. G., Pratkanis, A. R., Leippe, M. R., & Baumgardner, M. H. (1986). Under what conditions does theory obstruct research progress? *Psychological Review, 93,* 216–229.

Isakower, O. (1957). Preliminary thoughts on the analyzing instrument. *Journal of Clinical Psychoanalysis, 1,* 184–194.

Kanzer, M., & Glenn, J. (Eds.). (1980). *Freud and his patients.* New York: Jason Aronson.

Klein, M. I., & Tribich, D. (1982). Blame the child. *Sciences, 22,* 14–20.

Klumpner, G. H., & Frank, A. (1991). On methods of reporting clinical material. *Journal of the American Psychoanalytic Association, 39,* 537–551.

Kohut, H. (1979). The two analyses of Mr. Z. *International Journal of Psychoanalysis, 60,* 3–28.

Levenson, E. (1983). *The ambiguity of change.* New York: Basic Books.

McGuire, W. J. (1983). A contextualist theory of knowledge: Its implications for innovation and reform in psychological research. In L. Berkowitz (Ed.), *Advances in experimental social psychology* (Vol. 16, pp. 1–47). New York: Academic Press.

Michels, R. (1988). The future of psychoanalysis. *Psychoanalytic Quarterly, 57,* 167–182.

Murray, H. (1955). Introduction. In A. Burton & R. Harris (Eds.), *Clinical Studies of Personality* (Vol. 1). New York: Harper and Row.

Robbins, L. C. (1963). The accuracy of parental recall of aspects of child development and child rearing practices. *Journal of Abnormal and Social Psychology, 66,* 261–270.

Runyan, W. M. (1982). In defense of the case study method. *American Journal of Orthopsychiatry, 52,* 440–446.

Schwaber, E. A. (1986). Reconstruction and perceptual experience. *Journal of the American Psychoanalytic Association, 34,* 911–932.

Spence, D. P. (1987). *The Freudian metaphor.* New York: Norton.

White, H. (1978). *Tropics of discourse.* Baltimore: Johns Hopkins University Press.

CHAPTER 4

Locating Text Archives for Psychotherapy Research

ERHARD MERGENTHALER AND HORST KÄCHELE

IN THE FIRST EDITION OF THE *Handbook of Psychotherapy and Behavior Change*, Luborsky and Spence (1971) were already calling for empirical studies based on primary data—that is, audio and video recordings of therapeutic sessions, with transcriptions. However, even though a number of tapes and transcripts were produced, many of them were used only once, and they are no longer accessible to the researchers.

A significant step was taken when Hartvig Dahl made a set of transcripts of psychoanalytic sessions available to a broader group of researchers. Finally, various types of empirical assessment could be applied to the same sessions (see Dahl, Kächele, and Thomä 1988). Dahl (1979) also developed one of the first guides for uniform transcription, which became widely used by researchers. Shortly afterward, in Europe, especially in the German-speaking countries, Kächele and Thomä started to audiotape psychoanalytic and psychotherapeutic sessions and then shared them with others for basic research. Linguists also became interested in this type of textual material. The transcription standards, developed for the German-language recordings by Mergenthaler, came into widespread use. As a result of interdisciplinary endeavors, guides to transcription were made to fulfill the most likely needs of both psychotherapy researchers and linguists. In addition, the guidelines were fully compatible with computer use. Recently, Mergenthaler and Stinson (1992) published the English version of the transcription standards.

The plan for an archive that would centralize the psychotherapy data sources was conceived in 1979 by Kächele and Mergenthaler. With the funding of the German Research Foundation the archive became reality. In

1989 Sherwood Waldron initiated the Psychoanalytic Research Consortium as an archive for psychoanalytic recordings and transcriptions from North America.

We will give a brief overview of existing facilities today, emphasizing how the archive is administered rather than listing what is currently available. The numbers quickly change and can be easily updated by a phone call or letter to the archive of interest. We will take somewhat more space for the lending policy and the means of ensuring privacy and authorship. For those who are interested in more detail, we have supplied addresses at the end of this chapter.

Major Archives

We know of three major archives for psychotherapy data. Two of them, the Psychoanalytic Research Consortium (PRC) and the Center for the Study of Neuroses (CSN), collect English material only. The Ulm Textbank (UTB) collects both English and German recordings and transcriptions. We will highlight some of the materials available in each of the archives.

THE ULM TEXTBANK

The Ulm Textbank (UTB) become the world's largest collection of reports, test protocols, tapes, and transcripts. As part of the University of Ulm, Germany, it is administered by the section on computer science in psychotherapy (directed by Erhard Mergenthaler) and is affiliated with the department of psychotherapy (the clinical director is Horst Kächele). The UTB offers a full spectrum of services: (1) intake of relevant material, (2) lending of transcripts, tapes, or data files on diskettes, (3) computer-aided analyses of textual data, and (4) counseling for the planning of empirical studies. In addition, methodologies are developed to economically administer an archive (with a text bank managing system) and to automatically analyze textual data. Based on the huge amount of text in the archive, textual characteristics of various linguistic phenomena are also identified.

The holdings of the Ulm Textbank comprise material of English and German origin. The German-language data base now includes extensive samples from four psychoanalytic cases. Individual sessions from nine other psychoanalytic therapies are also included. The data base of initial interviews includes about five hundred intake interviews and is referenced according to the sex of the patient or therapist and whether the diagnosis is neurosis or psychosomatic disturbance. This body of texts is steadily being enlarged, with special attention to the patient variables of sex, diagnosis, social class, and age, and the therapist variables of experience and kind of psychotherapy. The English portion of texts in the Ulm

Textbank is from the Penn Psychotherapy Project, and is made up of forty sessions representing two early and two late sessions each from ten improved and ten unimproved patients in psychodynamic therapy. For the following texts, requests may be sent to the Ulm Textbank; but they are not regular parts of the archive and restrictions may apply: these are 15 stratified random sessions each from fifteen analytic cases (a total of 225 hours); another 25 sessions from an analytic case were selected—10 "work," 10 "resistance," and 5 "middle" hours; finally, there are 185 sessions from a different analytic case.

The kind of text included in the Textbank is determined by the goals, questions, and scientific interests of the supporting and other institutions. The Department of Psychotherapy at Ulm University, emphasizes the establishment of an empirical basis for research in the field of psychotherapy and for teaching. Resources for teaching include demonstration materials for the education of medical students and verbatim transcripts for the clinical education and supervision of resident physicians and psychologists.

The UTB is open to those engaged in transcript- or record-based research. The intake of material is done at one of three levels chosen by the donor:

1. The material is given to the UTB for internal use, such as for developing characteristics for linguistic variables. The material cannot be lent, printed, or edited. Thus UTB can guarantee full confidentiality for this kind of material.
2. The material is given to the UTB as available for lending. However, when copies are requested, the donor is contacted by the UTB and asked for permission. The interested scholar must supply proof of institutional affiliation and a description of the study for which the material is wanted.
3. The material is given to the UTB to use and lend as it wishes. The conditions of level 2 remain but there is less administrative work.

Whatever level a donor has chosen, he or she will be informed when a study using the material has been completed. If possible, copies of publications that result from studies based on a donor's materials will be provided.

Those who are interested in borrowing from the UTB must submit an overview of what they intend to do with the material. The staff of the UTB evaluates applications with special regard to confidentiality and ethics. If the request is acceptable, a form is sent to the applicant to be signed and returned before any material is sent. Essentially the borrower agrees that the use of the loaned material is restricted to the named person and to the specified research purposes. No copies may be made from the material loaned, and it must be returned in full when the research is done. If a publication results, a reprint must be given to the UTB. Before studies are printed, quotations from the material loaned have to be checked for confidentiality by the staff of the UTB.

One of the most often used services of the UTB is the computer-aided analysis of textual material. The Textbank has a variety of methods that can be tailored to the researcher's needs. Another service is advice to those planning new studies. Using the long experience of the staff, studies can often be quickly and effectively planned. Information about the collection is available, including a catalog of all available material and a list of all studies that have used the material to date.

The services of the UTB are available at very low cost. Aside from a small charge to cover the cost of materials, charges are made only for the labor-intensive tasks, such as the transcription of tape recordings.

THE PSYCHOANALYTIC RESEARCH CONSORTIUM

The Psychoanalytic Research Consortium (PRC), according to its chairman, Sherwood Waldron, is a nonprofit corporation, operating since 1989, whose purpose is to collect recordings of psychoanalysis and other psychoanalytically oriented psychotherapies and to catalog and safeguard the tapes and other materials relating to these treatments. The PRC also prepares suitable selections of such materials for distribution to qualified psychoanalytic researchers.

Researchers must obtain approval for access to materials; the process is comparable to that of the Ulm Textbank. The PRC's standards for the preparation of materials are also comparable to those of the Textbank. Transcription standards are the same, and techniques for preserving confidentiality are similar. There are equivalent restrictions on the use and publication of materials.

The PRC has access to recordings of more than twenty-five analyses by nine different analysts. The text of one analysis of 324 hours is completely available on computer. The other materials are transcribed to varying degrees. A number of psychotherapies conducted by analysts are also available. Because the PRC is an autonomous institution, it is dependent upon user fees for operating funds.

CENTER FOR THE STUDY OF NEUROSES

In contrast to the Ulm Textbank and the Psychoanalytic Research Consortium, the Center for the Study of Neuroses does not lend textual material; the center's purpose is to encourage scientists at various sites to participate in collaborative research endeavors. Project proposals must be approved by the directors and the coordinating committee of the Program for the Study of Conscious and Unconscious Mental Processes at the

University of California at San Francisco; the program is supported by the John D. and Catherine T. MacArthur Foundation. Work must be done with a designated liaison scientist, whose responsibility it is to facilitate collaboration and to ensure the proper use of materials.

Materials include running notes, process notes, videotapes, and audiotapes. In addition, the archive has three fully transcribed and time-coded brief therapies with patients suffering from pathological grief, plus transcripts from thirty other cases of pathological grief. Additional materials available are experimental data, physiological data, psychological testing scores, and recordings of research sessions, evaluation sessions, and follow-up sessions.

OTHER COLLECTIONS AND ARCHIVES

There exist several other collections of recordings and transcriptions. Both UTB and PRC will forward inquiries to another archive if its material fits the researcher's needs.

Methodologies for Analyzing
Transcript Data

Language can be viewed semiotically as a system of symbols whose structure is determined by rules based on the relationship between form and content. Accordingly, it is possible to distinguish between formal, grammatical, and substantive measurements. Each of these types of measurement can be further subdivided according to whether it can be applied to a speaker's text or to the entire speech activity in a conversation (the dialogue). It is therefore possible to speak of monadic or dyadic values and to distinguish among these types of measurements according to the kind of data they utilize. Best known are simple frequencies of occurrence, which form the basis for ratios and distributions.

It should also be noted that some of the approaches for formal and grammatical measurements presume substantive knowledge of, for example, the denotative meaning of a word. The contrast with substantive measurements stems from the fact that the required knowledge comes not from the psychoanalytic research field itself but from the realms of linguistics or information science.

The formal measurements can generally be determined simply. In computer-aided approaches, only the capacity to segment a sequence of symbols (letters, numbers, and special symbols) into words and punctuation is necessary. Such formal measurements and indications of their applicability include text size (tokens), vocabulary (types), type-token ratio, and redundancy.

The simplest and most elementary formal measurement is that of the number of words spoken by the analyst and patient. Kächele (1983) found that in a successful psychoanalytic treatment there was no correlation across 130 sessions in the number of words spoken by analyst and patient. In a rather unsuccessful treatment by the same analyst, these word counts were significantly correlated.

The redundancy of a text is a measure adopted from information theory. Spence (1968) proposed some important ideas about psychodynamic redundancy, without testing his ideas empirically. In addition, he formulated a series of hypotheses about the course that redundancy takes in psychoanalytic treatment. Kächele and Mergenthaler (1984) confirmed one of these hypotheses, that the repetitiousness of a patient's speech increased over the course of treatment. The therapist's redundancy, in contrast, remained constant.

Grammatical measures address such features as interjections and word class (part of speech). The grammatical measures require that the researcher have linguistic knowledge of the language being studied—for example, the grammar of English. The programming and precoding tasks in the computer-aided procedures are formidable. Moreover, many kinds of questions still cannot be correctly processed automatically. An example is lemmatization, which can assign 50 to 95 percent of all word forms, depending on the kind of text, to the correct lemma. The psychoanalytic interview contains speech with the many syntactically deviant forms (such as incomplete words and sentences) that characterize spoken and spontaneous speech, and therefore poses unique challenges. Accordingly, there exist almost no computer-aided studies of psychoanalytic texts using grammatical measures.

The dependence of word choice on word type and semantic class was demonstrated by Busemann (1925) in investigations of children's speech. He spoke of an "active" and a "qualitative" style with regard to verbs and adjectives. He showed that these differences in style are only slightly dependent on the subject being discussed and that they stem from personality variables. Using a computer-aided approach to the text of a psychoanalytic interview, Mergenthaler and Kächele (1985) showed that the realization of a word form within the text may depend on the subject matter. However, this microanalytic view does not exclude the possibility that, viewed at the macro level, personality-dependent variables are effective in the way described by Busemann (1925).

Substantive measures also require detailed expert knowledge of a theory and its area of application. Computer-aided procedures are able to provide only approximate results and are limited to narrowly defined constructions (Lolas, Mergenthaler, and von Rad 1982). New approaches in information science, especially in the field of artificial intelligence, could achieve a breakthrough by establishing data bases in conjunction with a system of rules. However, practical tools are not yet available.

In a pioneering content analytic study, Dahl (1972) was able to trace the downhill course of 363 hours during a two-and-one-half-year segment of an unsuccessful psychoanalysis and to convincingly categorize 25 sessions as 10 extreme "work" hours, 10 extreme "resistance" hours, and 5 hours directly in the middle of the range. Then, using single words derived from the Harvard III dictionary categories, he was also able to demonstrate word clusters that manifestly appear to reflect oedipal and other unconscious conflicts (Dahl 1974). Reynes, Martindale, and Dahl (1984) used the Regressive Imagery Dictionary (RID) (Stone et al. 1966) to compare this same patient's 10 working hours and 10 resistance hours. The working hours were characterized by increases in the dictionary categories that assessed primary process language, and the resistance hours were characterized by increases in the secondary process category scores. This finding agrees with Freud's attribution of defensive functions to the secondary processes (Bucci 1988).

Large continuous segments as well as selected sections of treatment transcripts may thus be examined using computer-aided text analysis as a tool in psychoanalytic process research. Further progress in basic research requires that methods be developed more extensively and that techniques from related scientific disciplines, such as information science and linguistics, be integrated.

Available Software

Computer-aided analysis of psychotherapy transcripts requires software that can at least distinguish the speech of the therapist and the patient. Furthermore, turn at speaking, hour, and type of treatment may be useful criteria for defining the units of analysis. Other desired segmentation criteria might be the onset and offset of dreams, early memories, or specific episodes. Text-analytic software, developed for the social sciences or for literary research (such as, General Inquirer, OCP), does not allow for this kind of segmentation. These programs support structures like chapter, paragraph, or line. The analyses performed with these systems are generally restricted to delimited areas like concordances (OCP) or content analysis (General Inquirer).

The development of TAS/C (Mergenthaler 1987), a text archive and analysis system, arose from the needs of psychotherapy research; the program represents a useful selection of methods and segmentation techniques. As input TAS/C accepts transcripts made in conformance with Dahl or Mergenthaler/Stinson standards. TAS/C is a system that allows for maintaining a text archive and analyzing the texts stored. It accommodates the dialogue structure of a text and is capable of managing marked segments, such as dreams, memories, and episodes. According to the scheme outlined in the previous section, TAS/C can be used to do formal, grammatical, and content-analytic studies. There are also tools for developing content-analytic dictionaries, for disambiguating texts, and for printing. Interfaces to statistical and graphical software exist. As a technical environment, TAS/C needs a computer to run the UNIX operating system. The program is also available for personal computers using a 386 or 486 processor.

Summary

Text archives have become increasingly crucial to the rapid maturation of dynamic psychotherapy research. We have listed the main archives and have given a few examples of the applications of their materials, particularly to linguistic analyses. Although computer analyses have often been used for limited linguistic analyses, many of these have bearing on important dynamic issues as well.

Addresses

Ulm Textbank, University of Ulm - Klinikum
Am Hochstrass 8
89081 Ulm, Germany

Psychoanalytic Research Consortium, Inc.
1235 Park Avenue, Suite 1B
New York, NY 10128

Center for the Study of Neuroses
Langley Porter Psychiatric Institute
University of California at San Francisco
401 Parnassus Avenue
San Francisco, CA 94143—0984

References

BUCCI, W. (1988). Converging evidence for emotional structures: Theory and method. In H. Dahl, H. Kächele, & H. Thomä (Eds.), *Psychoanalytic process research strategies* (pp. 29—49). New York: Springer-Verlag.

BUSEMANN, A. (1925). *Die Sprache der Jugend als Ausdruck der Entwicklungsrhythmik.* Jena.

DAHL, H. (1972). A quantitative study of a psychoanalysis. In R. R. Holt & E. Peterfreund (Eds.), *Psychoanalysis and contemporary science* (pp. 237–257). New York: Macmillan.

DAHL, H. (1974). The measurement of meaning in psychoanalysis by computer analysis of verbal context. *Journal of the American Psychoanalytic Association, 22,* 37–57.

DAHL, H. (1979). Word frequencies of spoken American English. Essex, CT: Verbatim.

DAHL, H., KÄCHELE, H., & THOMÄ, H. (EDS.). (1988). *Psychoanalytic process research strategies.* New York: Springer-Verlag.

KÄCHELE, H. (1983). Verbal activity level of therapists in initial interviews and long-term psychoanalysis. In W. Minsel & W. Herff (Eds.), *Methodology in psychotherapy research* (pp. 125–129). Frankfurt: Lang.

KÄCHELE, H., & MERGENTHALER, E. (1984). Auf dem Wege zur computerunterstuetzten Textanalyse in der psychotherapeutischen Prozessforschung. In U. Baumann (Ed.), *Psychotherapie: Makro-/Mikroperspektive* (pp. 223–239). Goettingen: Hogrefe.

LOLAS, F., MERGENTHALER, E., & VON RAD, M. (1982). Content analysis of verbal behaviour in psychotherapy research: A comparison between two methods. *British Journal of Medical Psychology, 55,* 327–333.

LUBORSKY, L., & SPENCE, D. P. (1971). Quantitative research on psychoanalytic therapy. In A. E. Bergin & S. L. Garfield (Eds.), *Handbook of psychotherapy and behavior change: An empirical analysis* (pp. 408–438). New York: Wiley.

MERGENTHALER, E. (1987). *TAS/C user manual.* University of Ulm: Ulm Textbank.

MERGENTHALER, E., & KÄCHELE, H. (1985). Changes of latent meaning structures in psychoanalysis. *Sprache und Datenverarbeitung, 9*(2), 21–28.

MERGENTHALER, E., & STINSON, C. H. (1992). Psychotherapy transcription standards. *Psychotherapy Research, 2*(1), 58–75.

REYNES, R., MARTINDALE, C., & DAHL, H. (1984). Lexical differences between working and resistance sessions in psychoanalysis. *Journal of Clinical Psychology, 40,* 733–737.

SPENCE, D. P. (1968). The processing of meaning in psychotherapy: Some links with psycholinguistics and information theory. *Behavioral Science, 13,* 349–361.

STONE, P., DUNPHY, D., SMITH, M. S., & OGILVIE, D. (1966). *The general inquirer: A computer approach to content analysis.* Cambridge: M.I.T. Press.

CHAPTER 5

Selecting Single Case Research Designs for Clinicians

PETER FONAGY AND GEORGE MORAN

THE PSYCHOANALYTIC METHOD PROVIDES ACCESS to unique data that may not be accessible outside of this long-term, intimate, and confidential relationship. The method provides a relatively standardized observational framework, with an observer trained to minimally disrupt the flow of emerging material while remaining attuned to his or her own, as well as the patient's, emotional reactions. The data and findings from the psychoanalytic method have been traditionally written about through case reports, a methodology representing the hallmark of nineteenth-century clinical medicine, which used clinical observation and phenomenology as its primary research tools.

Psychotherapeutic approaches that arose out of twentieth-century social science, however, have repudiated clinical case reports, both as part of the positivist critique of introspection and also on methodological grounds. For example, social scientists have charged that using the vehicle of the case report, clinicians often attribute patients' positive outcomes to the effects of their own clinical work, without taking into account a host of possible confounding variables. These factors threaten the internal validity (Cooke and Campbell 1979) of the case report, that is, the validity with which statements can be made about whether there is a causal relationship between the therapeutic intervention and the changes observed.

On their part, psychoanalysts have taken an appropriately cautious approach to methodological innovations which carry the potential to endanger the fragile psychoanalytic process. Yet this stance has left psychoanalysts dependent on a process that has largely been discredited in many fields of social science.

Accordingly, what is now needed is a means to enhance the internal validity of the data gathered in the clinical setting, so that the canons of objective scientific method can be met, while at the same time preserving the subtlety and complexity of subjective clinical phenomena. In the 1950s, the lack of methodological know-how to achieve these ends presented an insuperable barrier to systematic research. Today many significant methodological advances are available, which go a long way toward achieving, for the study of the individual case, the requirement of a logic of proof which Nagel (1959), Grünbaum (1986), and others have identified as lacking.

The aims of this chapter are to describe the types of case study methods that are now available to psychoanalysis and psychoanalytic psychotherapy and to review their assets and liabilities. Four major systematic approaches to the treatment of individual case data from psychoanalyses will be examined: (1) qualitative case studies, (2) quantitative studies of series of case records, (3) patient series or quasi-experimental designs, and (4) experimental designs. In subsequent sections we will examine special issues concerning the nature of research questions suitable for individual case study and the specific requirements of dependent variables and of statistical procedures imposed by the single case study paradigm. Before examining in detail specific types of individual case studies, it may be useful to consider a number of basic issues common to all the approaches listed.

Types of Research Designs

GROUP-BASED EXPERIMENTAL DESIGNS

Readers of psychiatric and psychological journals will be most familiar with group-based experimental designs; these have generally been adopted as the most appropriate means of conducting research in the mental health field. Common to all experimental procedures is the general principle of holding constant all factors except the independent variable under study. Random assignment of subjects to groups is assumed to equate them and thus to reduce the plausibility of group differences in terms other than the experimental treatment applied. To outline the limitations of this design is beyond the scope of this chapter. However, there have not been many well-developed alternatives to the experimental design.

NATURALISTIC DESIGNS

In naturalistic designs a large representative group of patients is observed undergoing one or more treatments and their outcome is correlated with both patient and treatment characteristics. These are a viable alternative favored by administrators of therapy programs despite their less than optimal scientific yield. While naturalistic designs can give a clear indication of the efficacy of a treatment procedure (for example, the proportion of patients who may be expected to improve substantially), the design cannot tell us whether treatment is necessary for improvement or demonstrate which components of a complex treatment contain the therapeutic ingredient. For these questions to be addressed, random assignment of subjects to treatment and non-treatment groups, or to different types of treatment group, is necessary.

It is not always the case that naturalistic designs have administrative implications while experimental designs can answer scientific questions. Among psychoanalytic investigations, the Menninger study (Wallerstein 1986) provides an impressive counterexample. The nonrandom assignment of subjects to psychotherapy and psychoanalysis makes this a naturalistic design. The study highlighted the value of therapeutic support to patients in the most seriously disturbed group.

The Menninger study falls into a subcategory of naturalistic designs called quasi-experimental designs (Cooke and Campbell 1979) in which subjects are assigned to two or more groups but the assignment is nonrandom. Patient series and psychotherapy process studies are also examples of naturalistic designs where dependent variables of interest, usually therapeutic outcome, are correlated with patient characteristics at the outset of treatment, therapist variables, or some measure of the evolution of the psychotherapy process.

INDIVIDUAL CASE DESIGNS

All the designs we have considered so far are group designs, where an individual contributes but one data point to an aggregate (mean, median, and so on) that describes the group at a particular time. In stark contrast are individual case designs where the focus of interest is the way a particular individual changes as a result of a process unfolding over time. In consequence, individual research designs, when they are quantitative, include numerous measurements over time (or qualitative observations, in the case of nonquantitative studies).

The individual case design requires that the causal process studied, as well as its effect, be documented with objective records, and wherever possible, operationalized and measured. The degree of control we decide to exercise over the causal process determines whether an individual case study is experimental or naturalistic.

In either case, the feature of the design that allows us the opportunity for scientific study is replication (the repeated occurrence) of a homogeneous category of phenomena which can be measured meaningfully. Fortunately, the psychoanalytic situation provides us with an ideal laboratory for the study of these kinds of data, be they patient-based (such as mood, reflectiveness, or cognitive style); therapist-based (such as empathy or directiveness); or relationship-based (such as the nature of the transference or countertransference). Depending on the particular research questions, these variables may be best treated as independent variables (indicators of the conditions the effect of which we may wish to examine), or as dependent variables (the indicators we expect to be affected by the unfolding conditions).

THE SINGLE CASE METHOD

Some of the most influential clinically relevant contributions in psychological treatment are based upon analyses of individual cases—not just in psychiatry (for example, Little Hans, Anna O, Little Albert) but also in neuropsychology (Luria 1966; Shallice 1979, 1989) and personality theory (Allport 1961). The belief that knowledge based upon groups of individuals is somehow more likely to be generalizable (that is, applicable beyond the specific locus of its discovery) than is the case for knowledge based upon individual cases is fatally flawed.

The belief derives largely from the remarkable achievements of the statistician A. R. Fisher, who worked in the 1920s and 1930s; through the development of the theory of sampling he made it possible for scientists, including psychologists, to make inferences about the populations they were studying on the basis of information gained from relatively small groups. As the criteria for the drawing of a genuinely random sample are very rarely, if ever, met by clinical investigations, the issue of what inferences may be drawn from a finding becomes primarily logical rather than statistical (Edgington 1966).

Information must be made available to permit the readers of a research report to make a decision about the applicability of findings concerning how conditions were specified, as well as the characteristics of the patient(s) in treatment. This constraint should apply equally to group and individual studies. Wherever possible and whatever the research question, large numbers need to be studied to ensure generality. This injunction implies the need for studies of large numbers of individuals, not large groups.

Individual case studies attempt to establish the relationship between intervention and other variables of interest through repeated systematic observation and measurement (Chassan 1967, 1979). There is little intrinsically incompatible between the psychoanalytic approach and the logic of the single case design tradition (see, for example, Hayes 1982; Kazdin

1982; Barlow and Hersen 1984; Kratochwill 1985) despite its origins in Skinnerian applied behavioral analysis (see Sidman 1960). The observation of variability across time within a single case combines a clinical interest to respond appropriately to changes within the patient, and a research interest to find support for a causal relationship between intervention and changes in variables of theoretical interest. The attention to repeated observations, more than any other single factor, permits knowledge to be drawn from the individual case and has the power to eliminate plausible alternative explanations.

Types of Individual Case Studies

THE QUALITATIVE CASE STUDY

Case study research aims to make a contribution to knowledge which goes beyond the primarily illustrative purpose of the case report. For clinical material to be considered as evidence, it must be subjected to further scrutiny according to the criteria that follow.

Current developments in psychoanalysis proposed with the intention "to support an empirical generalization or to tell a causal story" (Edelson 1988, 296) tend to invoke methodological principles derived from techniques of qualitative research (Kvale 1986; Good and Watts 1989). Three principles are particularly apposite. First, qualitative research should attempt to support conclusions using data from multiple sources (what Campbell and Fiske [1959] called triangulation) as a way of improving credibility. For example, in the narrowest sense, analysts' reports of cases can be supplemented by interviews with patients conducted by an independent clinician following the treatment. In a similar vein, patients' own written accounts of their treatments are sometimes revealing. A broader interpretation of triangulation is the supplementing of clinical psychoanalytic data with anthropological observations from other fields, such as literature or the visual arts.

Second, qualitative research should aim to formulate hypotheses clearly enough to permit the derivation of appropriate counterexamples to the hypothesis. For example, there exists a generalization that psychosomatic patients show a lack of capacity to generate and appreciate affect and elaborate it in fantasy ("alexythymia," Sifneos 1974; "pensée opératoire," Marty and de M'Uzan 1963). This generalization is of value only insofar as we could conceive of a large number of psychosomatic cases with a capacity to fantasize as disconfirming the original observation. If, when confronted with a counterexample, we should resort to the claim that alexythymia is specific to a limited subset of affects or fantasies, we inevitably greatly weaken the value of the generalization.

Third, quantitative research should clarify the personal connection between the researcher and the possible threats to objectivity which may then ensue. Edelson (1986) proposes six requirements for an empirical psychoanalytic case study:

1. There is a clear statement of the hypothesis (the proposed generalization).
2. The phenomena are made intersubjectively accessible via, for example, a durable record of utterances.
3. Negative instances of the generalization—that is, the type of observation that would be regarded as inconsistent with the generalization—are clearly specified.
4. Evidence that the hypothesis has not contaminated the data is supplied.
5. Formulations alternative to the hypothesis are offered; although they could also account for the findings, they are shown to be inferior in that they are not as fertile or they lead to a less detailed, precise, or complete narrative of causation.
6. The range of individuals and situations to which the hypothesis applies is made explicit.

The Committee on Scientific Activities of the American Psychoanalytic Association (1988) has recently put forward its own proposals for improving the standards of individual case studies (see chapter 3). Enhanced reporting of the clinical process with dialogues accompanied by commentaries—as opposed to narratives—are recommended as the preferred format for conveying clinical data. These steps toward improving the generalizability of case study data are long overdue in that they place the responsibility of upholding systematic clinical writing principles upon the entire psychoanalytic community.

Organizing material according to particular themes or conditions presents further problems: optimally, categories should be defined explicitly enough for the reliable allocation of clinical material to categories by independent judges. Normally, even simple clinical concepts such as oedipal rivalry may not be unambiguously identifiable. The set of categories should be exhaustive, so that every instance belongs to a category. Each category should be internally coherent; exhaustiveness is relatively easy to achieve with the injudicious use of heterogeneous "wastebasket" categories. In practice, attempts at categorizing psychoanalytic material are rarely subjected to such criteria.

Although not many case studies in the literature meet the minimal standards of qualitative research, there are nevertheless impressive examples of centers where psychoanalytic research has met the stringent standards of qualitative methodology. The multifaceted clinical studies emerging from decades of work at the Menninger Foundation (Wallerstein 1986a) for example, approach in caliber the stringent qualitative features proposed earlier. The forty-two patients in this unique treatment program were followed and reported on with sufficient rigor to make the findings from each individual case a unique addition to the clinical literature on the psychoanalytic treatment of severely disturbed patients. The Hampstead Child Psychoanalytic Index, containing the complete analytic treatment records of over 140 cases, is a superb example of a more theoretically oriented approach (Sandler, Kennedy, and Tyson 1980).

QUANTITATIVE STUDY OF CASE RECORDS

Quantitative analysis of individual case records is not an alternative to qualitative analysis; in fact, good qualitative analysis invariably precedes good quantitative analysis. Decisions concerning what to measure are qualitative decisions. Some procedure is always necessary to turn observations of behavior into a numerical index, and the index can only be as good as the procedure on which it is based. Good and Watts (1989) conceive of the procedure of quantification as a function (F) which takes as its input the set of raw observations present in the case record and gives as its output a set of values (V) which we may consider a representation of the raw observations. For example, in enumerating the frequency of negative references to an analyst, the quantification procedure will consist of operational definitions of what does or does not constitute a negative reference; for example, does an utterance have to refer to the therapist directly, or need it refer only to a figure who shares some characteristics with the therapist?

In the case of psychoanalytic research, (F) is usually a complex process. If raw data consist of a video recording of a child-analytic session, then (F) needs to be quite an elaborate coding scheme for categorizing relevant behaviors and (V) will be a set of frequencies (how often the behaviors occur) or co-occurrence relationships (the likelihood of one behavior's following another).

The epistemological worth of quantification boils down to how good a representation (F) provides of the subject matter of study: Does the representation permit the making of valid comparisons and the drawing of inferences? Since (F) is primarily a qualitative process, the validity of the quantitative analysis will be directly dependent upon the validity of the qualitative analysis that preceded it. It makes no sense, therefore, to claim that some kind of inherent incompatibility exists between the psychoanalytic method and quantitative investigations. Quantification is not the only route to causal explanation; nor does it give direct access to it. Careful qualitative analysis may well offer the researcher sufficient control to rule out the influence of potentially confounding variables. Without detailed qualitative analysis, categories will remain ambiguous and thus inherently incapable of excluding contaminants.

The advantages of quantification are clear: numerical representations of data provide access to statistical techniques and reduce the complexity of observations to a relatively small number of indicators. Quantitative data are also easier to inspect in searching for patterns of relationships or finding a useful format for presentation. How can we avail ourselves of these advantages in individual case studies?

Quantitative analysis of an individual case record sets out to demonstrate a lawful relationship between two or more sets of variables which are generally, but not invariably, regarded as causally connected. The establishment of such a causal relationship in $N = 1$ research tends to be based upon logical argument concerning concomitant variation rather than experimental manipulation. It is narrowminded to argue that experimental manipulation represents the sole path to causal accounts. Edelson (1989), for example, links the methodological difficulties faced by psychoanalytic theory, in attempting nonexperimentally to justify causal inferences, to those of evolutionary theorists who attempt nonexperimentally to justify conjectures about events occurring eons ago and over vast spans of time. There are many other nonexperimental sciences—astronomy, economics, geophysics—all of which appear to experience little difficulty in arriving at causal explanations via the careful measurement of naturally evolving processes.

Types of Quantitative Case Study

REPLICATION BY SEGMENTATION

Broadly speaking, two techniques have been developed to study relationships between patients' responses and other variables of importance in clinical psychoanalysis. One, which will be considered later, aims to provide a methodical model of the fluctuations observed throughout the entire period of the analysis; the second relies on the segmentation of the analytic observation into comparable epochs. In the latter method, an aspect of the psychoanalytic process, normally the conjunction of two purportedly causally related events (for example, a symptom and its unconscious determinant), is repeatedly extracted from segments of a treatment transcript. The time frame adopted (the epochs) can be adjusted to suit the phenomenon of interest. Normally, epochs of interest are identified on the basis of the dependent variable studied, and comparable positive and negative epochs are selected to permit statistical comparison. Statistically, the epochs tend to be treated as if they were independent random samples. The method can identify the likelihood of the co-occurrence of two phenomena; if one of the phenomena has a specific point of onset, the epoch preceding the event may be contrasted with randomly selected epochs to strengthen the causal argument by demonstrating a temporal relationship.

The approach to studying associations between events, which was originated by Lester Luborsky (1967), has recently been formalized as "the new research paradigm" in an excellent volume by Rice and Greenberg (1984). There are four components to this replication by segmentation paradigm:

1. The therapeutic record (transcript) is sampled and segmented into different episodes or events.
2. The segments are selected on the basis of particular kinds of recurring events (as in Luborsky's classic episodes of momentary forgetting).
3. A particular, measurable, dimension assumed to be causally related to the recurring events is identified and measured.
4. The hypothesis is formulated and tested concerning a possible association between the measures identified in (3) and the events noted in (2).

An example from Luborsky's laboratory may help to clarify this method. Peterson, Luborsky, and Seligman (1983) studied shifts in mood as the event of interest in the two-hundred-session psychotherapy record of a young man suffering from major depression. Operational criteria were drawn up for mood shifts using the method of triangulation (the subject noted the shift spontaneously, and independent judges confirmed it). The predictor variable of interest was the mode of cognitive functioning of the subject—specifically, the nature of the patient's attributions for bad events. Four hundred words before and after the mood shift were examined in four segments around a sudden increase in depression, five segments around a sudden reduction in depression, and three randomly selected episodes which did not involve mood changes. The authors were able to demonstrate a statistically significant relationship between internal, stable, and global attributions and shift to depressed mood.

The study illustrates how an ecologically valid case study, consisting primarily of unconstrained verbalization, may be used in a quasi-experimental context to study the evolution of basic psychological processes. In other investigations using the same verbatim material, the authors examined a variety of content characteristics, including the subject's statements about anxiety, hopelessness, guilt, hostility to self, loss of self-esteem, and oedipal conflicts in relation to mood shifts. The possibility of alternative accounts of mood shifts in terms of other variables were in this way ruled out. Thus the approach succeeds in dealing with a number of threats to internal validity. Reliability was demonstrated across judges, and the relationship between mood shifts and cognitive function was shown across sessions. The method speaks equally forcefully to clinical practice and experimental research.

There are, however, limitations to this method of studying a continuous process in terms of discontinuous observations. The primary interest of the authors was to demonstrate that cognitive style preceded shifts in mood. They showed this by demonstrating that the patient was significantly more internal, stable, and global in his attributions before a change in mood in the direction of depression than before a change in mood in the direction of elation. However, there may well be, for example, cyclical variations in mood over longer periods—say, months—within which there are also more frequent variations in mood—say, within days or even within the analytic hour. In the present case it is unclear whether the qualities of attribution belong to variability of mood as a function of short-term fluctuations or whether the attributions measured belong to the underlying, slower rate of change of mood. If the latter is the case, the attributions observed may be the consequence rather than the cause of changes in mood.

The most comprehensive application of the replication by segmentation paradigm is perhaps in the Mount Zion psychotherapy research project (Weiss and Sampson 1986), where the theoretical framework proposed by Weiss was systematically subjected to a long-term series of studies. For example, Gassner et al. (1986) were able to show that episodes identified as containing previously warded-off mental content were not characterized by anxiety, as might have been predicted by classical psychoanalytic theory. Rather, these episodes tended to follow periods during which the patient was insightful, free associating, able to articulate and explore his experience. In another study on the same case material, Silberschatz, Sampson, and Weiss (1986) found that where independent raters identified the analyst as responding in ways that disconfirmed the patient's pathogenic beliefs about people and relationships, the patient responded by being somewhat more insightful, more relaxed, less fearful, and less anxious and by expressing more love.

The replication by segmentation paradigm creates almost limitless possibilities for testing psychoanalytic hypotheses. A number of cautionary points, however, should be made. Statistical validity (the validity with which the studies permit conclusions about covariation between the assumed independent and dependent variables) is threatened by the low statistical power of most of the studies reported using this method. Even assuming that the effects we are looking for are large and that the average segment containing the item of interest differs from the negative set by at least one standard deviation (SD), at least ten episodes are necessary in each group to show a significant effect (Kraemer 1981). If the effect is subtle (for example one-third of an SD), around 150 observations per group will be required for the secure detection of the effect. There are very few events that occur with this frequency.

A further threat to statistical validity is posed by the fact that the epochs are not, on the whole, randomly selected and independent of one another, as the statistical tests applied assume. This could affect the generalizability of the conclusions to other members of the target population; but the problem can be easily remedied, either by using more appropriate statistical techniques or by requiring authors to submit two or three independent individual case studies where the same finding is observed.

Internal validity can be similarly threatened if the definition of the constructs and the operationalization of their measurement is biased. Vulnerability to bias is greatest precisely at the point where the limits around the critical segment are drawn. Certain definitions may lead the researcher to draw a sample from the material in such a way that possible counterexamples are excluded. Peterson, Luborsky, and Seligman (1983), for instance, systematically excluded shifts of mood that occurred within fifteen minutes of a previous shift, arguing that these were reactions to the previous mood shift and thus entailed a different causal process. Yet, it is possible that such secondary shifts would not have been associated with the predicted cognitive changes. Thus, if the rapid shifts had been included, the significant associations reported might not have been observed. To the extent that such definitions are arbitrary, their effect on the hypothesis under consideration should be systematically tested to ensure internal validity.

A final threat to internal validity is posed by the need to match epochs or segments containing the observations of interest with others that do not. Our lack of knowledge concerning factors that are likely to affect the way patients' material naturally evolves within sessions precludes a thoroughly systematic effort to match positive and negative epochs on crucial variables. As knowledge accumulates in the field, this source of threat to internal validity should correspondingly diminish.

TIME SERIES ANALYSIS

Time series studies of individual case reports are more ambitious in their aims than methods that rely on replication by segmentation. In contrast to the latter method, which artificially removes processes that change at a slow rate, time series analysis preserves all sequential dependencies in the series. Time series analysis is a flexible statistical procedure adapted from econometrics to the behavioral sciences by McCleary and Hay (1980) and Gottman (1981). A time series is any form of measurement taken at roughly equal intervals over a large number of occasions. The number of observations required for a time series is at least a hundred points. Psychoanalytic data thus lend themselves well to study using this technique, whether sessions or weeks of treatment are adopted as units of analysis. Several models of time series analysis are available, each making different assumptions about the data and using different algorithms to provide the final statistics.

One of the most robust methods is auto-regressive-integrated-moving-average (ARIMA) modeling, which was devised by Box and Jenkins (1970). The analysis begins by examining the nature of the fluctuations and trends within each time series. For exploratory studies this alone may provide descriptive data of interest. The initial work can give an indication of the regularity of certain types of interpretation; these may be compared across treatments or analysts.

The technique becomes of particular interest when one is examining the interrelationship of two or more time series. ARIMA can reveal subtle interrelationships which might have been very difficult to detect through visual inspection of the data. For example, assume that we wish to investigate the interrelationship of therapeutic alliance and transference interpretations. We have ratings of the level of each variable available for each session of a three-hundred-hour treatment. Using this approach we may initially be looking simply for the likelihood of co-occurrence of the two events (transference interpretations and high alliance) in the same time unit, in this case a session. At a second stage we may investigate if the prior presence of one of the variables—say, transference interpretations—predicts an increase in the second—say, therapeutic alliance—in the next or subsequent sessions. In the third stage we may study what proportion of the variability in the strength of therapeutic alliance from session to session, which cannot be accounted for in terms of its regular fluctuations, may be determined by transference interpretations. A final stage might lead us to return to examining to what extent the fluctuations in therapeutic alliance are uniquely determined by transference interpretation, or whether other related predictive variables may provide superior accounts.

It may be easier to illustrate the method with an account of an actual study. Moran and Fonagy (1987b) studied the 184 weeks of the analysis of a diabetic teenager. She was referred for treatment for brittle diabetes which manifested in recurrent episodes of hypoglycemia and ketoacidosis. Her diabetic control, which was very poor during the initial phase of her analysis, was monitored daily, and aggregated estimates of the quality of her blood glucose control could be obtained for each week. No transcripts for the sessions were available; the weekly reports of the treatment were used as the unit of analysis. Qualitative study of these data revealed several clinically significant dimensions of unconscious conflict present throughout the analysis (for example, the girl's feeling of not being loved by her father and being angry with him, conflicts over oedipal striving, and so on). Simultaneously a number of analytic themes pertaining to key symptoms were identified (such as phobic anxiety, deliberate self-punitive acts, and damaged self-representation).

Each analytic theme was defined conceptually and operationally with reference to the case material, and raters were trained to a criterion. Three independent judges rated all weekly reports for all symptoms and conflicts on 5-point scales with the anchors "definitely present" and "definitely absent." The ratings of the weekly reports on an analytic theme constituted a "series." Some of the ratings of analytic themes did not reach adequate levels of interrater agreement. The definition of intrapsychic conflict proved to be reliably rated with the exception of conflicts over death wishes.

The reliably rated analytic themes showed significant associations with the patient's quality of diabetic control. This finding, of course, is of limited interest, since the correlation may be totally accounted for by the gradual improvements in diabetic control concurrent with an increased appearance of psychic conflict in the material and a general decrease in other symptomatology. To remove association due to such a common trend, all the series were differenced. This process involved subtracting adjacent observations: for each week the data point became the change from the value observed in the previous week. In this way the covariation of week-to-week changes of analytic material and diabetic control could be examined. To strengthen causal arguments, in addition to looking at correlations between diabetic control and the analytic themes at the same time point, we also computed cross-lagged correlations, which yielded an indication of the extent to which analytic themes may be predicted by—or, indeed, may predict—changes in diabetic control.

The finding of greatest interest was that although the presence of themes of conflict in the analytic material tended to foreshadow improvements in diabetic control, improved diabetic control appeared to increase the likelihood of manifest psychological symptomatology one to three weeks later. To this point, the pattern of data provided support for our psychoanalytically based explanation of brittle diabetes (Moran 1984): that the transgressions of the diabetic regimen underlying brittle diabetes are neurotic adaptations to the anxiety and guilt aroused by unconscious conflict. Interpretation of these conflicts in the treatment studied tended to bring about an improvement in diabetic control, presumably by reducing the need for transgressions. The consequent improved control, however, led to temporary increases in anxiety and guilt.

Time series analysis is an exceptionally powerful technique. A threat to internal validity in the study just described is the possibility that a common natural fluctuation of some psychological variables and diabetic control may account for the correlations observed. For example, the patient's menstrual cycle could be the cause of such a common cyclical trend. This and other similar sources of bias may be overcome by creating transfer functions between two or more time series. A transfer function is a linear equation that relates the past of one time series to the present and future of another. In the present case, transfer functions were created for diabetic control and oedipal conflict which revealed that diabetic control could be predicted to a highly significant extent by ratings of oedipal conflict one to three weeks prior to the point at which diabetic control was assessed. The transfer function incorporating oedipal conflict accounted for 46 percent of the variance in diabetic control.

As this description illustrates, time series analysis pertains to causal explanations to the extent that we recognize a time-bound relationship between cause and effect. Establishing the facts of chronology, even if it does not remove the need for a more direct experimental test, does provide persuasive indirect evidence of at least the possibility of a causal link. The suggestion is strengthened if the measurements taken can in no way be biased by the expectation of a causal link. This can be achieved if, for example, the observations are rated in random order, as were the weekly reports in our example. Establishing a relationship between two variables in time is of itself, however, of little interest. Concomitant variation does not imply causation. To be of interest, such a demonstration has to be part of a broader psychoanalytic causal story.

The range of phenomena to which the time series approach can be applied is limited. The requirements for the inclusion of a variable are even more stringent than those that apply to the replication by segmentation paradigm. Thus, for a valid time series analysis, first, the dimensions looked at must occur throughout the series at varying intensities. Second, they must nevertheless be relatively homogeneous in form so that ratings at different times are comparable. Third, they must be contained within the time unit under investigation (for example, if we wish to examine determinants of resistance using the time unit of a session we must assume that there is a level of resistance that characterizes a particular session).

The applicability of the technique is further limited by its complexity and by the number of steps required. In-depth examination of time series analysis introduces a number of concepts that may be unfamiliar even to researchers with a good grasp of conventional statistical techniques. The application of such techniques, however, involves statistical packages that are fortunately available for microcomputers. The central requirement for conducting time series analysis (large numbers of equally paced observations) fits so well with the nature of psychoanalytic data that we consider this type of analysis to be one of the most valuable approaches to individual case data.

The time series approach to $N = 1$ design may seem complicated at first. It is, however, arguably the most easily accessible of the research designs we outline in this chapter. An analyst who keeps notes (session by session or week to week) of a patient's treatment readily accumulates 100 to 200 observations. Given access to such a resource, the research analyst may ask: "How do the different themes of the analytic work interact with one another? Is my clinical observation correct, that interpreting the anti-analytic destructive intent underlying my patient's acting out reduces the frequency or intensity of the acting out more than would be expected from the natural cyclical nature of such behaviors?"

The following "easy" steps may help satisfy the analyst's curiosity. Ask two colleagues to look at case records. One may be asked to rate the extent to which the patient manifested acting out during each time period (session or week) and the other to look at the interpretation of two aspects of the transference at each time unit. One aspect may be libidinal transference (the control theme), the other hostile aggressive transference. These ratings result in three time series. The analyst may at this stage seek statistical advice or may choose to enter the data into one of the many available statistical packages. In either case, the data will probably need differencing (adjacent observations subtracted), and correlations between the transference measures and the acting out measures will have to be computed. If significant associations are found, the analyst may wish to go no further than to report these. The analyst may, however, wish to see if there is a time-bound dynamic relationship between interpretation of the negative transference and acting out. This is discovered through computing lag correlations. Negative correlations between interpretation of the negative transference at t_1 and acting out at t_0 are expected (which would imply that interpreting the transference reduces the chance of acting out in the time period following the interpretation). The adventurous analyst may wish to construct a formal model of the relationship between the variables of interest using a transfer function—one may well be available in the statistical package being used.

PATIENT SERIES OR QUASI-EXPERIMENTAL DESIGNS

Individual case design methodology of the form discussed in the previous section may be extended to study more than one patient and to examine the differences, or the similarities, between patients. Qualitative patient series designs have a long and distinguished tradition in psychoanalysis (see Freud and Breuer [1895] 1955; Zetzel 1968) and have inspired many other well-known examples (such as Beck 1976).

The basic underpinning of more systematic, primarily quantitative, patient series research designs is most elegantly formulated by Cronbach (1975) in his principle of intensive local observation. The key features of this are (1) maintaining a clear focus on the individual rather than the average group member; (2) carefully examining how uncontrolled factors may cause specific departures from the common trend; (3) integrating personal characteristics, uncontrolled conditions, and events that occur during therapy and measurement into a causal account; and (4) delaying generalization and emphasizing the exceptions as well as the rules.

Although the emphasis in patient series design tends to be on the individual, in clinical research these designs are often applied as extensions of full experimental designs such as clinical trials. The researcher may, for example, be interested in personal characteristics that increase the likelihood of a patient's response to a particular treatment condition. Here we include patient series design because it encompasses an important category of individual case studies where the results from two or more patients are studied using either replication by segmentation or time series methodology.

Graff and Luborsky (1977) offer an interesting example in their visual display analysis of some fascinating time series data. As part of a study that examined the transcripts of four psychoanalyses of varying success, they plotted and contrasted averaged ratings of transference and resistance across the entire span of both successful and unsuccessful analyses. The plots clearly revealed that in a successful analysis the average ratings of both transference and resistance increased in the early phase of the analysis. The intensity of transference ratings continued to increase while the resistance ratings leveled off. In the end phase of the successful analysis, resistance declined while transference remained intense. By contrast, in the unsuccessful analysis resistance was more intense than transference from the start; transference was not firmly established by the middle phase; and resistance failed to decline in the terminal phase.

In an extension of this study, Luborsky et al. (1979) used the replication by segmentation technique to examine the responses to transference interpretations in three of these patients. Approaching the data by rating the 250-word segments before and after the transference interpretation on nine operationalized variables, including resistance, involvement, understanding, and transference, they were able to demonstrate characteristic differences between the patients who showed slight, moderate, and marked improvements. The patient whose analysis was relatively unsuccessful had only one significant response to transference interpretation: increased resistance. The patient with the intermediate outcome showed increased involvement and increased transference after transference interpretations. The patient showing the most positive overall response to psychoanalysis also showed the most marked increase in involvement, understanding, and transference as well as increases on other variables in response to transference interpretations. The results indicate that responses to transference interpretations may be a good indicator of potential for change.

Thus patient series extensions of individual case designs can yield interesting additional insights by using the pattern of associations observed in individual case studies as raw data and highlighting the differences between cases in the nature of the associations observed. Thus the technique has high ecological validity (it resembles real life). Naturally it suffers from the drawbacks of all ex post facto designs in that it permits more than one interpretation of the data obtained. For instance, the patterns of transference and resistance observed by Graff and Luborsky in unsuccessful analyses may have been the cause of differences in treatment success or simply the manifestation of an attribute which makes an individual unsuited to psychoanalysis for an entirely different reason (say, separation-individuation conflicts or overwhelming aggression). For confident causal assertions to be made from patient series designs, patients should be carefully matched to reduce to a minimum the likelihood of alternative accounts. Because it is doubtful that such matching can ever be adequately performed, increasing the sample size (that is, the number of patients in the series) is the safest route to improvements in generalizability.

EXPERIMENTAL DESIGNS

The designs we have examined so far represent an improvement upon the traditional methods of data collection in psychoanalysis in one way only, that is, by introducing increased rigor into data collection and data analysis. The information that is tapped by these more systematic methods was, of course, present in the data in the first place. But causal accounts are undoubtedly strengthened by careful attention to the reliability of categorization provided by good qualitative analysis, and by a focus on chronological associations (ensured by quantitative designs and the strengthening of external validity) which quasi-experimental interpretations can provide. A major step toward improving internal validity is taken when the psychoanalytic researcher decides to manipulate (that is, deliberately change) particular aspects of the conditions to which the patient is exposed; it is this type of manipulation that is assumed by experimental individual case studies.

Common to all experimental studies is the general principle of holding constant all factors except the independent variable under study. But it is unlikely that psychoanalysts would ever find themselves able to relegate their commitment to their patients' welfare to a point that would permit the artificial manipulation of the treatment condition. We may then

whether transference interpretations in the early phase of the psychoanalysis of children are helpful. In a study of this type, additional cases would be needed to counterbalance order effects—patients who have transference interpretations only at later stages of their treatment. In addition to discovering the value of particular techniques at particular phases of therapy, broader scale applications may help us to identify important patient group by technique interactions, which may in turn help us to be more specific in our therapeutic efforts. For example, are Kohutian approaches to interpretation (Kohut 1977, 1984) valuable particularly with narcissistic patients, or are they equally pertinent to other types of personality disordered patients?

REPLICATION SERIES DESIGNS

Replication is a key component of the experimental individual case study. To ensure the generalizability of the findings it is important to show that (1) they are reliable and cannot be accounted for by coincidence of circumstances, (2) they apply to a range of individuals, and (3) they may be demonstrated in a range of therapeutic settings and with different therapists.

Classical single case experimentation (Sidman 1960) differentiates between direct replication and systematic replication. In direct replication the same therapist attempts the same therapy with a different patient. For this type of replication it is important initially to ensure as much similarity between the patients as possible. In this way failures of replication are easier to interpret. Three replications are generally regarded as sufficient for generalizability (Barlow and Hersen 1984). Systematic replication is replication by different therapists in new settings with other patients and should be attempted only if direct replication has already been performed. The principle is to change as few variables at a time as is possible. In other words, initial systematic replications should mimic the original clinical approach as far as possible, and only when replication has been successfully performed should variations in technique or patient group or other parameters be attempted.

Fonagy and Moran (1990), in their treatment of growth-retarded diabetic patients, were able to report three successful replications of their A-B design. They initially treated a boy of eight, then a boy of twelve, and finally a girl of twelve. A contingent relationship between therapy and growth was demonstrated each time. Now it remains for other clinical settings to attempt systematic replication.

Replications are, however, impossible without an adequate description of the original treatment offered. Psychoanalysis on the whole has been slow to respond to the call for treatment to be sufficiently standardized to permit at least the assessment of the quality of replication (Luborsky 1984). Manuals for psychoanalytically oriented psychotherapeutic treatments are becoming available (for example, Kernberg et al. 1989; see part 3 of this book). In the case of full psychoanalysis, however, many object to manualization, claiming that the treatment they offer is too complex to be accommodated in a manual. At the Anna Freud Centre we (Fonagy et al. 1989) have for the past several years been working on a manual for child psychoanalysis which we hope will adequately describe the nature of the treatment offered.

General Issues Concerning Individual
Case Studies

DEPENDENT VARIABLES

Meissner (1989) identifies at least four separate data bases used by psychoanalysis: (1) an historical data base concerned with the patient's past; (2) an observational data base concerned with the patient's behavior, use of language, and tone of voice; (3) an associative data base concerned with the verbal productions of the patient; and (4) an introspective data base concerned with the analyst's thoughts, not necessarily verbalized. We do not agree with Meissner's conclusion that the nature of these data bases is incompatible with verification.

For example, Meissner questions the verifiability of the subjective experience of historical events, which, as we would all agree, is more important than the objective historical event itself. More recently, however, researchers have developed sophisticated techniques for the empirical study of precisely this aspect of personal historical material. Note, for example, the careful work of Brown and Harris on the impact of life events (Brown and Harris 1989) and that of Main and her colleagues on the recollection of childhood attachment experiences (Fonagy, Steele, and Steele 1991; Main, Kaplan, and Cassidy 1985; Main 1991).

Other contributors to this book offer a range of parameters that may be used in the context of individual case studies (for example, chapters 1 and 2). There are some general considerations of specific relevance to the designs we have considered here. Broadly speaking, there are two sources of data: (1) indirect data obtained from process notes, transcriptions, or recordings of psychotherapeutic treatment and (2) direct measures obtained specifically for the purpose of the study from patient, therapist, or independent observer before, during, or after treatment intervention.

Within each of these categories there exist three levels of measurement: global measures, individual target measures, and process measures. Global, or standard, measures have been developed for other populations with well-researched psychometric properties (see chapters 17 and 23). Standardized instruments such as personality inventories, diagnostic interviews, symptom checklists, and the like may not be as useful for the kind of repeated administration required by individual case investigators.

Individual target measures, such as ones used by behavior therapists to look at treatment progress, might be of limited value. As Bucci (1989) pointed out, the relevance of apparent symptomatic change in psychoanalysis is questionable. Improvement may reflect no more than dependency and compliance, while worsening may signal an increase in the person's capacity to tolerate feelings or autonomy. The aim of psychoanalysis is rarely limited to symptomatic improvement and tends to encompass character change. Nonetheless, we maintain that the monitoring of symptoms, if accompanied by a broader set of measures and a degree of psychoanalytic and methodological sophistication, can provide a valuable indicator of underlying psychological mechanisms (see, for example, Metcalfe 1956). Psychoanalytic treatment has its own targets which can be quantified, given time and effort on the part of the researcher. Target measures may include defenses, resistance, key conflicts, and the manifestation of essential psychological capacities (empathy, control of affects). These may be sampled inferentially, based on transcripts of sessions or via independent testing.

Process measures represent the heart of the individual case study. Quantification of what happens in the patient–analyst exchange has long been of powerful interest to clinicians and, more recently, to researchers as well. Process measures can most readily meet the requirement of being present in variable quantity throughout treatment. In combination with target measures (symptomatic indicators and the monitoring of key psychoanalytic variables), measurement of the process of therapy is most likely to advance clinical practice. The problem with individualized process measures in the past has been that inadequate attention was paid to their psychometric properties (Rust and Golombok 1989) and the validity of measures taken was spurious and untested. Nevertheless, with the advent of new, more systematic approaches to process research (Rice and Greenberg 1984), the accumulation of research with such measures will minimize this problem in the long term.

There remain only a number of specific cautions:

1. Because measures taken will require repeated administration, nonreactivity is essential (that is, the act of measurement should not impinge on the variable being measured, nor cause change with subsequent measurement using the same instrument).

2. Data collection should begin early, preferably before the start of treatment.
3. Data should be collected under consistent conditions to avoid confounding factors.
4. Multiple measures should be used in order to build up a cross-situational breadth, enhance construct validity, and detect side effects.
5. The measures should tap independent data sources to meet the criterion of triangulation (to be able to arrive at the same conclusion from a number of starting points).
6. The frequency of administration should be sufficient to tap fluctuations in the measure relevant to the study.

STATISTICS

There are many special considerations that apply to statistical analyses of individual case studies, and we cannot deal with them here. The interested reader should consult the excellent work by Kazdin (1984) for a review of the most commonly used statistical analyses for single case experimental design. A number of more general points, in reference to psychoanalysis and statistics, are worth considering here:

Most standard statistical tests, particularly of the parametric kind (such as analysis of variance and regression analysis), are inappropriate for the analysis of individual case data (where the error components of scores are not independent). In addition, there is general agreement that, notwithstanding suggestions to the contrary, the chi-squared tests and the t and F tests are also not suitable (Morley 1989).

The traditional way of looking at data from individual case studies has been simple visual analysis, where time is displayed on the abscissa (X-axis) and the dependent variable is displayed on the ordinate (Y-axis). Phase changes (if any) are indicated by vertical lines; differences in these (if any) are assumed to be visually detectable. If too many observations are made, or if the data are too "noisy" for visual inspection, there are various smoothing functions available; by combining adjacent points, these provide clarity, even if of a somewhat artificial kind. Data can be further clarified by removing underlying trends (by differencing using adjacent observations) and by weeding out extreme scores. After such cosmetic operations, the nature of the associations is more likely to be obvious in the visual display. Only if this is not the case should we feel forced to resort to statistical analysis.

There are a number of very simple techniques available for looking at the differences between phases of treatment. The randomization test (Edgington 1984), for example, does not rely on the same assumptions as conventional tests, such as random sampling of subjects from a population.

The test directly estimates how often a more extreme set of scores than the obtained pattern of results occurs if the data are rearranged in all possible combinations. There are also some very elegant nonparametric tests of trend based on Kendall's S statistic. Not only do these permit the identification of a trend for change in a particular direction, but they also enable the investigator to test the combined significance of such trends using the J statistic (Leach 1979). This technique may be particularly relevant to the replication by segmentation strategy. We have already mentioned time series analysis techniques, which in our view are the statistical treatment of choice for time series individual treatment designs, notwithstanding their relative complexity. They may also be useful for the analysis of experimental designs described in the last section. Some other, simpler, tests are described by Morley and Adams (1989).

EVALUATION

There are a number of advantages to the empirical study of psychoanalytic data using individual case methodology. First, the methodology itself is atheoretical and shares techniques with the disciplines of psychology, linguistics, and sociology. This should aid us in establishing a means of communicating our findings to the broader scientific community. Second, the individual case study method also has the power to communicate to the nonscientific community the benefits of our work in a manner which is condoned by opinion leaders (leading psychiatrists, media commentators, and judges, for example), on whom our public standing largely depends. Third, the method represents a development of—if not necessarily an improvement upon—traditional case study methodology. It may thus deliver fresh insights into the nature of conscious and unconscious functioning. Fourth, the method is uniquely suited to psychoanalytic clinical practice in certain respects, including the relatively long term nature of psychoanalytic investigations, the attention to uncontrollable as well as controllable conditions, the attention to events occurring during treatment and measurement, and the influence of specific features of history (see Cronbach 1975). Fifth, as this method is closer to psychoanalytic practice than other modes of systematic research, we hope that it may draw more analysts into the empirical research arena.

We do not underestimate the difficulties involved:

1. Critics may still argue that the small number of cases studied implies that psychoanalysis can speak only about an unrepresentative, homogeneous group of middle-class patients.
2. Ensuring internal validity is likely to conflict with other clinical aims, for

example, implementing the treatment as fast as possible, avoiding interference from measurement, and the like.
3. Ethical considerations, as well as legal ones, require attention.
4. Each measure needs to be examined for clinical relevance. The investigating clinician needs to develop measures suitable to his or her purpose.

Finally, some may claim that the performance of any independent
study alongside clinical work presents an irretrievable confound. Philosophical arguments can be marshaled both for and against the validity of
systematic investigation. Ultimately, what will speak to analysts in both
camps are clinically useful findings which will edify and assist them in their
daily work.

Summary

We have described and compared five individual case study methods: the
qualitative case study, studies of segments of therapeutic material, time
series studies, quasi-experimental designs, and experimental designs. Each
approach has its special place and value in relation to specific kinds of
potential psychodynamic research questions.

The qualitative single case study simply entails a more systematic
approach to analytic material than is routinely the case. It is a well-
established methodology within psychoanalysis and has received considerable recent attention. There can be no doubt that our traditional narrative
approach to reporting clinical material permits highly selective accounts.
This tendency would be adequately countered by the establishment of
minimal standards for qualitative reporting. It is probably most appropriate
when the integration of diverse ideas about a specific clinical problem or
developmental stage is the primary aim of the inquiry. A recently established research project at the Anna Freud Centre on the developmental
phase of early adulthood, under the leadership of Anne-Marie Sandler, is
an instance where this research approach is to be applied.

The quantitative analysis of an individual treatment record through
identifying repeated occurrences of some specific event is also well established. Here, a sample is drawn by gathering all or some segments of a
treatment record that contain an event of interest to the researcher. The
method has proved very fruitful in studying the nature of symptoms as
well as aspects of the therapeutic relationship. As very few events in an
analysis are unique, this approach offers almost limitless possibilities for
examining whether a specific class of events is associated with other
characteristic occurrences in the analytic material. The method is less useful

when there are few occurrences of the target event (for example, break-down within an analysis). There are statistical and methodological limitations inherent to segmenting what is a continuous real-time process. The approach is most valuable where there are clear and specific hypotheses to be tested (for example, that new information concerning childhood experiences is more likely to emerge following appropriate interpretations of the transference). It is less appropriate at the exploratory stage of quantitative analysis of case reports.

Time series analysis is a statistically more sophisticated technique which also requires substantial preparatory work. Information on all the parameters of interest is required for a large number of time units (sessions or weeks of treatment). Once the researcher has access to such data, he or she may freely explore the dynamic interplay between the parameters right through the treatment. Time series analysis harnesses relatively recent methodological advances in social science and permits the construction of sophisticated models of the psychoanalytic process. Its usefulness is limited to the investigation of phenomena that occur throughout an analysis (transference, various affects, interpretation, and so on). It is best suited to answering questions for which the time sequence of events may be expected to provide information concerning causal relationships.

Quasi-experimental designs allow for the comparison of groups of patients using the methodology derived from the quantitative study of individual case records. Intensive individual studies are collected and the researcher aims to account for differences between the individual patterns observed. Thus, successful analyses may be contrasted with unsuccessful analyses in terms of the evolving pattern of transference interpretations and resistance. Alternatively, we may wish to contrast borderline with neurotic patients in terms of their response to confrontational interventions. Because matching patients is an important part of the procedure, this approach is most appropriate when the variable used to group patients is unambiguous. This type of quasi-experimental design is just an extension of single case studies. It retains the individual focus of the designs discussed, while improving upon the generalizability of findings through increased sample size.

The experimental design has yet to be established in psychoanalytic research. Unlike any of the other individual designs, it requires some degree of systematic manipulation of the treatment. This would usually take the form of delaying treatment for an independently determined period in order to see if there is a tendency for spontaneous change. In contrast with the previous methods, the problems most readily addressed using this approach concern questions of efficacy rather than process. Experimental designs are typically the most persuasive to funding organizations. It is unknown whether the introduction of such a deliberately manipulative aspect changes the analytic process to a point beyond which findings may no longer be generalizable to traditional psychoanalysis.

Individual case designs have substantial advantages over traditional experimental studies. Problems of sampling and questions of generalizability trouble group designs as much, if not more, than individual case studies and their aggregation into quasi-experimental studies. Large group designs commonly have difficulties with recruitment and low participation rates, patient attrition, and poorly matched groups. For example, there can be little doubt that individuals who agree to participate in a randomized control trial (RCT) tend to be less seriously disturbed and more socially disadvantaged than the average patient; thus the generalizability of findings from RCTs may appropriately be questioned (Owens, Slade, and Fielding 1989). Attempts at statistically balancing variability by aggregating data from different individuals may provide data that can be generalized only to groups, not to individuals. Experimental designs also may blatantly flaunt the criterion of ecological validity. Findings should be pertinent to how things happen in the real world. Substantial deviations from normal clinical practice, which larger group designs may reflect, also bring with them many ethical problems.

Individual case designs are, however, not without substantial limitations. The small number of individuals involved must lead to questions concerning representativeness. Careful selection of participants and systematic replication is of considerable value. The issue of generalizability may be directly tackled by making sure that both genders are represented, a wide age range is covered, and, where appropriate, a diverse set of diagnostic groups is used. It is unlikely, however, that in any specific case all, or even the most important, relevant factors will be systematically sampled. For this reason, large group studies drawn from random samples will remain essential to enable researchers to manipulate single variables while assuming that random assignment to groups will provide a control over other pertinent factors.

Quasi-experimental large group designs may be an intermediate stage between experimental group studies and $N = 1$ research. In such studies, careful monitoring of the status of individuals with respect to factors suspected to be of relevance, together with appropriate statistical control procedures, may achieve considerable clarification of important issues to do with treatment.

Individual case studies in psychoanalysis will remain essential. Given the length and intensity of analytic treatment, large group studies will always require a level of funding where cost/benefit ratios are untenable for most funding agencies. The minimal methodological requirements placed upon RCTs have put such studies way beyond the reach of most clinical groups. Psychoanalytic research simply does not yet have the infrastructure to participate in research programs of this sort and may not be in such a position for some time. In order to establish its scientific credibility in the meantime, psychoanalysis will have to rely upon individual case data studied in a manner consistent with the canons of late twentieth century social science.

References

ALLPORT, G. D. (1961). *Pattern and growth in personality.* New York: Holt, Rinehart and Winston.

BARLOW, D. H., & HERSEN, M. (1984). *Single case experimental designs: Strategies for studying behavior change* (2nd ed.). New York: Pergamon Press.

BECK, A. T. (1976). *Cognitive therapy and emotional disorders.* New York: Meriden.

BOX, G. E. P., & JENKINS, G. M. (1970). *Time series analysis: Forecasting and control.* San Francisco: Holden-Day.

BROWN G., & HARRIS T. (1989). *Life events and illness.* London: Unwin Hyman.

BUCCI, W. (1989). A reconstruction of Freud's tally argument: A program for psychoanalytic research. *Psychoanalytic Inquiry, 9,* 249–281.

CAMPBELL, D. T., & FISKE, D. W. (1959). Convergent and discriminative validation by the multi-trait-multimethod matrix. *Psychological Bulletin, 56,* 81–105.

CHASSAN, J. B. (1967). *Research design in clinical psychology and psychiatry.* New York: Appleton-Century-Crofts.

CHASSAN, J. B. (1979). *Research design in clinical psychology and psychiatry* (2nd ed.). New York: Appleton-Century-Crofts.

COMMITTEE ON SCIENTIFIC ACTIVITIES OF THE AMERICAN PSYCHOANALYTIC ASSOCIATION (1988). *How can we best present our clinical experience? Suggestions for alternate methods of case reporting.* Unpublished manuscript.

COOKE, T., & CAMPBELL, D. (1979). *Quasi-experimentation.* Boston: Houghton Mifflin.

CRONBACH, L. J. C. (1975). Beyond the two disciplines of scientific psychology. *American Psychologist, 30,* 116–127.

DEUTCH, L. (1987). Reflections on the psychosomatic treatment of patients with bronchial asthma. *Psychoanalytic Study of the Child, 42,* 239–261.

EDELSON, M. (1988). *Psychoanalysis: A theory in crisis.* Chicago: University of Chicago Press.

EDELSON, M. (1989). The nature of psychoanalytic theory: Implications for psychoanalytic research. *Psychoanalytic Inquiry, 9,* 169–192.

EDGINGTON, E. S. (1966). Statistical inference and non-random samples. *Psychological Bulletin, 66,* 485–487.

EDGINGTON, E. S. (1984). Statistics and single case analysis. In M. Hersen, R. M. Eisler, & P. M. Monli (Eds.), *Progressive behavior modification* (Vol. 16). New York: Academic Press.

FONAGY, P. (1982). Psychoanalysis and empirical science. *International Review of Psychoanalysis, 9,* 125–145.

FONAGY, P. (1989). On the integration of psychoanalysis and cognitive behaviour therapy. *British Journal of Psychotherapy, 5,* 557–563.

FONAGY, P., & MORAN, G. S. (1990). Studies on the efficacy of child psychoanalysis. *Journal of Consulting and Clinical Psychology, 58,* 684–695.

FONAGY, P., KENNEDY, H., EDGCUMBE, R., TOUGET, & MORAN, G. (1992). *The Hampstead manual of child analysis.* Unpublished manuscript, Anna Freud Centre.

FONAGY, P., STEELE, H., & STEELE, M. (1991). Maternal representations of attachment during pregnancy predict infant-mother attachment patterns at one year. *Child Development, 62,* 891–905.

FREUD, S. (1917/1963). Introductory lectures on psycho-analysis: 3. General theory of the neuroses. In J. Strachey (Ed.), *The standard edition of the complete psychological works of Sigmund Freud* (Vol. 16, pp. 243–463). London: Hogarth Press.

FREUD, S. (1937/1958). Constructions in analysis. In J. Strachey (Ed.), *The standard edition of the complete psychological works of Sigmund Freud* (Vol. 23, pp. 257–269). London: Hogarth Press.

FREUD, S., & BREUER, J. (1895/1955). Studies on hysteria. In J. Strachey (Ed.), *The standard edition of the complete psychological works of Sigmund Freud* (Vol. 2, pp. 1–305). London: Hogarth Press.

GASSNER, S., SAMPSON, H., BRUMER, S., & WEISS, J. (1986). The emergence of warded-off contents. In J. Weiss & H. Sampson (Eds.), *The psychoanalytic process: Theory, clinical observation and empirical research.* New York: Guilford Press.

GOOD, D. A., & WATTS, F. N. (1989). Qualitative research. In G. Parry & F. N. Watts (Eds.), *Behavioural and mental health research: A handbook of skills and methods* (pp. 211–232). Hillsdale, NJ: Erlbaum.

GOTTMAN, J. M. (1981). *Time-series analysis: A comprehensive introduction for social scientists.* Cambridge: Cambridge University Press.

GRAFF, H., & LUBORSKY, L. (1977). Long-term trends in transference and resistance: A quantitative analytic method applied to four psychoanalyses. *Journal of the American Psychoanalytic Association, 25,* 471–490.

GRÜNBAUM, A. (1986). Precis of the foundations of psychoanalysis: A philosophical critique, with commentary. *Behavioral and Brain Sciences, 9,* 217–284.

HARRIS, F. N., & JENSON, W. R. (1985a). AB designs with replication: A reply to Hayes. *Behavioral Assessment, 7,* 133–135.

HARRIS, F. N., & JENSON, W. R. (1985b). Comparisons of multiple-baseline across persons designs and AB designs with replication: Issues and confusions. *Behavioral Assessment, 7,* 121–128.

HAYES, S. C. (1981). Single case experimental design and empirical clinical research. *Journal of Consulting and Clinical Psychology, 49,* 193–211.

HAYES, S. C. (1982). The role of the individual case in the production and consumption of clinical knowledge. In P. C. Kendall & J. N. Butcher (Eds.), *Handbook of research methods in clinical psychology.* New York: Wiley.

HAYES, S. C. (1985). Natural multiple baselines across persons: A reply to Harris and Jenson. *Behavioral Assessment, 7,* 129–132.

KAZDIN, A. E. (1982). *Single case research designs: Methods for clinical and applied settings.* New York: Oxford University Press.

KAZDIN, A. E. (1984). Statistical analyses for single case experimental designs. In D. H. Barlow & M. Hersen (Eds.), *Single case experimental designs: Strategies for studying behavioral change.* New York: Pergamon Press.

KERNBERG, O. F., SELZER, M. A., KOENIGSBERG, H. W., CARR, A. C., & APPELBAUM, A. H. (1989). *Psychodynamic psychotherapy of borderline patients.* New York: Basic Books.

KOHUT, H. (1977). *The restoration of the self.* New York: International Universities Press.

KOHUT, H. (1984). *How does psychoanalysis cure?* Chicago: University of Chicago Press.

KRAEMER, H. (1981). Coping strategies in psychiatric clinical research. *Journal of Consulting and Clinical Psychology, 49,* 309–319.

KRATOCHWILL, T. R. (1985). Case study research in school psychology. *School Psychology Review, 14,* 204–215.

KVALE, S. (1986). Psychoanalytic therapy as qualitative research. In P. D. Ashworth (Ed.), *Qualitative research in psychology.* Pittsburgh: Duquesne University Press.

LEACH, C. (1979). *Introduction to statistics: A non-parametric approach for the social sciences.* Chichester: Wiley.

LUBORSKY, L. (1967). Momentary forgetting during psychotherapy and psychoanalysis: A theory and research method. *Psychological Issues,* (Monograph 18/19), pp. 177–217.

LUBORSKY, L. (1984). *Principles of psychoanalytic psychotherapy: A manual for supportive-expressive treatment.* New York: Basic Books.

LUBORSKY, L., BACHRACH, H., GRAFF, H., PULVER, S., & CRITS-CRISTOPH, P. (1979). Preconditions and consequences of transference interpretations: A clinical-quantitative investigation. *Journal of Nervous and Mental Disease, 167,* 391–491.

LURIA, A. R. (1966). *Higher cortical functions in man.* New York: Plenum Press.

MAIN, M. (1991). Metacognitive knowledge, metacognitive monitoring and singular (coherent) vs. multiple (incoherent) models of attachment: Findings and directions for future research. In P. Harris, J. Stevenson-Hinde, & C. Parkes (Eds.), *Attachment across the life cycle.* New York: Routledge.

MAIN, M., KAPLAN, N., & CASSIDY, J. (1985). Security in infancy, childhood and adulthood: A move to the level of representation. In I. Bretherton & E. Waters (Eds.), *Growing points of attachment theory and research* (Monographs of the Society for Research in Child Development, Series no. 204), 50 (1–2).

Marty, P., & de M'Uzan, M. (1963). La pensée opératoire. *Revue Française de Psychanalyse, 27* (Suppl.), 1345–1356.

McCleary, R., & Hay, R. A. (1980). *Applied time series analysis for the social sciences.* Beverley Hills, CA: Sage.

Meissner, W. W. (1989). A note on psychoanalytic facts. *Psychoanalytic Inquiry, 9,* 193–219.

Metcalfe, M. (1956). Demonstration of a psychosomatic relationship. *British Journal of Medical Psychology, 29,* 63–66.

Moran, G. (1984). Psychoanalytic treatment of diabetic children. *Psychoanalytic Study of the Child, 38,* 265–293.

Moran, G., & Fonagy, P. (1987a). *Insight and symptomatic improvement.* Paper presented at the Workshop on Psychotherapy Outcome Research with Children, National Institute of Mental Health, Bethesda, MD.

Moran, G., & Fonagy, P. (1987b). Psychoanalysis and diabetes: An experiment in single case methodology. *British Journal of Medical Psychology, 60,* 370–378.

Moran, G., & Fonagy, P. (1991). Brittle diabetes: Empirical investigations. In R. Szur (Ed.), *Scientific explorations in child psychotherapy.* London: Free Associations Press.

Morley, S. (1987). Single case methodology in behaviour therapy. In S. J. Lindsay & G. E. Powell (Eds.), *A handbook of clinical adult psychology.* London: Gower Press.

Morley, S. (1989). Single case research. In G. Parry & F. N. Watts (Eds.), *Behavioural and mental health research: A handbook of skills and methods.* Hillsdale, NJ: Erlbaum.

Morley, S., & Adams, M. (1989). Some single statistics for exploring single case time-series data. *British Journal of Clinical Psychology, 28,* 1–18.

Nagel, E. (1959). Methodological issues in psychoanalytic theory. In S. Hook (Ed.), *Psychoanalysis, scientific method and philosophy* (pp. 38–56). New York: New York University Press.

Owens, R. G., Slade, P. D., & Fielding, D. M. (1989). Patient series and quasi-experimental designs. In G. Parry & F. N. Watts (Eds.), *Behavioural and mental health research: A handbook of skills and methods* (pp. 189–213). Hillsdale, NJ: Erlbaum.

Peck, D. F. (1985). Small *N* experimental designs in clinical practice. In F. N. Watts (Ed.), *New developments in clinical psychology.* Chichester: BPS-Wiley.

Peterson, C., Luborsky, L., & Seligman, M. E. P. (1983). Attributions and depressive mood shifts: A case study using the symptom-context method. *Journal of Abnormal Psychology, 92,* 96–103.

Rice, L., & Greenberg, L. (1984). *Change episodes in psychotherapy: Intensive analysis of patterns.* New York: Guilford Press.

Rust, J., & Golombok, S. (1989). *Modern psychometrics.* London: Routledge.

Sandler, J., Kennedy, H., & Tyson, R. (1980). *The technique of child analysis.* Cambridge, MA: Harvard University Press.

SHALLICE, T. (1979). Case study approach in neuropsychological research. *Journal of Clinical Neuropsychology, 1,* 183–211.

SHALLICE, T. (1989). *From neuropsychology to cognitive neuroscience.* Hillsdale, NJ: Erlbaum.

SIDMAN, M. (1960). *Tactics of scientific research.* New York: Basic Books.

SIFNEOS, P. E. (1974). A reconsideration of psychodynamic mechanisms in psychosomatic symptom formation in view of recent clinical observations. *Psychotherapy and Psychosomatics, 24,* 151–155.

SILBERSCHATZ, G., SAMPSON, H., & WEISS, J. (1986). Testing pathogenic beliefs versus seeking transference gratifications. In J. Weiss & H. Sampson (Eds.), *The psychoanalytic process: Theory, clinical observation and empirical research.* New York: Guilford Press.

STYLES, P. (1984). Client disclosure and psychotherapy session evaluations. *British Journal of Clinical Psychology, 23,* 311–312.

WALLERSTEIN, R. S. (1986). *Forty-two lives in treatment: A study of psychoanalysis and psychotherapy.* New York: Guilford Press.

WATSON, P. J., & WORKMAN, F. A. (1981). Non-concurrent multiple baseline across individuals design: An extension of the traditional multiple baseline. *Journal of Behavior Therapy and Experimental Psychiatry, 12,* 257–259.

WEISS, J., & SAMPSON, H. (1986). *The psychoanalytic process theory: Clinical observation and empirical research.* New York: Guilford Press.

ZETZEL, E. R. (1968). The so-called good hysteric. *International Journal of Psychoanalysis, 49,* 256–260.

CHAPTER 6

Psychoanalysis as Science: Challenges to the Data of Psychoanalytic Research

ROBERT S. WALLERSTEIN

SINCE FREUD'S DAY MANY PSYCHOANALYTIC psychotherapists have lived with the comfortable conviction that the road to explanation and the road to cure are indeed the same. To quote an enthusiastic advocate of this position, "It may turn out that every psychoanalyst who *merely* follows the method he was taught to follow will discover that he has been doing research, just as Monsieur Jourdain, of Molière's *Le Bourgeois Gentilhomme*, suddenly discovered that he had been speaking prose for forty years without knowing it" (Ramzy 1963, 74). Starting with Freud, the traditional case study method has indeed provided an extraordinary range of insights into the structure of mind, the forces at work in mental illness, and the processes of change and cure. In contrast, systematic formal research has had far less impact on either theory or practice (see Wallerstein and Sampson 1971). Nevertheless, however fruitful its data, and however brilliant the explanatory power of the theory derived from that data, for a host of reasons—which are enumerated in this chapter and others—the clinical case study method can no longer suffice as the sole avenue to the accrual of psychoanalytic knowledge. It must be supplemented by more rigorous and systematic research efforts, on and about the psychoanalytic process as it actually unfolds, if we are to have a basis for the credibility of our claims to status as a science.

Few theoretical issues have, in fact, been more passionately argued among both adherents from within and observers and critics from without

This chapter is condensed and abstracted from Wallerstein (1986) by Nancy Miller and Lester Luborsky.

than the status of our discipline as a science. Its position has had to be widely defended against critics among philosophers of science, like Ernest Nagel and Sidney Hook (Hook 1959), who argued that psychoanalytic theory did not satisfy the most basic requirements of a true science; and against Karl Popper (1963), who described psychoanalysis as ·a pseudoscience, since the elasticity of its postulates did not allow for the possibility of falsification, and therefore of true testing of its theoretical tenets.

Equally passionate criticisms have come from within. The central empirical dilemma was cogently posed in a paper by Philip Seitz (1966), "The Consensus Problem in Psychoanalytic Research," which demonstrated that expert analysts could not achieve reliable agreement about interpretations, based on inferences about complex internal states. David Rapaport noted that "there is [as yet] no established canon [in psychoanalysis] for the interpretation of clinical observations" (1960, 113). Even earlier, Glover maintained that there is "no effective control of conclusions based on interpretation, [and this fact] is the Achilles heel of psycho-analytical research" (1952, 405).

The fact that skilled psychoanalytic clinicians can construct differing but equally plausible and compelling formulations of psychoanalytic case material, yet at the same time have no systematic method for establishing the truth claims of any of the alternatives, has helped in part to propel the growing popularity of the hermeneutic perspective in psychoanalysis. Its main idea is that the truth value of a formulation can be derived only from the consistency with which the proposition appears within the data of the actual session.

That stance has also been sparked, in part, by a growing dissatisfaction with the powerful, once unquestioned, theoretical hegemony of the ego psychology tenets advanced by Hartmann, Kris, Loewenstein, Rapaport, and others within American psychoanalysis. In the past several decades the monolithic supremacy of Freud's metapsychology has given way to an array of divergent revisionist positions, encompassing many varieties of hermeneutic, phenomenological, subjectivistic, and/or linguistically based conceptualizations of the nature of psychoanalysis.

What these diverse perspectives have in common is an acceptance of the dichotomy between a psychology based on reasons and one based on causes as Home noted:

In discovering that the symptom had meaning, and basing his treatment on this hypothesis, Freud took the psychoanalytic study of neurosis *out of the world of science* into the world of the humanities, because a meaning is not the product of causes but the creation of a subject. This is a major difference; for the logic and method of the humanities is radically different from that of science, though no less respectable and rational, and of course much longer established (1966, 43).

Drawing upon the *verstehende Psychologie* of the German romantic school of philosophy spearheaded by Wilhelm Dilthey at the turn of the century, and with more current European philosophy of science contributions in the works of Gadamer (1975), Habermas (1971), and Ricoeur (1970), this argument has seemed to lend an aura of convincing plausibility to much current psychoanalytic theorizing. Some, like Home (1966), Rycroft (1966), and Klauber (1968) in England, seem persuaded that psychoanalysis should not be considered a scientific discipline at all, but rather a humanistic discipline like history, literary criticism, or biblical exegetical interpretation (from which the term *hermeneutic* derived in the first place).

In the United States, Gill (1976), Klein (1976), and Schafer (1976) have preferred to see psychoanalysis as still constituting a science, albeit one governed by its own set of evidential standards, including differing criteria of proof intrinsic to the special and subjective nature of its data base. Still others, like Modell (Abrams 1971), Sandler and Joffe (1969), and Wallerstein (1976) have worked toward trying to reconcile the idiosyncratic search for meaning and reasons with a concomitant effort to fit such data into the causal framework of a natural science of mind.

The hermeneutic argument has variously tried either to cope with the question of how psychoanalytic propositions are validated and proved (as in the writings of Ricoeur [1977] and of Steele [1979]) or, alternatively, to reject such questions of evidence as themselves reflecting unacceptable distortions of the essential nature of the psychoanalytic endeavor (Schafer 1981; Spence 1982; Sherwood 1969).

Paul Ricoeur, for example, has posited that since everything—"theory, method, treatment, and interpretation of a particular case" (1977, 865)—is to be verified at once, the way is open to charges of circularity in the validating process, exposing all propositions ultimately to the risk of being irrefutable and therefore unverifiable. His response to questions of validation has been to piece together a "confirmatory constellation," which includes criteria of coherence, inner consistency, and narrative intelligibility, as constituting the means of "proof" in psychoanalysis. He further developed the hermeneutic idea that while knowledge of the parts is required to understand the whole, the parts in turn can be understood only as aspects of the whole, which envelops them with meaning (see Steele 1979).

Others within the hermeneutic camp have tried to avoid the language of proof and evidence altogether, as representing a misrepresentation of what constitutes the essential core of the psychoanalytic dialogue. The distinction posed by them focuses on the quest for narrative fit, rather than for so-called historical truth. Psychoanalysis becomes, in this view, only the telling—and repeated retelling—of stories, stories of a particular life, until analyst and analysand come to a consensus based ultimately on a better story, one that encompasses more of what had been previously repressed and disavowed, and therefore one that makes better sense of the puzzling array of symptoms, behaviors, and dispositions with which the analysand had initially come for treatment.

This position has been advanced by Donald Spence (1982), who challenged the assumption that patients' words are sufficient to lead to the unraveling of the historical truth. Spence suggests that rather it is in the happenstance of the patient's choosing particular linguistic constructions that we have in sharable language the subjective form of the event or the memory to be explained. Pushed to its logical extreme, such a view suggests that the narrative or story that we create not only shapes our view of the past, but in constituting a creation of the present, actually *becomes* the past.

Such logic leads—according to Spence—to a transformation of the usual analytic conventions; rather than working on reconstruction, one moves toward new construction; rather than describing acts of discovery, one enters into acts of creation; rather than locating historical truth, one can only approximate narrative fit; rather than viewing analysis as a science of recovery of the past, one reconstitutes it into a dialogue of choice and creation in the present and future. Ultimately, Spence's view reconfigures the psychoanalyst from historical scientist and archivist into poet and aestheticist.

The hermeneutic approach to psychoanalysis arose in response to the field's difficulties in establishing its credibility as a natural science in the face of the mounting positivist philosophical attack (Hook 1959; Blight 1981). Some clinicians came to conceptualize psychoanalysis as an uneasy amalgam of the two strands of Western intellectual history embodied in Freud (see Holt 1972). There is, on the one hand, the clinical psychological theory, which seeks to interpret the reasons for human actions; on the other hand, there is the general metapsychological theory, existing within a natural science framework, which seeks to establish the causes of human behaviors. In the early 1970s George Klein (1976) attempted to sever and cast out the general metapsychological theory—representing what he viewed as an outmoded mechanistic construction which positivist critics had already demolished—from the clinical theory, which he felt to be the proper whole of psychoanalysis, hermeneutic in method and logic, and humanistic in its image of man.

This staking out of a new ontological position for psychoanalysis has clearly appealed to many; in relation to the place of research in our field, it has buttressed the widespread view that the traditional psychoanalytic case study method initiated by Freud is not only a sufficient form of research but also the only kind of research that is appropriate and relevant to the psychoanalytic enterprise. Accordingly, all research efforts grounded in the natural science model are viewed as inappropriate and irrelevant.

Counterarguments to the hermeneutic position have evolved around three sets of issues that hermeneuticists claim distinguish psychoanalysis from natural science. These include issues of the *logic* of the theory, issues of its *epistemological* base, and issues of its *methods* of discovery and validation.

In regard to the logic of psychoanalysis as a theory, Habermas (1971) made two pivotal and differentiating contentions. The first was that, as opposed to the causality of nature, operative in all natural science, psychoanalysis operates via the "causality of fate" (pp. 256, 271), a phrase taken from Hegel. What this suggests is that the neurotic's undoing of pathogenic repressions in the analytic process *dissolves* the causal connection previously linking the pathogenic conflict to the neurotic illness. Hebermas's second contention is that causal accounts in psychoanalysis are always embedded in, and determined by, the uniqueness of history and of context, whereas causal accounts in natural science are always generic and free of relationship to either history or context (p. 273).

In his incisive critique of this hermeneutic argument, Adolf Grünbaum (1984) has pointed out the illogic of Habermas's first contention, since therapeutic gain is achieved precisely by making use of a causal contention (completely akin to the logic of natural science) rather than by overcoming the connection; in regard to issues of history and context dependency, Grünbaum has demonstrated that no such logical distinction exists. Natural science provides many examples of the connectedness of causality and historical context. (As a homely example, the response of a rubber band to stretching is completely dependent on its past history of having been stretched.)

The epistemological argument for the hermeneutic position advanced in Spence's book (1982) was based on his distinction between the "privileged competence" of analysands in relation to understanding their internal mental states, versus the merely "normative competence" of trained psychoanalysts, who bring only their theory-grounded understanding to the report of the analytic interaction. (The treating analyst, who is party to the entire prior history and current context of the analysis, can, over time, come to share in the analysand's privileged competence.) If this argument is true, psychoanalysis would have a radically different epistemological base from that of other sciences, which rest on observations made by trained observers, using methods relevant to the data of observation, in ways that test them against the predictions of the theory.

Grünbaum has adduced many persuasive arguments to counter this claim of epistemological separateness. He notes, for example, that we can and do interpret against the patient's judgments and in the face of the patient's denials; that the patient's acknowledgment is only one of the criteria used in assessing the heuristic or veridical status of our interventions; that the patient's agreement can serve as a form of compliance, contaminated by suggestion; and that no human memory, let alone the neurotically conflicted patient's, is infallible. Grünbaum has adequately demonstrated that the patient's so-called cognitive monopoly is "demonstrably untenable" (1984, 38).

Moreover, Robert Holt (1961, 1962) has demonstrated how the *methods* used in humanistic disciplines such as literary criticism and history are at bottom identical with those of natural science. The time-honored idiographic-nomothetic methodological dichotomy actually does not hold; nor does the hermeneutic criterion of internal consistency differ at all from predictive validity as a truth criterion in the hard sciences. As Holt noted, "The test of predictive validity is nothing more than establishing the degree of internal consistency within the combined body of (1) the data (and theory) on which the prediction was based, and (2) establishing it in the newly obtained data" (1961, 52).

Karl Popper has, in fact, argued that total inductive justification is logically impossible, since *some* theory or conception must precede, and give meaning to, any observation; therefore

> objective knowledge is also conjectural knowledge. . . . all theoretical or generalizing sciences make use of the *same* method, whether they are natural sciences or social sciences. . . . the "method of hypothesis," the active attempt to grasp a situation, and to solve a problem by advancing a hypothesis and trying to test it. (Blight 1981, 189)

In the end, natural science and history use the same method to solve different kinds of problems.

And the dichotomization between reasons and causes has little to support it, other than suggesting that there are simply different domains of inquiry which are approached by the same scientific methods. That is, reasons can be causes when such reasons make a difference to the occurrence of events for which they are the reasons with only differences of degree distinguishing these. Given all of this, the hermeneutic argument can be seen to have collapsed, to no longer be a real alternative to an empirical approach to psychoanalysis.

A newer and more powerful challenge to the scientific credibility of psychoanalysis has, however, arisen from the natural science side, represented by the comprehensive philosophical examination of Freud's works by Grünbaum. Grünbaum's thesis (1984) is that the claim of psychoanalysis as a method yielding verifiable data about mental functioning rests on one "cardinal epistemological defense" (1984, 127), which he has dubbed "The

Tally Argument" (from Freud's statement [(1917) 1963] that "conflicts will only be successfully solved and . . . resistances overcome if the anticipatory ideas [the patient] is given, tally with what is really in him" [p. 452]). Grünbaum suggests that Freud's Tally Argument rests on the conjunction of two causally necessary conditions: (1) that *only* psychoanalytic treatment can yield veridically correct insights into the unconscious conflicts determining the neurosis and (2) that these correct insights are in turn causally necessary for the therapeutic conquest of the neurosis.

Since unique therapeutic effectiveness cannot be empirically claimed for psychoanalysis, and since we have ceased linking the standing of the theory to the outcome of the therapy, Grünbaum declared that the "epistemic warrant" for the truth claims of psychoanalytic propositions has vanished. That is, without the security afforded by the Tally Argument's direct linking of insight to cure, there is no sound basis for dealing with results that have been contaminated by the suggestive influence of the analyst, operating "under the pretense that analysis is *non* directive" (p. 130).

To restore the "probative value" of the theory, that is, its potential for making testable truth claims (rather than being restricted only to contributing heuristic, hypothesis-generating ideas) would require, according to Grünbaum, *extraclinical* testing of the theory. He therefore calls for prospective, controlled, experimental, and statistical epidemiological studies.

Responses to Grünbaum's judgment about the contamination of psychoanalytic data by Edelson (1984), Glymour (1974), Holt (1984), and me (Wallerstein 1986) suggest that contamination by suggestion is not necessarily an "all or none affair" (Holt 1984, 11). Various strategies exist both for assessing the presence and impact of suggestion and for minimizing its distorting influence. And many investigators have stressed the importance of testing hypotheses within the psychoanalytic situation.

Thomä and Kächele (1975) note that, in addition, extraclinical testing carries its own severe inherent limitations. They state:

> If the psychoanalytic method is not employed, and the process takes place outside of the treatment situation, only those parts of the theory can be tested that do not need a special interpersonal relationship as a basis of experience, and whose statements are not immediately related to clinical practice. (p. 63)

They conclude that psychoanalytic practice must be "the crucial place where the proof of its explanatory theories is to be rendered—we would not know where else they could be fully tested." Cognitive psychologist Matthew Erdelyi (1985) has described this as the issue of "ecological validity."

Study of the outcome and the process of psychoanalytic therapy is, therefore, in the words of Thomä and Kächele (1975), "the crucial place where the proof of [our] explanatory theories is to be rendered" (p. 63). This arena has drawn a number of committed investigators over the years, including Thomä, Kächele, and their co-workers in Ulm, Germany; Hartvig Dahl, Merton Gill, Mardi Horowitz, Otto Kernberg, Lester Luborsky, Hans Strupp, and Joseph Weiss in the United States; Peter Fonagy and George Moran in the United Kingdom; and others.

How can we then best test psychoanalytic propositions *within* the therapy situation in accord with the canons of empirical natural science? Benjamin Rubinstein, in a series of brilliant methodological articles (1975, 1980a, 1980b), has comprehensively laid out the range of issues, their possibilities, and the constraints in relation to the use of prediction as an effective theory-testing tool within psychoanalysis. Rubinstein's work has been concerned with problems of inference and confirmation in clinical and theoretical psychoanalytic work. Prediction can be to future events or to past events, things that might have occurred as antecedents to present events. Predictions (in psychoanalytic discourse) are characteristically probabilistic, that such and such is therefore more likely to happen, rather than universal and fixed, that it always happens in a singular, specifiable way. This means that psychoanalytic predictions are mainly to a class of events, not to a specific event. To quote Rubinstein:

> What we implicitly predict when testing a hypothesis about an unconscious motive is *not* the occurrence of a particular event but merely of any one or several of a particular class of events, namely, the class constituted of events qualifying as derivatives of the motive. . . . If such events are in fact observed, we regard the presence of the motive as to that extent confirmed. (1980b, 406)

Predictions therefore are imprecise (1980a, 12) and often implicit. "We merely implicitly predict that, if a posited unconscious motive is in fact present, then such and such will happen. Accordingly, we can become aware of this use of prediction only if, wondering about possible similarities between psychoanalysis and other sciences, we look for it actively" (Rubinstein 1980b, 405).

Rubinstein noted:

> Although not all scientific predictions can be tested by experiment, they can all be tested. A celebrated example from astronomy is the testing of Einstein's relativity theory by observing during a solar eclipse a deflection, predicted by the theory, of light from a distant star when passing by the sun. The important point is that experimentally and non-experimentally testable predictions have the same logical form, namely, the form of the statement "If A happens, then

B will also happen." Expressed in general terms, the only difference is that in the case of experimental testing a *person* makes A happen, while in nonexperimental testing *nature*, so to speak, does it. (1980b, 400)

On this basis there is now sufficient warrant for empirical testing in ways that are alert to the subtlety and complexity of subjective clinical phenomena while simultaneously loyal to the canons of objective scientific method.

I want to end with a credo, using words borrowed from Jacob Arlow (1982), an eminent clinician and theoretician (not an empirical researcher):

> We are approaching a postapostolic era in psychoanalytic history. In a few years, we will no longer have with us colleagues who had direct or indirect contact with the Founding Fathers. Our confidence in our work will have to rely not on the memories of bygone heroes but on solid observational data, meticulously gathered in the analytic situation and objectively evaluated, for *it is upon this set of procedures that the claim of psychoanalysis to a place among the empirical sciences is based.* (p. 18; italics added)

Summary

Three theoretical-clinical debates have heated up in the last two decades; the outcome of each has posed a threat to sound empirical research using data from psychoanalytic sessions. Each has been described and then refuted. These three are: (1) the hermeneutic position, that there is no proof possible from outside the session for anything discovered inside the session; (2) the contaminated-by-suggestion concept of Grünbaum, that clinical data are severely limited for use in research because they are inevitably contaminated by the therapist's suggestions; and (3) the common position that clinical case studies constitute an adequate basis for advancing the field. I trust that the counterpositions marshaled in this chapter clear the way for the healthy development of psychoanalytic research in the decades to come.

References

ABRAMS, S., reporter. (1971). Models of the psychic apparatus. *Journal of the American Psychoanalytic Association, 19,* 131–142.

ARLOW, J. A. (1982). Psychoanalytic education: A psychoanalytic perspective. *Annual of Psychoanalysis, 10,* 5–20.

BLIGHT, J. G. (1981). Must psychoanalysis retreat to hermeneutics? Psychoanalytic inquiry in the light of Popper's evolutionary epistemology. *Psychoanalysis and Contemporary Thought, 4,* 147–205.

CHAPTER 7

Psychodynamic Diagnosis in the Era of the Current DSMs

WENDY JACOBSON AND ARNOLD M. COOPER

THE CREATION OF THE DSM-III SYSTEM revealed a tension between research psychiatrists and psychodynamically oriented clinicians, who represented the majority of American psychiatrists. The new DSMs served the research need for reliable diagnostic categories far better than previous diagnostic manuals and spurred a revolution in nosological and epidemiological studies. These studies have been weighted toward achieving nosological reliability, often at the cost of validity. However, the preference of DSM-III and DSM-IIIR for defining diagnostic categories by discrete, observable behaviors with minimal use of clinical theory and inference did not optimally serve the clinical need for good descriptions of patients that would lead to rational treatment decisions (Offenkrantz et al. 1982; Offenkrantz, unpublished). In contrast, although psychoanalysts have not yet developed a scientifically reliable diagnostic system, the psychoanalytic diagnostic method, properly conducted, yields a most detailed and careful clinical assessment. Analysts' diagnostic efforts have been heavily weighted toward assessing character or personality type, aspects of psychological structural integrity, and expectable treatment behaviors and transference responses. However, the absence of an empirically tested, valid, and reliable operational psychodynamic nomenclature has handicapped psychodynamic process and outcome research.

In this chapter we will present the main diagnostic systems that are, and have been, available for psychodynamic clinicians. We will suggest that the current DSM family of diagnoses is a newly sophisticated version of one portion of the traditional diagnostic system for psychoanalysis and dynamic psychotherapy, but that it does not address fully other aspects of diagnosis significant for psychodynamic research and the clinical assessment of patients. We will review the limitations and constraints of the current DSM system, as suggested by psychoanalysis; these point to the need for both the refinement of existing DSM categories and the inclusion of supplementary measures for the psychodynamic assessment of patients for clinical care as well as research.

Complementary Diagnostic Traditions: The Descriptive and the Dynamic

Medical diagnosis from its earliest days gathered data on the presenting phenomenology of individual patients and fit that data into a classificatory system based on a theory. Where our forebears used the conception of humors, modern medicine turned to physiology and more recently to molecular genetics to explain the relationship between manifest symptoms and underlying pathology. In psychiatry and the mental health professions, the organizing diagnostic system for the past century has been a dual one. The descriptive or phenomenological system of Kraeplin, Freud, Bleuler, and others classified individuals by their shared symptom picture and course. The explanatory psychoanalytic system of Freud, like the basic science of physiology in medicine, organized psychiatric disorders according to theories of the significance of symptoms based on their underlying, core dysfunction. Using these two forms of classification—the phenomenological/descriptive and the explanatory/dynamic—a clinician or researcher can infer useful integrating diagnostic propositions (Frances and Cooper 1981).

The stated goal for the DSM-III and DSM-IIIR manuals (*Diagnostic and Statistical Manual of Mental Disorders*, 3d ed. and 3d ed. revised [American Psychiatric Association 1980, 1987]) was to develop a descriptive, behavior-based approach to diagnosis which would be as free as possible of theoretical assumptions. As much as possible, the new nomenclature was to be based on findings from the empirical research literature and was intended to encourage research. DSM-III introduced two important innovations not found in its predecessors (the first and second editions of the DSM [American Psychiatric Association 1952, 1968]). First, it operationalized diagnostic criteria, fostering enhanced reliability. Second, it introduced a multiaxial system, providing an improved conceptual framework for studying state–trait interactions and biological and social influences on psychopathology.

The new DSM system has had a vast impact upon mental health professionals and has provided a major stimulus to psychiatric research worldwide. The delineation of the personality disorder axis (Axis II) in the DSM[1] has led to increased diagnosis (Loranger 1990)[2] and empirical study of these disorders. Also of interest to psychodynamic clinicians is Axis V, the global assessment of functioning. This instrument, a slight modification of Luborsky's (1962; Luborsky et al., in press) Health-Sickness Rating Scale, assesses the patient's degree of impairment from symptoms and overall effectiveness of social and occupational functioning on a numeric scale. It is the first scaled, dimensional measure of the patient's life functioning to be included alongside the more usual categorical diagnoses.

Although input and cooperation from analysts was requested during the formulation of DSM-III and DSM-IIIR, for various and complex reasons very little of the psychodynamic diagnostic approach found its way into the new classificatory system. Wilson (1993) describes the professional context out of which DSM-III emerged, outlining the ideological, economic, intellectual, and scientific forces which have led in recent decades to a shift in general psychiatry away from a broadly conceived, biopsychosocial model—one informed by psychoanalysis, sociology, and biology—to a far narrower, research-based medical model. Wilson questions the wisdom of this narrowing of clinical gaze, and we do also. While participation has again been sought from the psychoanalytic community, it is also clear that the intention of the framers of DSM-IV is highly conservative (Frances et al. 1990), and they will make few changes that are not empirically based. Their position does not address the initial error of excluding psychodynamic data and inference as basic to clinical assessment. It seems unlikely that this omission will be corrected in the near future.

Limitations of Current DSM Diagnoses

The DSM-III system has many strengths. As noted previously, the multiaxial system is a great advance, the requirement for operational criteria is a transformation from the dark ages for research, and the delineation of a separate axis for personality disorders has been a boon to their study.

[1]DSM-III's preference for classifying observable rather than inferred phenomena fits with calling Axis II disorders ones of "personality" (the preferred psychiatric term) rather than "character" (the preferred psychoanalytic one). Though definitions of these terms overlap (Moore and Fine 1990; Frosch 1990), *personality* refers to an objective, observable pattern of behavior, deriving from the Greek "persona," or mask, worn in classical Greek theater. Personality refers to a social role. Character, in contrast, refers to a permanent structure which underlies this social role. Some aspects of an individual's character are not necessarily visible, but must be inferred (Auchincloss and Michels 1983; Michels as reported in Lindy 1990).

[2]Loranger (1990) notes that this finding relates in part to the different diagnostic practices of pre- and post-DSM-III eras (in the former, parsimony of diagnosis was the rule, while the current system encourages multiple diagnoses).

However, the new DSM's preference for a behavior-based, descriptive approach that stays close to observable data and minimizes clinical inference is itself a theoretical position, although a narrow one—that of logical positivism (Faust and Miner 1986; Schwartz and Wiggins 1986; Millon 1987; Schwartz 1991). This theoretical perspective favors behavioral or biological orientations (Michels as reported in Peltz 1987; Frances et al. 1990) over other, potentially more useful, perspectives in the realm of psychopathology (Schwartz and Wiggins 1988).

Critics have questioned the value of the logical positivist perspective for psychiatric diagnosis. While the new DSM nomenclature has been widely lauded by researchers for embracing the scientific standard of operationalism, which holds that a concept has no scientific merit beyond what can be reliably measured, Millon (1987) notes that reliance on an exclusively logical positivist operationalism was questioned decades earlier by leading philosophers of science (Leahey 1980). Polanyi (1958) and Kuhn (1970), among others, demonstrated convincingly that all scientific observations must themselves be construed as representing theoretical constructs, obtaining their meaning through placement in a network of concepts. In the long term, "it is theory that provides the glue that holds a classification together and imparts to it its scientific and/or clinical relevance" (Millon 1987, 111). Moreover, systematic evidence suggests that as sciences mature, they typically progress from an observation-based stage to one characterized by abstract, higher order systems based on theoretical constructs. Millon (1987) notes that "the characteristic which distinguishes a scientific classification is its success in grouping its elements according to theoretically consonant explanatory propositions." Accordingly, "the classes comprising a scientific nosology are not mere collections of overtly similar attributes . . . but a linked or unified pattern of known or presumed relationships among them" (pp. 111–12).

The creators of the new DSM have seriously handicapped psychiatric diagnosis by omitting some of the most useful and widely affirmed concepts in modern psychiatry—unconscious mental processes, intrapsychic conflict, and defenses. Constructing a diagnostic system without the use of these inferred, theoretical concepts limits the nosology to suboptimal clinical and research usefulness. It is as if physicists were to decide that they could not discuss black holes or even electrons because these are inferences derived from theory, not themselves empirically observed.

There is considerable potential for misdiagnosis when psychodynamic considerations are excluded. Take, for example, the narcissistic personality disorder. Narcissistic pathology broadly relates to difficulties with the regulation of self-esteem and the sense of self. A variety of behavioral presentations may be used to defend against painful levels of humiliation. An overt presentation, where the patient is palpably grandiose, devaluing, exploitative, and entitled, is one possibility, but so is a more covert presentation. A patient may be shy, charmingly dependent, unable to express anger, and easily shamed and humiliated, but covertly envious and rageful, entertaining fantasies of exhibitionistic grandiosity and denigration of supposed heroes. The difference between presentations does not define which patient is more narcissistic, but rather whether aggressive or passive masochistic defenses are being used to protect against recognition of low self-esteem and limited capacity for object relations (Cooper 1987; Cooper and Ronningstam 1992). In short, there are both "quiet" and "noisy" narcissists.

The DSM-III description of narcissistic personality disorder emphasized only the "noisy" version, and, for the most part, this trend continues in DSM-IIIR. In the latter document, a glimmer of change is evident: the description of narcissistic personality refers to a "pervasive pattern of grandiosity (in fantasy *or* behavior)" (American Psychiatric Association 1987, 349; italics added). This reference to the role of fantasy and (subtly and implicitly) to the possibility that a feature (grandiosity) might not be overtly expressed signals a covert acknowledgment of the importance and the unavoidability of psychodynamic considerations in personality disorder diagnosis.

In other current DSM diagnoses, there is some emphasis, although superficial, on conflicts, meanings, motives, object relations, and unconscious phenomena as important alongside overt behaviors. For example, in the DSM-IIIR description of avoidant personality disorder, lacking close friends is explained on the basis of needing unusually strong assurance of uncritical acceptance; avoidants yearn for relationships but cannot permit themselves to have them (Busch and Cooper, unpublished). This is in contrast, say, to DSM-IIIR schizoids, who do not want relationships at all. In DSM-IIIR, individuals with histrionic personality disorder "often act out a role such as . . . 'victim' or 'princess' *without being aware of it*" (American Psychiatric Association 1987, 348; italics added). The current DSM system is struggling under the weight of its exclusion of inferential, psychodynamic data.

Psychodynamic Diagnosis

Historically, psychoanalysis began with an interest in diagnostic specificity which was later obscured by a more narrow focus on analyzability (Bachrach 1978; Bachrach and Leaff 1978; Erle and Goldberg 1979). During the 1950s, as enthusiasm for psychoanalytic treatment expanded rapidly, notions regarding diagnostic assessment began to merge with pressures to assess and predict capacity to be treated by psychoanalysis. With diagnosis per se in relative eclipse, analyzability became increasingly important as a means of predicting outcome in psychoanalysis. The many large-scale analyzability studies (Kernberg et al. 1972; Appelbaum 1977; Wallerstein 1986; Sashin, Eldred, and van Amerogen 1975; Erle 1979; Erle and Goldberg 1984; Weber, Solomon, and Bachrach 1985; Weber, Bachrach, and Solomon 1985a, 1985b; Bachrach, Weber, and Solomon 1985) which began to be undertaken in this era, however, failed to produce either well-defined diagnostic categories which could predict outcome reliably or clear conceptualizations of which types of patients would do well in analysis (Bachrach 1978; Bachrach and Leaff 1978; Bachrach et al. 1991).

Recent developments in the therapeutic approach to patients with severe personality disorders (patients previously thought untreatable by analysis) has led to renewed interest in diagnostic specificity. Kohut's (1971, 1977, 1984) self-psychological approach to the preoedipal developmental and self-concept disturbances in narcissistic conditions and Kernberg's (1968, 1975, 1976, 1984) different integration of ego psychology and object relations to explain the pathological internalized object relationships of borderline and narcissistic conditions have helped with treatment conceptualization with these sicker populations. For example, Kohut believed that the narcissistic personality disorder required a different kind of participation from the analyst—one in which the analyst should allow an untouched, idealizing, regressive transference to develop during several years of the initial treatment process. Kernberg emphasizes that the analyst who has diagnosed borderline personality organization in a patient should be prepared to provide sharp limit setting and alterations within the analytic setting if necessary.

Because the psychoanalyst does not conduct a routine therapy for all patients, and because advances in psychoanalytic technique have increased the range of analyzable patients, the role of differential diagnosis has assumed renewed pragmatic significance. Clinical assessments are concerned with determining the particular psychotherapeutic mix (varying combinations of analysis or less intensive exploratory therapy, pharmacotherapy, and other psychotherapies) that is most likely to be successful with a particular patient. Thus diagnoses such as borderline personality, infantile personality, and severe narcissistic personality are important because they are believed to carry specific implications for the structure of defenses and transferences that help to determine treatment decisions. Greater knowledge of the transference responses in narcissistic and borderline patients has led to enhanced therapeutic skill. Despite the fact that a psychoanalytic nomenclature based on replicable, empirical findings has been slow to develop, on the clinical level the notion of using specific interventions for specific classes of patients is far more widely accepted today than it was years ago.

Psychodynamic diagnosis, while taking full account of descriptive diagnostic data, attends as well to unconscious mental processes and the severity of maladaptation. It classifies core aspects of character, personality, and adaptation to life as they are revealed in different modes of relating and representing self and others, both consciously and unconsciously. A psychoanalytic assessment focuses on the nature of intrapsychic conflicts, the predominant defenses, and the nature of internalized self-other representations and their affective interaction. Psychoanalytic diagnosis is derived from the phenomenology of the interaction between analyst and patient, as well as from historical data of the life narrative.

Psychoanalytic theory posits that processes outside a person's conscious awareness, as well as those within conscious awareness, powerfully affect and motivate thinking and behavior. Adult personality will be the resultant of the person's past and present experiences; innate, constitutional givens (intellectual and physical endowment, drives, temperament); and conscious and unconscious adaptive efforts to resolve predominant conflicts and fantasies. On the basis of decades of clinical experience, psychoanalysts have identified a number of different and commonly encountered patterns of conflict, underlying affects, and defenses. The individual manages these patterns using a variety of defensive, or coping, strategies (defense mechanisms). All defensive maneuvers are employed in the service of achieving an adaptive compromise of conflict between the underlying wishes and fantasies and the needs of adaptation to outer and inner requirements and standards. Observed behavior can best be understood when the balance among these multiple determinants is taken into account. For example, in the obsessive-compulsive character disorder, powerful, unresolvable conflicts over fearful obedience and angry defiance cause ambivalent oscillations that inhibit the capacity to act (Cooper 1987). Fantasies of dreadful retribution for loss of control of rageful affects lead to tight behavioral control.

Because significant determinants of behavior may be unconscious, similar behaviors at different times, or by different people, may reflect different underlying mental content (thoughts, feelings, motives, wishes, impulses, meanings). Conversely, two different behaviors may reflect similar underlying mental content (Stricker and Gold 1988). Take a simple example of the latter: at a time of parting, some individuals may signal their thoughts and feelings with a rough pat and averted gaze, while others hug intensely and lock gaze. Characteristics that may seem to reflect severe incapacity may represent defensive masking of abilities and achievements. For example, some individuals have a need to appear stupid; pseudostupidity may be used defensively to mask competitive impulses that are perceived as dangerous, or to deny that one knows family secrets. Conversely, a person may appear well integrated outwardly, but hide considerable psychopathology.

Though variables such as the defensive masking of core conflicts and fantasies, which occurs both consciously and unconsciously, are difficult to assess and classify reliably and validly even for experienced clinicians, these processes are part of the "physiology" of the mind as opposed to the brain (Reiser 1984, 1989). Evolving a diagnostic system that incorporates these important psychodynamic variables alongside behavioral descriptions poses a major challenge for the field.

In addition to describing predominant fantasies, conflicts, and defenses, psychodynamic diagnosis also assesses the severity of the maladaptive functioning which results from the particular mix of features in the individual case. This assessment includes noting the quality of object relations, operations of conscience, and ability to regulate inner tensions under a variety of circumstances, both stressful and relaxed. Severity assessments are critical because they strongly influence treatment technique.

A psychodynamic diagnostic hierarchy that reflects considerations of severity might range from the relatively high level adaptations found among some hysterical or obsessional personality disorders, to the mid-range of impairment found in many depressive-masochistic (Simons 1987), passive-aggressive, and narcissistic-masochistic (Cooper 1984, 1988, 1989, 1993) disorders, to the primitive-level disruptions found in severe narcissistic, borderline, antisocial, and paranoid disorders (Stricker and Gold 1988). Easser and Lesser (1965) differentiated the high-level hysteric from the low-level hysteroid, and Zetzel (1968) distinguished four subtypes on the hysterical continuum.

The psychoanalytic shorthand of "oedipal" and "preoedipal" disturbances represents another very rough severity hierarchy—one that has enjoyed considerable appeal, probably because it condenses considerations of severity with broad descriptions of conflictual content and developmental experience. Oedipal-level pathology refers to patients whose early dyadic (primary caretaker–child) relationships are believed to have been relatively undisturbed. These patients are thought to suffer from unresolved conflicts over sexuality, competition, and aggression that are reasonably well modulated in intensity of expression. Preoedipal pathology, in contrast, refers to patients who are believed to have experienced in their primary caretaking dyads early, severe distortions and disruptions which left them with structural fixations or deficits—overwhelming affects, weakness of defenses, and intense, unmodulated sexual and aggressive conflicts. The average clinical case presents a mixture of both, making these designations too broad to be useful for research. In the modern psychoanalytic view, these rough descriptions of mental organization are related not to specific developmental stages but to the quality of cumulative developmental life experience (Emde 1981, 1988; Western 1990).

Psychodynamic diagnostic assessments regarding both the type and the severity of disturbance rely heavily on assessing the quality of the patient's relationships and styles of interacting with others, especially the therapist. The psychodynamic diagnostician assesses how the patient's particular mode of relatedness—the depth, intensity, stability, and affective tone of the relationship—crystallizes into repetitive transference patterns with the therapist in the treatment situation. In addition, the diagnostician assesses the patterns of emotional response that the patient evokes (the countertransference). Knowledge of transference and countertransference responses informs predictions about treatment course and outcome.

Despite this rich framework of attributes, no classification has yet been devised to systematize psychodynamic variables. Though psychodynamic constructs have enjoyed considerable clinical utility and appeal, the field has not yet taken the next important scientific step, that of developing operationalized psychodynamic criteria specific enough to yield diagnoses of high predictive validity. This absence of an operational, psychodynamically informed nomenclature has had implications for the ability of psychoanalysis to demonstrate efficacy in comparison with other treatments, a task that has been pressed with increasing urgency in recent years (Klerman 1990). Psychoanalysis has never claimed to be a therapy only, and its ideas have been germinal for an enormous amount of research and a variety of treatments. However, psychoanalysis is also a treatment and, as such, needs to establish its comparability with competing treatments. To be in a position to do this, analytic investigators need a system of diagnostic assessment that is more inclusive than the current DSM.

Supplementary Measures to Specify Psychodynamic Diagnosis in Research

The limitations of the DSM system that are suggested by psychoanalytic theory point to the need both for the refinement of existing DSM categories[3] and for the inclusion of additional information relevant to the psychodynamic assessment of patients for clinical work, teaching, and research. Relevant supplementary remedies include specification of defensive operations, assessment of core intrapsychic and interpersonal conflicts, and assessment of internal psychological resources and psychiatric severity. Used in conjunction with current DSM categories, research studies that include

---

[3]Particularly for the personality disorders, major revisions may be needed. Consensus does not yet exist as to the number or validity of current Axis II syndromes (Hirschfeld 1993). In addition, there is active debate in the nosological literature regarding the diagnostic format that would best represent these entities (Gunderson 1992). Many investigators feel that alternative models (dimensional, prototypical) would be preferable to the current polythetic categorical model (see chapter 8).

these diagnostic measures are likely to yield important findings in their own right, as well as ones that could influence future editions of the DSM.

DEFENSE MECHANISMS

As has been noted, current DSM diagnoses do not help the clinician or researcher to distinguish more superficial defenses from the painful conflicts, object relations, or self-representations against which defenses are constructed. They also do not take severity into account. To help remedy this situation, investigators and practitioners have urged the incorporation of an axis of defense mechanisms in the DSM system. This axis would specify and quantify the psychological defense mechanisms from the pathological and immature to the healthy, adaptive, and mature. The pioneering work of Vaillant (1986, 1987; Vaillant and Drake 1985), Perry and Cooper (1986), Horowitz et al. (1984), and others has established significant evidence that the ego mechanisms of defense can be studied in empirically rigorous, clinically relevant fashion. These variables have been shown to be powerful predictors of morbidity and mortality when longitudinally assessed (Vaillant 1977; Vaillant and Perry 1980, 1985; Perry and Vaillant 1989). Ironically, a more solid empirical basis exists for including assessment of defense mechanisms than for many current Axis II disorders themselves (Vaillant 1987; Skodol and Perry 1993). A provisional axis of defensive operations is undergoing international field trials. Although it is unlikely that this psychodynamically based axis will be included in the forthcoming DSM-IV, nevertheless a number of well-developed, valid, and reliable indices for the assessment of defensive strategems are available for immediate use (see chapter 15 for an extensive review).

CORE CONFLICTS

As noted, current DSM diagnoses yield minimal information about the patient's intrapsychic conflicts or about how such conflicts typically are expressed in maladaptive interpersonal relationships. One feasible approach to taking this missing data into account systematically is to add the Core Conflictual Relationship Theme (CCRT) method to the diagnostic assessment (Luborsky and Crits-Christoph 1990; chapter 17). Numerous studies have demonstrated that the CCRT can be applied flexibly to clinical data derived from standardized diagnostic interviews, underscoring the utility of the method in assisting the clinician to formulate validly the patient's most pervasive area(s) of conflict. Core conflictual relationship themes are expressed repeatedly in the patient's conscious and unconscious wishes, in expectations regarding the reactions of others to these wishes, and in consequent self-responses to these anticipated reactions. Stable self and object representations have been demonstrated reliably to be pervasive across relationships with different types of people and have been shown to manifest the same consistency in dreams as in waking narratives. By supplementing DSM diagnoses with the CCRT, new insights regarding the covariance of two important orthogonal classes of information can be derived.

A considerable number of newer measures of conflictual patterns have been developed (see Luborsky and Crits-Christoph 1990, table 17-1). Though some are complicated to use and others need additional psychometric development, as a group these measures are well worth reviewing in preparation for clinical studies.

An additional instrument to consider is the Structural Analysis of Social Behavior (SASB), developed by Benjamin (1974, 1982, 1987), which is one of the oldest, richest, most reliable, and most sophisticated of these methods. The SASB can be used to yield dynamic formulations about conflicts manifested interpersonally. Calling upon an impressive body of empirical data, Benjamin (in press) describes the interpersonal and intrapsychic patterns characteristic of each of the Axis II disorders according to DSM-IIIR criteria. Because symptoms of personality disorder are dynamically interpreted in an interpersonal context, Benjamin has demonstrated that multiple diagnoses are far less likely to occur with her method. Theoretically and empirically based, the SASB method yields data regarding probable developmental experiences, typical transference patterns, and helpful therapeutic strategies for each DSM disorder.

INTERNAL PSYCHOLOGICAL RESOURCES AND PSYCHIATRIC SEVERITY

A large body of research literature suggests that an assessment of the severity of psychiatric illness has considerably more predictive power than any DSM-IIIR diagnostic category alone. In large part this is because high severity interferes with the patient's capacity to internalize the benefits, and tolerate the inevitable frustrations, of treatment. A number of psychotherapy outcome studies suggest that overall adequacy of personality functioning is a far more potent predictor of favorable outcome than is individual diagnostic category (Luborsky 1984; Luborsky et al. 1988; Luborsky and Crits-Christoph 1990; Bachrach and Leaff 1978; Diguer, Barber, and Luborsky 1993).

As already noted, the importance of this finding is underscored by the inclusion of a revised Axis V (Global Assessment Scale) in DSM-IIIR. This measure assesses both the extent of impairment from symptoms and the overall efficacy of social and occupational functioning. However, good adaptation in these different realms is often, but not necessarily, correlated. For example, reasonably effective occupational or social functioning not infrequently masks significant psychological morbidity and dysfunction. Accordingly, while Axis V serves as a potent predictor psychometrically, it is not specific enough in the individual case.

Devising a scale consisting of more purely internal measures remains an area of inquiry ripe for potential investigation. (See, for example, Bellak, Hurvich, and Gediman [1973] and Bellak and Goldsmith [1984] on ego function assessment, and Karush et al. [1984] and Cooper et al. [1966] on the adaptive balance profile.) Patients should benefit substantially from the development of experience-based measures which can attend with far greater precision to psychodynamically relevant variables, particularly severity measures.

In summary, with the current availability of psychometrically sophisticated measures, assessing psychodynamic variables such as defense mechanisms, intrapsychic and interpersonal conflict, and internal psychological resources should enhance significantly standard psychiatric approaches to diagnosis. Refined specification of the type and quantity of disturbance would compensate for many of the deficiencies of current DSM diagnoses. For instance, it should be possible to diagnose reliably how much and how primitive the projection used by a given patient is at baseline, and then to study systematically how such a variable relates prospectively to the selection and course of treatment, therapeutic change, and outcome over time.

Conclusion

There is a need for a more psychodynamically informed nosology. Psychoanalysis began with an interest in diagnostic specificity which was obscured by a narrower focus on responsiveness to treatment. With recent analytic theoretical advances, psychoanalysis has regained an interest in diagnostic specificity. The DSM-III family of diagnoses is a newly sophisticated descriptive portion of the traditional diagnostic system for psychoanalysis; its general clinical utility and research usefulness would be greatly enhanced by the inclusion of inferential psychodynamic data and observations. Current descriptions suffer from reliance on too narrow a theoretical base, and hence lack optimal research and clinical usefulness. In addition, present categories are insufficiently attentive to markers of severity.

There is now a great need to define the clinical questions, operationalize relevant variables, and collect the data upon which future classifications will be based. Those who are frustrated by the shortcomings of the current nomenclature may find it helpful to remember that it is a system in evolution, but one that holds out hope for achieving a nosology that is reliable, valid, and clinically relevant. Indeed, the system is at a relatively early stage of development. An important opportunity now exists for expanded collaborative work to devise a more theoretically based, psychometrically sound, and clinically relevant diagnostic classification. Optimal diagnostic criteria have yet to be determined. Patients will benefit from a more sophisticated and inclusive diagnostic effort.

References

AMERICAN PSYCHIATRIC ASSOCIATION. (1952). *Diagnostic and statistical manual of mental disorders.* Washington, DC: American Psychiatric Association.

AMERICAN PSYCHIATRIC ASSOCIATION. (1968). *Diagnostic and statistical manual of mental disorders* (2nd ed.). Washington, DC: American Psychiatric Association.

AMERICAN PSYCHIATRIC ASSOCIATION. (1980). *Diagnostic and statistical manual of mental disorders* (3rd ed.). Washington, DC: American Psychiatric Association.

AMERICAN PSYCHIATRIC ASSOCIATION. (1987). *Diagnostic and statistical manual of mental disorders* (3rd ed., rev.). Washington, DC: American Psychiatric Association.

APPELBAUM, P. (1977). *The anatomy of change.* New York: Plenum Press.

AUCHINCLOSS, E., & MICHELS, R. (1983). Psychoanalytic theory of character. In J. Frosch (Ed.), *Current perspectives on personality disorders.* Washington, DC: American Psychiatric Press.

BACHRACH, H. (1978). Analyzability: A clinical-research perspective. *Psychoanalysis and Contemporary Thought, 3,* 85–116.

BACHRACH, H., GALATZER-LEVY, R., SKOLNIKOFF, A., & WALDRON, S. (1991). On the efficacy of psychoanalysis. *Journal of the American Psychoanalytic Association, 39,* 871–916.

BACHRACH, H., & LEAFF, L. (1978). Analyzability: A systematic review of the clinical and quantitative literature. *Journal of the American Psychoanalytic Association, 26,* 881–920.

BACHRACH, H., WEBER, J., & SOLOMON, M. (1985). Factors associated with the outcome of psychoanalysis (clinical and methodological considerations): Report of the Columbia Psychoanalytic Center research project (4). *International Review of Psychoanalysis, 12,* 379–389.

BELLAK, L., & GOLDSMITH, L. (1984). *The broad scope of ego function assessment.* New York: Wiley.

BELLAK, L., HURVICH, M., & GEDIMAN, H. (1973). *Ego functions in schizophrenics, neurotics and normals.* New York: Wiley.

BENJAMIN, L. S. (1974). Structural Analysis of Social Behavior. *Psychological Review, 81,* 392–495.

BENJAMIN, L. S. (1982). Use of the Structural Analysis of Social Behavior (SASB) to guide intervention in psychotherapy. In D. Kiesler & J. Anchin

(Eds.), *Handbook of interpersonal psychotherapy* (pp. 190–212). New York: Pergamon Press.

Benjamin, L. S. (1987). Use of the SASB dimensional model to develop treatment plans for personality disorders. 1. Narcissism. *Journal of Personality Disorders, 1,* 43–70.

Benjamin, L. S. (in press). *Interpersonal diagnosis and treatment of personality disorders.* New York: Guilford Press.

Busch, F., & Cooper, A. M. (unpublished). Personality disorders in DSM-IIIR: A psychodynamic perspective.

Cooper, A. M. (1984). The unusually painful analysis: A group of narcissistic-masochistic characters. In G. Pollock & J. Gedo (Eds.), *Psychoanalysis: The vital issues* (pp. 45–67). New York: International Universities Press.

Cooper, A. M. (1987). Histrionic, narcissistic, and compulsive personality disorders. In G. Tischler (Ed.), *Diagnosis and classification in psychiatry: A critical appraisal of DSM-III* (pp. 290–299). New York: Cambridge University Press.

Cooper, A. M. (1988). The narcissistic-masochistic character. In R. Glick & D. Meyers (Eds.), *Masochism: Current psychoanalytic perspectives* (pp. 117–138). Hillsdale, NJ: Analytic Press.

Cooper, A. M. (1989). Narcissism and masochism: The narcissistic-masochistic character. *Psychiatric Clinics of North America, 12,* 541–552.

Cooper, A. M. (1993). Psychotherapeutic approaches to masochism. *Journal of Psychotherapy Practice and Research, 2,* 51–63.

Cooper, A. M., Karush, A., Easser, B., & Swerdloff, B. (1966). The adaptive balance profile and prediction of early treatment behavior. In G. Goldman & D. Shapiro (Eds.), *Developments in psychoanalysis at Columbia University* (pp. 183–214). New York: Hafner.

Cooper, A. M., & Ronningstam, E. (1992). Narcissistic personality disorder. In A. Tasman & M. Riba (Eds.), *American Psychiatric Press review of psychiatry* (Vol. 11, pp. 80–97). Washington, DC: American Psychiatric Press.

Diguer, L., Barber, J. P., & Luborsky, L. (1993). Three concomitants: Personality disorders, psychiatric severity, and outcome of dynamic psychotherapy of major depression. *American Journal of Psychiatry, 50,* 1246–1248.

Easser, B., & Lesser, S. (1965). Hysterical personality: A re-evaluation. *Psychoanalytic Quarterly, 34,* 390–405.

Emde, R. (1981). Changing models of infancy and the nature of early development: Remodeling the foundation. *Journal of the American Psychoanalytic Association, 29,* 179–219.

Emde, R. (1988). Development terminable and interminable: 1. Innate and motivational factors from infancy. *International Journal of Psychoanalysis, 69,* 3–42.

Erle, J. (1979). An approach to the study of analyzability and analysis: The course of forty consecutive cases selected for supervised analysis. *Psychoanalytic Quarterly, 48,* 198–228.

ERLE, J., & GOLDBERG, D. (1979). Problems in the assessment of analyzability. *Psychoanalytic Quarterly, 48,* 48–84.

ERLE, J., & GOLDBERG, D. (1984). Observations on the assessment of analyzability by experienced analysts. *Journal of the American Psychoanalytic Association, 32,* 715–737.

FAUST, D., & MINER, R. (1986). The empiricist and his new clothes: DSM-III in perspective. *American Journal of Psychiatry, 138,* 1198–1202.

FRANCES, A., & COOPER, A. (1981). Descriptive and dynamic psychiatry: A perspective on DSM-III. *American Journal of Psychiatry, 138,* 1198–1202.

FRANCES, A., PINCUS, H., WIDIGER, T., DAVIS, W., & FIRST, M. (1990). DSM-IV: Work in progress. *American Journal of Psychiatry, 147,* 1439–1448.

FROSCH, J. (1990). *Psychodynamic psychiatry: Theory and practice* (Vols. 1 & 2). Madison, CT: International Universities Press.

GUNDERSON, J. G. (1992). Diagnostic controversies. In A. Tasman & M. Riba (Eds.), *American Psychiatric Press review of psychiatry* (Vol. II, pp. 9–24). Washington, DC: American Psychiatric Press.

HIRSCHFELD, R. M. A. (1993). The Williamsburg Conference on personality disorders: What have we learned? *Journal of Personality Disorders, 7,* supp., 4–8.

HOROWITZ, M., MARMAR, C., KRUPNICK, J., WILNER, N., KALTREIDER, N., & WALLERSTEIN, R. (1984). *Personality styles and brief psychotherapy.* New York: Basic Books.

KARUSH, A., EASSER, B., COOPER, A., & SWERDLOFF, B. (1964). The evaluation of ego-strength: 1. A profile of adaptive balances. *Journal of Nervous and Mental Disease, 139,* 332–349.

KERNBERG, O. F. (1968). The treatment of patients with borderline personality organization. *International Journal of Psychoanalysis, 49,* 600–619.

KERNBERG, O. F. (1975). *Borderline conditions and pathological narcissism.* New York: Jason Aronson.

KERNBERG, O. F. (1976). *Object relations theory and clinical psychoanalysis.* New York: Jason Aronson.

KERNBERG, O. F. (1984). *Severe personality disorders.* New Haven: Yale University Press.

KERNBERG, O. F., BURSTEIN, E., COYNE, L., APPELBAUM, A., HOROWITZ, L., & VOTH, H. (1972). Psychotherapy and psychoanalysis: Final report of the Menninger Foundation Psychotherapy Research Project. *Bulletin of the Menninger Clinic, 36,* 3–275.

KLERMAN, G. (1990). The psychiatric patient's right to effective treatment: Implications of *Osheroff v. Chestnut Lodge. American Journal of Psychiatry, 147,* 409–418.

KOHUT, H. (1971). *The analysis of the self.* New York: International Universities Press.

KOHUT, H. (1977). *The restoration of the self.* New York: International Universities Press.

KOHUT, H. (1984). *How does analysis cure?* Chicago: University of Chicago Press.

KUHN, T. (1970). *The structure of scientific revolutions.* Chicago: University of Chicago Press.

LEAHEY, T. (1980). The myth of operationalism. *Journal of Mind and Behavior, 1,* 127–143.

LINDY, D. (1990). Research on personality disorders: Psychoanalytic contributions, criticisms, and perspectives. *Bulletin: The Association for Psychoanalytic Medicine, 29,* 21–30.

LORANGER, A. (1990). The impact of DSM-III on diagnostic practice in a university hospital. *Archives of General Psychiatry, 47,* 672–675.

LUBORSKY, L. (1962). Clinicians' judgments of mental health: A proposed scale. *Archives of General Psychiatry, 7,* 404–417.

LUBORSKY, L. (1984). *Principles of psychoanalytic psychotherapy.* New York: Basic Books.

LUBORSKY, L., & CRITS-CHRISTOPH, P. (1990). *Understanding transference: The Core Conflictual Relationship Theme method.* New York: Basic Books.

LUBORSKY, L., CRITS-CHRISTOPH, P., MINTZ, H., & AUERBACH, A. (1988). *Who will benefit from psychotherapy? Predicting therapeutic outcomes.* New York: Basic Books.

LUBORSKY, L., DIGUER, L., LUBORSKY, E., McLELLAN, A. T., WOODY, G., & ALEXANDER, L. (IN PRESS). Psychological health as a predictor of the outcomes of psychotherapy. *Journal of Consulting and Clinical Psychology.*

MILLON, T. (1987). Concluding commentary. *Journal of Personality Disorders, 1,* 110–112.

MOORE, B. E., & FINE, B. D. (1990). *Psychoanalytic terms and concepts.* New Haven: Yale University Press.

OFFENKRANTZ, W. (UNPUBLISHED). *Report of the American Psychoanalytic Association ad hoc committee to evaluate DSM-III.*

OFFENKRANTZ, W., ALTSCHUL, S., COOPER, A., FRANCES, A., MICHELS, R., ROSENBLATT, A., SCHIMEL, J., TOBIN, A., & ZAPHIROPOULOS, M. (1982). Treatment planning and psychodynamic psychiatry. In J. Lewis & G. Usdin (Eds.), *Treatment planning in psychiatry* (pp. 1–41). Washington, DC: American Psychiatric Association.

PELTZ, M. (1987). Panel report: Psychoanalytic contributions to psychiatric nosology. *Journal of the American Psychoanalytic Association, 35,* 693–711.

PERRY, J. C., & COOPER, S. H. (1986). A preliminary report on defenses and conflicts associated with borderline personality disorder. *Journal of the American Psychoanalytic Association, 34,* 863–893.

PERRY, J. C., & VAILLANT, G. E. (1989). Personality disorders. In H. I. Kaplan & B. J. Sadock (Eds.), *Comprehensive textbook of psychiatry* (5th ed., Vol. 2, pp. 1352–1387). Baltimore: Williams & Wilkins.

POLANYI, M. (1958). *Personal knowledge.* Chicago: University of Chicago Press.

REISER, M. (1984). *Mind, brain, body: Toward a convergence of psychoanalysis and neurobiology.* New York: Basic Books.

REISER, M. (1989). The future of psychoanalysis in academic psychiatry: Plain talk. *Psychoanalytic Quarterly, 58,* 185–209.

SASHIN, J., ELDRED, S., & VAN AMEROGEN, S. (1975). A search for predictive factors in institute supervised cases: A retrospective study of 183 cases from 1959–1966 at the Boston Psychoanalytic Institute and Society. *International Journal of Psychoanalysis, 56,* 343–359.

SCHWARTZ, M. A. (1991). The nature and classification of the personality disorders: A reexamination of basic premises. *Journal of Personality Disorders, 5,* 25–30.

SCHWARTZ, M. A., & WIGGINS, O. P. (1986). Logical empiricism and psychiatric classification. *Comprehensive Psychiatry, 27,* 101–114.

SCHWARTZ, M. A., & WIGGINS, O. P. (1988). Perspectivism and the methods of psychiatry. *Comprehensive Psychiatry, 29,* 237–251.

SIMONS, R. (1987). Psychoanalytic contributions to psychiatric nosology: Forms of masochistic behavior. *Journal of the American Psychoanalytic Association, 35,* 583–608.

SKODOL, A. E., & PERRY, J. C. (1993). Should an axis for defense mechanisms be included in DSM-IV? *Comprehensive Psychiatry, 34,* 108–119.

STRICKER, G., & GOLD, J. E. (1988). A psychodynamic approach to the personality disorders. *Journal of Personality Disorders, 2,* 350–359.

VAILLANT, G. E. (1977). *Adaptation to life.* Boston: Little, Brown.

VAILLANT, G. E. (1986). *Empirical studies of ego mechanisms of defense.* Washington, DC: American Psychiatric Association.

VAILLANT, G. E. (1987). An empirically derived hierarchy of adaptive mechanisms and its usefulness as a potential diagnostic axis. In G. Tischler (Ed.), *Diagnosis and classification in psychiatry: A critical appraisal of DSM-III* (pp. 464–476). New York: Cambridge University Press.

VAILLANT, G. E., & DRAKE, R. E. (1985). Maturity of ego defenses in relation to DSM-III Axis II personality disorder. *Archives of General Psychiatry, 42,* 597–601.

VAILLANT, G. E., & PERRY, J. C. (1980). Personality disorders. In H. I. Kaplan, A. H. Freedman, & B. J. Sadock (Eds.), *Comprehensive textbook of psychiatry* (3rd ed., Vol. 2, pp. 1562–1590). Baltimore: Williams & Wilkins.

VAILLANT, G. E., & PERRY, J. C. (1985). Personality disorders. In H. I. Kaplan & B. J. Sadock (Eds.), *Comprehensive textbook of psychiatry* (4th ed., pp. 958–986). Baltimore: Williams & Wilkins.

WALLERSTEIN, R. (1986). *Forty-two lives in treatment.* New York: Guilford Press.

WEBER, J., BACHRACH, H., & SOLOMON, M. (1985a). Factors associated with the outcome of psychoanalysis: Report of the Columbia Psychoanalytic Center research project (2). *International Review of Psychoanalysis, 12,* 127–141.

WEBER, J., BACHRACH, J., & SOLOMON, M. (1985b). Factors associated with the outcome of psychoanalysis: Report of the Columbia Psychoanalytic Center research project (3). *International Review of Psychoanalysis, 12,* 251–262.

WEBER, J., SOLOMON, M., & BACHRACH, H. (1985). Characteristics of psychoanalytic clinic patients: Report of the Columbia Psychoanalytic Center research project (1). *International Review of Psychoanalysis, 12,* 13–26.

WESTEN, D. (1990). Toward a revised theory of borderline object relations: Contributions of empirical research. *International Journal of Psychoanalysis, 71,* 661–693.

WILSON, M. (1993). DSM-III and the transformation of American psychiatry; A history. *American Journal of Psychiatry, 150,* 399–410.

ZETZEL, E. (1968). The so-called good hysteric. *International Journal of Psychoanalysis, 49,* 256–260.

CHAPTER 8

Diagnosis of Personality Disorder: Psychodynamic and Empirical Issues

NANCY E. MILLER

Dsm-III AND DSM-IIIR HAVE HAD A MOMENTOUS IMPACT in generating new research on the diagnosis of psychopathology. Yet psychoanalysts have questioned the utility and relevance of the new criteria, particularly as they pertain to the diagnosis of the disorders of personality (Frances and Cooper 1981). Although the major psychiatric disorders (Axis I) constitute important categories of modern psychodynamic practice and research, and many chapters in this volume reflect that emphasis, in the realm of diagnosis, it is the Axis II disorders encompassing highly complex trait constellations that have proven so problematic to clinicians and researchers alike.

Because disorders of character continue to be of paramount interest to psychoanalysts, and because the methodologic issues entailed remain daunting and relatively unknown to practitioners interested in research, this chapter will serve as a critical guide to these fast-breaking developments. Substantive and methodologic concerns pertaining to the descriptive approach favored by DSM-III, DSM-IIIR and DSM-IV and to the theory-based psychodynamic perspective will be reviewed respectively. Gaps in systematic knowledge and questions keyed to issues of clinical relevance and empirical validity will be highlighted for each. The psychometric properties of Axis II criteria and related assessment indices will also be touched upon.

While analysts have not contributed as substantially as they might to empirical study of these complex conditions, that situation is changing rapidly (as the existence of this volume attests), given the recent development of psychometrically sound indices sensitive to psychodynamic constructs and available for immediate supplementary use in conjunction with Axis II criteria. New and innovative measures of developmental level, defensive operations, intrapsychic and interpersonal conflict, transference and countertransference phenomena, internalization and the like carry considerable potential for ushering in a more clinically relevant, theoretically generative, and empirically sound era in personality disorder classification and assessment research.

Given that Axis II will be further revised in light of new scientific evidence, it will be increasingly important that psychodynamic investigators invest more substantially in defining the clinical questions, operationalizing relevant variables, and collecting the data upon which the next decisions regarding personality disorder classification will be invariably based. This discussion represents an important first step in that direction.

The Revolution in Personality Disorder Research

Throughout much of this century, disorders of personality manifested such poor levels of reliability when studied empirically that investigators largely overlooked their importance. That situation changed radically in 1980, with the publication of DSM-III and with the introduction of a multiaxial system that included the separation of personality disorder as a discrete axis of classification and provided operational criteria for the delineation of a new taxonomy (Loranger et al. 1987).

In an astonishingly brief period, the new nosology has led the way toward redressing the imbalance in the empirical literature on disorders of character, such that these chronic, pervasive, and maladaptive disorders are now far more widely perceived as conditions worthy of sustained research and clinical attention. In the interim, longitudinal follow-up data have begun to reveal the degree of enduring chronicity, high morbidity, and significant mortality associated with disorders of character in their own right (Perry 1988; 1991, and in press; McGlashan 1986a; Vaillant 1977; Vaillant and Drake 1985; Stone, Hurt, and Stone 1987). Over 5 percent of individuals with personality disorder end their lives through suicide (Miles 1977).

In retrospect, it is clear that the publication of DSM-III marked a watershed in the empirical study of the disorders of personality, and that the introduction of the multiaxial system has had a revolutionary impact in generating a new arena of methodologically sophisticated research (Loranger et al. 1987). The dizzying speed with which this explosion of attention has taken place can be matched only by the burgeoning impact such scrutiny has had on mental health research in this country and abroad. For example, as the federal government's lead agency supporting studies of psychopathology, the NIMH convened the first research meeting in its history on disorders of personality in 1990, following rapid dissemination of the new nomenclature (Shea and Hirschfeld [in press]). The initiation of the multidisciplinary *Journal of Personality Disorders* has served to showcase the research sophistication of a new generation of active investigators, many of whom are psychodynamically inclined. Interest has rapidly spread beyond the boundaries of the United States, generating the founding of the International Society for the Study of Personality Disorders, and stimulating the convening of the world's first research-driven International Congress on Disorders of Personality. In collaboration with the U.S. Alcohol, Drug Abuse, and Mental Health Administration, the World Health Organization has launched an ambitious project aimed at enhancing the scientific basis of diagnosis, via development of a cross-national instrument for the assessment of personality disorder, keyed to the most recent revisions of DSM (IV) and ICD (X), with the intent of facilitating comparisons of clinical and research findings across diverse nations and cultures. Participating sites in the International Pilot Study of Personality Disorder, begun in 1988, include facilities in Austria, England, Germany, India, Japan, Kenya, Luxembourg, the Netherlands, Norway, Switzerland, and the United States (Loranger et al. 1991).

Initially assigned to a separate axis in DSM-III to encourage consideration of the effect personality disorder had on a course and treatment of Axis I syndromes (Widiger and Frances 1985; Akiskal et al. 1983), substantial evidence now confirms that the co-morbid presence of personality disorder complicates course and adversely alters the rate and outcome of treatment response (Weissman, Prusoff, and Kleinman 1978; Frank et al. 1984 and 1987; Hirschfeld and Klerman 1979; Hirschfeld et al. 1983; Shea et al. 1987). These lifelong maladaptive patterns of feeling and interacting with others even appear to contribute to poorer responsiveness to antidepressant medication (Akiskal et al. 1980; Charney, Nelson, and Quinlan 1981; Klein 1977; Pfohl, Stangl, and Zimmerman 1984). Moreover, the clinical reports of Freud (1959), Abraham (1960), and the first generation of psychoanalysts, suggesting that characterologic features appear to etiologically predispose patients to the development of depressive disorder, have now been systematically confirmed (Akiskal 1981; Akiskal et al. 1977; Akiskal et al. 1978; Akiskal et al. 1980; Akiskal et al. 1983; Cassano, Maggini, and Akiskal 1983).

The act of including personality disorders in a position of prominence within the official nomenclature has resulted in a marked increase in the diagnosis of personality disorder (Loranger 1990) and provided the field with a set of detailed criteria upon which standardized assessment instruments have been based. While difficulties with both the diagnostic criteria and the assessment procedures remain (these will be detailed below), nevertheless, a high level of research activity continues to characterize this renaissance of empirical interest in the disorders of character.

By and large, psychoanalysis has not actively participated in this empirical revolution, although potentially it has much to contribute. The reasons for its relative isolation are complex, reflecting, in part, the influence of scientific and fiscal pressures which fueled the drive toward accountability in psychiatric assessment and treatment during the past quarter century. Wilson (1993) has detailed how the convergence of these trends in general psychiatry cumulatively shaped the paradigmatic shift away from a descriptive, clinically based, psychodynamic model of pathology, toward a more empirically driven research-based model.

The Importance of Theory

By the late 1970s, given the absence of sufficient predictive precision characterizing dynamic formulations, the radical solution of the DSM-III architects was to excise all theoretic underpinnings from Axis II, in an ambitious effort to wean psychiatric diagnosis from its unreliable moorings and to reestablish it on a more empirically based footing. The DSM-III work group opted to depend on a descriptive approach that remained close to the observable data, valued reliability, provided specified criteria, operationalized terminology, minimized inference, and ruled out theory.

The effort to eliminate all theoretic constructs from the Axis II classification constituted cause for alarm, not only to analysts but also to scholars of diverse perspectives studying normal personality variance (Costa and McCrae 1990), as well as to researchers engaged in systematic investigation of the full range of character pathology (Cloninger 1982; Akiskal 1992; Millon 1987b). Rather than being formulated on the basis of any consistent theory of personality or of personality disorder, the Axis II categories have largely been selected as classifications of convenience, culled from those clinical observations of work group members and consultants which appeared to carry heuristic value. In general, the criteria adopted reflected no conceptual rationale to assist the clinician in integrating and making meaningful sense of component syndromal variables (Millon 1987a).

In reference to the personality disorders, Livesley (1987) has rightly emphasized that the question of whether theoretic constructs or empirical findings should form the basis of a classification system and determine the selection of criteria is based on the false premise that these two methods are mutually exclusive. He suggests that theoretical issues should determine the hypotheses initially studied and the initial specification of traits selected in constructing a classification. Subsequent empirical findings could then be introduced to further refine the system (Widiger and Trull 1987). That kind of interplay between theory and research should prove to be far more generative and clinically useful in the long run than dependence upon naive empiricism alone. The most thoughtful investigators in personality research today concur, urging that empirical and theoretical approaches to diagnosis not be viewed as antagonistic, but rather be accepted as mutually facilitative processes which, in tandem, could have the potential to yield far more valuable scientific discoveries (Cloninger 1987; Epstein 1987; Millon 1987a, 1987b; Gunnderson 1987; Akiskal 1992; Widiger 1991a, chapter 7).

Problems of DSM-IIIR Personality Disorder Classification

While the emphasis of DSM-IIIR on descriptive phenomenology has been very useful in enhancing reliability and in stimulating research, it has too often failed in assisting practitioners to make those distinctions most crucial to clinical practice (Perry 1992). Despite the search for "infallible indicators" meant to yield definitive determination of the presence or absence of a particular disorder, marked variability still remains, in terms of number of underlying dimensions; degree of inference required; level of criterion specificity; number of criteria needed to reach threshold; temporal stability of criteria; and differing base-rates, both among criteria and among disorders (Shea 1992; Clark 1992; and Loranger et al. 1991). At the same time, the marked absence of agreement regarding core theoretic constructs has been repeatedly demonstrated, for instance, by virtue of the considerable variation found among clinicians regarding which personality disorder they assume a particular symptom reflects (Blashfield and Haymaker 1988).

Because coherent theoretic constructs have not guided architects of the new DSMs in defining the most parsimonious core personality disorder configurations, more recent shifts in the DSM format meant to enhance validity have only served to underscore the insufficient clarity characterizing many Axis II criteria (see Widiger 1991a and 1992 for an extensive review). For example, the initial DSM-III Axis II nomenclature was highly inconsistent in format, using monothetic criteria sets (wherein all the features are required to be present) for some disorders, like avoidant and schizoid; using a mixture of monothetic and polythetic criteria for others (wherein specific features are required, but where multiple options are permissible for each), as in paranoid and narcissistic disorders; and allowing certain criteria sets to remain entirely polythetic (wherein a set of optional criteria are provided, as in borderline or schizotypal conditions). Investigators soon learned, however, that the inclusion of monothetic criteria sets proved overly restrictive, resulting in too high a proportion of patients being jettisoned into "trashcan" categories (Widiger and Frances 1985). Accordingly, when the time came to revise DSM-III, work group members addressed that problem by determining that Axis II be converted to a polythetic format, wherein sets of optional criteria would be made available.

This benign attempt to adjust the nomenclature in a more salutory direction, however, resulted in an overcorrection of equally, if not more, serious proportions. Whereas the former DSM-III rules for inclusion were overly restrictive, the new DSM-IIIR adjustment has led to problems of excessive prevalence and multiple diagnoses. For example, following the switch to DSM-IIIR, Morey (1988), reported an 800 percent increase in the rate of schizoid personality disorder and a 350 percent increase in narcissistic personality disorder. With the advent of the new format, a substantial increase in morbidity among personality disorder diagnoses was noted, such that the average number of personality disorder diagnoses per patient now is reported as ranging from 2.8 to 4.6, with some patients meeting criteria for seven or more personality disorders.

The move to a polythetic format also led to a significant increase in the heterogeneity of phenomenology manifest within each diagnostic case. For example, Widiger (1991a, 1991b, 1992) illustrates that there are now ninety-three different ways to meet the DSM-IIIR criteria for borderline personality disorder. Accordingly, a patient can qualify for a diagnosis of borderline personality disorder without manifesting impulsivity, unstable intense relationships, or affective lability (Oldham et al. 1992). Similarly, an individual can be diagnosed with avoidant personality yet have many close friends.

Because the new nomenclature lacks theoretic coherence in defining a universe of pathology and its subdivisions, highly diverse symptoms are assigned equal weight, as though each were assumed to possess empirically equivalent diagnostic value (Millon 1987a). Moreover, given the atheoretic selection of symptoms, little attention has been devoted to assessing the predictive power of various criterion combinations.

These problems of excessive prevalence and clinical heterogeneity substantially decrease the value of Axis II as a guide to differential diagnosis in clinical decision making. Unlike the Axis I disorders, the personality disorder diagnoses tend to be less discrete, encompassing complex trait constellations and inferred dispositions (Millon 1987b). Livesley's (1987) review found substantial overlap in the description of different disorders, and other investigators have highlighted the limited discriminability of most Axis II criteria (Morey 1988).[1]

---

[1]A variety of psychodynamically sensitive, reliable, and psychometrically sophisticated measures are presently available, which, if used in conjunction with Axis II diagnoses, can

Finally, substantial evidence demonstrates that mixed personality disorders constitute the rule rather than the exception in diagnoses formulated using DSM-IIIR Axis II (Frances et al. 1990; Pfohl et al. 1987; Stangl et al. 1985). For instance, borderline personality disorder is rarely found alone and is empirically difficult to distinguish from others in the "flamboyant cluster" of histrionic, antisocial, and narcissistic personality disorders (Barasch, Kroll, and Carey 1983; Kroll et al. 1981); avoidant personality appears to overlap considerably with dependent personality (Reich, Noyes, and Troughton 1987).

In the event that several personality disorders are positively identified for a single individual, questions arise as to which should take hierarchical and treatment precedence in a system where all have seemingly equivalent status (Oldham and Skodol 1992). Inasmuch as many of the Axis II criteria sets are lacking in empirical support, the current personality disorder nomenclature as it is presently constituted stands in need of substantial and thoughtful adjustment (Widiger 1992).

Prototypic or Dimensional Models as Potential Solutions

Investigators have enumerated various potential solutions for the problems of excessive prevalence, heterogeneity, and multiple diagnosis (Blashfield 1984), the most prominent of which include either requiring a core defining feature or converting Axis II from a categorical to a dimensional format (Livesley 1991; Widiger 1992).

While the notion of anchoring diagnosis to a fundamental feature would most certainly increase the homogeneity of patients qualifying for that diagnosis, the daunting problem that remains is the determination of which feature to require, particularly in the absence of sufficient empirical evidence: Should the nomenclature include the item most often seen in prototypic cases, select the item with the highest positive predictive power, or choose the variable construed to be theoretically central to the disorder's pathology? (Widiger 1991b). Even if the Axis II work group

---

assist in reducing, eliminating, or further clarifying some of the problems alluded to above. For example, the theoretically and empirically based SASB method, developed by Lorna Benjamin (1974), has been used to describe the interpersonal and intrapsychic patterns characteristic of each of the Axis II disorders according to DSM-IIIR and DSM-IV criteria (Benjamin 1993). Benjamin's studies reveal, for instance, that while anger in borderline personality disorder is usually triggered by abandonment, narcissistic anger is most often stimulated by entitlement failure. Accordingly, by systematically considering a descriptive symptom such as "rage" in the context of object relationship themes as formulated by the SASB, the "overlap" problem (Livesley 1987; Morey 1988) incurred by DSM-IIIR diagnosis can be significantly curtailed.

were to decide to develop an algorithm integrating these approaches, at some level value judgments would certainly enter into the equation.

Because the disorders of personality are far less discrete than Axis I disorders, at times even appearing essentially continuous with one another, a number of investigators have suggested that a dimensional model might ultimately prove to be best suited for Axis II (Livesley 1991; Widiger 1991a, 1992; Cloninger 1987, in press; Frances 1982; Frances and Cooper 1981). Using dimensional models, the diversity of personality traits and the great range of possible combinations among them could be more adequately reflected. Rather than judging the presence or absence of a given trait or disorder, as in the current categorical approach (Kendall 1982), a dimensional model could specify the degree to which a particular pathologic personality trait is present or the degree to which a particular personality style might be perceived as inflexible or maladaptive (Widiger and Frances 1985).

With a dimensional system, the difficulty lies in determining how to decide which set of dimensions optimally defines the most suitable domain. At present, there are numerous potential models to select from, including theoretical dimensions, such as psychodynamic levels of personality organization (Kernberg 1975); dimensions reflecting different aspects of personality, such as temperamental qualities (Kretschmer 1936; Cloninger 1987, in press); interpersonal dimensions (Leary 1957; Benjamin 1974, 1993); and empirically based models of normal personality function.[2] No unanimity has yet been attained, regarding which realm(s) should be optimally favored in moving to a more dimensional system.

In his comprehensive review of the substantive criticisms leveled at the categorical approach to the diagnosis of personality disorder, Widiger (1991) has recommended that the DSM-IV provide formal recognition to the dimensional format of classification, or at least, offer this as a feasible alternative to the standard DSM-IIIR categories. From a psychoanalytic perspective, it would make good sense if the framers of DSM-IV were to encourage both categorical and dimensional systems of classification to

---

[2]While there is a strong history of empirical work on dimensional approaches to understanding the distribution of normal personality traits (Eysenck 1967; Costa and McCrae 1990), the DSM-IIIR disorders have evolved from work with clinically ill individuals, thus having had little to do with widely used models of personality structure (Overholser 1992). Although it is possible to interpret personality disorders within the framework of taxonomies generated from factor analysis, cluster analysis, and/or multidimensional scaling studies (Widiger 1992), to date the relationship between personality disorders and personality dimensions remains poorly understood. Cloninger's psychobiologic model remains the sole exception, having evolved from data based on clinical populations (Cloninger, Svrakic, and Pryzbeck, in press). In general, however, considerably more work with psychiatric populations will be necessary before the clinical relevance of such models can be adequately appraised (Perry 1990).

yet been undertaken, it remains difficult to sort out to what extent competing reports of clinical efficacy may be the result of studying patient samples with divergent levels of severity and qualitatively different forms of psychopathology.

Psychodynamic Developmental Hypotheses Pertinent to Personality Disorder Diagnosis

Most analysts share the assumption that human behavior is shaped by unconscious wishes and that complex psychological functions pass through a relatively invariant developmental sequence of epigenetic stages such that the fixations and/or regressions occurring at any one particular level ultimately affect subsequent ones, leaving their imprint upon the structure of psychopathology ultimately manifested in adult life (Stricker and Gold 1988). While this developmentally based framework characterizing the hierarchical classification of the character disorders has been clinically generative and heuristically useful to analysts, further systematic refinement of the working hypotheses underlying the framework would enable psychodynamically informed diagnoses to play an increasingly important prognostic role in psychiatric research. Given that a diagnosis is useful only to the extent to which it enables the analyst to formulate valid predictions about etiology, pathogenesis, course, outcome, and/or differential treatment response, enhanced attention to the specificity and accuracy of the assumptions underlying psychodynamic theories of function can only serve to integrate, validate, and advance the field scientifically.

In this respect, Gunderson (1987) has drawn attention to the fact that, regardless of their differences, all dynamic theories view adult forms of psychopathology as unfolding hierarchically along developmental lines, wherein those manifesting the greatest severity of illness are viewed as being "impaled" at the earliest ages on the developmental continuum.[4] Although much recent work (Emde 1981, 1988; Westen 1990; Vaillant 1977; Lichtenberg 1983), suggests that personality pathology as manifested in adulthood does not directly represent events transpiring at any single developmental stage, practitioners continue to compress a vast

---

[4]As Gunderson (1987) suggests, for example, some theorists (Giovacchini 1973; Modell 1963; Frosch 1970; and Searles 1977), believe that the developmental problems of borderline psychopathology are centered at the symbiotic phase of development, prior to the differentiation of self from object. Others view later stages as more critical to pathogenesis. Kernberg's "borderline personality organization," for example, is subdivided into discrete forms of "personality disorder," each of which is closely associated with specific subphases of separation-individuation. Adler (1981) proposes a different hierarchy, in conceptualizing narcissistic personality as also presenting along a continuum of severity.

clinical literature into a diagnostic shorthand which broadly condenses levels of pathologic severity together with infant and childhood developmental stages. Such notions remain clinically and conceptually appealing, in terms of both conferring hierarchical status and serving as markers of change in the course of monitoring therapeutic progress.

It is not widely known, however, that a significant number of follow-up studies conducted over extended periods have found that the probability of associating the etiology of a specific disorder with impairment at a specific developmental epoch is quite low. Basing his conclusions on systematic findings from a variety of sources, Gunderson (1987) suggests that it is the cumulative impact of dysfunctional parenting over time and the continuous presence of traumatic experience over considerable stretches which appears most crucial to outcome in the long term. More recently, in the context of a prospective and retrospective study of the origins of self-destructive behavior in borderline patients, van der Kolk et al. (1991) reported that while histories of physical and sexual abuse appeared to contribute to the initiation of self-destructive behaviors, only the long-term history of parental neglect and the chronic lack of secure attachment were significantly associated with maintaining these symptoms into adulthood.

It is possible, on the one hand, that analysts have ascribed too much etiologic significance to narrow developmental epochs in the construction of dynamic theories of pathogenesis, while on the other, that they may have accorded insufficient attention to efforts at formulating dynamic diagnoses of sufficient precision. This would suggest that long-term studies of the accuracy, predictive power, and generalizability of dynamic, phase-specific theories of pathogenesis should constitute important next steps in enhancing the scientific value of psychodynamic contributions to diagnosis (Gunderson 1987; Strauss et al. 1985).

Constitutional Givens, Psychodynamic Assumptions and Personality Disorder Diagnosis

A variety of clinical dynamic assumptions which relate to the predictive validity of personality disorder diagnosis could be refined with additional scientific scrutiny. Among these, for instance, might be assessment of the means by which innate and/or constitutional givens tend to color the structure of pathology and the flexibility of adaptational capacities. While individual differences in strength of the drives and in choice of defense mechanisms are frequently cited in the clinical literature, with few exceptions (e.g. Vaillant 1985; Vaillant and Drake 1985; Levin 1991) analysts have not exercised interest in, nor had the training necessary to take advantage of, impressive advances in related fields, such as psychobiology, neuropsychology, child development, and genetics (Siever and Davis 1991). Complementary data from these disciplines might be fruitfully integrated in the service of generating increasingly more sophisticated operationalizable hypotheses regarding dynamically important etiologic mechanisms pertinent to diagnosis.[5]

Kernberg has been one of the few contemporary thinkers to struggle directly with the problem of constitutional givens in constructing his theory of personality pathology (1968, 1975, 1984; Kernberg et al. 1988). He has conjectured that constitutionally determined excesses in aggressive drive derivatives, particularly when coupled with more than usual deprivation and frustration in early life, may comprise important risk factors for the development of borderline character disorder. Since the publication of Kernberg's hypothesis, a number of systematic family history studies have positively confirmed the presence of genetic components associated with the aggressive dimension of behavior in borderline personality disorder (Schulz et al. 1989; Silverman et al. 1991; Links, Steiner, and Huxley 1988, in Siever and Davis 1991). Since reliable evidence suggests that approximately half of the variance in personality traits is inherited (Kilzieh and Cloninger 1993), more extensive collaboration with colleagues in basic research should serve an increasingly important role in enhancing understanding of the basic dynamics of pathogenesis underlying the clinical expression of personality disorder so important to the diagnostician (Reiser 1984; Siever and Davis 1991).

At the same time, tacitly accepted dynamic hypotheses continue to stand in need of further systematic refinement. Gunderson (1987) for example, has drawn attention to the way in which Kernberg's assumption regarding the role of hypertrophied aggressive drive in borderline disorder overlaps with similar notions of causality postulated to account for conditions as disparate as schizophrenia, depression, and obsessive-compulsive disorder. He suggests that, even if all these hypotheses were accurate, there would still be a need for greater specificity—a need for clarifying the means by which particular pathologic processes unfold in the course of developing into disparate disorders with highly divergent outcomes. By embracing a scientific methodology that permits analysts to test their working hypotheses over time, cumulative answers to questions like these will contribute to the enhanced predictive power of an increasingly sophisticated, dynamically informed nosology (Edelson 1988).

[5]Considerable achievements, for example, in the study of temperament (Goldsmith 1982; Tellegen et al. 1988; Thomas and Chess 1977) have not as yet been widely integrated into psychodynamic theoretic consideration of a constitutional/genetic diathesis for personality disorder (Gunderson 1987; Siever and Davis 1991).

The field is poised to take advantage of newly available methods and technologies in order to more systematically refine the assumptions that shape everyday dynamic formulations and diagnostic decisions. For instance, while the collection of longitudinal data on course and outcome has long been viewed as one essential approach to validating diagnostic accuracy in personality disorder research, only recently have more systematic methods and better scientific tools become available (Strauss et al. 1985; Miller 1986; Drake and Vaillant 1988). Within the past decade or so, a number of already classic prospective and retrospective studies of personality disorder have been published, with psychoanalytically trained investigators prominently involved in many. These studies are worth consulting as potential models, in having innovatively combined descriptive and psychodynamic constructs and methods in the course of following the fate of personality disorder over time (see Drake, Adler, and Vaillant 1988; Perry 1988, in press; McGlashan 1986a; Vaillant 1977; Stone, Hurt, and Stone 1987).

Worthy of note, for example, is Drake, Adler, and Vaillant's (1988) finding of a 23 percent rate of personality disorder in a normal community sample of men (as opposed to a clinic sample), followed from age fourteen through age forty-seven. More impressively, variables from biological, environmental, and ego strength domains assessed across childhood were found to make substantial and independent contributions to predicting the presence of personality disorder in these men at age forty-seven. Although 79 percent of these individuals (versus 14 percent of the other normal subjects) manifested clear and continuing evidence of impairment, few ever received psychiatric attention. The public health implications of the early onset, extensive chronicity, and severity of these disorders, as well as the degree to which such disorders tend to be overlooked, merit further serious exploration.

These and other longitudinal findings underscore the urgent need for enhanced attention to specificity in psychodynamic research and classification. Independent studies, for example, have confirmed the presence of a subgroup of schizotypal patients who, when systematically culled from more inclusively defined borderline samples, are found to manifest significantly worse outcomes over time (McGlashan 1986b) and to respond more poorly to psychodynamically oriented psychotherapy (Stone 1983). In the years to come, the enhanced specificity, validity, and prognostic efficacy of once broadly inclusive psychodynamic designations should make an increasingly valuable contribution to clinical work.

Conclusion

With the advent in the 1970s and 1980s of major theoretical and technical advances in understanding and treating the more severe disorders of character (Kohut 1971, 1977; Kernberg 1968, 1975, 1981, 1984; Kernberg et al. 1988; Akhtar 1992), psychoanalysts have begun to express renewed appreciation of, and clinical interest in, diagnostic specificity (see chapter 7). At the same time, the development of detailed diagnostic criteria for all classified mental disorders has been viewed as a major innovation, substantially improving the reliability of psychiatric diagnosis and significantly stimulating new research. Probably in no class of psychiatric disorder has the research-enhancing effect of definition by explicit criteria been more evident than in the realm of the disorders of character. Quite suddenly in the 1980s these impairments, for decades of interest only to analysts, began to attract burgeoning and dramatic research interest. The temporal convergence of these two orthogonal historic developments offers clinicians and researchers alike a unique window of opportunity for collaborative work in developing a more theoretically based, psychometrically sound, valid and clinically relevant system of diagnostic classification.

On the one hand, the limitations and constraints of the DSM-III system as presently constituted point to the need for considerable readjustment of existing Axis II categories, as well as to the need for the inclusion of information more clinically relevant to the intrapsychic and interpersonal assessment of patients. On the other hand, the absence of a systematic, psychodynamically informed nomenclature for the personality disorders has had important implications, in limiting the generalizability of psychoanalysts' findings and in inhibiting the development of a body of empirical data demonstrating treatment efficacy.

As the chapters of this book amply reveal, by the close of the 1980s, key dynamic variables had been operationalized and important scientific measures had been developed, all of which are presently available for use in studies of the personality disorders. By including such operationalized psychodynamic constructs in conjunction with the DSM diagnostic criteria, investigators can better draw attention to developmental precursors and to intrapsychic and interpersonal organizing principles, and can play a larger role in enhancing the theoretic coherence of forthcoming revisions of the Axis II classification (Gunderson 1987; Frances and Cooper 1981).

As systematic study of the disorders of personality enters the twenty-first century, ideal diagnostic criteria and optimal assessment procedures have yet to be devised, and constitutional, genetic, psychosocial, and environmental etiologies have yet to be fully clarified. Nevertheless, the thoughtful addition of theoretically based psychodynamic research indices pertaining to variables such as intrapsychic conflict, defensive operations, developmental level, the therapeutic alliance, transference and counter-transference phenomena and the like, together with the ready collaboration of colleagues in closely related fields of basic research, promises to yield extensive benefits in enhancing the diagnosis and treatment of these chronic, complex, and costly disorders.

References

ABEND, S., PORDER, M., & WILLICK, M. (1983). *Borderline patients*. New York: International Universities Press.

ABRAHAM, K. (1960). Notes on the psychoanalytic investigation and treatment of manic-depressive insanity and allied conditions. In *Selected papers on psychoanalysis* (pp. 137–156). New York: Basic Books.

ADLER, G. (1981). The borderline-narcissistic personality disorder continuum. *American Journal of Psychiatry, 138,* 46–50.

AKHTAR, S. (1992). *Broken structures: Severe personality disorders and their treatment.* Northvale, NJ: Jason Aronson.

AKISKAL, H. S. (1981). Subaffective disorders: Dysthmic, cyclothymic, and bipolar II disorders in the "borderline" realm. *Psychiatric Clinics of North America, 4,* 25–46.

AKISKAL, H. S. (1992). Delineating irritable and hyperthymic variants of the cyclothmic temperament, *Journal of Personality Disorders, 6,* 326–342.

AKISKAL, H. S., BITAR, A. H., PUZANTIAN, V. R., ROSENTHAL, T. L., & WALKER, P. W. (1978). The nosological status of neurotic depression. *Archives of General Psychiatry, 35,* 756–766.

AKISKAL, H. S., DJENDEREDJIAN, A. H., ROSENTHAL, R. H., & KHANI, M. K. (1977). Cyclothymic disorder: Validating criteria for inclusion in the bipolar affective group. *American Journal of Psychiatry, 134,* 1227–1233.

AKISKAL, H. S., HIRSCHFELD, R. M. A., & YEREVANIAN, B. I. (1983). The relationship of personality to affective disorders: A critical review. *Archives of General Psychiatry, 40,* 801–810.

AKISKAL, H. S., ROSENTHAL, T. L., HAYKAL, R. F., LEMMI, H., ROSENTHAL, R. H., & SCOTT-STRAUSS, A. (1980). Characterological depression: Clinical and sleep EEG findings separating "subaffective dysthymias" from "character spectrum disorders." *Archives of General Psychiatry, 37,* 777–783.

BARASCH, J., KROLL, J., & CAREY, K. (1983). Discriminating borderline from other personality disorders. *Archives of General Psychiatry, 40,* 1297–1302.

BENJAMIN, L. S. (1974). Structural Analysis of Social Behavior. *Psychological Review, 81,* 392–495.

BENJAMIN, L. S. (1993). *Interpersonal diagnosis and treatment of personality disorders.* New York: Guilford Press.

BLASHFIELD, R. K. (1984). *The classification of psychopathology: Neo-Kraepelinian and quantitative approaches.* New York: Plenum Press.

BLASHFIELD, R. K., & HAYMAKER, D. (1988). A prototype analysis of the diagnostic criteria for DSM-IIIR personality disorders. *Journal of Personality Disorders, 2,* 272–280.

BLEULER, E. (1911/1950). *Dementia praecox, of the group of schizophrenias.* New York: International Universities Press.

CAREY, G., & GOTTESMAN, I. (1978). Reliability and validity in binary ratings. *Archives of General Psychiatry, 35,* 1454–1459.

CASSANO, G. B., MAGGINI, C., & AKISKAL, H. S. (1983). Short-term, subchronic and chronic sequelae of affective disorders. *Psychiatric Clinics of North America, 6,* 55–68.

CHARNEY, D. S., NELSON, C. J., & QUINLAN, D. M. (1981). Personality traits and disorder in depression. *American Journal of Psychiatry, 138,* 1601–1604.

CLARK, L. A. (1992). Resolving taxonomic issues in personality disorders: The value of large-scale analyses of symptom data. *Journal of Personality Disorders, 6,* 360–376.

CLONINGER, C. R. (1987). A systematic method for clinical description and classification of personality variants: A proposal. *Archives of General Psychiatry, 44,* 573–588.

CLONINGER, C. R., SVRAKIC, D. M., & PRYZBECK, T. R. (IN PRESS). A psychobiological model of temperment and character. *Archives of General Psychiatry.*

COSTA, P. T., & McCRAE, R. R. (1990). Personality disorders and the five-factor model of personality. *Journal of Personality Disorders, 4,* 362–371.

CRONBACH, L. J. (1970). *Essentials of psychological testing.* New York: Harper and Row.

DEUTSCH, H. (1942). Some forms of emotional disturbance and their relationship to schizophrenia. *Psychoanalytic Quarterly, 11,* 301–321.

DRAKE, R. E., ADLER, D. A., & VAILLANT, G. E. (1988). Antecedents of personality disorders in a community sample of men. *Journal of Personality Disorders, 2,* 60–68.

DRAKE, R. E., & VAILLANT, G. E. (1988). Longitudinal views of personality disorders. *Journal of Personality Disorders, 2,* 44–48.

EDELSON, M. (1988). *Psychoanalysis: A theory in crisis.* Chicago: University of Chicago Press.

EMDE, R. (1981). Changing models of infancy and the nature of early development: Remodeling the foundation. *Journal of the American Psychoanalytic Association, 29,* 179–219.

EMDE, R. (1988). Development terminable and interminable: 1. Innate and motivational factors from infancy. *International Journal of Psychoanalysis, 69,* 3–41.

EPSTEIN, S. (1987). The relative value of the critical and empirical approaches for establishing a psychological diagnostic system. *Journal of Personality Disorders, 1,* 100–109.

EYSENCK, H. J. (1967). *The biological basis of personality.* Springfield, IL: Charles C Thomas.

Frances, A. (1982). Categorical and dimensional systems of personality diagnosis: A comparison. *Comprehensive Psychiatry, 23,* 516–527.

Frances, A., & Cooper, A. (1981). Descriptive and dynamic psychiatry: A perspective on DSM-III. *American Journal of Psychiatry, 138,* 1198–1202.

Frances, A. Pincus, H., Widiger, T., Davis, W., & First, M. (1990). DSM-IV: Work in progress. *American Journal of Psychiatry, 147,* 1439–1448.

Frank, E., Kupfer, D. J., Jacob, M., & Jarrett, D. (1987). Personality features and response to acute treatment in recurrent depression. *Journal of Personality Disorders, 1,* 14–26.

Frank, E., Jarrett, D. B., Kupfer, D. J., & Grochocinski, V. J. (1984). Biological and clinical predictors of response in recurrent depression: A preliminary report. *Psychiatry Research, 13,* 315–324.

Freud, S. (1959). Heredity and the etiology of the neuroses. In *Collected papers,* 138–154. New York: Basic Books.

Frosch, J. (1970). Psychoanalytic considerations of the psychotic character. *Journal of the American Psychoanalytic Associations, 18,* 50.

Giovacchini, P. (1973). Character disorders: With special reference to the borderline state. *International Journal of Psychoanalytic Psychotherapy, 2,* 7–36.

Goldsmith, H. H. (1982). Genetic influences on personality from infancy to adulthood. *Child Development, 54,* 331–355.

Green, C. J. (1987). Instrument review: Diagnostic interview for borderline patients. *Journal of Personality Disorders, 1,* 115–118.

Gunderson, J. G. (1987). Interfaces between psychoanalytic and empirical studies of borderline personality. In J. S. Grotstein, M. F. Soloman, & J. A. Lang (Eds.), *The borderline patient: Emerging concepts of diagnosis, psychodynamics and treatment,* Vol. 1. Hillsdale, NJ: Analytic Press.

Hirschfeld, R. M. A., & Klerman, G. L. (1979). Personality attributes and affective disorder. *American Journal of Psychiatry, 136,* 67–70.

Hirschfeld, R. M. A., Klerman, G. L., Clayton, P. J., Keller, M. B., McDonald-Scott, P., & Lankin, B. H. (1983) Assessing personality: Effects of the depressive state on trait measurement. *American Journal of Psychiatry, 140*(6), 695–699.

Hoch, P. H., & Polatin, P. (1949). Pseudoneurotic forms of schizophrenia. *Psychiatric Quarterly, 23,* 248–276.

Hyler, S. E., & Rider, R. O. (1986). Manual for the PDQ-R (Personality Diagnostic Questionnaire) Personality Questionnaire. New York: New York State Psychiatric Institute.

Kendall, R. (1982). The choice of diagnostic criteria for biological research. *Archives of General Psychiatry, 39,* 1334–1339.

Kernberg, O. (1968). The treatment of patients with borderline personality organization. *International Journal of Psychoanalysis, 49,* 600–619.

Kernberg, O. (1975). *Borderline conditions and pathological narcissism.* New York: Jason Aronson.

KERNBERG, O. (1981). Structural interviewing. *Psychiatric Clinics of North America, 4,* 169–195.

KERNBERG, O. (1984). *Severe personality disorders.* New Haven: Yale University Press.

KERNBERG, O., SELTZER, M., KOENIGSBERG, H., CARR, A., & APPLEBAUM, A. (1988). *Psychodynamic psychotherapy of borderline patients.* New York: Basic Books.

KILZIEH, N., & CLONINGER, C. R. (1993). Psychophysiological antecedents of personality. *Journal of Personality Disorders, 7,* 100–117.

KLEIN, M. H. (1993). Issues in the assessment of personality disorders. *Journal of Personality Disorders, 7,* 18–33.

KLEIN, D. (1977). Psychopharmacological treatment in delineation of borderline disorders. In P. Hartocollis (Ed.), *Borderline personality disorders* (pp. 365–383). New York: International Universities Press.

KOHUT, H. (1971). *The analysis of the self.* New York: International Universities Press.

KOHUT, H. (1977). *The restoration of the self.* New York: International Universities Press.

KRETSCHMER, E. (1936). *Physique and character.* London: Routledge & Kegan Paul.

KROLL, J., SIMES, L., MARTIN, K., LARI, S., PYLE, R., & ZANDER, J. (1981). Borderline personality disorder: Construct validity of the concept. *Archives of General Psychiatry, 38,* 1021–1026.

LEARY, T. C. (1957). *Interpersonal diagnosis of personality: A functional theory and methodology for personality evaluation.* New York: Ronald Press.

LEVIN, F. M. (1991). *Mapping the mind.* Hillsdale, NJ: Analytic Press.

LICHTENBERG, J. (1983). *Psychoanalysis and infant research.* Hillsdale, NJ: Analytic Press.

LINKS, P. S., STEINER, M., & HUXLEY, G. (1988). The occurrence of borderline personality disorder in the families of borderline patients. *Journal of Personality Disorders, 2,* 14–20.

LIVESLEY, W. J. (1987). Theoretical and empirical issues in the selection of criteria to diagnose personality disorders. *Journal of Personality Disorders, 1,* 88–94.

LIVESLEY, W. J. (1991). Classifying personality disorders: Ideal types, prototypes, or dimensions? *Journal of Personality Disorders, 5,* 52–59.

LORANGER, A. (1990). The impact of DSM-III on diagnostic practice in a university hospital. *Archives of General Psychiatry, 47,* 672–675.

LORANGER, A. W., HIRSCHFELD, R. M. A., SARTORIUS, N., & REYIER, D. A. (1991). The WHO/ADAMHA international pilot study of personality disorders: Background and purpose. *Journal of Personality Disorders, 5,* 296–306.

LORANGER, A. W., SUSMAN, V. L., OLDHAM, J. M., & RUSSAKOFF, L. M. (1987). The personality disorder examination: A preliminary report. *Journal of Personality Disorders, 1,* 1–13.

LORANGER, A. W., LENZENWEGER, M. F., GARTNER, A. F., SUSMAN, V. L., HERZIG,

J., ZAMIT, G. K., GARTNER, J. D., ABRAMS, R. C., & YOUNGER, R. C. (1991). Trait-state artifacts and the diagnosis of personality disorders. *Archives of General Psychiatry, 48,* 720–728.

McGLASHAN, T. H. (1986a). The Chestnut Lodge follow-up study: 3. Long-term outcome of borderline personalities. *Archives of General Psychiatry, 43,* 20–30.

McGLASHAN, T. H. (1986b). Schizotypal personality disorder: The Chestnut Lodge follow-up study: 5. Long-term follow-up perspectives. *Archives of General Psychiatry, 43,* 329–334.

MILES, C. (1977). Conditions predisposing to suicide. *Journal of Nervous and Mental Disease, 146,* 231–246.

MILLER, N. E. (1986). The prediction of psychopathology across the life-span: The value of longitudinal research. In L. Erlenmeyer-Kimling & N. E. Miller (Eds.), *Life-span research on the prediction of psychopathology.* Hillsdale, NJ: Erlbaum.

MILLON, T. (1987). Manual for the MCMI-II (Millon Clinical Multiaxial Inventory) (2nd ed.). Minneapolis, MN: National Computer Systems.

MILLON, T. (1987a). Concluding commentary. *Journal of Personality Disorders, 1,* 110–112.

MILLON, T. (1987b). Special feature: Personality disorder criteria: Empirical or theoretical? *Journal of Personality Disorders, 1,* 71–72.

MODELL, A. (1963). Primitive object relationships and the predisposition to schizophrenia. *International Journal of Psychoanalysis, 44,* 282–291.

MOREY, L. (1988). Personality disorders under DSM-III and DSM-IIIR: An examination of convergence, coverage and internal consistency. *American Journal of Psychiatry, 145,* 573.

O'BOYLE, M., & SELF, D. (1990). A comparison of two interviews for DSM-IIIR personality disorders. *Psychiatry Research, 32,* 85–92.

OLDHAM, J. M., & SKODOL, A. E. (1992). Personality disorders and mood disorders. In A. Tasman & M. B. Riba (Eds.), *Review of psychiatry* (Vol. 11, pp. 418–435). Washington, DC: American Psychiatric Press.

OVERHOLSER, J. C. (1992). Aggregation of personality measures: Implications for personality disorder research. *Journal of Personality Disorders, 6,* 267–277.

PERRY, J. C. (1988). A prospective study of life stress, defenses, psychotic symptoms and depression in borderline and antisocial personality disorders and bipolar type II affective disorder. *Journal of Personality Disorders, 2,* 49–59.

PERRY, J. C. (1990). Challenges in validity of personality disorders: Beyond description. *Journal of Personality Disorders, 4,* 273–289.

PERRY, J. C. (1991) Use of longitudinal data to validate personality disorders. In J. M. Oldham (Ed.), *Personality disorders: New perspectives on diagnostic validity.* Washington, DC: American Psychiatric Press.

PERRY, J. C. (1992). Problems and considerations in the valid assessment of personality disorders. *American Journal of Psychiatry, 149,* 1645–1653.

PERRY, J. C. (1993). Longitudinal studies of personality disorders. *Journal of Personality Disorders*, 63–85.

PFOHL, B., BLUM, N., ZIMMERMAN, M., & STANGL, D. (1989). Manual for the SIDP-R (Structured Interview for DSM-IIIR Personality). Iowa City, IA: Department of Psychiatry, University of Iowa.

PFOHL, B., CORYELL, W., ZIMMERMAN, M., & STANGL, D. (1986). DSM-III Personality disorders: Diagnostic overlap with internal consistency of individual DSM-III criteria. *Comprehensive Psychiatry, 27,* 21–34.

PFOHL, B., STANGL, D., & ZIMMERMAN, M. (1984). The implications of DSM-III disorders for patients with major depression. *Journal of Affective Disorders, 7,* 309–318.

REICH, J., NOYES, R., JR., & TROUGHTON, B. A. (1987). Dependent personality disorders associated with phobic avoidance in patients with panic disorders. *American Journal of Psychiatry, 144,* 323–326.

REICH, J., NOYES, R., JR., CORYELL, W., & O'GORMAN, T. W. (1986). The effect of state anxiety in personality measurement. *American Journal of Psychiatry, 143,* 760–763.

REISER, M. (1984). *Mind, brain, body: Toward a convergence of psychoanalysis and neurobiology.* New York: Basic Books.

RENNENBERG, B., CHAMBLESS, D. L., DOWDALL, D. J., FAVERBACH, J. A., & GRACELY, E. J. (1992). The structured clinical interview for DSM-IIIR, Axis II and the Millon Clinical Multiaxial Inventory: A concurrent validity study of personality disorders among anxious outpatients. *Journal of Personality Disorders, 6,* 117–124.

ROBINS, L. N. (1985). Epidemiology: Reflections on testing the validity of psychiatric interviews. *Archives of General Psychiatry, 42,* 918–924.

ROBINS, L. N., HELZER, J. E., CROUGHAN, J., & RATCLIFF, K. S. (1981). National Institute of Mental Health Diagnostic Interview Schedule: Its history, characteristics, and validity. *Archives of General Psychiatry, 38,* 381–389.

SCHULZ, P. M., SOLOFF, P. H., KELLY, T., MORGENSTERN, M., SCHULZ, S. C., & DIFRANCO, R. (1989). A family history of borderline subtypes. *Journal of Personality Disorders, 3,* 217–229.

SEARLES, H. (1977). Dual and multiple identity processes in borderline ego functioning. In P. Hartocollis (Ed.), *Borderline personality disorders* (pp. 441–456). New York: International Universities Press.

SHEA, M. T. (1992). Some characteristics of the Axis II criteria sets and their implications for assessment of personality disorders. *Journal of Personality Disorders, 6,* 377–381.

SHEA, M. T., & HIRSCHFELD, R. M. A. (EDS.). (IN PRESS). NIMH Conference on Personality Disorders. *Journal of Personality Disorders.*

SHEA, M. T., GLASS, D. R., PILKONIS, P. A., WATKINS, J., & DOCHERTY, J. P. (1987). Frequency and implications of personality disorders in a sample of depressed outpatients. *Journal of Personality Disorders, 1,* 27–42.

SIEVER, L. J., & DAVIS, K. L. (1991). A psychobiological perspective on the personality disorders. *American Journal of Psychiatry, 148,* 1647–1658.

SILVERMAN, J. M., PINKHAM, L., HOVATH, T. B., COCCARO, E. F., KLAR, H., SCHEAR, S., APTER, S., DAVIDSON, M., MOHS, R. C., & SIEVER, L. J. (1991). Affective and impulsive personality disorder traits in the relatives of patients with borderline personality disorder. *American Journal of Psychiatry, 148,* 1378–1385.

SKODOL, A. E., OLDHAM, J. M., ROSNICK, L., KELLMAN, H. D., & HYLER, S. E. (1991). Diagnosis of DSM-IIIR personality disorders: A comparison of two structured interviews. *International Journal of Methods in Psychiatric Research, 1,* 13–26.

SKODOL, A. E., ROSNICK, L., KELLMAN, D., OLDHAM, J. M., & HYLER, S. E. (1988). Validating structured DSM-IIIR personality disorder assessments with longitudinal data. *American Journal of Psychiatry, 145,* 1297–1299.

SPITZER, R. L. (1983). Psychiatric diagnosis: Are clinicians still necessary? *Comprehensive Psychiatry, 24,* 399–411.

SPITZER, R. L., & ENDICOTT, J. (1979). *Schedule for Affective Disorders and Schizophrenia (SADS)* (3rd ed.). New York: New York State Psychiatric Institute.

STANGL, D., PFOHL, B., ZIMMERMAN, M., BOWERS, W., & CORENTHAL, C. (1985). A Structured interview for the DSM-III personality disorders: A preliminary report. *Archives of General Psychiatry, 42,* 591–596.

STONE, M. (1983). Psychotherapy with schizotypal borderline patients. *Journal of the American Academy of Psychoanalysis, 11,* 87–111.

STONE, M. H., HURT, S. W., & STONE, D. K. (1987). The PI 500: Long-term follow-up of borderline inpatients meeting DSM-III criteria. *Journal of Personality Disorders, 1,* 291–298.

STRAUSS, J. S., HAFEZ, H., LIEBERMAN, P., & HARDING, C. M. (1985). The course of psychiatric disorder, III: Longitudinal principles. *American Journal of Psychiatry, 142,* 289–296.

STRICKER, G., & GOLD, J. E. (1988). A psychodynamic approach to the personality disorders. *Journal of Personality Disorders, 2,* 350–359.

TELLEGEN, A., LYKKEN, D. T., BOUCHARD, D., JR., WILCOX, J. T., SEGAL, N. L., & RICH, S. (1988). Personality similarity in twins reared apart and together. *Journal of Personality and Social Psychology, 54,* 1031–1039.

THOMAS, A., & CHESS, S. (1977). *Temperament and development.* New York: Brunner/Mazel.

VAILLANT, G. E. (1977). *Adaptation to life.* Boston: Little, Brown.

VAILLANT, G. E. (1985). An empirically derived hierarchy of adaptive mechanisms and its usefulness as a potential diagnostic axis. *Acta Psychiatrica Scandinavica, 71,* 171–180.

VAILLANT, G. E., & DRAKE, R. E. (1985). Maturity of ego defenses in relation to DSM-III Axis II personality disorder. *Archives of General Psychiatry, 42,* 597–601.

VAN DER KOLK, B. A., PERRY, J. C., & HERMAN, J. L. (1991). Childhood origins of self-destructive behavior. *American Journal of Psychiatry, 148,* 1665–1671.

WEISSMAN, M. M., PRUSOFF, B. A., & KLERMAN, G. L. (1978). Personality and the prediction of long-term outcome of depression. *American Journal of Psychiatry, 135,* 797–800.

WESTEN, D. (1990) Toward a revised theory of borderline object relations: Contributions of empirical research. *International Journal of Psychoanalysis, 71,* 661–693.

WIDIGER, T. A. (1991a). Critical issues in the design of DSM-IV, Axis II. In R. Michels (Ed.), *Psychiatry,* Vol. 1. Philadelphia: J. B. Lippincott.

WIDIGER, T. A. (1991b). Personality disorders: Dimensional models proposed for DSM-IV. *Journal of Personality Disorders, 5,* 386–398.

WIDIGER, T. A. (1992). Categorical versus dimensional classification: Implications from and for research. *Journal of Personality Disorders, 6,* 287–300.

WIDIGER, T. A. (IN PRESS). The DSM-IIIR categorical personality disorder diagnoses: A critique and alternative. *Psychological Inquiry.*

WIDIGER, T. A., & FRANCES, A. (1985). Axis II personality disorders: Diagnostic and treatment issues. *Hospital & Community Psychiatry, 36,* 619–627.

WIDIGER, T. A., & TRULL, T. J. (1987). Behavioral indicators, hypothetical constructs and personality disorders. *Journal of Personality Disorders, 1,* 82–87.

WILSON, M. (1993). DSM-III and the transformation of American psychiatry: A history. *American Journal of Psychiatry, 150,* 399–410.

WING, J. K., COOPER, J. E., & SARTORIUS, N. (1974). *The measurement of classification of psychiatric symptoms.* London: Cambridge University Press.

ZIMMERMAN, M., & CORYELL, W. H. (1990). Diagnosing personality disorders in the community: A comparison of self-report and interview measures. *Archives of General Psychiatry, 47,* 527–531.

CHAPTER 9

Assessing Psychological Development Level

DIANNA HARTLEY

Psychoanalysis has, from its inception, been a developmental theory. In 1905 Freud articulated his first developmental formulation, based on the unfolding of the libidinal or psychosexual phases (the oral, anal, and phallic periods). Since then, our understanding both of normal human development and of developmental psychopathology has been enormously enriched by the work of other psychoanalysts and developmental psychologists. It has become clear that the developmental or organizational level of the patient's personality has important implications for making a comprehensive diagnosis, setting treatment goals, establishing a therapeutic alliance, choosing appropriate therapeutic interventions, evaluating treatment outcome, and understanding long-range prognosis. The degree of structure in the treatment and the kind of relationship offered by the therapist differentiate current approaches to the psychological treatment of patients who are seen to be organized at different levels and to have different developmental needs.

The developmental point of view is not concerned simply with the recovery of memories, which is more a historical than a developmental approach. Instead, it focuses on the gradual, sequential emergence and transformation of maturational factors and on the complex and continuing interaction between past and present experience. The sequence may be observed in children studied longitudinally or be reconstructed during the treatment of adults. Recent findings from infancy research, social and cognitive developmental psychology, and lifespan development can productively be incorporated into theories of the therapeutic action of psychoanalysis and psychotherapy. This chapter will present a brief overview of the conceptual, clinical, and empirical issues associated with measuring intrapsychic developmental level as it relates to the assessment of psychopathology and to the process and outcome of psychodynamic psychotherapies with adolescent and adult patients.

The Emergence of Developmental Models

Freud ([1905] 1953) initially believed that many forms of psychopathology either had their roots in fixations at particular psychosexual stages or represented regressions from higher levels of functioning. In 1914 he added the concepts of primary narcissism, autoeroticism, and secondary narcissism to his libidinally based theory of psychopathology. This framework was further elaborated by Abraham (1924), who divided the oral phase into sucking and biting periods, the anal phase into destructive-expulsive (sadistic) and mastering-retaining (anal erotic) subphases, and the phallic period into the true phallic and later genital phases, so that each stage included a libidinal and an aggressive component. Meissner (1985) presents a comprehensive and succinct resume of the stages of psychosexual development.

In the psychosexual model, Freud ([1905] 1953) assumed that the phases of sexual organization were normally passed through smoothly, but that such phenomena as excessive stimulation or libidinal adhesiveness could cause neurotic difficulties. For example, excessive gratification or deprivation during the oral phase (up to eighteen months) was associated with the pathological traits of excessive optimism or pessimism, demandingness, dependency, envy, and possessiveness. Effective solutions to the problems of this phase resulted in the capacities to give and take with others, to trust, and to rely on oneself. Maladaptive traits related to the anal phase (one to three years) were those associated with obsessive-compulsive neuroses, including conflicts over orderliness, obstinacy, ambivalence, defiance, and sadomasochistic tendencies. Positive resolution served as the foundation for autonomy, initiative, and cooperation. Issues of the phallic stage (three to five years) focused on castration anxiety and penis envy; mastery of these issues provided the basis for sexual identity, curiosity, and self-regulation of internal processes. The genital stage was associated mostly with adolescence and involved some reworking of all previous stages. Successful reintegration meant that one had the capacity for genital sexual satisfaction, a consistent sense of identity, and the ability to pursue goals and values.

While Freud used this framework for understanding the origins of psychopathology and, to some extent, for evaluating the outcome of psychoanalysis, techniques of practice were derived not from theory but rather from other aspects of his experience. In cases of neurosis, treatment was aimed at bringing excluded components of infantile sexuality into the personality organization.

As the attention of psychoanalysis turned from the psychosexual model to that of ego psychology, Hartmann (1939) proposed a theoretical framework for the emergence and development of the ego organization that marked the beginnings of psychoanalysis as a general theory of human development, not just of psychopathology. Following Anna Freud (1936), Hartmann, Kris, and Loewenstein (1946) postulated an initial undifferentiated matrix, which contains the individual's endowment and from which both the id and the ego originate. They also introduced the concept of "average expectable environment," affirmed the importance of parental contribution to development, and outlined a scheme for the phase-specific maturation of autonomous ego functions in the conflict-free sphere. They wrote of a progression from the undifferentiated stage to the gradual differentiation of self from the world in the first half year of life. In the second half year, the child's relationship to his or her own body and objects in the world shifts and the action of the reality principle becomes discernible. In this stage objects are experienced as existing to fulfill the child's needs. In the second year, an ego-id differentiation phase emerges, marked by ambivalence. The final phase of formation of the psychic organization is that of ego-superego differentiation, the result of social influences, identification with parental values, and resolution of the oedipal conflict. Hartmann, Kris, and Loewenstein did not intend to introduce a new theory of psychopathology, reconceptualize the therapeutic process, or lead to revisions of technique.

Another major developmental schema was that of Erikson (1950), who, in contrast to his predecessors, emphasized the ways in which social norms interact with biological drives to produce the identity of the individual. He described eight developmental stages, each triggered by biologically determined life events that disturbed the equilibrium between drives and social adjustment. Each new challenge might or might not be mastered through the development of new skills and attitudes. If not, then certain aspects of personality would be arrested at that stage and mastery of later stages would also be compromised. The stages and their biological triggers included:

- Trust versus mistrust (oral stage)
- Autonomy versus shame and doubt (bowel and bladder control)
- Initiative versus guilt (locomotion)
- Industry versus inferiority (latency)
- Identity versus role confusion (puberty)
- Intimacy versus isolation (physical maturity)

- Generativity versus stagnation (social maturity)
- Integrity versus despair (physical decline)

Erikson paid closer attention than classical psychoanalysts to the fact that development occurs in a set of cultural and family traditions which heavily influence the individual's personality style. He also extended the theoretically formative period from early childhood into later phases of life. In contrast to the marked determinism of early psychoanalytic theorists, his view tended to be more optimistic, both in seeing the individual as more plastic throughout the life cycle and in seeing altruistic values as close to biological needs in importance. The need for a coherent self-concept, fulfilled in a coherent, supportive social milieu, was fundamental in his theory.

Theories Based on Clinical and Normative Infant Observation

While both Hartmann and Erikson added environmental, interpersonal, and social elements to their conceptualizations of development, their ideas remained rooted in drive theory. Meanwhile, another group of theorists began to challenge the basic assumptions of what Greenberg and Mitchell (1983) have called the drive-structural model and to move toward what they call the relational-structural model.

René Spitz (1945, 1965) was among the first analysts to base his developmental theories on direct work with infants and children, rather than on clinical material from adult patients. He was also a pioneer in ascribing primary importance to the role of the mother and the mother–infant interaction in a theory of developmental stages. He stressed that from the beginning of life, the human partner of the child "quickens" the child's innate abilities and mediates all perception, behavior, and knowledge.

Spitz described development in terms of "organizers" of the psyche, which were similar to critical periods in the development of animals. During these critical periods, various currents are integrated with functions and capacities that emerge from the process of maturation, resulting in a restructuring of the psychic system on a higher level of complexity. The first organizer in the first two or three months is the smiling response; the second is the eight-month anxiety, which indicates differentiation among objects and a "libidinal object proper"; and the third, at about ten to eighteen months, is the use of "no" to express displeasure. Spitz's work was seminal in its use of direct observation of infants; its blend of psychoanalysis and experimental psychology; its recognition of the signal function of the primary caretaker; its view of developmental processes as increasingly complex hierarchical integrations; and its integration of affective, cognitive, and interpersonal components. While the more recent research of Emde (1988a, 1988b) and Stern (1985) indicate that Spitz may have exaggerated the passivity of the infant, his formulations are otherwise quite compatible with theirs; the congruence indicates both the validity of Spitz's research paradigm and the robustness of his conclusions. Based on his findings, he proposed methods of ameliorating developmental imbalances in childhood and modifications of adult psychotherapy to deal with developmental deficits relatively directly through the relationship with the therapist.

Melanie Klein's ideas also evolved from her intensive work with children (Klein 1948; Segal 1973). She described two major developmental constellations, the paranoid-schizoid position and the depressive position. Included in her descriptions of both constellations are object relations; prevalent anxieties, conflicts, and characteristic defensive operations; processes of introjection and projection; and processes of integration and synthesis.

The paranoid-schizoid position is marked by the defenses of splitting, denial, projection, and projective identification; by part—object relationships; and by basic fears about the survival of the self, which take the form of persecutory anxiety, stemming from sadistic impulses. If these fears are not excessive, the next developmental phase, the depressive position, begins in the second half of the first year, when children's increasing sense of reality leads to awareness that "good" and "bad" external objects are whole objects with good and bad parts. They comprehend that they aggressively attack the persons they also love and that they themselves therefore also have bad parts. With that shift, the predominant fear changes from external attack on the self to harm of the good internal and external objects by the self. Characteristic positive defense mechanisms include reparation, ambivalence, and gratitude; potential negative developments are omnipotence, manic triumph, harsh critical self-accusations, and polarized idealization and/or devaluation of others. The paranoid-schizoid and the depressive positions are reconstituted at various times in the course of a person's life and are implicated in conflicts related to all psychosexual levels.

In treatment, Kleinians prefer to work exclusively with interpretations, primarily transference interpretations aimed at the level of the patient's maximum anxiety, for the full range of disorders. They work analytically even with more severe disorders, stressing early interpretation of negative transferences derived from the paranoid-schizoid position. Kleinians also have contributed enormously to our understanding and use of the projective and introjective aspects of countertransference (Racker 1968; Ogden 1982, 1986; Spillius 1988; Spillius and Feldman 1989).

A particularly fertile framework, which has emerged from the observation of both normal and severely disturbed infants and young children, has been advanced by Mahler and her associates (Mahler, Pine, and Bergman 1975), who focused on the process of establishing separateness and individuality in the first three years of life. They propose a normal autistic first phase, marked by the infant's lack of awareness of a caretaker. It should be noted here that this aspect of their theory has been called into question by more recent infant observational work, which suggests that babies are immediately responsive to mother's voice, even prior to birth (Lichtenberg 1983), and certainly that there is an active interaction of mother and infant from the earliest postnatal days (Stern 1985). In the Mahlerian scheme, awareness of the presence of another person signals entry into the second phase, called normal symbiosis, in which the infant and caretaker seem to function as an omnipotent system. Next begins the separation-individuation process, spanning several years; this stage is characterized by three subphases, identified as hatching (differentiation of body image), practicing (physically moving away, upright locomotion, and "refueling"), and rapprochement (intense ambivalence, manifested by swings between seeking separateness and reunion). The last phase, object constancy, involves the achievement of a sense of identity and stable internalized representations of others.

Mahler (1974) described her work as enabling clinicians treating adults to make more accurate reconstructions of the preverbal period, thereby making patients more accessible to analytic interventions. Although she did not explicitly recommend changes in technique or in the theory of the therapeutic process, others have drawn on her work for that purpose, including Blanck and Blanck (1979), Fleming (1975), and Settlage (1977). Pine (1985) has presented a comprehensive explication of the value of this framework for working with the full range of patients—children and adults; psychotic, borderline and neurotic conditions—in various forms of psychotherapy and psychoanalysis.

More recently the work of Stern (1985) has challenged many of the ideas of previous approaches to developmental schemas. Stern intends his work to be normative rather than pathomorphic and prospective rather than retrospective. He stresses the reorganization of subjective perspectives on self and other with the emergence of new capacities as the child matures. His model consists of four senses of self, each with an associated domain of relatedness. The first "sense of emergent self" involves the process of coming into being and forming connections. With the rise of a single organizing subjective perspective and coherent physical self, the developmental leap into a "sense of core self" and "domain of core relatedness" occurs. Next, the "discovery" of subjective mental states beyond physical events opens up the "sense of subjective self" and the "domain of intersubjective relatedness." The capacities involved in this mode include sharing the focus of attention, apprehending the intentions and motives of others, and sensing congruence or lack of congruence between one's own state and that of another person. Finally, the sense that oneself and other people have storehouses of knowledge and experience which can be shared symbolically ushers in the "sense of verbal self" and the "domain of verbal relatedness," which involve the ability to objectify the self, to be self-reflective, and to use language to communicate.

Unlike other theoreticians, who include ideas of fixations and regressions, Stern views all senses of self and all domains of relatedness as active throughout subsequent development, although the formative phase for each sense of self is a sensitive period. He also thinks of other lifelong clinical issues, such as autonomy, mastery, intimacy, orality, and so forth, as important throughout all phases of development, not just during phase-specific periods. He makes broad recommendations for the diagnosis and treatment of adult patients based on his model for the developmental progression of the sense of self.

Based on systematic observational studies, Greenspan (1981, 1989) has traced how sensory modalities, affect dispositions, cognitive potentials, and object relations are integrated in the course of the first four years of life. By focusing on perturbations in the prerepresentational stage of life and difficulties in the early development of visual-spatial, auditory-verbal, and/or sensory-affective modalities, he has drawn links between the neonate's constitutional givens and the child's early relationships, which culminate in a developmental model of psychopathology, psychotherapeutic technique, and therapeutic change.

Recent Theories Based on Clinical Observation of Adults

Rather than focus on the development of the psychic apparatus at very early periods, Jacobson (1964) reconstructed a wide variety of sequences over the life span. Drawing on Hartmann, Kris, and Lowenstein (1946), she began with the concept of the undifferentiated matrix, but included in her theory the emergence not only of id, ego, and superego but also of aggressive and libidinal drives as well as of self and object representations. She advanced the idea that the infant acquires self and object images with good (libidinal) or bad (aggressive) valences depending on experiences of gratification or frustration with caretakers. Early libido and aggression were thought to shift continuously from object to self with weak boundaries between them. Early distribution (good-bad) and direction (self-other) shape all future growth as stable self and object representations emerge. Fusion with objects is replaced by introjections and identifications, processes by which traits and actions of object images become internalized parts of self images. Jacobson paid considerable attention to superego formation through a sequence initially polarized around pleasure and unpleasure, then organized by issues of strength and weakness, and finally viewed as the internalization of ethical values which regulate behavior, drive discharge, and self-esteem. Jacobson used her developmental perspective to account for a broad spectrum of psychological disorders. She also felt that developmental deficits called for changes in methods of treatment, and she spelled out specific modifications in frequency of visits and therapist's stance for severely depressed patients.

Strongly influenced by Jacobson, Kernberg (1976, 1980, 1984) has outlined a general theory of the basic units of internalized object relations; the developmental stages in their differentiation and integration; the implications of these stages for psychic structure; the relationship between developmental failure and various types of psychopathology, primarily personality disorders; and recommendations for supportive and expressive approaches to psychotherapeutic treatment.

The lowest level of character pathology in his formulations is marked by the lack of integration of self or object representations, projections of primitive superego nuclei, splitting, impulsivity, lack of empathy, and undermodulated expressions of libido and aggression. Included are infantile personalities, antisocial personalities, "as-if" characters, and patients with multiple sexual deviations and addictions. At the intermediate level he emphasizes defective superego integration, severe mood swings, contradictory feelings and behavior, a mixture of repression and other defenses (such as dissociation and undoing), and mixed pregenital and genital aims in relationships. This level includes passive-aggressive personalities, sadomasochistic personalities, and oral characters, as well as some infantile and narcissistic personalities. The highest level includes hysterical characters, obsessive-compulsive characters, and depressive-masochistic characters. These are characterized by well-integrated but severe superegos, stable self and object representations, excessive but successful repression, a wide variety of affective states, and genital-level sexual striving.

A second major developmental model which incorporates views of normal development, psychopathology, and fundamental modifications of psychotherapeutic technique has emerged recently from analyses of adult patients; this is the self psychology of Kohut (1971, 1977, 1984) and his associates (Goldberg 1985). They view the self, with both inherited and environmental determinants, as the core of personality, and they trace separate lines of development that move through a series of archaic structures toward maturity and cohesiveness. In response to lapses in parental empathy, original primary narcissism differentiates into two archaic configurations: the "grandiose self" involves an exaggerated and exhibitionistic image of the self that becomes the repository for infantile perfection; and the "idealized parental imago" transfers perfection to an admired omnipotent object. With further development, the grandiose self, the component associated with power and success, leads to self-esteem, ambition, and self-confidence. Likewise, the idealized parental image, associated with idealized goals, becomes integrated with the ego ideal to represent mature values and standards. In psychopathology, the grandiose self results in exhibitionism, shame, envy, depression, poor self-esteem, and hypochondriasis. Loss of the idealized object leaves the individual vulnerable to depression, depletion, failure of values, and fragmentation. Kohut stressed the need throughout life for empathic interaction with self-objects. Kohut suggests that specific behaviors of the therapist—mirroring the patient and allowing himself or herself to be idealized—compensate for earlier developmental failures and are crucial to effective treatment of those with narcissistic disorders.

Gedo's (1979) hierarchical epigenetic model of self-organization, based on a careful critique of traditional and more recent theory and research, is the most comprehensive existing scheme for assessing and working with the developmental level of adult patients. He synthesizes metapsychological theory, infant observation research, and clinical experience to construct an outline of psychological functioning that convincingly links development, psychopathology, and psychotherapy. The model includes five modes of psychological integration and functioning, each organized around a key developmental achievement: birth, differentiation of body boundaries, consolidation of self organization, formation of superego, and formation of repression barrier. Within each mode, he addresses typical conflicts (dangers and defenses), perceptual-cognitive development, and goals in relation to objects. In the epigenetic view, the formation of structure is the result of successive transactions between the person and the environment, with the outcome of each phase dependent on the outcomes of all previous phases, so that each phase integrates previous phases into a new level of organization. Gedo and Goldberg (1973) have made recommendations for specific kinds of interventions that are most useful for patients when they are functioning in a particular mode according to their model.

Empirical Research on Developmental Level

Although clinical assessment of an individual's level of development on a variety of dimensions has been an area of concern since the earliest days of psychoanalysis and psychotherapy, empirical research is a relatively recent undertaking. Most extant scales are based on concepts from object relations theory, blended with various other frameworks specific to the developers.

THE WASHINGTON UNIVERSITY GROUP

One of the earliest and best known conceptual/empirical systems for assessing level of ego development is that of Loevinger (1976). She sees ego development both as a developmental sequence and as a dimension of individual differences in any age cohort. Definitions given for each stage describe what persons at that stage have in common, regardless of chronological age. The stages include:

- The presocial (undifferentiated)
- The symbiotic
- The impulsive (oriented to present, need-gratifying relationships with intense affects
- The self-protective (short-term rewards and punishments, opportunistic hedonism, externalization of responsibility)
- The conformist (group identification, conformity to rules, stereotypical thinking)
- The conscientious (long-term goals and values, internalized rules, sense of responsibility, complex thinking, fine shades of emotion)
- The autonomous (emotional interdependence, valuing of individual differences, awareness of conflict, tolerance for ambiguity)
- The integrated (transcendence of conflict, self-actualization)

Detailed manuals explaining the concepts and scoring procedures thoroughly enough to allow self-training are available (Loevinger and Wessler 1970; Loevinger, Wessler, and Redmore 1970).

Investigators working in this framework have looked for associations between stages of ego development and forms of psychopathology. Hauser and his group, looking at adolescents, found that psychiatric patients, compared with normal and diabetic populations, showed arrests in ego development at preconformist levels (Hauser et al. 1983; Noam et al. 1984; Jacobson et al. 1986). Vincent and Vincent (1979), using an inpatient adult population, reported that those with character disorder diagnoses were more likely to score at preconformist levels than neurotic, psychotic, and normal groups. Vincent and Castillo (1984), looking at the relationship between ego development and DSM-III Axis II diagnoses in an adult outpatient sample, found that most patients below the conformity level were clustered in the "dramatic, emotional, or erratic" category, the only departure from the distribution in Loevinger's normative sample. They found no patients at the highest levels. Interestingly, 88 percent of their psychotic patients were at the conformity level or above. These studies suggest that most psychopathology can occur at any developmental stage as operationalized by this measure, and that the interaction of ego development, life-cycle phase, and psychopathology is not simple.

THE MICHIGAN GROUP

As part of the Menninger Foundation's Psychotherapy Research Project, Mayman (1968) presented a new projective assessment procedure, the Early Memories Test, and a scale to evaluate the thematic content according to psychosexual development, including constellations of feeling states, interpersonal conflicts, coping patterns, relationship expectations, and self experience. This scale uses psychosexual stages (oral, anal, phallic, oedipal) as basic divisions, but goes beyond Freud's concepts to assess ego and object relational modes with subtle differentiations. Unfortunately, the original scale, while clinically compelling, was apparently not used in any quantitative studies and nothing is known about its psychometric properties or construct validity.

Several of Mayman's students in the early 1970s (A. Krohn, E. R. Ryan, and J. Urist) designed other scales to evaluate levels of object representation as specific points on a developmental continuum from various clinical material, including dreams, Rorschach responses, and early memories.

Krohn's Object Representation Scale for Dreams (Krohn and Mayman 1974; Hatcher and Krohn 1980) was designed to assess increasing levels of capacity for interpersonal relatedness by examining the degree to which people are experienced as whole, consistent, alive, and complex, as opposed to absent, desolate, fragmented, and malignant. This scale has been applied to early memories and Rorschach responses as well as to dreams, and interrater reliability for judges—typically clinical psychology graduate students trained in the use of the scale—is adequate (Pearson correlations reported from .80 to .91; percent agreement within one step from 74 percent to 93 percent). Significant relationships have been found between scores on this scale and capacity to engage in psychotherapy for neurotic-level patients, though not for borderlines (Hatcher and Krohn 1980); inpatient treatment alliance and outcome in a psychoanalytic hospital setting (Frieswyck and Colson 1980); outcome in psychoanalytic psychotherapy (Greif 1989); and general mental health (Grey and Davies 1981).

Urist's Mutuality of Autonomy Scale (Urist 1977; Urist and Schill 1982) draws theoretically from Mahler, Kernberg, and Kohut and assesses the developmental progression from symbiosis to object constancy, or from primary narcissism to empathic object relatedness. The scale is in the of a 7-point continuum: (1) reciprocity-mutuality, (2) collabora cooperation, (3) simple interaction, (4) anaclitic-dependent, (5) reflec mirroring, (6) magical control-coercion, and (7) envelopment-incorporation. Typically, the highest, lowest, and average scores from a Rorschach protocol are used in data analyses. Reliabilities reported range from .80 to .94 (coefficient alpha) or 58 to 95 percent one-step agreement, using graduate students or experienced clinicians. The scale has been significantly associated with ratings of interpersonal relationships made by treaters (Urist 1977; Urist and Schill 1982); with outcome in psychoanalysis and psychotherapy (Kavanagh 1985) and in psychoanalytically oriented hospital treatment (Blatt et al. 1988); and with a differential diagnosis of borderline personality disorder and schizophrenia (Spear and Sugarman 1984).

Ryan's Object Relations Scale (Ryan and Bell 1984; Ryan and Cicchetti 1985) is comprised of 20 points divided into four main categories which assess prototypes of severe disturbances such as psychoses and borderline disorders (group A), prototypes of depressed or pathologically narcissistic states (group B), prototypes of neurotic disturbances in relatedness (group C), and prototypes of mutual interactions (group D). Reliabilities are reported in the .80s range (intraclass correlations) or one-step agreement of at least 80 percent. Ryan and Bell (1984) found significant increases in the scores of hospitalized psychotic patients from admission to follow-up. Also, those who maintained higher levels of object relations stayed out of the hospital longer. Ryan and Cicchetti (1985), looking at predictors of various components of therapeutic alliance, found that the Object Relations Scale accounted for the greatest part of the variance (about 30 percent) on their alliance measures.

THE YALE GROUP

The approach of Blatt and his associates at Yale integrates concepts from cognitive developmental psychology (Piaget 1954; Werner 1948) and object relations theory. Blatt has produced two relevant scales: the Developmental Analysis of the Concept of the Object (Blatt et al. 1976), which uses the theoretical formulations of Werner to judge human responses to the Rorschach; and the Conceptual Level Scale (Blatt et al. 1979) for scoring open-ended descriptions of people in the subject's life, based on an integration of Piagetian ideas and object relations theory.

Blatt et al. (1976) developed a manual for rating Rorschach human responses in three major areas: differentiation, articulation, and integration. Categories include accuracy of the response, differentiation, articulation, motivation, object-action integration, content of action, and nature of interaction. In a longitudinal study of a normal population tested at ages

11–12, 13–14, 17–18, and 30, they found increases in the number of differentiated, articulated, integrated human figures and an increase in positively toned interactions. Comparing the responses of a sample of severely disturbed adolescents and young adults with those of the normal seventeen-to-eighteen-year-olds, they found that the patients showed more responses at lower developmental levels. Surprisingly, however, the lower-level responses occurred when accuracy was adequate; when the response was inaccurate (did not match well with the actual form of the inkblot), the patients showed higher developmental levels than the normals. This finding has subsequently been replicated (Ritzler et al. 1980; Lerner and St. Peter 1984).

Subsequent work has focused on psychotic and depressed populations, with Blatt's (1974, 1990; Blatt and Shichman 1983) notion of two primary configurations of personality as a conceptual framework. He postulates an anaclitic line that involves the development of stable, mutually satisfying relationships, and an introjective line that involves the development of a stable, realistic, positive self-identity. Anaclitic disorders result from preoccupation with relationships, feelings, intimacy, and sexuality and are associated with avoidant defenses, while those with introjective disorders are concerned with maintaining a viable sense of self, are more ideational, have problems with aggression, and use counteractive defenses. Blatt and Lerner (1983) examined the quality of object representations in patients selected as prototypical of different disorders and described differences in both the structure and the content of their human responses. Blatt et al. (1988) found that among inpatients in intensive psychotherapy, introjective patients changed primarily in cognitive processes while anaclitic patients changed primarily in the interpersonal and object representational realms. Kavanagh (1985), using this scale along with the Urist (1977) Mutuality of Autonomy Scale, found that patients in the Menninger Psychotherapy Research Project increased in the degree of mutuality and benevolence of their Rorschach percepts and that patients in psychoanalysis had a greater increase in accurately perceived full human forms than those in psychotherapy. Blatt (1992) reanalyzed the Rorschachs from the Menninger sample and found that, despite the equivalence in degree of change on a general measure (Health-Sickness Rating Scale, Luborsky 1962), there was a patient-by-treatment interaction in which anaclitic patients improved more in psychotherapy while introjective patients improved more in psychoanalysis.

Blatt et al. (1979) developed another method of assessing the content and structure of object representations using spontaneous descriptions of significant people. Their Conceptual Level Scale measures the cognitive structural organization of the descriptions as (1) sensorimotor-preoperational, (2) concrete perceptual, (3) external iconic, (4) internal iconic, or (5) conceptual. In a study of depression among normal college students, they found a significant correlation between conceptual level and depression, and also that conceptual level varied with the theorized developmental level of depressive concerns. The lowest conceptual levels were associated with dependency issues, intermediate levels with self-criticism, and the highest level with no depressive issues. Recently, Marziali and Oleniuk (1990), using a modification of this method that allowed descriptions to be rated for proportion of material at each level, found no differences between borderline outpatients and a nonpsychiatric control group on parental descriptions; but they found significant differences in descriptions of a current relationship, with the borderlines showing more lower-level representations and the nonpatients showing more higher-level representations. They conclude that in adults, multiple levels of representations of others are retained, but in different proportions.

In a study designed to examine patients' descriptions of their therapists, Geller, Behrends, and Hartley (1982) determined that the Conceptual Level Scale was not unidimensional and that it confounded content and structural dimensions. They derived nine subscales from it for use in their study. Their manual (Hartley, Geller, and Behrends 1986) includes 5-point anchored scales for assessing complexity, deillusionment, embodiment, need gratification/frustration, psychological being, self–other differentiation, structural cohesiveness, temporality, and uniqueness. In a study rating relationship episodes from early and late sessions in successful and unsuccessful psychotherapy cases from the Penn Psychotherapy Project (Luborsky et al. 1980), I (Hartley 1987) found moderate reliability for the most recent version of the Developmental Level of Object Representation Scale (one-step agreement 82–95 percent; Pearson correlations .42–.69; intraclass correlations .53–.81). Patients with good outcomes showed significant increases in self–other differentiation and temporality, while patients with poor outcomes showed decreases on both dimensions. Similar trends were found for deillusionment and psychological being. Significant main effects for early versus late sessions were found on need gratification/frustration, with both groups decreasing their scores. Patients with good outcomes were found to be significantly higher than those with poor outcomes on structural cohesiveness and temporality.

THE MCGILL GROUP

A group at McGill University has recently produced the Quality of Object Relations Scale for ordering patients along a developmental continuum (Piper, de Carufel, and Szkrumelak 1985; de Carufel and Piper 1988; Piper 1989; Piper et al. 1990). Their scale integrates notions from psychosexual and object relations models of development. Their levels are ordered as narcissistic, depressive, obsessional, oedipal, and genital. Ratings focus on the affects that surround the relationship, the value attached to the object, the autonomy afforded the object, the reaction to real or imagined loss of the object, the stability of the relationship, and the kinds of gratification derived from the relationship. Scores on this scale, derived from two unstructured one-hour interviews, include assigning 100 points along the five levels of the scale and an overall rating ranging from 1 to 9. Agreement and reliability reported are moderate, and the authors are working on ways to improve them. These ratings have been predictors of several outcome and process variables in short-term psychoanalytic psychotherapy; they also differentiated improvers from nonimprovers in long-term and brief individual and group therapies. Results indicate an additive effect for quality of object relations (QOR) and outcome in therapy, that is those with higher QOR have better outcomes in interpersonal, transference-oriented brief therapy.

The original scale has been revised (de Carufel 1989) and now includes six positions: oral-narcissistic, oral-objectal, anal, phallic pre-oedipal (male and female), oedipal, and genital. Within each position are thirteen dimensions categorized along three supradimensions: investment of object, affects surrounding relationship, and representations of self and object. This version of the scale has not yet been used, but it promises more flexible and more encompassing ratings and an opportunity to study construct validity in more detail.

OTHER APPROACHES

Westen and his associates (Westen, Barends, et al. 1988; Westen 1989; Westen, Ludolph, Block et al. 1990; Westen, Ludolph, Lerner et al. 1990) have developed a manual for coding dimensions of object relations and social cognition from interview data, which they are preparing to use for coding psychotherapy transcripts. They include four scales: complexity and differentiation of representations of people, affective tone of relationship paradigms, capacity for emotional investment in relationships and morals, and understanding of social causality. Each scale is derived from clinical and social-cognitive-developmental research. The manual gives extensive theoretical background, general principles, anchor point descriptions, and specific scoring guidelines for each point. Reliability, using advanced graduate students and research assistants with bachelor's degrees range from .71 to .96 (Pearson's R).

Although the scale has not been used in treatment research, scores derived from Thematic Apperception Test (TAT) stories have been shown to discriminate among borderline, other psychiatric patients, and normal controls in a female adolescent population. The borderline group demonstrated more malevolent representations, less emotional investment in relationships and values, and less accurate and logical attributions of causality than other groups. However, the complexity of the borderlines' representations was *greater* than those of the other two groups. This parallels the findings of the Blatt group: that inaccurately perceived human figures on the Rorschach tend to be more highly articulated in more disturbed borderline patients, suggesting the necessity for independent assessment of cognitive and object relational components of psychological functioning.

Gedo's (1979; Gedo and Goldberg 1973) conceptual framework has stimulated the construction of two scales. Horowitz and his associates (1984) developed the Organizational Level of Self and Object Schematization Scale (Horowitz 1987). In a pilot study, they obtained a reliability coefficient of .74 (intraclass correlation) for two judges. In a study of process and outcome of brief therapy for bereavement reactions, they found a significant correlation between organizational level and change in the areas of work and interpersonal functioning. They also concluded that more "exploratory" behaviors in psychotherapy (such as differentiating real from fantasized meanings of the loss) led to better outcomes in better organized patients, while more "supportive" interventions (such as encouraging a change of understanding of self in relation to the deceased person and a change of patient's defective or inflated self-image to a more realistic one) was more helpful for those at lower levels. This finding parallels those of the Menninger Psychotherapy Project: that patients with more ego strength benefited more from more expressive therapies while those lower on this dimension improved more in more supportive therapies (Kernberg et al. 1972; Wallerstein 1986).

Wilson and his associates (Wilson, Passik, and Faude 1989; Wilson et al. 1989; Wilson, Passik, and Kuras 1989) have operationalized Gedo's model in two scoring systems. The Scale for Failures in Self Regulation assesses verbal and nonverbal manifestations of self-regulatory failure from clinical narratives (usually TAT stories). Reliability is reported to fall between .80 and .90, using advanced graduate student raters who were familiar with the development of the scale. The scale manifests three underlying components: structural-nonverbal (lack of time continuum and story resolution, primitive relatedness), impulsivity (extreme forms of affect or impulse), and thematic-verbal (emptiness, helplessness, aloneness). Using factor scores, they found significant differences between a sample comprised of opiate addicts and subjects with eating disorders and one of normal controls.

Their second measure, the Epigenetic Approach to the TAT (EPITAT) (Wilson, Passik, and Kuras 1989), is also used with narratives like TAT stories or Relationship Episodes. It is more directly based on Gedo's conceptual framework and is organized with five modes for each of ten psychological dimensions. The dimensions include: affect tolerance, affect expression, personal agency, centration-decentration, threats to the self, defenses and defensive operations, empathic knowledge of others, use of an object, adaptive needs, and temporality. Graduate student raters familiar with the theoretical orientation of the scale obtained reliabilities between .85 and .92 (Pearson correlations). Principal component analyses and correlational studies support the notion that the EPITAT measures ten relatively independent dimensions, that scores change with level of arousal, and that the test reliably discriminates between normal subjects and inpatients.

A group headed by Wallerstein (Zilberg et al. 1991; DeWitt et al. 1991) has developed a set of scales for assessing psychological capacities, based on the idea that certain psychological and relational capabilities evolve over the course of development. The scale does not follow a particular developmental model, but instead, using concepts from various psychoanalytic schools, represents prototypical good and poor outcomes of development likely to be seen in an adult outpatient population.

Clinical Implications of Concepts of Developmental Level

The conceptual and theoretical literature reviewed here suggests two central questions. First, how do infant, childhood, and later development affect adult psychological functioning and psychopathology? Second, given developmental deviance, how is psychotherapy effective in correcting the resulting difficulties and helping the individual resume psychological growth?

Most of the theorists mentioned were clinicians who spelled out the ramifications of obstacles at various developmental stages. Freud and Abraham saw fixations or regressions to certain levels or zones of libidinal gratification as producing particular neuroses and perversions. Later theorists—particularly Klein, Jacobson, Mahler, and Kernberg—specified how problems negotiating developmental tasks in the first three to four years of life are reflected in psychotic, borderline, and neurotic levels of functioning in adolescent and adult patients.

It is apparent from the conceptual and empirical reviews that these notions are not easily related to diagnostic categories from DSM-IIIR. Patients with the same diagnosis on Axis I, or even on Axis II, may show quite different pictures in terms of their developmental level. Developmental level is a dynamic, not a static, variable and it is necessary to think in terms of a range of functioning; modal, best, and worst points must be combined to portray any individual. Further conceptual work is needed to clarify relationships among cognitive phases, defensive organization, object relations, and moral development.

Eagle (1984), Greenberg and Mitchell (1985), and Gedo (1979) have demonstrated contemporary shifts in theory and clinical practice away from drive models toward object relational models of development and therapeutic action. Generally, these theories call for redefining transference and countertransference in terms of interactions and of developmental deficits and needs which may be stable or transient; for rethinking the relative contributions of insight, empathy, and other relationship variables to the outcome of psychotherapy; and for emphasizing necessary attention to patients' developmental fluctuations across a range of functioning in all treatments, regardless of diagnosis.

Summary and Best Bets for Further Research

Theories linking development, psychopathology, and psychotherapy are persuasive; but so far little evidence, other than clinical experience, argues for their acceptance. This is an area in which theory has far surpassed research, although, as we have seen, promising beginnings have been made. Much work remains; no measure or system of measures is even close to being well established psychometrically or conceptually. While reliabilities are adequate for all the scales reviewed, the links between theoretical definition and operational definition are often fuzzy, and the nomological network needed to confirm construct validity does not exist. Moreover, the area of dimensionality is not adequately addressed. Some scales assign a single number to assess developmental level, but anchor-point descriptions obviously are multidimensional; others have several items, but the number of underlying dimensions has not been verified.

In terms of diagnosis, it seems apparent that existing scales can be used to discriminate among psychotic, borderline, and neurotic or normal populations and that ratings made on these scales agree with clinician assessments of general mental health and interpersonal functioning.

Despite the necessity for further psychometric work, the EPITAT (Wilson, Passik, and Kuras 1989), the Scales for Assessing Object Relations (Westen et al. 1988), and the Scales for Developmental Level of Object Representations (Hartley, Geller, and Behrends 1986) are conceptually similar and show promise for use both for broad diagnostic or outcome studies and for smaller scale studies of psychotherapy process, since they can be applied to the kinds of narratives that occur in therapy. Although the Mutuality of Autonomy Scale (Urist and Schill 1982) assesses only one dimension, it has good psychometric properties and has been relatively widely used. The Quality of Object Relations Scale (Piper et al. 1990), although its initial complexity is reduced to simple ratings for data analysis purposes and although it requires a great deal of material for a rating, is also a promising measure.

With regard to psychotherapy, domains of investigation include the following: (1) how the ability to benefit from psychotherapy in general or from particular forms of therapy is linked to developmental level; (2) whether specific kinds of interventions are more appropriate than others for a patient functioning chronically or momentarily at a given developmental level; and (3) whether psychotherapy, conceived as a process for helping patients resume development, produces measurable changes in developmental level. Pretherapy developmental level has been found to be correlated with outcome in both inpatient and outpatient treatments. However, this is not a consistent finding, and more differentiated studies are needed to clarify discrepant conclusions. Changes in developmental levels have been positively correlated with other measures of change in assessing outcome of psychoanalytically oriented hospital treatment, psychoanalytic psychotherapy, and psychoanalysis. The number of studies assessing this dimension is so small, however, that the association cannot be assumed to be firmly established or understood without additional process studies. Similarly, when developmental level has been used to predict patients' ability to engage in the process of psychotherapy, positive correlations have emerged. On the other hand, the number of studies is extremely small, and the only process variable examined has been therapeutic alliance—and that with relatively gross estimates. Only the Horowitz group (1984) has addressed the question of using different kinds of interventions based on the patient's developmental level. While their findings do support this notion, again the variables were defined and operationalized at a rather global level, that is, supportive versus exploratory therapist actions.

The most clearly stated model linking development, psychopathology, and psychotherapy is that of Gedo (1979; Gedo and Goldberg 1973). Using this framework it would be possible to develop measures of developmental level and of therapy process and outcome that would address the diagnostic and treatment questions posed above in a combination of large-group and $N = 1$ studies. While most of the studies completed to date indicate that patients at higher developmental levels benefit most from therapy, we need to differentiate and integrate new ideas into research designs to discover how developmental level affects the possibilities and limitations of specific psychotherapeutic interventions.

References

ABRAHAM, K. (1924/1953). A short history of the development of the libido. *Selected papers*. New York: Basic Books.

BLANCK G., & BLANCK, R. (1979). *Ego psychology, Vol. 2. Psychoanalytic developmental psychology*. New York: Columbia University Press.

BLATT, S. J. (1974). Levels of object representation in anaclitic and introjective depression. *Psychoanalytic Study of the Child, 29,* 107–157.

BLATT, S. J. (1990). Interpersonal relatedness and self-definition: Two personality configurations and their implications for psychopathology and psychotherapy. In J. Singer (Ed.), *Repression and dissociation: Implications for personality theory, psychopathology and health*. Chicago: University of Chicago Press.

BLATT, S. J. (1992). Comparison of therapeutic outcome in psychoanalysis and psychotherapy: The Menninger Psychotherapy Project revisited. *Journal of the American Psychoanalytic Association, 40,* 691–724.

BLATT, S. J., BRENNEIS, C. B., SCHIMEK, J. G., & GLICK, M. (1976). Normal development and psychopathological impairment of the concept of the object on the Rorschach. *Journal of Abnormal Psychology, 85,* 364–373.

BLATT, S. J., FORD, R. Q., BERMAN, W., COOK, B., & MEYER, R. (1988). The assessment of change during the intensive treatment of borderline and schizophrenic young adults. *Psychoanalytic Psychology, 5,* 127–158.

BLATT, S. J., & LERNER, H. (1983). The psychological assessment of object representations. *Journal of Personality Assessment, 47,* 7–28.

BLATT, S. J., & SHICHMAN, S. (1983). Two primary configurations of neurotic psychopathology. *Psychoanalysis and Contemporary Thought, 6,* 187–254.

BLATT, S. J., WEIN, S. J., CHEVRON, E., & QUINLAN, D. (1979). Parental representations and depression in normal young adults. *Journal of Abnormal Psychology, 78,* 388–397.

DE CARUFEL, F. L. (1989, JUNE). *Object Relationship Scale*. Paper presented at the annual meeting of the Society for Psychotherapy Research, Toronto.

DE CARUFEL, F. L., & PIPER, W. E. (1988). Group psychotherapy or individual psychotherapy: Patient characteristics as predictive factors. *International Journal of Group Psychotherapy, 38,* 169–188.

DEWITT, K., HARTLEY D., ROSENBERG, S., ZILBERG, N., & WALLERSTEIN, R. (1991). Scales of psychological capacities: Development of an assessment approach. *Psychoanalysis and Contemporary Thought, 14,* 343–361.

EAGLE, M. (1984). *Recent developments in psychoanalysis*. New York: McGraw-Hill.

EMDE, R. (1988a). Development terminable and interminable: 1. Innate and motivational factors from infancy. *International Journal of Psychoanalysis, 69,* 23–42.

EMDE, R. (1988b). Development terminable and interminable: 2. Recent psychoanalytic theory and therapeutic considerations. *International Journal of Psychoanalysis, 69,* 283–296.

Erikson, E. H. (1950). *Childhood and society.* New York: Norton.

Fleming, J. (1975). Some observations on object constancy in the psychoanalysis of adults. *Journal of the American Psychoanalytic Association, 23,* 743–760.

Freud, A. (1936). *The ego and the mechanisms of defense.* New York: International Universities Press.

Freud, S. (1905/1953). Three essays on the theory of sexuality. In J. Strachey (Ed.), *The standard edition of the complete psychological works of Sigmund Freud* (Vol. 7, pp. 125–243). London: Hogarth Press.

Freud, S. (1914/1957). On narcissism. In J. Strachery (Ed.), *The standard edition of the complete psychological works of Sigmund Freud* (Vol. 14, pp. 67–102). London: Hogarth Press.

Frieswyk, S., & Colson, D. (1980). Prognostic considerations in the hospital treatment of borderline states: The perspective of object relations theory and the Rorschach. In J. Kwawer, H. Lerner, P. Lerner, & A. Sugarman (Eds.), *Borderline phenomena and the Rorschach test* (pp. 229–256). New York: International Universities Press.

Gedo, J. E. (1979). *Beyond interpretation.* New York: International Universities Press.

Gedo, J. E., & Goldberg, A. (1973). *Models of the mind.* Chicago: University of Chicago Press.

Geller, J. D., Behrends, R. S., & Hartley, D. (1982). Images of the psychotherapist: A theoretical and methodological perspective. *Imagination, Cognition and Personality, 1,* 123–146.

Goldberg, A. (Ed.). (1985). *Progress in self psychology* (Vol. 1). New York: Guilford Press.

Greenberg, J. R., & Mitchell, S. A. (1983). *Object relations in psychoanalytic theory.* Cambridge, MA: Harvard University Press.

Greenspan, S. I. (1981). *Psychopathology and adaptation in infancy and early childhood: Principles of clinical diagnosis and preventive intervention.* New York: International Universities Press.

Greenspan, S. I. (1989). *The development of the ego: Implications for personality theory, psychopathology, and the psychotherapeutic process.* Madison, CT: International Universities Press.

Greif, D. M. (1989, June). *Developmental level of object representations and psychotherapy outcome.* Paper presented at annual meeting of the Society for Psychotherapy Research, Toronto.

Grey, A., & Davies, M. (1981). Mental health as level of interpersonal maturity. *Journal of the American Academy of Psychoanalysis, 9,* 601–614.

Hartley, D. (1987, June). *Developmental level of object representations and psychotherapy outcome.* Paper presented at annual meeting of the Society for Psychotherapy Research, Ulm, Germany.

HARTLEY, D., GELLER, J., & BEHRENDS, R. S. (1986). *A manual for assessing the developmental level of object representations.* Unpublished manuscript, University of California, San Francisco.

HARTMANN, H. (1939). *Ego psychology and the problem of adaptation.* New York: International Universities Press.

HARTMANN, H., KRIS, E., & LOWENSTEIN, R. M. (1946). Comments of the formation of psychic structure. *Psychoanalytic Study of the Child, 2,* 11–38.

HATCHER, R., & KROHN, A. (1980). Level of object representation and capacity for intense psychotherapy in neurotics and borderlines. In J. Kwawer, H. Lerner, P. Lerner, & A. Sugarman (Eds.), *Borderline phenomena and the Rorschach test.* New York: International Universities Press.

HAUSER, S. T., JACOBSON, A., NOAM, G., & POWERS, S. (1983). Ego development and self-image complexity. *Archives of General Psychiatry, 4,* 325–332.

HOROWITZ, M. J. (1987). *States of mind* (2nd ed.). New York: Plenum Press.

HOROWITZ, M. J., MARMAR, C., WEISS, D. S., DeWITT, K. N., & ROSENBAUM, R. (1984). Brief psychotherapy of bereavement reactions: The relationship of process to outcome. *Archives of General Psychiatry, 41,* 438–448.

JACOBSON, A., BEARDSLEE, W., HAUSER, T., NOAM, G., POWERS, S., HOULIHAN, J., & RIDER, E. (1986). Evaluating ego defense mechanisms using clinical interviews: An empirical study of adolescent diabetic and psychiatric patients. *Journal of Adolescence, 9,* 303–319.

JACOBSON, E. (1964). *The self and the object world.* New York: International Universities Press.

KAVANAGH, G. (1985). Changes in patients' object representations during psychoanalysis and psychoanalytic psychotherapy. *Bulletin of the Menninger Clinic, 49,* 546–564.

KERNBERG, O. (1976). *Object relations theory and clinical psychoanalysis.* New York: Jason Aronson.

KERNBERG, O. (1980). *Internal world and external reality.* New York: Jason Aronson.

KERNBERG, O. (1984). *Severe personality disorders.* New Haven: Yale University Press.

KERNBERG, O., BERSTEIN, E., COYNE, L., APPLEBAUM, A., HOROWITZ, L., & VOTH, H. (1972). Psychotherapy and psychoanalysis: Final report of the Menninger Foundation's psychotherapy research project. *Bulletin of the Menninger Clinic, 36,* 1–278.

KLEIN, M. (1948). *Contributions to psycho-analysis.* London: Hogarth Press.

KOHUT, H. (1971). *The analysis of the self.* New York: International Universities Press.

KOHUT, H. (1977). *The restoration of the self.* New York: International Universities Press.

KOHUT, H. (1984). *How does analysis cure?* Chicago: University of Chicago Press.

KROHN, A., & MAYMAN, M. (1974). Object representations in dreams and projective tests. *Bulletin of the Menninger Clinic, 38*, 445–466.

LERNER, H. D., & ST. PETER, S. (1984). Patterns of object relations in neurotic, borderline, and schizophrenic patients. *Psychiatry, 47*, 77–92.

LICHTENBERG, J. D. (1983). *Psychoanalysis and infant research.* New York: Analytic Press.

LOEVINGER, J. (1976). *Ego development.* San Francisco: Jossey-Bass.

LOEVINGER, J., & WESSLER, R. (1970). *Measuring ego development: 1. Construction and use of a sentence completion test.* San Francisco: Jossey-Bass.

LOEVINGER, J., WESSLER, R., & REDMORE, C. (1970). *Measuring ego development: 2. Scoring manual for women and girls.* San Francisco: Jossey-Bass.

LUBORSKY, L. (1962). Clinicians' judgments of mental health: A proposed scale. *Archives of General Psychiatry, 7*, 407–417.

LUBORSKY, L., MINTZ, J., AUERBACH, A., CHRISTOPH, P., BACHRACH, H., TODD, T., JOHNSON, M., COHEN, M., & O'BRIEN, C. P. (1980). Predicting the outcome of psychotherapy: Findings of the Penn Psychotherapy Project. *Archives of General Psychiatry, 37*, 471–481.

MAHLER, M. S. (1974). Symbiosis and individuation. *Psychoanalytic Study of the Child, 29*, 89–106.

MAHLER, M., PINE, F., & BERGMAN, A. (1975). *The psychological birth of the human infant.* New York: Basic Books.

MARZIALI, E., & OLENIUK, J. (1990). Object representations in descriptions of significant others: A methodological study. *Journal of Personality Assessment, 54*, 105–115.

MAYMAN, M. (1968). Early memories and character structure. *Journal of Projective Techniques and Personality Assessment, 32*, 303–316.

MEISSNER, W. W. (1985). Theories of personality and psychopathology: Classical psychoanalysis. In H. I. Kaplan & B. J. Sadock (Eds.), *Comprehensive textbook of psychiatry.* Baltimore: Williams and Wilkins.

NOAM, G., HAUSER, S., SANTOSTEFANO, S., GARRISON, W., JACOBSON, A., POWERS, S., & MEAD, M. (1984). Ego development and psychopathology. *Child Development, 55*, 184–194.

OGDEN, T. (1982). *Projective identification and psychotherapeutic technique.* New York: Aronson.

OGDEN, T. (1986). *The Matrix of the mind: Object relations and the psychoanalytic dialogue.* New York: Aronson.

PIAGET, J. (1954). *The construction of reality in the child.* New York: Basic Books.

PINE, F. (1985). *Developmental theory and clinical process.* New Haven: Yale University Press.

PIPER, W. E. (1989, JUNE). *Instrumentation in the study of object relationships.* Paper presented at the annual meeting of the Society for Psychotherapy Research, Toronto.

PIPER, W. E., AZIM, H. F. A., MCCALLUM, M., & JOYCE, A. S. (1990). Patient suitability and outcome in short-term individual psychotherapy. *Journal of Consulting and Clinical Psychology, 58,* 475–481.

PIPER, W. E., DE CARUFEL, F. L., & SZKRUMELAK, N. (1985). Patient predictors of process and outcome in short-term individual psychotherapy. *Journal of Nervous and Mental Disease, 173,* 726–733.

RACKER, H. (1968). *Transference and countertransference.* New York: International Universities Press.

RITZLER, B., WYATT, D., HARDER, D., & KASKEY, M. (1980). Psychotic patterns of the concept of the object on the Rorschach. *Journal of Abnormal Psychology, 89,* 46–55.

RYAN, E. R., & BELL, M. D. (1984). Changes in object relations from psychosis to recovery. *Journal of Abnormal Psychology, 93,* 209–215.

RYAN, E. R., & CICCHETTI, D. V. (1985). Predicting the quality of alliance in the initial psychotherapy interview. *Journal of Nervous and Mental Disease, 12,* 717–725.

SEGAL, H. (1973). *Introduction to the work of Melanie Klein.* New York: Basic Books.

SETTLAGE, C. F. (1977). The psychoanalytic understanding of narcissistic and borderline personality disorders. *Journal of the American Psychoanalytic Association, 25,* 805–834.

SPEAR, W., & SUGARMAN, A. (1984). Dimensions of internalized object relations in borderline and schizophrenic patients. *Psychoanalytic Psychology, 1,* 113–129.

SPILLIUS, E. B. (ED.). (1988). *Melanie Klein today: Developments in theory and practice: Vol. 1. Mainly theory; Vol. 2. Mainly practice.* London and New York: Tavistock/Routledge.

SPILLIUS, E. B., & FELDMAN, M. (EDS.). (1989). *Psychic equilibrium and psychic change: Selected papers of Betty Joseph.* London and New York: Tavistock/Routledge.

SPITZ, R. (1945). Hospitalism: An inquiry into the genesis of psychiatric conditions in early childhood. *Psychoanalytic Study of the Child, 1,* 53–73.

SPITZ, R. (1965). *The first year of life.* New York: International Universities Press.

STERN, D. (1985). *The interpersonal world of the infant.* New York: Basic Books.

URIST, J. (1977). The Rorschach test and the assessment of object relations. *Journal of Personality Assessment, 41,* 3–9.

URIST, J., & SCHILL, M. (1982). Validity of the Rorschach Mutuality of Autonomy Scale: A replication using excerpted responses. *Journal of Personality Assessment, 46,* 450–454.

VINCENT, K. R., & CASTILLO, I. M. (1984). Ego development and DSM-III Axis II: Personality disorders. *Journal of Clinical Psychology, 40,* 400–402.

VINCENT, L., & VINCENT, K. (1979). Ego development and psychopathology. *Psychological Reports, 44,* 408–410.

WALLERSTEIN, R. (1986). *Forty-two lives in treatment.* New York: Guilford Press.

WERNER, H. (1948). *Comparative psychology of mental development.* New York: International Universities Press.

WESTEN, D. (1989). Are "primitive" object relations really preoedipal? *American Journal of Orthopsychiatry, 59,* 31–345.

WESTEN, D., BARENDS, A., LEIGH, J., MENDEL, M., & SILBERT, D. (1988). *Manual for coding dimensions of object relations and social cognition from interview data.* Unpublished manuscript, University of Michigan.

WESTEN, D., LUDOLPH, P., BLOCK, M. J., WIXOM, J., & WISS, C. (1990). Developmental history and object relations in psychiatrically disturbed adolescent girls. *American Journal of Psychiatry, 147,* 1061–1068.

WESTEN, D., LUDOLPH, P., LERNER, H., RUFFINS, S., & WISS, F. C. (1990). Object relations in borderline adolescents. *Journal of the Academy of Child and Adolescent Psychiatry, 29,* 338–348.

WILSON, A., PASSIK, S., & FAUDE, J. (1989). Failures of self-regulation. In J. Masling (Ed.), *Empirical studies in psychoanalytic theory* (Vol. 3). Hillsdale, NJ: Erlbaum.

WILSON, A., PASSIK, S., FAUDE, J., ABRAMS, J., & GORDON, E. (1989). A hierarchical model of opiate addiction: Failures of self-regulation as a central aspect of substance abuse. *Journal of Nervous and Mental Disease, 177,* 390–399.

WILSON, A., PASSIK, S., & KURAS, M. (1989). An epigenetic approach to the assessment of personality: The assessment of instability in stable personality organizations. In C. Spielberger & J. Butcher (Eds.), *Advances in personality assessment* (Vol. 8). Hillsdale, NJ: Erlbaum.

ZILBERG, N., WALLERSTEIN, R., DEWITT, K., HARTLEY, D., & ROSENBERG, S. (1991). A conceptual analysis and strategy for assessing structural change. *Psychoanalysis and Contemporary Thought, 14,* 317–342.

CHAPTER 10

Patient Pretreatment Predictors of Outcome

PAUL CRITS-CHRISTOPH AND MARY BETH CONNOLLY

T HIS CHAPTER PRESENTS A BRIEF REVIEW of the empirical evidence on patient pretreatment predictors of the outcome of psychodynamic psychotherapy.[1] What do we hope to accomplish with such a review? First, we hope to shed light on important considerations for designing future studies of psychodynamic psychotherapy. How should patients be screened and selected for research protocols? In terms of outcome studies, should treatment groups be matched on certain factors that might influence outcome? For predictive studies, should certain variables be controlled for, in assessing the predictive strength of some new variable? With these questions in mind, a review of predictive factors could help the field in the design of new studies.

Second, we need to clarify crucial clinical considerations regarding suitability for dynamic or psychoanalytic psychotherapy: Do research findings conform to the clinical lore, for example, that healthier, psychologically minded people do best in dynamic therapy? Are the predictions strong enough to be translated into clinical decisions regarding which particular treatment should be recommended to a given patient?

[1]This review relies heavily on the recent book by Luborsky et al. (1988) which presents factors that influence the outcome of psychotherapy; that work encompassed a broad range of orientations, not just dynamic psychotherapy. Additional studies have been included here in order to concentrate on the issues and variables most relevant to the practice of dynamic psychotherapy.

Clinical Literature on Patient Outcome Predictors

The clinical literature on the patient factors that relate to success in formal psychoanalysis has been reviewed by Bachrach and Leaff (1978) and Bachrach et al. (1991). Their review was based upon twenty-four papers in the analytic literature, yielding 390 separate references to specific prognostic factors. Of these, 90 percent were based upon clinical formulations of important predictors of outcome; the remaining 10 percent were based upon quantitative studies. The authors conclude:

> Taken together these studies suggest that persons most suitable for classical psychoanalysis are those whose functioning is generally adequate; they have good ego strength, effective reality testing and subliminatory channels, and are able to cope flexibly, communicate verbally, think in secondary-process terms, and regress in the service of the ego with sufficient intellect to negotiate the tasks of psychoanalysis; their symptoms are not predominantly severe, and their diagnoses fall within a "neurotic" spectrum. Such persons are able to form a transference neurosis and therapeutic alliance, are relatively free of narcissistic pathology, have good object relations with friends, parents, and spouses, and have been able to tolerate early separations and deprivations without impairment of object constancy; they are therefore able to experience genuine triangular conflict. They are motivated for self-understanding, change, and to relieve personal suffering. They are persons with good tolerance for anxiety, depression, frustration, and suffering and are able to experience surges of feeling without loss of impulse control or disruption of secondary-process mooring of thought. Their character attitudes and traits are well-suited to the psychoanalytic work, i.e., psychological mindedness. Superego is integrated and tolerant. They are mainly in their late twenties or early thirties and have not experienced past psychotherapeutic failure or difficulties. Of all these qualities, those relating to ego strength and object relations are most important. (Bachrach and Leaff 1978, 885–86)

In the literature on brief psychodynamic therapy, based upon the clinical experience of the authors, patient characteristics have been enumerated as positive or negative indicators for such treatment. Sifneos (1987), for example, lists the following criteria for suitability for brief dynamic therapy: (1) intelligence; (2) psychological mindedness; (3) a history of meaningful relationships; (4) appropriate affect during the initial interview; (5) capacity to formulate one major and specific complaint; (6) motivation for change beyond symptom relief; (7) no diagnosis of psychosis, major affective disorders, or substance abuse; and (8) absence of suicidal tendencies, acting out, or severe character pathology. Other brief dynamic therapists (see review by Barber and Crits-Christoph [1991]) list similar criteria, particularly the exclusion criteria of psychosis, severe personality disorders, and acting out tendencies. Thus, in many ways the patient characteristics deemed prognostic for brief dynamic therapy are similar to those designated as important for psychoanalysis.

Research Literature on Patient Variables that Predict Outcome

NATURE OF THE DATA BASE

The data base for this review consists of published studies which attempted to predict the outcome of psychodynamic psychotherapy. Only studies in which the treatment administered was clearly described as some form of psychodynamic therapy were included. This criterion excluded many of the predictive studies in the general psychotherapy literature reviewed by Luborsky et al. (1988). Even restricting the studies reviewed to those that label the treatment as psychodynamic in no way guarantees that the treatment delivered was purely dynamic or of high quality. Most of the studies reviewed here were performed prior to the advent of treatment manuals and scales to assess adherence to recommended procedures. Thus, the additional variation in outcome introduced through variations in quality of treatment delivered, or through other variables such as amount or length of treatment, nature of the patient population, and type of outcome measure used, limit what can be learned through our review. Nonetheless, it remains of interest to assess whether any consistent trends have emerged from these empirical studies.

This review is structured according to broad categories of predictors, such as measures of psychological health-sickness and anxiety, so that trends can be summarized across studies. In some cases, however, the categories include measures that may not be highly correlated. Therefore, the findings from different studies may have different meanings. In addition, the number of studies available within each category typically is small. For these reasons, we chose not to conduct a formal meta-analysis, in which correlations are averaged across studies. Since the majority of studies reviewed here predate most of the major methodological advances in the field of psychotherapy research (including treatment manuals, structured diagnostic interview methods, and the like), findings from individual studies are not discussed in detail. Rather, the aim is to see, within this limited data base, whether general trends emerge across studies that are consistent with the clinical literature on patient factors said to predict outcome.

Seven studies were reviewed for their use of psychological health-sickness as a predictor of the outcome of psychodynamic psychotherapy. The results of this review are grouped into four categories: global measures of health-sickness, Barron Ego Strength Scale, Klopfer Rorschach Prognostic Rating Scale, and chronicity of illness.

Global Measures of Psychological Health-Sickness and Severity of Maladjustment.

Two studies found a significant positive correlation between health-sickness and outcome using the Health-Sickness Rating Scale, or HSRS (Luborsky 1975). These studies were Luborsky (1962) ($r = .54$, with improvement ratings, $p < .01$, $n = 24$), and Luborsky et al. (1980) ($r = .30$ with residual gain, $p < .01$; $r = .25$ with improvement ratings, $p < .05$, $n = 73$). Another study of psychological health-sickness was done by Free et al. (1985); they studied fifty-nine patients treated with twelve weeks of brief focal psychodynamic therapy. In this study, patients who had shown the highest level of adaptive functioning before therapy showed more improvement on the HSRS ($r = -.30$, $p < .05$), the Quality of Interpersonal Relationships Subscale ($r = -.36$, $p < .05$), and target symptoms ($r = .32$, $p < .05$). A final study by Horowitz et al. (1984) investigated fifty-two bereaved patients treated with twelve sessions of time-limited dynamic psychotherapy. In this study, developmental level of self-concept was measured using the Self-Concept Rating Scale rated by independent clinical judges. Outcome was assessed with the Patterns of Individual Change Scales (PICS), which is a clinician-rated instrument assessing symptoms, social functioning, and self-regard, and with a symptom checklist (the SCL-90). Initial scores on the Self-Concept Rating Scale significantly predicted the work and interpersonal functioning scales on the PICS at termination ($r = .38$, $p < .05$) but not the SCL-90 termination scores.

Barron Ego Strength Scale.

In the context of the Menninger Psychotherapy Project, Kernberg et al. (1972) found a significant relationship between ego strength and the outcome of psychoanalytic psychotherapy ($r = .35$, $p < .05$, $n = 42$). In two other studies, Luborsky et al. (1980) and Endicott and Endicott (1964), the Barron's Ego Strength Scale was not significantly related to outcome.

Rorschach: Klopfer Rorschach Prognostic Rating Scale (RPRS).

Endicott and Endicott (1964), in their investigation of twenty-one patients, found that improved patients (outcome was assessed through a clinical rating made by the therapist) had a significantly higher RPRS than did unimproved patients (point-biserial $r = .43$, $p < .05$). Luborsky et al. (1980) did not find a significant correlation between RPRS and outcome.

Chronicity of Illness.

Karush et al. (1968) found that greater chronicity of illness was not significantly related to treatment outcome.

DIAGNOSIS

Karush et al. (1968) found that both psychotic and nonpsychotic subjects improved on judges' ratings of behavior changes made from case records (79 percent and 75 percent of patients, respectively). Structural change occurred in 50 percent of nonpsychotic patients but in only 29 percent of psychotic patients. The method for assessing structural change in this study appears to have been based upon clinical judgments culled from discussion with the therapists. Details of the methodology are not provided.

ANXIETY

Kernberg et al. (1972) found a significant relationship between initial anxiety, as rated by judges from a summary of an extensive clinical intake interview, and psychotherapy outcome, as measured by clinical judges' ratings of all clinical data at termination, using a paired comparisons procedure ($r = .50$, $p < .001$, $n = 42$). Luborsky et al. (1980) also investigated the predictive value of initial anxiety using the Prognostic Index interview (Auerbach and Luborsky 1968) but did not find a significant relationship to outcome, as assessed through residual gain scores on a composite (patient and independent clinician) measure of general adjustment, and through a composite measure of ratings of improvement by patient and therapist.

MOTIVATION

Keithly, Samples, and Strupp (1980) found a positive correlation between patient motivation, as rated by judges from a taped intake interview, and outcome. Motivation consisted of three separate scales: (1) ratings of the patient's ability to become emotionally involved in treatment, (2) ratings of the patient's degree of autonomy in seeking therapy and a positive expectation that he or she would be helped by treatment, and (3) ratings of the patient's willingness to acknowledge distress and actively talk about it in therapy. Multiple regression analyses relating all three motivation measures to therapists' ratings of global change ($R = .65$) and patients' ratings of global change ($R = .66$) were statistically significant.

Using the thirty-eight-item Motivation for Psychotherapy Scale rated by three judges from a pretherapy evaluation interview, Horowitz et al. (1984), however, did not find a significant relationship between motivation and outcome as measured by reported symptoms and by work and interpersonal function.

INTEREST IN, AND CAPACITY FOR, HUMAN RELATIONS

Piper, de Carufel, and Szkrumelak (1985) reported a significant positive correlation between the quality of relationships with the important objects of the patient's life (as rated by the therapist from a pretreatment interview) and two outcome measures, a self-rating of target change ($r = .53$, $p < .05$, $n = 21$) and a self-report of overall usefulness of therapy ($r = .72$, $p < .001$, $n = 21$). Quality of patients' object choice was also significantly related to two outcome measures, including initial self-rated target severity and therapist's rating of overall usefulness of treatment.

Moras and Strupp (1982) found that independent clinician ratings of patient adequacy of interpersonal relations were significantly predictive of improvement on the MMPI depression subscale ($r = -.42$, $p < .01$) over the course of time-limited dynamic therapy.

INTELLIGENCE

Luborsky et al. (1980) did not find a significant relationship between the Wechsler Adult Intelligence Scale and psychotherapy outcome (residual gain and rated benefits measures).

PERSONALITY TRAITS AND COPING STYLES

Buckley et al. (1984) studied the use of ego defenses in twenty-one patients. Therapists' ratings of undoing, rationalization, and isolation were significantly related to better outcome ($r = .57$, $p < .01$; $r = .55$, $p < .01$; $r = .43$, $p < .05$, respectively). Patients' ratings of reaction formation, projection, and blame were also significantly positively correlated with outcome ($r = .59$, $p < .01$; $r = .46$, $p < .05$; $r = .44$, $p < .05$, respectively). Piper, de Carufel, and Szkrumelak (1985), on the other hand, found that a more mature defensive style was significantly related to better outcome ($r = .47$ for target change ratings made by the patient and $r = .50$ for target change ratings made by therapist, $p < .05$, $n = 27$) in psychodynamic therapy of six months' duration. Defensive style was assessed in this study through ratings by the therapist made from a semi-structured interview.

Beutler and Mitchell (1981) reported that internalizing depressive patients obtained more benefit from psychoanalytic psychotherapy than impulsive externalizing patients ($p < .05$). The distinction between depressed-internalizing and impulsive-externalizing patients was made from a modification of Welsh's internalization ratio from the MMPI, obtained at intake on all patients. Outcome assessment consisted of ratings of target complaints obtained pre- and posttreatment.

MISCELLANEOUS TEST FINDINGS

MMPI Scales.

Endicott and Endicott (1964) found that two validity scales of the MMPI, the F scale and the K scale, were significantly correlated with psychotherapy improvement as measured by a therapist rating of clinical improvement ($r_{pb} = -.34$ and $r_{pb} = .39$, $p < .05$, $n = 21$).

Free-Drawing Test.

Fiedler and Siegel (1949) found a significant negative correlation between primitivity of drawing on the Free-Drawing Test and psychotherapy outcome as assessed via a clinical rating made from therapists' progress notes. The results of this study indicate that certain patients who will not benefit from psychotherapy may be differentiated by their drawings of a human head.

Rorschach.

A study by Siegel (1951) revealed a significant positive relationship between Rorschach scores and psychotherapy outcome. In this study Rorschach results were analyzed on three levels: (1) specific personality traits, corresponding to separate scoring categories, (2) larger trait syndromes, judged from the entire protocol, and (3) blind predictions of improvement and nonimprovement. In another study, Endicott and Endicott (1964) found that several Rorschach variables correlated with improvement in the psychotherapy group. Significant point-biserial correlations included improvement with mean number of responses, shading, and color (r_{pb} = .41, r_{pb} = .40, r_{pb} = .40, respectively, p < .05, n = 21).

PATIENT BACKGROUND AND DEMOGRAPHICS

Several demographic variables demonstrated no clear trend as outcome predictors, including sex (Jones and Zoppel 1982), religion (Rosenbaum, Friedlander, and Kaplan 1956), and previous psychotherapy (Klein 1960). Rosenbaum, Friedlander, and Kaplan (1956) found that higher socioeconomic status was related to better outcome while religious activity was negatively related to better outcome. Outcome was assessed in this study with therapists' clinical ratings of improvement. The study also investigated a number of other variables (such as quality of interpersonal relations) in relation to outcome, but since the measures were not obtained pretreatment, the results are not reviewed here.

THE MATCH BETWEEN PATIENT AND THERAPIST

A study by Jones (1982) revealed no significant relationship between patient-therapist racial match and outcome as rated by the therapist. Luborsky et al. (1980) found that patient-therapist similarities on a sum of ten demographic variables were significantly related to better outcome (residual gain r = .23, rated benefits r = .24, p < .05). This study also revealed that match on marital status alone was predictive of outcome (r = .23, p < .05, and r = .24, p < .05, for residual gain and rated benefits, respectively).

THE PENN PSYCHOTHERAPY PROJECT

The Penn Psychotherapy Project (Luborsky et al. 1980; Luborsky et al. 1988) offers an extensive study of pretreatment predictors of outcome for dynamic psychotherapy. Some of the findings from this study have been described in this chapter.

Additional findings included that three variables from the Prognostic Index (PI) interview correlated with rated benefits: emotional freedom (r = .30, p < .01), overcontrol (r = −.24, p < .05), and duration of illness (r = .23, p < .05). PI factors that did not significantly correlate with outcome included attractiveness for psychotherapy, manifest anxiety, anxiety tolerance, interests, secondary gain, and extrapsychic factors.

A large number of other predictors did not significantly correlate with outcome. These included measures of pretreatment adjustment status (including Minnesota Multiphasic Personality Inventory, Symptom Checklist, target complaints), patient psychological tests (tests of intelligence, field dependence-independence, life change), and demographic information (sex, age, race, marital status).

Conclusions and Recommendations

The most striking finding from this review of patient predictors of outcome of psychodynamic therapy is that so few studies were located. This is in contrast to the large number (181 patient or patient–therapist match findings) of predictive studies reviewed by Luborsky et al. (1988). Most of the predictive studies excluded from this review were studies of other forms of psychotherapy (such as client-centered) or unspecified psychotherapy. Other predictive studies were dropped because outcome measures were contaminated by initial levels (as when raw change scores were used). It is clear that significantly more research is needed on which patient pretreatment factors influence the outcome of psychodynamic therapy.

Several trends emerged for different categories of predictive measures. The most consistent findings were for measures of psychological health-sickness, interest, and capacity for human relations. As expected, based upon clinical wisdom, "healthier" patients did manifest better outcomes in dynamic therapy. Another finding of interest was that IQ was not predictive of outcome on these studies (although it was for the studies reviewed by Luborsky et al. [1988]).

Other categories of predictive variables, including ego strength, initial anxiety, motivation, demographic information, and the Rorschach Prognostic Rating Scale, yielded inconsistent results. In most cases, however, there were not enough studies performed to detect a consistent trend. Other promising directions for further research are the predictive success of "emotional freedom" and patient-therapist demographic similarity (Luborsky et al. 1980).

Although statistically significant predictions were reported for some studies, the size of the relationships with outcome was modest at best (the correlations ranged from .2 to .5). This level of prediction, however, does have implications for the design of future studies. For example, the consistency and size of findings for measures of severity of illness (such as psychological health-sickness) strongly suggest that this variable should be seriously taken into account in treatment outcome studies (by covariance analysis or matching) and in predictive studies.

A clinician whose role is to recommend a mode of treatment to patients may want to consider the results of these predictive studies—for example, if a patient scores high on psychological health-sickness, recommend psychodynamic therapy; if the patient scores low, recommend a different intervention, such as medication. The level of prediction outcome achieved by the studies reviewed here, however, is not yet high enough to apply to the individual case in clinical practice.

To date, then, there appears to be little support for many of the predictive factors specified by clinical writers. A notable exception is the health-sickness dimension, which has been widely referred to in the clinical literatures of both psychoanalysis and the briefer psychodynamic therapies, and which has also achieved consistent and impressive support in the research literature.

The health-sickness dimension actually consists of a variety of correlated components, including variables such as ego strength, chronicity of illness, developmental level of self-concept, and general level of functioning, all of which have been specifically mentioned by clinical writers. Thus, the research findings for psychological health-sickness, when broken down to a finer level of analysis, can be seen as supporting a number of specific factors mentioned in the clinical literature.

What is clear at this point, based on findings both from research and from clinical experience, is that no one factor is likely to explain an appreciable amount of the variance in outcome. Almost all studies reviewed presented only zero-order correlations of single predictors with outcome. Not only does this approach fail to illuminate the role of third variables and overlap among predictors, but it also fails to take into account the potential impact of a set of variables (like those explored in multiple regression analysis). Future studies designed with the goal of making clinical recommendations should be oriented toward the *cumulative* predictive power of a set of patient factors, rather than the predictive strength of individual factors. Once some useful patient predictors are found, these variables could be combined into an overall composite score assessing suitability for dynamic psychotherapy. The work of Butler, Thackrey, and Strupp (1987) on a suitability scale is a step in this direction. Greater attention also needs to be paid to the *interaction* of predictive variables. An example suggested by Luborsky (1962)—and in Luborsky et al. (1988, 305)—is ratings of high affect (such as depression or anxiety) in combination with high general psychological health.

Finally, there may be inherent limits to the predictive power of patient pretreatment factors: more powerful influences on outcome may emerge from closer study of discrete aspects of the psychodynamic process of treatment (see part 4). A more complete understanding of outcome would therefore result from investigating the interaction and combination of pretreatment characteristics and process variables. For example, certain interventions may lead to a more favorable outcome for patients with higher levels of psychological functioning but not for those with lower levels (see Horowitz et al. 1984; Azim et al. 1988). Such studies might not only succeed in explaining more of the variance in outcome but also do greater justice to the complexity of clinical wisdom about change in psychodynamic therapy.

References

AUERBACH, A., & LUBORSKY, L. (1968). *The Prognostic Index Interview manual.* Unpublished manuscript.

AZIM, H., PIPER, W., MCCALLUM, M., & JOYCE, A. (1988, JUNE). *Antecedents and consequences of transference interpretations in short-term psychotherapy.* Paper presented at the annual meeting of the Society for Psychotherapy Research, Santa Fe, NM.

BACHRACH, H., GALATZER-LEVY, R., SKOLNIKOFF, A., & WALDRON, S. (1991). On the efficacy of psychoanalysis. *Journal of the American Psychoanalytic Association, 39,* 871–916.

BACHRACH, H., & LEAFF, L. (1978). "Analyzability": A systematic review of the clinical and quantitative literature. *Journal of the American Psychoanalytic Association, 26,* 881–920.

BARBER, J., & CRITS-CHRISTOPH, P. (1991). Comparison of the brief dynamic therapies. In P. Crits-Christoph & J. Barber (Eds.), *Handbook of short-term dynamic therapy.* New York: Basic Books.

BEUTLER, L. E., & MITCHELL, R. (1981). Differential psychotherapy outcome among depressed and impulsive patients as a function of analytic and experiential treatment procedures. *Psychiatry, 44,* 297–306.

BUCKLEY, P., CONTE, H. R., PLUTCHIK, R., WILD, K. V., & KARASU, T. B. (1984). Psychodynamic variables as predictors of psychotherapy outcome. *American Journal of Psychiatry, 14*(6), 742–748.

BUTLER, S. F., THACKREY, M., & STRUPP, H. H. (1987, JUNE). *Capacity for Dynamic Process Scale (CDPS): Relation to patient variables, process, and outcome.* Paper presented at the annual meeting of the Society for Psychotherapy Research Meeting, Ulm, Germany.

ENDICOTT, N. A., & ENDICOTT, J. (1964). Prediction of improvement in treated and untreated patients using the Rorschach Prognostic Rating Scale. *Journal of Consulting Psychology, 28,* 342–348.

FIEDLER, F. E., & SIEGEL, S. M. (1949). The free-drawing test as a predictor of nonimprovement in psychotherapy. *Journal of Clinical Psychology, 5,* 386–389.

FREE, N. K., GREEN, B. L., GRACE, M. C., CHERNUS, L. A., & WHITMAN, R. M. (1985). Empathy and outcome in brief focal dynamic therapy. *American Journal of Psychiatry, 142,* 917–921.

HOROWITZ, M. J., MARMAR, C., WEISS, D. S., DEWITT, K. N., & ROSENBAUM, R. (1984). Brief psychotherapy of bereavement reactions. *Archives of General Psychiatry, 41,* 438–448.

JONES, E. (1982). Psychotherapists' impressions of treatment outcome as a function of race. *Journal of Clinical Psychology, 38,* 722–731.

JONES, E., & ZOPPEL, C. (1982). Impact of client and therapist gender on psychotherapy process and outcome. *Journal of Consulting and Clinical Psychology*, *50*, 259–272.

KARUSH, A., DANIELS, G., O'CONNOR, J., & STERN, L. (1968). The response to psychotherapy in chronic ulcerative colitis: 1. Pretreatment factors. *Psychosomatic Medicine*, *30*(3), 255–276.

KEITHLY, L. J., SAMPLES, S. J., & STRUPP, H. H. (1980). Patient motivation as a predictor of process and outcome in psychotherapy. *Psychotherapy and Psychosomatics*, *33*, 87–97.

KERNBERG, O., BURSTEIN, E., COYNE, L., APPLEBAUM, A., HOROWITZ, L., & VOTH, H. (1972). Psychotherapy and psychoanalysis: Final report of the Menninger Foundation's psychotherapy research project. *Bulletin of the Menninger Clinic*, *36*, 1–275.

KLEIN, H. A. (1960). A study of changes occurring in patients during and after psychoanalytic treatment. In P. Hoch & J. Zubin (Eds.), *Current approaches to psychoanalysis*. New York: Grune & Stratton.

LUBORSKY, L. (1962). The patient's personality and psychotherapeutic change. In H. H. Strupp & L. Luborsky (Eds.), *Research in psychotherapy* (Vol. 2). Washington, DC: American Psychological Association.

LUBORSKY, L. (1975). Clinicians' judgments of mental health: Specimen case descriptions and forms for the Health-Sickness Rating Scale. *Bulletin of the Menninger Clinic*, *35*, 448–480.

LUBORSKY, L., CRITS-CHRISTOPH, P., MINTZ, J., & AUERBACH, A. (1988). *Who will benefit from psychotherapy?* New York: Basic Books.

LUBORSKY, L., MINTZ, J., AUERBACH, A., CRITS-CHRISTOPH, P., BACHRACH, H., TODD, T., JOHNSON, M., COHEN, M., & O'BRIEN, C. P. (1980). Predicting the outcome of psychotherapy: Findings of the Penn Psychotherapy Project. *Archives of General Psychiatry*, *37*, 471–481.

MORAS, K., & STRUPP, H. (1982). Pretherapy interpersonal relations, patient's alliance, and outcome in brief therapy. *Archives of General Psychiatry*, *39*, 405–409.

PIPER, W. E., DE CARUFEL, F. L., & SZKRUMELAK, N. (1985). Patient predictors of process and outcome in short-term individual psychotherapy. *Journal of Nervous and Mental Disease*, *173*, 726–733.

ROSENBAUM, M., FREIDLANDER, J., & KAPLAN, S. (1956). Evaluation of results of psychotherapy. *Psychosomatic Medicine*, *18*, 113–132.

SIEGEL, S. M. (1951). Personality factors in psychotherapeutic improvement as identified by the Rorschach test. *American Psychologist*, *6*, 341–342 (Abstract).

SIFNEOS, P. E. (1987). *Short-term dynamic psychotherapy: Evaluation and technique* (2nd ed.). New York: Plenum Press.

PART III

DEFINING THE TREATMENT

CHAPTER 11

Effects of Training Experienced Dynamic Therapists to Use a Psychotherapy Manual

STEPHEN F. BUTLER AND HANS H. STRUPP

THE CREDO OF ALL SCIENTIFIC ENDEAVORS is specificity. If phenomena and processes are to be scientifically investigated and understood, then scientists must define, and if possible quantify, the object of their study. Relatively early in the scientific investigation of psychotherapy, it became apparent that global descriptions of psychotherapeutic techniques would not suffice. Thus, the insistence on more specific descriptions of treatment modalities reflected a general recognition of the need for disciplined scientific study of psychotherapy (Strupp and Bergin 1969; Bergin and Strupp 1972). In addition to these research concerns, insurance companies, and governmental agencies have demanded specification of treatments they pay for and desired a way to determine the qualifications of practitioners. To answer the call for greater specificity, psychotherapy researchers have developed treatment "manuals."

The questions remain whether therapists can be trained to implement and adhere to the principles and strategies outlined in these manuals, and which training procedures are most effective. In this chapter, we briefly review the best known, most commonly used of the treatment research manuals that codify therapeutic practices from a psychodynamic/interpersonal perspective and examine the results of training therapists to adhere to the manualized treatment.

Manualized Psychodynamic and Interpersonal Therapies

The three best known psychodynamic/interpersonal therapies that have manuals—interpersonal therapy, or IPT (Klerman et al. 1984), supportive-expressive therapy, or SE (Luborsky 1984), and time-limited dynamic psychotherapy, or TLDP (Strupp and Binder 1984)—conceptually differ from each other substantially. The most recent addition by Kernberg and his colleagues, a manual with a disorder-specific focus, will be discussed in chapter 13.

INTERPERSONAL THERAPY

Interpersonal therapy is a brief (twelve- to sixteen-week) individual psychotherapy developed for the treatment of ambulatory, nonpsychotic, nonbipolar depression. Although IPT emphasizes interpersonal and social factors in the understanding and treatment of depression, it also endorses a "medical" emphasis on the signs and symptoms of clinical depression.[1]

IPT aims to facilitate recovery by helping the patient deal more effectively with current interpersonal problems associated with the onset of depressive symptoms. The therapy is divided into stages. The initial sessions (up to four) are devoted to "dealing with the depression and diagnosing the interpersonal problems." This stage includes a careful evaluation of the patient's symptomatology; symptoms are given a name, that is, the syndrome depression. Naming the patient's dysphoric experience and teaching him or her about its symptoms, predicted course, and outcome, is expected to reduce the mystique of the experience. Rather than dealing with some unfathomable malady, patients learn that this is a "common disorder," that most people recover promptly with treatment, and that he or she is sick and entitled to the "sick role." The therapist then completes an "interpersonal inventory," which establishes the precise nature of the interpersonal problems that have precipitated the onset of the depressive episode. The IPT manual specifies rationales for classifying these interpersonal problems into one of four categories: grief, interpersonal disputes, role transitions, and interpersonal deficits.

In the intermediate stage (sessions 5 to 8), the therapist focuses on one or two of the categorized problem areas. In this stage, the therapist's

[1]IPT was included in the NIMH Treatment of Depression Collaborative Research Program (Elkin et al. 1985) as the manualized interpersonal therapy to be contrasted in a clinical trials design with cognitive therapy and clinical management with Imipramine/placebo. Results indicated no significant differences post termination.

first job is to facilitate discussion of topics pertinent to the identified problem area(s). The therapist then attends to the patient's affective state and to the therapeutic relationship in order to maximize the patient's intimate self-disclosure and to prevent the patient from sabotaging the treatment. The termination stage (sessions 9 to 12) consists of explicit discussion about termination, acknowledgment of grief, and support of the patient's sense of independent competence. The manual also provides guidelines for exploratory techniques, encouragement of affect, clarification, analysis of communications, use of the therapeutic relationship, and various "behavior change techniques."

In the research literature, IPT is usually included in discussions of manualized dynamic psychotherapies because the manual borrows a great deal from traditional psychoanalytic technique. However, the IPT approach is decidedly antianalytic in that it expressly forbids the therapist to make transference interpretations, a key analytic technique. IPT emphasizes interpersonal relationships, but its focus is on relationships outside the therapeutic one. The patient is "instructed, at the onset of the treatment, to express to the therapist complaints, apprehensions, and/or other averse feelings" (Klerman et al. 1984, 149). Unrealistically positive feelings toward the therapist are not systematically examined. Discussion of negative feelings toward the therapist is used as commentary to the patient on his or her interpersonal problems and is taken into account only for the purpose of avoiding serious disruption in the patient—therapist relationship. Primarily, however, therapists are advised to maintain a focus on relationships external to the therapeutic dyad. IPT recognizes, but does not address, personality or characterological problems which may form part of the person's predisposition to depressive symptomatology.

SUPPORTIVE-EXPRESSIVE THERAPY

Luborsky's (1984) supportive-expressive (SE) therapy traces its conceptual lineage to the Menninger model (see Menninger and Holzman 1973), which distinguishes between "supportive" and interpretive or "expressive" techniques. The supportive aspects of therapy represent the therapist's efforts to enhance the patient's positive experience of both the therapy and the therapeutic relationship, as opposed to providing understanding.[2] The manual makes explicit recommendations for facilitating supportive conditions under various circumstances.

Expressive techniques constitute interpretive psychoanalytic inter-

[2]Luborsky draws a parallel with the supportive aspects of therapy and what has commonly been referred to as "nonspecific curative factors" in psychotherapy (see Butler and Strupp 1986, for a critical review of the specific/nonspecific dichotomy).

ventions intended to promote the patient's understanding of his or her symptoms, anxieties, and internal conflicts. As insights are repeatedly worked through in the course of the treatment and made increasingly accessible to awareness, the patient eventually achieves an enhanced capacity to recognize, anticipate, and control his or her conflictual feelings and behavior. As in classical analysis, the central method for achieving understanding of unconscious motivation is analysis of the transference, wherein the patient reexperiences central, early intrapsychic conflicts manifested in relationship problems, in the here-and-now, with the therapist. Expressive techniques, presented as a series of principles and illustrated by case examples, are listed in the manual under the headings of Listening, Understanding, and Responding and Listening Again.

In addition, procedures for formulating the Core Conflictual Relationship Theme (CCRT) are outlined. This method provides principles for identifying two complimentary aspects of conflict: (1) the patient's conscious, preconscious, and unconscious wishes, needs, and intentions in regard to significant others, including the therapist, and (2) the patient's expectations of consequences of trying to get one's wish from that person. The CCRT is a valid and reliable method for understanding and organizing the patient's most essential intrapsychic conflicts within himself or herself and in relationships with other human beings, and it serves as a guide for the therapist's interpretative responses to the patient.

The relative use of supportive or expressive techniques is dependent on an assessment of the patient's ability to profit from expressive techniques. Patients likely to require "extra special provision of supportive conditions" (Luborsky 1984, 73) include those with character disorders, those with alloplastic symptoms (low anxiety tolerance, difficulties being reflective), those for whom it is important to prevent regression, and those who require the strengthening of defenses (versus analysis of defense, which may provoke undue anxiety, thereby weakening defenses).

Expressive techniques require a degree of psychological mindedness on the part of the patient, a capacity to achieve understanding of his or her core conflicts, and the commitment to persist in working through these relationship problems both with the therapist in the here-and-now and in regard to past relationships. A trial therapy period is recommended to help the therapist plan the relative proportions of supportive and expressive techniques.

By encouraging the therapist to draw "on appropriate proportions of supportiveness versus expressiveness" (Luborsky 1984, 56), SE treatment is flexible enough to deal with a wide range of problems, from mild situational maladjustments to borderline psychotic conditions. In general, the greater the psychiatric severity, the more supportive and less expressive the therapy.

TIME-LIMITED DYNAMIC PSYCHOTHERAPY

Time-limited dynamic psychotherapy was developed by Strupp and Binder (1984) as an approach to individual psychotherapy that emphasizes the analysis of the patient—therapist relationship (transference) as the central task for the psychotherapist.[3] The basic principles of this approach reflect empirical findings (Strupp 1980a, 1980b, 1980c, 1980d) which suggest that the major deterrents to the formation of a good working alliance are the patient's characterological distortions and maladaptive defenses, and—equally important—the therapist's personal reactions to such patterns. TLDP specifies principles and strategies for assessing and managing potential problems in the therapeutic relationship. The interpersonal problems that emerge with the therapist are assumed to be similar in form to the chronic, maladaptive interpersonal patterns that underlie the patient's difficulties in living, expressed as symptoms such as anxiety and depression.

The therapist's task consists of identifying the problematic interpersonal patterns as these evolve in the therapeutic relationship, and repeatedly helping the patient to understand, rather than act out, these conflictual interpersonal scenarios. Therapeutic change is hypothesized to occur as a result of the patient's developing awareness of self-defeating patterns, as well as his or her subjective experience of a different outcome within the therapeutic relationship.

To achieve this goal, the therapist uses the role of participant observer, participating, to a limited extent, in the patient's conflictual patterns and then interpreting, rather than enacting, the unrealistic scenario. The TLDP manual discusses various technical considerations for examining the therapeutic relationship, understanding the role of countertransference, making interpretive links to current and past relationships, understanding interpersonal meaning, and identifying and dealing with resistances.

Like SE, TLDP outlines a procedure for systematically organizing a dynamic focus or Cyclic Maladaptive Pattern (CMP; Schacht, Binder, and Strupp 1984; Butler and Binder 1987), which is used to help focus a time-limited therapy. The CMP constitutes a working model of the central pattern of interpersonal roles in which patients unconsciously cast themselves and others, and the resulting maladaptive interaction sequences, self-defeating expectations, and negative self-appraisals.

The CMP procedure organizes maladaptive patterns into a four-step cycle:

---

[3]TLDP is rooted in psychoanalytic conceptions and reformulations by interpersonal theorists (for example, Sullivan, 1953; Anchin and Kiesler 1982).

1. *Acts of Self:* actions of the self toward others
2. *Expectations of Others' Reactions:* imagined reactions of others to one's own actions
3. *Acts of Others Toward Self:* observed acts of others viewed as occurring in response to the acts of self
4. *Acts of Self Toward Self (introject):* how one treats oneself (self-controlling, self-punishing, self-congratulating, self-destroying, and so on)

These four categories characterize the rigidity, chronic repetitiveness, and self-perpetuating nature of neurotic and characterological problems. The therapist uses the CMP to point out, rather than act out, the patient's maladaptive scenarios.

A Comparison of Manualized Therapies

In relation to the other manualized psychodynamic/interpersonal therapies, IPT is more symptom-focused (addressed specifically to depression), more structured, and more didactic. IPT minimizes the role of attention to transference. The patient—therapist relationship is discussed only to address impediments to the progress of therapy. Even under these circumstances, the emphasis remains didactic rather than interpretive.

SE and TLDP are more flexible than IPT both in terms of the range of patients considered suitable as well as in terms of the time frame considered therapeutically appropriate (both can be adapted to a time-limited format or to a longer term, more open-ended approach). SE and TLDP deemphasize DSM-IIIR diagnoses, focusing instead on an assessment of the patient's ability to engage in the therapeutic task. Nevertheless, both have been demonstrated to be highly amenable for use in studies utilizing DSM diagnoses across a spectrum of disorders. In contrast to IPT, SE and TLDP are minimally didactic and do not rely on advice giving.

SE and TLDP do have differences. In TLDP, there is no distinction between supportive and exploratory aspects of the therapist's task. Rather, relationship problems with the therapist, such as not feeling supported, are identified and become the focus of the therapist's explorations. In addition, there is a greater reliance on an interpersonal framework in TLDP. As a result, TLDP views the concepts of transference and countertransference in more interpersonal and transactional terms than SE, which takes a more traditional psychoanalytic view of transference, countertransference, intra-psychic conflict, and wishes.

Training and Adherence

The training procedures specified for each of these manualized therapies are described in the manuals or subsequent publications (Luborsky 1984; Strupp et al. 1987; Rounsaville et al. 1986). All three manuals presume that trainees are already trained in the fundamentals of psychodynamic psychotherapy, and each approach calls for didactic training during which trainees read the manual. In IPT and TLDP, the didactic portion includes the use of videotaped illustrations of technique. This didactic portion of the training is followed by case supervision, focusing on trainees' efforts to implement principles and procedures as outlined in the manuals. All three approaches endorse using tape recordings of the sessions for supervision, reviewing previous sessions, and making recommendations based on the manuals' prescriptions.

Accompanying each manual is an instrument designed to assess the degree to which trainees "adhere" to the principles and procedures presented in the respective manual. Studies demonstrate that adherence scales can be rated reliably (Strupp, Butler, and Rosser 1988) and can differentiate the dynamic therapy in question from other forms of treatment, such as cognitive therapy, drug counseling, or clinical management (DeRubeis et al. 1982; Luborsky et al. 1982; Woody et al. 1983). To date, no effort has been made to differentiate two manual-guided dynamic therapies from each other.

IPT skills are assessed using the Therapist Strategy Rating Form (Chevron and Rounsaville 1983), which includes fourteen items rating therapists' skill in using IPT strategies. The form is designed to evaluate the problem area for the patient, the strategies the therapist is using to help the patient, and the quality with which the strategies are implemented (Rounsaville et al. 1988). The instrument yields an assessment of quality of problem-oriented strategies, general IPT skills, overall quality, and degree of patient receptiveness.

Luborsky (1984) included a rating scale for SE as an appendix in his manual. This scale provides four overall performance ratings in SE plus overall ratings of therapist skill and degree of help provided; there are also ratings assessing the extent of supportiveness, the degree to which understanding is facilitated, and the adequacy of the therapist's response in terms of expressive aims (this includes appropriate use of the CCRT).

To assess therapists' adherence to the principles and strategies of TLDP, the Vanderbilt Therapeutic Strategies Scale (Butler, Strupp, and Lane 1987) was developed. The instrument consists of two sections: (1) Psychodynamic Interviewing Style, which assesses strategies considered essential to the skillful conduct of any interpersonally based, dynamic psychotherapy, and (2) TLDP Specific Strategies, which lists therapist behaviors considered specific to TLDP. The instrument consists of twenty-one items and is intended for use by nonparticipant observers of taped sessions. The scale is accompanied by a rater manual (Butler and the Center for Psychotherapy Research Team 1986), which operationally defines each item and anchor point.

TRAINING EXPERIENCED THERAPISTS

Adherence to the Manual.

Efforts to train experienced therapists in IPT have been summarized in a recent review by Rounsaville et al. (1988). The most extensive collection and analysis of data on IPT has occurred as part of the NIMH Collaborative Depression Study (Rounsaville, Chevron, and Weissman 1984). Eleven psychologists and psychiatrists, with an average of fifteen years' experience, were selected from a pool of twenty-eight applicants to undergo IPT training. Performance on the first IPT training case yielded an average rating on the TSRF of "excellent." The average level of adherence did not change significantly during the course of the study, which involved two or three training cases and an additional five to ten cases in the efficacy phase. The investigators suggest that this failure to improve represents a "ceiling effect," resulting from the inclusion of highly skilled therapists only. Individual variation among the ratings was observed, but due to objectives of the larger project, unacceptable therapists were dropped rather than studied. For the small number of these highly experienced and skilled therapists who did not meet acceptable standards on an initial case, "subsequent supervised casework led to improvement in some but not in others" (Rounsaville et al. 1988, 684).

Luborsky et al. (1985) trained psychiatrists and psychologists in SE to treat a population of opiate addicts. Details are not given, but the five therapists in the SE condition were selected from a larger pool of applicants on the basis of an interview with Lester Luborsky, who chose therapists "judged to be best for this population" (p. 603). Under supervision, the therapists' execution of SE was clearly distinguishable from the other conditions in the study (CB and "drug counseling"). A measure of "purity" was used which assessed the degree to which the therapist performed the "intended" therapy, as *distinct* from techniques and strategies characterizing the other modalities. As a group, SE therapists obtained higher ratings of SE qualities than therapists in the other conditions, a result that suggests a training effect. In addition, there were significant within-group differences among the SE therapists themselves regarding the "purity" with which they conducted therapy. Statistical analyses suggested that, for all therapy conditions, the higher the therapist's level of purity, the better the patient's outcome in the areas of drug use, employment, and psychological status. This relation was significant even within caseloads of individual therapists (Luborsky et al. 1985).

At the Vanderbilt Center for Psychotherapy Research, data collection has been completed in an investigation of the effects of specialized training in TLDP. This is the only investigation to date which has attempted to compare experienced therapists' pretraining performance with performance after training in a manual-guided, dynamic/interpersonal therapy.

Sixteen dynamically oriented clinical psychologists and psychiatrists were observed on two cases before training and on two cases after training. These were seasoned, experienced therapists who treated adult outpatients complaining of anxiety, depression, and interpersonal difficulties. Adherence ratings were made on the third session for both pre- and posttraining cohorts (Butler et al. 1991). These ratings revealed that, prior to training, therapists were not adhering to TLDP. That is, they were not systematically attending to the therapeutic relationship in the early sessions. Pre- and posttraining group comparisons yielded significant differences on both the Psychodynamic Interviewing Style subscale and on the TLDP Specific Strategies subscale, suggesting enhanced general dynamic technique, greater attention to maladaptive interpersonal patterns, and heightened focus on the therapeutic relationship.

While the group mean adherence to TLDP increased posttraining, there was evidence of considerable variation in posttraining adherence. Figure 11.1 presents a graph of the mean TLDP adherence ratings pre- and posttraining for all sixteen therapists individually. Despite the higher posttraining group mean, this statistic obscures a marked variation in individual adherence posttraining. Indeed, some therapists' adherence scores were virtually unchanged posttraining. This finding is consistent with reports of training in IPT and SE, which also yield varying degrees of adherence. It seems clear that experienced therapists respond differentially to training programs designed to alter the way in which they characteristically conduct therapy.

A recent meta-analytic study of therapist effects in psychotherapy outcome studies (Crits-Christoph et al. 1990) provides an interesting counterpoint to this finding of variability of adherence. The authors found that the size of therapist effects on outcome in a given study (that is, the degree to which outcome is attributed to individual therapists) was *minimized* by using experienced therapists and a treatment manual. Thus, if experienced therapists using a treatment manual tend to reduce the effect size of the therapist variable on outcome, it stands to reason that they are "delivering the treatment" more uniformly than inexperienced therapists not using a manual.

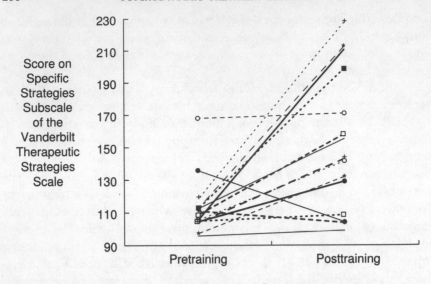

FIGURE 11.1
Mean adherence score for each therapist.

The apparently disparate conclusions of these findings and the findings of variable adherence in the investigations reviewed here can be explained by the different aims of Crits-Christoph et al.'s (1990) meta-analysis and this chapter. That is, we are more interested in highlighting the effects of training on the adherence of experienced therapists to manual prescriptions *irrespective of the effect of such adherence on outcome*.[4] In comparison with inexperienced therapists or studies not using a manual, the studies discussed here might yield small therapist effects on outcome as well. Indeed, data from the IPT work cited here and Luborsky et al.'s (1985) study were included in Crits-Christoph et al.'s (1990) review. Furthermore, in the Treatment of Depression Collaborative Research Program (Rounsaville, Chevron, and Weissman 1984; Elkin et al. 1989), in which observations of IPT were made, fully 20 percent of candidates were excluded from analysis for failure to adhere (Rounsaville et al. 1988). These therapists were not included in the Crits-Christoph et al. review, thus artificially constricting the range of variability and reducing, by an unknown quantity, therapist effects.

[4]As we have argued elsewhere (Strupp, Butler, and Rosser 1988), the use of outcome as the ultimate criterion for therapists' performance is problematic. In the Vanderbilt II study, for instance, we observed that a relatively poorly conducted therapy seemingly resulted in a large treatment effect for a patient with severe character disorder. Exploration of this outcome with the patient after treatment revealed that during therapy, he and his estranged father had nearly simultaneous heart attacks. In the patient's mind, this profound life experience largely overshadowed the effect of his weekly discussions with the therapist. People change or fail to change for a multitude of reasons which are not yet well understood.

The crucial point here is the consistent finding across studies of the differential response manifested by experienced therapists to training: some therapists appear to adhere very well, others have more difficulty, and some appear to be not influenced by training at all.

Factors Associated with Adherence.

Although all systematic investigations suggest that instruction in manual-guided dynamic therapies results in adherence at the group level, the findings also suggest that the nature of this adherence is not uniform. For example, examination of the IPT therapies revealed variable performance ratings within the group of therapists judged as "competent" with IPT. Although severity of patient's pretreatment symptoms was not related to adherence, one factor that did prove important was patient difficulty. Using the hostility scale of the Vanderbilt Psychotherapy Process Scale (Suh, O'Malley, and Strupp 1986) as a measure of this, Rounsaville et al. (1988) reported a strong relationship between patient hostility and therapist adherence. When patients were more difficult, therapists performed more poorly. Negative pretherapy patient expectations of outcome were also correlated with lower levels of therapist adherence. Interestingly, supervisors in this study tended to judge deviations from manual guidelines as acceptable in an effort to work with difficult patients. General therapist qualities, such as greater warmth and lower negative therapist attitude, as measured by the Vanderbilt Psychotherapy Process Scale (VPPS), also correlated both with therapist adherence to IPT and patient outcome. The authors suggest this may represent evidence of a "good therapist" factor, reflecting the possibilities that (1) more competent therapists are more flexibly capable of adapting their techniques to conform to the dictates of a training manual, and (2) specific IPT adherence ratings conceptually incorporate general clinical skills. They conclude that they "cannot rule out the possibility that greater adherence to manual guidelines is simply one of many features that characterize inherently good psychotherapists whose efficacy would be superior whether or not they received manual-guided training" (Rounsaville et al. 1988, 685).

Similar issues were present in efforts to understand the factors influencing adherence to SE. In addition to the effect of SE qualities and purity on outcome, Luborsky et al. (1985) found therapist personal qualities and quality of the helping alliance also related significantly to posttreatment outcome. Specifically, peer ratings of therapist's level of personal adjustment and interest in helping the patient were associated with outcome. Such therapist characteristics were reliably rated with high agreement by independent peers who had worked with the therapists. Furthermore, examination of the patient–therapist relationship with the Helping

Relationship Questionnaire (Alexander and Luborsky 1984), suggested that the presence of an early, mutual sense of potential benefits to be gained from the therapy was strongly related to outcome. Taken together, these findings suggested to Luborsky and his colleagues that "the major agent of effective psychotherapy is the personality of the therapist, particularly the ability to form a warm, supportive relationship" (Luborsky et al. 1985, 609).

Luborsky's purity measure also correlated with outcome measures.[5] While it is possible that the most effective therapists "happened" to deliver the purer therapy, examination of purity within therapist also yielded an association between purity and outcome. Thus, purity and the "manner in which the therapist delivered the therapy" (p. 608) reflect important and, perhaps, somewhat independent predictors of outcome. Luborsky and colleagues concluded that the formation of a helping alliance may be the most crucial determinant of effectiveness, and the helping alliance appears to depend on the therapist's personal adjustment. Furthermore, a good helping alliance may make adherence possible. That is, once the alliance is established, good therapists then execute the intended therapy. However, it is equally likely that once a patient experiences the alliance as helpful, he or she somehow "enables the therapist to adhere to his intended technique" (p. 610).

To shed light on the relationship between adherence to TLDP and competence, ratings of competence were made by expert TLDP trainers. These experts rated the same posttraining sessions used in the adherence ratings. Each session was rated on overall competence, patient difficulty, relevance of discussion, use of language, attunement to the patient, attunement to patterns, focus of the dialogue, timing/meaningfulness of interventions, openness to feedback, and avoidance of blaming. Generally high correlations were observed between these competence ratings and the Interviewing Style subscale of the Vanderbilt Therapeutic Strategies Scale, which suggests concurrence between the general aims of the two measures, namely to capture the quality of a given therapist's approach. However, the experts' ratings of competence were not consistently related to ratings of TLDP adherence on the Specific Strategies subscale. The authors (Butler et al. 1991) concluded that adherence ratings made by student raters trying to achieve high interrater reliability do not necessarily tap the competence or skill with which the therapist performs. This is similar to Rounsaville et

[5]It should be made clear that "purity" is not necessarily the same as adherence. As Luborsky et al. (1985) point out, it is theoretically possible to adhere to the manual-based criteria yet have a low purity rating, if a therapist's performance was also characterized by techniques of another therapy. That is, a therapist who adhered both to SE and to cognitive-behavioral therapy in the same session would be rated low on "purity." Purity reflects the extent to which a therapist adheres to a procedure *exclusively*.

al.'s (1988) finding of a weak relationship between adherence and skill. As Schaffer (1982) has proposed, the presence or absence of types of therapist behavior may represent a dimension of therapeutic performance that is separate from skill.

The finding that some instances of adherence were more skillfully conducted than others was consistent with clinical observations of project therapists' efforts to rapidly assess and address issues in the therapeutic relationship. Despite their experience, for some therapists, interventions were often forced and mechanical, rather than evolving smoothly from the flow of the patient's material. In many cases, efforts to address the relationship were premature, with attempts made before a pattern had been explored in sufficient depth to permit concrete and plausible connections between the patient's concerns outside of therapy and specific events in therapy.

For example, in the third session of one of the posttraining therapies (Butler and Strupp 1989), a female patient disclosed concerns about her ability to remain sexually faithful in significant heterosexual relationships. Rather than exploring the patient's fears further, the male therapist immediately began probing to determine whether there was a "pattern" in her selection of men. In the midst of the patient's anxious confusion about this question, the therapist abruptly raised the issue of her feelings for him. Though she denied any feelings for the therapist, he continued to force the issue. After a while the patient said, "I don't feel I've really opened up much yet," and switched the conversation away from her sexual concerns toward her panic symptoms. Although the therapist was attempting to adhere to TLDP by detecting an interpersonal pattern and then relating it to the therapeutic relationship, his effort was concrete and mechanical, and too vague, insensitive, and ill-timed to foster any security in self-exploration on the part of the patient.

A somewhat more skillful attempt also involved a third session. The patient and therapist discussed the patient's fantasy that people watching the videotape of their session would laugh at her. This was followed by the report of a previous therapist who had laughed at her. The therapist empathized with her humiliation and connected this with what she said earlier about repeated experiences of humiliation and devaluation from her father. He then asked, "Do you imagine that I might be feeling something like that too, in my reaction to you?" After an initial denial, the patient admitted to wondering whether the therapist might see her problems as "not that serious," and feel that she should be able to straighten things out for herself. Further exploration revealed fresh data regarding her masochistic inclination to aggressive self-attack in failing to meet perfectionistic standards, followed by more intimate vignettes of experiencing herself as being a disappointment to her harsh and critical father.

While both examples illustrate instances selected by raters as accurately identifying examples of technical adherence to TLDP, in comparison with the first therapist, the second one more skillfully explored psychodynamic themes, relating these to fantasies about the therapist's expected reaction, and going on to explore the patient's internalization of the harsh, paternal, critical other. Thus, comparable efforts at technical adherence obviously do not necessarily reflect comparable skill in the execution of these techniques and strategies.

These two cases are also useful in clarifying the nature of obtained correlations between adherence and similar process variables examined by the IPT and SE researchers. For instance, as with IPT, independent VPPS ratings revealed TLDP adherence to be significantly related to therapist exploration ($r = .42, p < .01$). However, the TLDP study, unlike Rounsaville et al. (1988), found nonsignificant correlations between TLDP adherence and the VPPS subscales of negative therapist attitude ($r = .01$) and therapist warmth and friendliness ($r = -.15$). An explanation for these discrepant results may be that a number of trained, IPT therapists were subsequently excluded from the Rounsaville et al. (1988) study based on expert evaluators' judgments that the therapists were "not performing IPT at a level that was acceptable for clinical trials" (p. 684). It is likely that exclusion of these less skillful therapists, who were not excluded in the TLDP study, accounts for the apparent difference in findings. Interestingly, examination of selected VPPS ratings for the two therapy sessions just discussed suggested that the less skillful therapist was rated as less warm and friendly than 62 percent of the sample, while the more skillful therapist was rated as more warm and friendly than 81 percent of the therapists in this sample. These data, while not conclusive, support the notion that comparable adherence scores may be associated with variable process ratings such as those provided by the VPPS.

SUMMARY

In general, it appears that, as a group, experienced therapists can be taught to conform to a manual-guided therapy as measured by reliable instruments designed to assess adherence. However, studies to date suggest that considerable variability exists in the degree of adherence evidenced by a particular therapist, or even within a particular patient–therapist combination. Finally, and perhaps most important, the data point to a complex relationship between technical adherence and competence or skill, which in turn may be related to interpersonal manner (see Schaffer 1982). For instance, Luborsky et al.'s (1985) purity of adherence to SE appeared to be dependent upon the establishment of a helping alliance, which in turn appeared to be related to "personal qualities" of the therapist.

Rounsaville and colleagues found no relationship between IPT adherence and outcome (Rounsaville, Weissman, and Prusoff 1981), and only a weak relationship between adherence and skill (Rounsaville et al. 1988). However, ratings of therapist competence made by supervisors were predictive of greater patient improvement (O'Malley et al. 1988). Furthermore, there was a tendency for competent therapists to deviate from manual guidelines in their attempts to work with more difficult patients (Rounsaville et al. 1988).

Thus, it seems clear that technical adherence, skill, and interpersonal manner are not isomorphic, though they may be interrelated in important ways. Precisely how they are related is less clear. Schaffer (1982) differentiates the therapist's contribution into three conceptual dimensions: (1) type of therapist behavior, referring to specific techniques used, (2) "skillfulness," defined as persuasiveness, timeliness, neutrality, and degree of discrepancy from the patient's point of view, and (3) interpersonal manner, involving empathy, warmth, and genuineness. Schaffer sees these as independent dimensions. On the other hand, we have proposed a more integrated model of interpersonal and technical skill. For example, Strupp (1986) noted: "The therapist's skill is significantly manifested by an ability to create a particular interpersonal context and, within that context, to foster certain kinds of learning" (p. 126). Clearly, adherence to the technical prescriptions of a manual is perhaps the least difficult part of the therapist's contribution to conceptualize and measure.

The current generation of manuals has provided an initial step toward the ultimate goal, namely, to operationalize competently conducted psychotherapy. We believe that an important method to accomplish this work will be the systematic comparison of good and poor therapists. Rather than to minimize therapist effects (Crits-Christoph et al. 1990), the task should be to describe and understand what differentiates the good therapist from the poor one. What are the implicit rules we use to exclude "poor" therapists from our studies? How do these qualities interact with various patient characteristics to yield the observed outcomes? The answers to such questions await creative uses of existing methods and measures as well as the development of new methodologies and measures. The challenge to psychotherapy research, however, is clear.

Implications for Research on Training

An important potential use of dynamic/interpersonal psychotherapy manuals is in the design and execution of training programs. There are few good data from traditional training programs regarding training methods, content, and effectiveness. Questions remain of how best to train therapists, whom to train, and how to determine when a therapist is performing adequately. The studies cited above have focused on training experienced therapists to adhere to a specific form of therapy. While this research addresses important issues, it is equally important to investigate the training of inexperienced and novice therapists (see Butler and Rock 1990). Conclusions from studies using experienced therapists may not be generalizable to inexperienced therapists. One observation made during TLDP training was that experienced therapists often seemed quite comfortable with their chosen techniques and style. Thus, the impetus for making genuine changes in their preferred mode of interacting with patients was often lacking. Novice therapists are undoubtedly more amenable to suggestions regarding technique and style.

What should therapists know and be able to do? Before we can specify the training necessary to achieve competence, we must be able to articulate what comprises competent performance. The lack of a suitable criterion for therapeutic competence is an impediment to psychotherapy research in general and renders scientifically based evaluation and modification of training programs extremely difficult, if not impossible. Understanding the therapist's contribution to therapy involves a consideration of the therapist's adherence, skill, and personal qualities. Adherence alone cannot be considered the totality of therapeutic competence. Nor can adherence be the sole goal of training.

However, going beyond descriptions of adherence requires describing particular activities more precisely (cf. Schaffer 1982). It is easy to suggest that a trainee should "establish a working alliance" with a patient. It is much more difficult to delineate precisely what actions on the part of the therapist might best help the therapist achieve such a goal. The precise delineation of desirable therapist actions is essential if psychotherapy training is to advance toward empirically based procedures. Clearly, from this perspective, psychotherapy research and psychotherapy training research are thoroughly interdependent (Strupp, Butler, and Rosser 1988).

An example of enhanced precision in investigating the personal qualities of the therapist is evident in a series of studies conducted at Vanderbilt. Scrutiny of the performance of experienced therapists who had undergone personal psychoanalysis suggested that these therapists were not superior to nonprofessional counselors in resisting and responding therapeutically to countertransferential reactions, especially patients' chronic hostility and negativism (Strupp 1980d).

Reexamining these data, Henry, Schacht, and Strupp (1986) attempted to precisely describe the problematic interaction sequences. Using the Structural Analysis of Social Behavior (SASB) method developed by Benjamin (1982), these authors were able to operationally define the concepts of *complementarity* and *multiple communications.* The former refers to

a given interaction sequence in which the communication of one participant is thought to "pull for" a complementary communication from the
other. Multiple communications simultaneously communicate more than
one interpersonal message (such as acceptance and rejection). Henry,
Schacht, and Strupp's analyses showed that cases with good outcome had
greater positive complementarity, less negative complementarity, and
greater total complementarity. Multiple communications were almost exclusively associated with therapies having poor outcome. This study serves
as a demonstration of the potential value of analyzing the complex interplay between therapists' and patients' personalities in therapy. By systematically identifying and investigating these interactions, we may be able
to move beyond simple notions of therapist warmth and genuineness and
more precisely describe important aspects of the therapist's personal contribution to the therapeutic process.

Traditionally, personal therapy has been used to "teach" therapists in
training to deal with their countertransference reactions. While adequate
levels of personal adjustment and clinical sensitivity are certainly essential
for therapists, personal therapy alone may not improve the therapist's
technical ability to recognize and manage the emergence of transference
difficulties (for example, hostility, resistance, or erotic feelings). Specialized
training to recognize subtle negative complementarity and multiple communications, perhaps through a system like SASB, may be a more efficient
approach to teaching therapists what to look for and what to do when
confronted with countertransference issues. We believe that efforts to
manualize dynamic therapy must move to a new level, one designed to
improve the interpersonal skills thought to underlie technical adherence.[6]

References

ALEXANDER, L., & LUBORSKY, L. (1984). Research on the helping alliance. In L.
    Greenberg & W. Pinsof (Eds.), *The psychotherapeutic process: A research
    handbook.* New York: Guilford Press.

ANCHIN, J. C., & KIESLER, D. J. (EDS.). (1982). *Handbook of interpersonal psychother-
    apy.* New York: Pergamon Press.

BENJAMIN, L. S. (1982). Use of Structural Analysis of Social Behavior (SASB)
    to guide intervention in therapy. In J. C. Anchin & D. J. Kiesler (Eds.),
    Handbook of interpersonal psychotherapy. New York: Pergamon Press.

BERGIN, A. E., & STRUPP, H. H. (1972). *Changing frontiers in the science of
    psychotherapy.* Chicago: Aldine-Atherton.

---

[6]We wish to acknowledge the seminal contributions of Thomas Schacht and William
Henry in the development of these ideas.

Butler, S. F., & Binder, J. L. (1987). Cyclical psychodynamics and the triangle of insight: An integration. *Psychiatry, 50,* 218–231.

Butler, S. F., & the Center for Psychotherapy Research Team (1986). *Working manual for the Vanderbilt Therapeutic Strategies Scale.* Unpublished manuscript, Vanderbilt University, Nashville, TN.

Butler, S. F., Henry, W. P., Strupp, H. H., & Lane, T. W. (1991). Measuring adherence and skill in time-limited dynamic psychotherapy. Submitted.

Butler, S. F., & Rock, D. (1990, June). Characteristics of expertise in psychotherapy. Paper presented to the annual meeting of the Society for Psychotherapy Research, Wintergreen, VA.

Butler, S. F., & Strupp, H. H. (1986). Specific and nonspecific factors in psychotherapy: A problematic paradigm for psychotherapy research. *Psychotherapy, 23,* 30–40.

Butler, S. F., & Strupp, H. H. (1989, June). Issues in training therapists to competency: The Vanderbilt experience. Paper presented to the annual meeting of the Society for Psychotherapy Research, Toronto.

Butler, S. F., Strupp, H. H., & Lane, T. W. (1987, June). The Time-Limited Dynamic Psychotherapy Therapeutic Strategies Scale: Development of an adherence measure. Paper presented at the annual meeting of the Society for Psychotherapy Research, Ulm, Germany.

Chevron, E. S., & Rounsaville, B. J. (1983). Evaluating the clinical skills of psychotherapists: A comparison of techniques. *Archives of General Psychiatry, 40,* 1129–1132.

Crits-Christoph, P., Baranakie, K., Kurcias, J. S., Beck, A. T., Carroll, K., Luborsky, L., McLellan, A. T., Woody, G. E., Thompson, L., Gallagher, D., & Zitrin, C. (1990, June). Meta-analysis of therapist effects in therapy outcome studies. Paper presented to the annual meeting of the Society for Psychotherapy Research, Wintergreen, VA.

DeRubeis, R. J., Hollon, S. E., Evans, M. D., & Bemis, K. M. (1982). Can psychotherapies for depression be discriminated? A systematic investigation of cognitive therapy and interpersonal therapy. *Journal of Consulting and Clinical Psychology, 50,* 774–756.

Elkin, I. E., Parloff, M. B., Hadley, S. W., & Autry, A. H. (1985). NIMH Treatment of Depression Collaborative Research Program: Background and research plan. *Archives of General Psychiatry, 42,* 305–316.

Elkin, I., Shea, T. M., Watkins, J. T., Imber, S. D., Sotsky, S. M., Collins, J. F., Glass, D. R., Pilkonis, P. A., Leber, W. R., Docherty, J. P., Fiester, S. J., & Parloff, M. B. (1989). National Institute of Mental Health Treatment of Depression Collaborative Research Program: General effectiveness of treatments. *Archives of General Psychiatry, 46,* 971–982.

Henry, W. P., Schacht, T. E., & Strupp, H. H. (1986). Structural Analysis of Social Behavior: Application to a study of interpersonal process of differential therapeutic outcome. *Journal of Consulting and Clinical Psychology, 54,* 27–31.

KLERMAN, G. L., ROUNSAVILLE, B., CHEVRON, E., NEU, C., & WEISSMAN, M. M. (1984). *Interpersonal psychotherapy of depression.* New York: Basic Books.

LUBORSKY, L. (1984). *Principles of psychoanalytic psychotherapy: A manual for supportive expressive treatment.* New York: Basic Books.

LUBORSKY, L., McLELLAN, A. T., WOODY, G. E., O'BRIEN, C. P., & AUERBACH, A. (1985). Therapist success and its determinants. *Archives of General Psychiatry, 42,* 602–611.

LUBORSKY, L., WOODY, G. E., McLELLAN, A. T., O'BRIEN, C. P., & ROSENWEIG, J. (1982). Can independent judges recognize different psychotherapies? An experience with manual-guided therapies. *Journal of Consulting and Clinical Psychology, 50,* 49–62.

MENNINGER, K. A., & HOLZMAN, P. S. (1973). *Theory of psychoanalytic technique.* New York: Basic Books.

O'MALLEY, S. S., FOLEY, S. H., ROUNSAVILLE, B. J., & WEISSMAN, M. M. (1988). Therapist competence and patient outcome in interpersonal psychotherapy of depression. *Journal of Clinical and Consulting Psychology, 56,* 496–501.

ROUNSAVILLE, B. J., CHEVRON, E. S., & WEISSMAN, M. M. (1984). Specification of techniques in interpersonal psychotherapy. In J. B. Williams & R. L. Spitzer (Eds.), *Psychotherapy research: Where are we and where should we go?* New York: Guilford Press.

ROUNSAVILLE, B. J., CHEVRON, E. S., WEISSMAN, M. M., PRUSOFF, B. A., & FRANK, E. (1986). Training therapists to perform interpersonal psychotherapy in clinical trials. *Comprehensive Psychiatry, 27,* 364–371.

ROUNSAVILLE, B. J., O'MALLEY, S., FOLEY, S., & WEISSMAN, M. M. (1988). The role of manual-guided training in the conduct and efficacy of interpersonal psychotherapy for depression. *Journal of Consulting and Clinical Psychology, 56,* 681–688.

ROUNSAVILLE, B. J., WEISSMAN, M. M., & PRUSOFF, B. A. (1981). Psychotherapy with depressed outpatients: Patient and process variables as predictors of outcome. *British Journal of Psychiatry, 13,* 67–74.

SCHACHT, T. E., BINDER, J. L., & STRUPP, H. H. (1984). The dynamic focus. In H. H. Strupp & J. L. Binder (Eds.), *Psychotherapy in a new key.* New York: Basic Books.

SCHAFFER, N. D. (1982). Multidimensional measures of therapist behavior as predictors of outcome. *Psychological Bulletin, 92,* 670–681.

STRUPP, H. H. (1980a). Success and failure in time-limited psychotherapy: A systematic comparison of two cases (Comparison 1). *Archives of General Psychiatry, 37,* 595–603.

STRUPP, H. H. (1980b). Success and failure in time-limited psychotherapy: A systematic comparison of two cases (Comparison 2). *Archives of General Psychiatry, 37,* 708–716.

STRUPP, H. H. (1980c). Success and failure in time-limited psychotherapy: With special reference to the performance of a lay counselor (Comparison 3). *Archives of General Psychiatry, 37,* 831–841.

STRUPP, H. H. (1980d). Success and failure in time-limited psychotherapy: Further evidence (Comparison 4). *Archives of General Psychiatry, 37,* 947–954.

STRUPP, H. H. (1986). Psychotherapy: Research, practice and public policy (How to avoid dead ends). *American Psychologist, 41,* 120–30.

STRUPP, H. H., & BERGIN, A. E. (1969). Some empirical and conceptual bases for coordinated research in psychotherapy: A critical review of issues, trends and evidence. *International Journal of Psychiatry, 7,* 18–90.

STRUPP, H. H., & BINDER, J. L.(EDS.). (1984). *Psychotherapy in a new key.* New York: Basic Books.

STRUPP, H. H., BUTLER, S. F., BINDER, J. L., SCHACHT, T. E., & ROSSER, C. L. (1987, JUNE). Time-limited dynamic psychotherapy: Development and implementation of a training program. Paper presented to the annual meeting of the Society for Psychotherapy Research, Ulm, Germany.

STRUPP, H. H., BUTLER, S. F., & ROSSER, C. L. (1988). Training in psychodynamic therapy. *Journal of Consulting and Clinical Psychology, 56,* 689–695.

SUH, C. S., O'MALLEY, S. S., & STRUPP, H. H. (1986). The Vanderbilt process measures: The Psychotherapy Process Scale (VPPS) and the Negative Indicators Scale (VNIS). In L. S. Greenberg & W. M. Pinsof (Eds.), *The psychotherapeutic process: A research handbook* (pp. 285–324). New York: Guilford Press.

SULLIVAN, H. S. (1953). *The interpersonal theory of psychiatry.* New York: Norton.

WOODY, G. E., LUBORSKY, L., MCLELLAN, A. T., O'BRIEN, C. P., BECK, A. T., BLAINE, J., HERMAN, I., & HOLE, A. (1983). Psychotherapy for opiate addicts: Does it help? *Archives of General Psychiatry, 40,* 639–645.

CHAPTER 12

Benefits of Adherence to Psychotherapy Manuals, and Where to Get Them

LESTER LUBORSKY AND JACQUES P. BARBER

AN ABRUPT SPEED UP OCCURRED in the evolution of psychotherapy research and practice with the advent of manuals. Within the brief span of fifteen years the field has advanced from having no manuals to having a manual for every properly equipped therapy. For dynamic psychotherapies the new manuals included these: *Principles of Psychoanalytic Psychotherapy* (Luborsky 1984), *Psychotherapy in a New Key: A Guide to Time-Limited Dynamic Psychotherapy* (TLDP) (Strupp and Binder 1984), and *The Treatment of Borderline Patients* (Kernberg et al. 1989). For other forms of psychotherapy, the new manuals included *Interpersonal Psychotherapy of Depression* (IPT) (Klerman et al. 1984) and *Cognitive Therapy of Depression* (Beck et al. 1979).

These manuals are different from the scores of older descriptions of psychotherapies—even those called manuals. To be a true manual, a treatment guide must have three characteristics: (1) a presentation of the main principles behind the techniques of the form of psychotherapy, (2) concrete examples of each technical principle, and (3) scales to guide independent judges in evaluating samples of sessions to determine the degree of conformity to the manual. This third criterion is the most crucial and distinctive. Even the very first descriptions of psychoanalytic technique, known generally as Freud's papers on technique (1911 [1958], 1912a [1958], 1912b [1958], 1913 [1958], 1914 [1958], and 1915 [1958]), only partly fit the definition: Freud's papers fulfill criterion 1 by providing principles of technique, and partially meet criterion 2 by presenting some examples of the principles; but they could not satisfy criterion 3 because they do not include a set of scales for judging degree of the adherence of the therapist to the manual's recommendations.

For many years, psychotherapy researchers complained about the lack of systematic knowledge about what therapists actually do in each form of psychotherapy. Yet the idea of measuring adherence to treatment manuals for different forms of psychotherapy is still recent. An early example of measurement of techniques used by therapists in a form of psychotherapy goes back to Weissman, Paykel, and Prusoff (1972). Although at that time they had no treatment manual, the team constructed an unpublished manual for interpersonal psychotherapy (Klerman and Neu 1976). At about the same time in 1976, the first, unpublished version of Luborsky's manual for supportive-expressive dynamic psychotherapy began to be used for training of psychiatry residents at the University of Pennsylvania. A manual for cognitive therapy came out in 1979 (Beck et al. 1979).

Illustration of the Content: The SE Dynamic Manual

The basic nature of manuals is best illustrated by providing detail about one of them in common use. This chapter will use the SE dynamic manual (Luborsky 1984). The principles and examples in this manual are consistent with Freud's recommendations for technique as well as with a representative selection of similar accounts of psychoanalytic psychotherapy. These principles are given not only in the SE manual but also in chapter 11.

The SE manual's main techniques, as its label warrants, are supportive and expressive. Supportive techniques and a supportive relationship provide a sense of security sufficient to allow the patient to try to undo the restrictions in functioning that were responsible for the symptoms and suffering and that necessitated the treatment.

The therapist's expressive techniques permit the patient to express thoughts and feelings. Both the patient and therapist listen to and reflect on these expressions, with the aim of understanding and changing what needs to be changed. Over the years much more has been written about expressive techniques than about supportive techniques, perhaps because how to be supportive has always seemed almost self-evident, while how to use the patient's expressions to provide accurate interpretations has always seemed to require special expertise. In general, expressive techniques are appropriate for patients with adequate ego strength and anxiety tolerance as well as with the capacity for greater understanding of their relationships and of themselves. Although supportive and expressive techniques can be separately identified, some techniques clearly have both components; an accurate interpretation is an expressive technique that can at the same time have strong supportive effects.

The manual helps the therapist extract from the session a version of the central relationship pattern called the Core Conflictual Relationship Theme, or CCRT (chapter 17). The manual offers guidance for making inferences about transference by formalizing the principles in the informal system that clinicians use.

The essence of the method is illustrated in figure 12.1, which is based on the psychoanalysis of Ms. Cunningham. On the periphery of the large central CCRT circle are smaller relationship episode (RE) circles containing the condensed accounts of each of the eleven relationship episodes in session 5. They are presented here in clockwise order, just as the therapist listened to them in the session. (A CCRT research judge "listens" like the therapist but has the luxury of going back over the episodes by rereading the transcript, not just by recalling the session.) One of the most relevant principles that clinicians use to decide on the formulation about the core relationship pattern, as well as on which parts of the pattern are likely to be experienced at the moment, is the recurrence of relationship components across relationship episodes. The three principal components of the pattern are the wishes (conscious or disavowed), the anticipated responses from others, and the responses of self. The large central circle contains the components that are most pervasive across episodes; these form a pattern that appears to correspond with what Freud (1912a [1958]) calls the "transference template" (Luborsky and Crits-Christoph 1990).

The therapist's interpretative style in this session is cautious and sparing but appropriately responsive to a few of the main themes of the patient's relationships. The patient's Wish B, to be reassured, is strongly expressed in her relationship episodes. The therapist undoubtedly noted the patient's wish to be reassured as it was expressed in RE 2 and RE 4 in terms of her wish to get reassurance from the husband and in RE 3 in terms of her father's wish for reassurance. The recurrence of themes in these REs and elsewhere in the session provides a clue to what might be experienced by the patient in the relationship to the therapist.

From these clues the therapist ventures an interpretation at the start of RE 6: "You didn't express wanting reassurance *here* yesterday." At that point the patient confirms that she had experienced the wish to get reassurance from him. The patient adds that she had said nothing about this earlier because she had not expected to get reassurance from him.

The therapist made another intervention that may be based on the same kind of cue from the patient. The cue is in RE 7 where the patient admits her inclination to be critical, to put the other person down (related to Wish A) before she can be friendly. On this basis, in RE 8 the therapist makes an intervention in which he questions the patient. The patient then reveals her criticism of him.

A further revelation appears in the next three REs: once Ms. Cunning-

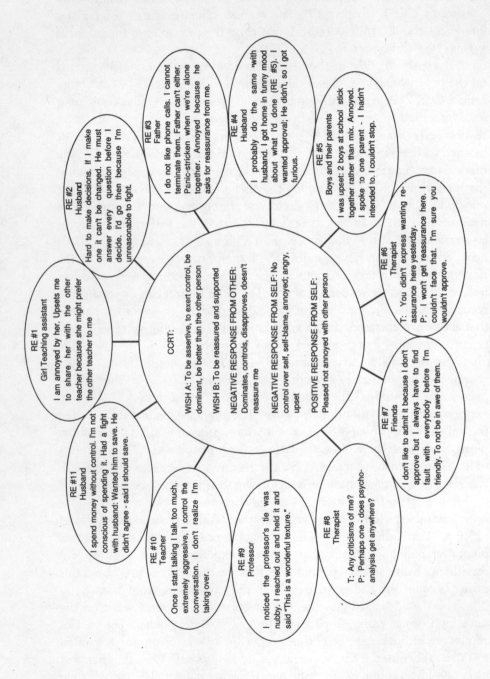

FIGURE 12.1

Relationship episodes and CCRT for specimen session 5.

ham begins to yield to the inclination to express herself assertively (Wish A), she becomes afraid that she will lose control and express herself too aggressively, without restraint. Such uncontrolled expressions are pervasive for her at this stage of treatment, with examples as reported in her REs: with the professor when she reached out to feel his tie (RE 9), with the teacher when she dominated the conversation (RE 10), and with her husband when she tried to control *his* spending but not her own (RE 11). But the therapist does not use this information for further interventions related to the transference, even though it probably is related to the patient's experience of the transference. That neglect by the therapist is to be expected and may be justified since an experience of the transference is hardly sufficient justification for an intervention.

This example from Ms. Cunningham's session 5 has illustrated how the principles in the manual guide the therapist's technique. We saw that the therapist was doing essentially what was recommended in the manual for psychoanalytic psychotherapy for expressive techniques: he was listening, understanding, and then deciding which aspects of his understanding should be used for interpretations. In these ways the therapist's understanding and responses followed the clinical principles that became formalized in the CCRT method.

We can also see from this example that the manual does not provide unduly restrictive guidelines for therapists intending to do psychoanalytic psychotherapy. In fact, most therapists who use the manual report being helped to understand the patient and to feel that the guidelines fit each patient. Nor does the manual provide only one set of techniques that are applied in exactly the same way to all patients. For example, for this patient, some of the supportive techniques listed in the manual are not appropriate and were therefore not used. For this patient, who had a high developmental level and was psychologically minded, the expressive techniques were the most appropriate and the most often used.

Clinical and Research Benefits of Manuals

When a promising new method is fashioned it is followed by a rush of research based on the method and a rapid increase in knowledge. Not only our field but many other fields as well show this typical sequence. A crescendo of contributions is continuing to come from the use of psychotherapy manuals.

1. Reliable measures of the degree of adherence to each manual are being developed and used in outcome studies. The use of adherence measures in treatment outcome studies has gradually increased, as shown by Moncher and Prinz (1991), who examined 359 outcome studies and found that 45 percent applied adherence measures. That percentage is undoubtedly continuing to increase.

Only three examples of adherence measures are given here, but each form of psychotherapy has had a parallel development.

Koenigsberg et al. (1985) constructed the thirty-five-item Therapist Verbal Intervention Inventory to assess the supportive and the expressive techniques (e.g., clarification, education, encouragement, advice, sympathy, limit setting, confrontation) used by psychoanalytic psychotherapists in their work with patients diagnosed with borderline personality disorder. The raters assess on a 5-point scale the relative emphasis placed upon a particular technique within the sampling unit, usually a fifteen-minute segment. Acceptable interrater reliabilities have been achieved for the assessment of fourteen therapeutic interventions characteristic of expressive psychotherapy. The tapes used in that study could not be used for assessing the reliability of the supportive items. As expected, the items with the lowest reliability were those addressing the internal world of the patient, the "internal reality," and those focusing on defensive operations.

Measures of adherence to interpersonal psychotherapy also were reliably judgable. For example, Rounsaville, Chevron, and Weissman (1984) used ratings by independent evaluators to verify that the therapist performed the treatment in accordance with the interpersonal psychotherapy manual. They found the evaluation ratings had good agreement (.71 to .87).

Svartberg (1989) developed the short-term anxiety provoking psychotherapy (STAPP) Therapist Competence Rating Form (STCRF) to assess therapists' competence in applying STAPP techniques. The scale refers to eleven techniques specific to STAPP; each of the eleven items, if applicable, is rated on a 3-point scale. Entire sessions are rated for competence in the presence and frequency of strategies and the skillfulness with which they are implemented. Thirty-one sessions from eight neurotic patients treated by five experienced therapists were rated. Reliability, as measured by internal consistency of the STCRF, was acceptable: alpha coefficients of .61 (rater 1), .82 (rater 2), and .71 (pooled). Similarly, the median item—mean STCRF score correlations were for rater 1, $r = .31$ ($p = .08$), for rater 2, $r = .61$ ($p < .001$), for pooled judges, $r = .50$ ($p < .001$).

2. *Different psychotherapies are found to be readily distinguished.* It was not known until the use of manuals how well clinicians could recognize and distinguish samples of different forms of psychotherapy. It had been expected by some, starting with Rosenzweig (1936), that psychotherapies would have strong common features so that differences among them might be hard to recognize. But the manuals' technology enabled clear discon-

firmation of this expectation. In one study (Luborsky et al. 1982), for example, the degree of distinctiveness among three psychotherapies was examined: dynamic (SE), cognitive-behavioral (CB), and drug counseling (DC) (described in Woody et al. 1983). In fifteen-minute samples of sessions, one judge was 65 percent accurate and another judge was 81 percent accurate (where 33 percent accuracy would be expected by chance). Still another judge who merely scored three therapist speech factors—percent nondirective statements, percent clarifying statements, percent questions—was able to correctly classify the types of sessions almost perfectly. In addition, some of the basic techniques of the treatment were rated distinctively, as they should have been according to the manual. For example, "finding cognitive distortions" and "directiveness," were distinctive for cognitive-behavioral therapy; "understanding feelings and basic transference relationships" were significantly more evident in the supportive-expressive psychotherapy; and "monitoring current problems" was more evident in drug counseling.

An informative similarity among the three treatments also appeared in the frequency of "giving support." Although "giving support" is described in the supportive-expressive manual as a necessary facet of the treatment, it is not presented in the cognitive-behavioral manual. Regardless of this difference in manuals, the three treatments were virtually identical in providing a middle range of degree of support; the three treatments were judged not to differ significantly in this characteristic.

DeRubeis et al. (1982) also showed that independent judges could distinguish cognitive therapy and interpersonal therapy. Two more recent studies, by Hollon et al. (1988) and Hill, Grady, and Elkin (1992), are large-scale studies that provide a fine-grained examination of reliability and that discriminate between treatments achieved by the adherence measures. In the Hollon study the reliabilities of the Collaborative Study Psychotherapy Rating Scale ranged from adequate to strong and the discrimination between the treatments was particularly powerful.

The Hill, Grady, and Elkin (1992) study replicated the Hollon results. They showed that: (1) treatments could be discriminated; (2) similar reliabilities were found with a new set of raters; and (3) therapists adhered to their therapy's treatment manuals rather than to other treatment manuals.

3. *Therapists differ in degree of adherence to each manual's recommendations.* The VA-Penn research (Luborsky et al. 1985) reported differences in adherence to manuals for dynamic therapy, cognitive therapy, and drug counseling for each of nine therapists, three for each treatment. Each of the therapists treated four to six patients. To examine conformity we developed a score called purity. Purity was defined as the ratio of the use of techniques from the intended treatment manual divided by the use of the

intended techniques plus the techniques from other manuals. The ratio scores for purity differed considerably from therapist to therapist, ranging from high adherence (therapist 1 with a ratio of 1.00), to low adherence (therapist 6 with a ratio of .49).

4. *Therapists generally find the manuals helpful.* Therapists find the manual useful after they have applied it in practice. A kind of user satisfaction survey has appeared for the four best-known manuals. Rosengard (1991) has compared the manuals listed at the outset of this paper (except Kernberg et al. 1989). Twenty-four users filled out a questionnaire about these four manuals; the majority believed that all four manuals were well structured and would be highly useful in the training of therapists.

5. *Adherence is variably associated with the outcome of the treatment in different studies.*

VA-Penn studies: During the examination of differences in adherence with the purity measure it was noticed for the first time that purity and outcome were related (Luborsky et al. 1985). As will be shown in table 12.1, the purity score was significantly correlated with various outcome measures at the end of treatment. These correlations were based on taking the three treatments together. For the treatments separately, the correlations were larger for the supportive-expressive psychotherapy than for the cognitive-behavioral psychotherapy and the drug counseling.

At this point, we decided to see whether the association of purity and outcome was also evident *within* each therapist's caseload. We set this analysis up as a 3 × 3 table in which the cases in each therapist's caseload were divided into three purity levels, and these were broken against the three outcome levels. The chi-square was highly significant ($p < .001$). This analysis certainly strengthens the group finding, for it indicates that the trend exists even within each therapist's caseload.

TDCRP study: Since this first observation the psychotherapy research field has actively taken up the question of the relationship of adherence to outcome. Elkin (1988) has examined the data from the giant Treatment of Depression Collaborative Research Program (TDCRP); but the team did not find a significant correlation between adherence and outcome (table 12.2) in the psychotherapy and placebo conditions. With imipramine, greater adherence was related to *less* improvement. Elkin (1988) suggested that Luborsky et al.'s ratings might have included more of a competence component than the ratings in her study. Another possibility could be that Elkin's therapists showed greater adherence. But if we could somehow take together the significant results of the Penn Study and the nonsignificant results of the depression collaborative study, we would have something like the Spanish recipe for horse and canary pie: mix one horse and one canary. As Jacob Cohen (in Luborsky et al. 1971) emphasizes, studies with

TABLE 12.1 *Correlations between Ratings of Adherence to Therapy Qualities and Seven-Month Outcomes: VA-Penn Study*

Therapy Qualities	Drug Use	Outcomes	
		Psychiatric Severity	Beck Depression
SE Qualities N = 14	.44*	.46*	.37*
CB Qualities N = 15	.12	.29†	.29†
DC Qualities N = 12	.18	−.10	.04
Purity	.47**	.42**	.38**

Note: SE = supportive-expressive therapy; CB = cognitive-behavioral therapy; DC = drug counseling.
*$p < .05$ level or better
**$p < .01$ level or better
†$p < .10$ level or better

TABLE 12.2 *Studies of Adherence in Relation to Therapy Outcome*

Studies	Adherence Scale	Relation to Outcome
VA-Penn: SE therapy (Luborsky et al. 1985)	Purity measure 4-item scale N = 14	.42 ($p <$) $p < .001$ within therapist's caseload (χ^2)
VA-Penn: CB therapy (Luborsky et al. 1985)	Purity measure 4-item scale N = 15	.69 legal .66 SCL
TDCRP: CB & IPT (Elkin 1988)	Purity measure N = 193	.10 n.s. HRSD .08 n.s. HSCL-90
Penn: Cognitive therapy (DeRubeis & Feely 1990)	Session 2 N = 25	.53 concrete factor n.s. abstract factor
Vanderbilt: TLDP (Butler et al. 1991) (Henry et al. 1992)	Vanderbilt Therapeutic Strategies Scale	n.s.
Yale: Interpersonal therapy (O'Malley et al. 1988)	supervisor's rating of skill Session #4	.56
Yale: (Rounsaville et al. 1981)	Psychotherapist's Treatment Schedule Form, percent times using a technique	n.s.
Short-term anxiety-provoking (STAPP) (Svartberg 1989)	11-item scale therapeutic strategies; STAPP Therapist Competence Rating Form N = 13	− .55 with change in SCL − 90 ($p < .06$)
STDP & BAP (Winston et al. 1987)	Fidelity Scale	n.s.
Cognitive & dynamic Gaston (in press)	Therapeutic strategies 17 item scale N = 6 N = 10	CT: greater on problematic reactions DT: less on exploration with improved patients

significant results are to be weighted more heavily than those with nonsignificant results because there are fewer reasons for significant results than for nonsignificant results.

Cognitive therapy study (DeRubeis and Feeley 1990): Four tapes were rated, one each from each quadrant of therapy for each of twenty-five depressed patients. The use of concrete cognitive therapy techniques at session 2 predicted subsequent change in depression ($r = .53$), providing evidence that therapists' adherence to the basic techniques of cognitive therapy (concrete factor) is associated with subsequent improvement in depression. In explanation of the significant correlation, it may be relevant that most therapists used in this study were in training; therefore the sample contains a wider range of adherence than that used by Elkin (1988).

TDLP Vanderbilt study: The adherence measure in this unpublished study (Henry et al. 1992; Butler et al. 1991) was not significantly related to outcome.

IPT study: O'Malley et al. (1988) found with thirty-five patients from the TDCRP training phase that the supervisor's ratings of overall therapist skill and therapist's self-ratings of effectiveness were correlated with patient's ratings of change and total termination scores on the Hamilton rating scale for depression and the Social Adjustment Scale (.56 with supervisor's ratings of skill). Thus, it is especially informative to note that supervisor's ratings of the quality of applying interpersonal therapy techniques are especially predictive. This observation leads to the possibility that the quality of therapists' interventions, not just therapists' adherence to the manual, might be critical for the prediction of outcome.

IPT study: Some aspects of interpersonal therapy are associated with outcome (Rounsaville et al. 1981). For example, the more time the therapists think they spent on exploratory techniques, the worse the outcome; the more time spent on decision analysis and advice, the better the outcome. In contrast, the use of reflective techniques (clarification, insight development, and encouraging affect) did not predict outcome. However, this is not a true adherence study; it is a correlational study of certain techniques with outcomes.

Short-term anxiety-provoking therapy study: Svartberg (1989) developed an eleven-item competence measure for the twenty sessions of Sifneos's STAPP. Svartberg and Stiles (1992) found that competence was *inversely* related to the patient's improvement. Furthermore, they showed that in this small sample alliance and competence did not interact in causing change; on the contrary, they seemed to play independent roles. However, this scale, unlike the others, measures not adherence but competence.

STDP and BAP study: Two forms of brief psychotherapy, short-term dynamic psychotherapy (STDP) and brief adaptation-oriented psychotherapy (BAP), were examined by fidelity scales (Winston et al. 1987). There was no significant correlation between fidelity and outcome.

It is a good general observation about our field, and many others, that it is necessary to replicate and rereplicate until there are enough studies to discern a trend. In table 12.2 the results of ten studies are summarized. Four studies showed positive significant correlations and the rest were nonsignificant. At this point it is difficult to see the basis for significant versus nonsignificant results. One factor that may be influential in explaining these differences is the degree to which each adherence measure taps competence as well as adherence. The original Penn adherence scale ("purity measure") may have reflected competence as well as adherence. The treatment of Depression Collaborative Research Program Scale (CSPRS) was probably more restricted to adherence. The new version of the Penn Adherence Scale (Barber et al. 1992) has a way to examine the matter: it includes separate rating scales for every item both for adherence and for quality of therapeutic technique. Waltz et al. (in press) offer an encompassing framework of options for the assessment of adherence and competence. They recommend assessing both adherence and competence, a combination that few studies include.

Positive significant correlations between adherence and outcome can be understood in either direction of causality. It could be that the "good behavior" of the therapist in terms of conformity to the manual provides rewards for virtue in terms of better outcomes for the patient. Or it could be that when the patient is progressing well the therapist can show a greater capacity and freedom to behave in accordance with what is recommended in the manual. Some of the supervisors who have trained therapists in the use of the manual believe that the causal direction in the correlation is to be interpreted mainly but not entirely in the former way. The therapists who adhered to the manual were the ones who had the capacity to carry out the therapy in the recommended style, while the therapists who did not adhere were less able to do this and, in that sense, were less competent.

Future Research with Psychotherapy Manuals

The research on adherence to the manuals that has just been described needs to be expanded:

1. There is a need for further investigations of treatment differences in adherence. Manuals were developed in part to define psychotherapies more precisely. Systematic comparisons of psychotherapies will enable us to gain much better understanding of the differences among therapies.

2. The field needs more precise measurement tools of the degree to which each therapist provided the patient with what was recommended in the manual. Differences in adherence among therapists have already enlightened us, but much more has to be understood about such observations.

3. We need research to determine to what degree treatments that are guided by manuals are carried out more precisely and with greater conformity than treatments that are not guided by manuals.

4. More studies are needed on the relation of the therapist's adherence to treatment outcomes. As our review has shown, the studies vary: some show a high relationship and others find no association. The differences in results are not easy to figure out. The variation does not seem to be related to the type of treatment, but might be related to the degree to which adherence measures assess slavish adherence or skillful adherence. We may learn whether this distinction makes a difference through a study in progress (Barber et al. 1992), where the judges rate these dimensions separately.

5. To learn more about why adherence is sometimes associated with greater benefits to the patient, an analysis of the components of a manual for which adherence has been highly associated with benefits may be informative.

6. Another obvious need is to continue to study the process of learning to perform manual-guided psychotherapy, which is reviewed in chapter 11. Manuals can serve as helpful tools in facilitating such studies. Because manuals specify the techniques of a psychotherapy, they can be used for training psychotherapists both for clinical practice and for participation in psychotherapy research studies.

7. It will be important to learn whether manual-guided treatments, when adhered to, really offer more benefits to their patients than other treatments. The typical nonsignificant difference effect found in comparisons of different forms of psychotherapy (Luborsky, Singer, and Luborsky 1975; chapter 24) had been conjectured to result from the lack of use of manuals; most psychotherapies' techniques are broad, indistinct, and significantly overlapping. We can discover whether manual-guided treatments overlap less and whether they do differ significantly in the benefits they provide patients. Perhaps aided by the guidance of manuals, the mystery of the nonsignificant difference effect among psychotherapies may begin to reveal some of its secrets.

8. More needs to be learned about whether in some cases manuals can hinder the therapist. In our opinion, the question usually arises only before manuals are tried. Many years' experience with the use of the SE dynamic manual strongly suggests the contrary: manuals are generally helpful and do not restrict the therapist's exercise of skill. One of the reasons it took so long to develop psychotherapy manuals, as opposed to

behavioral therapy manuals, was that it was difficult to specify the techniques a psychotherapist should use. The SE dynamic manual, for example, offers certain broad principles and therefore may not be of enough help in specific situations in psychotherapy. An illustrative *inapplicable* cartoon might be drawn showing a patient and therapist sitting in front of a manual displayed on a music stand, just as musicians do in following the score of a musical piece. But that cartoon would only be shown for its humorous contrast with what is actually done in the use of a psychotherapy manual—the therapist draws on a remembrance of the manual's main guidelines as they are helpful in dealing with the challenges of the unfolding session.

References

BARBER, J. P., CRITS-CHRISTOPH, P., LUBORSKY, L., CRITS-CHRISTOPH, K., & SMAILIS, J. (1992, JUNE). *Initial data on the development of an adherence scale for supportive-expressive dynamic psychotherapy.* Presented at the annual meeting of the Society for Psychotherapy Research, Berkeley, CA.

BECK, A. T., RUSH, J. A., SHAW, B. F., & EMERY, G. (1979). *Cognitive therapy of depression.* New York: Guilford Press.

BUTLER, S., HENRY, W., STRUPP, H., & LANE, T. (1991). Measuring adherence and skill in time-limited dynamic psychotherapy. Submitted.

DeRUBEIS, R., & FEELEY, M. (1990). Determinants of change in cognitive therapy for depression. *Cognitive Therapy and Research, 14,* 469–482.

DeRUBEIS, R., HOLLON, S., EVANS, M., & BEMIS, K. (1982). Can psychotherapies for depression be discriminated? A systematic investigation of cognitive therapy and interpersonal therapy. *Journal of Consulting and Clinical Psychology, 50,* 744–756.

ELKIN, I. (1988, JUNE). *Relationship of therapist's adherence to treatment outcome in the NIMH Treatment of Depression Collaborative Research Programs.* Paper presented at the annual meeting of the Society for Psychotherapy Research, Sante Fe, NM.

FREUD, S. (1911/1958). The handling of dream-interpretation in psychoanalysis. In J. Strachey (Ed.), *The standard edition of the complete psychological works of Sigmund Freud* (Vol. 12, pp. 89–96). London: Hogarth Press.

FREUD, S. (1912a/1958). The dynamics of transference. In J. Strachey (Ed.), *The standard edition of the complete psychological works of Sigmund Freud* (Vol. 12, pp. 97–108). London: Hogarth Press.

FREUD, S. (1912b/1958). Recommendations to physicians practicing psychoanalysis. In J. Strachey (Ed.), *The standard edition of the complete psychological works of Sigmund Freud* (Vol. 12, pp. 109–120). London: Hogarth Press.

FREUD, S. (1913/1958). On beginning the treatment: Further recommendations in the technique of psychoanalysis. In J. Strachey (Ed.), *The standard edition of the complete psychological works of Sigmund Freud* (Vol. 12, pp. 121–144). London: Hogarth Press.

FREUD, S. (1914/1958). Remembering, repeating and working through: Further recommendations on the technique of psychoanalysis. In J. Strachey (Ed.), *The standard edition of the complete psychological works of Sigmund Freud* (Vol. 12, pp. 147–156). London: Hogarth Press.

FREUD, S. (1915/1958). Observation on transference-love: Further recommendations on the technique of psychoanalysis. In J. Strachey (Ed.), *The standard edition of the complete psychological works of Sigmund Freud* (Vol. 12, pp. 157–171). London: Hogarth Press.

HENRY, W., STRUPP, H., SCHACHT, T., BINDER, J., & BUTLER, S. (1992). *Effects of training in time-limited dynamic therapy: 4. Changes in therapeutic outcome* Unpublished manuscript, Vanderbilt University, Nashville, TN.

HILL, C., O'GRADY, K., & ELKIN, I. (1992). Applying the Collaborative Study Psychotherapy Rating Scale to rate therapist adherence to cognitive-behavioral therapy, interpersonal therapy and clinical management. *Journal of Consulting and Clinical Psychology, 60,* 73–79.

HILL, C., O'GRADY, K., & PRICE, P. (1988). A method for investigating sources of rater bias. *Journal of Counseling Psychology, 35,* 346–350.

HOLLON, S., EVANS, M. D., AUERBACH, A., DeRUBEIS, R., ELKIN, I., LOWERY, A., KRISS, M., GROVE, N. M., TUASON, V. B., & PIASECKI, J. (1988). Development of a system for rating therapies for depression: Differentiating cognitive therapy, interpersonal psychotherapy, and clinical management pharmaco-therapy. Unpublished manuscript.

KERNBERG, O., SELZER, M., KOENIGSBERG, H., CARR, A., & APPELBAUM, A. (1989). *The treatment of borderline patients.* New York: Basic Books.

KLERMAN, G., & NEU, C. (1976). *A manual for interpersonal treatment of depression.* Unpublished manuscript. New Haven: Yale University.

KLERMAN, G., WEISSMAN, M., ROUNSAVILLE, B., & CHEVRON, E. (1984). *Interpersonal psychotherapy of depression.* New York: Guilford Press.

KOENIGSBERG, H. W., KERNBERG, O., HAAS, G., LOTTERMAN, A., ROCKLAND, L., & SELZER, M. (1985). Development of a scale for measuring techiques in the psychotherapy of borderline patients. *Journal of Nervous and Mental Disease, 173,* 424–431.

LUBORSKY, L. (1984). *Principles of psychoanalytic psychotherapy: A manual for supportive-expressive treatment.* New York: Basic Books.

LUBORSKY, L., CHANDLER, M., AUERBACH, A. H., COHEN, J., & BACHRACH, H. M. (1971). Factors influencing the outcome of psychotherapy: A review of quantitative research. *Psychological Bulletin, 75,* 145–185.

LUBORSKY, L., & CRITS-CHRISTOPH, P. (1990). *Understanding transference: The CCRT method.* New York: Basic Books.

LUBORSKY, L., CRITS-CHRISTOPH, P., McLELLAN, T., WOODY, G., PIPER, W., IMBER, S., & LIBERMAN, B. (1986) Do therapists vary much in their sucess? Findings from four outcome studies. *American Journal of Orthopsychiatry 56,* 501–512.

LUBORSKY, L., McLELLAN, A. T., WOODY, G. E., O'BRIEN, C. P., & AUERBACH, A. (1985). Therapist success and its determinants. *Archives of General Psychiatry, 42,* 602–611.

LUBORSKY, L., SINGER, B., & LUBORSKY, L. (1975). Comparative studies of psychotherapies: Is it true that "everybody has won and all must have prizes"? *Archives of General Psychiatry, 32,* 995–1008.

LUBORSKY, L., WOODY, G. E., McLELLAN, A. T., O'BRIEN, C. P., & ROSENZWEIG, J. (1982). Can independent judges recognize different psychotherapies? An experience with manual-guided therapies. *Journal of Consulting and Clinical Psychology, 50,* 49–62.

MONCHER, F., & PRINZ, R. (1991). Treatment fidelity in outcome studies. *Clinical Psychology Review, 11,* 247–266.

O'MALLEY, S., FOLEY, S., & ROUNSAVILLE, B., (1988). Therapist competence and patient outcome in interpersonal psychotherapy of depression. *Journal of Consulting and Clinical Psychology, 56,* 496–501.

ROSENGARD, P. (1991). *A comparative analysis of four psychotherapy manuals and a proposed model for psychotherapy manuals.* Frankfurt: Lang.

ROSENZWEIG, S. (1936). Some implicit common factors in diverse methods of psychotherapy. *American Journal of Orthopsychotherapy, 6,* 412–415.

ROUNSAVILLE, B. (IN PRESS). Training therapists to perform interpersonal psychotherapy in clinical trials.

ROUNSAVILLE, B., CHEVRON, E., & WEISSMAN, M. (1984). Specification of techniques in interpersonal psychotherapy. In R. Spitzer & J. Williams (Eds.), *Psychotherapy research: Where are we and where should we go?* New York: Guilford Press.

ROUNSAVILLE, B., WEISSMAN, M., & PRUSOFF, B. (1981). Psychotherapy with depressed outpatients: Patient and process variables as predictors of outcome. *British Journal of Psychiatry, 135,* 67–74.

STRUPP, H., & BINDER, J. (1984). *Psychotherapy in a new key: A guide to time-limited dynamic psychotherapy.* New York: Basic Books.

SVARTBERG, M. (1989). Manualization and competence monitoring of STAPP. *Psychotherapy, 26,* 564–571.

SVARTBERG, M., & STILES, T. C. (1992, JUNE). *The relations of therapeutic alliance and therapist competence to client change in short-term anxiety provoking psychotherapy: A pilot study.* Paper presented at the meeting of the Society for Psychotherapy Research, Berkeley, CA.

WALTZ, J., ADDIS, M., KOERNER, K., & JACOBSON, M. (IN PRESS). Testing the integrity of a psychotherapy protocol: Assessment of adherence and competence. *Journal of Consulting and Clinical Psychology.*

WEISMAN, M., PAYKEL, E., & PRUSOFF, B. (1972). Checklist quantification of a psychological therapy: Pilot studies of utility. *Journal of Nervous and Mental Disease, 154,* 125–136.

WINSTON, A., FLEGENHEIMER, W., POLLACK, J., LAIKIN, M., KESTENBAUM, R., & McCULLOUGH, L. A brief psychotherapy fidelity scale—reliability, validity and relation to outcome. Abstracts from the Society for Psychotherapy Research 18th Annual Meeting, June 16–20, 1987, Ulm, West Germany.

WOODY, G., LUBORSKY, L., McLELLAN, A. T., O'BRIEN, C., BECK, A. T., BLAINE, J., HERMAN, I., & HOLE, A. V. (1983). Psychotherapy for opiate addicts: Does it help? *Archives of General Psychiatry, 40,* 639–645.

CHAPTER 13

Developing a Disorder-Specific Manual: The Treatment of Borderline Character Disorder

---

OTTO F. KERNBERG AND JOHN F. CLARKIN

THROUGHOUT OUR CLINICAL RESEARCH effort, we have aimed to develop a specific (psychodynamic) treatment adapted to the particular needs of the borderline patient.[1] Although our conception of the borderline patient is more extensive, it overlaps with that of DSM-III and DSM-IIIR. Borderline personality organization (BPO) can be distinguished from neurotic and psychotic levels of organization by the three structures of identity versus identity diffusion, primitive versus more mature defenses, and reality testing. Since the three structural variables are difficult to operationalize, our treatment efforts focus on the narrower group of patients designated in DSM-III and DSM-IIIR as borderline personality disorder (BPD). Patients with this constellation of behaviors can be reliably assessed with semistructured interviews. Since BPO is a broader concept, we assume that BPD patients are also characterized by BPO, but not vice versa.

The Treatment

THEORY OF THE PATHOLOGY OF BORDERLINE PATIENTS

Any treatment specified for a particular patient population must articulate the congruence between the unique patient pathology and the

---

[1] In addition to the present authors, the research team includes A. Appelbaum, S. Bauer, L. Gornick, P. Kernberg, H. Koenigsberg, L. Rockland, M. Selzer, T. Smith, and F. Yeomans.

treatment parameters (format of treatment, strategies and techniques, focus of the sessions, and the like). Thus we will begin by describing a model or formulation of borderline pathology, from which will flow the conceptualization of the treatment.

In our view, borderline personality organization constitutes a broad spectrum of character pathology or personality disorders which have in common a lack of integration of the concept of self and of the concept of significant others, that is, the syndrome of identity diffusion. This syndrome is characterized by chronic difficulties in assessing in an integrated way one's own motivations, behavior, and interpersonal interactions, and, by the same token, the motivation and integrated aspects of those others who are centrally significant in one's life. Identity diffusion underlies the chronic interpersonal difficulties of patients with borderline personality organization, their chaotic interactions in intimate relationships, and their failure in empathy and accurate assessment of their own and others' intentions and actions. Identity diffusion differentiates patients with borderline personality organization—who constitute the most severe spectrum of personality disorders—from patients with neurotic personality organization, that is, less severe character pathology or personality disorders. The latter have an integrated sense of self and the capacity for integrated conceptions of significant others, that is, they have normal identity formation.

A second major characteristic of borderline personality organization is the dominance of primitive defensive mechanisms, especially the mechanism of splitting. Primitive defensive mechanisms have in common a way of dealing with unconscious intrapsychic conflict by the mutual dissociation of contradictory aspects or motivations involved in such intrapsychic conflicts; there is a corresponding tendency toward oscillations between contradictory ego states respectively characterized by idealized "all good" and persecutory "all bad" experiences of self and others. These primitive defensive mechanisms (splitting, projective identification, omnipotence, omnipotent control, primitive idealization, devaluation, and denial) also involve behavioral components that tend to induce serious chaos and confusion in interpersonal relations. Clinically these defense mechanisms are reflected in the apparent unpredictability, impulsivity, manipulativeness, blaming tendencies, arrogance, and helplessness typical of borderline patients, and, above all, in the lack of impulse control and of modulation of primitive affects, particularly anxiety, depression, and rage.

A third characteristic of patients with borderline personality organization is their maintenance of the capacity for reality testing, that is, the capacity for differentiating, when confronted with their behaviors, intrapsychic from external origins of stimuli, for differentiating self from others, and for maintaining empathy with ordinary social criteria of reality. Reality testing differentiates borderline personality organization from psychotic disorders, including atypical psychotic conditions that may look like personality disorders.

Our view of the etiology of these psychostructural characteristics of borderline personality organization dovetail with Margaret Mahler's (Mahler, Pine, and Bergman 1975) conception that early stages of psychosocial development predate the integration of the concepts of the self and of significant others, that is, the stage of object constancy.

THEORY OF PSYCHODYNAMIC TREATMENT

On the basis of these formulations we have constructed a theory of psychodynamic treatment that derives from the theory of psychoanalytic technique. Our treatment modifies this technique in the light of a general strategy geared to the resolution of the specific disturbances of borderline patients. The basic objective of this psychodynamic psychotherapy is the diagnosis and psychotherapeutic resolution of the syndrome of identity diffusion, and, in the process, (1) the resolution of primitive defensive operations characteristic of these patients and (2) the resolution of their primitive internalized "part object" relationships into "total" object relationships characteristic of more advanced neurotic and normal functioning.

Primitive internalized object relations are constituted by part self representations relating to part object representations in the context of a primitive, all good or all bad, affect state. They are part object relations precisely because the representation of self and the representation of object have been split into an idealized and a persecutory component—in contrast to the normal integration of good or loving with bad or hateful representations of self and significant others. These primitive or part object relations emerge in the treatment situation in the form of primitive transferences characterized by the activation of such self and object representations and their corresponding affects as a transference "unit" enacted defensively against an opposite primitive transference unit under completely opposite affect valence or dominance.

STRATEGIES OF THE TREATMENT

In essence, the psychotherapeutic strategy in the psychodynamic treatment of borderline patients consists of a three-step procedure. *Step 1* is the diagnosis of an emerging primitive part object relationship in the transference, and the interpretive analysis of the dominant unconscious fantasy structure that corresponds to this particular transference activation. For example, the therapist may point out to the patient that their momentary relationship resembles that of a sadistic prison guard and a paralyzed, frightened victim.

Step 2 of this strategy is to identify the self and the object representation of this particular primitive transference, and the typically oscillating or alternating attribution of self and object representation by the patient to himself or herself and to the therapist. For example, the therapist may point out, in expanding the previous intervention, that it is as if the patient felt like a frightened, paralyzed victim, while attributing to the therapist the behavior of a sadistic prison guard. Later on, in the same session, the therapist may point out to the patient that by now, the situation has become reversed in that the patient behaves like a sadistic prison guard while the therapist has been placed in the role of the frightened victim.

Step 3 of this interpretive intervention would be delineating the linkage between the particular object relationship activated in the transference and an entirely opposite one activated at other times but constituting the split off idealized counterpart to this particular persecutory object relationship. For example, if at other times the patient has experienced the therapist as a perfect, all giving mother, while the patient's experience of self is as a satisfied, happy, loved baby who is the exclusive objective of mother's attention, the therapist might point out that the persecutory prison guard is really a bad, frustrating, teasing, and rejecting mother. At the same time, the victim is an enraged baby who wants to take revenge but is afraid of being destroyed because of the projection of his or her own rage onto mother. The therapist might add that this terrible mother–infant relationship is kept completely separate from the idealized relationship out of the fear of contaminating the idealized one with the persecutory one, and out of the fear of the destruction of all hope that, in spite of the rageful, vengeful attacks on the bad mother the relationship with the ideal mother might be recovered.

The successful integration of mutually dissociated or split off, all good and all bad, primitive object relations in the transference includes the integration not only of the corresponding self and object representations, but also of primitive affects. The integration of intense, polarized affects leads, over time, to affect modulation, to an increase in the capacity for affect control, to a heightened capacity for empathy with both self and others, and to a corresponding deepening and maturing of all object relations.

This psychotherapeutic strategy also involves a particular modification of three basic tools derived from standard psychoanalytic technique. First, the strategy involves interpretation—that is, the establishment of hypotheses about unconscious determinants of the patient's behavior—as the major technical tool of the treatment. In contrast to standard psychoanalysis, however, in this treatment interpretation involves mostly the preliminary phases of interpretive interventions, that is, a systematic clarification of the patient's subjective experience, the tactful confrontation of the meanings of those aspects of subjective experience—verbal communication, nonverbal behavior, and total interaction with the therapist—that express further aspects of the transference, and a restriction of the unconscious aspects of interpretation to the unconscious meanings in the here-and-now only. In standard psychoanalysis interpretation centers on unconscious meanings in both the here-and-now and the there-and-then of the unconscious past; in the psychodynamic psychotherapy of borderline patients psychodynamic interpretations of the unconscious past are reserved for relatively advanced stages of the treatment. At these later stages, the integration of primitive transferences has transformed primitive into advanced transferences (more characteristic of neurotic functioning and more closely reflective of actual experiences from the past).

Another difference with standard psychoanalysis is the modification of transference analysis in each session to reflect the therapist's ongoing attention to (1) the long-range treatment goals with a particular patient and (2) the dominant current conflicts in the patient's life outside the sessions. In order that the treatment not gratify excessively the patient's transference—thus undermining the patient's initial motivation and treatment objectives—the therapist has to remain in touch with long-range treatment goals. Also, in order to prevent the splitting off of external reality from the treatment situation—and severe acting out expressed by such dissociation—transference interpretation has to be linked closely to the present realities in the patient's life. In short, then, in contrast to psychoanalysis (where a systematic focus on the transference is a major treatment strategy), in the psychodynamic psychotherapy of borderline patients transference analysis is modified by attention to initial treatment goals and current external reality.

Third, insofar as interpretations require a position of technical neutrality (the therapist's equidistance from the forces in mutual conflict in the patient's mind), that stance is an important aspect of the psychodynamic psychotherapy of borderline patients, as well as of standard psychoanalysis. However, given the severe acting out of borderline patients inside and outside the treatment hours, technical neutrality may have to be limited by unavoidable structuring (limit setting) of the treatment situation, which (at least temporarily) reduces technical neutrality and requires its reinstatement by means of interpretations of the reasons for which the therapist moved away from the position.

The therapeutic strategy determines a set of tactical considerations regarding the interventions in each treatment hour. The particular coloring given to this psychotherapy by the tactics differentiates it both from standard psychoanalysis and from supportive psychotherapy. In contrast to supportive psychotherapy, the therapist refrains, as much as possible, from technical interventions such as affective and cognitive support, guidance and advice giving, direct environmental intervention, and any other technical maneuver that would reduce technical neutrality—with the exception of necessary structuring or limit setting within or outside of the treatment hours. In supportive psychotherapy, transference interpretations are not used for enhancing the therapeutic alliance, ensuring patient compliance, or resolving symptoms. In contrast, in psychodynamic treatment both positive and negative transferences are interpreted (with the exception of milder aspects of the positive transference, which may be left untouched, particularly in early stages of the treatment, in order to foster the therapeutic alliance). Our treatment approach includes a systematic effort to interpret primitive idealizations of the therapist because of their counterpart to dissociated primitive negative transferences.

In each session, it is important to assess the patient's capacity to differentiate fantasy from reality and to interpret unconscious meanings only after the confirmation of the patient's and therapist's shared views of reality. This confirmation may require the consistent and tactful confrontation of the patient with immediate reality. The patient's attribution of fantastic meanings to the therapist's interpretive interventions also needs to be clarified and interpreted. It is important to assess the secondary gain of severe symptoms and behaviors, to interpret such secondary gain, and, if necessary, to reduce or eliminate the secondary gain by limit setting—which goes along with the assessment and interpretation of any slippage of technical neutrality. The analysis of unconscious sexual conflicts must include the analysis of contamination of sexuality with aggression in order to help the patient free sexual behavior from control by aggressive impulses.

Another crucial aspect of tactical interventions is the need to interpret primitive defenses systematically as they emerge in each hour. In contrast to earlier writers, we believe that primitive defenses do not "strengthen" the frail ego of the borderline patient but are the very cause of chronic ego weakness. Interpretation of primitive defenses is a major tool for increasing ego strength and reality testing and facilitates the interpretation of primitive transferences.

Given the severe tendencies toward acting out on the part of borderline patients, dangerous complications in their treatment may derive from their characterologically based, "nondepressive" suicide attempts, drug abuse, self-mutilating and other self-destructive behaviors, and aggressive behaviors that may be life-threatening to themselves and others. An important aspect of each session—and not just a part of the overall structuring of the treatment—is the assessment of whether there are emergency situations that require immediate intervention. On the basis of our general treatment strategy and experience in the treatment of severely ill borderline patients, we have constructed the following set of priorities of inter-

of our trainees doing the treatment. These tapes can be used both for observing and identifying with competent peers and for illustrating faulty therapeutic interventions.

In addition, one needs ongoing supervision to treat borderline patients. We have not standardized the supervision but rather have encouraged different supervisors to use their creativity in fostering the growth of the trainees. Supervisors are encouraged to review the audiotapes of the therapy sessions either with the trainees or prior to supervision sessions. Supervisors do meet regularly with each other to share experiences and to make sure the basics are in place. In addition, supervisor-therapist pairs are provided with feedback from the clinical researchers who rate the therapists for adherence to the manual. We have the impression that the rating scales and audiotapes have made the supervisors more aware of the details of the treatment.

RATING ADHERENCE TO TREATMENT

To assess the reliable delivery of the manualized dynamic therapy, we developed two scales. One scale assesses the negotiation of the treatment contract early in the work with the BPD patient, a process that is an adaptation to the particular pathology of BPD. The other is a general scale for the assessment of degree of adherence to themes and strategies or techniques throughout the treatment.

Rating of Contract Setting.

The severity of self-destructive symptoms (such as chronic suicidal behavior, chronic self-mutilating behavior, drug or alcohol abuse, eating disorders), secondary gain of treatment, or severe antisocial behavior may threaten the psychodynamic psychotherapy from the very beginning. Accordingly, we have developed a method of contract setting that includes an assessment of major difficulties which could militate against a stable treatment situation, and which could foster premature dropout or force the therapist away from a position of technical neutrality and into a more supportive modality of treatment.

The assessment of which behaviors are under the patient's control and which behaviors are not, and the determination of what may be realistically expected from the patient, and what not, are important tasks in the early sessions of psychotherapy. The thoughtful review and integration of these data are directly reflected in the therapist's decisions regarding the minimum conditions under which he or she feels it will be possible to treat the patient. In the course of this process, the therapist must identify potential obstacles that may require a firm commitment by the patient before the psychotherapy may proceed.

Clinical experiences (which still remain to be tested empirically) indicate that the more careful and systematic the contract setting, the lower the risk of premature dropout. Therapists differ in their efforts to state the treatment contract and to negotiate the contract with the patient around the fifth or sixth session, as specified by the manual. While the process seemed rather simple as described in the seminar, it was much more difficult when the therapist was in the room with a borderline patient.

We therefore assessed the ability of the therapist to articulate various aspects of contract setting, hoping to improve supervision and teaching of this procedure. We devised a scale to evaluate the contract session, incorporating a rating of the therapist's statement of his or her responsibilities, the therapist's statement of the patient's responsibility in the treatment, and the negotiation of mutual expectations. This scale has yielded adequate interrater reliability (intraclass correlation coefficients from .74 to .92). The therapist's comments regarding how the patient might sabotage the treatment, based upon prior behavior in other treatments, are also rated. Agreement about changing those behaviors in treatment is addressed. Preliminary data suggest that the overall quality of the contract setting is related to the patient's remaining in treatment.

Rating of Adherence.

Adherence to the psychodynamic approach was conceptualized to consist of two factors. First is the therapist's use of the core techniques of clarification, confrontation, and interpretation, while maintaining therapeutic neutrality and abstaining from supportive techniques. Second, treatment techniques are to be focused systematically, in a hierarchical fashion, on salient themes presented by the borderline patient. We assume that in following the set of thematic priorities for the therapist's interventions outlined before, the therapist is providing one indication of skillful adherence to this psychodynamic approach. Thus, our rating of adherence involves a measure of the degree to which the therapist uses dynamic techniques as focused on a hierarchy of themes brought by the patient.

Ratings were made on transcripts of entire sessions. A unit for rating was defined as patient material directly preceding the therapist's intervention. For each unit, the rater scored the most prominent patient theme, the nature of the therapist's intervention, and the theme of the patient toward which the therapist focused intervention.

Acceptable reliability figures (kappas ranging from 1.0 to .83) have been achieved for categories of patient's themes such as breach of contract, transference themes, other affect-laden themes, and childhood material.

Kappas for type of therapist intervention ranged from .76 to .60 for informs, clarifies, interprets, and confronts. In assessing adherence, we found that most therapists used the dynamic techniques with salient themes. We were also able to identify therapists who, in certain sessions, were at variance with the manual.

RATING OF THERAPEUTIC ALLIANCE

We are impressed with the ability of various alliance measures to predict continuation in treatment and outcome in dynamic treatment and other forms of treatment. However, we are skeptical of the ability of existing measures of alliance, most developed with patients with neurotic character structure, to be applicable to the borderline patient, who typically is quite angry and disdainful of the therapy in its early stages. At the extreme, we expected borderline patients to rate the alliance as negative, while at the same time coming to each session and fighting with the therapist in an intensely emotional, involved manner. In addition, we hypothesized that the alliance of the borderline patient would be quite variable and fluctuate (even to extremes) not only within sessions but between them.

With such cautions in mind, we have begun to explore the alliance and its measurement. Several self-report methods—the Penn Helping Alliance Scales (Alexander and Luborsky 1986) and the California Psychotherapy Alliance Scales (CALPAS) (Marmar, Weiss, and Gaston, in press)—have been studied. Given the potential discrepancy between what the BPO patients report and how they actually behave, we felt the need for a system of self-reports matched with ratings of actual sessions. This has led us to use the CALPAS, with which sessions with borderline patients can be reliably rated. There appears to be a range of scores for borderline patients; but as a group they manifest poorer alliances than do neurotic patients, as expected.

SCORING THE CCRT OF BORDERLINES

We were interested in the Core Conflictual Relationship Theme (CCRT) concept and methodology (Luborsky 1977). We hypothesized that CCRTs of borderline patients would be more fragmented than those of neurotic patients, and we thought that changes in such themes might give us a measure of patient change.

Preliminary work (Schlefer et al. 1989) indicates that one can isolate and rate CCRTs with patients in psychodynamic treatment. The most prevalent themes manifested involved wishes to avoid conflict and to be close to others; the most frequent expected responses from the other were "rejecting," and "opposes me"; and the most frequent response of self was feeling "angry" and "out of control." These themes seem consistent with borderline pathology as noted in the DSM-IIIR criteria.

Aside from the content of the CCRT themes, most striking to us was the form of their productions: the CCRTs of these patients were characterized by confusion between self and object, between negative and positive impulses, and between wish and action. There were also contradictions between the same components within one relationship episode (RE) and between REs created within the same session. Our impression is that borderline themes and levels of differentiation are different from those of neurotic patients, but a direct comparison of borderline and nonborderline patients in dynamic therapy is needed.

We plan to use the CCRTs as an ancillary change measure for individual borderline patients, and as a focus of attention, or lack of attention, by respective therapists. That is, while our treatment manual does not relate to CCRTs as such and how they are to be addressed, using session transcripts we will investigate how they are used by the therapist who follows our manual. The fact that the CCRTs of borderlines seem to reflect borderline pathology both in content and process would make them a natural focus for intervention, especially when the RE is one involving the therapist personally (transference).

Findings and Problems

While research findings are preliminary, data are available regarding the teaching of the treatment; the measurement of borderline pathology; and the measurement of process variables in the treatment, including adherence to the treatment and the therapeutic alliance. There has been an interactive effect between the articulation of the manual, the teaching of the manual, the beginning performance of the therapists, the ratings of their behavior, and subsequent feedback to them about their relative strengths and weaknesses.

Since our pilot study constituted a one-cell nonrandomized investigation, the differential effectiveness of this approach for the borderline patient cannot yet be assessed. We have been able to estimate the percentage of patients who remain in treatment, and of those, the percentage of patients who show changes in general symptoms, in specific borderline symptoms, and in social or vocational behavior. We have also begun to contrast the treatment course of patients who seemed to profit from the psychodynamic treatment with that of those who did not. Of the patients remaining in treatment, there are some who have made substantial improvement, some who have made slow but important changes, and some who have changed little, if at all. Interesting questions are whether these process projectories could have been predicted and whether treatment gains are maintained over time.

The dropout rate of borderline patients, especially dropouts occurring within the first five to ten sessions, is still a major problem. By twelve weeks of treatment, our dropout rate is 35 percent, which compares favorably with the 48 percent rate reported by Goldberg et al. (1986) in their outpatient medication study and the 67 percent rate reported by Skodol, Buckley, and Charles (1983) in another outpatient study. Our experience suggests that the dropout of BPD patients from treatment should be seen not as one isolated event, but rather as an event embedded within a larger sequence of help-seeking (and -rejecting) episodes. It seems quite understandable that patients characterized by affective instability, impulsivity, and anger would create, and destroy, a series of help-seeking episodes. One might hypothesize that the patients who remained in treatment did so not necessarily because of the nature of the treatment itself but rather through some interaction between the personality qualities of the particular therapist and the patient's current readiness for treatment. For example, one who has remained in the current study had been in a number of prior outpatient treatments and, in fact, had signed out of our inpatient service against medical advice. After six months of struggling without treatment, she took the initiative to return to the hospital and stated that she was ready for treatment. A number of our other patients who dropped out early did not seem ready for treatment in their sequence of help-seeking episodes.

Another serious problem faced by any clinical research team interested in psychodynamic treatment is the difficulty inherent in operationalizing and measuring character change. One of the major aims of the pilot study was to explore ways in which change could be reliably charted in borderline patients across time. We have found instruments that enable us to measure symptomatic change in borderline patients, though one must note that borderlines tend to overestimate their symptom severity (Hurt et al. 1985). In addition, there are instruments one can use to measure the social and occupational functioning of borderline patients. More difficult is measuring the changes in specific borderline behavior—in particular, those behaviors noted in the eight criteria of Axis II. We have begun to approach this problem by an expansion to the SCID-II semistructured interview, and by rating each of the eight criteria on a dimensional scale. When such ratings are assessed in a systematic, sequential manner, scores on the eight criteria over time can be used to evaluate change.

Finally, even if one can measure change in overall symptoms, social and work function, and borderline symptoms, there is still the issue of measuring hypothesized internal structures of the borderline patient. As noted earlier in this chapter, we have begun the development of a self-report instrument to measure the three structures of BPO. One would not depend solely upon a self-report instrument, however, to measure something as subtle and complex as structure and structural change.

We have discussed elsewhere (Hurt and Clarkin 1990) a comparison of the psychodynamic and cognitive/behavioral treatments of borderline patients as articulated in manuals by Kernberg et al. (1989) and Linehan (1983). As opposed to the psychodynamic emphasis on the use of confrontation and interpretation in the evolving transference relationship between patient and therapist, the cognitive/behavioral approach relies on support, education, and the development of alternative coping skills. One area of striking similarity is in the careful articulation and framing of the treatment at the beginning. Both manuals specify that patient and therapist roles be clearly stated, and consequences when the roles are not defined are spelled out. This step seems especially important for the area of self-destructive and suicidal behavior. In both approaches it is carefully noted that the therapist cannot prevent the patient from attempting suicide, and that the therapist's involvement in crises leading up to self-destructive behavior will be limited. There are also interesting similarities in the intensity and length of treatment. Not only the dynamic treatment but also the behavioral approach recognizes the severity of the pathology and recommends intense and long-term treatment.

There remain, of course, significant differences. From our perspective, the psychodynamic approach protects therapeutic neutrality except in specific instances. In contrast, the behavioral approach uses many supportive and directive strategies. It remains to be seen how such differences in treatment might affect the process and outcome on specific subgroups of BPD patients.

Previous writings (Kernberg 1984) would suggest that not all borderline patients are well suited for response to a psychodynamic approach and that some would be better assisted in a supportive approach. The question of which patients, according to what criteria, are most suited for each approach has not been adequately researched. Our impressions are as follows. Patients with overt anger toward the therapist and therapy are especially difficult for beginning therapists (probably, of all therapeutic persuasions) to handle. To absorb the anger, not attack back, and interpret the patient's behavior demand self-control and skill. If the therapist is skilled and an adequate working alliance develops, psychodynamic treatment can proceed. Overtly angry patients may terminate without warning. The therapist must anticipate and actively interpret threats, both overt and subtly implied, to the treatment. Patients who are impulsive and self-destructive (impulse cluster) need immediate, focused attention on those symptoms. While behavioral approaches attend to such behaviors immediately and directly, the psychodynamic approach addresses them through manifestations in the transference. The nature of which impulsive cluster patients can work best in the dynamic treatment mode needs to be more systematically determined. Clinical experience indicates that the severity of antisocial features constitutes a major limiting factor to the effectiveness of psychodynamic psychotherapy for borderline patients; current work is focusing on the relation of outcome to this dimension.

In the recent history of psychotherapy research, there has been an overrepresentation of the investigation of brief treatments that are cognitive and behavioral in orientation. There are probably reasons for this disproportionate representation, grounded in the relative ease in manualizing and teaching brief treatments using strategies that are relatively concrete and well specified. The underrepresentation of long-term treatments of psychodynamic orientation is a tribute to the difficulties in manualizing and teaching this highly complex and sophisticated approach.

It remains to be seen whether we can successfully teach a dynamic approach that calls on a therapist's technical expertise and clinical acumen. As noted earlier in the chapter, we have varied the experience level of our therapists in order to investigate the level of skill and expertise necessary as a prerequisite for learning this approach. The data collected thus far favor more experienced therapists, but some less experienced therapists have learned the therapy adequately.

References

ALEXANDER, L. B., & LUBORSKY, L. (1986). The Penn Helping Alliance Scales. In L. S. Greenberg & W. M. Pinsof (Eds.), *The psychotherapeutic process: A research handbook.* New York: Guilford Press.

GOLDBERG, S. C., SCHULTZ, S. C., SCHULTZ, P. M., RESNICK, R. J., HAMER, R. M., & FRIEDEL, R. L. (1986). Borderline and schizotypal personality disorders treated with low-dose thiothixene versus placebo. *Archives of General Psychiatry, 43,* 680–686.

HURT, S. W., & CLARKIN, J. F. (1990). Borderline personality disorder: Prototypic typology and the development of treatment manuals. *Psychiatric Annals, 20*(1), 1–6.

HURT, S. W., CLARKIN, J. F., FRANCES, A., ABRAMS, R., & HUNT, H. (1985). Discriminate validity of the MMPI for borderline personality disorder. *Journal of Personality Assessment, 49,* 56–61.

HURT, S. W., CLARKIN, J. F., WIDIGER, T., FYER, M., SULLIVAN, T., STONE, M., & FRANCES, A. (1990). Evaluation of DSM-III decision rules for case detection using joint conditional probability structures. *Journal of Personality Disorder, 4,* 121–130.

KERNBERG, O. (1984). *Severe personality disorders: Psychotherapeutic strategies.* New Haven: Yale University Press.

KERNBERG, O., SELZER, M., KOENIGSBERG, H., CARR, A., & APPELBAUM, A. (1989). *Psychodynamic psychotherapy of borderline patients.* New York: Basic Books.

LINEHAN, M. M. (1983). *Dialectical behavior therapy for treatment of parasuicidal women: Treatment manual.* Seattle: University of Washington Press.

LUBORSKY, L. (1977). Measuring a pervasive psychic structure in psychotherapy: The Core Conflictual Relationship Theme. In N. Freedman & S. Grand (Eds.), *Communicative structures and psychic structures* (pp. 367–395). New York: Plenum Press.

MAHLER, M., PINE, F., AND BERGMAN, A. (1975). *The psychological birth of the human infant.* New York: Basic Books.

MARMAR, C. R., WEISS, D. S., & GASTON, L. (IN PRESS). Towards the validation of the California Therapeutic Alliance Rating System. *Journal of Consulting and Clinical Psychology.*

OLDHAM, J., CLARKIN, J. F., APPELBAUM, A., CARR, A., KERNBERG, P., LOTTERMAN, A., & HAAS, G. (1985). A self-report instrument for borderline personality organization. In T. H. McGlashan (Ed.), *The borderline: Current empirical research.* Washington, DC: American Psychiatric Press.

SCHLEFER, E., SELZER, M., CLARKIN, J. F., YEOMANS, F., & LUBORSKY, L. (1989, MAY). Rating CCRTs with borderline patients. Paper presented at the annual meeting of the American Psychiatric Association, San Francisco.

SKODOL, A., BUCKLEY, P., & CHARLES, E. (1983). Is there a characteristic pattern to the treatment history of clinical outpatients with borderline personality disorder? *Journal of Nervous and Mental Disease, 171,* 405–410.

SPITZER, R., WILLIAMS, J., & GIBBONS, M. (1985). *Instruction manual for the structured clinical interview for DSM-III-R (SCID, 7/1/85 revision).* New York: Biometrics Research Department, New York State Psychiatric Institute.

YEOMANS, F., SELZER, M., & CLARKIN, J. F. (1992). *Treating the borderline patient: A contract-based approach.* New York: Basic Books.

PART IV

MEASURING KEY PROCESSES

CHAPTER 14

The Therapeutic Alliance and Its Measures

ADAM HORVATH, LOUISE GASTON, AND LESTER LUBORSKY

THE IMPORTANCE OF THE THERAPIST–CLIENT relationship has been discussed since the earliest days of psychotherapy. Over the years different theoretical models have been proposed to explain the role of the relationship within the therapeutic work. However, along with the recognition of the value of this factor, there are also controversies about its function in therapy. The two main issues most often debated are (1) the importance of the relationship as compared with the technique of therapy (for example, Brenner 1979; Gelso and Carter 1985), and (2) the specific client and/or therapist qualities or behaviors that play a role in developing a successful therapeutic ambiance (such as Barrett-Lennard 1985; Bordin 1976; Frank 1961; Frieswyk et al. 1986; Gaston 1990; Horvath and Greenberg 1989; Luborsky 1976, 1990; Strong 1968; Strupp and Hadley 1979).

In this chapter we try to present a balanced view by providing evidence for the utility of the alliance concept while acknowledging controversies. We first review concepts that describe the therapeutic relationship. Then we explicate the concept of the therapeutic alliance and review methods of measuring the alliance. Next we present the research linking the quality of the alliance to the outcome of therapy. Finally, we examine the clinical implications of these findings.[1]

---

[1]The terms therapeutic alliance, working alliance, and helping alliance have been used to refer to specific aspects of the therapeutic relationship or to the relationship as a whole. As the use of these terms in the literature has not been consistent, we will use "the alliance" generically to refer to all of the above constructs, unless otherwise specified.

Conceptualizations of the Therapeutic Relationship

THE PSYCHODYNAMIC PERSPECTIVE

In a paper first published in 1912, Freud remarked on the need for the analyst to maintain a stance of "serious interest" and "sympathetic understanding" toward the patient so that the healthy part of the patient's ego can form a positive attachment to, and develop a collaborative relationship with, the analyst. Later he elaborated on this idea by suggesting that, as a result of such a stance on the part of the analyst, the patient would be encouraged to link the therapist with the "images of people by whom he was accustomed to be treated by affection" (Freud [1913] 1958, 139–40).

In his early papers Freud described this attachment as a form of beneficial transference. He thought that positive transference had the effect of "[the client] clothing the doctor with authority" and saw this aspect of the relationship as the source of the client's "belief in his [analyst's] communications and explanations" (Freud [1913] 1958, 99). The source of such attachment is the unconscious projection of the client's idealized relationship; thus, positive transference, like its negative counterpart, is subject to interpretation as part of the central task of the analytic process. However, in his later writings, Freud appeared to have modified this positive transference view of the therapeutic alliance to include the possibility of a beneficial client–therapist attachment grounded in reality: "[The analyst] and the patient's weakened Ego, *basing themselves on the external world,* have to band themselves together. . . . This pact constitutes the analytic situation" (Freud 1940, 173; italics added). The implication of this later perspective is that, while interpretation of the client's projections or unresolved prior experiences is central to therapy, it is the ability of the intact portion of the client's ego (that is, the conscious, reality-based part of the self) to develop a covenant with the "real" therapist that makes it possible to continue with the task of healing.

Sterba (1934) further developed the idea that the intact, healthy, or reasonable part of the client's ego forms a conscious contract with the therapist; he referred to this bond as *ego alliance.* Later, Greenson (1965), in an influential paper, elaborated on the concept of this reality-based collaboration between therapist and client and coined the term *working alliance.* He called for a distinction between this aspect of the therapist–client dynamic and transference neurosis, and he proposed a model that has three components: transference, the working alliance, and the real relationship (Gelso and Carter 1985). Subsequently, Zetzel (1956) clarified some of the differences between transference and alliance, suggesting that, in effect, the nonneurotic part of the client—therapist relationship (the alliance) permits the client to step back and use the therapist's interpretations to draw distinctions between the remnants of past relationships and the real association between himself or herself and the therapist. She argued that, in successful analysis, the client is oscillating between periods when the relationship is dominated by transference and periods when the relationship is dominated by the working alliance. She coined the term *therapeutic alliance*. More recently, Frieswyk and his colleagues (1986) emphasized the distinction between alliance and transference, reserving the term *alliance* for the conscious collaborative aspect of the relationship which is based primarily on rational agreement between therapist and client.

A slightly different conceptualization of the therapeutic alliance was offered by Bibring (1937), who suggested that it represents a "new-object relationship." This position was further developed by Gitleson (1962) and Horwitz (1974) and, more recently, Bowlby (1988). In essence, the object relationists claim that the client, as part of the change process, develops the capacity to form a positive, need-gratifying relationship with the therapist. This attachment is qualitatively different from those based on early childhood experiences and represents a new class of events for the client. They suggest that it is one of the central tasks of the therapist to maintain a positive, reality-grounded stance toward the patient and thus to create an opportunity for the client to reflect on the discrepancies between the distorted and the realistic experiences of the relationship. Luborsky notes that the "alliance may serve the patient [with] what may be called a transitional object or a transitional teddy bear—a supportive helpful person . . . capable of providing a necessary help in achieving the client's goals" (1990, 15). Still others (e.g., Gaston, 1990, 1991), suggest that the alliance subsumes a number of distinct components, some of which are intrapersonal (for example, the patient's working capacity) while others are essentially interpersonal (for example, working strategy consensus).

While these writers argued for distinctions between the alliance and transference there are also analysts who maintain that all aspects of the therapist—client relationship are manifestations of the transference neurosis and should be interpreted as such. They maintain that the client's apparent collaboration or "alliance" represents an unconscious wish to gain the therapist's approval as a parental figure or is a form of covert competition. This logic leads some (for example, Brenner 1979; Curtis 1979) to conclude that the use of a construct such as the alliance may be misleading and can result in a dangerous watering down of the central thrust of the analytic work—the interpretation of transference.

The focus of the controversy appears to be the question of whether (or to what degree) the alliance is an intrapersonal or interpersonal phenomenon. To put it differently, to what degree is the alliance an interactional variable dependent upon the motivation, skill, and fit of the client and the therapist, as opposed to the notion that the quality of the therapeutic relationship is, at least initially, predestined by the client's unresolved intrapersonal difficulties? The intrapersonal (transference) position may be paraphrased thus: the client brings to the therapy a host of unresolved relationships with significant others—usually from childhood—that form the core of the neurotic predicament. In therapy the emotions and thoughts associated with the original conflict are displaced (transferred) to the benign unintrusive persona of the therapist. Thus the relationship "entails a misperception or misinterpretation of the therapist . . . [and] is an *unreal* relationship in this sense" (Gelso and Carter 1985, 170). Some interpret these notions quite narrowly (for example, Brenner 1979) and see the alliance as aim-softened transference and, therefore, not a relationship, properly speaking, but essentially an intrapsychic phenomenon. Others (for example, Westerman 1990) offer a more flexible position and argue that all relationships, in the broadest sense, are prejudiced by previous interpersonal experiences. Following this logic, to ignore the intrapersonal factor in the alliance leads to a misunderstanding of the clinical situation.

Yet a different model, based on a similar view of the transference, has been proposed by arguing that the alliance is not a separate or distinct variable but is an alternative perspective on the same phenomenon as the positive transference (Hatcher 1990). Proponents of this view tend to maintain that the therapeutic relationship is both interpersonal (that is, a real event arising out of the synergy of therapist and client) and intrapersonal (that is, anchored by the client's previous unresolved relationships). Within this view it is implicit that the development of the alliance is linked to technical changes (such as interpretation, insight) occurring in therapy. Using this perspective, identifying indicators of a good alliance is a way of highlighting some of the successful technical accomplishments in therapy. Thus the alliance is an alternative, but not a substitute perspective to the concept of positive transference. The key issue debated among these researchers is how much past relationships influence the alliance; we will present empirical data bearing on this issue later in this chapter.

Notwithstanding the fact that some questions remain, there seems to be a general movement toward a compromise position. We believe that we are witnessing the development of a growing consensus: a comprehensive definition of the alliance needs to take account of the influence of prior experiences (that is, positive and negative transference) and, at the same time, to delineate the alliance as a distinct aspect of the relationship.

THE CLIENT-CENTERED POSITION

Rogers (1951, 1957) postulated that the therapist's willingness to be empathic, to be congruent, and to accept the client unconditionally were not only essential but sufficient conditions for therapeutic success. These necessary and sufficient relationship conditions were predicated on the therapist's position or attitude rather than on the client's responsiveness, liking of the therapist, or willingness to collaborate in the therapy. It is important to note that while client-centered theory is often regarded as the quintessential humanistic position idealizing the "I and Thou" aspect of therapy, Rogers's propositions virtually ignore the client's role in the relationship. The approach presumes a fated response to the benevolent attitude of the therapist.

The impact of the therapist's conditions on the client's gains has been the focus of a large number of investigations. Initial findings were highly positive. However, subsequent research reviews (for example, Mitchell, Bozart, and Krauft 1977) indicate that it is the *client's perception of the therapist's attitudes* that exhibits a moderate but consistent relationship to a positive outcome of therapy rather than the therapist's intent or behavior toward the client. Moreover, beneficial effects do not appear to hold constant across different therapeutic modalities.

SOCIAL-INFLUENCE PERSPECTIVES

While Rogers concentrated on the role of the therapist, Strong and his colleagues (LaCrosse 1980; Strong 1968) developed a theory of therapeutic relationship that focuses on the client's cognitions. This theory—based on the work of social psychologists Hovland, Janis, and Kelly (1953) and Cartwright (1965)—postulates that the therapist's beneficial influence is proportional to the degree to which the client perceives the therapist as expert, attractive, and trustworthy. Since the strength of the therapist's influence is proportional to the client's attributions, the client's beliefs are directly related to the benefits she or he is likely to accrue from therapy.

From the historical perspective, social influence theory can be viewed as a reaction to Rogers's exclusive emphasis on the therapist's attitudes; it is an attempt to balance the perspective by highlighting the client's role in the relationship. Early research on the relation between the social influence dimensions—attractiveness, expertness, and trustworthiness—and therapy outcome suggests that, in analogue studies, the client's attributions of therapist qualities are influential (LaCrosse 1980). However, the results of subsequent clinical trials indicate that the impact of these variables on outcome may be quite modest and inconsistent across therapy modalities (Adler and Greenberg 1989; Horvath 1981).

PANTHEORETICAL CONCEPTUALIZATIONS

During the last decade and a half, evidence has accumulated indicating that a variety of apparently dissimilar therapies produce roughly similar increments in client improvements (Luborsky, Singer, and Luborsky 1975; Smith, and Glass, 1977; Stiles, Shapiro, and Elliot 1986). The resulting growing awareness of the importance of the generic as well as the theory-specific factors in therapy led to the examination of the common relationship ingredients across theoretically diverse treatments. Within this context, there have been efforts to expand and broaden the psychodynamic concept of the alliance.

One of the earliest contributions involved the identification of two different, sequential aspects of the client—therapist relationship by Luborsky (1976). He used theoretical distinctions drawn by Greenspan and Cullander (1975) to identify two types of helping alliance. Type 1 was described as "a therapeutic alliance based on the patient's experiencing the therapist as supportive and helpful with himself as a recipient" (p. 94); the Type 2 alliance is ". . . based on a sense of working together in a joint struggle against what is impeding the patient. . . . on shared responsibility for working out treatment goals. . . . a sense of 'we-ness' " (p. 94). He applied these concepts to taped therapy sessions from the Penn Psychotherapy Research Project and found that the strength of Type 1 and Type 2 alliance was associated with the likelihood of improvement in psychodynamic therapy.

Bordin (1975) proposed a new definition of the working alliance in order to capture the relational elements in all change-inducing relationships. His concept of the alliance builds on Greenson's (1967) earlier work but considerably extends the scope of the construct. In a sequence of papers Bordin (1975, 1976, 1980, 1989) attempted to clarify the distinctions between the unconscious projections of the client (that is, transference) and the alliance. His formulation shifted the emphasis to the client's positive collaboration with the therapist against the common foe of the client's pain and self-defeating behavior. He proposed that alliance has three constituent elements: tasks, bonds, and goals. The definitions of these components may be summarized as follows: tasks are the in-counseling behaviors and cognitions that form the substance of the counseling process. In a well-functioning relationship both parties must perceive these tasks as relevant and efficacious; furthermore, each must accept the responsibility to perform these acts. A strong working alliance is characterized by the therapist and the client mutually endorsing and valuing the goals (outcomes) that are the target of the intervention. The concept of bonds embraces the complex network of positive personal attachments between client and therapist, which include mutual trust, acceptance, and confidence.

The pantheoretical perspective of the alliance incorporates both client and therapist as active collaborators and emphasizes the importance of the fit between the participants. Moreover, it aims to clarify the role of the alliance in therapy. The relationship does not replace therapist interventions as the active ingredient in healing; the working alliance is what "makes it possible for the patient to accept and follow treatment faithfully" (Bordin 1980, 2).

These formulations also offer an alternative to the traditional dichotomous perspective of content and process factors in therapy. Based on this perspective it may be argued that these two aspects are not separate but interdependent and that the positive developments in each facilitate the growth of the other (Greenberg and Horvath 1991). We draw three implications from this synergic aspect of the model.

1. Clients' attachments to therapists are, in part, based on their assessment of the relevance and potency of the interventions offered. This suggests that clients do not move through therapy mechanically responding to a benevolent attitude on the part of the therapist, as Rogers proposed. Instead they actively (though often only implicitly) evaluate the quality of the interventions and compare their in-therapy experiences to their expectations, to their sense of involvement, gain, and insight.

Recent research on clients' cognitions during therapy offers partial support to the idea that clients' assessments of therapy are inner directed rather than merely responses to therapist factors (Hill and O'Grady 1985; Horvath, Marx, and Kamann 1990; Martin, Martin, and Slemon 1989). Suggesting that clients' assessment of the relevance of therapeutic tasks is important, however, does not mean that a therapist whose style of therapy is congruent with a client's expectations will necessarily have a stronger alliance. Rather, the therapist has to be able to: (a) communicate to the client the important links between therapy-specific tasks and the overall goals of treatment and (b) maintain an awareness of the client's commitment to these activities and effectively intervene if resistance is present.

2. Clients' assessment of the quality of the tasks in therapy is partially predicated on a sense of agreement on what are important and reasonable expectations of therapy (goals). Although it is likely that therapists and clients almost invariably have some agreement on the global, long-term goals of the process, it has been argued that the short- and medium-term expectations of client and therapist may be quite different: "Clients seek speedy relief from the pain that brought them to the therapist, whereas the therapist perceives therapy as a process which will lead to the eventual but not necessarily immediate relief of the client's suffering" (Horvath, Marx, and Kamann 1990, 620). The therapist's goals and expectations are dictated by his or her theory and may not be readily available to the client. Part of the therapist's task is to negotiate short- and medium-term expectations, link these to the client's wish to obtain lasting relief from suffering, and obtain the client's active consent to pursue these objectives. The client, on the other hand, will have to deal with postponements of gratification by using both cognitive (such as an

endorsement of the tasks of therapy) and affective components (such as a personal bond) of the relationship.

3. Cognitive and affective components of the alliance, in turn, are influenced by and influence the client's ability to forge strong personal bonds with the therapist. As Luborsky's (1976) research suggests, the client's initial response to the person of the therapist might well be dominated by a judgment concerning whether the helper seems caring, sensitive, sympathetic, and helpful (that is, the Type 1 helping alliance). Such judgments may be influenced by external features (for example, attractiveness), contextual information (for example, expertness), and the client's prior experiences in similar relationships (LaCrosse 1980). Subsequently, the influence of these initial impressions is augmented or even supplanted by the more cognitive (evaluative, collaborative) components of the alliance.

Measuring the Alliance

There are at least eleven methods available to measure the strength of the alliance in therapy. Some of these were developed for a specific research project; others were designed for more general use. The later, psychometrically more sophisticated instruments are reviewed in this chapter.

Horvath and Symonds (1991) identified five clusters of related alliance measures used in the majority of the investigations published to date. These were:

1. California Psychotherapy Alliance Scales, CALPAS (Gaston 1991) and CALTRAS (Marmar, Weiss, and Gaston 1989)
2. Penn Helping Alliance Scales, PENN, HAQ, HAcs, HAr (Alexander and Luborsky 1987; Luborsky et al. 1983)
3. Therapeutic Alliance Scale, TAS (Marziali 1984a)
4. Vanderbilt Therapeutic Alliance Scale, VPPS, VTAS (Hartley and Strupp 1983)
5. Working Alliance Inventory, WAI (Horvath 1982).

Each of these instruments is available in several versions, and most have been adapted for use as an observer's rating scale or as a self-report measure. In addition to assessing the global level of alliance, these scales also provide measurements of alliance components (subscales).

RELIABILITY

Overall, the reliability of these measures appears to be good; the average reliability index for all measures was estimated as .86. Instruments rated by therapists are the most reliable .93, but the client's scales are also stable, at .88. The average interclass correlation reported for observers' ratings is a respectable .82 (Horvath and Symonds 1991).

SIMILARITIES AND DIFFERENCES IN CLINICAL/OPERATIONAL DEFINITIONS

Given the large number of instruments, the reader might wonder whether all of these scales measure the same underlying construct. There are several ways to approach this complex question. Perhaps the most obvious question is to ask whether and to what degree the definitions undergirding each of these instruments are equivalent. A more empirical approach to this problem is to estimate the covariance among the measures. Last, one could investigate whether all of these instruments predict outcome equivalently.

It seems that two aspects of the alliance, (a) personal attachments or bonds and (b) collaboration or willingness to invest in the therapy process, are common elements among the instruments. Beyond these core components, the following constructs are monitored by two or more instruments: therapists' and clients' positive/negative contributions (e.g., CALTRAS, TAS); shared or agreed on goals for the therapy (e.g., CALPAS, CALTRAS, WAI, PENN); capacity to form a relationship (e.g., PENN, VTAS, CALPAS, CALTRAS); acceptance or endorsement of therapy tasks (e.g., CALPAS, CALTRAS, WAI), and active participation in therapy (e.g., PENN, CALPAS, CALTRAS, VTAS) (Gaston 1990; Hansell 1990; Hartley 1985; Horvath 1992; Marziali 1984b). It should be noted, however, that the weight or emphasis given to these components varies among measures.

What is the proportion of commonality among these instruments? Tichenor and Hill's (1989) data suggest that there is a 12 to 71 percent overlap among four observer-rated scales (CALPAS, PENN, VTAS, and WAI). In another study (Safran and Wallner 1991), two self-report scales were compared (WAI and CALPAS). The overall shared variance was reported as 76 percent. However, at the subscale level, overlap ranged from 0 to 67 percent, with an average value of 37 percent. Information available on another group of self-report measures (PENN, VPPS, and TAS) suggests that there is a wide range of commonalities at the subscale level (0 to 69 percent), with an average overlap for client-rated instruments of approximately 21 percent and for therapists' scales of 18 percent (Bachelor 1990).

The data presented above are difficult to interpret: ordinarily we look for generous overlap between measures as evidence that they assess the same process. However, most instruments also strive to capture distinct components of the alliance with each subscale; thus low subscale correlations within instruments are thought to be desirable. It can be argued, therefore, that low correlations across subscales of these instruments are to be expected, and a more proper test of similarity would entail comparison of parallel subscales only. Unfortunately, there is insufficient commonality among the subscales across instruments to undertake such assessment at this time.

As noted before, these instruments represent different theoretical perspectives. The PENN scales arose out of a psychodynamic perspective and are influenced by Luborsky's work on the alliance (Luborsky et al. 1985); VPPS represents a dynamic/eclectic framework that has been informed by the work of Strupp and his colleagues at Vanderbilt University (Strupp 1974); the TAS and CALPAS scales are influenced by both traditional psychodynamic concepts of the alliance and the subsequent work of Bordin (Gaston 1990); the WAI was designed to capture Bordin's pantheoretical perspective and was validated using his definitions of the alliance dimensions of goals, tasks, and bonds (Horvath and Greenberg 1989). Two of the scales (PENN and WAI) are theoretically homogeneous, and the remaining instruments represent a more eclectic position. The "homogeneous" scales tend to have higher interscale correlations, whereas blended scales (particularly the CALTRAS) appear to have more independent subscales (Horvath 1992).

It is important to note that, across all instruments, therapist alliance scales have provided significantly poorer predictions of all types of outcomes than other sources of assessments (Horvath and Symonds 1991). This appears to be true irrespective of the outcome indices predicted. There may be two reasons for this. The fault could lie in the fact that the therapists' scales are direct rewordings of client instruments. Thus far no effort has been made to specifically identify the therapist's experience of the alliance. Alternatively, some therapists may significantly misjudge the client's sense of the relationship; countertransference might account for a significant portion of these errors. We need to pay more careful attention to the therapists' process and discover the basis of their judgments to gain better understanding of the difficulties therapists experience in evaluating the status of the relationship.

There are other differences among these measures. Not all outcomes are equally well predicted by each, as will be discussed later in this chapter (Bachelor 1990; Safran and Wallner 1991). There are also disparities in length and complexity of the measurement task.

Obviously, no single alliance measurement has emerged as clearly superior to all others. Researchers and clinicians will have to make choices of instrumentation, taking into account all of the factors—theoretical, empirical, and practical—in making their selection. We would, however, caution against the use of untried or custom-made measures. The variability of instrumentation has already made it difficult to corroborate other researchers' findings; any further proliferation of assessment methods might lead us toward a virtual Babel and away from a clearer understanding of the complexities of therapy.

Relation of the Alliance to Therapy Outcome

During the last two decades, over a hundred research reports have been published on the alliance. A broad range of issues has been addressed with respect to both the nature of the alliance and its function in therapy. There are several recent reviews of this research (Gaston 1990; Horvath and Symonds 1991; Luborsky 1990).

THE STRENGTH OF ASSOCIATION BETWEEN ALLIANCE AND OUTCOME

Recently the quantitative research linking the relationship between alliance and outcome has been synthesized using meta-analytic techniques (Horvath and Symonds 1991). On the basis of the twenty-four studies included in the review, Horvath and Symonds report that the average effect size (ES) linking quality of alliance to therapy is $r = .26$. While the absolute value of this ES may seem modest, one way of interpreting a relationship of this magnitude is to note that the quality of the alliance may account for a 26 percent *difference* in rate of success in therapy (Rosenthal 1984). Moreover, the actual influence of the alliance may well be greater; to avoid overestimating the importance of the alliance, the authors based their calculation on the assumption that all relations observed but not reported by researchers or reported as "not significant" were in reality $r = .0$. This assumption is probably overly pessimistic in light of the range and distribution of the effect sizes reported.

FACTORS ATTENUATING ALLIANCE—OUTCOME RELATIONS

Type of Treatment.

Alliance research covers a broad variety of treatments and client problems. The impact of the alliance has been examined in therapies using behavioral (DeRubeis and Feeley 1991; Krupnick 1990), cognitive (Rounsaville et al. 1987; Safran and Wallner 1991), gestalt (Greenberg and Webster 1982), and psychodynamic (Eaton, Abeles, and Gutfreund 1988; Horowitz and Marmar 1985; Luborsky 1976; Luborsky and Auerbach 1985; Marmar et al. 1986; Marziali, Marmar, and Krupnick 1981; Piper, DeCarufel, and Szkrumelack 1985; Saunders, Howard, and Orlinsky 1989; Windholtz and Silberschatz 1988) treatments. It appears that strong alliance makes a positive contribution in all of these treatments (Horvath and Symonds 1991). However, in a recent study (DeRubeis and Feeley 1991) offer a warning that the alliance may be less predictive of outcome in highly structured forms of interventions (such as behavior therapy). Yet because the two studies reporting these results used similar process measures, it may be that the research design was not sensitive to all components of the alliance. Replication using instruments more sensitive to the cognitive aspects of the alliance may be required before firm conclusions can be drawn.

Predicting Different Outcomes.

Alliance measurements have been used to predict a variety of therapy outcome indices, ranging from drug use (Luborsky et al. 1985), through social adjustment (Rounsaville et al. 1987), to client's and therapist's subjective ratings of global improvement (Eaton, Abeles, and Gutfreund 1988). In general, the alliance measures appear to be better at predicting outcomes tailored to the individual client, such as the Target Complaint (TC) measure (Battle et al. 1966), than assessments of symptomatic change, such as the Symptom Checklist (SCL-90). The average correlation of alliance rating and outcome rated on the TC was .30 (N of 8 studies); the same correlation for the SCL-90 was .09 (N of 6 studies) (Horvath 1991b). At first glance it may appear that the self-rated outcome might be a "softer" index of improvement and thus easier to forecast than the more standardized rating scales. This is not the case, however; one of the most successful predictions of therapeutic gain was documented by Luborsky and his colleagues (1985). They found a .65 correlation of alliance and behavioral indices such as drug use, employment, and legal status.

Length of Treatment.

The impact of the alliance has been demonstrated in treatments ranging from four to over fifty sessions in length. Horvath and Symonds (1991) examined the correlation between the length of therapy and the alliance–outcome relation; they found a small, statistically nonsignificant negative correlation, and they concluded that length of treatment does not affect the degree to which the alliance influences outcome.

Early vs. Late Alliance.

The point in treatment that therapeutic relationship was assessed, however, did appear to influence the alliance–outcome relation. Early alliance appears to be a slightly more powerful prognosticator of outcome (ES = .3, N = 11) than alliance measures averaged across sessions or taken toward the middle of treatment (ES = .2, N = 8). Although the differences between these values are small, subsequent investigations (DeRubeis and Feeley 1991; Piper et al. 1991b; Piper, Azim, Joyce, and McCallum 1991a) appear to confirm this trend. One possible explanation for the apparent anomaly that we can better predict success on the basis of the quality of the early phases of the relationship may be explained by the course of the alliance over time. Longitudinal analyses of the levels of the alliance in more and less successful therapy (e.g., Horvath and Marx 1991; Safran et al. 1990) appear to confirm a rupture/repair cycle in successful therapies, as predicted by Zetzel (1956) and Bordin (1989). This variation in alliance levels may account for the more modest correlation between outcome and averaged or midphase alliance; the significant index of success in this phase of therapy may be the successful resolution of these ruptures rather than the level of the alliance in any given session.

The Effect of Responder Bias.

Notwithstanding the apparently robust link between good alliance and positive outcome, there is the possibility that the observed process—outcome relations do not in fact support the link between alliance and outcome but are the product of a "halo" phenomenon or confound (Orlinsky and Howard 1986; Saunders, Howard, and Orlinsky 1989; Waskow and Parloff 1975). This situation can arise as a result of the client's natural favorable bias toward the outcome of a therapy whose process they appraised highly. Conversely, if the clients valued the results of the intervention positively, they might tend to recall favorably process elements that were associated with the therapy. (Similarly, though less likely, such situations can contaminate the findings of studies using observers' or therapists' reports to assess both relationship and outcome.) These possibilities can be examined directly: if the relation between alliance and outcome is due in large part to such a halo effect, the correlation between client's evaluation of outcome and alliance should be significantly greater than the relation between alliance and outcome measures each obtained from different sources. These correlations were examined using fifty-four separate outcome/alliance relations reported in the literature. In fact, there appear to be no reliable differences to support the halo effect hypothesis (Horvath and Symonds 1991). Nor was there support for the possibility that observers' or therapists' evaluations of the alliance positively predisposed them to evaluate outcome likewise. In some cases the opposite situation appears to be more likely, for example, observers' alliance scores were better predictors of clients' evaluations than their own judgment of the outcome. Likewise, therapists' alliance scores tend to predict their own outcome evaluation least well and observers' scores most effectively. The evidence available thus far indicates that the role of the alliance in therapy is indeed more than a "self-fulfilling prophecy" or a reflection of clients' generic disposition toward therapy.

Alliance and Early Outcome.

A related question is often raised with respect to the validity and the value of generic relationship factors: Are these variables merely facsimiles for early results of therapy? The question can be specifically posed thus: Are early indications of good alliance in therapy simply the epiphenomena associated with the signs of therapeutic progress (DeRubeis and Feeley 1991; Luborsky 1990)?

If the alliance turns out to be even partially a by-product of therapeutic gains, this would seriously challenge both the theoretical and the practical utility of the concept. Viewing the alliance as an artifact scenario leads to several testable hypotheses: (a) if the alliance is indeed a by-product of successful therapy, its development ought to follow therapeutic progress in a parallel fashion (that is, in an idealized successful treatment situation, its quality ought to grow from poor to better); (b) conversely, early, particularly first session, measures of the alliance ought to be clearly less efficient predictors of outcome than measures obtained later in therapy; and (c) last, the most direct test of the epiphenomenon hypothesis is the determination of whether the alliance can account for a significant proportion of final outcome *after* the variance associated with therapeutic gains measured at the same time as the alliance has been statistically removed.

Evidence is emerging in the literature that none of these hypotheses is likely true. We shall review these in the same order as the hypotheses were listed. First, Safran et al. (1990) have found that positive outcome was associated with successful repairs of alliance ruptures (breakdown of the relationship) rather than with a linear or parallel development throughout therapy. Horvath and Marx (1991) likewise described the course of the alliance in successful therapy as a series of developments, decays, and repairs. Second, Kokotovic and Tracey (1990) reported that very early (first session) alliance measures were predictive of therapy dropouts. Horvath (1992) found that both early and late alliance measures were better predictors of final outcome than those obtained in the middle of therapy. Finally, Gaston and her colleagues (1991) computed partial correlations (controlling for therapy gains) associated with alliance and posttherapy outcome. She found that alliance predicted 36 percent to 57 percent of the variance in posttherapy outcome over and above short-term improvements.

Pretherapy Factors. It is reasonable to assume that both clients and therapists bring unique capacities to bear on the development of the therapeutic alliance.[2] Moreover, it is likely that some of these client/

---

[2]For the sake of conceptual clarity, only variables actually measured prior to the commencement of therapy will be presented under this heading. Other factors which are

therapist variables interact to produce particularly propitious or poor alliance patterns. Unfortunately, there is a dearth of information available on the impact of the therapists' pretreatment characteristics or the effect of specific therapist/client variable combinations on the development of the alliance. This gap reflects an important hiatus in our knowledge, which is particularly serious in light of the fact that therapists might be frequently misjudging the true status of the alliance.

Research on the relation of client factors and subsequent strength of the alliance is, however, available. In fact, the impact of a large number of diverse client characteristics has been monitored. Recently, Horvath (1991) summarized eleven of these studies. In order to make the interpretation of the broad spectrum of variables easier, client factors were sorted into three categories: (a) interpersonal capacities or skills, (b) intrapersonal dynamics, and (c) diagnostic features. The interpersonal category included measures of quality of the clients' social relationships (e.g., Moras and Strupp 1982), family relations (e.g., Kokotovic and Tracey 1990), and indices of stressful life events (e.g., Luborsky et al. 1983). The intrapersonal category subsumes indices of clients' motivation (e.g., Marmar, Weiss, and Gaston 1989), psychological status (e.g., Ryan and Cicchetti 1985), quality of object relations (e.g., Piper et al. 1991b), and attitudes (e.g., Kokotovic and Tracey 1990). Diagnostic feature refers to the severity of the client's problem in the beginning of treatment (e.g., Luborsky et al. 1983) or to prognostic indices (e.g., Klee, Abeles, and Muller 1990). It appears that both intrapersonal and interpersonal client variables have a similar, significant impact on the alliance. The average correlation coefficient (weighted by sample size) between these variables and alliance was $r = .3$ and $r = .32$, respectively. Thus, clients who have difficulty maintaining social relationships (e.g., Moras and Strupp 1982), or have poor family relationships (e.g., Kokotovic and Tracey 1990) are less likely to develop strong alliances. Similarly, patients who have little hope for success (e.g., Ryan and Cicchetti 1985), have poor object relations (e.g., Piper et al. 1991b), are defensive (e.g., Gaston et al. 1988), or are not psychologically minded (e.g., Ryan and Cicchetti 1985), are often associated with poor alliance in therapy. Severity of symptoms, on the other hand, had apparently only a small impact on the therapy relationship.

In a recent study, Piper and his colleagues (Piper et al. 1991b) estimated clients' enduring relationship pattern (quality of object relations, or QOR) by two assessment interviews conducted by experienced clinicians. They also measured six aspects of current interpersonal functioning, the level of the alliance, and three posttreatment and follow-up outcome

---

measured during therapy but might capture pretreatment characteristics (such as working capacity or therapist's skill) will be discussed elsewhere.

indicators. Their results support the importance of the client's pretherapy intrapersonal process in the development of the alliance; QOR had a statistically significant relation with alliance as well as outcome. (These correlations were similar in magnitude, $r \approx .23$.) The correlation between the clients' alliance rating and the outcome indices was somewhat greater than QOR's, but QOR was a superior predictor to the therapists' alliance ratings. Current interpersonal relationships were poor predictors of both alliance and outcome. Unfortunately, no information was provided on the partial correlations among QOR, alliance, and outcome to help us decide the important question whether QOR and alliance were predicting overlapping or distinct portions of the outcome. Also, the alliance measures used in this investigation appear to have been specifically developed for the project; thus the results cannot be safely generalized.

Another unanswered question with respect to the impact of the client pretreatment factors is whether these variables affect the alliance only at the beginning phase of treatment or throughout therapy. This question has important practical implications. Therapist interventions would depend on whether the deleterious effects of poor object relations affect only the initial building of the alliance or also its subsequent maintenance.

THEORETICAL AND CLINICAL IMPLICATIONS

Critical Phases.

There may be two important phases in the life of the alliance over the course of therapy. The first is the initial development of the alliance, which takes place within the first five sessions and probably peaks during session 3 (Horvath 1981; Saltzman et al. 1976). During this early phase satisfactory levels of collaboration and trust must be established; the client needs to join the therapist as a participant in the therapeutic journey and develop faith in the procedures that provide the framework of the therapy. The second critical phase occurs as the therapist begins to challenge old neurotic patterns. The client experiences the therapist's more active interventions as a reduction in sympathy and support; this likely reactivates the client's past dysfunctional relational beliefs and behaviors, thus weakening or rupturing the alliance. Such deterioration of the relationship must be repaired if therapy is to continue successfully.

According to this model, alliance may fail at different times and impact therapeutic success in different ways. Difficulties in developing a supportive relationship and arriving at a mutual endorsement of the therapeutic procedures can occur in the beginning of therapy. In such cases it is unlikely that the client will adhere to the therapeutic regime and premature termination is likely (Kokotovic and Tracey 1990). Later, failure to experience the interruptions in the alliance may be a sign either that the therapy is coasting (that is, dysfunctional thoughts, affects, or behavior patterns are not challenged or are ignored) or that the client responds to the therapist in an unrealistic, idealized manner and fails to use the therapeutic encounter to deal with core conflictual issues (that is, there is positive transference but no alliance present). Therapy may also fail if the challenges to the alliance in the second phase are too severe or are not attended to properly, so that the rupture does not heal (Safran et al. 1990).

The model we propose draws on the concepts proposed by Luborsky (1976), Bordin (1975, 1976), Horvath (1991), and Safran and colleagues (1990), as well as recent empirical findings. There appears to be evidence to confirm the significance of what we referred to as the first phase: a number of researchers have found that failure to develop these initial levels of the alliance has a deleterious impact on outcome and may disrupt therapy (Frank and Gunderson 1990; Kokotovic and Tracey 1988, 1990; Saunders, Howard, and Orlinsky 1989).

Support for the nature and impact of the second critical phase is emerging. Safran and his colleagues (1990) suggest that "most therapy cases . . . are characterized by at least one or more ruptures in the therapeutic alliance over the course of therapy" (p. 154). Luborsky (1976) found that the strength of type 2 alliance was related to the quality of outcome in dynamic therapy. Similarly, Foreman and Marmar (1985) report that therapists were able to improve the level of alliance in cognitive therapy by addressing the conflicted in-therapy relationships. Gaston and Ring (1992) found that therapists who focused on a client's problematic relationships improved the alliance, in contrast with those who focused on problems. Last, Reandeu and Wampold (1991) examined verbal transactions of high and low alliance therapist-client dyads and found that high alliance clients responded to the therapist's challenging interventions with nonreactive high involvement statements, whereas low alliance clients used avoidance (low involvement) responses in these situations. Although all of these studies are based on small samples, there appears to be a consistent finding that focusing on the conflictual relationship on the therapist's part and involvement as opposed to avoidance on the client's part contribute to better alliance.

Therapist Interventions That Affect the Alliance.

Although there is a considerable body of research on the therapeutic impact of the quality of the alliance, relatively little has been written about specific techniques to improve the relationship. This state of affairs is hardly surprising. Therapy involves complex behaviors and such a multitude of contingencies that there is a natural reluctance to provide narrow guidelines for specific therapist action (Butler and Strupp 1986). Nonetheless, it has been argued that without such specifications we may not be able to advance our understanding of the therapeutic process beyond the knowledge that most therapies are helpful compared with receiving no treatment at all (Luborsky, Singer, and Luborsky 1975; Stiles, Shapiro, and Elliot 1986). Moreover, research is unlikely to provide guidance to clinical practice unless the relations between clearly defined therapist actions in specific contexts and the effect of these interventions on process or outcome can be demonstrated (Soldz 1990). There have been several recent advances toward these goals. Overcoming considerable technical difficulties associated with such tasks, concise therapy manuals have been developed (Beck et al. 1979; Klerman et al. 1984; Luborsky 1984), permitting rigorous contrasts to be made among theoretically diverse interventions. Complex in-therapy processes have also been successfully specified, opening the door to empirical research effects of interpretation and transference (Luborsky 1977; Weiss et al. 1986). In this tradition, there is a body of research literature developing on therapist behaviors that impact on the alliance.

There is empirical corroboration of Freud's original proposition that a friendly sympathetic attitude toward the client is beneficial for the initial development of the alliance (Adler 1988; Horvath 1981; Kokotovic and Tracey 1990). This notion is further supported by the finding that early alliance measures are significantly correlated with measures of empathy as well as outcome. However, some of the research on early alliance also suggests that the endorsements of the tasks involved in therapy and a sense of collaboration with the therapist are the factors most closely associated with positive outcome (Adler 1988; Horvath and Greenberg 1989). These results may also indicate that the client's perception of the therapist's acceptance and support is closely linked with the technical aspects of treatment. It may be the case that while, on one hand, the clients "clothe the therapist with authority" (Freud [1913] 1958, 99–108), they also need to be reassured that this power is shared before they feel safe to commit themselves deeply to the therapeutic journey.

Safran and his colleagues (1990) developed a theoretical model of the function of the alliance during therapy. Their schema is congruent with Luborsky's work on the Core Conflictual Relationship Theme (1977) and also with Bordin's (1976) model of the alliance. Briefly, Safran suggests that the client brings into the therapeutic situation dysfunctional interpersonal relationship schemas that are reactivated during therapy. If the therapist responds in a manner that confirms the schemata, the cycle is maintained or even exacerbated. If, on the other hand, the pattern is recognized and the client's negative feelings toward the therapist are facilitated, it is possible to disrupt the cycle and help the client to gain a better grasp of his or her pathogenic ideas. (Safran and colleagues also provide a model of alliance rupture and resolution based on these propositions, the details of which are beyond the scope of this chapter.)

There is some empirical support for this model; Reandeu and Wampold (1991) found that clients who responded with high engagement to strong therapists' interventions developed better alliances than those patients who withdrew or used avoidance maneuvers. The occurrence of alliance fluctuations across time has been documented in a small-scale study (Horvath and Marx 1991). Other investigators, however, did not report such cycles over time (Gomes-Swartz 1978; Hartley and Strupp 1983; Krupnick 1990; Marmar, Weiss, and Gaston 1989; Morgan et al. 1982). The failure of subsequent investigators to observe these variations may be due to the fact that while Horvath and Marx monitored individual alliance scores over time, the other investigators averaged scores across individuals, possibly masking asynchronous fluctuations.

The clinical implications of this model are worth noting. It follows from this schema that negative client sentiments, avoidance, or even high levels of compliance may be signs of disruption in the alliance. Safran argues that the therapist should attend carefully to these signals and provide support and empathy for the client so that he or she can bring these conflicted feelings into full awareness. The proposition that direct attention to the vicissitudes of the in-therapy relationship has a salutary impact fits well with Bordin's (1976) notion that the alliance directly taps into the past pathogenic relationships of the client. There is also preliminary empirical evidence, provided by Foreman and Marmar (1985), that therapists may be able to strengthen the alliance by focusing on the therapy relationship directly. These investigators found that initially poor alliances improved as a result of such action. Although they interpret their findings with caution, noting that the clients in the study had broadly heterogeneous symptoms prior to therapy, other investigators (Coady 1988; Marziali 1984a) also noted that therapists' attention to negative in-therapy experiences improved the alliance.

The research findings on the impact of interpretation on the alliance present a more complex picture. Gaston and Ring (1992) investigated the effect of frequency of interpretation on the alliance and failed to find evidence of significant benefits. Crits-Cristoph, Cooper, and Luborsky (1988) investigated the impact of the accuracy of interpretations and likewise came short of finding beneficial association with change. Recently, Piper, Azim, Joyce, and McCallum (1992a), in a well-controlled study, discovered a curvilinear relationship between frequency of interpretations and the quality of the alliance.

These findings should not surprise us. It is likely that neither frequency nor accuracy of interpretation itself has a direct beneficial effect. More likely, the timing of the interpretation relative to the phase of the therapy as well as the depth and focus of the intervention would have to be taken into account in determining its impact. Some indirect evidence supporting this level of complexity is provided by Mallinckrodt and Nelson (1991), who contrasted the alliance ratings of more and less trained therapists. The therapists with higher levels of training had higher ratings on the Task and Goal scales of the Working Alliance Inventory but were not rated differentially on the Bond scale. These results may suggest that more and less trained therapists were equally liked, trusted, and perceived as empathic; however, the better trained, more experienced therapists—who presumably were more adept at the timing and pacing of their interventions—were better able to engage the clients in selecting appropriate goals and as collaborators in therapy.

References

ADLER, J. V. (1988). A study of the working alliance in psychotherapy. Unpublished doctoral dissertation, University of British Columbia.

ADLER, J. V., & GREENBERG, L. S. (1989). The working alliance and outcome in psychotherapy: A client-report study. Unpublished manuscript, University of British Columbia.

ALEXANDER, L. B., & LUBORSKY, L. (1987). The Penn Helping Alliance Scales. In L. S. Greenberg & W. M. Pinsoff (Eds.), The psychotherapeutic process: A research handbook. New York: Guilford Press.

BACHELOR, A. (1990, JUNE). Comparison and relationship to outcome of diverse dimensions of the helping alliance as seen by client and therapist. Paper presented at the annual meeting of the Society for Psychotherapy Research, Wintergreen, VA.

BATTLE, L. C., IMBER, S. D., HOEHN-SARIC, R., STONE, A. R., NASH, E. H., & FRANK, J. D. (1966). Target complaints as criteria of improvement. American Journal of Psychotherapy, 20, 184–192.

BECK, A., RUSH, A. J., SHAW, B. F., & EMERY, G. (1979). Cognitive therapy for depression. New York: Guilford Press.

BIBRING, E. (1937). On the theory of the results of psychoanalysis. International Journal of Psycho-Analysis, 18, 170–189.

BORDIN, E. S. (1975, AUGUST). The working alliance: Basis for a general theory of psychotherapy. Paper presented at the annual meeting of the American Psychological Association, Washington, DC.

BORDIN, E. S. (1976). The generalizability of the psychoanalytic concept of the working alliance. Psychotherapy: Theory, Research and Practice, 16, 252–260.

BORDIN, E. S. (1980, JUNE). Of human bonds that bind or free. Paper presented at the annual meeting of the Society for Psychotherapy Research, Pacific Grove, CA.

BORDIN, E. S. (1989, APRIL). *Building therapeutic alliances: The base for integration.* Paper presented at the annual meeting of the Society for the Exploration of Psychotherapy Integration, Berkeley, CA.

BOWLBY, J. (1988). *A secure base: Clinical applications of attachment theory.* London: Routledge.

BRENNER, C. (1979). Working alliance, therapeutic alliance, and transference. *Journal of the American Psychoanalytic Association, 27,* 136–158.

BUTLER, S. F., & STRUPP, H. H. (1986). Specific and nonspecific factors in psychotherapy: A problematic paradigm for psychotherapy research. *Psychotherapy: Theory, Research and Practice, 23,* 30–40.

CARTWRIGHT, D. S. (1965). Influence leadership and control. In J. G. March (Ed.), *Handbook of organizations.* Chicago: Rand McNally.

COADY, N. (1988, JUNE). *Prediction of outcome from interpersonal process: A study of the worker-client relationship.* Paper presented at the annual meeting of the Society for Psychotherapy Research, Santa Fe, NM.

CRITS-CRISTOPH, P., COOPER, A., & LUBORSKY, L. (1988). The accuracy of therapists' interpretations and the outcome of dynamic psychotherapy. *Archives of General Psychiatry, 56,* 490–495.

CURTIS, H. C. (1979). The concept of the therapeutic alliance: Implications for the "widening of scope." *Journal of the American Psychoanalytic Association, 27,* 159–192.

DeRUBEIS, R. J., & FEELEY, M. (1991). Determinants of change in cognitive therapy for depression. *Cognitive Therapy and Research, 14,* 469–482.

EATON, T. T., ABELES, N., & GUTFREUND, M. J. (1988). Therapeutic alliance and outcome: Impact of treatment length and pretreatment symptomology. *Psychotherapy: Theory, Research and Practice, 25,* 536–542.

FOREMAN, S., & MARMAR, R. C. (1985). Therapist actions that address initially poor therapeutic alliances in psychotherapy. *American Journal of Psychiatry, 142,* 922–926.

FRANK, A. F., & GUNDERSON, J., G. (1990). The role of the therapeutic alliance in the treatment of schizophrenia. *Archives of General Psychiatry, 47,* 228–236.

FREUD, S. (1912/1958). The dynamics of transference. In J. Strachey (Ed.), *The standard edition of the complete psychological works of Sigmund Freud* (pp. 99–108). London: Hogarth Press.

FREUD, S. (1913/1958). On the beginning of treatment: Further recommendations on the technique of psychoanalysis. In J. Strachey (Ed.), *Standard edition of the complete psychological works of Sigmund Freud* (pp. 122–144). London: Hogarth Press.

FREUD, S. (1940). The technique of psychoanalysis. In J. Strachey (Ed.), *Standard edition of the complete psychological works of Sigmund Freud* (pp. 172–182). London: Hogarth Press.

FRIESWYK, S. H., ALLEN, J. G., COLSON, D. B., COYNE, L., GABBARD, G. O., HORWITZ, L., & NEWSOM, G. (1986). Therapeutic alliance: Its place as process and outcome variable in dynamic psychotherapy research. *Journal of Consulting and Clinical Psychology, 1*, 32–39.

GASTON, L. (1990). The concept of the alliance and its role in psychotherapy: Theoretical and empirical considerations. *Psychotherapy, 27*, 143–153.

GASTON, L. (1991). Reliability and criterion-related validity of the California Psychotherapy Alliance Scales—patient version. *Psychological Assessment, 3*, 68–74.

GASTON, L., MARMAR, C., GALLAGHER, D., & THOMPSON, L. (1991). Alliance prediction of outcome beyond in-treatment symptomatic change as psychotherapy progresses. *Psychotherapy Research, 1*, 104–112.

GASTON, L., MARMAR, C. R., THOMPSON, L. W., & GALLAGER, D. (1988). Relation of patient pretreatment characteristics to the therapeutic alliance in diverse psychotherapies. *Journal of Consulting and Clinical Psychology, 4*, 483–489.

GASTON, L., & RING, J. M. (1992). Preliminary results on the Inventory of Therapeutic Strategies. *Journal of Psychotherapy Research and Practice, 1*, 1–13.

GELSO, C. J., & CARTER, J. A. (1985). The relationship in counseling and psychotherapy: Components, consequences, and theoretical antecedents. *Counseling Psychologist, 2*, 155–243.

GITLESON, M. (1962). The curative functions in psychotherapy. *International Journal of Psycho-Analysis. 43*, 194–205.

GOMES-SWARTZ, B. (1978). Effective ingredients in psychotherapy: Prediction of outcome from process variables. *Journal of Consulting and Clinical Psychology, 46*, 1023–1035.

GREENBERG, L. S., & HORVATH, A. O. (1991, JULY). *The role of the therapeutic alliance in psychotherapy research.* Paper presented at the annual meeting of the Society for Psychotherapy Research, Lyon, France.

GREENBERG, L. S., & WEBSTER, M. C. (1982). Resolving decisional conflict by Gestalt two-chair dialogue: Relating process to outcome. *Journal of Counseling Psychology, 29*, 468–477.

GREENSON, R. R. (1965). The working alliance and the transference neuroses. *Psychoanalysis Quarterly, 34*, 155–181.

GREENSON, R. R. (1967). *Technique and practice of psychoanalysis.* New York: International Universities Press.

GREENSPAN, S., & CULLANDER, C. (1975). A systematic metapsychological assessment of the course of an analysis. *Journal of the American Psychoanalytic Association, 23*, 107–138.

HANSELL, J. (1990, JUNE). *The relationship of the California Psychotherapy Alliance Scales to other measures of the alliance.* Paper presented at the annual meeting of the Society for Psychotherapy Research, Wintergreen, VA.

HARTLEY, D. (1985). Research on the therapeutic alliance in psychotherapy. In

R. Hales & A. Frances (Eds.), *Psychiatry update annual review* (pp. 532–549). Washington DC: American Psychiatric Association.

HARTLEY, D. E., & STRUPP, H. H. (1983). The therapeutic alliance: Its relationship to outcome in brief psychotherapy. In J. Masling (Ed.), *Empirical studies in analytic theories* (pp. 1–37). Hillsdale, NJ: Erlbaum.

HATCHER, R. (1990, JUNE). *Transference and the therapeutic alliance.* Paper presented at the annual meeting of the Society for Psychotherapy Research, Wintergreen, VA.

HILL, C. F., & O'GRADY, K. (1985). List of therapist intentions illustrated in a case study and with therapists of varying theoretical orientations. *Journal of Counseling Psychology, 32,* 3–22.

HOROWITZ, M., & MARMAR, C. (1985). The therapeutic alliance with difficult patients. In R. Hales & A. Frances (Eds.), *Psychiatry update annual review* (pp. 573–584). Washington, DC: American Psychiatric Association.

HORVATH, A. O. (1981). *An exploratory study of the working alliance: Its measurement and relationship to outcome.* Unpublished doctoral dissertation, University of British Columbia.

HORVATH, A. O. (1982). Working Alliance Inventory (Revised). Instructional Psychology Research Group, *82,* Simon Fraser University, Burnaby, Canada.

HORVATH, A. O. (1991, JULY). *What do we know about the alliance and what do we still have to find out?* Paper presented at the annual meeting of the Society for Psychotherapy Research, Lyon, France.

HORVATH, A. O. (1992). *Measurement of the working alliance: A review.* Paper submitted for publication.

HORVATH, A. O., & GREENBERG, L. S. (1989). The development and validation of the Working Alliance Inventory. *Journal of Counseling Psychology, 36,* 223–233.

HORVATH, A. O., & MARX, R. W. (1991). The development and decay of the working alliance during time-limited counselling. *Canadian Journal of Counselling, 24,* 240–259.

HORVATH, A. O., MARX, R. W., & KAMANN, A. M. (1990). Thinking about thinking in therapy: An examination of clients' understanding of their therapists' intentions. *Journal of Consulting and Clinical Psychology, 58,* 614–621.

HORVATH, A. O., & SYMONDS, B. D. (1991). Relation between working alliance and outcome in psychotherapy: A meta-analysis. *Journal of Counseling Psychology, 38,* 139–149.

HORWITZ, L. (1974). *Clinical prediction in psychotherapy.* New York: Jason Aronson.

HOVLAND, C. I., JANIS, I. L., & KELLEY, H. H. (1953). *Communication and persuasion: Psychological studies of opinion change.* New Haven: Yale University Press.

KLEE, M. R., ABELES, N., & MULLER, R. T. (1990). Therapeutic alliance: Early indicators, course, and outcome. *Psychotherapy: Theory, Research and Practice*, 27, 166–174.

Klerman, G. L., Weissman, M. M., Rounsaville, B. J., & Chevron, E. S. (1984). *Interpersonal psychotherapy of depression*. New York: Basic Books.

Kokotovic, A. M., & Tracey, T. J. (1988, August). *The working alliance in the early phase of counseling*. Paper presented at the annual meeting of the American Psychological Association, Chicago.

Kokotovic, A. M., & Tracey, T. J. (1990). Working alliance in the early phase of counseling. *Journal of Counseling Psychology*, 37, 16–21.

Krupnick, J. (1990, June). *The relationship of therapeutic alliance and outcome in interpersonal psychotherapy and cognitive behavior therapy*. Paper presented at the annual meeting of the Society for Psychotherapy Research, Wintergreen, VA.

LaCrosse, M. B. (1980). Perceived counselor social influence and counseling outcomes: Validity of the Counselor Rating Form. *Journal of Counseling Psychology*, 27, 320–327.

Luborsky, L. (1976). Helping alliances in psychotherapy. In J. L. Cleghhorn (Ed.), *Successful psychotherapy* (pp. 92–116). New York: Brunner/Mazel.

Luborsky, L. (1977). Measuring a persuasive psychic structure in psychotherapy: The Core Conflictual Relationship Theme. In N. Freedman & S. Grand (Eds.), *Communicative structures and psychic structures* (pp. 367–395). New York: Plenum Press.

Luborsky, L. (1984). *Principles of psychoanalytic psychotherapy*. New York: Basic Books.

Luborsky, L. (1990, June). *Therapeutic alliance measures as predictors of future benefits of psychotherapy*. Paper presented at the annual meeting of the Society for Psychotherapy Research, Wintergreen, VA.

Luborsky, L., & Auerbach, A. (1985). The therapeutic relationship in psychodynamic psychotherapy: The research evidence and its meaning for practice. In R. Hales & A. Frances (Eds.), *Psychiatry update annual review* (pp. 550–561). Washington, DC: American Psychiatric Association.

Luborsky, L., Crits-Cristoph, P., Alexander, L., Margolis, M., & Cohen, M. (1983). Two helping alliance methods for predicting outcomes of psychotherapy: A counting signs vs. a global rating method. *Journal of Nervous and Mental Disease*, 171, 480–491.

Luborsky, L., McLellan, A. T., Woody, G. E., O'Brien, C. P., & Auerbach, A. (1985). Therapist success and its determinants. *Archives of General Psychiatry*, 42, 602–611.

Luborsky, L., Singer, B., & Luborsky, L. (1975). Comparative studies of psychotherapies: Is it true that "everybody has won and all must have prizes"? *Archives of General Psychiatry*, 32, 995–1008.

Mallinckrodt, B., & Nelson, M. L. (1991). Counselor training level and the formation of the therapeutic working alliance. *Journal of Counseling Psychology*, 38, 14–19.

MARMAR, C. R., HOROWITZ, M. J., WEISS, D. S., & MARZIALI, E. (1986). The development of the therapeutic alliance rating system. In L. S. Greenberg & W. M. Pinsof (Eds.), *The psychotherapeutic process: A research handbook* (pp. 367–390). New York: Guilford Press.

MARMAR, C., WEISS, D. S., & GASTON, L. (1989). Toward the validation of the California Therapeutic Alliance Rating System. *Psychological Assessment: A Journal of Consulting and Clinical Psychology, 1,* 46–52.

MARTIN, J., MARTIN, W., & SLEMON, A. (1989). Cognitive mediational models of action-act sequences in counseling. *Journal of Counseling Psychology, 36,* 8–16.

MARZIALI, E. (1984a). Prediction of outcome of brief psychotherapy from therapist interpretive interventions. *Archives of General Psychiatry, 41,* 301–305.

MARZIALI, E. (1984b). Three viewpoints on the therapeutic alliance scales: Similarities, differences and associations with psychotherapy outcome. *Journal of Nervous and Mental Disease, 172,* 417–423.

MARZIALI, E., MARMAR, C., & KRUPNICK, J. (1981). Therapeutic alliance scales: Development and relationship to psychotherapy outcome. *American Journal of Psychiatry, 138,* 361–364.

MITCHELL, K. M., BOZART, J. D., & KRAUFT, C. C. (1977). Reappraisal of the therapeutic effectiveness of accurate empathy, non-possessive warmth, and genuineness. In A. S. Gurman & A. M. Razin (Eds.), *Effective psychotherapy.* New York: Pergamon Press.

MORAS, K., & STRUPP, H. H. (1982). Pretherapy interpersonal relations, patients' alliance and the outcome in brief therapy. *Archives of General Psychiatry, 39,* 405–409.

MORGAN, R., LUBORSKY, L., CRITS-CRISTOPH, P., CURTIS, H., & SOLOMON, J. (1982). Predicting the outcomes of psychotherapy by the Penn Helping Alliance Rating Method. *Archives of General Psychiatry, 39,* 397–402.

ORLINSKY, D. E., & HOWARD, K. I. (1986). The psychological interior of psychotherapy: Explorations with the Therapy Session Report Questionnaires. In L. S. Greenberg & W. M. Pinsof (Eds.), *The psychotherapeutic process: A research handbook.* New York: Guilford Press.

PIPER, W. E., AZIM, H. F. A., JOYCE, A. S., & McCALLUM, M. (1991). Transference interpretations, therapeutic alliance and outcome in short-term individual therapy. *Archives of General Psychiatry, 48,* 946–953.

PIPER, W. E., AZIM, H. F. A., JOYCE, A. S., MacCALLUM, M., NIXON, G. W. H., & SEGAL, P. S. (1991). Quality of object relations vs. interpersonal functioning as a predictor of therapeutic alliance and psychotherapy outcome. *Journal of Nervous and Mental Disease, 179,* 432–438.

PIPER, W. E., DeCARUFEL, F. L., & SZKRUMELACK, N. (1985). Patient predictors of process and outcome in short-term individual psychotherapy. *Journal of Nervous and Mental Disease.*

REANDEU, S. G., & WAMPOLD, B. E. (1991). Relationship of power and involvement to working alliance: A multiple-case sequential analysis of brief therapy. *Journal of Consulting and Clinical Psychology, 38,* 107–114.

Rogers, C. R. (1951). *Client centered therapy.* Cambridge, MA: Riverside Press.

Rogers, C. R. (1957). The necessary and sufficient conditions of therapeutic personality change. *Journal of Consulting and Clinical Psychology, 22,* 95–103.

Rosenthal, R. (1984). *Meta-analytic procedures for social research.* Beverly Hills, CA: Sage.

Rounsaville, B. J., Chevron, E. S., Prusoff, B. A., Elkin, I., Imber, S., Sotsky, S., & Watkins, J. (1987). The relation between specific and general dimensions of the psychotherapy process in interpersonal psychotherapy of depression. *Journal of Consulting and Clinical Psychology, 55,* 379–384.

Ryan, E. R., & Cicchetti, D. V. (1985). Predicting quality of alliance in the initial psychotherapy interview. *Journal of Nervous and Mental Disease, 173,* 717–725.

Safran, J. D., Crocker, P., McMain, S., & Murray, P. (1990). The therapeutic alliance rupture as a therapy event for empirical investigation. *Psychotherapy, 27,* 154–165.

Safran, J. D., & Wallner, L. K. (1991). The relative predictive validity of two therapeutic alliance measures in cognitive therapy. *Psychological Assessment: A Journal of Consulting and Clinical Psychology, 3,* 188–195.

Saltzman, C., Leutgert, M. J., Roth, C. H., Creaser, J., & Howard, L. (1976). Formation of a therapeutic relationship: Experiences during the initial phase of psychotherapy as predictors of treatment duration and outcome. *Journal of Consulting and Clinical Psychology, 44,* 546–555.

Saunders, S. M., Howard, K. I., & Orlinsky, D. E. (1989). The therapeutic bond scales: Psychometric characteristics and relationship to treatment effectiveness. *Psychological Assessment: A Journal of Consulting and Clinical Psychology, 1,* 323–330.

Smith, M. L., & Glass, G. V. (1977). Meta-analysis of psychotherapy outcome studies. *American Psychologist, 32,* 752–760.

Soldz, S. (1990). Therapeutic interaction: Research perspectives. In R. A. Wells & V. J. Giannetti (Eds.), *Handbook of the brief psychotherapies* (pp. 27–54). New York: Plenum Press.

Sterba, R. F. (1934). The fate of the ego in analytic therapy. *International Journal of Psycho-Analysis, 115,* 117–126.

Stiles, W. B., Shapiro, D., & Elliot, R. (1986). Are all psychotherapies equivalent? *American Psychologist, 41,* 165–180.

Strong, S. R. (1968). Counseling: An interpersonal influence process. *Journal of Counseling Psychology, 15,* 215–224.

Strupp, H. H. (1974). On the basic ingredients of psychotherapy. *Psychotherapy and Psychosomatics, 24,* 249–260.

Strupp, H. H., & Hadley, S. W. (1979). Specific vs. nonspecific factors in psychotherapy. *Archives of General Psychiatry, 36,* 1125–1136.

TICHENOR, V., & HILL, C. E. (1989). A comparison of six measures of working alliance. *Psychotherapy, 26,* 195–199.

WASKOW, I. E., & PARLOFF, M. B. (EDS.). (1975). *Psychotherapy change measures.* Rockville, MD: National Institute of Mental Health.

WEISS, J., SAMPSON, H., & THE MOUNT ZION PSYCHOTHERAPY RESEARCH GROUP. (1986). *The psychoanalytic process.* New York: Guilford Press.

WESTERMAN, M. A. (1990, JUNE). *The therapeutic alliance.* Paper presented at the annual meeting of the Society for Psychotherapy Research, Wintergreen, VA.

WINDHOLTZ, M. J., & SILBERSCHATZ, G. (1988). Vanderbilt Psychotherapy Process Scale: A replication with adult outpatients. *Journal of Clinical and Consulting Psychology, 56,* 56–60.

ZETZEL, E. R. (1956). Current concepts of transference. *International Journal of Psychoanalysis, 37,* 369–376.

CHAPTER 15

Defenses and Their Effects

J. CHRISTOPHER PERRY

THIS CHAPTER REVIEWS THEORETICAL CONTRIBUTIONS on defense mechanisms, surveys empirical findings to date, touches upon clinical issues, and culminates with an exploration of the future for research on defenses. Excellent reviews and critiques of historically important contributions are available elsewhere (Vaillant 1977, 1986; Perry and Cooper 1987; Horowitz 1988; Cooper 1989; Vaillant 1992). To help psychodynamics flourish in the scientific arena, it is better to emphasize measurement and evidence over theory. However, because research on defense mechanisms involves theory-informed measurement (percepts aided by concepts, to paraphrase Kant), it has produced some happy scientific results. Furthermore, new challenges promise to bring the study of psychopathology closer to that of the process of change in psychotherapy. Defenses underlie many psychopathological phenomena which resist change directly but are susceptible to change when the underlying mechanisms are addressed. This tenet of dynamic psychiatry is empirically testable.

Theoretical Contributions on Defense Mechanisms

EARLY THEORETICAL DEVELOPMENTS

In 1894 Sigmund Freud first described the phenomena of defensive operations, which he referred to by the general term repression (see chapter 16). He offered exciting observations suggesting that individuals develop some psychological symptoms because of unconscious operations against consciously unacceptable but salient wishes and impulses. Thus, from the inception of psychoanalytic observation and theory, both defense and conflict were given central roles. In subsequent years Freud described a number of specific mechanisms, such as repression, isolation, displacement, dissociation, and humor. By 1906 he shifted back toward using the generalized term repression, and he never systematized his thinking about defenses.

By 1926 in formulating his second theory of anxiety, Freud hypothesized that forbidden impulses trigger signal anxiety which then brings specific defenses into play, to keep unacceptable impulses out of conscious awareness. Symptoms thus represented a compromise between the unconscious pressures exerted by the impulses (the id) and the inhibitory prohibitions against them (the superego) which were mediated by defenses of the ego. It was left to Anna Freud to more fully describe the range of defenses in *The Ego and the Mechanisms of Defense* ([1937] 1966), in which she groups defenses by the sources of the anxiety which they defended against: instinct, the external world, and the superego.

FURTHER DEVELOPMENTS IN DRIVE, DEFENSE, AND EGO FUNCTIONING

While defenses were said to guard against the emergence of instinct, drive, and/or derivative wishes, Waelder ([1930] 1976) revealed how defenses could serve multiple functions, including securing some gratification of the forbidden impulse while at the same time defending against it. Certain defensive character traits, such as paranoid projection, may include wish-fulfilling fantasies simultaneously with resultant symptoms. Schafer (1968) later emphasized that in its use of defenses the ego is motivated to seek gratification and reduce or eliminate pain, while still playing its defensive role in warding off forbidden wishes. Hartman, Kris, and Lowenstein (1964) suggested that some ego functions could be relatively neutralized (that is, conflict-free), and therefore were not directed against forbidden impulses. They suggested that defenses as well as other ego functions could be directed against either impulses or the external world, thereby enhancing the individual's adaptation to reality. These dual defensive functions, which deal both with intrapsychic conflict and with adaptation to the constraints of the external world, were also utilized by Haan (1963) as a rationale for separating coping mechanisms from related defense mechanisms.

DEFENSES AND OBJECT RELATIONS

Klein (1946) added to the classical view that defenses counter drives when she posited that infants introject parental body parts early in the process of superego development, prior to internalizing the parents as whole, separate objects. She suggested that certain defenses were triggered by impulses associated with internalized self representations (for example, fantasies of parts of the self, body products) which are then projected onto objects. Thus, defenses like splitting, projective identification, idealization, and omnipotence involve distorted perceptions of the self or of the external world, linked to internal drive states.

This view of the relation between defense and object representation has been elaborated by Kernberg (1967, 1975, 1983), who suggested that defenses can be divided into three overall levels of organization: psychotic, borderline, and neurotic, each of which is associated with certain predominant defenses. At each level of organization, defenses in part serve to protect the individual from anxiety-producing internalized self and object images. Kernberg is perhaps best known for his description of borderline personality organization, in which splitting mechanisms predominate over repression, the latter being more characteristic of neurotic personality organization. Splitting of self and object representations into polar opposites (for example, positive versus negative introjects) is also reinforced by denial, projective identification, idealization, omnipotence, and devaluation (Kernberg 1967, 1975). Splitting and related defenses keep aggressive and libidinal object images apart, thereby minimizing anxiety, but at the price of preventing the individual from synthesizing emotional meaning into more realistic representations or schemas of self and others.

DEFENSES AND SELF PSYCHOLOGY

In their focus on the treatment of narcissistic disorders, Kohut (1984) and other proponents of the self psychology perspective have described a variety of functions for defenses commonly associated with narcissistic psychopathology, such as idealization, devaluation, and omnipotence. For example, in defending against oedipal-level hostile impulses, these defenses may be viewed as resistances to therapeutic exploration. In certain narcissistic individuals, however, they may be better understood as reparative efforts to strengthen an "enfeebled self." Thus, self psychologists caution that such defenses, despite their pathological effect on external adaptation, may sometimes better be dealt with in early and midphase treatment by empathic mirroring rather than by interpretive interventions.

CURRENT VIEWS AND ASSUMPTIONS ABOUT DEFENSES

While many aspects of psychodynamic theory have eluded scientific examination, empirical work on defenses has been quite extensive. Researchers have provided operationalized, nonoverlapping definitions, often including prototypical examples, to aid in making low-inference clinical judgments for identifying each specific defense. Good measurement reliability has stimulated considerable scientific work in this area.

Currently there is consensus among researchers regarding the following aspects of the defense mechanism construct.

1. An overall definition of a defense is that it is the individual's automatic psychological response to internal or external stressors or emotional conflict. Defenses are triggered by the occurrence of what Freud called "signal anxiety" arising whenever internal wishes or drives conflict with internalized prohibitions or external reality constraints.

2. Defenses generally act automatically, that is, without conscious effort. Often the individual is totally unaware of the defensive operation, although in some instances he or she may have partial awareness. A common use of displacement exemplifies this: an individual suddenly becomes irritated at a small annoyance and then realizes that this response has been misdirected from a more significant source of annoyance over which he or she felt frustrated or powerless. The classic example is the individual coming home after an argument with the boss and then getting irritated at the spouse over an issue that usually would not evoke much emotion.

3. Character traits are in part made up of specific defenses which individuals use repetitively in diverse situations. Individuals tend to specialize, using a prototypical set of defenses across a variety of stressors. While defenses can be viewed as underlying dispositions (traits) which are manifest under certain stressful states, nevertheless the defenses used at any given time may vary in degree or specificity with the stressor, making some state effects expectable. Whether there is a specificity between type of stressor and individual defense is an empirical question.

4. A recent review tallied forty-two different individual defense mechanisms offered by various authors (Perry and Cooper 1987). Although there is no clear rationale for selecting a definitive list of defenses (Vaillant 1977), a process of consensus has favored those defenses manifesting clear, nonoverlapping definitions, reliability, and demonstrated empirical findings.

5. Defenses affect adaptation. Each defense presumably is highly adaptive in certain situations. For example, the use of projection in battle situations may help the individual resolve ambiguous situations in ways that minimize personal harm. Similarly, the abused child's use of splitting of others' images allows the child to coexist with the abusive caretaker on whom he or she is highly dependent for survival. While each defense may be adaptive in certain situations—for instance, when originally learned—nonetheless there is a clear hierarchy of defenses in relation to the overall adaptiveness of each one. Defenses at the lower end are usually maladaptive, save in a few situations, while those at the higher end are adaptive

in a broader array of circumstances. Another aspect of adaptiveness is flexibility, rather than rigidity, in selecting the defense that is most adaptive in a given instance.

6. When defenses are least adaptive, they protect the individual from awareness of stressors and/or associated conflicts at the price of constricting awareness, freedom to choose, and flexibility in maximizing positive outcomes. When defenses are most adaptive, they maximize the expression and gratification of wishes and needs, minimize negative consequences, and provide a sense of freedom of choice.[1]

7. Despite the use of developmental terms to describe groups of defenses, such as immature or mature, the question of whether defenses emerge in a certain normative developmental sequence represents an empirically open issue. Developmental terms are used for reasons of history and convenience only. Candidates for their replacement should be based on other empirical findings. For example, it has been posited that a developmental sequence links certain defenses across the continuum of adaptiveness. For instance, acting out in early life (for example, rebelling against authority) may evolve into reaction formation later (taking the side of authority) and may finally develop into altruism (helping the unfortunate obtain fairness from those in authority). The unfolding of such sequences deserves sustained longitudinal study and may hold important implications regarding the phase and range of therapeutic change (see chapter 9).

Clinical Assessment Methods and Research Findings

CLINICAL ASSESSMENT METHODS

Clinical methods for measuring defenses have generally used interview data rated by a clinician using a definition (with or without an accompanying scale) for each defense. Complex psychodynamic constructs are often difficult to measure reliably, and each researcher has approached this problem differently. Apart from the ability of two clinicians to agree on whether a given subject uses a given defense (measurement reliability), the issue of the construct validity of the defense remains in question. Following is a brief description of the major clinical methods, their reliabili-

---

[1]Some authors distinguish the most adaptive defenses by the special term coping mechanisms, whereas many in the dynamic tradition retain the defense designation, because the so-called coping mechanisms still share many characteristics with other defenses. This question of terminology, defense versus coping, raises questions more of preference than of science.

ties, and selected methodological issues. Major clinical findings addressing the validity and utility of studying defenses are subsequently discussed.

RESEARCH FINDINGS

Weintraub and Aronson (1963) applied methods of formal speech analysis to hypotheses about defensive functioning. They recorded a ten-minute monologue speech sample from subjects which they then rated for twelve formal characteristics. Several of these (the use of negations, qualifications, explanations, retractions, and evaluations) may relate to defenses such as denial, undoing, and rationalization. While reliabilities of the scales were good, the lack of external criteria of measurement validity in this or subsequent studies makes it unclear whether the method measures defensive functioning, cognitive functioning, or some combination of the two.

Haan (1963) used written summaries of an average of twelve hours of individual interviews for rating ten defense mechanisms and ten related coping mechanisms (such as repression versus suppression, intellectualization versus intellectuality). The interviewer and a blind judge rated the presence of the defenses on a 1–5 scale based on operationalized definitions. All raters were clinically experienced. The mean reliability coefficients of the individual defense ratings were .66 for male and .50 for female subjects. Given the extensive data base, those defenses which are most meaningful should declare themselves by their repetitive occurrence, thus aiding their reliable identification. It is not clear how applicable the method would be to situations where fewer interviews were available, or where interview summaries were not available.

Bellak, Hurvich, and Gediman (1973) developed the Ego Function Assessment, which uses clinical interviews to assess twelve aspects of ego functioning. Scale 8 summarizes the overall effectiveness of defensive functioning on a 13-point scale, although it does not assess specific defenses. Using an accompanying structured interview, the rater probes defensive functioning primarily by looking for evidence of symptom formation and failure to contain anxiety. The original reliability of the scale was high ($r = .81$), although another study obtained a lower estimate ($r = .13$) (Dahl 1984a).

Semrad, Grinspoon, and Fienberg (1973) developed a forty-five-item instrument, the Ego Profile Scale, which clinicians rate on the basis of clinical observation, yielding scores for nine defenses. On a separate sample, Ablon, Carlson, and Goodwin (1974) found that the interrater reliability coefficients of the nine defense patterns ranged from .49 to .89. A factor analysis of the instrument suggested that the nine patterns could be collapsed into seven factors. The instrument was designed for use with inpatients, where prolonged behavioral observation was possible; its applicability to outpatient settings has not been tested.

Vaillant (1971, 1976, 1977) devised a glossary of eighteen defense mechanisms to rate life vignettes obtained from interviews in which subjects discussed how they dealt with important events in their lives. He has applied this method to two long-term follow-up studies of males first obtained during adolescence: a sample of college men (Vaillant 1976) and a sample of inner-city boys who were the control subjects in the Gluecks' study of delinquency (Vaillant, Bond, and Vaillant 1986). Vaillant (1976) selected twenty life vignettes from each subject who had been interviewed during middle age and divided them into six clusters, from which blind raters determined the subject's three major defenses. The mean reliability for the defense ratings was .56 (range − .01 to .95) for the blind raters but somewhat higher when their combined ratings were compared with the nonblind ratings of the author (mean $r = .73$, range .53 to .96). Although the reliability may be somewhat lower if applied to unselected life vignettes, this method clearly captures clinically significant long-term defensive functioning. It is probably most valid when life vignettes are gathered close to the time of actual occurrence, thereby minimizing bias due to recall. However, it is not known whether a single clinical interview yields a representative and large enough sample of life vignettes to produce a stable picture of an individual's overall defensive functioning. In prospective studies, the use of life vignette data from serial interviews may offer a good external criterion for validating cross-sectional measures of defensive functioning.

Jacobson et al. (1986b) studied defense mechanisms among three groups of adolescents: diabetics, nonpsychotic psychiatric patients, and healthy high school students. They assessed twelve defenses and a measure of overall defense success from transcripts of open-ended interviews. Each defense has both a definition and a 5-point rating scale, providing clinical examples of the minimal, moderate, and maximal ratings. The intraclass interrater reliability coefficients were greater than .60 for seven defense scales. This method uses clinical data and employs a highly specific rating scheme that measures defensive functioning in degrees. It is a promising instrument for both teaching and research.

Perry and Cooper (1986a, 1986b, 1989) studied defenses among a sample of individuals with borderline or antisocial personality disorder or bipolar type II affective disorder. They had a group of nonprofessionals rate twenty-two defenses by observing a videotaped dynamic interview of each subject. Their instrument, the Defense Mechanism Rating Scales (DMRS), includes a definition for each defense, a description of its function, comments on how to discriminate it from other defenses, and an accompanying 3-point rating scale anchored with examples of probable and definite uses of the defense. The reliability of the individual defenses was acceptable when group consensus ratings were compared (median intraclass reliability = .57, range .37 to .79). When defenses were combined into five summary defense scales (action, borderline, disavowal, narcissistic, obsessional) reliabilities were significantly higher (median value .74). Subsequently Perry added eight mature defenses to the rating manual and employed all thirty defenses in rating written summaries of prospectively gathered life vignette data on the same sample. Comparable interrater reliabilities were obtained using professional raters. The DMRS rating manual, currently in its fifth edition (Perry 1990a), is available from the author, while the DMRS definitions are available elsewhere (Vaillant 1992).

The DMRS can also be used for quantitative scoring of psychotherapy or other interview transcripts. Each of two raters listens to an audiotape while following along with the transcripts. Each defense is identified with a notation in the left margin denoting when the defense started and stopped operating. Comparing the profiles of defense scores for a session, the interrater reliability of this quantitative procedure generally yields an intraclass $R > .70$ per session (Perry, Kardos and Pagano, in press). Furthermore, each defense can be weighted by its place in the overall hierarchy of defenses (divided into seven levels, with 1 = least adaptive and 7 = most adaptive). When an average weighted score is calculated across all the defenses identified, the result is an overall maturity of defenses score, with an interrater reliability of intraclass $R = .89$. The author's impression, which should be empirically tested, is that rating transcripts alone without listening to the audiotape of the subject results in a loss of many nonlexical cues, especially those relating to affect. This would bias against the recognition of certain defenses, especially those dealing with inhibition and diversion of affect (such as isolation, displacement, and reaction formation). Comparison of the quantitative profile of defenses within or between subjects can detect differences in the frequency and degree of a defense's use, apart from its presence or absence.

DEFENSES AND ADAPTATION: THE DEFENSE HIERARCHY

A number of researchers have tested Semrad's suggestion that ego mechanisms could be organized hierarchically in relationship to their overall adaptiveness (Semrad 1967). Vaillant (1971) first proposed a theoretical hierarchy, grouping individual defenses into four categories from least to most adaptive: psychotic, immature, neurotic, and mature. This categorization did not include the so-called borderline level defenses proposed by Kernberg. Five studies have since tested the hierarchical model of defensive functioning using clinical methods.

Vaillant tested this hierarchy on two different longitudinal samples, using the life vignette method of assessing characteristic defenses and comparing them with global measures of adult development or mental health. The samples were a cohort of college-age men and a second cohort of inner-city men both followed into middle adulthood (Vaillant 1976; Vaillant, Bond, and Vaillant 1986). Battista (1982) examined the association between defenses using Vaillant's definitions and global mental health ratings on a sample of inpatients. Jacobson et al. (1986b) studied the association between defenses and Loevinger's measure of ego development in a sample of diabetic and control adolescents. Perry and Cooper (1989) studied a sample with borderline or antisocial personality or bipolar type II affective disorders. They examined the association between defenses and global functioning—the Global Assessment Scale (GAS)—at two time periods: an initial estimate at intake and an average of multiple assessments over several years of follow-up, presumably yielding a more stable estimate. Table 15.1 displays the correlations from these studies. The defenses are presented in order of the median (actual or interpolated) value of each defense's correlation with the measure of mental health used, across the six estimates from the five studies.

These studies used different time frames, different assessment methods of defenses and mental health, different age and socioeconomic cohorts, and both normal and psychiatrically disordered subjects. Overall, the similarity of the pattern of findings across the studies is strong.

The three psychotic-level defenses (delusional projection, psychotic denial, and distortion) had the largest negative relationship to global functioning, with a median of − .57 for the category as a whole. Although the findings are based on one study alone, they are highly congruent with the defenses' place in the hierarchy. Because of the wholesale distortion of external reality involved, these defenses are associated with very poor external adaptation. The term *psychotic* is accurate regarding reality testing in this category, but it conceptually confounds defense and diagnosis. This category of defenses largely fails in regulating the individual's response to stress and conflict, and therefore "level of defensive dysregulation" might appropriately replace the term *psychotic*.

Every defense classified a priori at the immature level also showed a negative association with global functioning, albeit not as strong as psychotic defenses. The median correlations were: acting out, − .32; neurotic denial, − .29; fantasy, − .28; projection, − .25; hypochondriasis (also known as help-rejecting complaining, − .23; and passive aggression, − .19. The overall median correlation for the immature category is − .28. Interestingly, the only positive correlation with global mental health at the immature level was obtained by passive aggression in the adolescent sample of Jacobson et al. (1986b), suggesting the possibility that this defense does not have such negative implications during adolescence as during later

TABLE 15.1. *Hierarchical Relationship of Defenses to Global Mental Health or Adaptation Study*

	Battista 1982	Vaillant 1976	Vaillant & Drake 1985	Jacobsen et al. 1986b	Perry & Cooper 1989	
					Early	Later
Psychotic						
Delusional projection	− .66					
Psychotic denial	− .57					
Distortion	− .48					
Immature						
Avoidance				− .44		
Acting out	− .22	− .37	− .26	− .26	− .37	− .42
Neurotic denial	− .40	− .24	− .41		− .27	− .04
Fantasy	− .60	− .28	− .57	− .30	− .01	.00
Projection	− .22	− .41	− .50	− .26	− .24	− .21
Hypochondriasis	− .04	− .23	− .53		− .21	− .37
Passive aggression	− .07	− .19	− .47	.11	− .18	− .29
Image-Distorting						
Splitting of others' images					− .42	− .34
Splitting of self images					− .31	− .36
Devaluation					− .24	− .18
Omnipotence					− .09	− .19
Manic denial					− .13	− .09
Bland denial					− .15	− .03
Projective identification					− .02	− .11
Primitive idealization					.01	− .10
Neurotic						
Displacement	− .16	− .16	.12	− .19	− .15	− .18
Dissociation					− .15	− .12
Asceticism				− .05		
Reaction formation		− .13			.15	− .04
Repression	.04	.04	.04	− .30	.09	.05
Rationalization					.13	− .04
Undoing					.08	.11
Isolation					.17	.10
Intellectualization	.29	− .14	.06	.34	.22	.21
Mature						
Sublimation	.26	.04	.45	.39		
Altruism	.19	.10	.46	.30		
Humor			.33			
Anticipation	.50	.34	.40			
Suppression	.25	.57	.55	.30		

developmental epochs. In further subdividing the immature level, Perry and Cooper (1989) designated acting out, passive aggression, and hypochondriasis as action defenses because they act on others, and denial, projection, and rationalization (from the neurotic category) as disavowal defenses because they act to disclaim wishes, ideas, affects, or actions.

The image-distorting category, a term suggested by Bond et al. (1983), includes the so-called borderline and narcissistic defenses. It was next in overall negative association to mental health, with a median for the category of − .12. Although based on only two estimates, both from the sample of Perry and Cooper (1989), the stability of the category over time strengthens the findings. Interestingly, the defenses most associated with borderline personality (splitting of self and others' images) had the strongest negative correlations, while those most associated with narcissistic personality (omnipotence, devaluation, idealization) had less negative effects. Rather than hold on to the diagnostic terms for these defenses, thereby confounding defense and diagnosis, borderline and narcissistic defenses can be aptly renamed major and minor image-distorting defenses, respectively. This division accurately reflects the degree of emotional distortion in self and/or object images or in the representations entailed by each; the difference in overall adaptiveness; and their empirical separation by factor analysis.

The category of neurotic defenses had an overall median association with global functioning of .04. Most individuals use some of these mechanisms, regardless of what other defenses they use in addition. The high prevalence of neurotic defenses, combined with their placement in the middle ground of adaptiveness, does not allow them to differentiate individuals by global functioning well. Within the category, there are some differential associations, however. The median correlations are: displacement, − .16; dissociation, − .14; asceticism, − .05; reaction formation, − .04; repression, .04; rationalization, .05; undoing .10; isolation, .14; and intellectualization, .22. Interestingly, the obsessional defenses, which minimize affect while keeping ideas intact (isolation, undoing, and intellectualization), appear somewhat more adaptive, while defenses that misdirect or alter the experience of affects and wishes (displacement, dissociation, reaction formation) are slightly less adaptive overall. Each of these defenses involves some inhibition of awareness of idea, affect, wish, or object. If one were to drop the historically burdened term *neurotic*, "level of mental inhibitions" would be an appropriate replacement.

For the five mature defenses studied, the overall median correlation with global functioning is .33. The medians for the individual defenses are: sublimation, .26; altruism, .29; humor, .33; anticipation, .40; and suppression, .43. These defenses clearly occupy the highest adaptive level. In each case the original stressor is dealt with in a way that creatively handles wishes, affects, and conflict, resulting in personally or socially valuable responses. If a name were to be found to supplant the older developmental term mature, "high adaptive level" would be appropriate.

Defenses can be grouped on the basis of conceptual relationship (for example, repression and dissociation are both associated with hysterical behavior), empirical association, and the ability to predict some other characteristic such as global functioning or response to treatment. For example, action defenses and major image-distorting defenses both correlate negatively with global functioning, but splitting and projective identification present serious problems of regression in treatment. There is a need for comprehensive study of the individual defenses to make a final determination of the most valid way to group them. Until that is done, the hierarchy of defenses will be open to some additional changes.

DIAGNOSTIC STUDIES AND OTHER FINDINGS

Several studies have examined the degree of association between diagnostic groups and defense mechanisms. These efforts have particularly focused on personality disorders, because Axis II focuses on personality traits more than symptoms (the opposite being true for Axis I), and defenses are often studied as dynamic traits.

AXIS II PERSONALITY DISORDERS

Vaillant and Drake (1985) independently rated a follow-up sample of inner-city men at age forty-seven for the presence of a personality disorder and for their defenses (rated from life vignettes gathered retrospectively from the previous ten years). Sixty-six percent of those men with any Axis II diagnosis used mostly immature defenses (projection, fantasy, hypochondriasis, passive aggression, acting out, and dissociation/denial), as opposed to 10 percent of those without an Axis II disorder. Conversely, the use of mature defenses such as humor, sublimation, and suppression correlated negatively with the presence of a personality disorder. Overall defense maturity also correlated highly ($r = .78$) with the Health-Sickness Rating Scale. The following specific personality disorders were highly associated with certain defenses:

Paranoid: projection 100 percent, acting out 75 percent
Schizoid: fantasy 33 percent
Antisocial: acting out 75 percent, dissociation/denial 63 percent
Narcissistic: dissociation/denial 83 percent, acting out 61 percent, projection 39 percent
Dependent: dissociation/denial 56 percent

Passive aggressive: passive aggression 64 percent, dissociation/denial 43
    percent
Avoidant: passive aggression 25 percent, dissociation/denial 25 percent

Unlike the other disorders, avoidant personality disorder did not
demonstrate a large association with particular defenses, which suggests
that it may be dynamically more heterogeneous than the others. Conversely, narcissistic personality disorder demonstrated a defense profile
similar to that of antisocial personality, although the former scored far
lower on a sociopathic symptom scale than the latter. This suggests a
common dynamic to both disorders.

Perry and Cooper (1986b) independently assessed the relationship
between groups of defenses and diagnoses in their study of personality and
affective disorders. Borderline psychopathology was significantly associated with the major image-distorting defenses (splitting and projective
identification) ($r = .36$, $n = 73$, $p = .01$) and with the action defenses
(acting out, hypochondriasis, passive aggression) ($r = .26$). Antisocial
psychopathology correlated with minor image-distorting defenses (omnipotence, idealization, devaluation) ($r = .23$) and with disavowal defenses
(denial, projection, and rationalization) ($r = .22$). The presence of bipolar
type II affective disorder was associated with obsessional defenses (isolation, intellectualization, and undoing) ($r = .37$). However, defenses were
not powerful discriminators of the three study diagnoses. Multivariate
analyses based on each subject's defenses alone were not able to separate
them significantly.

Perry and Cooper (1986b) also tested the hypothesis that the border-
line-level defenses outlined by Kernberg (1967, 1975) represented two
independent dimensions. When they subjected ratings of the eight defenses to a factor analysis, the predicted two factors emerged: (1) a borderline factor (now renamed major image-distorting), consisting of splitting of
self and object images and projective identification, and (2) a narcissistic
factor (now renamed minor image-distorting), consisting of omnipotence,
idealization, and devaluation. Mood-incongruent denial (manic or depressive denial) also loaded on the narcissistic factor. One defense, bland denial,
occurred infrequently and did not load on either factor.

Dahl (1984b) examined differences between hospitalized patients
with borderline personality and other disorders using the Bellak Ego Function Assessment. The defensive functioning of the borderline group was
significantly higher than that of the schizophrenic group but was not
different from the group with affective psychoses. Borderline patients
scored lower than those with other personality disorders and neuroses, a
finding in line with Kernberg's (1967) original assertion. Using the same
instrument, Goldsmith, Charles, and Feiner (1984) also found that defensive

functioning and level of object relations were the two ego functions that most differentiated borderline from neurotic patients.

AXIS I DISORDERS AND EPISODES

Ablon, Carlson, and Goodwin (1974) followed the course of improvement in hospitalized patients with unipolar or bipolar affective disorders using serial assessment of defensive functioning with the Ego Profile Scale (Semrad, Grinspoon, and Fienberg 1973). Two-thirds of the patients demonstrated a shift away from using distortion, denial, and projection as they improved clinically. Manic patients tended to show an increase in somatization and hypochondriasis just before switching out of manic episodes.

Perry (1988, 1990b) examined the association of defensive functioning and Axis I episodes in following up the sample of personality and affective disorders. Defenses were assessed by the qualitative method from videotaped interviews at intake. Action and major image-distorting (borderline) defenses predicted subsequent increases in depressive symptoms and gradual recurrences of major depressive episodes. Major image-distorting defenses also predicted the occurrence of psychotic and psychoticlike symptoms (such as illusions, ideas of reference) over the follow-up. Perry (1990b) subsequently rated defenses from the subject's response to life events over the follow-up period using the life vignette method, which yields a quantitative profile of each defense. The results indicated that action defenses correlated positively with total duration of dysthymia and agoraphobia and negatively with the number of hypomanic and manic episodes. Major image-distorting defenses correlated with the total duration of agoraphobia and of panic disorder. Obsessional defenses correlated positively with the total duration of hypomanic and manic episodes and negatively with major depression and panic disorder episodes. These findings also support the general hierarchy of defenses, in that the two lowest defense levels on the hierarchy predicted a more severe symptomatic course in most cases, while the obsessional defenses predict a less severe course. Again, midlevel defenses in the hierarchy did not predict any course.

OTHER NONDIAGNOSTIC FINDINGS

Haan (1963) found that IQ was generally positively related to coping mechanisms (mature defenses) and negatively related to the use of nonmature defense mechanisms. Prospectively, mature coping mechanisms correlated with demonstrated increases in certain aspects of IQ on retesting, whereas defense mechanisms correlated with a drop in aspects of IQ. Weinstock (1967) examined adult defenses in the same sample alongside ratings of the subjects' families made during childhood and adolescence. Family conflict in early childhood correlated with the subject's later use of regression, denial, repression, and doubt. Subjects appeared to learn these defenses by imitating how their parents handled conflicts. In contrast, mature coping mechanisms, such as suppression, sublimation, tolerance of ambiguity, and the ability to regress in service of the ego, correlated with a more stable early childhood, followed by some family conflict emerging during adolescence. In general the relation between coping mechanisms and family environmental variables appeared more complex and less clearly attributable to imitation and modeling than was true for defense mechanisms.

Snarey and Vaillant (1985) examined the relation between upward social mobility in Vaillant's inner-city male sample and defense mechanisms at midlife. Three defenses were associated with upward mobility, even after other social variables were taken into account. The authors posited that these defenses (intellectualization and the two mature defenses of altruism and anticipation) aid the individual in problem solving and forming helping relationships, which may in turn promote career advancement. Interestingly, intellectualization in the subjects was also associated with later upward social mobility in the subjects' children, demonstrating a cross-generational effect for this defense.

Vaillant (1983) examined the childhood antecedents of the overall maturity of defenses among his inner-city sample. Surprisingly, childhood variables (IQ, feelings of adequacy, not being hyperactive) were only weakly associated with adult maturity of defenses. Even childhood environmental strengths which correlated with adult mental health failed to correlate with maturity of defenses. Subsequent analysis suggested that maturity of defenses is not simply synonymous with adult mental health, but may play a role in its generation. Vaillant, Bond, and Vaillant (1986) examined the correlations between maturity of adult defenses and each of three adult measures: psychosocial maturity, social competence, and adult global functioning. The correlations were significantly stronger among those who had the bleakest childhoods (respectively, .77, .68, .82) than among those with intermediate (.66, .51, .78) or warm (.46, .38, .70) childhoods. While the conclusions from this finding would be stronger if defenses had been measured closer to childhood, nonetheless the consistent, differential associations suggest that maturity of defenses has a causal influence on later adult mental health, especially among those with bleak childhoods. In the prospective sample of college men, Vaillant and Vaillant (1990) did find that maturity of defenses at ages twenty through forty-seven was correlated with physical health (.19), psychosocial adjustment (.41), and observer-rated satisfaction assessed at age sixty-three through sixty-five. The predictive association between maturity of defenses and later psychosocial adjustment remained strong (.37), even after the effects of other strong predictor variables, such as mood altering drug use, alcohol abuse, and childhood strengths, were partialed out.

In a study of treatment for obesity, Ellsworth and colleagues found, using Vaillant's method, that patients with sustained weight loss by eighteen months had higher maturity of defenses than did patients with temporary weight loss. Specifically, the more successful patients used more anticipation and altruism, while the less successful used more passive aggression over the course of the study. The sustained weight loss group had greater numbers of fat cells than the temporary weight loss group, suggesting that the former group had equal if not greater physiological pressures than the temporary weight loss group. The authors suggested that relying on anticipation "may avoid the environmental, social and psychological (especially affective) pressures that initiate or maintain eating" (1986, 779).

In Ulm, Germany, Schwilk and Kächele (1989) have examined the association between defenses and adjustment among survivors of bone marrow transplantation treatment of leukemia. All subjects were assessed retrospectively using the Defense Rating Inventory (Ehlers 1983) for periods prior to, during, and after treatment. While this study is still in progress, preliminary use of cluster analysis divided patients into two groups. In the first group, avoidance and resignation predominated, resulting in a depressive retreat during treatment and recovery. In the second group, patients using projection and omnipotence were better able to counteract the life-threatening illness and treatment. Some obsessional defenses were evident as well during subsequent recovery. These findings suggest that defenses relatively low on the scale of general adaptiveness may have special value that differentiates them when certain life-threatening stresses are encountered.

SUMMARY OF CLINICAL ASSESSMENT STUDIES

The diagnostic studies cited suggest that there are important associations between the immature, major and minor image-distorting defenses and personality disorders, whereas mature defenses are negatively associated with these disorders. In particular, borderline patients were characteristically found to have lower defensive functioning than patients with other nonpsychotic disorders that have been studied. Defenses lower in the hierarchy assessed at intake or over the follow-up predict a more symptomatic course over follow-up of several Axis I episodes. In addition, there may be characteristic changes in defensive functioning over the course of symptomatic episodes, such as with affective disorders. More studies are needed to assess whether there are differential relationships between defenses and type of Axis I disorder.

These data suggest several things. First, there are important associations between dynamic defenses and descriptive personality diagnosis, but few are highly specific. For example, projection is somewhat specific to paranoid personality; acting out, which one would expect in antisocial personality, is equally prevalent in antisocial and paranoid disorders.

Second, the most prevalent of all defenses among personality disorders is denial (formerly called dissociation by Vaillant). Perry and Cooper (1989) similarly found that the disavowal defenses (predominantly denial) were the most commonly observed defenses in response to life events over follow-up, accounting for 38.3 percent of all defenses rated. This suggests that the factors that produce denial appear to be generic to whatever produces personality disorders.

Third, whenever two disorders share defenses in common, the disorders appear to share some dynamic etiological factors. Both Vaillant and Drake (1985) and Perry and Cooper (1986b) found a relationship between antisocial and narcissistic psychopathologies. Future studies would do well to study the two disorders together.

In summary of the nondiagnostic studies, defenses appear to be a component of mental health but are not synonymous with it. Overall maturity of defenses correlates differentially with mental health, depending on the quality of childhood. These associations deserve further study. Elucidating the factors leading to the genesis of defenses and enhancing their subsequent modification should have exciting and powerful influences on devising more specific and effective psychotherapeutic treatments.

Other Assessment Methods

SELF-REPORT INSTRUMENTS

Several self-report instruments have been developed to assess defense mechanisms. The advantage of the paper-and-pencil test approach is that it is saves the clinician's time, avoids subjective inference in rating, and is potentially highly reliable. However, there is a need to demonstrate that such instruments are valid measures of what they purport to measure. Because defenses involve a degree of unawareness of their operation, self-report can measure only conscious derivatives of a defense. Unless self-report measures correlate highly with clinical measures of their respective defenses, it will be difficult to interpret their relevance to clinical defensive phenomena, although they may measure other aspects of personality.

THE DEFENSE MECHANISM INVENTORY (DMI)

Glesser and Ihilevich (1969) constructed the DMI to assess five aspects of defensive functioning from subjects' responses to stories on a forced-choice questionnaire. The defense constructs are (1) turning against objects (encompassing identification with the aggressor and displacement), (2) projection, (3) principalization (encompassing isolation, intellectualization, rationalization), (4) turning against self, and (5) reversal (reaction formation, denial, negation, and repression). The immediate and short-term stability of the scales is good (Glesser and Ihilevich 1969; Weissman, Ritter, and Gordon 1971). Studies comparing the DMI to other measures have been summarized elsewhere (Ihilevich and Glesser 1986; Cramer 1988).

The ipsative scoring procedure for the DMI unfortunately introduces an artificial level of intercorrelation among scales, precluding quantitative scoring for comparing subjects (Cooper and Kline 1982). Cramer (1988) found the best support for the validity of the reversal and turning against the self scales. The evidence for principalization was dubious, and Cramer suggests that the scale may measure the tendency to value intellectuality rather than to use the purported defenses. Projection failed to correlate with measures of paranoid psychopathology, although some other correlates were in the expected direction. Finally Cramer found little evidence that turning against objects was a defense, but suggested that it is a tendency to lack inhibition or control. Massong et al. (1982) found few expected correlations between the DMI and another self-report measure of defenses. Unfortunately, the relationship of the DMI scales to clinical measures of defenses is largely unknown.

THE DEFENSE STYLE QUESTIONNAIRE

Bond et al. (1983) developed a self-report instrument, the Defense Style Questionnaire (DSQ), designed to assess conscious derivatives of twenty-four defense mechanisms. A factor analysis revealed four stable dimensions or defense styles and included the following defenses and designations:

Style 1: A maladaptive reaction pattern style included the immature defenses of acting out, passive aggression, regression, withdrawal, inhibition, and projection.
Style 2: The image-distorting style included the defenses of omnipotence/devaluation, primitive idealization, and splitting.
Style 3: A self-sacrificing style consisted of pseudo-altruism and reaction formation.

Style 4: An adaptive or mature style consisted of humor, suppression, and sublimation.

The maladaptive action pattern style correlated most negatively with independent measures of ego strength and ego development, while the second and third styles correlated somewhat negatively, and the adaptive style correlated positively. These findings are consistent in direction and strength with the hypothesized levels of defense the questionnaire tries to measure. In a subsequent clinical study (Bond et al. 1989), the first three styles correlated negatively with the Health-Sickness Rating Scale (− .23, − .23, − .20), as expected.

Bond and Vaillant (1986) reported that the first three defense styles were more highly associated with psychiatric patients than with normal controls. However, there was no clear relationship between any style and particular diagnostic groups. They suggested that defensive functioning appears to be independent of Axes I, II, and IV of DSM-III and therefore should be considered for its independent contribution to patient diagnosis.

Vaillant, Bond, and Vaillant (1986) administered the DSQ to Vaillant's sample of inner-city men, comparing clinical ratings of defenses at age forty-seven with the DSQ administered seven years later, at age fifty-four. Fifty percent of the DSQ items correlated significantly with the clinically measured style they purportedly represented, although not necessarily most highly with the identical defense measured clinically. Bond also compared defenses rated from the DSQ with clinical ratings using the DMRS (Bond et al. 1989). Unfortunately, single raters were used rather than consensus ratings, as intended, for the DMRS, resulting in diminished reliability. They found that immature defenses rated from clinical interviews correlated significantly with the maladaptive (.36), image-distorting (.32), and self-sacrificing (.23) defense styles; otherwise, the two methods were not comparable. When some patients were retested after six months of treatment, the DSQ styles were fairly stable (coefficients ranging from .68 to .73), with a tendency for treated patients to show less use of maladaptive and image-distorting styles and more of the mature styles. Bond (1990) found that borderline patients did not differ from patients with other personality disorders and from nonpersonality disordered patients on the four DSQ styles, whereas the borderline patients did use more immature and image-distorting defenses as measured clinically by the DMRS. This suggests greater discriminant validity for the clinical method than for the self-report.

Others have examined the stability of the factor structure of the DSQ. Steiner (1990) obtained the same four factors as Bond in a sample of eating disordered women, although data were not presented. Reister et al. (1989), using a German translation on a large sample, found that many items were noncontributory. When the questionnaire was reduced to thirty-five items, however, four clinical factors emerged. The immature and mature factors resembled Bond's, but splitting loaded with the immature defense style instead of with omnipotence and devaluation, which formed a separate narcissistic factor; instead of a self-sacrificing style, the authors found defenses controlling affects and impulses. Andrews, Pollock, and Stewart (1989) administered the eighty-eight-item revised DSQ (Bond 1986) to a large sample of nonpsychiatric controls and outpatients. They found a three-factor solution in which the image-distorting defenses loaded either with the immature defenses (splitting, devaluation) or the neurotic defenses (omnipotence/idealization). The maladaptive style correlated moderately with neurotic defense style, Eysenck's Neuroticism measure, an external locus of control, and an overall symptom score from the SCL-90. The neurotic defense style correlated less strongly with the other measures, while the mature style correlated negatively with them. The authors relabeled some of the DSQ items to make them consistent with the glossary of defenses in DSM-IIIR, and derived a short form (thirty-six items) of the DSQ. Flannery and Perry (1990) studied normal adults and found that only the maladaptive defense style resembled Bond's, whereas three other factors were not similar. The maladaptive style correlated very highly with reports of life stress and anxiety and depressive symptoms, as did some of the image-distorting defenses. A mixed self-sacrificing and mature factor correlated negatively with depressive symptoms. These studies suggest that the maladaptive style is the most stable and valid on the DSQ, and there is less support for the adaptive or mature style.

Pollock and Andrews (1989) found a differential association between specific anxiety disorders and defenses. Panic disorder with or without agoraphobia was associated with displacement, somatization, and reaction formation; social phobia was associated positively with devaluation and displacement, and negatively with humor; and obsessive disorder was associated positively with undoing, acting out, and projection, and negatively with humor.

Steiner (1990) compared the DSQ defense styles among different eating disorders. Patients with depression or normal-weight bulimia endorsed more immature defenses than did those with restrictive anorexia or bulimia/anorexia, who in turn endorsed more immature defenses than normal adolescents. Older anorectic patients showed lower defense maturity, suggesting that longer illness was associated with worse defensive functioning. Steiger et al. (1989) found that patients with any eating disorder subtype exhibited more maladaptive and image-distorting but fewer mature style defenses than controls, suggesting that the subtypes share a common dynamic substrate. An exception was that binging anorectics showed extreme maladaptive defense scores. Maladaptive defenses were correlated with developmental histories of less parental care and empathy and higher levels of overprotection, especially from fathers.

PROJECTIVE MEASURES OF DEFENSES

The Rorschach Test and Defenses.

Despite widespread use of the Rorschach test, few empirical studies of defense mechanisms have used it. Most of the research has been reviewed elsewhere (Perry and Cooper 1987).

Researchers have used three general strategies for rating defenses from the Rorschach test. The first relies on formal Rorschach scores, the second relies on thematic interpretation of the content of responses, and the third employs a mixture of the first two.

In general, studies focusing on exclusive use of formal scores have proven disappointing. These include early work by Haan (1964), which demonstrated few relations of formal scores to clinical measures of defense and coping. Bahnson and Bahnson (1966) devised a sixteen-item index of repression which included card rejections, long reaction times, and numerous determinant ratios to study the role of repression in the etiology of malignant neoplasm. Having inadequate control groups unfortunately prevented them from drawing definitive conclusions about their measure of repression.

Content-oriented measures of defense show the strong influence of Schafer's seminal monograph (Schafer 1954). Baxter, Becker, and Hooks (1963) developed criteria for scoring denial, projection, isolation, undoing, and displacement in a study of the defenses of parents of neurotics and good and bad premorbid schizophrenic patients. Differences in defensive style were found between parents of the two groups of schizophrenic parents, but not between these parents and those of neurotics. Holt (1960, unpublished manuscript) has provided definitions of some of the classical defenses (such as projection, isolation, negation, and rationalization) and other defenses (including minimization and repudiation) as a part of his effort to assess primary process thinking. His category of defense effectiveness, which includes these defenses, has been an important aspect of research in this area. In contrast to the preceding two measures of defense, both of which exclude repression, Levine and Spivack (1964) developed a complex measure for the assessment of repressive style. Because the measure relies extensively on verbal expressive style, it may be confounded by other factors that influence verbal expressiveness, such as guardedness, low verbal intelligence, and depression.

Several researchers have assessed defenses by using both formal scores and content interpretation. Gardner et al. (1959) studied the relationships between the cognitive styles of leveling and sharpening and their defensive counterparts, repression and isolation. They defined their content variables for repression (including childlike material, poor integrative effort, little variety of content) in general terms and used them to select protocols that reflected extreme reliance on either of these defenses. This method has generated some intriguing findings on the relation between perceptual styles and defenses (such as scanning and projection). Luborsky, Blinder, and Schimek (1965) found striking relationships between isolation and venturing to look around more (as measured by eye fixation photography) and between repression and the tendency to look around less. Using a similar approach to defenses, Bellak, Hurvich, and Gediman (1973) developed global criteria to rate defensive failure and pathological interference by certain defenses (repression, isolation, and projection) with adaptive behavior, using Rorschach responses in schizophrenics, neurotics, and normals. This approach employed intuitive judgment by highly experienced Rorschach clinicians without recourse to explicit objective criteria. It was also employed in the Menninger Psychotherapy Outcome Study (Applebaum 1977).

Lerner and Lerner (1980) developed an instrument, the Lerner Defense Scales (LDS), which assesses five defense mechanisms related to borderline personality organization as described by Kernberg (1975). The LDS scores only human responses on the Rorschach, which may limit its usefulness in individuals who perceive few human responses. Borderline patients used more splitting, devaluation, idealization, projective identification, and omnipotence than schizophrenics, and more splitting, projective identification, and denial than neurotics (Lerner, Albert, and Walsh 1987).

Cooper, Perry, and Arnow (1988) developed the Rorschach Defense Scales (RDS), which measures fifteen defenses across the range of psychotic, borderline, and neurotic defenses. The median intraclass reliability coefficient of the scales is .62 (range .45 to .80). The instrument primarily uses verbal content but secondarily includes aspects both of formal scoring and of the subject—examiner relationship. In an outpatient sample of personality and affective disorders, the authors found that borderline psychopathology was positively associated with manifestations of devaluation, projection, splitting, and hypomanic denial, but negatively associated with intellectualization and isolation. The latter two obsessional defenses were associated with the bipolar type II affective disorder group. Interestingly, no significant relationships were found between specific defenses and antisocial psychopathology. The authors found concurrent evidence for the importance of splitting in borderline personality, since splitting scored on the Rorschach correlated significantly with clinical ratings of splitting from independently obtained diagnostic interviews. Lerner, Albert, and Walsh (1987) also found that the RDS scales for splitting, devaluation, and omnipotence had higher scores in borderline groups than in schizophrenic and neurotic comparison groups. Furthermore, certain defenses from the RDS and LDS were highly correlated (splitting, .49; devaluation, .64), whereas others were less so (projective identification, .30; idealization, .13). While the LDS scales were highly intercorrelated, the RDS scales were not, which suggests better discriminant validity for the RDS.

Cooper, Perry, and O'Connell (1991) subsequently examined the ability of the RDS to predict outcome in a follow-up of their sample. Projection and devaluation predicted higher levels of both objective and self-report mood symptoms, whereas intellectualization and Pollyanna-like denial and isolation predicted lower levels. The same pattern pertained to predicting global functioning and impairment in psychosocial role functioning.

While the Rorschach has the disadvantage of requiring specialized training for administration and interpretation, it has the advantage of being less influenced by the examiner's technique than is a clinical interview. Although the Rorschach has been overvalued as an aid to descriptive diagnosis, studies using manual-based scoring systems for defenses may demonstrate new predictive possibilities for the test. This may include predicting regressive responses to psychodynamic therapies or helping to determine whether treatment resistance is associated with defensive organizations based on splitting or on higher neurotic-level defenses.

The Defense Mechanism Test (DMT).

The Defense Mechanism Test is a projective test devised by Kragh (1955; 1969; Kragh and Smith 1970) in Lund, Sweden, and it has been popular in European research. It consists of TAT-like pictures which are presented in a tachistoscopic device at increasing time exposures from the subliminal (say, .01 second) until the image is accurately perceived by the subject (say, at .5 second). After each presentation, subjects draw and describe their perceptions, which are later scored for ten defenses based on distortions that appear at different exposure times.

Cooper and Kline (1986) demonstrated that a necessary element in the visual presentation of the DMT is the presence of a threat to the main figure or hero in the picture. When the DMT is administered without a threat to the hero, far fewer signs of defensive activity occur. Manipulation of the type of affective threat presented to the subject influences the incidence of certain defensive responses. When elements denoting shame were introduced into the DMT picture sequence, significantly more isolation and reaction formation were scored than was the case when more pleasant affective cues were used (Westerlundh 1983).

Enthusiasm was generated early on for the DMT by the demonstration that DMT defense scores predicted the successful completion of training among pilots, and the likelihood of aviation accidents (Kline 1987). However, evidence is still inadequate to determine whether the DMT scoring system is a valid measure of defenses or of other forms of perceptual distortion. Nonetheless, the predictive usefulness has led to further refinement of an objective scoring method for the DMT (Cooper and Kline 1989).

The originator of the DMT referred to it as a test of percept-genesis of defenses, that is, that defenses in part generate distortions in perceptions that reflect early traumas. This notion contains an assumption in DMT interpretation, referred to as parallelism, that the relative place in the time series in which defenses show up reflects the age at which past traumata occurred. To date, parallelism has received support only from case reports (e.g., Kragh 1983). The assumption of parallelism is independent of whether the test measures defenses (Kline 1987).

Few studies have looked for evidence supporting the measurement validity of the DMT scoring of defenses. Von der Lippe and Torgersen (1984) examined the relation among women's DMT defense scores and character type, as measured by questionnaire and early history. The oral (dependent) character was related to lack of use of isolation, earlier recognition of oral themes (such as a woman breastfeeding), and the report of a cold, harsh upbringing. Obsessive character was associated with isolation and the report of a positive mother–daughter relationship. Hysterical character was only weakly related to repression, strongly related to introjection of the opposite sex, and related to a bad mother–daughter relationship. Cooper and Kline (1986) compared the DMT and 16-Personality Factor (16-PF) inventory for convergent evidence of the validity of the DMT defenses. The correlations were generally small but supported the validity of DMT isolation of affect, reaction formation, introjection of the opposite sex, and projection, while no evidence supported the validity of repression, denial, identification with the aggressor, polymorphous introjection, and turning against the self.

The DMT continues to be used largely in European research, where other measures of defenses have been heretofore lacking. New scoring systems have been developed (Cooper and Kline 1989), and a new computer-assisted method of presentation has been developed by Getzinger-Albrecht at the Forschungsstelle für Psychotherapie, Stuttgart, Germany. The DMT continues to hold promise, although more studies are needed to demonstrate the measurement validity of the individual defenses and the clinical usefulness of the DMT.

Challenges for the Study of Defenses

DEFENSES AND THE MULTIAXIAL DIAGNOSTIC SYSTEM

In the development of DSM-III and its revision, dynamically oriented psychiatrists urged that a sixth dynamic axis be included (Karasu and Skodol 1980). An axis for defenses appeared to be the most clinically useful possibility with consistent scientific support. However, efforts to create an axis for DSM-III and DSM-IIIR were hampered by the lack of preparatory work leading to a consensus on which defenses to include, how to define them, and how to rate them (Vaillant 1986), as well as a demonstration of the feasibility of a proposed axis in a field trial setting. Fortunately, things have progressed in the development of DSM-IV. A review specifically pertinent to DSM-IV is available elsewhere (Skodol & Perry 1993).

Why should defenses be included as an axis for DSM-IV? One of the accepted findings about DSM-III and DSM-IIIR is that it has been good at the descriptive task of diagnosis but offered little in elucidating the etiology and in guiding treatment of most of the neurotic disorders that bring people to treatment (Vaillant 1984). The majority of practicing psychiatrists and a sizable number of other mental health professionals conduct psychotherapy from a dynamically informed perspective, and some systematic diagnostic method is needed to help guide such treatments. A defense axis can offer such guidelines, and a few are listed here to whet the appetite. More extensive treatment of the topic is warranted.

1. Regardless of the patient's presenting symptomatic picture, the higher the overall level of defensive functioning (that is, high adaptive-level defenses predominating over those lower in the hierarchy), the better the prognosis.

2. When defenses from the level of mental inhibitions predominate, patients can be classified roughly as obsessional, hysterical, both, or other neurotic. When lower defense levels are equally present, patients can be classified further as masochistic (passive aggression, hypochondriasis), mixed borderline-hysteric (major image-distorting), and so on. Each of these has extensive treatment implications associated with a rich clinical literature.

3. When the major and/or minor image-distorting defenses are present, patients can be classified into borderline and narcissistic types, with their different treatment implications. Patients for whom splitting and projective identification are salient are vulnerable to regressing, especially in unstructured free associative settings, and may reenact childhood abuse scenarios in treatment relationships (Perry et al. 1990). Patients in whom idealization, devaluation, and omnipotence predominate may require modi-

fication of conflict-oriented interpretive treatments to emphasize the reparative value of such defenses (Cooper 1989).

4. Patients presenting with predominant disavowal defenses (denial, projection, and rationalization) are likely to have some features of personality disorders. These defenses impair the patient's acceptance of the seriousness of problems and capacity to take responsibility for handling the stressors and conflicts related to the presenting problem. Special efforts, such as using counterdenial and counterprojection, will be required to establish a positive therapeutic alliance (Perry and Cooper 1987).

The current proposal for a defense axis will have the clinician record individual defenses that are prominent or salient and note the predominating levels or styles that they make up. For instance, a patient presenting with life problems consistent with an obsessional and narcissistic character might have defenses such as isolation, intellectualization, undoing, reaction formation, displacement, omnipotence, devaluation, and idealization. The predominating styles would be obsessional, other neurotic, and minor image-distorting. These defenses would alert the clinician that standard interpretive techniques would likely threaten self-esteem regulation, leading to increased use of the narcissistic defenses, and possibly leading to a negative therapeutic reaction. Issues arising in therapy might be explored, interpreted, or supported depending on which style of defenses predominates at the time.

The proposed axis, with the support of the Fund for Psychoanalytic Research, is currently being tested at three sites: Cambridge Hospital, Payne Whitney Clinic at Cornell–New York Hospital, and hospitals associated with the University of Oslo. If the proposed defense axis demonstrates acceptable interrater reliability and other useful features, it should offer a persuasive argument for its inclusion in DSM-IV.

DEFENSIVE PROCESSES AND PSYCHOTHERAPY RESEARCH

The advent of quantitative methods of assessing defenses opens a new vein in psychotherapy process and outcome research. Because defenses are construed as basic psychological mechanisms underlying psychopathology, the possibility of identifying individual defenses as they occur during the conduct of psychotherapy is as exciting as measuring a physiological parameter during an experimental procedure. In psychotherapy, the therapist's interventions as well as the patient's external life problems and immediate experiences are naturalistic stressors for the patient. From a research perspective, identifying the patient's defensive responses may serve as a focus for examining the moment-to-moment processes of psychopathology in operation. Questions that warrant systematic study include the following:

1. Is the subject defending against an internal or external stressor; if so, what?
2. Is the defense associated with a core conflict?
3. Did the therapist's preceding intervention precipitate the defense or a major shift in the overall level of defensiveness?
4. What are the best ways for the therapist to address the defense to enable the patient to use higher- rather than lower-level defenses?
5. What therapist interventions help the individual generalize therapeutic advances in defensive functioning to stressors outside the context of therapy?

This is not a modest set of questions. It is a partial wish list designed to help us improve our understanding of defenses and their therapeutic treatment.

Conclusion

Of all the psychodynamic constructs, defense mechanisms have attained the most scientific support. There are reliable methods that can identify defensive phenomena from interview or life vignette data, projective testing, and self-reports. Although the comparability of data obtained by these different data sources and instruments requires further delineation, there is systematic evidence that individual defenses have meaningful relationships to psychopathology and adaptation. Defenses demonstrate a consistent hierarchical relationship to their general level of adaptiveness. Defenses are not synonymous with descriptive diagnosis, but reflect some of the dynamic underpinnings across related diagnoses. For instance, the use of omnipotence, idealization, and devaluation is common to narcissistic and antisocial personality disorders. In addition, individual defenses are associated with certain symptoms, symptom levels, psychosocial role impairments, and other evidence of compromise formations resulting from problems in handling stress and conflict. What little is known about the etiology of certain defenses supports roles for both biological and psychological factors, but much further study is required. The study of defenses in psychotherapy is still evolving from clinical report to systematic empirical study, but promises to aid in the devising of more focused and effective treatment interventions to improve adaptation.

References

ABLON, S. L., CARLSON, G. A., & GOODWIN, F. K. (1974). Ego defense patterns in manic-depressive illness. *American Journal of Psychiatry, 131*, 803–807.

ANDREWS, G., POLLOCK, C., & STEWART, G. (1989). The determination of defense style by questionnaire. *Archives of General Psychiatry, 46*, 455–460.

APPLEBAUM, S. (1977). *Anatomy of change.* New York: Plenum Press.

BAHNSON, J., & BAHNSON, T. (1966). The role of ego defenses: Denial and repression in the etiology of malignant neoplasm. *Annals of the New York Academy of Science, 125*, 826–844.

BATTISTA, J. R. (1982). Empirical test of Vaillant's hierarchy of ego functions. *American Journal of Psychiatry, 139*, 356–357.

BAXTER, J., BECKER, J., & HOOKS, W. (1963). Defensive style in the families of schizophrenics and controls. *Journal of Abnormal and Social Psychology, 5*, 512–518.

BELLAK, L., HURVICH, M., & GEDIMAN, H. (1973). *Ego functions in schizophrenics, neurotics and normals.* New York: Wiley.

BOND, M. (1986). Defense Style Questionnaire. In G. E. Vaillant (Ed.), *Empirical studies of the ego mechanisms of defense* (pp. 146–152). Washington, DC: American Psychiatric Press.

BOND, M. (1990). Are "borderline defenses" specific for borderline personality disorders? *Journal of Personality Disorders, 4*, 251–256.

BOND, M., GARDNER, S. T., CHRISTIAN, J., & SIGAL, J. J. (1983). Empirical study of self-rated defense styles. *Archives of General Psychiatry, 40*, 333–338.

BOND, M., PERRY, J. C., GAUTIER, M., GOLDENBERG, M., OPPENHEIMER, J., & SIMAND, J. (1989). Validating the self-report of defense styles. *Journal of Personality Disorders, 3*, 101–112.

BOND, M., & VAILLANT, J. S. (1986). An empirical study of the relationship between diagnosis and defense style. *Archives of General Psychiatry, 43*, 285–288.

COOPER, C., & KLINE, P. (1982). A validation of the Defense Mechanism Inventory. *British Journal of Medical Psychology, 55*, 209–214.

COOPER, C., & KLINE, P. (1986). An evaluation of the Defence Mechanism Test. *British Journal of Psychology, 77*, 19–31.

COOPER, C., & KLINE, P. (1989). A new objectively scored version of the Defence Mechanism Test. *Scandanavian Journal of Psychology, 30*: 228–238.

COOPER, S. H. (1989). Recent contributions to the theory of defense mechanisms: A comparative view. *Journal of American Psychoanalytical Association, 37*, 865–891.

COOPER, S. H., PERRY, J. C., & ARNOW, D. (1988). An empirical approach to the study of defense mechanisms: 1. Reliability and preliminary validity of the Rorschach Defense Scales. *Journal of Personality Assessment, 52*, 187–203.

COOPER, S. H., PERRY, J. C., & O'CONNELL, M. E. (1991). The Rorschach Defense

Scales: 2. Longitudinal perspectives. *Journal of Personality Assessment, 56,* 191–201.

CRAMER, P. (1988). The Defense Mechanism Inventory: A review of research and discussion of the scales. *Journal of Personality Assessment, 52,* 142–164.

DAHL, A. A. (1984a). A study of agreement among raters of Bellak's Ego Function Assessment test. In L. Bellak & L. A. Goldsmith (Eds.), *The broad scope of ego function assessment.* New York: Wiley.

DAHL, A. A. (1984b). Ego function assessment of hospitalized adult psychiatric patients with special reference to borderline patients. In L. Bellak & L. A. Goldsmith (Eds.), *The broad scope of ego function assessment.* New York: Wiley.

EHLERS, W. (1983). Die Abwehrmechanismen: Definition und Beispiele. *Praxis Psychother, Psychosom 28,* 55–56.

ELLSWORTH, G. A., STRAIN, G. W., STRAIN, J. J., VAILLANT, G. E., KNITTLE, J., & ZUMOFF, B. (1986). Defensive maturity ratings and sustained weight loss in obesity. *Psychosomatics, 27,* 772–781.

FLANNERY, R. B., JR., & PERRY, J. C. (1990). Self-rated defense style, life stress, and health status: An empirical assessment. *Psychosomatics, 31,* 313–320.

FREUD, A. (1937–1966). *The ego and the mechanisms of defense* (rev. ed.). New York: International Universities Press.

FREUD, S. (1894/1962). The neuro-psychoses of defence. In J. Strachey (Ed.), *The standard edition of the complete psychological works of Sigmund Freud* (Vol. 2, pp. 45–61). London: Hogarth Press.

FREUD, S. (1906/1962). My views of the part played by sexuality in the aetiology of the neuroses. In J. Strachey (Ed.), *The standard edition of the complete psychological works of Sigmund Freud* (Vol. 7, pp. 271–279). London: Hogarth Press.

FREUD, S. (1926/1959). Inhibitions, symptoms and anxiety. In J. Strachey (Ed.), *The standard edition of the complete psychological works of Sigmund Freud* (Vol. 20, pp. 77–175). London: Hogarth Press.

GARDNER, R. W., HOLZMAN, P. A., KLEIN, G. S., LINTON, H. B., & SPENCE, D. P. (1959). Cognitive controls: A study of individual consistencies in cognitive behavior. *Psychological Issues,* Monograph 4.

GLESSER, G. C., & IHILEVICH, D. (1969). An objective instrument for measuring defense mechanisms. *Journal of Consulting and Clinical Psychology, 33,* 51–60.

GOLDSMITH, L. A., CHARLES, E., & FEINER, K. (1984). The use of EFA in the assessment of borderline pathology. In L. Bellak & L. A. Goldsmith (Eds.), *The broad scope of ego function assessment.* New York: Wiley.

HAAN, N. (1963). Proposed model of ego functioning: Coping and defense mechanisms in relationship to IQ change. *Psychological Monographs, 77,* 1–23.

HAAN, N. (1964). An investigation of the relationship of Rorschach scores, patterns and behavior to coping and defense mechanisms. *Journal of Projective Techniques, 28,* 429–441.

HARTMANN, H., KRIS, A., LOWENSTEIN, R. M. (1964). *Essays on ego psychology: Selected problems in psychoanalytic theory.* New York: International Universities Press, Inc.

HOLT, R. (1960). *Manual for scoring primary process on the Rorschach.* Unpublished manuscript.

HOROWITZ, M. J. (1988). The mechanisms of defense. In *Introduction to psychodynamics: A new synthesis* (chap. 10, pp. 187–210). New York: Basic Books.

IHILEVICH, D., & GLESSER, G. C. (1986). *Defense Mechanisms: Their classification, correlates, and measurement with the Defense Mechanisms Inventory.* DMI Associates, 615 Clark Ave., Owosso, MI 48867.

JACOBSON, A. M., BEARDSLEE, W., HAUSER, S. T., NOAM, G. G., & POWERS, S. I. (1986a). An approach to evaluating ego defense mechanisms using clinical interviews. In G. E. Vaillant (Ed.), *Empirical studies of the ego mechanisms of defense.* Washington, DC: American Psychiatric Press.

JACOBSON, A. M., BEARDSLEE, W., HAUSER, S. T., NOAM, G. G., POWERS, S. I., HOULIHAN, J., & RIDER, E. (1986b). Evaluating ego defense mechanisms using clinical interviews: An empirical study of adolescent diabetic and psychiatric patients. *Journal of Adolescence, 9,* 303–319.

KARASU, B. T., & SKODOL, A. E. (1980). VIth Axis for DSM-III: Psychodynamic evaluation. *American Journal of Psychiatry, 137,* 607–610.

KERNBERG, O. F. (1967). Borderline personality organization. *Journal of the American Psychoanalytical Association, 15,* 41–68.

KERNBERG, O. F. (1975). *Borderline conditions and pathological narcissism.* New York: Jason Aronson.

KERNBERG, O. F. (1983). Object relations and character analysis. *Journal of the American Psychoanalytical Association, 31,* 247–271.

KLEIN, M. (1946). Some notes on schizoid mechanisms. *International Journal of Psycho-Analysis, 27,* 99–110.

KLINE, P. (1987). The scientific status of the DMT. *British Journal of Medical Psychology, 60,* 53–59.

KOHUT, H. (1984). *How does analysis cure?* Chicago: University of Chicago Press.

KRAGH, U. (1955). *The actual-genetic model of perception-personality.* Lund, Sweden: Gleerup.

KRAGH, U. (1969). *The Defense Mechanism Test.* Stockholm: Testforlaget.

KRAGH, U. (1983). Studying effects of psychotherapy by the Defense Mechanism Test: Two case illustrations. *Archives of Psychology, 135,* 73–82.

KRAGH, U., & SMITH, G. J. W. (1970). *Percept-genetic analysis.* Lund, Sweden: Gleerup.

LERNER, H., ALBERT, C., & WALSH, M. (1987). The Rorschach assessment of borderline defense: A concurrent validity study. *Journal of Personality Assessment, 51,* 334–348.

LERNER, P., & LERNER, H. (1980). Rorschach assessment of primitive defenses in borderline personality structure. In H. Kwawer, H. Lerner, P. Lerner, & A.

Sugarman (Eds.), *Borderline phenomena and the Rorschach test.* New York: International Universities Press.

LEVINE, M., & SPIVACK, G. (1964). *The Rorschach Index of Repressive Style.* Springfield, IL: Thomas.

LUBORSKY, L., BLINDER, B., & SCHIMEK, J. (1965). Looking, recalling, and GSR as a function of defense. *Journal of Abnormal Psychology, 70,* 270–280.

MASSONG, S. R., DICKSON, A. L., RITZLER, B. A., & LAYNE, C. C. (1982). A correlational comparison of defense mechanism measures: The Defense Mechanism Inventory and the Blacky Defense Preference Inventory. *Journal of Personality Assessment, 46,* 477–480.

PERRY, J. C. (1988). A prospective study of life stress, defenses, psychotic symptoms and depression in borderline and antisocial personality disorders and bipolar type II affective disorder. *Journal of Personality Disorders, 2,* 49–59.

PERRY, J. C. (1990a). *Defense Mechanisms Rating Scales,* fifth edition. J. C. Perry, Cambridge, MA.

PERRY, J. C. (1990b). Psychological defense mechanisms in the study of affective and anxiety disorders. In J. Maser & C. R. Cloninger (Eds.), *Co-morbidity in anxiety and mood disorders* (pp. 545–562). Washington, DC: American Psychiatric Press.

PERRY, J. C., & COOPER, S. H. (1986a). What do cross-sectional measures of defenses predict? In G. E. Vaillant (Ed.), *Empirical studies of the ego mechanisms of defense.* Washington, DC: American Psychiatric Press.

PERRY, J. C., & COOPER, S. H. (1986b). A preliminary report on defenses and conflicts associated with borderline personality disorder. *Journal of the American Psychoanalytic Association, 34,* 863–893.

PERRY, J. C., & COOPER, S. H. (1987). Empirical studies of psychological defenses. In R. Michels & J. Cavenar, Jr. (Eds.), *Psychiatry* (Vol. 1, chap. 30). Philadelphia: Lippincott.

PERRY, J. C., & COOPER, S. H. (1989). An empirical study of defense mechanisms: I. Clinical interview and life vignette ratings. *Archives of General Psychiatry, 46,* 444–452.

PERRY, J. C., HERMAN, J. L., VAN DER KOLK, B. A., & HOKE, L. (1990). Psychotherapy and psychological trauma in borderline personality disorder. *Psychiatric Annals, 20,* 33–43.

PERRY, J. C., KARDOS, M. C., & PAGANO, C. J. (IN PRESS). The study of defenses in psychotherapy using the Defense Mechanism Rating Scales (DMRS). In U. Hentschel & W. Ehlers (Eds.), *The concept of defense mechanisms in contemporary psychology: Theoretical, research, and clinical perspectives.* New York: Springer.

POLLOCK, C., & ANDREWS, G. (1989). Defense styles associated with specific anxiety disorders. *American Journal of Psychiatry, 146,* 1500–1502.

REISTER, G., MANZ, R., TRESS, W., SCHEPANK, H. (1989, SEPTEMBER). *Validation of the German version of Bond's Questionnaire on Defense Styles.* Paper delivered at the Biennial Meeting of the Society for Psychotherapy Research, European Division, Bern, Switzerland.

SCHAFER, R. (1954). *Psychoanalytic interpretation in Rorschach testing.* New York: Grune & Stratton.

SCHAFER, R. (1968). Mechanisms of defense. *International Journal of Psycho-Analysis, 49,* 49–62.

SCHWILK, C., & KÄCHELE, H. (1989, SEPTEMBER). *Defense mechanisms during severe illness.* Paper presented at the Third European Conference on Psychotherapy Research, Bern, Switzerland.

SEMRAD E. (1967). The organization of ego defenses and object loss. In D. M. Moriarity (Ed.), *The loss of loved ones* (pp. 126–134). Springfield, IL: Charles C Thomas.

SEMRAD, E., GRINSPOON, L., & FIENBERG, S. E. (1973). Development of an Ego Profile Scale. *Archives of General Psychiatry, 28,* 70–77.

SKODOL, A., & PERRY, J. C. (1993). (IN PRESS). Should an Axis for Defense Mechanisms be included in DSM-IV? *Comprehensive Psychiatry, 34*(2).

SNAREY, J. R., & VAILLANT, G. E. (1985). How lower- and working-class youth become middle-class adults: The association between ego defense mechanisms and upward social mobility. *Child Development, 56,* 899–910.

STEIGER, H., VAN DER FEEN, J., GOLDSTEIN, C., & LEICHNER, P. (1989). Defense styles and parental bonding in eating-disordered women. *International Journal of Eating Disorders, 8,* 131–140.

STEINER, H. (1990). Defense styles in eating disorders. *International Journal of Eating Disorders, 9,* 141–151.

VAILLANT, G. E. (1971). Theoretical hierarchy of adaptive ego mechanisms. *Archives of General Psychiatry, 24,* 107–118.

VAILLANT, G. E. (1976). Natural history of male psychological health: The relation of choice of ego mechanisms of defense to adult adjustment. *Archives of General Psychiatry, 33,* 535–545.

VAILLANT, G. E. (1977). *Adaptation to life.* Boston: Little, Brown.

VAILLANT, G. E. (1983). Childhood environment and maturity of defense mechanisms. In D. Magnusson & V. Allen (Eds.), *Human development: An interactional perspective.* New York: Academic Press.

VAILLANT, G. E. (1984). The disadvantages of DSM-III outweigh its advantages. *American Journal of Psychiatry, 141,* 542–545.

VAILLANT, G. E. (1986). Introduction: A brief history of empirical assessments of defense mechanisms. In G. E. Vaillant (Ed.), *Empirical studies of ego mechanisms of defense* (pp. viii–xvii). Washington, DC: American Psychiatric Press.

VAILLANT, G. E. (ED.). (1992). *Ego mechanisms of defense: A guide for clinicians and researchers.* Washington, DC: American Psychiatric Press.

VAILLANT, G. E., BOND, M., & VAILLANT, C. O. (1986). An empirically validated hierarchy of defense mechanisms. *Archives of General Psychiatry, 43,* 786–794.

VAILLANT, G. E., & DRAKE, R. E. (1985). Maturity of ego defenses in relation to DSM-III Axis II personality disorder. *Archives of General Psychiatry, 42,* 597–601.

VAILLANT, G. E., & VAILLANT, C. O. (1990). Natural history of male psychological health: 12. A 45-year study of predictors of successful aging at age 65. *American Journal of Psychiatry, 147,* 31–37.

VON DER LIPPE, A., & TORGERSEN, S. (1984). Character and defense: Relationship between oral, obsessive and hysterical character traits and defense mechanisms. *Scandinavian Journal of Psychology, 25,* 258–264.

WAELDER, R. (1930/1976). The principle of multiple function. In S. A. Guttman (Ed.), *Psychoanalysis: Observation, theory, application* (pp. 68–83). New York: International Universities Press.

WEINSTOCK, A. R. (1967). Family environment and the development of defense and coping mechanisms. *Journal of Personality and Social Psychology, 5,* 67–75.

WEINTRAUB, W., & ARONSON, H. (1963). The application of verbal behavior analysis to the study of psychological defense mechanisms: Methodology and preliminary report. *Journal of Nervous and Mental Disease, 134,* 169–181.

WEISSMAN, H. N., RITTER, K., & GORDON, R. M. (1971). Reliability study of the Defense Mechanism Inventory. *Psychological Reports, 29,* 1237–1238.

WESTERLUNDH, B. (1983). The motives of defense: Perceptogenetic studies: 1. Shame. *Psychological Research Bulletin, 23*(7), 1–13.

CHAPTER 16

Repression and the Unconscious

HOWARD SHEVRIN AND JAMES A. BOND

LET US IMAGINE THAT ELISABETH VON R., one of Freud's early patients who came to him suffering from mysterious difficulties in walking and standing (Breuer and Freud [1895] 1957), approached Freud with the following account of her troubles:

> "I know why I find standing up and walking so painful. It all began at my sister's deathbed as my brother-in-law stood beside me. It was then that the terrible thought first occurred to me, 'Now that my sister is dead, I can marry my brother-in-law.' Moreover, it is not really my brother-in-law I want to marry but my father, and since my mother is still living it would be good of her to die like my sister. But these are terrible desires to have and deserve punishment. These occasional rheumatic pains in my legs might serve as a punishment, making it hard for me to stand up or walk so that I can't go out and enjoy things— certainly not meet men. Why should any man marry a monster like me? I will stay home in pain, depriving myself of a happy life—a fit punishment for such awful desires. Please don't ask me to give up these desires; when I try to do that I get terribly depressed and feel there is nothing at all to live for. Better to stay home, crippled and unhappy, than to be totally depressed. I wish there were yet another alternative. Can you help me find it?"

Most readers might find this fictitious account unbelievable. Psychoanalytic readers might be equally incredulous but might consider several diagnostic alternatives: (a) for so much to be conscious, the patient must be psychotic despite her apparent reasonableness; (b) the patient is an obsessive, intellectualizing person who knows all this purely intellectually, and all the appropriate affect is isolated; (c) the patient's insistence on the centrality and importance of her own desires is indicative of a narcissistic disorder marked by an unconscious sense of entitlement; or (d) the patient has already been analyzed and that accounts for her understanding, but she is caught up in some unresolved transference bind with her previous analyst.

There is a fifth alternative unlikely to be considered: the patient is that rare, perhaps nonexistent person, someone who lacks a dynamic unconscious, who for whatever reason does not or cannot repress unwelcome desires and needs continually to deal with them in the full light of consciousness—a kind of psychodynamic idiot savant.

Why is the fifth alternative, although certainly imaginable, implausible? What is the basis for our disbelief?

From a common-sense point of view, our example provokes disbelief because experience tells us that people are not usually conscious of such painful personal truths. Yet from a thoroughly skeptical point of view, one could argue that common sense may suffer from overlooking the universality of report bias (Erdelyi 1985). While it may be correct to say that people hide painful truths from themselves, they also withhold painful truths about themselves from others, although they are aware of these truths. How do we know when we are dealing with the former and when we are dealing with the latter?

Our example provokes disbelief in psychoanalysts because a number of assumptions are inherent in the psychoanalytic method.[1] One crucial assumption is the axiomatic principle of psychological continuity: beyond any apparent surface discontinuity in the patient's conscious presentations of himself or herself is an underlying psychological continuity. The psychoanalytic method first directs us to be attuned to any discontinuities in the patient's account, any illogical leaps, omissions, or inconsistencies. Many psychoanalytic writers have developed terms for the phenomena. Rapaport ([1944] 1967) chose the label "discontinuities," Schafer (1983) referred to "signs of unintelligibility or less than desired intelligibility," Edelson (1984) called them "senseless mental contents," and Barratt (1988) talked about "internal opacities." This repeated attempt to label the same phenomena suggests how essential such phenomena are to psychoanalysis. Sometimes these discontinuities are obvious. The patient describes irrational fears, talks volubly about every relationship except one, or conveys in painstaking detail but without any appropriate feeling, a sexual problem. Thus, upon reading our imaginary account of Elisabeth von R., the psychoanalyst immediately tries to identify any possible discontinuity—it lacks affect, it sounds too intellectual-

---

[1]For a systematic examination of these assumptions and their crucial place in the psychoanalytic method, the reader is referred to Rapaport ([1944] 1967); Shevrin (1984, 1991).

ized, she knows too much, she is too insistent on the primacy of her own desires, or the like.

Discontinuity is a puzzling phenomenon that requires explanation. Certain phenomena are puzzling to all of us, regardless of our theoretical orientation or preferred method. For example, a phobia is puzzling to the phobic patient and to everyone else: the behavior therapist will apply one method, the cognitive therapist another, the biological psychiatrist a third, and the psychoanalyst a fourth. But all would agree that the phobia is puzzling. Why should a person fear something, knowing that it is not rationally to be feared?

The psychoanalytic method assumes that beneath the apparent discontinuity is an underlying continuity inaccessible to the patient. Our consciousness presents itself in patches, but there is an underlying garment that is whole. Thus, in the example, the underlying continuity may have to do with a hypothetical unresolved transference, or an unacknowledged sense of entitlement. These are clinical hypotheses.

From this apparent surface discontinuity and the assumption of an inaccessible psychic continuity, a significant corollary is derived: the psychological unconscious. Psychoanalysts are forced into disbelief when confronted with the Elisabeth von R. example because it violates the fundamental assumption of psychological continuity and its corollary of a psychological unconscious.

There are three other assumptions that serve to define the psychoanalytic method:

1. The *genetic assumption,* according to which current discontinuities and their unconscious causes have a history, although the assumption does not stipulate how far back that history may go
2. The *free association assumption,* which leads the analyst to believe that by eliciting any and all thoughts from the patient it will prove possible to arrive at a knowledge of the underlying continuity, although nothing is stipulated as to the particular content or form of these free associations
3. The *intervention assumption,* according to which all impediments to communication with the psychoanalyst on the part of the patient are to be pursued, although nothing is stipulated concerning the nature of these impediments or how they are to be pursued

Taken together, these assumptions constitute a unique method which makes it possible to explore the intimate, inner life of an individual in a way no other method can accomplish. Note that the genetic assumption says nothing, for example, about the significance of early childhood experience; the free association assumption says nothing about preferred means or content; and the intervention assumption says nothing about what types of content create impediments to communication from the patient to the psychoanalyst.

However, in their practice of the method based on these assumptions, analysts believe they have discovered that early childhood experiences play the preponderant role in the development of neurosis; that free associations are especially rich in feelings and experiences about sex and aggression with regard to relationships important to the patient, and that the feelings are often revealed by seemingly arbitrary connections (such as by slips); and that attending to impediments to communication reveals that feelings toward the psychoanalyst based on experiences from the past (transference) play an especially important role. The assumptions of the method sensitize the analyst to recognizing these kinds of discontinuities in the clinical material, which the analyst then explores and brings to the attention of the patient. Based on the accumulation of further data, the analyst tries to explain these discontinuities to the patient in the form of interpretations, and subsequently, to professional colleagues in the form of clinical theories.

The psychoanalytic method as briefly defined may assume that what is discontinuous is inaccessible, but this inaccessibility is not brought about in any particular way. Repression is only one of the possible ways of rendering something inaccessible to consciousness.

Let us take as an illustration the same Elisabeth von R. At one point in that early analysis, she recalled a thought that flashed through her mind as she stood at her sister's deathbed with her brother-in-law nearby: "Now he is free to marry me." In horror, she immediately banished the thought. Freud and she were convinced that the wish that lay behind the thought had caused the symptoms for which she had come for treatment; indeed, her symptoms were alleviated once she had recalled the banished thought.

The fact that a memory of this kind was elicited, that it had been deliberately banished, that a feeling of horror accompanied the thought, and that the symptoms disappeared, are data characteristic of a method that encourages an intimate sharing of an individual's inner life. It is unlikely that another method, such as behavior modification, cognitive therapy, or biological psychiatry would have uncovered data of this nature.

However, to identify Elisabeth von R.'s previously banished, unwelcome thought as the *cause* of her symptoms would constitute a clinical hypothesis in need of further empirical verification. From a purely clinical standpoint, the treatment outcome is entirely acceptable: a new understanding emerges, a symptom is alleviated, the patient is improved. Much clinical work in all fields is valued not because of its unequivocal truth value but because of its practical and heuristic benefits.

The scientific problem for psychoanalysis, however, remains to develop a reliable research methodology, sensitive to the nature of the data elicited, which can systematically and empirically test the predictive validity of such heuristically rich clinical hypotheses. Edelson (1984) argues, in his efforts to build a more empirically based foundation for psychoanalytic theory, that it is crucial that plausible alternative hypotheses be considered and ruled out, if possible.

In the present case, for example, it could be hypothesized that Elisabeth von R.'s thought, once banished, no longer existed in any psychological sense, but was present solely as some modification of the nervous system which could then produce symptoms lacking any relevance psychologically to the thought itself. Or, once banished, the thought might be a source of increased stress or tension and contribute to a variety of physiological and psychological disturbances. Or the outcome might be entirely the result of suggestion, a potential artifact of the psychoanalytic method.

Accordingly, repression and the unconscious can be seen to exist on different conceptual levels. Repression is essentially a clinical hypothesis formulated to account for the difficulties patients experience in recalling conflictual personally significant thoughts and memories as these arise in the psychoanalytic situation. The unconscious, on the other hand, does not have empirical standing within clinical psychoanalysis. Because the psychoanalyst uses the assumption of an unconscious at every turn, psychoanalytic data can only support the heuristic value of the assumption, not its validity.

An interesting implication can be derived from the conceptual disparity between repression and the unconscious. If the phenomena involved in repression are most commonly elicited by the psychoanalytic method, then they can best be studied within the clinical context of psychoanalysis. If the unconscious is a basic assumption necessary for the practice of psychoanalysis itself, then its existence is far better established by using methods other than the psychoanalytic.

In the review of the experimental and clinical research literature to follow, we shall see that efforts to study the nature of repression with nonanalytic methods have proven largely unsuccessful, while the existence of unconscious psychological processes has received, and continues to receive, increased support within psychology.

Accordingly, the best approach to studying the nature of repression and the unconscious might be a combination of clinical psychoanalytic and nonpsychoanalytic methods. Further support for this viewpoint follows in the concluding section of this paper, which reviews multimethod experimental studies.

Definitions of Repression

Generally speaking, in current psychoanalytic terminology, repression is defined as the *motivated forgetting* of some *ideational* content related to a conflictual unconscious wish.[2] In this definition, the motive is considered either to be entirely unconscious or to have a significant unconscious origin. The mental content is an idea, cognitive in character, rather than an affect. Affects are separated from a particular mental content through the defense called isolation. This usage of the term *repression* has not always been the rule.

Early on, Freud used *repression* as equivalent to any defensive activity. However, with increasing awareness of the variety of ways in which individuals can defend against what is emotionally unacceptable, in time, different defenses were identified, culminating in the classic contribution of Anna Freud ([1936] 1946). There have also been more recent attempts to inventory or catalogue the variety of defenses identified by analysts in the course of their work (Vaillant 1987; Perry and Cooper 1989); see also chapter 15). For our purposes, we will follow the currently acceptable "narrow" definition of repression, equivalent to the unconscious intentional forgetting of particular ideational contents related to a conflictual unconscious wish.

In his metapsychological paper on repression, Freud ([1915a]1957) identified three phases to the repressive process, which are roughly developmental in order: (1) primal repression, (2) repression proper, and (3) the return of the repressed. Although there is considerable unclarity about primal repression, it appears to serve two main functions—one developmental and the other logical. From a developmental standpoint, primal repression is presumed to constitute the first automatic repressive act directed against the "representative" of an instinct. It is this initial primary act of repression that creates the original "pull from underneath," from the direction of the instincts or impulses forming the basis of all subsequent repressions. One can designate this primal repression as logically required if one is to account for all later acts of repression identified as acts of repression proper. This concept of primal repression has the status of a theoretical fiction and has played little role in subsequent research and practice. The concept of repression proper is generally equated with the "after expulsion" of an idea that has already been in consciousness. In this

---

[2]There have been many efforts over the years to define repression. Systematic and scholarly explorations of these definitions can be found in LaPlanche and Pontalis (1973), which examines the various definitions offered by Freud, and Moore and Fine (1990), which draws upon more contemporary sources.

respect it is different from the original act of primal repression. When it is also borne in mind that what is thrust out of consciousness may not simply be the conflictual wish but also any derivative of it, one realizes that the scope of repression proper is considerable.

In his paper on repression, Freud offered the following account of repression proper: (1) an initial withdrawal of attention from a disturbing idea present in consciousness (initial avoidance), (2) the pull from underneath of the more deeply anxiety-arousing conflictual wishes; and (3) a permanent "countercathexis" against the idea, which has become part of the constellation of highly anxiety arousing unconscious ideas.

The pull from underneath requires further elaboration. The phrase implies that a repressed unconscious wish intrinsically seeks expression and gratification through whatever means might be available; any perception, sensation, or thought becomes fair game and, through displacement, can be linked to a repressed wish and thus itself can become subject to repression.

Once the notion of a derivative is relied upon to account for the various ways in which individual ideas, perceptions, memories, judgments, and so on, can in fact be indirectly and distantly related to the core of unconsciously anxiety arousing wishes, the door is opened for the "compromise formation" structural theory advanced by Arlow and Brenner (1964). From the standpoint of structural theory, the derivative enters into all compromise formations, insofar as it provides some modicum of gratification of the unconscious wish, is met with sufficient superego censure to result in a degree of bearable unpleasure, and remains sufficiently distant from the underlying wish so that the individual is protected against traumatic anxiety.

Brenner (1966) has argued persuasively against treating defenses such as repression as unique mechanisms; he considers them instead to be based on the full range of ego psychological processes put to defensive use. Thus, repression is based on forgetting, initiated and sustained by an unconscious motive to avoid anxiety which is related to an unacceptable wish. In Kernberg's (1984), Vaillant's (1990), and Perry and Cooper's (1989), efforts to create a hierarchically based taxonomy of defenses, repression is considered to be on a developmentally higher level.

Experimental Research on Repression

The effort to excise the phenomenon of repression from its *in vivo* psychoanalytic context and to study it *in vitro* in the laboratory has resulted in a variety of stillborn attempts, although recent efforts have shown more promise (Erdelyi 1985, 1990; Horowitz 1988; Singer 1990). The earliest efforts were based on a total misconception of the role of unpleasure in repression, relating it solely to unpleasantness of any kind in the ordinary meaning of that term, whereas in psychoanalysis unpleasure results from the desire to gratify a forbidden wish, awareness of which would result in conflict (Meltzer 1930). Even when efforts were made to induce anxiety in the laboratory, the basic defect remained because the anxiety was not related to individual underlying conflicts (Wolitzky, Klein, and Dworkin 1976).

Some researchers tried to simulate conflict and repression in the laboratory with the use of the Zeigarnik effect, based on the finding that uncompleted tasks were more likely to be forgotten than completed tasks. Uncompleted tasks could be designed to result in an ego-involving experience of failure at the required task (MacKinnon and Dukes 1964). But unless failure was related to underlying unconscious wishes and conflict over them, the results could not be expected to be decisive for the psychoanalytic concept of repression, and they were not. Laboratory manipulation of success and failure as a model for inducing repression was criticized and alternate explanations, not implicating repression, such as disturbed attention, response inhibition, and report bias were offered.

One might imagine that the substantial literature on perceptual defense would provide the most relevant and telling body of evidence in favor of repression on the basis of laboratory investigation (see Bowers 1984; Dixon 1971; Erdelyi 1974). Perceptual defense research has demonstrated that the recognition threshold for words varies as a function of word content. Moreover, individual differences have been reported; some subjects responded to emotionally laden words with an increase in threshold, while others responded with a decrease in threshold. However, before it could be decisively concluded that increases in threshold were a function of repression (rather than some disruption because of the sheer emotionality of the words), it was necessary to demonstrate both that there was some motivation on the part of the subjects for failing to recognize the words quickly enough and that this motivation derived from an unconscious conflictual wish. No such evidence has been brought forward.

Yet it was true that perceptual defense studies implied the existence of unconscious processes because they suggested that stimuli must first be identified unconsciously before recognition thresholds could be raised or lowered. Findings emerging from subliminal stimulation research offer greater opportunities for exploration than do perceptual defense studies insofar as they follow the fate of the subliminal input in subsequent responses such as images, dreams, and associations (see Shevrin 1988; Shevrin et al. 1992).

In a variety of cognitive experiments not directly concerned with repression, relevant findings have appeared (Erdelyi 1985). In addition to the perceptual defense findings that emotional stimuli may significantly affect thresholds, it has also been demonstrated with neutral material presented in perceptual displays that subjects can intentionally and selectively narrow the field of attention, omitting much that is plainly visible. Having reviewed a number of such cognitive studies involving selective attention and inattention, Erdelyi concludes: "This contemporary work tends to confirm the basic repression mechanism—if not the defense—posited by Freud, that is, 'a function of rejecting and keeping something out of consciousness' " (1985, 257). Erdelyi further concludes that some of the basic mechanisms that might be considered to be involved in repression have been demonstrated, such as retrieval inhibition, blocking, and dissociation. For example, subjects have been shown to be capable of intentionally blanking out a complex visual scene in order to attend to another superimposed scene. Also, it has been shown that aversive stimuli disrupt memory, but as Erdelyi states: "The compound fact—that the available mechanisms are in fact deployed for defense against aversive stimuli, as plausible as it may appear, has not been demonstrated experimentally" (1985, 258).

One interesting facet of Erdelyi's statement is the degree to which it is consistent with the expectations derived from structural theory, as proposed by Brenner (1982, chap. 5). According to structural theory, defensive activities utilize the full range of psychic functions and do not constitute a separate class of specialized defense mechanisms. In effect, any psychological process can be used in the service of defense. Experimental research has identified a variety of psychological processes operating unconsciously with respect to relatively neutral stimuli, all of which can be put to the particular service of a repressive defense once a motive has been identified for the defensive activity. While demonstrating that much can be processed unconsciously, cognitive experimental paradigms do not reveal the motive present at the time the psychological process elicited by the experiment is operating. Aware of this significant failing, Erdelyi notes that "scientific psychology has yet to develop a methodology of purpose" (1985, 259).

Systematic Clinical Research on Repression

How can an unconscious motive resulting in repression be identified? In Erdelyi's phrase, can the psychoanalytic clinical method, and the research based on it, provide a "psychology of purpose"?

Perhaps the most comprehensive research approach to the study of unconscious motivation and its bearing on defenses is Luborsky's program, based on the symptom-context method (chapter 1) and the Core Conflictual Relationship Theme (CCRT) (Luborsky 1984; Luborsky and Crits-Christoph 1990; see also chapter 17). The former method undertook to identify the conditions antecedent to a symptom, the latter to identify a significant transference paradigm in which wish (or motive) plays a significant role. When combined, these two methods could provide a powerful tool for investigating the role of unconscious motivation in symptom formation and empirically enable closer examination of the role of repression and unconscious processes.

With respect to the symptom-context method, Luborsky, Docherty, and Penick (1973) reviewed some fifty-three studies dealing with the onset conditions for a range of psychosomatic symptoms. They found that for every symptom there were psychological antecedents, although the relationship was often weak to modest. The same psychological antecedents were found for different symptoms. These antecedents were, in order of frequency across studies: resentment, frustration, deprivation, anxiety, and helplessness. In studies based on immediate observations, frustration tended to be a frequent antecedent, while in retrospective studies, separation anxiety appeared more frequently. While Luborsky and his colleagues were generally critical of the methodological rigor of the studies and noted difficulties in reliability in particular, they were pleasantly surprised by the · finding that in every study antecedent psychological conditions were found.

Although we can be similarly heartened by the fact that what are generally thought of as psychosomatic symptoms do indeed have psychological antecedents, how far do these findings take us in establishing unconscious motivation and the role of repression as they occur in the clinical setting? From the review, there would appear to have been no way to determine whether the frustration or helplessness were conscious or unconscious, or what aspect of the antecedents might have been unconscious. Similarly, the role of defenses in contributing to the appearance of the psychosomatic symptoms was not evaluated. The authors hypothesize that the link between the antecedent conditions and the symptom is a dynamic unconscious factor. It is also possible that some general effect of stress may be the cause: as frustration or separation anxiety increases in full consciousness, a condition of stress is induced that, once having passed a certain point, triggers a somatic symptom in a vulnerable system.

Perry and Cooper (1989) have developed the Defense Mechanism Rating Scales (DMRS), which are applied to measuring defense mechanisms operating in clinical interview and life vignette data (see also chapter 15). Although the authors identify a series of problems encountered in research on defense mechanisms (for example, no agreement on a defense inventory, no uniform diagnostic criteria, different data sources, and so on), the necessity to demonstrate that defense mechanisms operate unconsciously and that some mental content is kept from consciousness as a result, does not appear on their list, nor does the research itself attend to these two issues. Hypochondriasis, for example, is defined as a "defense against the anger the subject experiences whenever he feels the need for emotional reliance on others. . . . the subject expresses the anger as an indirect reproach by rejecting help as 'not good enough,' while continuing to ask for more of it" (Perry and Cooper 1989, 445). This makes psychodynamic sense, and the research itself emerges with interesting findings relating certain patterns of defenses with various diagnostic categories based on reliable clinical judgments. But as with the psychosomatic studies, alternate hypotheses asserting that these "defensive" processes could be occurring with full consciousness are not ruled out.

In a study attempting to pay careful attention to identifying what is and is not in consciousness, Horowitz and his coworkers (1975) sought to demonstrate that contents warded off early in a psychoanalysis appeared later on. The critical issue is finding the means by which the initial warding off was established. A group of clinicians read the process notes for the first ten sessions of a psychoanalysis and then examined hours 41 through 100 for newly emerging themes. They selected fifty of these themes which were then rated on a 5-point scale for the degree to which they were likely to have been warded off in the initial ten sessions, for instance, "He thinks of his father as greedy," rated at 4.50, versus "He fears looking ridiculous," rated at 1.70). A number of hypotheses were tested, such as the notion that patient discomfort would increase with the emergence of a warded-off content. By and large, the evidence is circumstantial and theory-dependent, although it forms a cogent and coherent pattern, *if* certain basic assumptions are granted—in particular, the assumption that the warded-off content was, in fact, unconscious, and that it was the emergence of this material into consciousness that caused the discomfort. Even within a psychodynamic theoretical context, however, it is possible to construct alternative hypotheses. For example, when in the early sessions the patient's father was idealized and in the later sessions he was vilified, it may not be the case that the negative feelings toward father were warded off only to emerge later, but rather that a positive paternal transference prevailed early on and was replaced later with a negative paternal transference. One could hypothesize that memories and attitudes toward father consistent with each transference valence were recruited without having to assume that memories and attitudes associated with the opposite valence were warded off. It should be possible (in principle) to determine through independent means the presence and content of any warded-off attitude. This endeavor would constitute a more rigorous test of the presence of unconscious warded-off contents.

Indeed, in Luborsky's research on momentary forgetting mentioned earlier, an experimental paradigm has been developed which can bring investigators closer to the actual occurrence of the defensive act. In these studies, a transient event, which appears to have direct bearing on repression, has been placed under intensive systematic scrutiny (Luborsky, Sackeim, and Christoph 1979). The phenomenon, although rare, is clear and reliably identifiable: as the patient is about to utter some thought, he or she suddenly forgets it. In about 70 percent of instances, the patient is able to recover the forgotten thought within two minutes.

When samples of several hundred words before and after the momentary forgetting (the context of the "symptom") were examined and compared with suitable control passages, three factors were found to characterize the antecedent conditions: (1) a cognitively disturbed state, marked by uncertainty in ideation and unclarity of expression; (2) a heightened insecure involvement with the therapist, marked by more explicit references to the therapist; and (3) an individually specific Core Conflictual Relationship Theme (CCRT), activated in the context of the relationship with the therapist. It is tempting to hypothesize that when a particular conflictual transference issue begins to emerge, as evidenced by greater engagement with the therapist and the appearance of material bearing on the Core Conflictual Relationship Theme, a thought related to the transference and laden with conflictual significance appears in consciousness, following which attention is quickly withdrawn. This sequence resembles Freud's postulated first step of repression characterized by the withdrawal of attention (Freud [1915a] 1957). In most of the Luborsky team's instances, however, the balance shifted back in favor of consciousness, and the thought was recovered. In instances where the thought was not recovered, one could hypothesize that the pull from underneath was stronger, that the thought succumbed to after expulsion, and that as Freud further hypothesized, a countercathectic force intervened to keep the thought from further entry into consciousness (Freud [1915a] 1957).

As Luborsky, Sackeim, and Christoph (1979) point out, their findings on momentary forgetting may support the hypothesis of motivated forgetting as one interesting construal of the data, but they cannot independently demonstrate its presence. They emphasize that their method does not allow for the independent assessment of the three factors (cognitively disturbed state, insecure involvement with therapist, and Core Conflictual Relationship Theme) and how they interact. Similarly, we cannot conclude on the basis of the research method what exactly was unconscious, except perhaps for the momentary forgetting itself. One does not know if the CCRT itself is unconscious, as implied by the concept of transference, or whether it may, in fact, be in the patient's conscious awareness.

The authors conclude, "The method of controlled naturalistic observation that we have employed has not settled some questions concerning the purposeful nature of forgetting" (Luborsky, Sackheim, and Christoph 1979, 347). Unimpressed with the outcome of previous experimental studies on repression, they have called for experimental designs in which stimuli would be uniquely tailored to the individual's psychology, and they have recommended the development of new methods to deal with the limitations of naturalistic observations in identifying the role of unconscious motivation.

Multiple-Method Research

As noted earlier, the clinical psychoanalytic method is best suited to elicit phenomena that can be accounted for by the theory of repression, but it is poorly suited to establishing the role of the unconscious in that process. While the theory stipulates that forgetting must be motivated by conflict associated with psychic pain, evidence for potential mechanisms which could be used for repressive purposes must be demonstrated empirically. The strength of the symptom-context method derives from its incorporation of a naturalistic clinical psychodynamic method which allows for the manifestation of symptoms to be elicited by the method itself. While it is rich in generating hypotheses, the symptom-context method, as used, for example, in clinical studies of momentary forgetting, cannot definitively establish a motive or yield information regarding the unconscious nature of a patient's behavior. Similarly, insufficient data are available regarding the patient's degree of conscious awareness regarding his or her own core conflicts at the outset of, or during the course of, psychodynamic treatment.

Accordingly a multiple-method approach, based on data entirely independent of clinical judgment yet converging with data produced with naturalistic clinical methods, could hold promise of being able to resolve some of the methodological shortcomings of research on the psychoanalytic concept of repression.

There have been attempts to incorporate other methods with the psychoanalytic clinical approach since the 1940s. One of the earliest studies, Mittleman and Wolff (1943), recorded fluctuations in finger temperature during psychoanalytic sessions. They found that temperature decreased during periods of negative or conflictual affect and increased with positive affect. However, skin temperature also increased when there was clinical evidence for a successful repressive pattern. Thus, increased finger temperature could not distinguish between a repressed and a nonconflicted state. As in the symptom-context and CCRT methods, the determination of what was unconscious was based on complex clinical interpretations.

In an interesting report of observations on the use of the galvanic skin response (GSR) collected during psychotherapy sessions, Toomin and Toomin (1975) described a promising physiological measure. They provided anecdotal clinical evidence that the GSR displays a different pattern depending on whether emotionally meaningful material is in, or approaching, consciousness or is deeply repressed. A sharp increase in GSR indicates that material is in, or close to, consciousness while a paradoxical flatness or drop in skin conductance is indicative of deeply repressed material. The potential value of this index lies in the fact that it could provide a measure independent of clinical inference or interpretation, thus, making a study of convergent validity feasible. For example, one might imagine a study about the nature of the wishes which are likely to be repressed and predict unique GSR patterns when such material emerges in the clinical exchange. To our knowledge, no subsequent research has exploited these clinical observations.

More recently, Glucksman, Quinlan, and Leigh (1985) reported on a psychotherapy case wherein changes in skin conductance were studied in connection with ratings of defenses, manifest symptoms, and affect. They found that increases in skin conductance accompanied increased symptom experience and occurrence, a decreasing sense of mastery, and increased negative affect. If the Toomin and Toomin observations are correct, this increase might indicate material that would be in, or approaching, consciousness, rather than pointing to the presence of deeply repressed material. The findings support previous work done on antecedent conditions of psychosomatic symptoms and extend this work to purely psychological symptoms such as phobias and anxiety states. At the same time, the study is subject to the criticisms noted earlier with respect to establishing the role of unconscious processes in the patient's behavior.

In our own research, we have developed a multiple-method approach aimed at investigating the relationship between symptom and unconscious conflict (see Shevrin 1988; Shevrin et al. 1992). The method is comprised of three independent sets of operations or methods: (a) a clinical psychodynamic assessment, (b) a cognitive laboratory procedure based on the use of subliminal and supraliminal stimuli, and (c) a signal analysis of event-related potentials (ERPs) obtained in response to the subliminal and supraliminal tachistoscopic word presentations.

Patients diagnosed with social phobias and pathological grief reactions are evaluated in depth and given a psychodynamically oriented test battery, including the WAIS, Rorschach, and TAT. Clinical evaluation interviews, usually four in number, are tape recorded and transcribed, as are the testing sessions. Psychoanalytically oriented clinicians, using their clinical judgment as they would in nonresearch cases, examine the interview and test protocols and arrive at a psychodynamic formulation. That formulation becomes the basis for selecting key words and phrases used by the patient which in the clinicians' judgments are related to the patient's conscious experience of the symptom and to the underlying unconscious conflict.[3] These words, plus two groups of suitable control words drawn from the Osgood Semantic Differential (Osgood, May, and Miron 1975), are then presented in a tachistoscope for a subliminal duration (1 msec) and for a supraliminal duration (30–40 msec), both at 10 ft/lamberts luminance. Each time a word is flashed at one or the other duration, an objectively measured EEG brain response—that is, an event-related potential—is obtained. We wanted to know if the words selected to relate to the unconscious conflict when presented subliminally and supraliminally would show different patterns of brain response than words related to the conscious experience of the symptom.

In this approach, the use of subliminal stimuli is of special methodological importance: when stimuli are presented at 1 msec under the conditions of luminance described, the stimuli are considerably below the recognition threshold and can be considered to be entirely unconscious; the subliminal condition meets the most stringent threshold criteria for determining subliminality (Cheesman and Merikle 1986). Thus, no inference needs to be made as to the unconscious status of the subliminal stimuli, as would occur in the clinical situation. At the same time, the signal analysis of brain responses provides objective measurements based on operations entirely independent of clinical judgments, the subliminal/supraliminal stimuli, or introspective reports. Accordingly, the method incorporates three independent methods derived from diverse domains which can meaningfully converge on hypotheses concerning unconscious conflict.

We found that when words selected by clinicians to be related to the unconscious conflict underlying the patient's symptom are presented subliminally, the brain can correctly identify them; however, when these same words are presented supraliminally, the brain can no longer correctly identify them. The opposite pattern is found for words related to the patient's conscious experience of a symptom. The brain more correctly identifies these conscious words supraliminally than subliminally. The control words show no partiality in correct brain identification, either for the subliminal or the supraliminal conditions.

In short, the patients appear to know unconsciously what they appear not to know consciously, but only for the words that have been selected by clinicians to be related to unconscious conflict. The hypotheses regarding unconscious conflicts developed by the clinicians are supported by convergent findings from the subliminal/supraliminal presentations and the

[3]Concerns with interjudge reliability of word selection were dealt with in this design in two ways: (1) Based on the Delphi method (Linstone and Turoff 1975), the judges' word ratings were combined; combined ratings are more reliable than individual ratings (Cronbach 1970, 167–173). (2) Given our convergent validity design, a statistical association was sought between the word selections and EEG brain responses; if the word selections were highly unreliable, it is unlikely that any statistically significant association would have been found.

concomitant brain responses. The assumptive and inferential nature of unconscious processing necessitated by the clinical method is compensated for by the operationally defined nature of unconscious processing which characterizes the subliminal approach.

Moreover, the unconscious conflict word stimuli are processed differently by the brain when they are presented supraliminally and are in full conscious awareness. It is reasonable to hypothesize that what accounts for the failure of the brain to identify the unconscious-related words supraliminally, when it has already identified them accurately subliminally, is some inhibitory or repressive process. Note again that the stimuli selected were uniquely tailored to fit the particular unconscious conflict manifested by each individual subject.

One might argue that what the clinicians have hypothesized to be unconscious might in fact have been in the patient's conscious awareness. If so, it becomes difficult to explain why the words hypothesized to be related to an unconscious conflict are processed so differently (when presented subliminally and supraliminally) from conscious words, that is, those related to the consciously experienced symptom. Why in particular are the conflictual words not correctly identified by brain responses when they are supraliminal and in consciousness, especially since they have already been so identified subliminally? It would seem that the less complicated and consistent explanation is that the hypothesized conflict was in fact unconscious.

It should also be noted that although the individual words were quite different from subject to subject, thus meeting a condition advocated by Luborsky, Sackeim, and Christoph (1979), the brain responses indicated that functionally they were treated the same way depending on whether they were related to the unconscious conflict or presented subliminally or supraliminally.

A multiple-method approach based on convergent operations holds some promise for investigating the nature of repression and unconscious processes, insofar as it both takes advantage of the strengths of the clinical psychoanalytic method in eliciting the requisite phenomena and compensates for the method's weaknesses in identifying the presence of unconscious activity.

Summary

The phenomena calling for the hypothesis of repression can best be elicited by the psychoanalytic method. As a result, efforts to investigate this hypothesis by laboratory means are unlikely to succeed because they cannot elicit the requisite phenomena. However, the psychoanalytic method, which is based in part on the assumption of a psychological unconscious, cannot distinguish what is unconscious from what is conscious. For this discrimination, more exacting laboratory methods are more suitable. The main implication of our analysis is that the relationship between repression and the unconscious can best be investigated with the combined use of clinical and laboratory methods.

A review of the experimental literature on repression supports the position that studies have largely failed to provide evidence in support of repression. Similarly, a review of the clinical research supports the position that studies have failed to identify when a particular content is unconscious. Finally, a number of multi-method studies are reviewed which promise as an approach to cast light on the relationship between repression and the unconscious.

References

ARLOW, J. A., & BRENNER, C. (1964). *Psychoanalytic concepts and the structural theory.* New York: International Universities Press.

BARRATT, B. B. (1988). Why is psychoanalysis so controversial? Notes from left field! *Psychoanalytic Psychology, 5*(3), 223–239.

BOWERS, K. S. (1984). On being unconsciously influenced and informed. In K. S. Bowers & D. Meichenbaum (Eds.), *The unconscious reconsidered.* New York: Wiley.

BRENNER, C. (1966). The mechanism of repression. In *Psychoanalysis: A general psychology.* New York: International Universities Press, 390–399.

BRENNER, C. (1982). *The mind in conflict.* New York: International Universities Press.

BREUER, J., & FREUD, S. (1895/1957). Studies on hysteria. In J. Strachey (Ed.), *The standard edition of the complete psychological works of Sigmund Freud* (Vol. 2, pp. 135–181). London: Hogarth Press.

CHEESMAN, J., & MERIKLE, P. M. (1986). Distinguishing conscious from unconscious perceptual processes. *Canadian Journal of Psychology, 40*(4), 343–367.

CRONBACH, L. J. *Essentials of psychological testing,* (3rd ed.). New York: Harper & Row, 1970.

DIXON, N. F. (1971). *Subliminal perception: The nature of a controversy.* London: McGraw-Hill.

EDELSON, M. (1984). *Hypothesis and evidence in psychoanalysis.* Chicago: University of Chicago Press.

ERDELYI, M. H. (1974). A new look at the new look: Perceptual defense and vigilance. *Psychological Review, 82,* 1–25.

ERDELYI, M. H. (1985). *Psychoanalysis: Freud's cognitive psychology.* New York: Freeman.

ERDELYI, M. H. (1990). Repression, reconstruction, and defense: History and integration of the psychoanalytic and experimental framework. In J. L.

Singer (Ed.), *Repression and dissociation*. Chicago: University of Chicago Press.

FREUD, A. (1936/1946). *The ego and the mechanisms of defense*. New York: International Universities Press.

FREUD, S. (1915a/1957). Repression. In J. Strachey (Ed.), *The standard edition, of the complete psychological works of Sigmund Freud* (Vol. 14, pp. 143–158). London: Hogarth Press.

FREUD, S. (1915b/1957). The unconscious. In J. Strachey (Ed.), *The standard edition, of the complete psychological works of Sigmund Freud* (Vol. 14, pp. 166–204). London: Hogarth Press.

GLUCKSMAN, M. L., QUINLAN, D. M., & LEIGH, H. (1985). Skin conductance changes and psychotherapeutic content in the treatment of a phobic patient. *British Journal of Medical Psychology, 58,* 155–163.

HOROWITZ, L. M., SAMPSON, H., SIEGELMAN, E. Y., WOLFSON, A., & WEISS, J. (1975). On the identification of warded off mental contents: An empirical and methodological contribution. *Journal of Abnormal Psychology, 84,* 545–558.

HOROWITZ, M. J. (ED.). (1988). *Psychodynamics and cognition*. Chicago: University of Chicago Press.

KERNBERG, O. F. (1984). *Severe personality disorders*. New Haven: Yale University Press.

LAPLANCHE, J., & PONTALIS, J. B. (1973). *The language of psychoanalysis*. New York: Norton.

LINSTONE, H. A., & TUROFF, N. (1975). *The Delphi Method: Techniques and applications*. Reading, MA: Addison Wesley.

LUBORSKY, L. (1984). *Principles of psychoanalytic psychotherapy*. New York: Basic Books.

LUBORSKY, L., & CRITS-CHRISTOPH, P. (1990). *Understanding transference: The Core Conflictual Relationship Theme method*. New York: Basic Books.

LUBORSKY, L., DOCHERTY, J. P., & PENICK, S. (1973). Onset conditions for psychosomatic symptoms: A comparative review of immediate observations with retrospective research. *Psychosomatic Medicine, 35*(3), 187–204.

LUBORSKY, L., SACKEIM, H., & CHRISTOPH, P. (1979). The state conducive to momentary forgetting. In J. Kihlstrom & F. Evans (Eds.), *Functional disorders of memory*. Hillsdale, NJ: Erlbaum.

MACKINNON, D. W., & DUKES, W. F. (1964). Repression. In L. Postman (Ed.), *Psychology in the making*. New York: Knopf.

MELTZER, H. (1930). Individual differences in forgetting pleasant and unpleasant experiences. *Journal of Educational Psychology, 21,* 399–409.

MITTLEMAN, B., & WOLFF, H. G. (1943). Emotions and skin temperature: Observations on patients during psychotherapeutic (psychoanalytic) interviews. *Psychosomatic Medicine, 5,* 211–231.

MOORE, B. E. & FINE, B. D. (1990). *Psychoanalytic terms and concepts*. New Haven: American Psychoanalytic Association and Yale University Press.

OSGOOD, C. C., MAY, W. H., & MIRON, M. S. (1975). *Cross-cultural universals of affective meaning.* Urbana: University of Illinois Press.

PERRY, J. C., & COOPER, S. H. (1989). An empirical study of defense mechanisms. *Archives of General Psychiatry, 46,* 444–452.

RAPAPORT, D. (1944/1967). The scientific methodology of psychoanalysis. *In M. M. Gill (Ed.), The collected papers of David Rapaport.* New York: Basic Books.

SCHAFER, R. (1983). *The analytic attitude.* New York: Basic Books.

SHEVRIN, H. (1984). The fate of the five metapsychological principles. *Psychoanalytic Inquiry, 4*(1), 33–58.

SHEVRIN, H. (1986). Subliminal perception and dreaming. *Journal of Mind and Behavior, Cognition and Dream Research* (Special Issue), 7, 379–395.

SHEVRIN, H. (1988). Unconscious conflict: A convergent psychodynamic and electrophysiological approach. In M. J. Horowitz (Ed.), *Psychodynamics and cognition.* Chicago: University of Chicago Press.

SHEVRIN, H. (1990). Subliminal perception and repression. In J. Singer (Ed.), *Repression and dissociation: Implications for personality, psychopathology and health.* Chicago: University of Chicago Press.

SHEVRIN, H. (1991, APRIL). *The nature of the psychoanalytic method: Clinical and research implications.* Paper presented at the First International Conference on Psychoanalytic Research, London.

SHEVRIN, H., WILLIAMS, W. J., MARSHALL, R. E., HERTEL, R. K., BOND, J. A., & BRAKEL, L. A. (1992). Event-related potential indicators of the dynamic unconscious. *Consciousness and Cognition, 1,* 340–366.

SINGER, J., (ED.). (1990). *Repression and dissociation: Implications for personality, psychopathology and health.* Chicago: University of Chicago Press.

TOOMIN, M. K., & TOOMIN, H. (1975). GSR feedback in psychotherapy: Some clinical observations. *Psychotherapy: Theory, Research and Practice, 12,* 33–38.

VAILLANT, G. (1987). Empirical studies of ego mechanisms of defense. *American Journal of Psychiatry, 48,* 131–135.

VAILLANT, G. (1990). Repression in college men followed for half a century. In J. Singer (Ed.), *Repression and dissociation: Implications for personality, psychopathology, and health.* Chicago: University of Chicago Press.

WOLITZKY, D. L., KLEIN, G. S., & DWORKIN, S. F. (1976). An experimental approach to the study of repression: Effects of a hypnotically induced fantasy. In D. P. Spence (Ed.), *Psychoanalysis and contemporary science.* New York: International Universities Press.

CHAPTER 17

Transference-Related Measures: A New Class Based on Psychotherapy Sessions

LESTER LUBORSKY, JACQUES P. BARBER,
JEFFREY BINDER, JOHN CURTIS, HARTVIG DAHL,
LEONARD M. HOROWITZ, MARDI HOROWITZ,
J. CHRISTOPHER PERRY, THOMAS SCHACHT,
GEORGE SILBERSCHATZ, AND VIRGINIA TELLER

WE INTRODUCE HERE A NEW CLASS of transference-related measures. These measures have in common a method for extracting from psychotherapy sessions the patient's underlying patterns of conflictual themes. Almost all of these measures emphasize the central relationship pattern (CRP) of conflictual relationships with others and with the self.

Freud's ([1912] 1958) assumption in his explanation of transference was that a central relationship pattern is formed in the early relationships with the parents; once formed, it constantly gets "reprinted afresh" throughout a person's life in close relationships, including the one with the therapist. The basic idea of this pattern was first presented by Freud in 1895 and then presented again in various ways throughout his career—most fully in his "transference template" concept in 1912. Then, for the past century dynamic clinicians have used this basic concept for understanding the parallels between the patient's experience of the relationship with the therapist and the patient's significant early parental relationships.

The heart of the observations is found in the pervasiveness of certain ideas throughout the session and particularly across the narratives in the session. This pervasiveness gives the greatest support to the concept of a pattern or schema that serves as a template for generating similar versions of itself.

Surely, a reliable operational method for extracting so central a pattern should be mightily useful in clinical work. Yet only recently have such measures been introduced into psychotherapy research and practice. There are cogent reasons for this delay, however. For one, dynamic psychotherapy practitioners were almost totally unaware of how little they agreed with each other, even for experts' formulations of the transference (Seitz 1966; DeWitt et al. 1983). In addition, clinicians have been skeptical of any guidelines that they construe as lessening the sensitivity of their clinical judgment.

Despite these "resistances" to the development of transference measures, the new genre of guided measures based on psychotherapy has been healthily multiplying ever since Luborsky (1976). There are now fifteen of them in various states of development and application (the seven italicized works are used in this chapter as a representative sample to illustrate the genre): The measures can be found in Luborsky (1976), Caston (1977), Curtis and Silberschatz (1991), Benjamin (1979), M. Horowitz (1979), Teller and Dahl (1981), Carlson (1981), Gill and Hoffman (1982), Schacht, Binder, and Strupp (1984), Grawe and Caspar (1984), Kiesler et al. (1985), Bond and Shevrin (1986), Maxim (1986), Kiesler (1987), Perry, Augusto, and Cooper (1989), and L. Horowitz et al. (1989).

The measures in this genre have certain characteristics in common:

1. They rely on relationship interactions and patterns in psychotherapy sessions to assess psychological conflicts.
2. They abstract from the relationship interactions the most pervasive patterns, and therefore the most central conflictual relationship patterns.
3. The pattern is evaluated by clinical judgment rather than by the patient's self-report alone.
4. The pattern is judgable by a system that gives at least moderate agreement of judges.

Some Central Relationship Pattern Measures

Only seven of the measures were selected for description here. But all fifteen are sketched in Luborsky and Crits-Christoph (1990, chap. 17) and described in more extensive detail about each procedure with an example of its application to the same case in Luborsky, Popp, Barber, Shapiro, and Miller (in press).

THE CORE CONFLICTUAL RELATIONSHIP THEME METHOD

What led to the Core Conflictual Relationship Theme (CCRT) method (Luborsky and Crits-Christoph 1990) was the desire to give uniform and reliable guidelines to clinicians to enable them to find the common elements across the relationship episodes told during psychotherapy. Three components of each relationship episode are scored: the wishes in relationship to the other person, the expected and actual responses of the other person, and the responses of the self. The method rests on four assumptions: (1) the database consists of the relationship episodes (narratives); (2) the components can be reliably extracted from these narratives; (3) the CCRT is composed of the most pervasive of the components across the narratives; and (4) the CCRT is a significant central relationship pattern that is related to the concept that clinicians call the transference pattern.

The method, therefore, consists of two main phases: the selection of narratives in the session about self–other relationships and the extraction of the CCRT from the narratives. Another dimension that is to be scored is the positive and negative quality of the responses of the self and the other in each narrative, which, taken together, corresponds to Freud's distinction between positive and negative transference.

The usual clinical mode of scoring the CCRT is termed "tailor-made" because it allows the clinician leeway to describe each component. An alternative, restricted version of the scoring is in terms of standard categories. These uniform categories are used by all scorers; they are given in Luborsky and Crits-Christoph (1990, chap. 2), along with more details of scoring procedures.

The guidelines for CCRT scoring have succeeded in creating a method that can reliably extract the central relationship pattern. Other facets of the method are also reliably scorable—the selection of the main other person in the narrative and the completeness and the location of the narrative (Crits-Christoph et al. 1990; Bond, Hansell, and Shevrin 1987). The use of standard categories in the scoring of the CCRT components makes the assessment of reliability a straightforward matter. Using Cohen's method (Cohen 1968), the weighted kappas for the wish and the negative response of self were .61 ($p < .01$), and for the negative response from other was .70 ($p < .001$).

The validity findings are also promising for showing validity through the correspondence of our CCRT findings with Freud's twenty-two observations about his transference concept (Luborsky and Crits-Christoph 1990, chap. 18). Among those observations for which we could examine an operational translation, some correspondence could be found for seventeen of Freud's twenty-two observations. This level of correspondence offers enough evidence to support the conclusion that the CCRT and the transference concept have much in common.

PLAN FORMULATION METHOD

The Plan Formulation method grew out of studies of a particular psychoanalytic theory of therapy developed by Weiss (1986) and empirically tested by Weiss, Sampson, and the Mount Zion Psychotherapy Research Group (1986). The method has enabled clinicians to construct comprehensive and reliable case formulations that include these components: the patient's goals for therapy; the inner obstructions (pathogenic beliefs) that prevent or inhibit the patient from attaining goals; the ways the patient is likely to test the therapist to disconfirm pathogenic beliefs; the insights that will be helpful to the patient; and traumas that led to the development of the pathogenic beliefs. The method has been applied to the study of psychoanalyses (Caston 1977, 1986; Curtis and Silberschatz 1989) and a variety of brief psychotherapies (Curtis and Silberschatz 1989; Curtis et al. 1988; Perry et al. 1989; Rosenberg et al. 1986). The Plan Formulation method has led to the development of measures of therapist accuracy (Silberschatz 1986; Silberschatz, Fretter, and Curtis 1986; Silberschatz et al. 1988) and therapy process and outcome (Nathans 1988; Silberschatz, Curtis, and Nathans 1989). These studies have demonstrated the value of the Plan Formulation method by showing that accurate interventions lead to patient progress and, as preliminary studies indicate, to favorable patient outcome.

In all of the studies reliabilities (intraclass correlations) have averaged in the .7 to .9 range for each of the plan components: goals, obstructions, tests, and insights (Curtis and Silberschatz 1989; Rosenberg et al. 1986). The method has also been reliably used by investigators outside of the Mount Zion Psychotherapy Research Group (Collins and Messer 1988).

CONFIGURATIONAL ANALYSIS METHOD AND THE ROLE-RELATIONSHIP MODELS CONFIGURATION

The Configurational Analysis method clarifies (1) the central conflicts, (2) the states of mind, (3) the internalized object relations in terms of role relationship models, and (4) controls and defenses, in that order. The aspects most relevant to transference are the states and role-relationship models.

The Configurational Analysis method (M. Horowitz 1979, 1987) appears to estimate some of the same basic relationship patterns as the CCRT, but it involves a more encompassing Role-Relationship Models Configurational (RRMC) method. For the Configurational Analysis method, the data from process notes and transcripts of sessions are examined from three interrelated points of view: states, relationship patterns, and information. The point of view that has stemmed from the CCRT is the Role-Relationship Models Configuration approach. The RRMC approach offers a conceptual model for intrapsychic conflict about relationships and the scripts for interactions between self and other. The five basic elements are (1) the roles and traits of self schemas; (2) the schema of the object person; (3) the aims from each toward the other, often beginning as the wish for action or expressed emotion from the self; (4) the response of the other; (5) the reactions of self. These have been illustrated and compared with the CCRT (Horowitz 1989, 1991a, b, c; Horowitz, Luborsky, and Popp 1991). In the RRMC method, four types of role-relationship models are placed in a configuration about a specific type of object relationship. There are desired, dreaded, compromise-maladaptive, and compromise-adaptive role-relationship models in a role-relationship models configuration.

Evidence has been provided for the reliability of the state analysis point of view (Horowitz 1987; Horowitz, Ewert, and Milbrat [in press]). Reliability has been determined to be satisfactory in terms of how independent judges relate the role-relationship model configurations from experts to the early videotapes of such sessions (Horowitz and Eells 1993). Two independent teams have been able to converge on similar role-relationship model configurations (Horowitz et al. 1984), and a current collaborative study between University of California at San Francisco and Yale research groups, has shown that independent teams can come up with approximately the same RRMC when viewing the same clinical material.

FRAME METHOD

The frame method is based on the identification of frames. A frame is a recurrent, structured sequence of events that represents a person's significant wishes and beliefs (Teller and Dahl 1981, 1986). The events may include mental and other behaviors, such as acting, perceiving, believing, knowing, wishing, and feeling. The most important relationship among the events is their sequential order, for example, expresses anger → feels rejected → withdraws. Dahl (1988) proposed that frames (1) are represented in the mind in nonverbal code in Bucci's (1985) dual code system of mental representations; (2) are structured sequences of emotions and defenses (Dahl 1978); (3) are the residues of early object relations (Gedo 1979); (4) endure over time; (5) appear across conflicts, objects, and situations; (6) can interact with each other; (7) can account for a wide spectrum of repetitive, neurotic, maladaptive behavior, and, in principle, normal, adaptive behavior; (8) permit specific predictions of wishes and beliefs; and (9) provide the framework for a theory of change independent of any particular theory of how to bring about the change (Dahl, in press).

Teller and Dahl (in press) described three methods for identifying frames. In method A judges use the patient's narratives first to construct prototypes and second to find instantiations (repetitions) both with different objects and in different situations. Method B uses the patient's own inductive generalizations about his or her behaviors as prototypes; judges then search for instantiations as in method A. Method C (Leeds and Bucci 1986) uses an objective procedure to discover the repetitive sequences of events. With this method Davies (1989) found frames in the play of three-year-olds that were consistent for each child separately and for one child with two other children, and that reflected the child's interactions with his or her mother. Additional reliability studies are in progress.

CYCLICAL MALADAPTIVE PATTERN METHOD

The Cyclical Maladaptive Pattern (CMP) method offers guidelines for formulating the pattern that provides a treatment focus for the therapist's interventions; the method was therefore first called the Dynamic Focus method in Schacht, Binder, and Strupp (1984). The shift to the CMP label was intended to stress the observation that the pattern shows a self-perpetuating cycle. The system's components, as illustrated in Henry, Schacht, and Strupp (1986), include (a) acts of self, (b) expectations of others, (c) consequent acts of others toward self, and (d) consequent acts of self toward self. These components appear to be similar to the components in the CCRT. Acts of self, for example, include the wishes. The expectations of others and consequent acts of others toward self are both included in the responses from others in the CCRT system. Consequent acts of self toward self are similar to the responses of self in the CCRT system.

To increase reliability and theoretical coherence, the CMP has been integrated into the measurement methods of the Structural Analysis of Social Behavior (SASB), with the new label SASB-CMP. Consequently, the reliability should be the same as that achieved by the SASB. This new generation system reorganizes the information into three categories: (a) interpersonal acts, (b) introjective acts, and (c) expectancies, by procedures described in Schacht, Binder, and Strupp (in press).

IDIOGRAPHIC CONFLICT FORMULATION METHOD

The Idiographic Conflict Formulation (ICF) method (Perry and Cooper 1985, 1986; Perry, Augusto, and Cooper 1989) includes the assessment of conscious and unconscious motives and supporting evidence. The ICF has five components: (1) wishes, (2) fears, (3) symptomatic and avoidant outcomes resulting from conflicting wishes and fears, (4) specific stressors to which the patient is vulnerable, and (5) the subject's best level of adaptation to the conflicts. Standardized lists of the two motive components are available, which include forty wishes and thirty-nine fears, to increase reliability and comparability of formulations by the ICF method. The wishes and fears are arranged according to Erikson's eight-stage hierarchy of psychological development, a structure that increases the heuristic value of the ICF. In one case comparison with the CCRT, using the standardized lists, the ICF identified a greater number of motives than the CCRT (Hoglend, Guldberg, and Perry 1992), but overall the results were very similar.

The reliability of the ICF was tested on two independent formulations made on twenty cases, using paired comparisons to determine the similarity of correctly matched versus mismatched pairs of ICFs (Perry, Augusto, and Cooper 1989). Using a 7-point scale (7 = essentially complete overlap), the mean similarity of correctly matched ICF pairs (4.41) was significantly higher ($p < .0001$) than that of mismatched ICFs, from subjects with the same major diagnoses (3.05) and from subjects with different diagnoses (2.91).

CONSENSUAL RESPONSE FORMULATION METHOD

In the Consensual Response Formulation method (L. Horowitz et al. 1989) a videotape of an evaluation interview is presented to a group of clinicians, each of whom writes a dynamic formulation. Then the formulations are divided into thought units. The most frequent thought units across clinicians are collected into a composite formulation called a consensual formulation. The focus of the method, therefore, is on the clinicians' consensual observations and inferences. One validity study found that formulations with a higher proportion of interpersonal content are associated with greater improvement (L. Horowitz et al. 1989). In another validity study, naive clinicians, reading only the consensual formulations, were able to anticipate correctly the interpersonal problems that were actually discussed in the treatment, giving a mean chi-square of 22.2 ($p < .001$). These results confirm the earlier finding (L. Horowitz et al. 1989) that patients with primarily interpersonal problems are more suitable for brief dynamic psychotherapy.

The replicability of the method was established by having another group of clinicians repeat the entire Consensual Response Formulation procedure. Corresponding formulations had an 80 percent overlap in content. In addition, 100 percent of the judges were able to match the replicated formulation correctly to the original formulation of the same case.

Comparisons among Alternative Central Relationship Pattern Methods

A good way to gain experience with the workings of a method is to apply it to a sample session. Such an example is presented in a special issue of *Psychotherapy Research* (Luborsky, Popp, Barber, Shapiro, and Miller, in press) for each of the methods listed above. Readers who aim to become even better acquainted with the methods are encouraged to read this special issue. Not only are the methods delineated in more detail, but the results of each method are given as well. Both clinical and statistical comparisons are given. The statistical one is based on independent judges' paired comparisons of the results of each method. These comparisons show a moderate degree of similarity across the results of the different methods.

Because the measures in this new class have only recently come on the scene, they show wide differences in their reliability and validity information (Barber and Crits-Christoph, in press). The CCRT and the Plan Formulation methods are the earliest examples of such methods, and each one has a long history of psychometric advances in terms of information provided about reliability and validity. In the same sense the Structural Analysis of Social Behavior (Benjamin 1974, 1979) is one of the most advanced, for it represents years of ingenious and substantial research development.

Inspection of these diverse methods reveals commonalities in their basic categories. One of these is their emphasis on conflicts, especially for impulse versus executive functions; for example, each has categories for wishes, needs, and goals versus expected responses from others and responses of self.

Yet quantitative research to examine the similarity in formulations guided by these measures has just begun. Five studies have so far compared one measure with other measures, usually on a single case, by the paired comparisons method. These studies are: Luborsky (1988) for the CCRT, Patient's Eperience of Relationship with the Therapist (PERT), and Frame; M. Horowitz, Luborsky, and Popp (1991) for the Role-Relationship Model and CCRT; Johnson et al. (1989) for the CCRT and Cyclical Maladaptive Pattern; Kächele, Luborsky, and Thomä (1988) for the CCRT and PERT; Perry et al. (1989) for the CCRT, Idiographic Conflict Summary, and Plan Formulation. The consistent finding from these studies is that there is a core of significant similarity among the measures.

A group in the Program on Conscious and Unconscious Mental Processes of the John D. and Catherine T. MacArthur Foundation applied psychoanalytic, psychodynamic, cognitive, and social learning theory approaches to the same cases as recorded in psychotherapy. All approaches aimed at repetitive maladaptive patterns that might be seen in both transference and outside-of-therapy relationships. The results indicated both a similarity in terms of the convergence of the inferences and a nesting of smaller schematic inferences in some methods as contained within the larger schematic inferences of other methods (Horowitz 1991a). For example, the Structural Analysis of Social Behavior Method could nest within the Core Conflictual Relationship Theme inferences, which in turn could nest within the larger frame of defensive layering and multiple self schemas of the Role Relationship Models Configuration Method.

Another large-scale study (Mackenzie 1989) compared twelve patients on four measures: the Inventory of Interpersonal Problems (L. Horowitz, Weckler, and Doren 1983), the Relationship Anecdotes Paradigms interview (Luborsky 1990), the Structural Analysis of Social Behavior (Benjamin 1974), and the Reportory Grid (Kelly 1955). The results of the four methods, when translated into common terms based on the SASB, showed that each method had areas of uniqueness as well as larger areas of overlap with other methods.

The decision by a researcher or clinician to use a measure may depend partly on the practical matter of the time it takes to apply the measure. In terms of time for scoring, the methods generally are expensive. The CCRT based on relationship episodes drawn from psychotherapy or from the Relationship Anecdote Paradigm interviews takes about one and one-half to three hours per session to score properly, according to the tailor-made plus standard categories procedure; there are ways to score the CCRT that cut down on time, such as applying standard categories only. But the CCRT is among the least time expensive of the central relationship pattern measures. And, when the CCRT or others of these measures are applied by the therapist in everyday practice, no extra time is involved.

Applications of Transference-Related Measures in Clinical Practice and in Research

The transference-related measures have a variety of clinical applications. The guidance of these measures allows clinicians to make reliable formulations. They tend not to be difficult to use clinically. To make a transference formulation by the CCRT method, for example, the therapist has only to examine the patient's communications in a session—especially those in the relationship episodes—then to note the wishes and responses that are in common across the different episodes. Some of the transference-related measures, including the CCRT measure, permit the therapist to make a rapid transference formulation. That transference formulation offers a focus for making interpretations that can be helpful therapeutically (Crits-Christoph, Cooper, and Luborsky 1990; Weiss and Sampson 1986).

These guided systems for inferring the central relationship pattern also have a valuable application in inpatient treatments. One of these applications of the CCRT is being developed by Luborsky et al. (in press). The use of the method begins with the initial staff conference, in which each member of the team presents an account of his or her interaction with the patient. The combined set of narratives serves as the basis for formulating the CCRT. Through this procedure the team comes to a generally shared formulation of the patient's central relationship problems; they can then provide more consistent and helpful treatment responses to the patient.

A basic research gain from the use of operational methods is to provide reliable measures so that systematic studies can be done of propositions about the central relationship pattern. From about 1895 to 1937 Freud identified a broad spectrum of twenty-two different aspects of his transference concept (as noted here and as reviewed in Luborsky and Crits-Christoph 1990, chap. 18). Freud ([1912] 1958) considered these aspects of his concept to be empirically based, not simply theoretically inferred. The observations deal with the origins and functions of the transference, as well as with the stimuli that activate the transference. The guided clinical pattern-recognition methods can be used to further investigate these facets of the concept; the CCRT and other methods have confirmed many of them.

Transference-related measures assess the now fashionable superordinate central relationship *schema*. The theory of such schemas has become an important part of research on the intersection of cognitive science and clinical science (Stein 1992). Both cognitive-behavioral and psychoanalytically oriented clinicians use techniques that are located at this intersection. Cognitive-behavioral clinicians tend to use smaller schemas having to do with belief systems; dynamic clinicians tend to use larger schemas related to central transference-related patterns.

Is there any serious danger from imposing a guided system on clinical inference making? The question raises the even more fundamental issue of whether any guided method results in a transference formulation that is deficient in capturing the essential pattern for the particular patient. Our conclusion at this point is that the danger is minimal and the gain is maximal. Clinicians already have systems of their own, and they derive these systems from their reading of Freud's or other expert clinicians' recommendations. The traditional unguided clinical systems differ more from clinician to clinician. The methods summarized here offer uniform guiding principles that permit clinicians to achieve some agreement.

A related version of the question is how much these guided measures can be considered to be a measure of the clinical concept of transference. An obstacle to coming to a conclusion on this form of the question is the absence of systematic studies comparing clinicians' unguided transference formulations with guided formulations based on the same sessions. So far we have only a few cases on which we have both unguided and guided transference formulations. One of these is Ms. Cunningham, described in Luborsky and Crits-Christoph (1990, chap. 4). The clinical formulations showed relatively poor agreement, while the CCRT formulations showed moderately good agreement. The capacity to achieve agreement in transference formulations is a desirable asset for both clinicians and researchers.

Another set of terms for which this same issue can be debated is salience versus frequency. *Salience* to a clinician tends to mean central or crucially meaningful. It might be argued that the CCRT was constructed to use only *frequency* of recurrence. But our thesis is that clinicians actually use both *salience* and *frequency*, sometimes unwittingly. Because salient events tend to be associated with related frequent events, it typically does not matter which of several aspects of the clinical data are selected as salient— an event selected because of salience tends also to be frequent. This thesis is easily illustrated by any of the episodes given to illustrate the CCRT, for example, the ones for Ms. Apfel (refer to figure 1.2). A clinician might select any of the five relationship episodes as a salient event, yet all of the episodes show redundancy in their themes.

We conclude with what seems to be a mystifying paradox about clinicians' slowness to accept more exact methods of inferring the transference. Clinicians generally should have been searching harder for improvements in their methods of formulation. Perhaps they have been unaware of the limits of their formulations and of their differences with each other. Perhaps they generally have confidence that they already know how to do this kind of formulation and feel that if they do not sense the transference at the moment, they need only to listen to the patient further. And, basically, clinicians are afraid to tamper with the conventional method of formulation. They fear that any formal system will diminish or distort their natural sensitivity. But experience now comes to the rescue: we now know that after some practice with the new methods, clinicians have tended to be reassured. They have come to see that the new methods offer a common language and common conceptual domain for their formulations. And we have learned that the new methods of making transference-related formulations retain their high quality even after they have been distilled into more uniform and reliably recognized components.

References

BARBER, J. P., & CRITS-CHRISTOPH, P. (IN PRESS). Advances in measures of dynamic formulation. *Journal of Consulting and Clinical Psychology*.

BENJAMIN, L. S. (1974). Structural Analysis of Social Behavior. *Psychological Review, 81*, 392–425.

BENJAMIN, L. S. (1979). Use of Structural Analysis of Social Behavior (SASB) and Markov chains to study dynamic interactions. *Journal of Abnormal Psychology, 88*, 303–319.

BOND, J., HANSELL, J., & SHEVRIN, H. (1987). Locating a reference paradigm in psychotherapy transcripts: Reliability of relationship episode location in the Core Conflictual Relationship Theme (CCRT) method. *Psychotherapy, 24,* 736–749.

BOND, J., & SHEVRIN, H. (1986). *The clinical evaluation team method.* Unpublished manuscript, University of Michigan.

BUCCI, W. (1985). Dual coding: A cognitive model for psychoanalytic research. *Journal of the American Psychoanalytic Association, 33,* 571–607.

CARLSON, R. (1981). Studies in script theory: 1. Adult analogs of a childhood nuclear scene. *Journal of Personality and Social Psychology, 40,* 501–510.

CASTON, J. (1977). Manual on how to diagnose the plan. In J. Weiss, H. Sampson, J. Caston, & G. Silberschatz, *Research on the psychoanalytic process: Vol. 1. A comparison of two theories about analytic neutrality* (Bulletin No. 3, pp. 15–21). San Francisco: Psychotherapy Research Group, Department of Psychiatry, Mount Zion Hospital and Medical Center.

CASTON, J. (1986). The reliability of the diagnosis of the patient's unconscious plan. In J. Weiss, H. Sampson, & the Mount Zion Psychotherapy Research Group, *The psychoanalytic process: Theory, clinical observations, and empirical research* (pp. 241–255). New York: Guilford Press.

COHEN, J. (1968). Weighted kappa: Nominal scale agreement with provision for scaled disagreement on partial credit. *Psychological Bulletin, 70,* 213–220.

COLLINS, W., & MESSER, S. (1988, JUNE). *Transporting the Plan Diagnosis Method to a different setting: Reliability, stability, and adaptability.* Paper presented at the annual meeting of the Society for Psychotherapy Research, Santa Fe, NM.

CRITS-CHRISTOPH, P., COOPER, A., & LUBORSKY, L. (1990). The measurement of accuracy of interpretations. In L. Luborsky & P. Crits-Christoph, *Understanding transference: The Core Conflictual Relationship Theme method* (pp. 173–188). New York: Basic Books.

CRITS-CHRISTOPH, P., LUBORSKY, L., POPP, C., MELLON, J., & MARK, D. (1990). The reliability of choice of narratives and of the CCRT measure. In L. Luborsky & P. Crits-Christoph, *Understanding transference: The Core Conflictual Relationship Theme method* (pp. 93–101). New York: Basic Books.

CURTIS, J. T., & SILBERSCHATZ, G. (1989). *The Plan Formulation Method: A reliable procedure for case formulation.* Manuscript submitted for publication.

CURTIS, J. T., SILBERSCHATZ, G., SAMPSON, H., WEISS, J., & ROSENBERG, S. E. (1988). Developing reliable psychodynamic case formulations: An illustration of the Plan Diagnosis Method. *Psychotherapy, 25,* 256–265.

DAHL, H. (1978). A new psychoanalytic model of motivation: Emotions as appetites and messages. *Psychoanalysis and Contemporary Thought, 1,* 373–408.

DAHL, H. (1988). Frames of mind. In H. Dahl, H. Kächele, & H. Thomä (Eds.), *Psychoanalytic process research strategies* (pp. 51–66). Heidelberg: Springer-Verlag.

DAHL, H. (IN PRESS). Emotions as wishes and beliefs: The key to understanding change events in psychotherapy. In J. Safran & L. Greenberg (Eds.), *Affective change events in psychotherapy*. New York: Academic Press.

DAVIES, J. (1989). The development of emotional and interpersonal structures in three-year-old children. Doctoral dissertation, Derner Institute for Advanced Psychological Studies, Adelphi University.

DeWITT, K. N., KALTREIDER, N., WEISS, D. S., & HOROWITZ, M. J. (1983). Judging change in psychotherapy: Reliability of clinical formulations. *Archives of General Psychiatry, 40*, 1121–1128.

FREUD, S. (1895/1955). Studies on hysteria. In J. Strachey (Ed.), *The standard edtion of the complete psychological works of Sigmund Freud* (Vol. 2, pp. 3–305). London: Hogarth Press.

FREUD, S. (1912/1958). The dynamics of the transference. In J. Strachey (Ed.), *The standard edition of the complete psychological works of Sigmund Freud* (Vol. 12, pp. 99–108). London: Hogarth Press.

GEDO, J. (1979). Theories of object relations: A metapsychological assessment. *Journal of the American Psychoanalytic Association, 27*, 361–373.

GILL, M., & HOFFMAN, I. (1982). A method for studying the analysis of aspects of the patient's experience of the relationship in psychoanalysis and psychotherapy. *Journal of the American Psychoanalytic Association, 30*, 137–167.

GRAWE, K., & CASPAR, F. (1984). Die Plan Analyse als Konzept und Instrument für die Psychotherapie Forschung. In U. Bauman (Ed.), *Psychotherapie: Makro- und Mikro-perspectiven* (pp. 177–197). Cologne: Hogrete.

HENRY, W. P., SCHACHT, T. E., & STRUPP, H. H. (1986). Structural Analysis of Social Behavior: Application to a study of interpersonal process in differential psychotherapeutic outcome. *Journal of Consulting and Clinical Psychology, 54*, 27–31.

HOGLEND, P., GULDBERG, C., & PERRY, J. (1992). Scientific approaches to making psychodynamic formulations. *Nordic Journal of Psychiatry, 46*, 41–48.

HOROWITZ, M. J. (1979, 1ST ED./1987, 2ND ED.). *States of mind: Configuration/ Analysis of individual personality*. New York: Plenum Press.

HOROWITZ, M. J. (1987). *States of mind: Analysis of change in psychotherapy* (2nd ed.). New York: Plenum Press.

HOROWITZ, M. J., (1989). Relationship schema formulation: Role relationship models and intrapsychic conflict. *Psychiatry, 52*: 260–274.

HOROWITZ, M. J. (1991a). Person schemas. In M. Horowitz (Ed.) *Person schemas and maladaptive interpersonal patterns*. Chicago: University of Chicago Press.

HOROWITZ, M. J. (1991b). States, schemas, and controls: General theories for psychotherapy integration. *Journal of Psychotherapy Integration, I*, 85–102.

HOROWITZ, M. J. (1991c). Converging sereio methods for interring person schemas. In M. Horowitz (Ed.) *Person schemas and maladaptive interpersonal patterns*. Chicago: University of Chicago Press.

HOROWITZ, M. J. & EELLS, T. (1993). Case formulations using role relationship models configurations: A reliability study. *Psychotherapy Research, 3*, 57–68.

HOROWITZ, M. J., LUBORSKY, L., & POPP, L., (1991). A comparison of the role relationship models configuration and the core conflictual relationship theme. In M. J. Horowitz (Ed.), *Person schemas and maladaptive interpersonal patterns.* Chicago: University of Chicago Press.

HOROWITZ, M. J., MARMOR, C., KRUPNUK, J., WILNER, N., & WALLERSTEIN, R., (1984). *Personality styles and brief psychotherapy.* New York: Basic Books.

HOROWITZ, M. J., MARMAR C., WEISS, D. S., MARKMAN, H., TUNIS, S., BECKER, T., & LUBORSKY, L. (IN PRESS). Relationship schema formulation: Role relationship models and intrapsychic conflict. *Psychiatry.*

HOROWITZ, L. M., ROSENBERG, S., URENO, G., KALEHZAN, B., & O'HALLORAN, P. (1989). Psychodynamic formulation, Consensual Response Method and interpersonal problems. *Journal of Consulting and Clinical Psychology, 57,* 599–606.

HOROWITZ, L. M., WECKLER, D., & DOREN, R. (1983). Interpersonal problems and symptoms: A cognitive approach. In P. C. Kendall (Ed.), *Advances in cognitive-behavioral research and therapy* (Vol. 2, pp. 82–127). New York: Academic Press.

JOHNSON, M., POPP, C., SCHACHT, T., MELLON, J., & STRUPP, H. (1989). Converging evidence for identification of recurrent relationship themes: Comparison of two methods. *Psychiatry, 52,* 275–285.

KÄCHELE, H., LUBORSKY, L. & THOMÄ, H. (1988). Ubertragung als Structur und Verlaufsmuster: Zwei Methoden zur Erfassung dieser Aspekte. In L. Luborsky & H. Kächele (Eds.), *Der zentrale Beziehungskonflikt.* Ulm: PSZ-Verlag.

KELLY, G. A. (1955). *The psychology of personal constructs* (Vol. 1). New York: Norton.

KIESLER, D. J. (1987). *Check List of Psychotherapy Transactions-Revised (CLOPT-R) and Check List of Interpersonal Transactions-Revised (CLOIT-R).* Richmond, VA: Virginia Commonwealth University.

KIESLER, D. J., ANCHIN, J. C., PERKINS, M. J., CHIRICO, B. M., KYLE, E. M., & FEDERMAN, E. J. (1985). *The Impact Message Inventory: Form II.* Palo Alto, CA: Consulting Psychologists Press.

LEEDS, J., & BUCCI, W. (1986, JUNE). *A reliable method for the detection of repetitive structures in a transcript of an analytic session.* Paper presented to the annual meeting of the Society for Psychotherapy Research, Wellesley, MA.

LUBORSKY, L. (1976). Helping alliances in psychotherapy: The groundwork for a study of their relationship to its outcome. In J. L. Claghorn (Ed.), *Successful psychotherapy* (pp. 92–116). New York: Brunner/Mazel.

LUBORSKY, L. (1988). A comparison of three transference-related measures applied to the specimen hour. In H. Dahl, H. Kächele, & H. Thomä (Eds.), *Psychoanalytic process research strategies* (pp. 109–115). New York: Springer.

LUBORSKY, L. (1990). The relationship anecdotes paradigms (RAP) interview as a versatile source of narratives. In L. Luborsky & P., Crits-Christoph, *Understanding transference; The Core Conflictual Relationship Theme method* (pp. 102–116). New York: Basic Books.

LUBORSKY, L., & CRITS-CHRISTOPH, P. (1990). *Understanding transference: The Core Conflictual Relationship Theme method.* New York: Basic Books.

LUBORSKY, L., POPP, C., BARBER, J., SHAPIRO, D., & MILLER, N. (EDS.) (IN PRESS). Seven transference-related measures—Each applied to the Ms. Smithfield interview. *Psychotherapy Research.*

LUBORSKY, L., & SCHAFFLER, P. (1990). Illustrations of the CCRT scoring guide. In L. Luborsky & P. Crits-Christoph, *Understanding transference: The Core Conflictual Relationship Theme method* (pp. 51–81). New York: Basic Books.

LUBORSKY, L., VAN RAVENSWAAY, P., BALL, W., STEINMAN, D., SPREHN, G., & BRYAN, C. (IN PRESS). How to focus psychiatric hospital treatment: Use of the CCRT-FIT method (Focused In-patient Treatment). In *Prospective psicoanalitiche nel lavoro instituzionale, 11,* 9–16.

MACKENZIE, R. (1989, MAY). *Comparing methods to assess patients for therapy.* Paper presented to the annual meeting of the American Psychiatric Association, San Francisco.

MAXIM, P. (1986). *The Seattle Psychotherapy Language Analysis Schema.* Seattle: University of Washington Press.

NATHANS, S. (1988). *Plan Attainment: An individualized measure for assessing outcome in psychodynamic psychotherapy.* Unpublished doctoral dissertation, California School of Professional Psychology at Berkeley.

PERRY, J. C., AUGUSTO, F., & COOPER, S. H. (1989). Assessing psychodynamic conflicts: 1. Reliability of the Idiographic Conflict Formulation method. *Psychiatry, 52,* 289–301.

PERRY, J. C., & COOPER, S. H. (1985). Psychodynamics, symptoms, and outcome in borderline and antisocial personality disorders and bipolar type II affective disorder. In T. H. McGlashan (Ed.), *The borderline: Current empirical research* (pp. 21–41). Washington, DC: American Psychiatric Press.

PERRY, J. C., & COOPER, S. H. (1986). A preliminary report on defenses and conflicts associated with borderline personality disorder. *Journal of the American Psychoanalytical Association, 34,* 865–895.

PERRY, J. C., LUBORSKY, L., SILBERSHATZ, G., & POPP, C. (1989). An examination of three methods of psychodynamic formulation based on the same videotaped interview. *Psychiatry, 52,* 302–323.

ROSENBERG, S., SILBERSCHATZ, G., CURTIS, J., SAMPSON, H., & WEISS, J. (1986). A method for establishing reliability of statements from psychodynamic case formulations. *American Journal of Psychiatry, 143,* 1454–1456.

SCHACHT, T. B., BINDER, J., & STRUPP, H. (1984). The dynamic focus. In H. Strupp & J. Binder, *Psychotherapy in a new key: A guide to time-limited dynamic psychotherapy* (pp. 65–109). New York: Basic Books.

SCHACHT, T., BINDER, J., & STRUPP, H. (IN PRESS). *Psychotherapy Research.*

SEITZ, P. (1966). The consensus problem in psychoanalytic research. In L. Gottschalk & A. Auerbach (Eds.), *Methods of research in psychotherapy* (pp. 209–225). New York: Appleton-Century-Crofts.

SILBERSCHATZ, G. (1986). Testing pathogenic beliefs. In J. Weiss, H. Sampson,

& the Mount Zion Psychotherapy Research Group, *The psychoanalytic process: Theory, clinical observations, and empirical research* (pp. 256–266). New York: Guilford Press.

SILBERSCHATZ, G., CURTIS, J. T., FRETTER, P. B., & KELLY, T. (1988). Testing hypotheses of psychotherapeutic change processes. In H. Dahl, H. Kächele, & H. Thomä (Eds.), *Psychoanalytic process research strategies* (pp. 129–145). Berlin: Springer-Verlag.

SILBERSCHATZ, G., CURTIS, J. T., & NATHANS, S. (1989). Using the patient's plan to assess progress in psychotherapy. *Psychotherapy, 26,* 40–46.

SILBERSCHATZ, G., FRETTER, P., & CURTIS, J. (1986). How do interpretations influence the process of psychotherapy? *Journal of Consulting and Clinical Psychology, 54,* 646–652.

STEIN, D. (1992). Schemas in cognitive and clinical sciences: An integrative construct. *Journal of Psychotherapy Integration, 2,* 45–63.

TELLER, V., & DAHL, H. (1981). The framework for a model of psychoanalytic inference. *Proceedings of the Seventh International Joint Conference on Artificial Intelligence, 1,* 394–400.

TELLER, V., & DAHL, H. (1986). The microstructure of free association. *Journal of the American Psychoanalytic Association, 34,* 763–798.

TELLER, V., & DAHL, H. (IN PRESS). The characteristics, identification, and application of Frames. In L. Luborsky, C. Popp, J. Barber, D. Shapiro, & N. Miller (EDS.), Seven transference-related measures: Each applied to the Ms. Smithfield interview. *Psychotherapy Research* (Special Issue).

WEISS, J. (1986). Theory and clinical observations. In J. Weiss, H. Sampson, & the Mount Zion Psychotherapy Research Group, *The psychoanalytic process: Theory, clinical observations, and empirical research* (pp. 3–138). New York: Guilford Press.

WEISS, J., SAMPSON, H., & THE MOUNT ZION PSYCHOTHERAPY RESEARCH GROUP. (1986). *The psychoanalytic process: Theory, clinical observations, and empirical research.* New York: Guilford Press.

CHAPTER 18

Countertransference and Qualities of the Psychotherapist

STEPHEN F. BUTLER, LYDIA V. FLASHER, AND
HANS H. STRUPP

SIGMUND FREUD ONCE QUIZZED HIS PROTÉGÉ Carl Jung, "What is the transference?" Jung's famous answer was, "Transference is the alpha and omega of psychoanalysis." Freud responded, "You have understood." What Jung had understood was the central role transference plays in making possible the treatment of psychological maladies by bringing into the present psychoanalytic situation conflicts with their origin in the patient's distant, and sometimes unremembered, past. Analysis of the transference may be said to define analytic/dynamic treatment and to distinguish it from other approaches to psychotherapy.

In contrast to transference, countertransference held a much less illustrious position in early psychoanalytic thinking. Indeed, its very existence has been only grudgingly accepted (Poggi and Ganzarain 1983; Epstein and Feiner 1979). Very little attention was devoted to the concept of countertransference following Freud's introduction ([1910] 1957) of the term until the late 1940s, when a few psychoanalytic writers began to explore the potential usefulness of the phenomenon and to expand its theoretical boundaries. The last decade or so has seen a reemergence of interest in countertransference and an increased appreciation of its vital role in the therapeutic setting.

In this chapter, we trace the evolution of the concept of countertransference, the theoretical assumptions underlying these shifts in meaning, and the reasons why countertransference has moved from the periphery of psychoanalytic theory to virtual center stage. In addition, we will examine early attempts to study the concept empirically and the problems inherent in such research.

Definitions and Fundamental Assumptions

Freud introduced the concept of countertransference with these words:

> We have become aware of the "counter-transference," which arises in the physician as a result of the patient's influence on his unconscious feelings, and we are almost inclined to insist that he shall recognize his countertransference and overcome it. . . . Anyone who fails to produce results in a self-analysis of this kind may at once give up any idea of being able to treat patients by analysis. ([1910] 1957, pp. 144–145).

Having introduced the concept, Freud in his later writings did little to flesh it out, leaving later theorists to speculate on what he meant by "overcoming" the countertransference (Tansey and Burke 1989). Subsequent suggestions to adopt the "emotional coldness" of the surgeon were juxtaposed with exhortations for the analyst[1] to "turn his own unconscious like a receptive organ toward the transmitting unconscious of the patient" (Freud [1912] 1958, p. 115). This ambiguity regarding the proper place for the analyst's feelings and reactions to the patient was further complicated by reports of Freud's actual behavior with patients, which revealed a more flexible attitude toward therapeutic technique than is evident in his theoretical writings (e.g., Gay 1988). Still, there is little direct information available regarding how Freud actually dealt with or "overcame" what he considered to be his own countertransference reactions.

Over the years, disagreements on countertransference have usually revolved around two pivotal issues: (1) restriction versus expansion of the term *countertransference* and (2) the drive model of psychodynamics versus the relational/interpersonal model (Greenberg and Mitchell 1983).

Restriction versus expansion of the meaning of countertransference was addressed in a classic paper by Kernberg (1965), who identified two "contrasting approaches" to countertransference. The "classical" approach defines countertransference as "the unconscious reaction of the psychoanalyst to the patient's transference" (p. 38). According to Kernberg, this restricted definition comes closest to Freud's use of the term and is consistent with his recommendation to overcome the countertransference response. Kernberg labeled the alternate approach "totalistic," which expanded the meaning of countertransference to encompass "the total emotional reaction of the psychoanalyst to the patient in the treatment

[1]Because the present discussion refers to literature from both classical psychoanalysis and psychodynamic psychotherapy, both *therapist* and *analyst* are used in an effort to be consistent with the original literature being addressed. Despite certain technical differences, these terms are considered by the present authors to be essentially interchangeable within the context and aims of this chapter.

situation" (p. 38), including both conscious and unconscious reactions to the patient.

Clearly, the therapist's emotional and behavioral responses to a particular patient reflect a panoply of root causes. The therapist's response can reflect the therapist's pathology, his or her transference to the patient's transference, and his or her empathic identification with the patient's struggle. Such identification can be essential for therapy to work; yet, at times, it can be an impediment to treatment. Another type of reaction transpires when the therapist's emotional response reproduces the patient's disavowed destructive or aggressive reactions, as in projective identification. Finally, the therapist might respond in a way any human being might be expected to respond, for example, with exasperation at the patient's manipulative or passive-aggressive behavior.

The discrepancy in views of countertransference reflects differences in fundamental assumptions associated with the drive model as opposed to an object relations view of motivation and treatment. In drive theory (Greenberg and Mitchell 1983), the organizing psychological principle is determined by the regulation of energy within the organism, such that the aim of action is the attainment of "freedom from the press of endogenously arising stimulation" (p. 44). Viewed from this perspective, countertransference is seen to arise endogenously, signaling "unresolved neurotic conflicts within the analyst" (p. 388). Patient and therapist, in this model, constitute largely self-contained organisms, confronting each other as stimuli for their respective independent neurotic concerns.

For object relations theorists, the psychoanalytic experience is inherently dyadic. The events unfolding within the consulting room are seen as the product of interaction between patient and therapist, which necessarily involves the entire range of "real" and "distorted" response in both participants. From this perspective, countertransference is considered inevitable in any therapeutic interaction.

Since the advent of Kernberg's (1965) paper, there appears to have been a greater acknowledgment of the totalistic view of countertransference. Recent accounts of the history of countertransference typically construe development of the concept as a progression from the classical view to the totalistic one (e.g., Greenberg and Mitchell 1983; Tansey and Burke 1989; Slakter 1987; Gorkin 1987).

Evolution of the Psychoanalytic View

As previously noted, countertransference responses were initially deemed to be solely the result of the therapist's pathogenic, pretherapy relationships and, therefore, not based on objective observations of the patient.

Consequently, countertransference was regarded as an obstacle to be overcome by the analyst in his or her own analysis. When Freud ([1910] 1957)
introduced the concept of countertransference, he underscored the importance of overcoming such reactions in the analyst, noting that "no psychoanalyst goes farther than his own complexes and internal resistances permit" (p. 145). Such reasoning led to the requirement of a personal analysis
in order to remove or minimize the distortions of countertransference.

Although Freud emphasized an empathic stance toward the patient
and a receptive, tolerant view of the analyst's own unconscious reactions,
his "cold surgeon" analogy and pejorative references to countertransference (Gorkin 1987) set the stage for "four decades of silence" (Tansey and
Burke 1989, p. 14) on the topic. The reasons for this negative stance likely
stemmed from Freud's sensitivity to charges that "unscientific subjectivity"
was intrinsic to psychoanalytic methodology.

This negative bias gradually began to shift as some psychoanalytic
writers considered the possibility that therapists' emotional responses to
patients might actually serve a useful purpose in promoting understanding
of patients. This expansion was, in large part, the result of attempts to
expand the scope of psychoanalysis to encompass more severely disturbed
patient populations.

In a radical paper, Winnicott (1949) distinguished "objective countertransference" from other types of countertransference feelings, defining
this as "the analyst's love and hate in reaction to the actual personality and
behavior of the patient based on objective observation" (p. 70). Winnicott
emphasized for the first time that, with severely disturbed patients, negative feelings on the part of the analyst are *inevitable*, rather than a product
of the analyst's psychopathology. The idea was advanced that this type of
response to the patient conveys important meaning and information to the
analyst.

Heimann (1950), influenced by Klein's (1946, 1955) seminal work on
projective identification, went further by proposing that the totality of the
analyst's emotional response to the patient constitutes an important tool,
permitting the analyst to follow the patient's emotions and unconscious
fantasies. She proposed that the countertransference was, in fact, the "patient's creation" (Heimann 1950, p. 83), and as such, reflected the *patient's*
pathology rather than the therapist's. Noting that the "analyst's unconscious understands that of his patient," Heimann (1950, p. 81) emphasized
this as a potentially superior form of knowing the patient's inner world.

Little (1951) also interpreted the concept of countertransference
broadly to include both conscious and unconscious reactions to the patient,
recommending the judicious use of "counter-transference interpretations"
wherein the analyst's subjective reactions are used to clarify the transference and further the therapeutic alliance. Reik (1948) also advocated careful

attention to inner signals which might reflect unconscious perceptions regarding the patient.

Racker's important contribution (1953, 1957) further developed the notion of countertransference as potentially induced by the patient, primarily as an identification with the patient or the patient's internalized objects. He postulated the presence of a lawful relationship between the patient's transference and the therapist's countertransference. Racker's "law of talion" (1957, p. 315) maintains that every positive transference situation is met with a positive countertransference, while every negative transference is answered by a negative countertransference (such as love for love, hate for hate). He recommended that the analyst be as aware as possible of countertransference responses and "avoid falling into a blind repetition of the vicious circle that constitutes the patient's primary problem in human relationships" (Tansey and Burke 1989, p. 26).

Reich (1951, 1960, 1966) reaffirmed the virtues of maintaining the classical view, noting that any strong or prolonged emotional reaction carried largely negative implications for treatment. Her use of the more restricted, classical definition of countertransference highlights the problem of diluting the concept by expanding it to mean virtually *any* reaction to the patient. Kernberg (1965), in his discussion of this issue, notes that the classical approach demands neither coolness nor lack of humanity, and it guards against excessive intrusion of the analyst's personality into the therapeutic endeavor. Nevertheless, defining countertransference as something basically wrong, Kernberg argues, fosters a "phobic attitude of the analyst toward his emotional reaction" (p. 59).

Modern Psychodynamic Views

In recent years, the psychoanalytic literature has focused increasing attention on countertransference reactions in assessment and treatment. To a large extent, this reflects continuing efforts to expand psychoanalytic treatment to more severely disturbed patients, including schizophrenic individuals (e.g., Searles 1979) and those with severe forms of character pathology, such as borderline and narcissistic personality disorders (e.g., Giovacchini 1979; Kernberg 1975), reflecting the recognition that such patients tend to elicit from therapists a more or less predictable set of intense responses.

In recent years, the view of countertransference as a ubiquitous phenomenon of essential significance to the therapeutic endeavor has become virtually universal among psychoanalytic theorists (e.g., Epstein 1979; Giovacchini 1989; Gorkin 1987; Langs 1976; Menninger and Holzman 1973; Tansey and Burke 1989). Differences do remain, however.

A useful framework for making distinctions among the various concepts of countertransference theories has been proposed by Epstein and Feiner (1988): they advance (1) the classical conception, wherein countertransference is viewed as unconscious resistance of the analyst to the transference of the patient (the analyst's blind spots), (2) the totalistic conception, wherein all feelings and attitudes of the therapist toward the patient are considered countertransference, and (3) the view of countertransference as the natural, role-responsive, necessary complement or counterpart to the transference of the patient, and to the patient's style of relatedness, suggesting that a transference reaction cannot be maintained without a corresponding, complementary countertransference response.

Winnicott's initial contribution to the countertransference literature was seminal in the evolution of the totalist view of countertransference, though in his later writings, he argued in favor of limiting the term to its original (classical) usage, reserving the term for "neurotic features [in the analyst] *that spoil the professional attitude* and disturb the course of the analytic process as determined by the patient" (1988, p. 266). Consistent with his earlier work, he proposes an exception to this rule—that is, work with psychotic patients. For this population, Winnicott encourages the use of "the analyst's total response to the patient's needs" (p. 268), stipulating that the appropriate use of the analyst's reactions depends upon the patient's diagnosis (neurotic versus psychotic).

Kohut's pivotal contributions to psychodynamic technique include his emphasis on the therapist's experience of empathy. Kohut's (1971) developmental model places the child in an empathic, responsive human milieu, where relatedness to others is seen as being as essential for psychological survival as oxygen is for physical survival (Greenberg and Mitchell 1983). Chronic failure of empathic responsiveness by the parents is posited as responsible for characterological pathology. Kohut posits that therapeutic change takes place not through interpretations, but rather through experience of the analyst's function as a new "selfobject," who makes up for the lost developmental momentum blocked by early selfobject failure. Initially, the patient overidealizes the therapist, but small, inevitable empathic failures on the analyst's part permit the patient eventually to see himself or herself and the analyst in more realistic terms. Since the fundamental work of the therapy relies on the therapist's internal experience of empathy with the patient, countertransference is used by Kohut to denote the various resistances and impediments on the part of the analyst to being used as a selfobject. This would include feeling aversion to being overidealized, withdrawing from the patient (declaring the patient "unanalyzable") because of the stress of empathizing with a severely disturbed patient, or even adhering to the traditional "analytic stance" (Kohut 1984, p. 87). Empathic failure on the part of the analyst is not necessarily viewed in a negative light. Rather, these instances present the opportunity for the patient to move from a pathological reliance on external mirroring from the selfobject to an internalization of the idealizing function.

Firmly ensconced within the totalistic approach, Kernberg's (1965) use of the term nevertheless conveys a rather traditional model of countertransference as an impediment to the true work of the analyst. Kernberg describes two uses of countertransference: the first is viewed as a diagnostic tool for understanding how the "patient's transference leads to distortions in the psychoanalytic situation" (1986, p. 53); the second considers countertransference reactions as potential impediments to the analyst's "creativity" and ability to continue "illuminating" the patient's material in spite of negative feelings directed toward the analyst. Kernberg defines these reactions as inevitable and unavoidable, thereby lessening the stigma and facilitating the capacity to neutralize the effects of negative responses, such as aggression, in the countertransference (Kernberg 1965).

Sandler ([1976] 1987) proposed that the analyst maintain "the capacity to allow all sorts of thoughts, day-dreams and associations to enter [his] consciousness while he is at the same time listening to, and observing, the patient" (p. 198). He notes that reactions that initially appear as blind spots often can be usefully viewed as compromise formations between the analyst's own tendencies and *"his reflexive acceptance of the role which the patient is forcing on him"* (p. 111).

Sullivan and his followers (e.g., Anchin and Kiesler 1982; Strupp and Binder 1984) formulated a more interpersonal theory whose assumptions were explicitly divorced from a drive model of motivation. Influenced by social psychologists, Sullivan's (1953) description of the therapist as "participant observer" cast the therapist into an interpersonal space of continuous give-and-take between therapist and patient. Here, the therapist's pathology or blind spots, while acknowledged, are deemphasized, and instead, the reciprocal, interpersonal forces that therapist and patient exert upon one another tend to be highlighted. The patient is seen to enact a particular "evoking style" (e.g., Kiesler 1982), which elicits an anticipated response in the significant other—whether inside or out of the consulting room. This expected response serves to confirm the patient's disavowed expectations about the object, which constitute the core of the patient's maladaptive, evocative style. The therapist's experience of an interpersonal "pull" (the countertransference) to respond to patients in certain stereotyped ways is viewed as *necessary* for continuance of the patient's self-defeating neurotic style. Sustained attention to these countertransference pulls constitutes the essential method whereby the therapist can avoid unwitting confirmation of the patient's maladaptive expectations, providing instead the opportunity for a "corrective emotional experience"—though without the manipulative connotation implied by Alexander and French (1946; see also Marmor 1986; Strupp and Binder 1984).

The utility of countertransference varies from serving as a diagnostic tool to constituting the fundamental source of therapeutic knowledge and intervention. Analysts differ on which conditions warrant the use of countertransference reactions, and about whether, when, and how to disclose one's countertransference reactions (e.g., Gorkin 1987; Tansey and Burke 1989). Possibly most important, however, is disagreement regarding the fundamental view of the patient and therapist as discrete entities having unidirectional influence on each other versus a view of both participants as part of a bidirectional field of continuous actions and reactions which are mutually influential.

Empirical Investigations of Countertransference

Psychoanalytic concepts have historically presented great difficulties to the empirical researcher, and countertransference is no exception. Measuring most variables in psychotherapy research presents the investigator with formidable methodological problems, as the demands of measurement inevitably require a compromise of the richness and complexity of the treatment situation and tremendously oversimplify patient and therapist variables (Luborsky and Spence 1978; Singer and Luborsky 1977; Strupp 1960).

Intrapsychic and unconscious phenomena, such as countertransference, have proven especially difficult to operationalize. For example, an early attempt to study countertransference in a natural setting was conducted as part of the Menninger Foundation's Psychotherapy Project. After treatment was completed, an evaluation team attempted to determine the extent to which countertransference had hindered therapy. Luborsky et al. (1958) examined countertransference using comprehensive assessments, including supervisors' reports, therapists' progress notes, and taped evaluation interviews with patients, therapists, relatives, and employers at termination. They concluded that it was difficult to rate countertransference feelings and to determine their influence. In another study investigating the level of inference required to evaluate countertransference problems, Strupp (1973) concluded that the high level of inference necessary to rate this phenomenon considerably reduced the reliability of the ratings.

Empirical attempts to examine more easily measured qualities of the therapist have tended to focus on the relation between static qualities or extratherapy variables and therapy outcome. In their review of this literature, Beutler, Crago, and Arizmendi (1986) note a generally weak relationship between such variables and outcome. For example, similarity of therapist and patient on age, gender, ethnicity, socioeconomic status, and values/attitudes yielded inconsistent results that were difficult to interpret. The most robust therapist dimensions included therapist's well-being, social influence attributes (expertness, trustworthiness, attraction, credibility), therapist's expectation of therapy success, and therapist's competency. These reviewers, however, expressed doubt that investigations of these static therapist qualities in a "simplistic model of unidirectional cause and effect assumptions" (p. 297) would ever produce more than weak, inconclusive results. They proposed a move toward understanding therapist variables in the context of actual interactions between therapist and patient.

The empirical literature on countertransference parallels the progression of clinical theory, moving from studies which assume a unidirectional cause-and-effect model toward those adhering to a more bidirectional, object relations/interactional approach. In the following section, selected investigations of countertransference will be examined, in order to demonstrate how modern research methods may be opening this area to unprecedented empirical investigation.

INVESTIGATIONS OF THERAPISTS' COUNTERTRANSFERENCE

One of the earliest empirical investigations of countertransference attempted to test the classical definition of countertransference by quantifying therapists' alleged misperceptions of patients (Fiedler 1951). Fiedler found that therapists rated as less competent were more likely to misperceive their patients. Another early study (Cutler 1958) examined the hypothesis that countertransference phenomena occur when the therapist's perceptions and responses to the patient are influenced by the therapist's personal needs. Cutler found that therapists cannot objectively report session material involving their own intrapsychic conflicts, and he reported therapist interventions to be less than optimal when patient material touched on areas of conflict for the therapist. Perry has reported similar findings, in terms of the therapist's difficulty identifying patient's defenses when these comprise issues of personal conflict for the therapist (see chapter 15).

Bandura (1956) hypothesized that therapists' anxieties would impair their ability to conduct effective psychotherapy. Therapists rated as less competent by supervisors tended to be viewed as more anxious by their peers. Later, Bandura, Lipsher, and Miller (1960) improved the methodology by using independent ratings of therapist behaviors from tape-recorded therapy sessions, rather than supervisors' global ratings. The results supported the idea that preexisting therapist characteristics influenced the therapist's performance in the session; the authors also found evidence of a bidirectional influence of patient and therapist behaviors.

In an early investigation by Strupp (1958, 1960), 237 psychodynamic and client-centered psychotherapists were asked to view a thirty-minute film of the initial interview with an adult male patient. They were then instructed to respond as vicarious interviewers. Strupp found significant relationships between therapists' negative attitudes toward the patient and their clinical judgments relevant to treatment. Therapists' conscious negative attitudes were also associated with less empathic and sometimes antagonistic or hostile hypothetical responses to the patient. Strupp concluded that, although therapists are often consciously aware of their dislike for a particular patient, typically they are unaware of the incipient effects of their feelings on their in-session behavior with the patient.

Yulis and Kiesler (1968) examined low-anxious versus chronically high-anxious therapists with respect to the degree of personal involvement manifested in their interventions. During interruptions of a tape of a patient, therapists were asked to choose one of a pair of statements they would have made had they been the therapist. Results confirmed the authors' expectations: consistently greater personal involvement was observed for low-anxious therapists, while high-anxious therapists avoided transference interpretations and were more likely to avoid patients' hostile feelings when these were directed toward the therapist.

The studies cited thus far suggest that negative therapist attitudes can negatively influence therapists' interactions with patients. The findings provide relatively crude demonstrations of the existence of the clinical concept of countertransference and also provide some clues about the nature of relevant therapist attitudes and characteristics as well as about how and when these might influence the process of therapy. On the other hand, these early efforts contain serious methodological flaws that limit their generalizability.

PATIENT CHARACTERISTICS AND COUNTERTRANSFERENCE

As noted earlier, a major turning point in thinking about countertransference emerged with Winnicott's (1949) notion that patients' behaviors influence therapists' reactions. Empirical investigations of the influence of general patient characteristics on the success of therapy have consistently shown that the patient's willingness and ability to become actively involved in the therapeutic interaction are related to outcome (Gomes-Schwartz 1978; Keithley, Samples, and Strupp 1980; Moras and Strupp 1982; Filak, Abeles, and Norquist 1986; see also Garfield [1986] and Orlinsky and Howard [1986] for extensive reviews of this topic). While important, such findings tell us little about the manner in which patient qualities affect therapist responses and the therapeutic process.

An early study by Russell and Snyder (1963) examined the effects of hostile patient affect and friendly patient demeanor on therapist anxiety and verbal responses. The results confirmed the hypothesis that hostile patient behavior was associated with significantly greater therapist anxiety.

Another approach to studying the interaction of patient and therapist behaviors was developed by Tourney and his colleagues (1966). Twenty-eight therapist and patient process variables were rated every five minutes during sessions with neurotic and schizophrenic patients. Analyses revealed a relationship between neurotic patients' expressions of hostility toward therapists and therapists' anxiety, hostility, and errors of commission.

This selective review illustrates some specific, early approaches to unraveling the nature of the patient's impact on the therapist's behavior. Like the studies of therapist's characteristics and attitudes, these studies are methodologically flawed, depend heavily on analogue designs, use inexperienced therapists, and implicitly assume a unidirectional causality.

The perspective on countertransference espoused by the Vanderbilt research group involves two aspects. One is the view that countertransference encompasses those reactions (attitudes, behavior, thoughts, feelings, and fantasies) that are *evoked* in a complementary fashion by the patient's transference enactments. The second is the view that the personal vulnerabilities that reflect a particular therapist's personality and developmental history influence how that therapist will tend to respond to patients.

Some of the early work by Strupp (1960) addressed the first of these components. He suggested that the therapist's negative attitudes (dislike), presumably evoked by a difficult patient, were associated with negatively tinged clinical judgments in diagnosis, treatment plan, and prognosis. As part of a later investigation, Strupp and Hadley (1979) studied the performance of highly experienced therapists, each of whom treated three patients in individual psychotherapy. The patients were young men with symptoms of anxiety, depression, and difficulties relating to peers. The researchers observed considerable variability in the treatment outcomes of these patients. In attempting to gain a better understanding of the success and failure of these psychotherapies, Strupp (1980a, b, c, and d) intensively studied the therapeutic process in good and poor outcome cases treated by the same therapist. It became clear that experienced therapists—even those who had undergone personal therapy or analysis—tended to respond to patient hostility with irritation, coldness, and other forms of counterhostility. Strupp (1980d) noted, "[In] our study, we failed to encounter a single instance in which a difficult patient's hostility and negativism were successfully confronted or resolved" (p. 954).

Later, Henry, Schacht, and Strupp (1986) reexamined the identical cases using the Structural Analysis of Social Behavior (SASB) method

(Benjamin 1974, 1982), a detailed, conceptually rigorous, and empirically validated measure of moment-by-moment patient–therapist interactions. Comparisons of the high- and low-change cases by Henry, Schacht, and Strupp (1986) revealed that in low-change cases, therapists made significantly fewer statements classified as "affirming and understanding" and fewer statements classified as "helping and protecting." On the other hand, therapists in the low-change cases made significantly more statements classified in the category "belittling and blaming." Patients in the low-change cases were significantly less "disclosing and expressing," more "trusting and relying" (in a passive, deferential sense), and more "walling off and avoiding." In the high-change cases, none of the patient communications and only 1 percent of therapist communications were judged to be hostile, in contrast to low-change cases, where the corresponding averages were 19 percent and 20 percent. Henry et al.'s analyses showed that poor outcome cases had less positive complementarity, more negative complementarity, and less total complementarity. Examination of multiple communications, defined as simultaneously communicating more than one interpersonal message (such as acceptance and rejection), revealed that such communications were almost exclusively associated with therapies having poor outcome.

Christensen (1987), in a study of fourteen adult outpatients, found that therapists who perceived hostility (such as "belittling and blaming" and "sulking and appeasing") in their childhood relationships with mother and father, as well as in their self-concept "at worst," were observed to engage in significantly more hostile behavior in the therapeutic interaction and to make more technical errors.

Further examination of the patient–therapist interactions in the same fourteen cases by Henry, Schacht, and Strupp (1990) revealed that poor outcome cases with no introject change were typified by therapist behaviors that tended to be "belittling and blaming" and "ignoring and neglecting." In addition, the authors found a strong correlation between therapist statements that were hostile and controlling and patient statements that were self-blaming and critical. Poor outcome cases were found to have a significantly higher level of complex communications (simultaneously affiliative and hostile or simultaneously focusing on self and other), significantly greater patient and therapist hostility, and less patient speaking (relative to therapist). Finally, those therapists whose pretherapy self-ratings indicated relatively greater self-punitiveness were more likely to be rated as treating their patients in a disaffiliative manner.

SUMMARY OF EMPIRICAL RESEARCH

The number of investigations of countertransference is small, and the quality of existing studies has only recently reached beyond the analogues of therapy situations, global measures, and inexperienced therapists used in the earliest studies. Despite these methodological shortcomings, virtually all the different theoretical countertransference perspectives have received support from the empirical literature. The classical view of countertransference is upheld by studies showing that the therapist's psychological well-being (including anxiety, negative attitude, presence of conflicts) has important implications for therapeutic performance. The totalistic view is also endorsed, as studies tend to show that the therapist's behavior is influenced by how the patient presents, particularly with respect to hostility. Perhaps most impressive is the recent identification of specific forms of interpersonal relatedness between patient and therapist that are significantly associated with good and poor outcome. This work begins to reveal the complex interplay between key aspects of the patient's and therapist's personalities.

Implications for Future Research

The empirical studies reviewed here reflect advances in research methods and theoretical conceptualizations that may have important implications for future investigations. Is it true, for instance, that patients diagnosed with borderline personality disorder induce distinctive kinds of countertransference reactions, or are there general therapist reactions to "difficult" patients which span diagnostic boundaries? Are particular therapist reactions significantly associated with different therapeutic modalities, or does the personality and conflictual style of the therapist contribute most substantially? In contrast to other medical services, psychotherapy's "technology" cannot be separated from the personality or "instrument" of the therapist (Butler and Strupp 1986).

While there are formidable difficulties in measuring phenomena as complex as countertransference, the literature suggests that the field is moving beyond measures of static, extratherapeutic variables to psychodynamic styles of patients and therapists and to actual process interactions between the participants in the therapeutic setting. In addition, the operational definitions of countertransference reactions have undergone conceptual development since the early investigations. More recently, productive designs have used measures of therapist errors (which may reflect countertransference reactions) and the theoretically appealing concept of interpersonal complementarity.

Another focus for future research lies in the arena of psychoanalytic and psychodynamic psychotherapy training. From the early days of psychoanalysis, a central emphasis in training focused on limiting and managing countertransference. To this end, personal analysis for the therapist was prescribed as the method of choice for teaching therapists to deal with countertransference problems and enactments. Operationalizing countertransference may permit relatively precise tests of the effectiveness of such training on the therapist's actions within sessions.

In recent research by the Vanderbilt group (Strupp et al. 1987; Butler, Lane, and Strupp 1988; Butler and Strupp 1989) on training a group of experienced therapists in time-limited dynamic psychotherapy, our attention was forcefully drawn to a number of problems. Although it was possible to demonstrate increased adherence to psychodynamic time-limited techniques following training, some therapists manifested their learning in a mechanical manner. Moreover, there was no straightforward relationship between training and effect on therapeutic process and outcome. It became clear that modes of traditional training (in this case, group supervision and didactic lectures) seem to go only a limited distance in changing therapists' behavior. We are in the process of developing a variety of new training approaches, which we hope will have greater efficacy in helping therapists to recognize, tolerate, work through, and use transference and countertransference phenomena.

Conclusion

Significant progress is being made in conceptualizing measures of countertransference, in devising research designs, and in forging technologies for dealing more effectively with countertransference problems in the course of treatment. Not only are these new perspectives useful for studying complex interpersonal dynamics in the therapy process, but they also permit more precise characterizations of the impact of therapists' level of object relatedness on their behavior with patients in the therapy session. Significant findings, together with the demonstrated utility of new interpersonally based methodologies, augur well for further gains in the empirical understanding of transference and countertransference in the future.

References

ALEXANDER, F., & FRENCH, T. M. (1946). *Psychoanalytic therapy: Principles and applications.* New York: Ronald Press.

ANCHIN, J. C., & KIESLER, D. J. (EDS.). (1982). *Handbook of interpersonal psychotherapy.* New York: Pergamon Press.

BANDURA, A. (1956). Psychotherapists' anxiety level, self-insight, and psychotherapeutic competence. *Journal of Abnormal and Social Psychology, 52,* 333–337.

BANDURA, A., LIPSHER, D. H., & MILLER, P. E. (1960). Psychotherapists' approach-avoidance reactions to patients expression of hostility. *Journal of Consulting Psychology, 24,* 1–8.

BENJAMIN, L. S. (1974). Structural Analysis of Social Behavior. *Psychological Review, 81,* 392–425.

BENJAMIN, L. S. (1982). Use of Structural Analysis of Social Behavior (SASB) to guide intervention in psychotherapy. In J. C. Anchin & D. J. Kiesler (Eds.), *Handbook of interpersonal psychotherapy* (pp. 190–212). New York: Pergamon Press.

BEUTLER, L. E., CRAGO, M., & ARIZMENDI, T. G. (1986). Research on therapist variables in psychotherapy. In S. L. Garfield & A. E. Bergin (Eds.), *Handbook of psychotherapy and behavior change* (3rd ed., pp. 257–310). New York: Wiley.

BUTLER, S. F., LANE, T. W., & STRUPP, H. H. (1988, JUNE). *Patterns of therapeutic skill acquisition as a result of training in time-limited dynamic psychotherapy.* Paper presented to the annual meeting of the Society for Psychotherapy Research, Santa Fe, NM.

BUTLER, S. F., & STRUPP, H. H. (1986). Specific and nonspecific factors in psychotherapy: A problematic paradigm for psychotherapy research. *Psychotherapy, 23,* 30–40.

BUTLER, S. F., & STRUPP, H. H. (1989, JUNE). *Issues in training therapists to competency: The Vanderbilt experience.* Paper presented to the annual meeting of the Society for Psychotherapy Research, Toronto.

CHRISTENSEN, J. (1987). *Pre-therapy interpersonal relations and introject as reflected in the therapeutic process.* Unpublished master's thesis, Vanderbilt University, Nashville, TN.

CUTLER, R. L. (1958). Countertransference effects in psychotherapy. *Journal of Consulting Psychology, 22,* 349–356.

EPSTEIN, L. (1979). The therapeutic function of hate in the countertransference. In L. Epstein & A. H. Feiner (Eds.), *Countertransference: The therapist's contribution to the therapeutic situation* (pp. 213–234). New York: Jason Aronson.

EPSTEIN, L., & FEINER, A. H. (EDS.). (1979). *Countertransference: The therapist's contribution to the therapeutic situation.* New York: Jason Aronson.

EPSTEIN, L., & FEINER, A. H. (1988). Countertransference: The therapist's contribution to treatment. In B. Wolstein (Ed.), *Essential papers on countertransference,* (pp. 282–303). New York: New York University Press.

FIEDLER, F. E. (1951). A method of objective quantification of certain countertransference attitudes. *Journal of Clinical Psychology, 7,* 101–107.

FILAK, J., ABELES, N., & NORQUIST, S. (1986). Clients' pretherapy interpersonal attitudes and psychotherapy outcome. *Professional Psychology: Research and Practice, 17,* 217–222.

FREUD, S. (1910/1957). The future prospects of psychoanalytic therapy. In J. Strachey (Ed.), *The standard edition of the complete psychological works of Sigmund Freud* (Vol. 11, pp. 139–151). London: Hogarth Press.

FREUD, S. (1912/1958). Recommendations to physicians practising psychoanalysis. In J. Strachey (Ed.), *The standard edition of the complete psychological works of Sigmund Freud* (Vol. 12, pp. 111–120). London: Hogarth Press.

GARFIELD, S. L. (1986). Research on client variables in psychotherapy. In S. L. Garfield & A. E. Bergin (Eds.), *Handbook of psychotherapy and behavior change* (3rd ed., pp. 213–256). New York: Wiley.

GAY, P. (1988). *Freud: A life for our time.* New York: Norton.

GIOVACCHINI, P. L. (1979). Countertransference with primitive mental states. In L. Epstein & A. H. Feiner (Eds.), *Countertransference: The therapist's contribution to the therapeutic situation* (pp. 235–265). New York: Jason Aronson.

GIOVACCHINI, P. L. (1989). Countertransference triumphs and catastrophes. Northvale, NJ: Jason Aronson.

GOMES-SCHWARTZ, B. (1978). Effective ingredients in psychotherapy: Predictions of outcome from process variables. *Journal of Consulting and Clinical Psychology, 46,* 1023–1035.

GORKIN, M. (1987). *The uses of countertransference.* Northvale, NJ: Jason Aronson.

GREENBERG, J. R., & MITCHELL, S. A. (1983). *Object relations in psychoanalytic theory.* Cambridge, MA: Harvard University Press.

HEIMANN, P. (1950). On countertransference. *International Journal of Psychoanalysis, 31,* 81–84.

HENRY, W. P., SCHACHT, T. E., & STRUPP, H. H. (1986). Structural Analysis of Social Behavior: Application to a study of interpersonal process of differential therapeutic outcome. *Journal of Consulting and Clinical Psychology, 54,* 27–31.

HENRY, W. P., SCHACHT, T. E., & STRUPP, H. H. (1990). Patient and therapist introject, interpersonal process, and differential outcome. *Journal of Consulting and Clinical Psychology, 58,* 768–774.

KEITHLEY, L., SAMPLES, S. J., & STRUPP, H. H. (1980). Patient motivation as a predictor of process and outcome in psychotherapy. *Psychotherapy and Psychosomatics, 33,* 87–97.

KERNBERG, O. (1965). Notes on countertransference. *Journal of the American Psychoanalytic Association, 13,* 38–56.

KERNBERG, O. (1975). *Borderline conditions and pathological narcissism.* New York: Jason Aronson.

KERNBERG, O. (1986). Countertransference, transference regression, and the incapacity to depend. In H. C. Meyers (Ed.), *Between analyst and patient.* Hillsdale, NJ: Analytic Press.

KIESLER, D. J. (1982). Interpersonal theory for personality and psychotherapy. In J. C. Anchin & D. J. Kiesler (Eds.), *Handbook of interpersonal psychotherapy* (pp. 3–24). New York: Pergamon Press.

KLEIN, M. (1946). Notes on some schizoid mechanisms. *International Journal of Psycho-analysis, 33,* 433–438.

KLEIN, M. (1955/1975). On identification. In *Envy and gratitude and other works, 1945–1963* (pp. 141–175). New York: Delacorte Press.

Kohut, H. (1971). *The analysis of the self.* New York: International Universities Press.

Kohut, H. (1984). *How does analysis cure?* (A. Goldberg, Ed.). Chicago: University of Chicago Press.

Langs, R. (1976). *The bipersonal field.* New York: Jason Aronson.

Little, M. (1951). Counter-transference and the patient's response to it. *International Journal of Psycho-analysis, 32,* 32–40.

Luborsky, L., Fabian, M., Hall, B. H., Ticho, E., & Ticho, G. (1958). Treatment variables. *Bulletin of the Menninger Clinic, 22,* 126–147.

Luborsky, L., & Spence, D. P. (1978). Quantitative research on psychoanalytic therapy. In S. L. Garfield & A. E. Bergin (Eds.), *Handbook of psychotherapy and behavior change: An empirical analysis* (pp. 331–368). New York: Wiley.

Marmor, J. (1986). The corrective emotional experience revisited. *International Journal of Short-Term Psychotherapy, 1,* 43–47.

Menninger, K. A., & Holzman, P. S. (1973). *Theory of psychoanalytic technique* (2nd ed). New York: Basic Books.

Moras, K., & Strupp, H. H. (1982). Pretherapy interpersonal relations, patients' alliance, and outcome in brief therapy. *Archives of General Psychiatry, 39,* 405–409.

Orlinsky, D. E., & Howard, K. I. (1986). Process and outcome in psychotherapy. In S. L. Garfield & A. E. Bergin (Eds.), *Handbook of psychotherapy and behavior change* (3rd ed., pp. 311–381). New York: Wiley.

Poggi, R. G., & Ganzarain, R. (1983). Countertransference hate. *Bulletin of the Menninger Clinic, 47*(1), 15–35.

Racker, H. (1953). A contribution to the problem of countertransference. *International Journal of Psycho-analysis, 34,* 313–324.

Racker, H. (1957). The meanings and uses of countertransference. *Psychoanalytic Quarterly, 26,* 303–357.

Reich, A. (1951). On countertransference. *International Journal of Psychoanalysis, 32,* 25–31.

Reich, A. (1960). Further remarks on countertransference. *International Journal of Psycho-analysis, 41,* 389–395.

Reich, A. (1966). *Psychoanalytic contributions.* New York: International Universities Press.

Reik, T. (1948). *Listening with the third ear.* New York: Farrar, Strauss, & Young.

Russell, P. D., & Snyder, W. U. (1963). Counselor anxiety in relation to amount of clinical experience and quality of affect demonstrated by clients. *Journal of Consulting Psychology, 27,* 358–363.

Sandler, J. (1976). Countertransference and role-responsiveness. *International Review of Psychoanalysis, 3,* 43–47. Reprinted in E. Slakter (Ed), *Countertransference* (pp. 105–114). Northvale, NJ: Jason Aronson, 1987.

Searles, K. F. (1979). *Countertransference and related subjects.* New York: International Universities Press.

Singer, B. A., & Luborsky, L. (1977). Countertransference: The status of clinical versus quantitative research. In A. S. Gurman & A. M. Razin (Eds.), *Effective psychotherapy: A handbook of research* (pp. 433–451). Oxford: Pergamon Press.

SLAKTER, E. (1987). *Countertransference,* Northvale, NJ: Jason Aronson.

STRUPP, H. H. (1958). The psychotherapist's contribution to the treatment process: An experimental investigation. *Behavior Science, 3,* 34–67.

STRUPP, H. H. (1960). *Psychotherapists in action.* New York: Grune and Stratton.

STRUPP, H. H. (1973). *Psychotherapy: Clinical, research, and theoretical issues.* New York: Jason Aronson.

STRUPP, H. H. (1980a). Success and failure in time-limited psychotherapy: A systematic comparison of two cases (Comparison 1). *Archives of General Psychiatry, 37,* 595–603.

STRUPP, H. H. (1980b). Success and failure in time-limited psychotherapy: A systematic comparison of two cases (Comparison 2). *Archives of General Psychiatry, 37,* 708–716.

STRUPP, H. H. (1980c). Success and failure in time-limited psychotherapy: A systematic comparison of two cases (Comparison 3). *Archives of General Psychiatry, 37,* 947–954.

STRUPP, H. H. (1980d). Success and failure in time-limited psychotherapy: Further evidence (Comparison 4). *Archives of General Psychiatry, 37,* 954–974.

STRUPP H. H. (1982). Foreword. In J. C. Anchin & D. J. Kiesler (Eds.), *Handbook of interpersonal psychotherapy* (pp. ix–xi). New York: Pergamon Press.

STRUPP, H. H., & BINDER, J. L. (1984). *Psychotherapy in a new key: A guide to time-limited dynamic psychotherapy.* New York: Basic Books.

STRUPP, H. H., BUTLER, S. F., BINDER, J. L., SCHACHT, T. E., & ROSSER, C. L. (1987, JUNE). *Time-limited dynamic psychotherapy: Development and implementation of a training program.* Paper presented to the Society for Psychotherapy Research, Ulm, Germany.

STRUPP, H. H., & HADLEY, S. W. (1979). Specific versus nonspecific factors in psychotherapy: A controlled study of outcome. *Archives of General Psychiatry, 36,* 1125–1136.

SULLIVAN, H. S. (1953). *The interpersonal theory of psychiatry.* New York: Norton.

TANSEY, M. J., & BURKE, W. F. (1989). *Understanding countertransference: From projective identification to empathy.* Hillsdale, NJ: Analytic Press.

TOURNEY, G., BLOOM, V., LOWINGER, P. L., SCHORER, C., AULD, F., & GRISELL, J. (1966). A study of psychotherapeutic process variables in psychoneurotic and schizophrenic patients. *American Journal of Psychotherapy, 20,* 112–124.

WINNICOTT, D. W. (1949). Hate in the countertransference. *International Journal of Psycho-analysis, 30,* 69–74.

WINNICOTT, D. W. (1988). Counter-transference. In B. Wolstein (Ed.), *Essential papers on countertransference* (pp. 262–269). New York: New York University Press.

YULIS, A., & KIESLER, D. J. (1968). Countertransference response as a function of therapist anxiety and content of patient talk. *Journal of Consulting and Clinical Psychology, 32,* 413–419.

CHAPTER 19

Assessing the Therapist's Interpretations

PAUL CRITS-CHRISTOPH, JACQUES P. BARBER, KATHRYN
BARANACKIE, AND ANDREW COOPER

INTERPRETATION HAS BEEN DESCRIBED WITHIN the clinical psychoanalytic literature as the "supreme agent in the hierarchy of therapeutic principles" (Bibring 1954, 763). Despite the clinical emphasis, however, there have been few empirical studies of interpretation. This chapter briefly reviews the status of interpretation in dynamic psychotherapy and psychoanalysis as reflected in both clinical and research literature. Major clinical writings will be discussed with an eye toward defining issues related to the timing, wording, accuracy, precision, and impact of types of interpretations, both transferential and extratransferential, and the multiple conceptualizations of this therapeutic tool will be traced. The results of studies of the immediate and long-term (treatment outcome) effects of interpretations will be reviewed, and methods that were developed to determine the quality and/or accuracy of interpretations will be assessed. Implications of research for clinical practice will be highlighted, and promising future directions for research on interpretation will be suggested.

The Clinical Literature on Interpretation

INTERPRETATION IN PSYCHOANALYSIS

At the beginning of this century, listening to the patient's flow of associations, Freud noticed that there were gaps in his patient's memory; thus he initially emphasized the uncovering of early memories and the reconstruction of the past as the main goals of treatment. But through trial and error he eventually recognized that both removal of amnesias and full reconstruction were marked with difficulties. When Freud directly asked his patients to fill in apparent gaps in their discourses, he found that they often deflected his efforts using various means. The repeated experience of this multifaceted resistance led Freud to the conclusion that the amnesias resulted from an active force, repression, an unconscious (hypothetical) mental mechanism activated by the patient's efforts to avoid pain (see also chapter 16). The ideas resisted by the patient were viewed, then, as derivatives of repressed thoughts, which in the process of entering conscious awareness are disguised by the gatekeeping power of repression. Thus, if one could translate the free associations back into their unconscious origins, or remove the distortions, then what was unconscious could fully emerge into conscious awareness.

The goal of interpretation, therefore, was to work toward distilling the (covert) repressed thought or feeling from the (overt) disguised free association. In the topographic view the therapist takes systematic steps to translate the language of the primary process into the language of secondary process. In order to achieve this goal, analysts interpret not only free associations but also more primary process phenomena such as slips of the tongue, dreams, and symptoms. Through the interpretation of these compromise formation phenomena, unconscious threatening/exciting desires are clarified. Interpretations are, therefore, the main vehicle through which patients are said to gain insight, which is considered to be one of the central change mechanisms hypothesized in traditional psychoanalysis, particularly from an ego psychology point of view (see also chapter 21).[1]

If interpretation constitutes the main method for inducing change during psychoanalysis, why not tell the patient right away that, for example, he wishes to have sex with his mother? Fenichel (1945) and others noted that the patient's problem is not ignorance but rather the active resistances that keep the patient from knowing and from experiencing any sense of conviction regarding the reality of the disavowed yearnings. Thus, Fenichel recommends the now widely accepted technical rule that defenses be interpreted before impulses and conflicts are analyzed. In this view, the role of interpretation is "to split the patient's ego into an observing and experiencing part so that the former can judge the irrational character of the latter" (1945, 25). Only after the patient can begin to observe and acknowledge his own strategems for fending off conflictual, anxiety-provoking thoughts and affects can the field be cleared for the patient to emotionally come to grips with the validity of hidden wishes.

[1]While this chapter discusses both clinical and empirical considerations regarding interpretive interventions, quite broadly, for the most part, it is oriented toward the treatment requirements of relatively higher order neurotic patients. The issues of nonverbal interpretation and of nonverbal aspects of verbal interventions are not included here.

In parallel to his focus on analyzing inner resistance, early on in his writings Freud ([1901–1905] 1957) emphasized the interpretation of transference. Since transference is an enactment of the patient's intimate relationships of the past, the goal of the interpretation of transference is to help the patient understand how these early relationships distort relationships in the present, and most particularly with the therapist. Interpretations are viewed as the main instrument for reconstructing past unsuccessful developmental experiences (Chrzanowski 1987). In the last few decades, however, this view has been increasingly criticized by theorists who either stress that the real past is not important (Strupp and Binder 1984), who state that the past cannot be known for its truth value (Spence 1982), or who assert that the analyst's role is not to correct patients but to allow them to understand the needs that cause them to be biased (Arlow 1987).

Early on, Bibring (1954) described five types of therapeutic intervention in terms that are still used. These include:

1. Suggestion: the uncritical acceptance by the patient of ideas and emotions from the therapist in his or her authoritative position
2. Abreaction: the relief from acute tension through emotional discharge
3. Manipulation: influence through actual experience (e.g., advice, guidance, or any technique used to promote treatment)
4. Clarification: restating in more precise phenomenological terms what the patient is already saying
5. Interpretation: going beyond the descriptive-phenomenological data and elucidating to the patient how behaviors have been determined by certain dangerous, but gratifying, wishes and thoughts, which formerly the patient had to keep secret from himself or herself and others

He noted that the first three are used commonly across a host of diverse forms of treatment. The last two techniques, however, he classified as uniquely psychodynamic, in that their aim was to enhance insight and increase self-understanding. Thus, in Bibring's view, relating the patient's behavior toward the therapist to that toward a parent would not be viewed as an interpretation unless some aspect of the patient's behavior outside conscious awareness were pointed out.

Lowenstein (1951), however, defined interpretation more broadly to include "those explanations, given to patients by the analyst, which add to their knowledge about themselves" (p. 4). He does not refer to the therapist's mention of the repetitive nature of the patient's interpersonal behavior with various people as an interpretation, but instead would describe this as preparation for interpretation. Complete interpretations would include references to unconscious ideas or complexes such as the oedipal one.

Lowenstein also discussed various parameters of interpretations, suggesting, for example, that interpretation should be given at a time when the patient is neither overwhelmed by emotional reaction to an event to be interpreted nor completely removed from the conflict. He also proposed to interpret both resistances and defenses before id derivatives, with material appearing in the transference taking primacy over material that does not. Accordingly, clinicians were cautioned not to analyze major neurotic symptoms at the outset of treatment, but rather were encouraged to systematically interpret neurotic defenses prior to dealing with characterological issues. Lowenstein emphasized the importance of carefully timing the delivery of an intervention, underscored the importance of repeating interpretations across different domains of the same theme ("working through"), and highlighted the importance of making brief interventions using everyday language.

Early in the technical development of psychoanalysis, Strachey (1934) introduced the concept of "mutative interpretation" to describe those interpretations which constitute the "ultimate operative factor in the therapeutic action" (p. 152). According to Strachey, mutative interpretations have the following characteristics: (1) they should be close to the patient's affect; (2) they should target material that is either developmentally early or strongly repressed—in other words, "deep," which might be preferable to superficial interpretations or to no interpretation, when derivatives of id impulses are the cause underlying the patient's increasing anxiety; and (3) they should be specific, concrete, and detailed. Importantly, mutative interpretations are those that induce changes in the theoretically hypothesized structures of the mind. To underscore this effect, Strachey distinguished two phases of the interpretive process that inform both the overall analysis and individual interpretations. During phase one, the patient becomes aware of an id-related impulse (an intense desire, wish, or idea) directed toward the therapist; phase two occurs when the patient realizes that the emotion or thought projected onto the therapist is directed to an object from the past (a fantasy object) and not to the real object.

Strachey emphasized the central role of transference interpretation versus extratransference interpretation, in that the former is both more likely to be closer to the patient's affective state and more likely to provide an opportunity for the patient to internalize aspects of the analyst's benign curiosity, acceptance, and analyzing function (see chapter 22).

More recently, Stone has suggested (Halpert 1984) that although the centrality of transference in interpretations has been repeatedly emphasized in the clinical literature, other interpretations have been assigned "an exclusively adjunctive or preparatory function" and have rarely been openly discussed. He posed the question to his panel whether such interpretive modes might not contribute in themselves to significant "structural change."

Gray responded in the negative. In his detailed clinical papers, Gray (1973, 1986) has suggested that the efficacy of interpretive work is significantly enhanced to the degree that it is focused mainly on intrapsychic conflict, expressed in the here-and-now, as manifested in the transference. He has outlined two varieties of interpretive focus: id interpretations and defense interpretations, each of which can be directed toward either transference or extratransference phenomena. Citing a variety of possible negative effects resulting from id interpretations of current extraanalytic relationships—particularly for neurotic patients, as opposed to those with borderline pathology—Gray has stated that "whenever a patient talks about a manifest outside relationship, there is always significant transference influence on the choice of subject brought up, and the form in which it is expressed" (quoted in Halpert 1984, 138). Gray has similarly noted the considerable disadvantages incurred when defense interpretations are focused on extratransference situations rather than on the more immediate activity of the patient's transference.

Others, including both Halpert and Blum (see Halpert 1984), have viewed transference and extratransference interpretation as having the potential to be "complimentary and synergistic." Blum has gone so far as to suggest that transference interpretation has long been idealized, beginning with Strachey. Noting that while some extratransference interpretations may indeed be regarded as confirmations and extensions of the transference, or preparatory to an interpretation, Blum has suggested that some may be "necessary and valuable" in their own right in effecting the analytic process.

Gill has suggested that the "priority" of transference interpretation, both in the work of psychoanalysis and in psychoanalytic psychotherapy, need not be confused with its "exclusivity"; that is, talking about transference is not to demean the utility of other interventions. Nevertheless, in his writings, Gill (1982) has focused consistently on the crucial role of transference interpretation in effecting change, distinguishing two main phases: (1) the interpretation of resistance to awareness of transference and (2) the interpretation of the resolution of transference. The initial phase entails interpretation of the here-and-now patient–therapist relationship. This continues in the latter phase, wherein genetic interpretations regarding similarities between the current transference attitude and repetitive maladaptive patterns of relatedness in the past are introduced. While Gill has also classified extratransference interpretations into those directed to the here-and-now and those referring to the there-and-then, he does not waver in according primacy to those interpretations focused on resistance to awareness of the transference. Theoretically and technically, Gill has moved away from the exclusive focus on the intrapsychic that Gray and others represent, to address more directly interpersonal phenomena. Accordingly, he stresses that interpretations must explicitly take into account how the nature of the interplay with the therapist makes the transference plausible to the patient.

Nevertheless, the relative balance accorded to the primacy of transference and genetic interpretation varies not only across major schools of psychoanalytic thought—whether object-relations, drive-discharge and conflict, or self psychology and the like—but within schools as well (Stewart 1987; Parkin 1987; Kohut 1977). Heimann's comment on this issue, notes Stewart, was prescient; Heimann noted that

> in spite of general agreement amongst analysts that the transference is the battleground, in other words, that the dynamic changes in the patient's ego depend on the working through of his emotional conflicts as they center upon the analyst, there are great differences in psycho-analytic technique as practiced. These have often been defined in terms of the timing of transference interpretations, of interpretations of the negative versus the positive transference, or deep versus superficial interpretations, or the number of interpretations altogether. In the past—perhaps not only in the past—the analyst's efficiency was measured by the amount of his silence. (1986, 305)

Although Heimann attributed differences in technique to the degree of appreciation of the role played by unconscious fantasy in mental life, there are probably a host of additional factors external to theory which may account for technical divergences, not the least of which are personal qualities of the analyst, characteristics of the patient, and the goodness of fit between them.

While an extensive clinical literature has evolved around the variables cited by Heimann, with the exception of a few studies of negative transference and number of interpretations, empirical focus on these important issues has been scanty at best, despite the profusion of testable clinical hypotheses and axioms. For example, concerning the issue of depth of interpretation, Strachey (1934) suggested that mutative interpretations pitched at the appropriate level and directed at the transference and its concomitant resistances constituted what was central to therapeutic efficacy (see also Glover 1955, 276–288). According to Etchegoyen's (1983) reading of Strachey's paper, so-called superficial interpretations were those interpretations that did not relate directly to the emerging impulse, while deep interpretations could be characterized by their induction of intolerable anxiety without movement toward resolving it. One common rule of technique suggests that therapist interpretations containing material slightly beyond the patient's recognition (that is, moderately deep) are more beneficial than interpretations that go far beyond the patient's awareness (that is, deep) or that stay very close to the patient's awareness (that is, superficial) (Fenichel 1945). Nevertheless, a significant minority of analysts would take issue with such a viewpoint.

King neatly touches upon the same issues when she suggests that there exist dichotomous viewpoints in the field which lead to different technical approaches to the interpretation and use of transference phenomena:

> The first is that in order to enable a transference neurosis to develop and the illness to be experienced in relation to the analyst (and therefore become accessible to treatment) transference interpretations should not be made in the early stage of treatment, lest they bias or inhibit the growth of the transference neurosis, rendering the neurosis of the patient less accessible to treatment. The second approach arises from the idea that an understanding of the transference is the "royal road to the unconscious" so that the quicker you can evoke the transference of early pathogenic material into the analytic relationship and towards the person of the analyst, the sooner you will have access to unconscious processes in the patient and be in a position to analyze his unconscious anxieties and conflicts. (1971, 5–6)

Fenichel (1945) addressed another important issue related to interpretation: criteria for estimating the accuracy of an interpretation. Like many authors before him, Fenichel viewed the patient's acceptance of an interpretation as likely to support its validity under ordinary circumstances. A negative answer, however, was not to be accepted easily; a plea of not guilty by a person accused of a crime is rarely seen as conclusive (Freud 1920). Fenichel emphasized that the issue is not whether but *how* the patient says yes or no. Since the role of the interpretation is to encourage the expression of unconscious material, the patient's subsequent associations, as well as his or her entire demeanor, should provide telling data regarding the validity of the interpretation. Brenner (1976) noticed that correct interpretations are followed typically by 'fresh analytic material' i.e., by memories, dreams, fantasies, symptoms, or transference reactions (p. 52). Other evidence for correct interpretations are recognition with surprise, a feeling of familiarity, the return of a forgotten memory, an affective reaction, a slip, a confirmatory dream, associations or acting out. He emphasized that improvement in symptoms is a necessary consequence of the efficacy and correctness of interpretation, albeit not a sufficient indication because there might be a "paradoxical worsening of symptoms" and because symptom remission may result from something other than the mutative interpretation. Nevertheless, he posited that absence of improvement in symptoms over time constitutes suggestive evidence that the interpretations have been incorrect.

Earlier, Kubie (1952) indicated that interpretations should be considered working hypotheses which could be corroborated or refuted by the patient's further associations; by changes in symptoms; or, at times, by the analyst's ability to predict the patient's future behavior. While these criteria are necessary they are not sufficient, and Kubie does not go far enough, despite his worthwhile description of the problems inherent in the validation of interpretations (see pp. 74–90 in Kubie 1952).

A major difficulty in attempting to validate the accuracy of an interpretation results from the psychoanalytic principle of overdetermination; that is, psychodynamic theory assumes that any one behavior represents the final common pathway of multiple causes. Any behavior can therefore be interpreted in a variety of ways, such that one can never be certain of the primacy of a particular interpretation's truth value. Moreover, multiple interpretations are possible. During the initial years in the development of psychoanalysis, the focus of interpretation was well defined; the aim was first to explain a patient's symptoms and later to recover childhood memories. Nowadays, the focus has broadened extensively (to include, for example, developmental arrest), making it far more complex to assess and study both the accuracy and the relative primacy of an interpretation.

If no good criteria exist for selecting among alternative, equally compelling interpretations, then how should a therapist proceed? Several responses may be ascertained from the literature. The first, and perhaps most prominent, response has been to avoid the issue. A different approach, derived from recent developments in the philosophy of science, suggests that therapists and clinical researchers should have two or more plausible, competing hypotheses in mind when generating an interpretation. The patient's overall response is then used to corroborate one of the hypotheses and refute the other(s). Another answer, represented by the growth in popularity of the hermeneutic approach, is that neither the "historical truth," the accuracy, nor the truth value of an interpretation matters much in the long run; what is important is the "narrative truth" or "consistency of the story" agreed upon by patient and therapist (e.g., Spence 1982; see also chapter 6).

Many authors have addressed the problems and consequences of "inexact interpretation." Some have claimed that inexact interpretations have a detrimental effect on the patient and on future treatment (as in the creation of a "pseudo-transference neurosis," Glover 1955, 130), while others have suggested that such interpretations nevertheless contribute to helping the patient. More recently, discourse regarding inexact interpretation has all but disappeared in the clinical literature. While there are many complex reasons for this, one important consideration has been the advent of shorter treatment. In the past several decades, several brief, time-limited psychodynamic treatments have emerged, which have brought with them certain shifts in focus, with particular emphasis on the need for greater precision in defining and interpreting the patient's main conflict or primary interpersonal themes (e.g., Crits-Christoph and Barber 1991; Davanloo 1980; Luborsky 1984; Malan 1976a and b; Mann 1973; Sifneos 1972; Strupp and Binder 1984; Weiss and Sampson 1986). By virtue of their considerable time constraints, these therapies can focus on only a few issues—typically only one neurotic conflict of acute onset can be dealt with. The more chronic ego syntonic and characterological problems are usually, though not always, more appropriately treated in longer-term approaches.

Given the brevity of these treatments, most authors underscore the importance of forestalling the development of a full-blown transference neurosis during the ongoing course of treatment; once such a phenomenon has crystallized, the option of continuing in short-term treatment is sharply curtailed. Attention to the therapeutic alliance, however, is particularly crucial, and all authors emphasize the importance of early and repeated interpretation of resistance ambivalence and negative transference. Sifneos (1972) and, to a far more confrontational extent, Davanloo, deliberately increase the patient's anxiety by sustained concentration on interpreting the patient's strategies of defense against disavowed wishes and fears.

Malan's interpretive focus on the "triangle of insight," repeatedly linking here-and-now interpretations of transferential phenomena with significant objects in the past (TP interpretations), as well as with significant relationships in the present, was later extensively used by Davanloo.

Malan (1976a and b) and other short-term theorists also relied heavily on the use of "trial interpretations" in both assessment and early treatment interviews, in order to yield data regarding the patient's degree of psychological mindedness and capacity to make use of interpretations, in order to deepen the therapeutic alliance and reduce resistance, and in order to generate a central conflictual formulation around which the treatment will focus.

Of the various short-term dynamic interventions which have recently evolved, Mann's twelve-session course focuses the most intensely on interpretations regarding the issues of time, finitude, limits, mortality, and loss in the context of the transferential relationship. The brevity and imposition of absolute and nonnegotiable time limits has brought Mann to focus far greater precision on the wording, tone, and format of the interpretive intervention itself. His focused, succinct interpretations, simultaneously encompassing both the patient's primary wish and most dreaded fear, in everyday language, has had an impact even on longer-term psychodynamic treatments.[2]

---

[2]In this regard, see Schafer's (1976) work on action language, regarding how choice of active or passive voice in parsing an interpretation may carry significantly different meanings for the patient.

This selective review of the concept of interpretation from the classical psychoanalytic literature helps to clarify the major issues surrounding the concept of interpretation. First, all authors view interpretation as central to the psychoanalytic task and process. Second, most authors try to circumscribe the scope of the concept by limiting it to the discussion of unconscious material, thereby excluding interventions such as pointing out the repetitive nature of the patient's interpersonal problems, which are intrapsychically derived. Third, most authors emphasize clinical sensitivity regarding the timing of interpretations, given the affective and defensive status of the patient, so that interpretations are not delivered too early, when the patient is highly defended. Fourth, the timing of interpretations is also emphasized with regard to closeness to consciousness of the warded-off material; that is, for an interpretation to be effective, the patient must have already been discussing closely relevant material. In this regard, Kleinian analysts appear to interpret "deeper" conflictual material earlier (Spillius 1988) than do, say, ego psychologists, who appear to focus more intently on defense analysis. Fifth, the correctness of an interpretation is not necessarily related to the patient's acceptance of the interpretation, but rather is related to his or her consequent affects, symptoms, or flow of associations. Sixth, most authors view transference interpretations as qualitatively more powerful and effective than extratransferential interpretations (Gray, in Halpert 1984), but depending on the nature of the patient's characterological disorder, authors differ on what constitutes the most appropriate treatment phase for the delivery of transference interpretations. Self psychologists, for example, tend to delay the introduction of transference interpretations with narcissistic patients far longer than do those working within an ego psychology model (Kohut 1977). Seventh, most authors subscribe to the view that certain kinds of interpretations should be made before others; for example, almost all drive-oriented therapists propose that the interpretation of resistance should precede the interpretation of id derivatives. Kleinians are among the exceptions here. Eighth, all authors seem to believe that a strong therapeutic alliance is a necessary condition for interpretations. Ninth, some authors emphasize the role of transference interpretation in shedding light on etiological underpinnings, for example, by describing the nature of how infantile relationships shaped current modes of being in relationships; all theoretical approaches tend to emphasize the importance of the patient's eventual emotional conviction that current transference wishes and character patterns have been decisively shaped by important relationships in the past.

Research on Interpretation

Studies of the role of interpretation in psychoanalytic psychotherapy or psychoanalysis have usually been of two types: process studies of the immediate (in-session) responses of patients to interpretations and outcome studies, relating the nature of the interpretation to the progress of treatment. More recently, a third direction of research has emerged: assessing the appropriateness or accuracy of therapists' interpretations.

PROCESS STUDIES OF INTERPRETATIONS

The earliest empirical work on interpretation was a series of studies on depth of interpretation (Harway et al. 1955; Howe 1962; Rausch et al. 1956; Dittman 1952; Speisman 1959). Harway et al. (1955) defined depth of interpretation as the extent of the disparity between the patient's own awareness of his or her emotions and motivations and the view expressed by the therapist of these issues.

Most studies concerning depth of interpretation focused on the development of a scale for assessing the concept. The instrument (Harway et al. 1955) consisted of a 7-point rating scale anchored with descriptions of therapist activity. The lowest point (nondeep) of the scale was anchored by the statement, "Therapist merely repeats the material of which the patient is fully aware," and the highest point was anchored with the statement, "Therapist response deals with inferences about material completely removed from the patient's awareness." Using clinicians as judges, Harway et al. found that when judges were given the whole session as a context for evaluating interpretations, as opposed to judging individual therapist responses, therapist statements were rated as deeper. No difference between transcripts and tape recordings of the same material, however, emerged. Presenting therapist statements in random order to judges was found to lower the reliability of depth ratings.

Only two studies employed the depth of interpretation scale to explore the impact of interpretations of different levels of depth on the immediate patient responses. Dittman (1952) found that the use of moderately deep interpretations, rather than superficial ones, was related to ratings of therapeutic progress during the first thirty sessions of a single patient's therapy. Speisman (1959) studied the relationship between depth of interpretation and verbal resistance in psychotherapy. Three categories each of positive resistance (pursuit of exploration) and of negative resistance (avoidance of the therapeutic task) were assessed through ratings of transcripts of patient statements (therapist statements were deleted from the text). For twenty-two patients in psychotherapy, Speisman observed that moderately deep interpretations were more effective than deep or superficial interpretations for maintaining minimal levels of patient resistance.

Luborsky et al. (1979) examined the immediate context of transference interpretations within three psychoanalyses. The results of the study indicated that each patient responded in his or her own consistent way to the transference interpretations. One patient typically showed a negative response to transference interpretations (that is, an increase in resistance); the second showed some positive response; the third showed a very positive response. This study, however, did not explore the relative accuracy of the transference interpretations, a factor that may account for the differences between patients.

Garduk and Haggard (1972) researched the immediate impact of interpretations compared with noninterpretations for four patients (two in psychoanalysis, two in psychotherapy). It was found that patients responded more slowly to interpretations and that they talked less after interpretations. After interpretation, patients expressed more defensive and oppositional associations, more transference-related material, higher affect, and increased understanding and insight. Each of these dimensions was assessed through 4-point rating scales applied to segments of transcripts of therapy sessions. Experienced psychoanalytically oriented clinicians served as judges.

The earlier process studies of interpretations must be interpreted cautiously in light of a number of methodological concerns, such as small sample size and the use of global, imprecise measures. Some research efforts, however, show promise in attacking these important clinical questions in more sophisticated ways.

For example, Azim et al. (1988) have investigated the use and the impact of transference interpretations as moderated by the quality of the patient's object relations. Forty patients received short-term psychoanalytically oriented psychotherapy. The results indicated that, when confronted with a resistant patient, the therapists responded according to the level of the patient's object relations. For patients with good object relations, therapists tended to interpret the transference; for patients with poorer object relations, therapists simply talked more, responding perhaps to the patient's vulnerability by increasing activity to lessen the patient's anxiety. In addition, patients with poor object relations responded with less dynamic work after transference interpretations compared with nontransference interpretations. Overall, a very high rate of transference interpretations was associated with decreased dynamic work, suggesting that too much emphasis on transference interpretation may increase resistance.

OUTCOME STUDIES OF INTERPRETATION

In one of the first outcome studies of interpretation cited in the literature, Sloane et al. (1975) reported a significant negative relationship between the number of therapist interpretations and clarifications and treatment outcome. This study, however, cannot be considered a true test of the relationship between interpretations and outcome, since interpretation and clarifications were not differentiated in the data analyses.

Several studies have been concerned with the relationship between treatment outcome and object related interpretations; that is, those interpretations that focus on intimate relationships in the patient's life. In the first investigation, Malan (1976) studied the brief psychotherapies of thirty patients. He selected for inclusion in the study only those interpretations that made reference to one or more of the following objects: (1) the therapist (T); (2) the patient's parents (P); and (3) significant others in the patient's life (O). The various combinations of objects yielded several types of object interpretations. The most important type, according to psychoanalytic theory (e.g., Bibring 1954; Strachey 1934), was thought to be the transference interpretation, or the TP link. Indeed, Malan did find that TP interpretations were significantly related to treatment outcome. No significant relationships were observed, however, between the other types of object interpretations and treatment outcome.

Several methodological deficiencies jeopardize the usefulness of Malan's findings. For example, therapist process notes were used as the source of data. Process notes have the disadvantage of containing biased and distorted recollections of the therapy. Additionally, the judges who coded interpretations into object categories were contaminated by prior knowledge of the patients' treatment outcomes. Finally, only a single measure was used to assess outcome.

Using Malan's original data, Marziali and Sullivan (1980) successfully replicated his results. Although they employed interpretation coders who were blind to therapy outcome, they failed to correct the other methodological problems in his study. Marziali (1984) then improved on Malan's design by studying audio recordings of the patients' therapy sessions, rather than therapist process notes. In addition, therapy outcome was assessed by five psychodynamic scales: capacity for friendship; capacity for intimacy; capacity to use support; self-esteem; and assertiveness. The judges who coded interpretations into object categories were also blind to outcome.

The author reported several significant findings. The *frequency* of TP interpretations was positively correlated with two of the outcome scales (intimacy and capacity to use support), as well as with the total of the five scales. The frequency of TPO interpretations (those interpretations that link therapist, parents, and significant others) was positively correlated with four of the outcome scales (friendship, self-esteem, assertiveness, capacity to use support), as well as with the total scale score.

Although this investigation was methodologically more sophisticated than the earlier studies, only some of the outcome scales were significantly related to TP and TPO interpretations. Furthermore, the use of an index such as frequency of interpretations may be problematic. The positive findings might have reflected the influence of the therapist's level of activity rather than the impact of object interpretations per se.

In another investigation, Piper et al. (1986) studied the audio recordings of twenty-one patients in brief psychotherapy. They selected for inclusion in the study interpretations that focused on the following objects: father; mother; siblings; unspecified family member; significant other; unspecified other; therapist; therapist–parent link; significant other–therapist link; and significant other–parent link.

With 10 different types of interpretations and 17 outcome scores, a total of 170 correlations were possible. Only 9 significant correlations (5.3 percent) were obtained, which is about the number that would have been expected as a function of chance. There are several possible explanations for the lack of positive results. First, an index such as proportion of object interpretations may have been unsuitable (Piper et al. 1986). While some patients may improve when particular types of object interpretations are emphasized more than others, there is no compelling reason to believe that all patients will respond in the same manner. Second, as suggested by the study of Azim et al. (1988), the impact of interpretations may depend upon the quality of the patient's object relations, and there may also be negative effects, with an overemphasis on transference interpretations in particular. Third, other aspects of interpretations, such as their timing, sensitivity, and accuracy, were not assessed in the Piper et al. (1986) investigation, and these factors may be crucial in understanding the role of interpretations.

McCullough et al. (in press) reported the most sophisticated study in this area. This team investigated therapist interventions in combination with patient affective versus defensive responding in relationship to treatment outcome. Sixteen patients were treated with either confrontational dynamic therapy (Laikin, Winston, and McCullough 1991) or a more cognitively oriented brief dynamic therapy (Pollock and Horner 1985). The main findings were that (1) a high frequency of transference interpretations followed by patient affect was associated with favorable outcome and (2) all interventions followed by defensiveness correlated negatively with outcome. An examination of patient and therapist variables separately, rather than interactionally, did not produce any significant findings. Although McCullough et al. found that a high frequency of transference interpretations followed by affect was a positive predictor of treatment outcome, they did not assess whether an extremely high rate of such interpretations could be counterproductive, as suggested by the Azim et al. (1988) study.

STUDIES OF ACCURACY OF INTERPRETATIONS

Although the reviewed studies have contributed to understanding the immediate and long-term impact of frequency of interpretations, the failure to control for the appropriateness and the accuracy of therapists' interpretations may well have obscured effects. Until recently, the concept of accuracy of interpretations has been ignored in psychotherapy research, largely because the valid assessment of interpretive accuracy is a task of great complexity.

According to Silberschatz, Fretter, and Curtis (1986), assessing the accuracy of interpretations requires: identifying the patient's main psychological issues and evaluating the interpretations specifically on whether they address those issues. The procedure used in their study was based on a theory of therapy developed by Weiss and Sampson (1986). The therapy transcripts of three patients in brief dynamic therapy were used. One set of judges formulated each patient's "plan," that is, the patient's strategies for disconfirming pathogenic beliefs. Pathogenic beliefs are unconscious beliefs generally developed in childhood; they usually involve a fear of danger tied to the pursuit of a certain goal or to the attempt to gratify a certain impulse. Another set of judges rated therapists' interpretations for their degree of accuracy, or plan compatibility. The plan compatibility scale assessed the extent to which an intervention facilitated the patient's unconscious plan. Patient progress was assessed by scoring the material before and after interpretations with the Experiencing Scale (Klein et al. 1970). The Experiencing Scale measures the extent to which a patient focuses on his or her feelings while simultaneously reflecting on those feelings.

The results of the study were the following: (1) no significant relationship was found between object interpretations and immediate patient progress and (2) a significant positive relationship was reported for each patient between plan compatibility of interpretations and immediate patient progress as measured by the Experiencing Scale. In addition, the investigators reported that the proportions of interpretations compatible with the plan were significantly higher in therapies of the patients with good outcome than in therapies of the patients with poor outcome.

Silberschatz, Fretter, and Curtis (1986) have thus provided initial empirical support for the importance of assessing the accuracy of interpretations. Some restraint, however, should be exercised in interpreting the results because the generalizability of the findings was restricted by the use of a small sample size ($N = 3$), which eliminated the opportunity for a systematic analysis of outcome data. In addition, the assessment of immediate patient progress was limited to only one measure, the Experiencing Scale. While this scale has been found useful in a variety of studies on the process of psychotherapy, it does not measure a construct directly relevant to a psychodynamic understanding of the treatment process. A complex process such as immediate patient progress would seem to call for a more comprehensive assessment.

In a related vein of research, a measure of the accuracy of therapists' interpretations based on the Core Conflictual Relationship Theme (CCRT) method has been developed and used in a study of the relationship of interpretive accuracy to outcome in dynamic psychotherapy (Crits-Christoph, Cooper, and Luborsky 1988). This measure was influenced by Auerbach and Luborsky's (1968) rating scale on therapist response to the patient's main communication. In the Crits-Christoph, Cooper, and Lubosky (1988) study, accuracy was assessed on therapists' interpretations culled from two early-in-treatment sessions of forty-three patients receiving moderate-length (about one year) dynamic therapy. The CCRT measure (Luborsky 1977; Luborsky and Crits-Christoph 1990) was scored by independent judges using transcripts of the two treatment sessions. The CCRT consists of three components of the patient's relationship pattern: (a) the patient's main wishes, needs, or intentions toward the other person; (b) the responses from the other person; and (c) the responses of the self. Accuracy of interpretation was rated on a 4-point scale assessing the degree to which each therapist interpretation addressed a CCRT wish, negative response from other, and negative response of self.

The results indicated that accuracy on the main wishes and responses from others was significantly related to outcome, even after controlling for the effects of general errors in technique and the quality of the therapeutic alliance. Accuracy on negative responses of self was not related to outcome. These results suggest that when therapists accurately focus more on the interpersonal aspects of patient material (the wishes toward others and their expected or actual responses), rather than simply patients' feeling states (the response of self), greater progress results. An additional hypothesis tested by the authors—that accurate interpretations would have their greatest impact in the context of a positive therapeutic alliance—was not confirmed. This result was surprising, given the common clinical belief that the background of a positive alliance is necessary for interpretive work. It is possible that the sample used in the study did not include enough patients with a distinctly negative alliance and that this restricted range on the alliance variable prevented a meaningful interaction between alliance and interpretive accuracy from emerging. In fact, patients dropping out of treatment before eight sessions, many of whom would be expected to have negative alliances, were not included in the study sample.

A study by Crits-Christoph, Schuller, and Connolly (1988) examined the immediate patient response to accurate versus inaccurate interpretations. Patient response was assessed with a 19-item scale of patient resistance (Schuller, Crits-Christoph, and Connolly 1991), which consisted of four subscales: abrupt change or shifting of topic, vague response or doubting the therapist, flat or halting speech, and oppositional response. For a sample of twenty patients, the results indicated that interpretations accurate on the wish component of the CCRT were followed by increases in the vague/doubting form of resistance, whereas interpretations accurate on the response of self component led to decreases in the vague/doubt subscale. It was suggested that an increase in vagueness and doubting may reflect a useful form of working through or an ameliorative struggle on the part of the patient. This is particularly the case when the patient is faced with both sides of a conflict or with a wish or intention previously denied and maintained outside of conscious awareness. With correct interpretation of the patient's affective states (response of self), the patient has a less immediate need to struggle and, instead, feels more comfortable in that the information is experienced as more ego syntonic. This less resistant response, however, may not make an important contribution to the eventual therapeutic outcome.

Studies by Joyce and Piper represent the most comprehensive investigation of interpretive accuracy yet reported. Using transcripts of sessions from a controlled clinical trial of short-term dynamic therapy (Piper et al. 1990), these researchers examined the immediate effects of both the object and accuracy of interpretations (Joyce 1991), as well as the relationship of these measures of interpretation to treatment outcome (Piper 1991). For the study of immediate effects, eight sessions (out of a total treatment length of twenty sessions) for sixty patients who completed treatment were rated by judges on a number of variables. All variables were averaged over the eight sessions rated. In general, the results of the study indicate that different facets of interpretation relate to different measures of immediate patient response. More specifically, it was found that (1) frequency of transference (therapist as object) interpretations was inversely related to the occurrence of Dynamic Work (a measure of the extent to which the patient had developed a "psychoanalytic focus" involving exploration of both defensive operations and dynamic expressions), (2) accuracy, or what the authors refer to as correspondence, of interpretations was positively correlated with the amount of Patient Involvement (a measure composed of ratings of patient disclosure and the Experiencing Scale), and (3) the accuracy of transference interpretation in particular was associated with Patient Involvement, Patient Confidence (measured by ratings of decrease in Limited Vocal Quality, a variable which has previously been shown to indicate a withdrawal or reluctance to contribute to the therapy process),

and Hesitant Acknowledgment (a factor composed of frequent confirmations of the therapist's interpretation but a decrease in the overall verbal
output of the patient). Accuracy (correspondence) of interpretations was
assessed in this study through judges' ratings of the extent to which the
therapist addressed the dynamic themes that were specified in the therapist's written formulation of the case made after the second session.

The study linking process to outcome (Piper 1991; see also Piper et
al., in press) used two main predictor variables: concentration of transference interpretations (proportion of therapist interventions which were
transference interpretations) and correspondence (accuracy) of transference
interpretations. Dependent variables included the therapeutic alliance and
measures of outcome at termination and follow-up (five months after
termination). Analyses were conducted separately for patients with high
quality of object relations versus low quality of object relations.

The results indicated that, for patients with high quality of object
relations, concentration of transference interpretations had a significant
curvilinear relationship to the therapeutic alliance and two posttherapy
outcome measures (general symptomatology and individualized objectives). As concentration increased to high levels, alliance and posttherapy
outcome rapidly worsened. As the authors point out, the meaning of this
finding is not clear, since either a high concentration of transference interpretations could have weakened the alliance and led to poor outcome, or
a poor alliance in a patient not improving could have prompted more
transference interpretations from the therapist. Although concentration did
not relate to alliance or posttherapy outcome in the group of patients with
low quality of object relations, correspondence did demonstrate a significant inverse relationship with alliance in this group. In addition, correspondence was inversely related to change on individualized objectives at
follow-up.

The results for correspondence in the high quality of object relations
group were quite complex. Although correspondence did not relate to
alliance or posttherapy outcome in this group, a significant interaction
between correspondence and concentration in predicting change in general
symptomatology at follow-up was found. At low levels of concentration,
correspondence was strongly positively related to outcome. At high levels
of concentration, however, there was no relationship between correspondence and outcome.

Overall, the results of the Piper (1991) and Joyce (1991) studies
support the view that the quality or accuracy of therapists' interpretations
facilitates immediate patient progress and eventual outcome. These studies
further suggest that accuracy is most relevant to patients with high quality
of object relations, and, in fact, that for patients with low quality of object
relations, interpretation of relationship themes may actually be counterpro-

ductive. Instead, for these patients, a purely supportive relationship with the therapist may be most beneficial. The findings by Horowitz et al. (1984) on an interaction between the use of exploratory versus supportive interventions and patients' developmental level of self-concept in predicting outcome is consistent with this explanation. The other important finding of the Piper (1991) study is that, for patients with high quality of object relations, interpretation of themes in the therapeutic relationship is important, but excessive use of such transference interpretations can actually hinder therapeutic progress.

These findings suggest that a careful theory-guided analysis of the process of dynamic therapy can yield robust results that are consistent with clinical wisdom. It is likely that the strength of the findings is related to the sampling of a relatively large number of sessions (eight). In addition, these studies document the necessity of examining multiple aspects of interpretations in order to unravel the complexity of dynamic therapy. One limitation of the Piper (1991) and Joyce (1991) studies, however, is that accuracy of interpretation was assessed through correspondence of interpretations with the therapist's own formulation of the case. Obviously, if the therapist's original formulation is off the mark, this measure at correspondence will not appropriately assess the quality of the therapist's intervention.

One final study (Crits-Christoph, Barber, and Kurcias, in press) on accuracy of interpretation examined the relationship between accuracy and the development of the therapeutic alliance over the course of dynamic therapy. Accuracy of interpretation was scored on two early-in-treatment sessions as described in the Crits-Christoph, Cooper, and Luborsky (1988) study. The therapeutic alliance was assessed using the Helping Alliance Counting Signs method (Luborsky et al. 1983) and was scored on the two early in treatment and two later-in-treatment sessions (approximately eight months into treatment that lasted an average of one year). It was found that accuracy on the wish plus response from other dimension of the CCRT correlated significantly with the change in the alliance from early to later in treatment. Further analyses revealed that accurate interpretations served to both improve a poor alliance and maintain an initially positive one. Thus, it was concluded that the quality of the relationship with the therapist is not simply a function of what the patient brings to therapy but is intimately connected to the nature of the technical interventions that are made by the therapist. This study stands as one of the few investigations which attempts to tease out directionality of relationships between measures of the therapy process by employing a design where therapist actions at time one are related to other process variables at a subsequent time in treatment. Although causality can not be "proven" with any correlational design, the use of a multiple time point design allows one to begin to rule out some alternative explanations of the findings.

IMPLICATIONS OF RESEARCH FOR CLINICAL WORK

Research on dynamic psychotherapy, while experiencing significant growth of late, still remains in its infancy. Only a handful of solid empirical studies on interpretation have been performed, and these studies have had different aims, methods, and results. It is premature, then, to conclude that the research literature has reached a consensus on some aspects of the use or the impact of interpretations. Accordingly, the time is not yet ripe for recommendations regarding clinical technique based on systematic research results. The existing data, however, do suggest some promising directions for additional research that may eventually have direct implications for the practice of dynamic psychotherapy.

FUTURE DIRECTIONS FOR RESEARCH

Future research on interpretations should proceed along two fronts: (1) testing prominent hypotheses related to interpretation as discussed in the clinical literature and (2) building on findings in the existing research literature. By developing along both lines, we should be able to examine the validity of clinical lore and yet allow for unexpected or novel findings.

The clinical literature as reviewed early in this paper, while often pointing in a variety of directions, offers a wealth of theoretical statements that can serve as the basis for empirical study. For example, there seems to be considerable consensus that transference interpretations are more potent than nontransference interpretations (cf. Gill 1982; Sifneos 1972; Strachey 1934). Silberschatz, Fretter, and Curtis (1986), however, suggest that accurately addressing the patient's themes is more important than whether the interpretation makes reference to the therapist. This issue should be pursued in correlational designs, as in the work of Marziali (1984), Piper (1991), and Piper et al. (1986), as well as in experimental designs—for instance, a comparison of a treatment that uses extratransference interpretations with one that uses primarily transference interpretations.

Many other aspects of interpretations which are thought to have great importance clinically have yet to be studied. As discussed by Spiegel and Hill (1989), the timing of interpretations is a case in point. Interpretations that are too early are not considered therapeutic, but no study has yet taken timing into account. There is likely to be difficulty, however, in establishing a method for reliably coding interpretations into categories of "too early," "just right," and "too late." Related to timing is the issue of the sequence of interpretations over the course of treatment. Is it better first to interpret resistance or, in Gill's (1982) words, resistance to the awareness of transference, before moving on to genetic interpretations? Moreover, if it is better to first interpret resistances or defenses, which particular types of resistances or defenses within these categories should be addressed initially before moving on? Studies posing these questions would have to look at interpretations in a large number of sessions of treatment rather than focus on just a few sessions, as most studies have done. Although it will be difficult in practical terms, it may be necessary to perform such studies to do justice to the complexity of psychodynamic psychotherapy.

In terms of building on findings in the existing research literature, we can make several suggestions. A fruitful direction might be to look at the interactions of dimensions that have emerged in different studies. For example, depth of interpretation could be examined in interaction with accuracy. Accurate interpretations that occur at a moderate depth might be predicted to be most beneficial. In addition, accuracy of interpretation could be examined in interaction with object of focus (e.g., Piper 1991) or with patient qualities (such as level of object relations, overall psychological health-sickness). Patient diagnosis, severity of illness, and nature of defensive constellations are other variables which might interact with interpretive accuracy. Highly defended (repressive style) patients may, for example, react less favorably to accurate interpretations than patients who have greater flexibility in their defenses. On the other hand, those with highly permeable defenses and who are prone to regression may also respond less favorably. Further investigation of the relationship between accuracy of interpretation and shifts in the therapeutic alliance is also warranted.

A wider range of variables should be investigated in understanding the immediate impact of interpretations. Investigators have studied affect, "experiencing," and resistance, and we need to know how much these constructs overlap or have different meanings. Other aspects of patient responses, such as the flow of associations and the activation of particular defenses, should be measured as well.

In regard to accuracy of interpretations, research should compare the clinical formulation methods on which the accuracy measures are based. Does the Plan Diagnosis method (Silberschatz, Fetter, and Curtis 1986) yield the same kind of information as the Core Conflictual Relationship Theme method (Luborsky and Crits-Christoph 1990)? It may be useful to bring other clinically based approaches to psychodynamic formulation (e.g., Perry, Cooper, and Michels 1987) into the research arena, in order to compare them to the existing, empirically based measures of dynamic themes.

New research directions would necessitate the development of new measures to tap the relevant clinical constructs. Clearly, more scale development is needed for assessing clinical variables of resistance and defense, although some progress has been made in these areas (e.g., Schuller, Crits-Christoph, and Connolly 1991; O'Connell et al. 1990). Also needed are scales to measure other relevant aspects of interpretations, such as their timing, degree of supportiveness or empathy conveyed, and degree of criticalness or countertransference displayed.

Countertransference might be investigated through assessments of the therapist's CCRT and other aspects of his or her personality. The particular fit or match between the patient's CCRT and the therapist's CCRT would be especially interesting to study and might provide a glimpse into the nature of countertransference phenomena. Far more difficult, but equally important, would be a phenomenological approach to study the sequence of affective perceptual clues, problem-solving stratagems, employed by highly respected clinicians in the course of creatively generating accurate interpretations. Similarly, studies distinguishing between quality of interpretation in therapists with good patient outcomes, versus those formulated by therapists with poorer patient outcomes, all other variables being equal, might be useful.

No one type of research design can provide all the answers concerning the role of interpretation in psychoanalysis or in related forms of psychotherapy. Single-case designs, which can be more sensitive to the complexity of the clinical situation; large-sample correlational research, which permits investigations of many independent variables simultaneously and which demonstrates the generalizability of a phenomenon; and experimental studies, which can better demonstrate causality and rule out third variables, all need to be done. While psychodynamic psychotherapy has a history of scanty attention from empirical investigators, we are moving into a new era in which this treatment is being studied by a much larger number of sophisticated researchers, and future possibilities are exciting. The field is rapidly beginning to expand on its results with the goal that empirical data may one day be seen as an equal partner, working hand in hand with the clinical literature to enhance the practice of psychodynamic psychotherapy.

References

Arlow, J. A. (1987). The dynamics of interpretation. *Psychoanalytic Quarterly*, 56, 68–87.

Auerbach, A. H., & Luborsky, L. (1968). Accuracy of judgements of psychotherapy and the nature of the "good hour." In J. Shlien, H. F. Hunt, J. P. Matarazzo, & C. Savage (Eds.), *Research in psychotherapy* (Vol. 3). Washington, DC: American Psychological Association.

Azim, H., Piper, W., McCallum, M., & Joyce, A. (1988, June). *Antecedents and consequences of transference interpretations in short-term psychotherapy*. Paper presented at the Society for Psychotherapy Research, Santa Fe, NM.

BIBRING, E. (1954). Psychoanalysis and the dynamic psychotherapies. *Journal of the American Psychoanalytic Association, 2,* 745–770.

BRENNER, C. (1976). *Psychoanalytic technique and psychic conflict.* New York: International Universities Press.

CHRZANOWSKI, G. (1987). Psychoanalytic interpretation in modern, clinical perspective: A flight from history. *Contemporary Psychoanalysis, 23*(3), 469–482.

CRITS-CHRISTOPH, P., & BARBER, J. P. (EDS.). (1991). *Handbook of short-term dynamic psychotherapy.* New York: Basic Books.

CRITS-CHRISTOPH, P., BARBER, J. P., & KURCIAS, J. (IN PRESS). The accuracy of therapists' interpretations and the development of the therapeutic alliance. *Psychotherapy Research.*

CRITS-CHRISTOPH, P., COOPER, A., & LUBORSKY, L. (1988). The accuracy of therapists' interpretations and the outcome of dynamic psychotherapy. *Journal of Consulting and Clinical Psychology, 56*(4), 490–495.

CRITS-CHRISTOPH, P., SCHULLER, R., & CONNOLLY, M. B. (1988). *The impact of the accuracy of therapists' interpretations on patients' levels of resistance in dynamic psychotherapy.* Unpublished manuscript. University of Pennsylvania.

DAVANLOO, H. (1980). *Short-term dynamic psychotherapy.* New York: Jason Aronson.

DITTMAN, A. (1952). The interpersonal process in psychotherapy: Development of a research method. *Journal of Abnormal and Social Psychology, 47,* 236–244.

ETCHEGOYEN, R. H. (1983). Fifty years after the mutative interpretation. *International Journal of Psycho-Analysis, 64,* 445–459.

FENICHEL, D. (1945). *The psychoanalytic theory of neurosis.* New York: Norton.

FREUD, S. (1901–1905/1953). Fragment of an analysis of a case of hysteria. In J. Strachey (Ed.), *The standard edition of the complete psychological works of Sigmund Freud* (Vol. 7, pp. 15–122). London: Hogarth Press.

FREUD, S. (1920). *A general introduction to psychoanalysis* (Authorized translation). New York: Boni and Liveright.

GARDUK, E., & HAGGARD, E. (1972). Immediate effects on patients of psychoanalytic interpretations. *Psychological Issues* (Monograph 28).

GILL, M. (1982). The analysis of transference: Vol. 1. Theory and technique. *Psychological Issues* (Monograph 53).

GLOVER, E. (1955). *Technique of psychoanalysis.* New York: International Universities Press.

GRAY, P. (1973). Psychoanalytic technique and the ego's capacity for viewing intrapsychic activity. *Journal of the American Psychoanalytic Association, 21,* 474–494.

GRAY, P. (1986). On helping analysands observe intrapsychic activity. In A. D. Richards & M. S. Willick (Eds.), *Psychoanalysis: The science of mental conflict. Essays in honor of Charles Brenner* (pp. 245–262). Hillsdale, NJ: Analytic Press.

HALPERT, E. (1984). Panel report: The value of extratransference interpretation (L. Stone, H. Blum, P. Gray, & N. Leites). *Journal of the American Psychoanalytic Association, 32,* 137–146.

HARWAY, N., DITTMAN, A., RAUSH, H., BORDIN, E., & RIGLER, D. (1955). The measurement of depth of interpretation. *Journal of Consulting Psychology, 19* (4), 247–253.

HEIMANN, P. (1956). Dynamics of transference interpretations. *International Journal of Psycho-Analysis, 37,* 303–310.

HOROWITZ, M. J., MARMAR, C., WEISS, D., DeWITT, K. N., & ROSENBAUM, R. (1984). Brief psychotherapy of bereavement reactions: The relationship of process to outcome. *Archives of General Psychiatry, 41,* 438–448.

JOYCE, A. (1991, JUNE). *Concentration and correspondence of transference interpretations in short-term individual psychotherapy.* Paper presented at the annual meeting of the Society for Psychotherapy Research, Lyon, France.

KING, P. H. M. (1971). The therapist-patient relationship. *Journal of Analytical Psychology, 18,* 1–18.

KLEIN, M., MATHIEU, P., GENDLIN, E., & KIESLER, D. (1970). *The Experiencing Scale: A research and training manual.* Madison: Wisconsin Psychiatric Institute.

KOHUT, H. (1977). *The restoration of the self.* New York: International Universities Press.

KUBIE, L. S. (1952). Problems and techniques of psychoanalytic validation and progress. In E. Pumpian-Mindlin (Ed.), *Psychoanalysis as science.* Stanford, CA: Stanford University Press.

LAIKIN, M., WINSTON, A., & McCULLOUGH, L. (1991). Intensive short-term dynamic psychotherapy. In P. Crits-Christoph & J. P. Barber (Eds.), *Handbook of short-term dynamic psychotherapy.* New York: Basic Books.

LOWENSTEIN, R. M. (1951). The problem of interpretation. *Psychoanalytic Quarterly, 20,* 1–14.

LUBORSKY, L. (1977). Measuring a pervasive psychic structure in psychotherapy: The Core Conflictual Relationship Theme. In N. Freedman & S. Grand (Eds.), *Communicative structures and psychic structures.* New York: Plenum Press.

LUBORSKY, L. (1984). *Principles of psychoanalytic psychotherapy: A manual for supportive-expressive treatment.* New York: Basic Books.

LUBORSKY, L., BACHRACH, H., GRAFF, H., PULVER, S., & CHRISTOPH, P. (1979). Preconditions and consequences of transference interpretations: A clinical-quantitative investigation. *Journal of Nervous and Mental Disease, 169,* 391–401.

LUBORSKY, L., & CRITS-CHRISTOPH, P. (1990). *Understanding transference: The Core Conflictual Relationship Theme method.* New York: Basic Books.

LUBORSKY, L., CRITS-CHRISTOPH, P., ALEXANDER, L., MARGOLIS, M., & COHEN, M. (1983). Two helping alliance methods for predicting outcomes of psychotherapy. *Journal of Nervous and Mental Disease, 17,* 480–491.

MALAN, D. M. (1976a). *The frontier of brief psychotherapy.* New York: Plenum Press.

MALAN, D. M. (1976b). *Toward the validation of dynamic psychotherapy.* New York: Plenum Press.

MANN, J. (1973). *Time-limited psychotherapy.* Cambridge, MA: Harvard University Press.

MARZIALI, E. (1984). Prediction of outcome of brief psychotherapy from therapist interpretive interventions. *Archives of General Psychiatry, 41,* 301–304.

MARZIALI, E., & SULLIVAN, J. (1980). Methodological issues in the content analysis of brief psychotherapy. *British Journal of Medical Psychology, 53,* 19–27.

MCCULLOUGH, L., WINSTON, A., FARBER, B. A., PORTER, F., POLLACK, J. LAIKIN, M., VINGIANO, W., & TRUJILLO, M. (IN PRESS). The relationship of patient–therapist interaction to outcome in brief psychotherapy. *Psychotherapy.*

O'CONNELL, M., KARDOS, M., PAGNO, C. J., PERRY, J. C., & YOUNG, D. (1990, JUNE). *Assessing changes in defensive functioning with the Defense Mechanism Rating Scales (DMRS).* Paper presented at the annual meeting of the Society for Psychotherapy Research, Wintergreen, VA.

PARKIN, A. (1987). The two classes of objects and the two classes of transference. *International Journal of Psycho-Analysis, 68,* 185–195.

PERRY, S., COOPER, A. M., & MICHELS, R. (1987). The psychodynamic formulation: Its purpose, structure, and clinical application. *American Journal of Psychiatry, 144,* 543–550.

PIPER, W. (1991, JUNE). *Concentration, correspondence, therapeutic alliance, and therapy outcome.* Paper presented at the annual meeting of the Society for Psychotherapy Research, Lyon, France.

PIPER, W., AZIM, H., JOYCE, A., & MCCALLUM, M. (IN PRESS). Transference interpretation, therapeutic alliance, and outcome in short-term individual psychotherapy. *Archives of General Psychiatry.*

PIPER, W., AZIM, H., MCCALLUM, M., JOYCE, A. (1990). Patient suitability and outcome in short-term individual psychotherapy. *Journal of Consulting and Clinical Psychology, 58,* 475–481.

PIPER, W., DEBBANE, E., BIENVENU, J., DE CARUFEL, F., & GARANT, J. (1986). Relationships between the object of focus of therapist interpretations and outcome in short-term individual psychotherapy. *British Journal of Medical Psychology, 59,* 1–11.

POLLOCK, J., & HORNER, A. (1985). Brief adaptation-oriented psychotherapy. In A. Winston (Ed.), *Clinical and research issues in short-term dynamic psychotherapy.* Washington, DC: American Psychiatric Press.

RAUSCH, H., SPERBER, Z., RIGLER, D., WILLIAMS, J., HARWAY, N., BORDIN, E., DITTMAN, A., & HAYS, W. (1956). A dimensional analysis of depth of interpretation. *Journal of Consulting Psychology, 20* (1), 43–48.

SCHAFER, R. (1976). *A new language for psychoanalysis.* New Haven, CT: Yale University Press.

SCHULLER, R., CRITS-CHRISTOPH, P., & CONNOLLY, M. B. (1991). The resistance scale: Background and psychometric properties. *Psychoanalytic Psychology, 8*, 195–211.

SIFNEOS, P. E. (1972). *Short-term psychotherapy and emotional crisis.* Cambridge, MA: Harvard University Press.

SILBERSCHATZ, G., FRETTER, P., & CURTIS, J. (1986). How do interpretations influence the process of psychotherapy? *Journal of Consulting and Clinical Psychology, 54,* 646–652.

SLOANE, R. B., STAPLES, F. R., CRISTOL, A. H., YORKSTON, N. J., & WHIPPLE, K. (1975). *Psychotherapy versus behavior therapy.* Stanford, CA: Stanford University Press.

SPEISMAN, J. (1959). Depth of interpretation and verbal resistance in psychotherapy. *Journal of Consulting Psychology, 23,* 93–99.

SPENCE, D. (1982). *Narrative truth and historical truth.* New York: Norton.

SPIEGEL, S., & HILL, C. (1989). Guidelines for research on therapist interpretation: Toward greater methodological rigor and relevance to practice. *Journal of Counseling Psychology, 36,* 121–129.

SPILLIUS, E. B. (ED.) (1988). *Melanie Klein today, development in theory and practice: Vol. 2: Mainly practice.* London: Routledge.

STEWART, H. (1987). Varieties of transference in interpretations: An object-relations view. *International Journal of Psycho-Analysis, 68,* 197–205.

STRACHEY, J. (1934). The nature of the therapeutic action of psycho-analysis. *International Journal of Psychiatry, 15,* 127–159.

STRUPP, H. S., & BINDER, J. L. (1984). *Psychotherapy in a new key: A guide to time-limited dynamic psychotherapy.* New York: Basic Books.

WEISS, J., SAMPSON, H., & THE MOUNT ZION PSYCHOTHERAPY GROUP (1986). *The psychoanalytic process: Theory, clinical observation and empirical research.* New York: Guilford Press.

CHAPTER 20

Primary Process Analogue: The Referential Activity (RA) Measure

WILMA BUCCI AND NANCY E. MILLER

CONSIDER THE FOLLOWING TWO EXCERPTS from an early session with a psychoanalytic patient:

. . . In fact, I was kind of horrified last night at myself. I had a course a— after I left here and a [sniff] it a, it's an art course for teachers [sniff] and we were working on rubbing things for texture. And at one point I noticed the professor's tie, which was a very nubby coarse woven one, and although it would have been too soft to rub, I just [chuckle] reached out and held it out and said, "Well, this has a wonderful texture," which it did. But I was horrified at myself, because I've never done anything like that before. And then I was sure his reaction was horror, too, that I had been so forward. I don't know what it was actually, but at the time I was sure it was just horror.

. . . I suppose it's also just wondering what the function of friendly advice is anyway. If you're a good friend of somebody—not that I'm saying this is the situation I'm in, but just makes me wonder—when you're a good friend of somebody, how much, from your point of view, you should advise your friend and how much you should keep quiet, because the person is what they are and, and your point of view is going to be different from theirs in any case.

In the first passage, the patient relates a specific incident, rich in concrete, sensory detail. She seems to be emotionally reexperiencing the event as she translates it into words. In contrast, the second segment illustrates a much more abstract, generalized kind of speech, which reflects logical processing more than emotional connection.

Introduction to Multiple Code Theory

Clinical impressions such as these can now be explored more systematically through Bucci's multiple code theory and measures of Referential Activity (RA) (Bucci 1993, in press) The multiple code theory is based on her earlier formulation of a dual code model (Bucci 1985, 1989) derived from work on imagery and cognition by Paivio (1971, 1986). She has posited that all information is registered in the mind in either verbal or nonverbal form. The verbal system (or code) is organized hierarchically and logically; the multimodal nonverbal codes consist of sensory, somatic, and motoric contents, with their own systematic organizing principles; emotions are major organizing structures in the nonverbal system. The different systems are joined by referential connections, such that dominant emotional schemas from the nonverbal system can be translated—through referential connections—into logically organized speech.

Bucci's studies demonstrate that when dominant emotional schemas are represented by clear, specific, and concrete imagery, connections between the realm of the private and subjective and the world of the sequential and logical are most direct. Referential connections are classified as most direct for specific concrete entities or properties, and the words that refer to them (such as *orange, apple, juicy, sweet*); referential connections are less direct for category terms such as *fruit*, and still less direct for higher order category terms such as *food*, or for abstract terms such as *human needs, truth*, or *justice*.

Research instruments can now reliably chart fluctuations in these referential connections, via the moment-to-moment study of variation in language style. Language rated as high in Referential Activity (RA) not only reflects the activation of imagery and emotion in the speaker's mind, but at the same time, is likely to evoke a corresponding emotional experience for the listener. One would expect, therefore, that transference-related phenomena should in any given treatment hour significantly converge with high RA utterances on the part of the patient.

To return to the clinical excerpts cited above, it is possible that some may consider the second passage to be more directly linked to subjective experience. Application of the RA measures, however, demonstrates that the patient's central latent schemas are captured most directly in the concrete, specific contents of the initial quote, even if this has gone unrecognized by the patient and the analyst.

The Nonverbal System and the Primary Process

Much in the characterization of these verbal and nonverbal codes is reminiscent of Freud's original distinction between the primary and secondary processes, evident as early as 1895 in his "Project for a Scientific Psychology," and elaborated later in chapter 7 of the *Interpretation of Dreams* (LaPlanche and Pontalis 1973). However, in those works, Freud distinguished modes of thought on the economic basis of the mobility of cathexis, such that primary process thought was characterized by the immediate discharge of free energy and ready shifts in attachment, whereas secondary process thought was characterized by bound energy, manifesting a more modulated, delayed form of discharge. Freud's energy model, which is rooted in nineteenth-century biology, has no role in the scientific context of today.

Moore and Fine (1968, 1990) note other related characteristics which can be more readily accommodated in current information-processing terms. In their glossaries they suggest that *primary process* can refer to "a primitive, irrational type of wishful thought, dominated by the emotions, close to the instinctual drives, embracing the disregard of logic, the coexistence of contradiction, the absence of temporal dimensions and negatives and the use of indirect representation, and concretization (imagery)." The multiple nonverbal systems (in some ways, an analogue of primary process thought) are based on perceptual similarities or representations that are associated because they look or feel alike, share common functions, occur at the same time and place, or the like. In addition, the nonverbal system is similarly organized by emotion, which tends to be processed across multiple modalities simultaneously.

On the other hand, secondary process mentation as described by the Moore and Fine glossaries (1968, 1990) is governed by the reality principle and operates using verbal denotative symbols characteristic of the exercise of purposeful attention, judgment, reasoning, and controlled action. While primary process focuses on perceptual identity, secondary process focuses on conceptual similarity. As is true of secondary process thought, Bucci's verbal system represents the mode of language and logic and is similarly organized hierarchically, in categories of increasing generality and abstractness. Bucci's formulation eliminates the energy concepts, and it accounts for essential aspects of the distinction between the primary and secondary processes of thought in the context of an emotional information processing model based on current research in cognitive science (Bucci 1993, in press). There is now good evidence (Bucci 1988) to suggest that the nonverbal system, like the verbal system, is a structured, organized means of representing information, which can operate in mature conscious thought; it has its own organizing principles, which are no less rule-governed, differentiated, or complex than those of the verbal system, and thus are neither primitive nor driven by instinctual drives. Accordingly, since connection to the nonverbal system in itself is not regressive, even the concept of regression in the service of the ego is rejected since it implies return to a more primitive, less articulated form of thought. The multiple code theory of regression is innovative in underscoring that it is the loss of the referential links, or *the loss of connections* within either system, that constitutes the regressive move. Processing in either system may become regressive, distorted, or pathological when the two systems become dissociated, such that infantile expectations and beliefs reemerge. For example, the analytic patient may be said to regress when the new referential structures that have been built in the course of treatment are lost or abandoned and the patient can no longer acknowledge or identify his or her emotions as such but reverts to intellectualization and acting out.

The goals of treatment are characterized not as imposing the secondary process on the primary process of thought, but rather as developing connections *between* nonverbal emotional structures and words, through which acknowledgment of the warded-off emotional schemas, and their reorganization, can then take place.

Translating Primary Process Constructs into Multiple Code Analogues

A number of interesting psychoanalytic constructs emerge afresh in the context of the multiple code formulation. Repression, as noted, would refer to the dysfunction of referential connections between nonverbal experience and words; but it can also refer to dissociation *within* the nonverbal system—that is, between representations of actions, images of objects, and visceral experience. For a young child, for example, the representation of the caretaker may include a belief that this person is necessary for survival, but may also include an expectation of being attacked by, or a wish to destroy, that person; the contents of the caretaker schema may thus be connected to diverse, conflictual visceral experiences of satisfaction, fear, and rage. Since defenses operate to inhibit connections within such emotional schemas, visceral sensations could become dissociated from the persons who elicit them, or from the actions that would consummate the wish. Fear or anger may be displaced onto other persons; directed at the self; experienced as pervasive anxiety, without an object; or experienced as somatic events only, without any recognized psychic meaning. In these terms, a useful analogue of the defenses could be generated, depending on the specific representational or connecting processes being diverted or blocked.

Such warded-off schemas then become reflected in repetitive patterns of behavior, which emerge in free association and are played out in the context of the therapeutic relationship. Free association can be seen in this context as a means of permitting nonverbal emotional schemas to lead the verbalization process, without the connections necessarily being apparent in the verbal system.

The transference provides an interpersonal context in which warded-off schemas, which may be infantile, distorted, dissociated, or conflictual, can be played out with a concrete and present object. The various measures of the transference (see chapter 17) may be seen as ways of identifying and characterizing these underlying emotional structures as they are manifest in language and behavior. Through experience in the here-and-now, and through concrete and specific language, the patient may make new referential connections to emotional structures that had previously been warded off. In this respect, *insight* can be defined as the verbal articulation of emotional structures through activation of referential connections. On the other hand, *intellectualization* refers to the articulation of emotional meanings, based on connections within the verbal system only. Conversely, in acting out, connections within maladaptive emotional structures lead directly to action, without mediation by the logic and reality filters of the verbal code. The goal of treatment is change in the emotional structures themselves, so that the world actually "looks different" and "feels different" and so that impulses operate differently, rather than being simply understood on an intellectual level. To bring about structural change, the activation of many specific instances of a pattern is necessarily repeated in different contexts, including memories, dreams, and the transference. Recoding within the nonverbal emotional structures represents a theoretical goal and hoped for outcome in psychoanalytic treatment.

Methods for Scoring Referential Activity

The methods for scoring RA include qualitative rating scales and objective measures based on quantifiable linguistic features. The scoring procedures for all RA measures are described in the RA manual (Bucci and Kabasakalian-McKay 1992).

RA RATING SCALES

The scales measure the concreteness, specificity, clarity, and imagery level of speech. They may be defined briefly as follows.

- *Concreteness:* degree of perceptual or sensory quality (not cognitive concreteness in a deficit sense). May include references to imagery in any sense modality, somatic or visceral experience, motoric activity, and emotion. A high level of concreteness in the manifest content does not rule out the possibility that abstract concepts are being represented; for instance, metaphorical expressions have their power through representing abstract ideas in concrete form.
- *Specificity:* a highly specific text is detailed and informative; it includes explicit descriptions of persons, objects, places, or events. It is possible to be specific in talking about many different types of material, including abstract as well as concrete contents—a person may tell exactly what he had for breakfast, or a logician may talk in considerable detail about the provisions of truth tables.
- *Clarity:* the rater's overall impression of the intelligibility of the narrative and the effectiveness with which the speaker's ideas come through the language. Texts can be rated as high in clarity even if the speaker moves from idea to idea, as in free association, providing that each idea is well focused and the transitions are signaled. Texts may also be rated as high in clarity if confusion, conflict, or ambiguity are being expressed, providing that the expression of these feelings is clear.
- *Imagery:* the rater's overall impression of the degree to which an emotional experience or image is present in the speaker's mind and has been communicated in the language so the listener or reader can experience it as well. The score may reflect, in part, the extent to which an image is actually evoked for the rater.

For all dimensions, the scoring is intended to apply to the manifest content of the text; no clinical inferences are involved. The rater scores how well the speaker actually translates experience into words, not what he or she may have meant to say.

OBJECTIVE FEATURES OF RA LANGUAGE STYLE

In addition to the scales, specific linguistic features provide objective indicators related to the RA dimension. These include:

- Metaphoric expressions, which use concrete images to represent complex emotions and ideas
- Linguistic features that impart a quality of immediacy, such as direct quotes and stylistic use of the present tense in describing past events ("So he comes into the room and he sits down, and he says to me . . .")

• Establishment of time and place and introduction of a character in relationship to oneself very early in a narrative (Dodd and Bucci 1987)

COMPUTER-ASSISTED RA (CRA) SCORING PROCEDURES

Qualities reflected in the RA scales may also be captured in categories of individual lexical items, making them amenable to computer-assisted procedures. This methodology permits automatized RA scoring of transcripts.

In addition the method of lexical analysis contributes to basic knowledge of the linguistic features of the RA dimension: high RA is associated with greater use of words referring to imagery in any sensory modality, action, or somatic experience;[1] greater use of words related to specific female and male roles;[2] use of third person singular pronouns (*he, she, him, her);* use of prepositions reflecting visual spatial relations (such as *in, on, outside*), which are likely to appear in description of images[3] as well as words rated as high in concreteness and imagery.[4] These categories incorporate the lexical elements likely to predominate in the concrete and imagistic stories about specific individuals that constitute the typical contents of high RA speech.

Empirical Research Findings

CONVERGENT AND DIVERGENT VALIDATION OF RA MEASURES

The RA measures, including scales, counts of objective features of language style, and computer-assisted procedures, have been applied to many types of texts, including brief monologues, early memories, TAT protocols, and transcripts of therapy sessions. They have been extensively validated, as both trait and state measures, through patterns of intercorrelation with related cognitive and clinical tasks. Persons with high RA language style, measured in a standardized monologue task, were found to have relatively fast reaction times in direct naming tasks, which reflect the referential function at its simplest level (Bucci and Freedman 1978; Bucci 1984). High RA speakers have greater subjective experience of imagery, as measured by the widely used Questionnaire upon Mental Imagery (QMI)

---

[1]Word lists reflecting such content areas have been developed by Martindale (1975).
[2]For example, *mother, father, husband, wife,* included in several categories of the *Harvard III Psychosociological Dictionary* (Stone et al. 1966).
[3]Word list being developed by Bucci and Mergenthaler at the University of Ulm, Germany.
[4]From a word list developed by Toglia and Battig (1978).

(Sheehan 1967); and they are rated as more highly intuitive, according to the Myers-Briggs Type Indicator (Briggs-Myers 1980), as reported by Ellenhorn (1989). They do better on ability measures that depend on reasoning about everyday events, such as the Comprehension subtest of the WAIS; but they show no advantage in tests of abstract verbal intelligence, such as the Similarities subtest, nor in simple word fluency measures. High RA speakers use more hand movements keyed to rhythm and intonation patterns of speech, indicating a connection to motoric representations on some level (Bucci and Freedman 1978). Variation in mothers' RA level relates to emotional and linguistic development in their children (Cahn 1987; Jaffe 1985). Higher RA levels, in both patient and therapist, measured prior to treatment, are associated with greater progress in resolving major conflict areas (Von Korff 1986).

STATE VARIATION IN RA

The studies of trait variation in referential function described above are important in building construct validity of the RA measures. However, the value of RA in process research lies primarily in its state variation, as responsive to changes both in situational context and in somatic and emotional state. RA is below the normal range for clinically depressed patients and improves with remission as measured by standardized monologue and naming tasks (Bucci and Freedman 1981; Bucci 1984). Systematic cyclical effects on RA are found in reported dreams of psychotherapy patients, with higher RA levels manifested prior to ovulation and lower levels in the premenstrual phase (Severino, Bucci, and Creelman, 1989). Significant correlations have been found between RA fluctuation and measures of emotional and physiological arousal, in a multimeasure psychotherapy study in which all sessions were videotaped, concurrent physiological data collected, and a wide range of clinical measures applied (Horowitz et al., in press).

RA FLUCTUATION AND TRANSFERENCE EVENTS

In a study of convergent validation of psychotherapy process measures, RA scoring plus several additional measures of transference-related phenomena were applied to the same tape-recorded transcript of a psychoanalytic session (Dahl, Kächele, and Thomä 1988). As expected, the location of the transference-related measures, as scored by independent researchers, converged significantly, occurring primarily in the high RA segments (Bucci 1988, 1993). The 37 percent of utterances classified as high RA accounted for eleven out of fourteen (79 percent) of the wish structures in this session identified by Dahl (1988) and for seven out of eleven (64 percent) of the Relationship Episodes (REs) identified by Luborsky and Crits-Christoph (1988) in scoring the Core Conflictual Relationship Theme (CCRT). The passage concerning the teacher's tie given in the opening of this chapter, which was the peak RA utterance of the hour, was the center of the major sequence of J × r codings (judgments [j] of allusions to the relationship [r] in narrative material that manifestly concerns some other theme [x]) in this session, as identified by Hoffman and Gill (1988). Data from all three methods support the postulate that high RA passages in a session are likely to refer to significant, latent emotional structures being played out in the relationship. The covariation among the RA and transference-related measures provides validation for both sets of constructs. The patient talks most concretely and specifically about events reflecting prototypical emotional schemas, activated in the here-and-now.

EFFECTS OF PLAN COMPATIBILITY ON RA

In a study of three brief psychotherapy treatments carried out by the Mount Zion Psychotherapy Research Group, Bucci et al. (1988) found significantly greater increases in RA, measured by residualized gain scores, following interventions judged as "plan compatible," that is, relevant to the patient's conscious or unconscious treatment goals (Weiss and Sampson 1986). Bucci et al. also found significantly higher patient RA levels in treatments judged as having successful outcomes as rated by independent clinical measures. While plan compatibility also related significantly to the Experiencing Scale (Klein et al. 1970),[5] no significant correlation was found between the RA and Experiencing measures; thus the study provided divergent validation for both measures.

NEW RESEARCH DIRECTIONS

New research directions include methodological developments in construction and application of the RA measures, as well as studies that elaborate the construct validity of these measures and further develop the theoretical framework of the multiple code model. To facilitate large-sample and longitudinal studies, new objective and automated procedures for scoring RA are being developed which will be applicable across a wide range of speakers and type of speech samples. These will yield reliable distinctions among different RA components. Other related projects include the scoring of scales and related dimensions directly from audiotapes

[5]The Experiencing Scale focuses on direct expression of conscious emotional experience, rather than on the specific and concrete narratives that serve as metaphors for latent emotional structures, as reflected in the RA approach (Bucci 1993).

or videotapes without transcribing; measures of vocal tone, pausing, gestures, and body movements related to the RA dimension; the identification of additional quantifiable features of RA language style, including studies of metaphors, which constitute paradigmatic features of high RA speech. Work on developing procedures for evaluating therapist RA suggests that the RA of the therapist may have its primary effect in determining how he or she listens, rather than what he or she says (McMath 1991). Thus, RA assessment of the therapist's utterances reflect the therapist's responsiveness to what the patient has been saying, and its impact with respect to increasing the patient's subsequent associative flow. A preliminary manual for applying RA measures to therapist speech has been developed.

Several ongoing studies address variations in RA associated with personality style, or diagnosis, in groups characterized as obsessive and hysteric; and in clinical groups, including chronic schizophrenics, persons with psychosomatic disorders, and hospitalized borderline patients. A final set of studies concerns the definition of free association as a progression of referential cycles, marked by changing levels of RA scales and validated by fluctuation in other research measures. These include the Experiencing Scale, which is high in the nonverbal dominance phase of the cycle; measures of the transference such as Luborsky's CCRT, Teller and Dahl's frame structures, and Hoffman and Gill's measure of covert and overt allusions to the relationship, which are associated with the peak referential phase of the cycle; and insight measures, which are associated with the verbal dominance phase (Bucci 1993).

The concept of the referential cycle itself has been validated in recent research by Hull (1990) in a study of a long-term treatment of a borderline inpatient. The degree of RA patterning—the degree to which a clear referential cycle emerged in a session—was found to be inversely correlated with symptom levels, measured through weekly administrations of the SCL-90R.

IMPLICATIONS OF RESEARCH

RA measures are easily scored without clinical expertise; they are applied to language style, rather than content; and automated procedures have been developed to facilitate large-sample research. The measures are interpretable in the context of a basic theory of psychoanalytic process, but they are neutral with respect to differences and controversies in clinical theory and technique. By deriving the RA pattern for a session, including RA cycles and peaks, immediate sense can be made of a session, including prediction to specific points in the hour where significant latent relationship structures are expressed.

Applying RA Measures to Clinical Material

The following discussion of a videotaped and transcribed assessment interview with a symptomatic twenty-three-year-old woman, provides a fuller sense of how RA measures can be directly applied to any clinical transcript. Seven transference-related measures have also been applied to this interview in a convergent validation project (Luborsky, Popp, Barber, Shapiro, and Miller, in press).

The RA scales were applied to the transcript of the specimen hour for both patient and therapist speech. The patient speech was also scored from the videotape, using the RA scales, and computer-assisted procedures were applied. Judges for segmentation and the RA scales were graduate students in clinical psychology.

Judges are trained by reading the RA manual (Bucci and Kabasakalian-McKay 1992), scoring the sets of practice materials that accompany the manual, and discussing scoring deviations in training groups until acceptable reliability is achieved. One or two practice sessions are usually required to achieve reliability for segmentation, and three or four for the RA scales; no clinical expertise is required for any of these procedures. For computer-assisted procedures, using preset word lists, we can expect matches for only a relatively small proportion of the words in any given text. Therefore segments of substantial size, including at least 100 words, are usually required to achieve a reliable result.

SEGMENTATION OF THE TRANSCRIPT

The type of segmentation procedure that is applied varies for different RA measures and different types of text; the procedures and their applications are defined, with illustrative examples, in the RA scoring manual.

Two major types of units are used for scoring RA: major theme units and idea units. Major theme units reflect obvious shifts in subject matter, where one topic is clearly ended and another introduced, and are often signaled either by a statement explicitly marking the change of subject or by an explicit narrative shift with a new scene and new cast of characters. These large segments are generally used for computer-assisted procedures.

Idea units are less obvious shifts in focus of the narrative, which capture a single "shot" or "frame," and are used for scoring the RA scales. Given the same instructions, some judges tend to mark finer divisions than others; there tends to be almost complete agreement on broader unit divisions. This result yields extremely high reliability for the broader unit divisions, and also allows the size of unit to be calibrated by adjusting the required proportion of judges agreeing to a given division. Reliability of segmentation for the idea units chosen for this session was .98, reported as coefficient alpha, based on an average intercorrelation of .92 for four judges (using McNemar's formula for computation of the correlation coefficient from number of shared elements; Kelly 1924). Segment boundaries agreed on by at least three of the four judges were used for this study, yielding seventy-four segments. Larger idea units (and fewer divisions) would have been achieved by selecting only those boundaries on which all four judges agreed.

RA SCALES APPLIED TO PATIENT SPEECH

The RA Scales.

The four RA scales, concreteness, specificity, clarity, and overall imagery level, were scored for each segment. Reliability for the overall RA score, which is an average of the four subscales, was .85 for the four judges, computed as coefficient alpha. For the individual subscales, reliability was .82 for concreteness, .87 for specificity, .65 for clarity; and .69 for imagery. Judges generally have the lowest reliability for the clarity scale; the somewhat reduced reliability for imagery probably reflects lack of variability for this dimension in this transcript.

As in previous work, significant intercorrelations were obtained among the four scales, with intercorrelations higher for concreteness with imagery and for clarity with specificity than for other pairs. For the session as a whole, patient RA showed a mean of 3.29, on a scale of 0–10. The mean for CLASP (average of clarity and specificity), which reflects organizational qualities of discourse, was 4.14. This was significantly above the mean of 2.43 for CONIM, (average of concreteness and imagery), which reflects level of sensory imagery as represented in speech ($p < .001$).

Fluctuations in Patient RA.

These scores were used to provide a picture of the fluctuation in the patient's access to emotional experience in the course of the interview. There are two RA peaks in this session. The first was about being raped by (described as her third rape out of five), and contracting veneral disease from, a man who had been caring for her while she was ill, in Southeast Asia:

PATIENT: . . . and I found out when I got, got back here three months later after getting it, four months after getting it, that it almost completely had eaten its way through my inner vaginal wall, which left quite a bit of damage in there, also quite a bit of emotional damage. I also found out when I got back here I was pregnant, and nobody knew, or especially, I did not know, if it was my husband's or my rapist's. I didn't know. Luckily my body took control of that one and aborted it naturally.

This was the closing half of the first peak segment, which received scores of 5.5 for CONIM and 6.5 for CLASP. The second peak concerned a situation in which the woman's current lover told her that "he had been sleeping with another woman in my truck or in our truck and on my futon." Both of these stories are highlighted by the RA scoring as potentially revealing of the patient's emotional structures. Both concern someone who has cared for her, who then victimizes or betrays her, and her part in this. CONIM is consistently below the midrange of the scale throughout the session, rising above this level only at the two peaks. CLASP scores generally fluctuated around the midrange of the scale (as is usually the case for nonclinical subjects in analogue studies), and showed the same two peaks.

SCORING RA DIRECTLY FROM VIDEOTAPE

The possibility of rating the RA scales reliably, on line, without using a written text, has obvious practical significance in bypassing the costly and time-consuming transcribing process. From a conceptual perspective, we were also interested in the extent to which the multichannel message of the video can be captured in the written text. This has bearing on potential clinical applications of the RA research: for example, whether therapists can be trained to become sensitive to fluctuations in patient RA in the session itself, and to what extent the effect of the patient's language as the therapist might experience it in vivo compares with the effect of the written word.

For this experiment, the first thirty-eight segments of the session were scored from the videotape by a group of seven trained judges. The videotape was stopped after each segment for twenty seconds; this provided sufficient time for scoring the four scales for all judges.

Reliability, computed as coefficient alpha for the seven judges, was .79 for concreteness, .85 for specificity, .69 for clarity, .81 for imagery, and .93 for overall RA. This is comparable to the reliability obtained for the four judges rating the transcripts. The scores for the seven judges were combined to yield the RA video scores. The pattern of intercorrelations between the subscales was the same as for the patient transcript scoring, and the derived CONIM, CLASP, and overall RA scores were computed.

The correlation for video versus transcript scoring was .48 for

CLASP, .59 for CONIM, and .59 for overall RA. All these correlations are significant ($p < .01$). The video scoring for overall RA and for the sub-scales identifies the same peaks and troughs as the transcript scoring procedure. The mean CONIM score for the thirty-eight segments rated from the video was 2.53—almost identical to the CONIM mean of 2.58 for the same segments rated from the transcript. While the video and transcript ratings for CLASP were significantly correlated, the video CLASP rating of 2.55 was significantly lower than the transcript mean of 4.37 for those segments.

In discussing the video scoring, raters noted dissociation and lack of synchrony between the verbal and nonverbal messages as a signifi-cant factor in understanding this patient. In the transcript scoring, this dissociation is reflected in the significant differences between the CLASP and CONIM scores; in the video scoring, it affects the level of the CLASP score itself. The conclusion of this experiment is that the video scoring does permit identification of the same major peaks as in the transcript, and suggests the same dissociation; but video scoring pre-sents a different overall result regarding the level of organization and intelligibility of the patient's speech. The degree to which this patient may confuse her therapist is captured more directly in the video than in the transcript scoring.

COMPUTER-ASSISTED RA SCORING PROCEDURES

Computer-assisted content analysis procedures were also applied to this session. The Text Analysis System (TAS), developed by Mergenthaler (1985), matches categorized word lists to a text and provides frequencies, proportions, and other results for each of the categories. For purposes of the CRA analysis, the transcript was divided into major theme units, as defined in the manual; most shifts were marked by explicit topic changes introduced by the therapist. This segmentation yielded nine major theme units (MTUs) for the entire session and seven MTUs for the proportion of the session used for video scoring.

The computer analysis largely succeeded in identifying the same peaks and troughs as were identified in the RA transcript and video scoring. Again, the patient shows greater access to emotional material when she talks about her victimization and her own contribution to this and greater dissociation when she talks about her relationship with her husband. These results represent a promising first step in computer modeling of RA. An extensive project is under way to develop more finely grained computer-assisted procedures which are suitable for appli-cation to small text segments and which can reliably distinguish the different RA scales.

THE MIRRORING OF THE RELATIONSHIP

The therapist's interventions were also scored for the RA scales following the same procedures (McMath 1991). The results provide an example of how the RA measures can be used to reflect the interaction between therapist and patient speech. While the therapist directed the choice of topic through his questioning, the patient determined the level of emotional expression, as indicated by the sequential relationships between their RA scores. There was a significant correlation between the overall RA level of the patient utterance and the immediately *following* therapist utterance ($r = .32$, $df = 80$, $p < .01$), but no significant correlation for the patient utterance with the immediately *preceding* therapist speech ($r = .14$, $df = 81$, n.s.).

The therapist was consistently low in imagery. His highest score was 3 out of a possible 10. His "minipeaks" occurred in only two utterances toward the end of the session, and in both instances involved use of the patient's own words, referring to her being "picked on" and "scapegoated" and wanting to heal herself. We suggest that the use of words that the patient has introduced is potentially a means by which the therapist may connect to, or enter, the patient's "referential space." In the following interchange, the therapist addresses the patient's wish to control her current lover, also using a key word that she had introduced:

PATIENT: MIKE tells me that I need to let go of him, and I speak of it as letting go, but as ALEX pointed out . . . "What are you letting go of? You never owned him in the first place." That very premise is a wrong premise or a premise that sets you up for a fall.
THERAPIST: Do you think you did own him?

This intervention is followed by the patient's largest RA increase in the session, and the second major RA peak.

The multiple code theory postulates that themes reflected in the RA peaks reflect underlying emotional structures to which the patient has the most immediate access, and which are likely to refer, at least implicitly, to the relationship; the therapist will be most effective in connecting to these. In contrast, the therapist is unlikely to connect to the patient's experiential system, or to facilitate referential connections, if he addresses the content of material in the RA troughs. In the following excerpt the therapist has intervened in response to the patient's very low RA description of her relationship with her husband:

THERAPIST: Uh-huh. Did you two have conflicts about anything?
PATIENT: Nope.

THERAPIST: Never argued, no conflicts?

PATIENT: No. Not that I can remember, not that I can remember [voice softens]. It was a very straightforward relationship. Um, one thing that might have also helped that is he knew JAKARTA a lot better than I did, and so he was sort of taking me around and showing me places, so it wasn't as if I was completely independent and knew the area myself well enough to go off.

When the therapist attempts to open this low RA material, the patient puts on her heaviest armor, becomes disorganized, and disorganizes him as well. In the following interchange, a few seconds later, the therapist reaches a low point in his own RA:

THERAPIST: Yeah. What do you think he didn't know about you here? What parts of yourself or your background?

PATIENT: It's hard for me to say now because I've come, become a lot more in touch with myself in the last few years, um, so it's very hard for me to say right now because, I, it's hard for me to delineate exactly what was then and what is now.

THERAPIST: Well, maybe you can, maybe you don't have to tell me so much, then, more now, what, what you've come to know about yourself that you think he—that either you didn't know then, or he didn't know.

A major issue for this patient is her difficulty in accessing emotional experience, as she herself says, at the close of the session:

PATIENT: I can talk about a lot of this stuff and have been able to talk a lot about this stuff very easily. When it comes down to emoting, in my emotional feelings on the subject is where I have trouble talking.

THERAPIST: Uh-huh.

PATIENT: Um. And feeling it 'cause I can talk about it to no end.

When the patient is in an RA trough, neither addressing the contents directly nor leaving the patient in control of the emotional level of the discourse facilitates the connecting of emotional experience to words. At such times, the therapist may need to turn away from the content of the material and focus instead on the retreat from symbolizing, and the reasons for this.

A final note: The goal of this brief report has been to provide an illustration of the types of analyses that are possible using the multiple coding and RA approaches. One additional inference from the RA analysis of this session is notable. The themes expressed in the patient's RA peaks concern her betrayal by someone whom she had trusted and who had cared for her, her participation in this victimization, and her attempts at control. The themes of victimization, complicity, and control emerge repeatedly in the dominant narratives of her adult life, and also emerge, in a more constricted way, in the narratives of her childhood. The relevance of these themes to the therapeutic relationship, in this special context, seem painfully clear as she herself collaborates in producing a specimen hour to be used by us all—researchers and clinicians—although this was not directly addressed in the session.

Summary

The multiple code hypothesis suggests that all information is organized in one of two major systems, either in a verbal one—which is logically, hierarchically organized—or in the multiple nonverbal codes—which are organized emotionally and based on perceptual similarities. These may be seen as analogues to primary and secondary process mentation, as described by Freud; but multiple code theory accounts for the distinction in current scientific terms, without reference to the energy concepts of the metapsychology. Emotional schemas from the nonverbal system are linked, through referential connections, to clear, specific, concrete imagery, expressed in organized and communicative speech.

Variations in language styles, or fluctuations in referential connections, can be reliably assessed with measures of Referential Activity (RA) including computer-assisted procedures that permit the automated scoring of psychotherapy transcripts. The RA measures have been applied to many types of texts and have been extensively validated as both trait and state measures.

In addition to their relationship to measures of physiological, hormonal, and affective change, what is most important for psychotherapy researchers is that RA fluctuation has been intimately linked to independent measures of transference-related events; to therapists' responsiveness and quality of interpretation; and to psychodynamic treatment outcome. Current studies are focused on variations in referential activity as associated with personality style and on free association as a progression of RA cycles.

An example of the type of clinical query that can now be entertained using this methodology is demonstrated in the assessment of how, through a particular use of language, the patient can evoke a corresponding affective response from her therapist in the countertransference. With the further development and refinement of this approach, which is based both in psychoanalysis and in cognitive science, many aspects of primary process discourse, long impervious to systematic investigation, will begin to yield their secrets.

References

BRIGGS-MYERS, I. (1980). *Gifts differing.* Palo Alto, CA: Consulting Psychologists Press.

BUCCI, W. (1984). Linking words and things: Basic processes and individual variation. *Cognition, 17,* 137–153.

BUCCI, W. (1985). Dual coding: A cognitive model for psychoanalytic research. *Journal of the American Psychoanalytical Association, 33,* 571–608.

BUCCI, W. (1988). Converging evidence for emotional structures: Theory and method. In H. Dahl, H. Kächele, & H. Thomä (Eds.), *Psychoanalytic process research strategies* (pp. 29–49). Heidelberg: Springer-Verlag.

BUCCI, W. (1989). A reconstruction of Freud's tally argument: A program for psychoanalytic research. *Psychoanalytic Inquiry, 9,* 249–281.

BUCCI, W. (1993). The development of emotional meaning in free association. In J. Gedo & A. Wilson (Eds.), *Hierarchical conceptions in psychoanalysis* (pp. 3–47). New York: Guilford Press.

BUCCI, W. (IN PRESS). A multiple code theory of free association and dreams. In P. Fonagy & O. Kernberg (Eds.), *The integration of research and psychoanalytic practice: The proceedings of the IPA's First International Conference on Research.*

BUCCI, W., & FREEDMAN, N. (1978). Language and hand: The dimension of referential competence. *Journal of Personality, 46,* 594–622.

BUCCI, W., & FREEDMAN, N. (1981). The language of depression. *Bulletin of the Menninger Clinic, 45,* 334–358.

BUCCI, W., KABASAKALIAN, R., & THE RA RESEARCH GROUP. (1992). *Instructions for scoring Referential Activity (RA) in transcripts of spoken texts.* Ulm, Germany; Ulmer Textbank.

BUCCI, W., LANGS, R. C., FRETTER, P., & DODD, M. (1988). The effect of interventions on unconscious communication and referential activity. Symposium presented at the annual meeting of the Society for Psychotherapy Research (SPR), Santa Fe, NM.

CAHN, A. (1987). *The effect of the Holocaust experience on the symbolizing function in survivors and their children.* Unpublished doctoral dissertation, Adelphi University.

DAHL, H. (1988). Frames of mind. In H. Dahl, H. Kächele, & H. Thomä (Eds.), *Psychoanalytic process research strategies* (pp. 51–66). Heidelberg: Springer-Verlag.

DAHL, H., KÄCHELE, H., & THOMÄ, H. (EDS.). (1988). *Psychoanalytic process research strategies.* Heidelberg: Springer-Verlag.

DODD, M., & BUCCI, W. (1987). The relation of cognition and affect in the orientation process. *Cognition, 27,* 53–71.

ELLENHORN, T. (1989). *The symbolic transformations of subjective experience in discourse.* Unpublished doctoral dissertation, Adelphi University.

HOFFMAN, I. Z., & GILL, M. M. (1988). A scheme for coding the patient's experience of the relationship with the therapist (PERT): Some applications, extensions, and comparisons. In H. Dahl, H. Kächele, & H. Thomä (Eds.), *Psychoanalytic process research strategies* (pp. 67–98). Heidelberg: Springer-Verlag.

HOROWITZ, M. J., STINSON, C., CURTIS, D., EWERT, M., REDINGTON, D., SINGER, J., BUCCI, W., MERGENTHALER, E., MILBRATH, C., HARTLEY, D. (IN PRESS). Expressing and warding off topics during psychotherapy: An intensive case study. *Journal of Personality.*

HULL, J. (1990). *Variations in the referential cycle in a symptomatic borderline inpatient.* Paper presented at the annual meeting of the Society for Psychotherapy Research, Wintergreen, VA.

JAFFE, L. (1985). *Maternal symbolic and psycholinguistic behaviors and the child's evolving capacity to tolerate separation.* Unpublished doctoral dissertation, Adelphi University.

KELLY, T. L. (1924). *Statistical method.* New York: Macmillan.

KLEIN, M. H., MATHIEU, P. L., GENDLIN, E. T., & KIESLER, D. J. (1970). *The Experiencing Scale: A research and training manual.* Madison: Wisconsin Psychiatric Institute.

LAPLANCHE, J., & PONTALIS, J. B. (1973). *The language of psychoanalysis.* New York: Norton.

LUBORSKY, L., & CRITS-CHRISTOPH, P. (1988). The assessment of transference by the CCRT method. In H. Dahl, H. Kächele, & H. Thomä (Eds.), *Psychoanalytic process research strategies* (pp. 99–108). Heidelberg: Springer-Verlag.

LUBORSKY, L., POPP, C., BARBER, J. P., SHAPIRO, D., & MILLER, N. (EDS.). (IN PRESS). Seven transference-related measures: Each applied to the Ms. Smithfield interview. *Psychotherapy Research.*

MARTINDALE, C. (1975). Romantic progression: The psychology of literary history. Washington, DC: Hemisphere.

MCMATH, T. (1991). *The effect of therapist interventions on patient referential activity.* Unpublished doctoral dissertation, Adelphi University.

MERGENTHALER, E. (1985). *Textbank systems: Computer science applied in the field of psychoanalysis.* Heidelberg: Springer-Verlag.

MOORE, B. E., & FINE, B. D. (EDS.). (1968). *A glossary of psychoanalytic terms and concepts.* New York: American Psychoanalytic Association.

MOORE, B. E., & FINE, B. D. (EDS.). (1990). *Psychoanalytic terms and concepts.* New Haven: American Psychoanalytic Association and Yale University Press.

PAIVIO, A. (1971). *Imagery and verbal processes.* New York: Holt, Rinehart and Winston.

PAIVIO, A. (1986). *Mental representations: A dual coding approach.* New York: Oxford University Press.

SEVERINO, S., BUCCI, W., & CREELMAN, M. (1989). Cyclical changes in emotional information processing in sleep and dreams. *Journal of the American Academy of Psychoanalysis.*

SHEEHAN, P. W. (1967). A shortened form of Betts' questionnaire upon mental imagery. *Journal of Perceptual and Motor Skills, 24,* 386–389.

STONE, P. J., DUNPHY, D. C., SMITH, M. S., & OGILVIE, D. M. (1966). *The general inquirer: A computer approach to content analysis.* Cambridge, MA: M.I.T. Press.

TOGLIA, M. P., & BATTIG, W. F. (1978). *Handbook of semantic word norms.* New York: Wiley.

VON KORFF, P. (1986). Referential activity and the therapeutic process. Unpublished doctoral dissertation, Adelphi University.

WEISS, J., SAMPSON, H., & THE MOUNT ZION PSYCHOTHERAPY RESEARCH GROUP. (1986). *The psychoanalytic process: Theory, clinical observation, and empirical research.* New York: Guilford Press.

CHAPTER 21

Evaluating Insight

PAUL CRITS-CHRISTOPH, JACQUES P. BARBER, NANCY E. MILLER, AND KATHERINE BEEBE

IN ANCIENT GREECE, PHILOSOPHERS and thinkers emphasized knowing oneself as a major ethical goal. Centuries later, Freud added a deeper meaning to knowing oneself when he developed and elaborated on the concept of unconscious ideas and motivations. Recognizing that the unconscious (repressed) aspects of human mental life have far-reaching implications for the determination of human behavior, particularly neurotic symptoms, Freud emphasized the curative role of gaining knowledge or insight into these subterranean realms of subjective experience.

Initially, Freud used hypnosis to help patients achieve insight by recovering traumatic memories of external events in the context of affective discharge. With the abandonment of the seduction model of etiology, however, Freud shifted his view of pathogenesis from an emphasis on external trauma to an internal focus on the vicissitudes of instinctual drives. This move was accompanied by Freud's mounting interest in the symbolic interpretation of dreams and their associations, and by his growing emphasis on the analyst's insight into the deeper meanings of the patient's material.

Insight in the Clinical Literature

Early analysts tended to directly convey their immediate understanding to the patient, relying heavily on the use of explanation, direction, and intellectual argument. By the time he wrote "On beginning the treatment," Freud ([1913] 1961) openly acknowledged the therapeutic failure of such an approach: "In the early stages of psychoanalytic technique, we took an intellectualist view of the situation: we set a high value on the patient's knowledge of what he had forgotten, and we made hardly any distinction, between our knowledge and his. It was a severe disappointment when the expected success was not forthcoming" (p. 141).

As Freud's method of eliciting clinical data from his patients shifted, so too did the goal of his therapeutic intervention. While in precursor versions of psychoanalysis he used hypnosis to elicit traumatic memories for the purpose of abreaction, with the development of free association the focus shifted to the mining of insight, to uncovering of the "deep structure" of the individual's subjective world (Erdelyi 1985). Thus, with the introduction of the structural model, Freud's therapeutic goal changed from "making the unconscious conscious" to emphasizing the building and integration of intrapsychic structure—"where the id was, there shall ego be." Analysis from then on not only attempted to help the patient remember forgotten events, but also tried to help the patient place forgotten memories into their causal context, where they might be better integrated into the now more expanded and maturely functioning ego. As Freud became increasingly convinced of the power and value of transference phenomena in the treatment setting, he concluded that without the affective immediacy of the transferential experience, the patient's newly derived insight would remain ineffectual.

Since Freud's time, insight has commonly been perceived as the cornerstone of the psychoanalytic theory of structural change. Valid insight, "seeing into" the deep structure of one's formerly repressed conflict motives, was said to yield a significantly better integrated, more flexible, and more maturely functioning ego. The mature ego could exercise optimal control over affect discharge and ego regression, while at the same time manifesting an enhanced capacity for self-observation. In the event, however, that such qualities of insight did not lead to symptomatic improvement or to psychic change, it was presumed that the insight was either erroneous, incomplete, insufficiently worked through, or too highly intellectualized.

Not uncommonly, to resolve this difficulty, analysts made reference to the elusive distinction between "emotional" and "intellectual" insight. Thus, for Strachey (1934) "emotional" insight represented the culmination of a successful mutative intervention (see chapter 19), leading to structural and symptomatic change. "Intellectual" insight, however, constituted a rationalization which he was convinced would never result in sustained improvement. Most practicing psychoanalysts believe that effective insight can be distinguished from purely intellectual insight; but for research purposes, the meaning of true, effective, emotional, or valid insight has proven to be far more elusive.

A telling example of the kind of complexity entailed can be found in Moore and Fine (1990), the American Psychoanalytic Association's glossary, which states that "often the cognitive awareness of insight is repressed again in the process of psychic reorganization, but the new emotional freedom is maintained." Although such a view is commonly accepted in the clinical community, from a research perspective the definition creates considerable difficulty. For example, what kinds of operational definitions and markers might an investigator formulate to positively identify the presence of "valid" insight in the absence of the patient's conscious cognitive knowledge?

Sandler, Dare, and Holder (1973) have critically discussed the problem, and they have pointedly depicted the serious tautological error inherent in the assumption that if insight is ineffective in producing change, then it is not true insight, whereas if insight does bring about positive change, it is thereby considered valid and effective. The authors suggest that the concept of emotional insight be radically divorced from the concept of cure—that is, that intellectual insight be distinguished from those forms of insight "which either release emotion or involve some aspects of 'feeling state' as part of the insight itself" (p. 111). Such a definition, shorn from its links with outcome, might free investigators to study more productively the relative importance of insight versus alternative explanatory variables which could prove to be equally powerful from the point of view of therapeutic efficacy.

At present, it is not clear whether insight will maintain hegemony theoretically and clinically as the most powerful tool in the armamentarium of the analyst. The recently popular interpersonal, as opposed to intrapsychic, psychoanalytic models have elevated alternative mechanisms of change and cure in treatment.

Not surprisingly, the quiet theoretical shifts over time are duly reflected in subtle changes manifest in the definition of *insight* in successive editions of the Glossary of Psychoanalytic Terms (Moore and Fine 1968, 1990). For example, the 1968 edition stressed economic aspects of drive theory: "Analytic insight differs from other cognitive understanding in that it cannot occur without being preceded by dynamic changes leading to . . . the release of energies." By 1990, all reference to the energy-releasing function of insight had been dropped, and the language employed is now more naturalistic and less mechanistic. The theoretical hegemony of insight is reaffirmed, however. Thus, the 1968 and 1990 definitions continue to emphasize that attainment of insight is essential for therapeutic change. This is a testable hypothesis, of course, not a reified fact.

While direct reference to metapsychology has been dropped in the later edition of the glossary, no mention of alternate theoretical or clinical views on insight—whether from an object relations, self psychology,

Kleinian, interpersonal, developmental, or other psychoanalytic perspective—has been included. This may reflect the theoretical fragmentation characterizing the field today; perhaps the present phase is transitional, preceding the coalescence of a more powerful, integrative psychodynamic paradigm.

The recent edition of the glossary notes that affect and cognitive awareness are both essential in stimulating the derepression and psychic reorganization of repressed conflictual material. Surprisingly, it nowhere refers to what some would consider an integral aspect in the course of developing insight, that is, the reexperiencing of the conflict in the heat and immediacy of the transference relationship.

Rather than perceiving insight as constituting the patient's sudden discovery of hidden or disavowed knowledge, analysts more often perceive the coming of insight as constituting a complex process inextricably associated with the subsequent working through of crucial affects and thoughts in the context of the transference relationship. This mode of integrating, on both affective and cognitive planes, psychic contents which had formerly been in opposition or rigidly compartmentalized over time is an area of clinical work illuminated by Kris (1956), who described insight clinically, in the transferential context of the "good hour." Ferenczi (1950) and Rank (1936) also emphasized the significance of the current transference relationship in shaping insight-fostering interpretations that are emotionally meaningful and therapeutically powerful.

Emphasis on the crucial curative role of insight continues to be stressed to this day in major publications and paper sessions sponsored, for example, by the American Psychoanalytic Association. In Blum's (1980) collection of papers on *Psychoanalytic Explorations of Technique*, the opening chapters are wholly devoted to technical and theoretical considerations regarding insight (e.g., see chapters by A. Freud, H. Blum, and P. Newbauer).

Nevertheless, contrary American voices have been raised over the years, beginning perhaps with the efforts of Alexander in the 1940s (Alexander and French 1946). Although his view was widely discredited at the time, Alexander advocated focusing predominantly on the "corrective emotional experience," as constituting the most profound vehicle of intrapsychic change, in contradistinction to analytic insight. While Sullivan in the U.S. and Balint in the U.K., among others, were also unambivalent in underscoring the primary therapeutic power of the dyadic relationship (though both differed from Alexander and from each other in their definition of that relationship), both theorists have been considered peripheral to the central thrust of American ego psychology. A much more solid harbinger of a qualitative shift in clinical and theoretical mores is the evocative, metaphoric, quietly revolutionary writing of Loewald (1960), who from the security of an esteemed position within American psychoanalysis, has highlighted the therapeutic impact of "the integrative experience," wherein the analyst, "makes himself available for the development of a new object-relationship between the patient and the analyst" (p. 17). Similarly, Stone's (1961) affirmation of the importance of the "real relationship" further objectified a substantial clinical undercurrent in American views of key treatment variables in psychoanalysis.

Over the course of the past several decades, with the growing popularity of the British object relations school in the United States, together with the rapid surge of growth in interpersonal and self psychology approaches, the relative emphasis on dyadic experiential and transference/countertransference considerations has overshadowed the more traditional emphasis on insight as the crucial determinant of change. Kohut (1977) for example, has repeatedly underscored the greater importance of the empathetic relationship with the therapist, in contradistinction to the relative role of interpretation and insight.

Schematically, in the intellectual history of psychoanalysis, the postulated mechanism of change was seen as resting either on the long esteemed variable of insight on the one hand, or on the cumulative impact of the analytic relationship on the other. Wallerstein (1986) highlighted these distinct, though now more often polarized, theoretical pulls and their clinical implications in his book, *Forty-two Lives in Treatment* (1986).

Initially, Wallerstein and Robbins (1956) conceptualized insight as the "ideational representation" of a change in ego function, which need not correlate with assessments of behavioral or structural change. According to this view, insight would seem to be reflected in the conscious awareness of intrapsychic changes in defensive operations, traits, wishes, and behaviors. Whether this change in conscious apprehension is an epiphenomenon remains unclear.[1] Nevertheless, at the outset of their Menninger investigation Wallerstein and Robbins framed a series of compelling questions regarding the theoretically causal and curative role of insight. Looking at insight in terms of its relationship to process and outcome variables, these investigators wondered whether (1) insight simply set the stage, and thus comprised only one of many preconditions for change to occur; (2) whether insight could be demonstrated to be a direct result of change; or (3) whether insight should simply be viewed as a correlate or accompaniment (rather than causative agent) of intrapsychic change.

As late as 1992, the point was still being made (Pulver 1992) that rather than viewing the curative factor as being either insight or the healing

---

[1]Recall our discussion of the 1990 glossary definition of insight, which underscores the enduring therapeutic impact of insight even in instances where such knowledge has once again been repressed.

aspects of the relationship, it is more likely that both variables constitute important components which interact in complex ways that are incompletely understood. Ultimately, systematic process research should yield more direct implications not only for shaping future generations of theory, but also for influencing the way psychoanalytic technique is used in clinical practice.

Research on Insight

Insight has been investigated in a variety of ways by researchers. This includes studies of the development of an insight measure, research on the correlates of insight as an individual difference variable, treatment outcome studies, research on insight as a process measure, and investigations on the prediction of outcome. We will review each of these areas briefly, placing emphasis on methods that have most relevance to research on psychodynamic psychotherapy.

THE MEASUREMENT OF INSIGHT

Many early studies (Dymond 1948; Feldman and Bullock 1955; Grossman 1951; Kelman and Parloff 1957; Mann and Mann 1959) measured insight through the assessment of congruence between self-descriptions and descriptions given by others. The methodological problems with this approach have been identified by Gage and Cronbach (1955) and Roback (1974), among others, and include halo effects and lack of information to rate the behaviors of others. In addition, it has been found that such ratings vary with the perceived similarity between the target and the observer, thereby raising questions about the accuracy of the ratings. Thus, the use of this methodology has declined. Similarly, self-report measures (e.g., Funder 1980; Smith 1957) have been employed, but their validity is questionable due to the effects of self-deception.

Tolor and Reznikoff (1960) developed their own insight scale, which was based on a definition of insight as the ability to understand the causal factors underlying attitudes and behavior. The scale consists of twenty-seven hypothetical situations which focus on the utilization of thirteen defense mechanisms. For each situation there are four possible interpretations of the behavior illustrated, one of which is the most insightful. Roback (1974) questions the scale's assumption that the ability to understand the motivation of others is dependent upon insight about one's self. Thus, this scale may have little relevance to a psychoanalytic understanding of insight based upon self-understanding of warded-off conflictual feelings and wishes.

A final method of assessing insight involves the use of observer ratings. A thorough review of this area has been presented by Broitman (1984). Probably the work that comes closest to clinical psychoanalytic conceptions of insight is reflected in the process studies reported by Weiss and Sampson (1986) in their review of the investigations by the Mount Zion Psychotherapy Research Group, which used ratings of insight from transcripts of psychoanalytic sessions. We shall return to these and other observer rating methods. In general, such observer rating methods have been found to have adequate interjudge reliability, but their validity remains in question when judges are not supplied with an operationalized definition of insight.

CORRELATES OF INSIGHT

A few studies have examined the relationship between insight and general adjustment. Mann and Mann (1959), who did not focus specifically on the conscious awareness of conflictual impulses, operationalized insight as the amount of congruence between the way one is perceived by others and the way one sees oneself. In a sample of ninety-six students, the authors found no relationship between insight and adjustment. Tolor and Reznikoff (1960) administered their insight test to trained and untrained psychiatric nurses (approximately matched on intelligence level) and to psychiatric patients. Trained nurses demonstrated the highest level of insight, untrained nurses the next highest, and psychiatric patients the lowest. Dymond (1948) assessed insight using subjects' agreement versus disagreement with interpretations of their interpersonal patterns selected from the Thematic Apperception Test. No reliability of this measurement method was reported, but insight was found to relate to level of empathic ability (empathic ability was defined as the degree to which subjects "took the role" of the characters in their TAT stories by providing rich descriptions of the characters' thoughts and feelings).

COMPARATIVE OUTCOME STUDIES

The importance of insight for behavior change has been investigated in a number of comparative outcome studies in which insight-oriented treatment is compared with other treatments. Luborsky (chapter 24) has reviewed these studies and concludes that although insight-oriented therapy produces change in most patients, other treatments typically obtain equal effects in relation to outcomes of treatment. The specific role of insight per se, however, in these therapies is not known. In fact, only in the more recent studies (e.g., Woody el al. 1983; Thompson, Gallagher, and Breckenridge 1987) have investigators attempted to control the adequacy of the treatment delivered through the use of treatment manuals and assessments of the extent to which therapists actually used techniques designed to elicit insight. Thus, much more research is needed to determine the usefulness of treatments that focus on the acquisition of insight. Of course, even if other therapies continue to produce effects equal to those of insight therapy, we will not have confirmation that insight does not lead to change; rather, such findings may suggest that there can be multiple routes to change.

STUDIES ON PREDICTION OF OUTCOME

The most relevant research from a psychodynamic perspective examines the relationship of individual differences in self-understanding and insight to outcome of treatment.

In the earliest investigation, Raskin (1949) reported a significant correlation ($r = .63$) between change in insight and treatment outcome for a sample of ten patients. Insight was measured by judges' classification of client statements as to whether the statements exhibited insight and understanding or not. Rosenbaum, Freidland, and Kaplan (1956) found that therapists' pretreatment ratings of patients' levels of insight were not related to outcome. An abstract by Zolik and Hollon (1960) reported that insight was significantly related to outcome, but no further details were provided. Although two of these three studies reported a significant relationship between insight and outcome, minimal systematic attention was given to measurement of the concept. Simple, global ratings of insight were used (often a single item), with no discussion of reliability or validity. In addition, the therapy used in these investigations was not well defined.

O'Malley, Chong, and Strupp (1983) predicted outcome from the subscales of the Vanderbilt Psychotherapy Process Scale, which included a measure of self-examination and exploration of feelings and experience. This subscale is a 7-item measure of the extent to which the patient attempted to self-explore during sessions. Ratings were made of three 5-minute segments (the first, last, and middle five minutes of the session) from each of the first three sessions of treatment of thirty-eight patients in brief dynamic therapy. The interjudge reliability was reported to be .94, and internal consistency (coefficient alpha) was .96. In relation to outcome, significant prediction of therapist-rated outcome measures was obtained, but not independent clinician- or patient-rated outcome measures. Since this scale does not measure the level or gain in actual insight, but rather simply the attempt to engage in self-examination, it is less relevant to testing hypotheses about insight per se.

An investigation performed by Morgan et al. (1982) used a 9-item insight rating scale, which was applied to two early in treatment and two late in treatment sessions of patients in dynamic psychotherapy of moderate (one year) length. Scale items included the following:

1. Patient recognizes specific phenomena (ideation, affect, behavior) relevant to the problems being discussed.
2. Patient recognizes habitual patterns of behavior.
3. Patient recognizes that he or she plays an active rather than a passive role in producing his or her symptoms and experiences. He or she becomes increasingly conscious of provoking behaviors that are related to production of symptoms and experiences.
4. Patient recognizes particular behaviors as indications of defensiveness or resistance.
5. Patient connects two problems which were previously unconnected, or sees their immediate relevance.
6. Patient becomes increasingly aware of previously unconscious (repressed) thoughts, feelings, or impulses.
7. Patient is able to relate present events to past events.
8. Patient is able to relate present experiences to childhood experiences.
9. Patient's awareness of psychological experience appears to be cumulative.

Each item is rated on a 10-point, Likert-type scale which measures the degree of insight; the scale was influenced by Reid and Finesinger's (1952) definition of emotional insight. The patient sample consisted of the ten most improved and ten least improved patients from the total sample of seventy-three patients in the Penn Psychotherapy Project (Luborsky et al. 1988). Experienced psychoanalysts trained in using the rating scales served as judges. Interjudge reliability of the scale items ranged from .75 to .90, and the internal consistency of the scale (coefficient alpha) was .92. The scale was reported to correlate strongly with operationalized measures of the therapeutic alliance and negatively with an empirical measure of patient resistance. No significant effects were found, however, in an analysis of variance comparing the ten most improved patients with the ten least improved or in comparing such variables in the early sessions versus the late ones. The interaction between treatment phase and outcome was not significant, thereby not supporting the hypothesis that the most improved patients in particular gained insight from early in treatment to late in treatment.

Although the studies have not used current operationalized measures because the research was begun in the 1950s, the intensive clinical studies of Wallerstein (1986), which bear on the relationship of insight to structural change, are worth mentioning here as a potential stimulus for further research. In this massive effort, Wallerstein conducted a careful, systematic clinical analysis of case material from the forty-two patients enrolled in the Menninger Psychotherapy Research Project. They were treated with either psychoanalysis or supportive-expressive psychotherapy. His follow-up assessments suggested that 45 percent of the sample attained a level of structural change that superseded the actual level of insight developed over the course of treatment. While 24 percent achieved levels of insight that seemed proportional to the degree of structural change evidenced, 7 percent attained a level of insight that outstripped discernible structural changes; 24 percent manifested minimal acquisition of insight and showed very little meaningful structural change, posttermination. Taken at face value, these results raise intriguing questions regarding the necessity of insight for structural change.

One problem with all the predictive studies cited so far is that their methods have exclusively relied upon unguided clinical assessments of insight, that is, upon data derived from clinicians who defined insight subjectively. In contrast, a major methodological advance (Crits-Christoph 1984; Crits-Christoph and Luborsky 1990) has been the development of more systematic methods of guided clinical judgment, to be used in the measurement of self-understanding. In general, methods of guided clinical judgment have been found to manifest significantly better predictive validity than unguided ratings (Holt 1978; see also chapter 17). In the Crits-Christoph (1984) method, judges assess the extent to which the patient has reliably demonstrated degrees of self-understanding or insight relative to an independent operationalized criterion: the Core Conflictual Relationship Theme (CCRT).

The CCRT represents a systematic approach to obtaining clinical formulations of patients' main conflictual relationship themes. The primary data are derived from narrative episodes about interactions with other people which are told by patients during actual psychotherapy sessions. These episodes can be reliably coded (using a manual) to yield formulations of the patients' main wishes; provisions are also included for coding the patients' view of the responses of the other person as well as the responses of the self, as contained in each episode. The final CCRT is systematically derived from the highest frequency elements scored over ten episodes, and usually is made up of several wishes, responses from other, and responses of self.

The self-understanding scale (of the CCRT) consists of items designed to measure patients' insight about core conflicts in different object-related domains. Self-understanding is assessed regarding: (1) the CCRT in general, (2) the CCRT in relation to the therapist, (3) the CCRT in relation to parents, and (4) the CCRT in relation to each of two significant others discussed by the patient within each session. Each judge independently rates the degree of self-understanding verbalized by the patient in a session, including each of the main wishes, the response(s) from other, and response(s) of self. Up to forty-five conflict-related ratings are scored for each session, including general, therapist, parent, person 1, and person 2 related conflicts, with a maximum of three wishes for each; similarly, three responses are coded from other, as are three responses of self. The final scores for each session are calculated by averaging across wishes, responses from other, and responses of self for each of the four categories: general, therapist, parents, and other people. In addition, a final composite self-understanding score is also obtained by combining these four scores. To rate the scale, judges are given transcripts of sessions, a list of the two significant others for each session, and the CCRT formulation for the patient. (Selection of the others and formulation of the CCRT have already been validly and reliably ascertained, using a different panel of trained judges.) Each item is then rated on a scale of 1 ("none") to 5 ("very much").

Using a subset ($n = 43$) from the original seventy-three patients of the Penn Psychotherapy Project (Luborsky et al. 1988), Crits-Christoph and Luborsky evaluated the relationship of the self-understanding of the CCRT scale to the outcome of brief psychodynamic psychotherapy. Each of two early treatment sessions (usually sessions 3 and 5) were scored for the CCRT and the self-understanding of the CCRT scale. Interjudge reliability (two judges pooled), using the intraclass correlation coefficient, emerged as follows: .77 for the general scale, .87 for the therapist scale, .89 for the parents scale, .87 for the significant others scale, and .89 and .85 for the total score.

The results of an analysis predicting treatment outcome revealed that level of self-understanding (averaging sessions 3 + 5) yielded two statistically significant findings: (1) self-understanding about the therapist was associated with a composite outcome measure of rated improvement ($r = .31$), and (2) self-understanding about significant others was correlated with a residual gain score on a global adjustment measure ($r = .34$). It is likely, however, that level of self-understanding relates to patients' level of general psychological mindedness. Acquisition or gain in insight, rather than level of insight, would be of greater theoretical interest. An initial attempt to assess gain in insight by examining the change from session 3 to session 5 resulted in no significant predictions. It is clear, however, that hypotheses about gain in insight over the course of dynamic therapy must be tested over considerably longer periods of time.

INSIGHT AND THE PROCESS OF THERAPY

Although insight is an inherent part of the process of dynamic therapy, few researchers have attempted to study insight within or across sessions of treatment. One exception is a study by Broitman (1984) in collaboration with the Mount Zion Psychotherapy Research Group. In a series of three single-case studies, Broitman investigated the impact of interpretations that were compatible and incompatible with the patient's unconscious "plan" (see chapter 19). The 9-item Morgan et al. (1982) Insight Scale, supplemented by an additional global rating of insight, was rated on segments of patient material before and after interpretations. Results indicated that for each patient, ratings of insight were highly correlated with the Experiencing Scale. The Experiencing Scale (Klein, Mathieu-Coughlan, and Kiesler 1986), a commonly used measure in psychotherapy research, assesses the patient's level of involvement in the therapy. Low scores indicate that the patient's discourse is superficial and impersonal, whereas high scores indicate that strong feelings are explored in greater depth and that the patient's immediate experience and affective resonance are being used as a referent for problems and self-understanding. Thus, the Morgan Insight Scale and the Experiencing Scale appear to measure the same dimension. Correlations between plan compatibility and insight for the three patients were all statistically significant and similar in magnitude to previously reported correlations (Silberschatz, Fretter, and Curtis 1986) between plan compatibility and experiencing.

Another process study of insight was performed by Hohage and Kubler (1988), who attempted to develop a scale for assessing emotional insight. Emotional insight, defined as the integration of different frameworks of self-perception, is scored by judges who code therapy transcripts for four dimensions. The first dimension is the *extent of experiencing*, which focuses on references to the "inner world" of the patient. A second dimension, labeled *emotional access*, captures the extent to which the patient is fully immersed in his or her subjective experiences during the hour, as demonstrated by intense or vivid feelings or spontaneity. *Cognitive access*, the third dimension, is represented by variables relating to objective observation, evaluation, or logical analysis of the patient's own experiences. A final rating of *ambiguity* is made, taking into account the amount of tension between being immersed (emotional access) and being at a distance (cognitive access).

Hohage and Kubler applied the Emotional Insight Scale to patient statements at the beginning and end of a psychoanalytic treatment. Results indicated a significant increase in emotional insight as displayed by all scales except the cognitive access scale. Although these results are promising in terms of documenting increases in the sort of work during therapy that should lead to increased self-understanding, the scale appears to measure a different construct from insight as defined from a classical psychoanalytic perspective—as formerly warded-off material becoming conscious. Instead, the scale appears to measure patients' access to their inner experiences.

IMPLICATIONS OF RESEARCH FOR CLINICAL PRACTICE

Researchers continue to struggle with the most basic definition and rudimentary measurement of the concept of insight. The difficulties encountered in operationalizing the concept, however, should serve as a challenge to clinicians to attend to these issues in their work and particularly in their clinical and theoretical writing. It is astonishing to consider how many of the great number of books and articles on the practice of dynamic therapy focus no attention on what is generally held to be the central curative factor of the treatment. Better articulation of the role of insight, its various forms, and the mechanisms through which it leads to change will set the stage for researchers to conduct more sophisticated and clinically relevant research on insight.

FUTURE RESEARCH DIRECTIONS

Assuming advances in the clinical and theoretical literature on insight, empirical research can begin to move forward. Because of the primitive status of research in this area, progress is needed in all phases of research, beginning with scale development. More work on the reliability and particularly the validity of instruments designed to assess the various types of insight is needed.

Specifically, it will be of interest to further examine the overlap between emotional insight and experiencing so that the nature of the constructs being measured is further clarified. With clinical rating instruments for assessing insight, it will be critical to determine the necessary level of clinical expertise, skill, and training of judges, as well as the optimal size of the rated unit of measurement (whole sessions or brief segments) and optimal time frame (within treatment) for sampling. Related to the size of the unit of measurement is the issue of whether insight occurs episodically at key moments (Elliot 1984) or whether it is a slowly evolving phenomenon that must be evaluated on a more global level. (See chapter 2 for an interesting approach to this question, using the Q-sort.)

Research is needed on the overlap and separate contributions of emotional insight and content-based insight. One hypothesis worth testing is that the greatest psychotherapeutic progress is made when a patient achieves an understanding of internal conflicts while experiencing a high level of emotional arousal (that is, that the desired content and process are concurrent). In addition to exploring interactions between emotional arousal and content insight, the relationship of these variables to treatment outcome could be assessed using advanced statistical methods such as causal modeling. This would help test alternative explanations such as whether the insight is only concomitant to, or a result of, behavior change, rather than a cause.

An especially interesting area for study would be to investigate which types of therapist interventions bring about the greatest gains in insight in which types of patients, experiencing which specific kinds of conflicts. In addition, are there certain types of interventions that impede insight? Comparisons of transference versus nontransference, accurate versus inaccurate, and deep versus superficial interpretations could be made in terms of the effects on insight.

Finally, in understanding what leads to outcome, it will be important to bring other dimensions into investigations of insight. It is likely that insight is more relevant to the prediction of outcome for some types of patients (such as high functioning) than others. In particular, patient diagnosis and characteristic styles of defenses employed should be investigated in this context. By examining insight as it interacts with patient variables and other treatment variables, we can enhance our understanding of what is crucial in the process of dynamic therapy and further identify the role of insight.

References

ALEXANDER, F., & FRENCH, T. M. (1946). *Psychoanalytic therapy: Principles and application.* New York: Ronald Press.

BLUM, H. P. (ED.). (1980). *Psychoanalytic explorations of technique: Discourse on the theory of therapy.* New York: International Universities Press.

BROITMAN, J. (1984). *Insight, the mind's eye.* Unpublished doctoral dissertation, Wright Institute, Berkeley, CA.

CRITS-CHRISTOPH, P. (1984, SEPTEMBER). *The development of a measure of self-understanding of core relationship themes.* Paper presented at an NIMH workshop on methodologic challenges in psychodynamic research, Washington, DC.

CRITS-CHRISTOPH, P., & LUBORSKY, L. (1990). The measurement of self-understanding. In L. Luborsky & P. Crits-Christoph, *Understanding transference: The Core Conflictual Relationship Theme method.* New York: Basic Books.

DYMOND, R. (1948). A preliminary investigation of the relation of insight and empathy. *Journal of Consulting Psychology, 12,* 228–233.

ELLIOT, R. (1984). A discovery-oriented approach to significant change events in psychotherapy: Interpersonal process recall and comprehensive process analysis. In L. Rice & L. Greenberg (Eds.), *Patterns of change: Intensive analysis of psychotherapy process* (pp. 249–286). New York: Guilford Press.

ERDELYI, M. H. (1985). *Psychoanalysis: Freud's cognitive psychology.* New York: Freeman.

FELDMAN, M., & BULLOCK, D. (1955). Some factors related to insight. *Psychological Reports, 1,* 143–152.

FERENCZI, S. (1950). *Further contributions to the theory and technique of psychoanalysis.* London: Hogarth Press.

FREUD, S. (1913/1961). On beginning the treatment. In J. Strachey (Ed.), *The standard edition of the complete psychological works of Sigmund Freud* (Vol. 12, pp. 121–144). London: Hogarth Press.

FUNDER, D. C. (1980). On seeing ourselves as others see us: Self agreement and discrepancy in personality ratings. *Journal of Personality, 48,* 473–493.

GAGE, N., & CRONBACH, L. (1955). Conceptual and methodological processes in interpersonal perception. *Psychological Review, 62,* 411–422.

GROSSMAN, D. (1951). The construction and validation of two insight inventories. *Journal of Consulting Psychology, 15,* 109–114.

HOHAGE, R., & KUBLER, J. C. (1988). The Emotional Insight Rating Scale. In H. Dahl, H. Kächele, & H. Thomä (Eds.), *Psychoanalytic process research strategies* (pp. 243–256). Heidelberg: Springer-Verlag.

HOLT, R. R. (1978). *Methods in clinical research: Vol. 2. Prediction and research.* New York: Plenum Press.

KELMAN, H., & PARLOFF, M. (1957). Interrelations among three criteria of improvement in group therapy: Comfort, effectiveness, and self-awareness. *Journal of Abnormal and Social Psychology, 54,* 281–288.

KLEIN, M. H., MATHIEU-COUGHLAN, P., & KIESLER, D. J. (1986). The Experiencing Scales. In L. Greenberg & W. Pinsof (Eds.), *The psychotherapeutic process: A research handbook.* New York: Guilford Press.

KRIS, E. (1956). On some vicissitudes of insight in psychoanalysis. *International Journal of Psycho-Analysis, 37,* 445–455.

KOHUT, H. (1977). *The restoration of the self.* New York: International Universities Press.

LOEWALD, H. W. (1960). On the therapeutic action of psychoanalysis. *International Journal of Psycho-Analysis, 41,* 16–33.

LUBORSKY, L., CRITS-CHRISTOPH, P., MINTZ, J., & AUERBACH, A. (1988). *Who will benefit from psychotherapy? Predicting therapeutic outcome.* New York: Basic Books.

MANN, J., & MANN, D. (1959). Insight as a measure of adjustment in three kinds of group experience. *Journal of Consulting Psychology, 23,* 91.

MOORE, B. E., & FINE, B. D. (EDS.). (1968). *A glossary of psychoanalytic terms and concepts.* New York: American Psychoanalytic Association.

MOORE, B. E., & FINE, B. D. (EDS.). (1990). *Psychoanalytic terms and concepts.* New Haven: American Psychoanalytic Association and Yale University Press.

MORGAN, R. W., LUBORSKY, L., CRITS-CHRISTOPH, P., CURTIS, H., & SOLOMON, J. (1982). Predicting the outcomes of psychotherapy using the Penn Helping Alliance rating method. *Archives of General Psychiatry, 39,* 397–402.

NEUBAUER, P. (1980). The role of insight in psychoanalysis. In *Psychoanalytic explorations of technique: Discourse on the theory of therapy* (pp. 29–40). New York: International Universities Press.

O'MALLEY, S. S., CHONG, S. S., & STRUPP, H. H. (1983). The Vanderbilt Psychotherapy Process Scale: A report on the scale development and process-outcome study. *Journal of Consulting and Clinical Psychology, 51,* 581–586.

PULVER, S. (1992). Psychic change: Insight or relationship. *International Journal of Psycho-Analysis, 73,* 199–208.

RANK, O. (1936). *Truth and reality.* New York: Alfred A. Knopf.

RASKIN, N. (1949). An analysis of six parallel studies of the therapeutic process. *Journal of Consulting Psychology, 13,* 206–221.

REID, J., & FINESINGER, J. (1952). The role of insight in psychotherapy. *American Journal of Psychiatry, 108,* 726–734.

ROBACK, H. (1974). Insight: A bridging of the theoretical and research literatures. *Journal of the Canadian Psychologist, 15,* 61–89.

ROSENBAUM, M., FREIDLAND, J., & KAPLAN, S. (1956). Evaluation of results of psychotherapy. *Psychosomatic Medicine, 18,* 113–132.

SANDLER, J., DARE, L., & HOLDER, A. (1973). *The patient and the analyst.* New York: International Universities Press.

SILBERSCHATZ, G., FRETTER, P., & CURTIS, J. (1986). How do interpretations influence the process of psychotherapy? *Journal of Consulting and Clinical Psychology, 54,* 646–652.

SMITH, F. E. (1957). Defensiveness, insight and the K scale. *Journal of Consulting Psychology, 23,* 275–277.

STONE, L. (1961). *The psychoanalytic situation: An examination of its development and essential nature.* New York: International Universities Press.

STRACHEY, J. (1934). The nature of the therapeutic action of psycho-analysis. *International Journal of Psycho-Analysis, 15,* 127–159.

THOMPSON, L., GALLAGHER, D., & BRECKENRIDGE, J. (1987). Comparative effectiveness of psychotherapies for depressed elders. *Journal of Consulting and Clinical Psychology, 55,* 385–390.

TOLOR, A., & REZNIKOFF, M. (1960). A new approach to insight. *Journal of Nervous and Mental Disease, 130,* 286–296.

WALLERSTEIN, R. S. (1983). Some thoughts about insight and psychoanalysis. *Israeli Journal of Psychiatry and Related Science, 20,* 33–43.

WALLERSTEIN, R. S. (1986). *Forty-two lives in treatment: A study of psychoanalysis and psychotherapy.* New York: Guilford Press.

WALLERSTEIN, R. S., & ROBBINS, L. L. (1956). Concepts: The psychotherapy research project of the Menninger Foundation. *Bulletin of the Menninger Clinic, 20,* 239–262.

WEISS, J., SAMPSON, H., & THE MOUNT ZION PSYCHOTHERAPY RESEARCH GROUP. (1986). *The psychoanalytic process: Theory, clinical observation and empirical research.* New York: Guilford Press.

WOODY, G., LUBORSKY, L., MCLELLAN, A. T., O'BRIEN, C. P., BECK, A. T., BLAINE, J., HERMAN, I., & HOLE, A. V. (1983). Psychotherapy for opiate addicts: Does it help? *Archives of General Psychiatry, 40,* 639–645.

ZOLIK, E. S., & HOLLON, T. N. (1960). Factors characteristic of patients responsive to brief psychotherapy. *American Psychologist, 15,* 287.

CHAPTER 22

Patients' Representations of Their Therapists and Therapy: New Measures

DAVID E. ORLINSKY AND JESSE D. GELLER

P ATIENTS FREQUENTLY REMARK ON HAVING thought about their therapists and therapy during the time between sessions. These representations include reminiscences, reflections, and feelings about what happened during sessions, and also imaginary conversations and activities with their therapists. Therapy thus appears to take place between sessions as well as during sessions, through the patients' inner representational activity.[1]

A renewed interest in the nature, origins, consequences, and modifiability of these internal representations has been evident among many psychoanalytically oriented therapists. On one hand, they have been influenced to varying degrees by the writings of Klein (1932) and the British object relations theorists (Fairbairn 1952; Guntrip 1969; Winnicott 1965), Kohut's self psychology (1971, 1977), the attachment theory of Bowlby (1969, 1980), and other recent writers (e.g., Dorpat 1979, 1981; Greenberg and Mitchell 1983; Kernberg 1976; Loewald 1962, 1976, 1988; Mahler 1979; McDevitt 1979; McDougall 1985; Meissner 1979, 1981; Searles 1977). Schafer's (1968) *Aspects of Internalization* was also important in drawing attention to these phenomena.

On the other hand, psychodynamic clinicians and theorists have been challenged to reexamine their models of the therapeutic action of psychotherapy, especially by patients who have failed to develop valued and cohesive representations of themselves as separate and different from

[1]Preparation of this paper by the first author was partially supported by research grant R 01 MH 42901 from the National Institute of Mental Health.

others, and who feel incapable of functioning independently. The result has been a new conceptualization of therapy in which insight is only one component in a complex interplay between empathy and the internalization of patient-therapist interactions (Geller 1988; Loewald 1988; Pine 1985).

This augmented model of therapeutic action, in turn, has thrown a new light on traditional forms of treatment. According to Singer and Pope (1978):

> Psychoanalysts often notice that patients in a sense adopt the therapist as a kind of imaginary companion, someone to whom they talk privately in their minds. . . . This pattern of behavior need not be viewed necessarily as an instance of excessive attachment or dependency. Often it is a natural phase of a new learning procedure in which the patient is gradually assimilating what in effect the analyst has been teaching him about a process of self-examination and heightened self-awareness. (p. 21)

Curiously, representations of the therapist and therapy have failed to attract much scientific attention even from psychodynamically oriented researchers. Scientific research on therapy typically has focused on therapeutic process and outcome. Traditionally, treatment process has been defined in terms of events that occur within therapy sessions (such as therapist interventions and patient–therapist interactions), and outcome has been formulated symptomatically or nosologically (that is, in terms of reduction in psychopathology). Unfortunately, since patients' representations of the therapist occur most noticeably outside therapy sessions, they have not been viewed as part of the therapeutic process; and, since they are not overtly related to symptoms or explicitly involved in adaptive functioning, they have found no place in outcome research. As commonly happens, the very conceptions that have usefully focused research attention in certain directions have deterred researchers from recognizing clinical phenomena that do not readily fit them.

Intrigued by clinical case reports (e.g., Cameron 1961; Dorpat 1974; Haskell, Blacker, and Oremland 1976; Pfeffer 1961) and related theoretical developments, Geller and his colleagues began about a decade ago to develop the Therapist Representation Inventory, (Geller, Cooley, and Hartley 1981), a method for exploring the patient's aggregate image of the therapist at a single point in time. Inspired in part by that work, Orlinsky and his colleagues extended earlier work on patients' and therapists' experiences in successive therapy sessions (Orlinsky and Howard 1975) by developing instruments to study patients' and therapists' experiences of therapy in the intervals between sessions, the Intersession Experience Questionnaires (Orlinsky and Lundy 1986; Orlinsky and Tarragona 1986).

From these beginnings, a new area of psychotherapy research has rapidly developed.[2]

The aim of this chapter is to introduce readers to this new area of research. Our discussion will focus successively on the clarification of theoretical concepts, the operationalization of those concepts in our research instruments, the psychometric characteristics of these instruments, initial results of their application in clinical settings, and a consideration of questions for further research.

Representation and Internalization: Theoretical Considerations

Most broadly defined, representational processes include all forms of cognitive or ideational experience other than immediate sensory data and innate response patterns. The concept of representation encompasses memories and expectations, habits and skills, images and fantasies, thoughts and symbols. Representations may be concrete or abstract, realistic or unrealistic, and may refer to things past, present, or future. They may also vary in both their degree of energy and their emotional valence. No branch of psychology, excepting the most radical form of operant behaviorism, has tried to function without some such concept as representation.

Two distinct though often convergent traditions in psychology place a particularly strong emphasis on the interplay of representation and the related concept of internalization. One is psychoanalysis; the other, that of developmental cognitive psychology, as exemplified variously in the works of Piaget (1950), Vygotsky (1962), and Bruner (1964). Our evolving approach to studying the construction, forms, and functions of patients' representations of their therapy and therapists is based on a selective integration of these two theoretical traditions.[3]

Since agreement within and between these traditions has yet to be

[2]Early reports of work with the two instruments include: Barchat (1989); Derby (1989); Epstein (1989); Farber and Geller (1988, 1989); Geller, Guisinger, and Schulberg (1989); Geller and Schaffer (1988); Honig (1989); Lehman (1990); Lundy (1989); Lundy and Orlinsky (1987); Montgomery (1988); Orlinsky and Tarragona (1988, 1989); Rohde, Geller, and Farber (1989); Rhodes et al. (1987); Tarragona (1989); Tarragona and Orlinsky (1987, 1988); Wzontek (1990). A promising and very different approach to research on internalization based on Benjamin's (1974) "Structural Analysis of Social Behavior" was reported recently by Quintana and Meara (1990).
[3]The most effective efforts to clarify internalization and related concepts have been offered by Schafer (1968), Meissner (1981), and Behrends and Blatt (1985). Another approach to personality that deals extensively with representational concepts is the personal construct theory of Kelly (1955); psychotherapeutic applications of that approach are reviewed in Bannister (1975).

achieved regarding either basic terms for describing internalization processes or the number and nature of underlying mechanisms involved, a preliminary clarification of working definitions and hypotheses is required.

CONCEPTIONS OF THE INTERNAL AND EXTERNAL

A basic source of confusion in discussions of internalization stems from the diverse ways in which *internal* and *external* are defined, which in turn depend on whether one starts from an objectivist or subjectivist perspective.

Theories of cognitive development have typically been formulated from an objectivist perspective. That is, the developing person is understood essentially from the viewpoint of an external observer. In this observational frame, behavioral processes are overt and representational processes covert, inferred largely from logical gaps in the sequential flow of behavior.[4]

The term *representation* typically refers to externally unobservable events reported by subjects, such as images, memories, thoughts, and the like. Such experiences are inherently transient. The related term *schema* refers to relatively enduring units of cognitive-affective structure whose activities give rise to representations. Schemas as such are not directly available to consciousness; rather, they are inferred elements from which subjective experiences are selectively generated. In the objectivist view, the term *internalization* refers to the processes that are responsible for the formation of schemas. When a result that was once produced by a sequence of externally observable behaviors becomes producible without carrying out the full sequence, it is presumed that covert representational activity based on cognitive schemas has been substituted for the missing behavioral steps. Thus, from this objectivist perspective, internalization has the meaning that Piaget (1950) referred to as "interiorization."

With respect to the growing child, cognitive development reveals a pattern of increasing interiorization. That is, the general thrust of development appears to entail an overall shift from motorically mediated (external) processes to symbolically mediated (internal) processes: from action, to imagination, to abstract thought; and so, also, from trial-and-error, to intuition, to reasoning. As development proceeds, the schemas and processes that generate a person's representational activity (that is, his or her "inner life") are thought to become progressively more differentiated and highly organized.

[4]There is a characteristic implication that behavioral processes are "external" and representational processes are "internal," that is, occur within the organism. The metaphorical nature of this distinction and its tendency to distort thinking has been clarified by Lakoff and Johnson (1980).

Psychoanalytic theory, on the other hand, is generally formulated from a subjectivist or phenomenological perspective, at least insofar as representations are concerned.[5] Persons are viewed, within the framework of their own experience, as active subjects who are involved, alternately or concurrently, with internal and external representations, that is, with "field[s] of representations falling respectively within and outside the subjective self" (Atwood and Stolorow 1980). The external world of the objectivist perspective is not directly knowable as such, but is constructed of consensual or collective object representations embedded in communications and sanctioned by communities (see, e.g., Berger and Luckmann, 1966).

In the psychoanalytic tradition, object representations having psychical "quality" (Freud [1900] 1953) define what the person experiences as external, in both waking and dreaming states, while self representations are based on what the person experiences as internal. Varied domains of self representation include: the body image; self-images based on actual performance and experiences in familial relationships, peer groups, and other social contexts; extensions of self-feeling to possessions, pets, and projects; social identities based on a sense of belonging to ethnic, religious, class, and cultural groups; the ego ideal; and dramatic personifications as protagonists in fantasy formations that indirectly express dynamically unconscious (repressed) wishes.

The psychological boundary between self representations and object representations is only gradually established during infancy, and it remains relatively permeable and reversible. The boundary is more permeable in early childhood, in drowsing and sleeping states, and in pathological somatic and psychological conditions. The sense of self (that is, the conviction that one is a distinct being in one's own right) is more firmly established in later childhood and adulthood, in fully alert consciousness, and in somatic and psychological health. The ambiguity of the boundary is reflected, for example, in Kohut's (1971) concept of the "selfobject," that is, others that are emotionally part of the self and that substitute for or support the individual's self-regulative capacities. The continued permeability of the boundary is also demonstrated by the capacity to identify with others and to externalize self components, even in adulthood.

From the psychoanalytic perspective, then, *internalization* refers to the processes by which self representations are modeled upon object representations. These processes are usually referred to (somewhat generically) as

[5]The phenomenological or subjectivist perspective is especially clear in object relations theory and psychoanalytic self psychology; it is less consistently stressed, for example, in the structural theory. The confounding of objectivist and subjectivist frameworks in Freud's writings has been pointed out by a number of commentators, including Bettelheim (1983), Holt (1973), and Schafer (1976).

"identification," and are thought to operate differently at various developmental levels. The more primitive variants of identification have been called incorporation and introjection, according to the definitions of Laplanche and Pontalis (1973), and viewed as "prototypes of identification." (Their definitions, which we follow, differ from those of Schafer, who uses the words *introject* and *introjection* in a different sense, and excludes the term *incorporation*).[6] Freud ([1921] 1955) described the more mature variants of identification as "imitation" and "empathy" in the following passage: "A path leads from identification by way of imitation to empathy, that is, to the comprehension of the mechanisms by means of which we are enabled to take up any attitude at all toward another mental life" (p. 110, n. 2).

The contrast between the two theoretical traditions can be summed up as follows. From the objectivist perspective, *inner* and *outer* locate objects and events in physical space with respect to the boundaries of the organism. Behavior reflects the external activity of the organism, and experience—all experience—is viewed as internal activity. On the other hand, from the phenomenological or subjectivist perspective, *inner* and *outer* refer to different domains of experience, "falling respectively within and outside the subjective self." Thus, to the objectivist, both self representations (phenomenologically internal) and object representations (phenomenologically external) would be viewed as spatially internal to the organism.

Freud's recognition of the difference between the two perspectives is suggested by the diagram he placed at the end of chapter 8 in *Group Psychology and the Analysis of the Ego* ([1921] 1955, p. 116). This drawing distinguishes clearly between external objects (external in the objectivist sense) and psychological objects (that is, object representations, which are internal in the objectivist sense but external in the phenomenological sense). In a way, this diagram also implies a potential synthesis of the two perspectives by putting them both into a single, more comprehensive framework; but, as with so many of his suggestions, Freud never returned to deal with this systematically. Armed with a clear recognition of the

---

[6]Schafer nevertheless points to an important phenomenon by his use of the term *introject* (noun) which ought not to be lost. Introjects are "imaginary 'felt presences' [experienced as] existing within the confines of the body or mind or both, but which are not experienced as an expression of the subjective self. . . . The subject conceives of this presence as a person, a physical or psychological part of a person (e.g., a breast, a voice, a look, an affect) or a person-like thing or creature" (1968, 72). This corresponds closely to the traditional psychoanalytic concept of the imago, as defined by LaPlanche and Pontalis (1973), which term may have fallen into disfavor due to its origin in and association with the writings of Jung. Introjects or imagos retain a special place among object representations due to their imaginal vividness, affective intensity, and intimate involvement with self representations. Similar constructs are to be found in the seminal works of Klein (1932) and Sullivan (1953).

differences in these two perspectives and of the different meanings of inner and outer in each, we can at least avoid confusion, and may further venture to explore the possibility of synthesis indicated in Freud's diagram.

An approach toward synthesis may be opened by relaxing the rigid dichotomy between objectivist and subjectivist perspectives that Western philosophers have tended to draw following the work of Descartes (MacMurray 1957; Ryle 1949; Toulmin 1990). Taking this step, Lakoff and Johnson (1980), among others, have proposed that the two perspectives ought to be viewed as complementary rather than antithetical frameworks. The synthesis which Lakoff and Johnson call *experiential* emphasizes intersubjectivity and eschews both the naive realism toward which objectivism leads and the romantic idealism which is often the end product of subjectivism. It allows the theorist to look both "within" the organism, at the complex and idiosyncratic worlds of felt meanings constructed by individuals, and yet to affirm the substantial independence of the socially constructed collective world of direct and indirect relationships. It is actually only in such an enlarged perspective that Freud's diagram in *Group Psychology* really makes sense.

INTERIORIZATION AND IDENTIFICATION AS STAGES OF INTERNALIZATION

In this expanded view, objective interiorization and subjective identification are both legitimate aspects of internalization. Internalization would be understood as a general process in which interiorization and identification figure as successive stages. A formula expressing this sequential arrangement may be written as follows: perceptual experience → psychological schemas → personality organization.[7]

"Perceptual experience" refers to activation of the perceptual apparatus by patterns of sensory input—that is, by the continuing flux of physical stimuli impacting on exosomatic and endosomatic sense organs. Stimuli impinging on endosomatic sense organs, especially those arising from organismic metabolism, were called drives by Freud ([1915] 1957) and were given special consideration because of their dynamic or motivational properties. However, stimuli impinging on exosomatic sense organs were also recognized as having dynamic significance through their ability to

---

[7]We do not mean to suggest a one-sided view of what we believe to be a reciprocal chain of causal influence. The formula was written as perceptual stimulation → psychological schemas → personality organization to represent the processes of internalization. Analysis of the parallel processes of externalization would lead to a reversal of the formula, as follows: personality organization → psychological schemas → perceptual stimulation. Defensive processes (repression, denial, isolation, projection, and so on) reflect the first of these externalizing transformations: personality organization → psychological schemas. Apperceptive processes (assimilation, in Piaget's sense) reflect the second, more peripheral transformation: psychological schemas → perceptual stimulation.

evoke pleasure/pain responses (Freud [1903] 1953, [1911] 1958) or, in traumatic situations, to overwhelm the individual's capacity to respond altogether (Freud [1920] 1955).

"Psychological schemas" refers to enduring cognitive and affective meaning structures that selectively embody patterns of information abstracted from perceptual experience. (Like genes, schemas may be posited theoretically before their physical basis has been discovered.) These are not unlike the ideational-affective "complexes" so much discussed in the early concept-building days of psychoanalysis. Complexes were thought to arise partly through innate predispositions and partly through the influence of emotionally significant events experienced during critical stages of development. Once formed, dynamically activated complexes subtly influence the individual's perceptions of current events and may prompt the reenactment of complex-relevant behaviors. An example of this type of externalization of psychological structure is the phenomenon of transference, which can be represented by reversing our formula: psychological schemas → perceptual experience. A special hypothesis of psychoanalysis is that psychological schemas grounded in early formative relationships of unresolved conflict later function as transference templates or "stereotypes" (Freud [1912] 1958), which Luborsky has operationalized in terms of his Core Conflictual Relationship Themes (Luborsky and Crits-Christoph 1990).

Finally, "personality organization" refers to the differentiation and integration of psychodynamically potent psychological schemas. Over the course of development, these schemas are progressively differentiated into hierarchically linked domains and subdomains: from a primal state of relatively undifferentiated experience to one in which self as body ego is distinguished from object world, to one in which consciousness is distinguished from the dynamically unconscious, then actual ego from ego ideal, and so forth (Freud [1921] 1955, pp. 130–131; [1930] 1961, chap. 1). At the same time, adaptive behavior is only possible if each differentiation is followed by a more complex and flexible integration of schematic domains and subdomains. In broad outlines, this process parallels the development of intelligence depicted by Piaget, although he did not apply his concepts very much to the area of personality (except in Piaget 1981). We note in passing that the scheme also suggests the two broad types of psychopathology highlighted respectively in classical and modern psychoanalysis: problems or failures of functional integration between domains and subdomains of personality organization, in the varied forms of intrapsychic conflict; and problems or failures of stable differentiation, in the forms of borderline, narcissistic, and schizophrenic disorders.

Returning to our formula, we see that interiorization (internalization in the objectivist sense) refers to the first transformation depicted: perceptual experience → psychological schemas. By contrast, identification (internalization in the subjectivist sense) refers to the second transformation: psychological schemas → personality organization. The formula can be given more specific content if we allow that the perceptual experiences which normally are most significant for survival arise in relationships with other persons. Attachment theory, interpersonal theory, self psychology, and object relations theory all emphasize the gradual transformation of the infant's absolute dependence on caregivers, and the child's reliance on protection and gratification by adults and peers, into lifelong adult needs for involvement, intimacy, and interdependence. The most significant and emotionally charged forms of perceptual experience for humans are those that involve close relationships of various kinds. Thus for our purposes the formula given above can be rewritten as: interpersonal involvements → self-other schemas → personality organization.

INTERIORIZATION

This revision allows us to see that the process of interiorization is not limited in relevance to purely cognitive theories. Interiorization, restated in the proposed terms, refers to the transformation: interpersonal involvements → self-other schemas. This formula encompasses the hypothesis implicit in virtually all versions of psychodynamic theory, that basic personality patterns are formed in the earliest and most emotionally significant relationships. These formative relationships are typically experienced during early childhood within the family circle, supplemented and modified to some degree during later childhood and adolescence. A related hypothesis holds that in certain conditions even adult relationships can shape or modify personality organization. Successful psychoanalyses and psychotherapies must be viewed as exemplifying relationships in adulthood that influence personality organization; otherwise, clinical analyses and therapies could have only diagnostic value. Other examples of the impact that interpersonal involvements can have on personality in adult life are the fulfillment of profoundly felt wishes in a love relationship and the process of mourning when a loved one is lost.

Psychodynamic theories further hypothesize that the quality and quantity of affect experienced by a person in a formative relationship have an influence on the form and function of internal representations subsequently generated from the schema in question. Quantitatively, the more intense the original affect, either by its singular impact or by accumulation through recurrent experiences in the involvement, the more psychodynamically active will the resulting schema be, and the more vividly and persistently will it press to be represented in consciousness. Stated in terms of classical drive theory, the more intensely cathected a wish, the more energetically will it press for discharge in consciousness and action. If the wish is threatening to the ego, the more vigorously will it be resisted by countervailing wishes for safety, and the larger will be the proportion of the ego's available energy that must be devoted to defense.

In addition, psychodynamic or affective-motivational models of psychological functioning (Geller 1984) hypothesize that the affective quality of the formative relationship will determine the psychodynamic functions of representations based on the self-other schema that has been formed. Thus representations of an involvement will tend to have a nourishing or sustaining function to the extent that the original involvement was gratifying. In times of adversity, people may call upon memories of past gratifying involvements, evoke fantasies about currently unavailable involvements, and anticipate future gratifications in order to help maintain a positive emotional balance. Even the sometimes painful experience of erotic longing may have a sustaining effect. Alternatively, schemas formed in a mainly hostile interpersonal context may generate vengeful persecutory representations, like the one that obsessed Melville's Captain Ahab, or fearful persecutory representations, like those that torment the paranoiac.

Schemas of involvements will generate representations that have a primarily defensive function to the extent that the involvements in which they were formed were experienced as disruptively frustrating or threatening. Freud ([1920] 1955) observed that recurrent representations of traumatic experiences reflect efforts at mastery. In part these efforts reflect a belated attempt to compensate the previous absence of "signal anxiety." However, many years earlier Freud noted that the rehearsal of traumatic events under normal circumstances also reflects efforts to discharge the anxiety they elicit and to assimilate them to the core of meaningful life experiences (Breuer and Freud [1895] 1955).

PERSONALITY DEVELOPMENT

Self-other schemas also mediate the developmental impact of experiences on the organization of personality. This latter function is depicted by the second transformation in our formula: self-other schemas → personality organization. Generally speaking, the *self* element in each self-other schema enriches the inner domain of potential self representations, while the schematized *other* element adds to the domain of potential object representations.

As individuals mature from infancy to adulthood, they are inducted by their societies into ever wider and more differentiated interpersonal involvements which vary in the degree of continuity or discontinuity in the roles accorded to self and other (see, e.g., Benedict 1938; Erikson 1963; Kakar 1978). To the extent that a subsequent involvement resembles a schema based on an earlier formative relationship, the new involvement evokes and is assimilated to the established schema, adding nuance and resonance to it. This subjective assimilation of new interpersonal involvements to the self-other schemas established in earlier formative relationships may be reflected in the process that Freud ([1912] 1958, p. 105) distinguished as the "transference of friendly or affectionate feelings which are admissible to consciousness," in contrast to the conflictual, resistance-evoking "prolongations of those feelings into the unconscious." This preconscious, positive transference was further described by Freud ([1913] 1958, p. 139) as "a proper rapport" with the patient, which is evoked by the analyst's patience and "serious interest," and which prompts the patient "to form . . . an attachment and link the doctor up with one of the imagos of the people by whom he was accustomed to be treated with affection" (p. 140). It is precisely this attachment in the patient, tinged with an "affectionate and devoted dependence" toward the analyst as a surrogate of former caregivers (Freud [1912] 1958, p. 105), that can help the patient overcome resistances grounded in unconscious, conflictual transferences, and thus ultimately to resolve them through the therapeutic processes of insight and working through. In essence, this attachment coincides with what Bordin (1979) called the "bond" component of the therapeutic alliance, and may be linked to the evidence that Orlinsky and Howard (1986b) summarized under the heading of the "therapeutic bond."

On the other hand, discontinuity between established self-other schemas and new involvements stimulates the differentiation of new self-other schemas, providing the individual with new schematized elements from which self and object representations may be generated. Of course, schemas often persist in the face of contradictory information. Compatibility or incompatibility with currently perceived conditions is a matter of degree, subject to the judgmental processes of reality testing. Given schemas in which much emotion has been invested, a relatively slight degree of incompatibility is readily denied or distorted. However, the denial or distortion of major discrepancies between expectation and perception would endanger the individual's adaptation, and is found only in relatively serious psychopathological conditions. The size of the discrepancy between experience and expectation that must exist before structural change occurs undoubtedly varies with circumstances. The essence of unconscious, conflictual transferences lies in their distorting influence on perception and their relative immunity to modification by new experience; but if one is involved in a relationship in which danger is anticipated, and yet somehow finds that the expectation was unfounded, then a realistic revision of the schema's emotional and motivational valence should ensue (Weiss and Sampson 1986). Where the defense of personal security is at stake, individuals are understandably circumspect with regard to such demonstrations. Once the seeds of suspicion are sown, they are exceptionally difficult to uproot. Thus, realistic revision of inappropriate and inefficient defensive schemas is a central problem in all forms of therapy (see Wachtel 1977) and usually can be accomplished only when the patient has considerable confidence in the protective and adaptive powers of the therapist.

The presence of newly differentiated schematic elements in turn engenders a corresponding integrative process. Reciprocal assimilation and accommodation ensue among the individual's diverse *self* elements and among the varied concrete and generalized *other* schemas from which the individual constructs a psychological object world. This dialectical process of alternating differentiation and synthesis has been recognized as the normal pattern of personality growth by a number of writers (e.g., Angyal 1941; Kegan 1982).

MODES OF IDENTIFICATION

Viewed in this context, identification in its broadest sense can be seen as referring to five distinct though interrelated types of phenomena, which may be distinguished by the following names: role identification, relational identification, reflexive identification, substitutive identification, and compensatory identification.

1. *Role identification* occurs when an individual becomes heavily invested emotionally in a particular role around which the *self* component in a self-other schema is formed. The individual is then said to have identified with that role, and through it with the social group or relationship of which it is a part (Parsons 1958). Using the concept in this way, Freud ([1921] 1955) observed, "Each individual is a component part of numerous groups, he is bound by ties of identification in many directions, and he has built up his ego ideal upon the most various models" (p. 129). Moreover, the more a particular role identity is emotionally cathected, the more salient it is in the individual's identity hierarchy (McCall and Simmons 1978). Identification in this sense is a general process of considerable importance in personality development.

2. *Relational identification* occurs when an individual comes to identify with the relationship itself rather than just with a specific role, thereby gaining a capacity to enact the role of the other as well as that of the self (Mead 1954; Parsons 1958). One may "take the role of the other" toward a third party, whom one then treats as the self of the original relationship—as, for example, when a little child plays at being mama vis-à-vis a doll or a younger child cast in the baby role. Thus one learns to do to others as one has been done to by another (not necessarily the same other). For example, one learns to become a parent in large part

through identification with one's own parents. Those who have been abused may become abusers of others, as indicated by the concept of "identification with the aggressor" (A. Freud 1967), although they may also become ardent defenders of the downtrodden and oppressed. This, too, is a general process with broad implications for development.

3. *Reflexive identification* is perhaps even more significant from the perspective of personality organization. This form of identification extends beyond taking the role of the other and enables individuals to take up both roles in a relationship, that is, to split the self and so act toward themselves as others have acted toward them. Laplanche and Pontalis (1973) refer to this as internalization in the strict sense—as, "for example, [when] the relation of authority between father and child is said to be internalised in the relation between super-ego and ego" (p. 227). The structural and developmental significance of reflexive identification is readily grasped, exemplified in such major ego functions as those of regulating impulses and self-esteem.

4. *Substitutive identification* is a fourth type of identification, and is typically instigated so that the self may enjoy the libidinal position of a specific other. This involves the production of behavior by the *self* component of a self-other schema which mimics behavior or attributes normally associated with the other in question. Freud ([1921] 1955, chap. 7) gives several examples of this phenomenon: the identification of a little girl motivated by oedipal feelings with her sick mother, and the identification of students with a schoolmate involved in a love affair they too wish to have. A more complex example of substitutive identification arises in the situation of group formation, when each member identifies with the selves of others based on their parallel emotional attachments to a common leader or "leading idea" (Freud [1921] 1955, chap. 8).

5. *Compensatory identification* denotes a fifth type of identification in which the *self* component of a self-other schema is transformed to resemble a lost or rejecting other. It inverts the emotional situation of mourning as a means of assuaging the suffering involved (Freud [1917b] 1957).[8] If the pain seems too great to bear, and especially if strong dependent or ambivalent feelings mark the lost attachment, then compensatory identification is a likely outcome. This allows the individual to preserve the positive emotional character of the lost involvement ("My beloved loves me") even though perceived reality contradicts it ("My loved one has left me"), without seriously compromising the individual's reality testing, as would an outright denial. By transforming the schematized

---

[8]This is the specific case discussed by Behrends and Blatt (1985). In actual cases, identification and detachment through mourning may not be mutually exclusive outcomes. Readers are referred to Geller (1988) for a more extensive theoretical treatment of this topic.

object into a self component, the transitive attachment of self-to-object is converted into a reflexive mode of self-involvement. Thus the lost involvement is restored to the individual's control—although, as Freud ([1917] 1957) indicated in analyzing the dynamics of neurotic depression, the transformation may ultimately diminish rather than enhance the individual's subjective sense of self-determination and well-being.

IDENTIFICATION IN PSYCHOTHERAPY

What do these various forms of identification imply about the workings of psychoanalytic therapy? Psychotherapy, of course, is a special type of interpersonal involvement in which the defining roles are those of patient and therapist (Orlinsky 1989). Individuals who become emotionally involved in the role of patient are likely to become identified with that role and to make being a patient a prominent part of their identities. This may happen, but it is not particularly therapeutic unless the patient role is significantly discontinuous with *and* emotionally preferable to the patient's previous role identifications. Under those stringent circumstances, identification with the patient role can offer the individual an emotional haven and workspace in which to develop new, more benign self-other schemas. For seriously disturbed or otherwise psychologically deprived individuals (for example, those with narcissistic or borderline personality disorders), a stable supportive relationship in which the functions and identities of patient and therapist are clearly differentiated is, in and of itself, likely to be a therapeutic experience. Unfortunately, it is precisely in such cases that therapists cannot rely on evoking a nonconflictual, preconscious positive transference and that a therapeutic bond is so difficult to establish, so emotionally taxing to sustain, and so constantly in need of repair. Accordingly, we consider role identification an important therapeutic factor primarily with seriously impaired individuals.

Relational and reflexive forms of identification, on the other hand, are likely to play a more prominent part in the treatment of individuals with relatively well developed interpersonal skills. Both forms of identification involve the patient's taking the therapist's attitude and behavior as a model, either for the patient's relations with others (relational identification) or for the patient's self-relatedness (reflexive identification). Through relational identification, patients can enhance the quality of their interpersonal relations by extending to others a measure of the attentiveness, patience, empathy, and nonjudgmental acceptance that their therapists have shown toward them. This may be most effectively cultivated in group therapy, couple therapy, and family therapy, where the therapist can not only model but actively supervise and reinforce patients' efforts in this direction.

However, reflexive identification is perhaps the most important transformation in any successful treatment, because through this patients may develop a therapeutic self schema directly applicable to themselves. By acquiring a self-caring and self-analytic attitude, patients can become more attentive, patient, empathic, and nonjudgmentally accepting toward themselves, as their therapists had been. In some cases this may lead to a modification of harsh and infantile superego attitudes (Strachey 1934) through the internalization (in the strict sense of LaPlanche and Pontalis) of the more benign authority of the therapist. Moreover, the habit of seeking insight through self-analysis, based on a reflexive identification with the therapist, also equips patients with a valuable adaptive skill that can be applied in difficult life situations (although it is equally true that excessive or intellectualizing self-analysis can serve a defensive function). Though it is seen to occur in any treatment modality, reflexive identification may be most powerfully encouraged in the context of "individual" (dyadic) treatments. Follow-up studies of psychoanalytic cases have remarked on the appearance of this self-analytic function in successful cases (e.g., Pfeffer 1961; Schlessinger and Robbins 1983).

On the other hand, the therapeutic importance of substitutive identification is probably most salient in group psychotherapy, where the morale enhancing effect of group cohesion is a prominent curative factor (e.g., Yalom 1975). Group members gain a powerful narcissistic premium by heightening their perceptions of basic identity with one another, both directly in regard to their common lot and indirectly through a common attachment to their therapist (Freud [1921] 1955, chap. 8). Of course, through analytic work group members may also gain insight and may also have the benefits associated with relational and reflexive modes of identification with the therapist.

Only compensatory identification, the type involved in neurotic depression (Freud [1917b] 1957), seems to have no positive therapeutic function. Indeed, it may be mainly seen in situations of therapist illness, premature therapist-initiated termination or other administrative disruptions of therapy, in which patients feel abandoned or rejected. Being unable to accept this painful situation, or to express direct feelings of anger toward the therapist, the patient may instead protect the therapist by forming an unconscious compensatory identification, expressing anger at the therapist indirectly against a remodeled self schema (in the form of guilt, depression, and self-punitive behavior). This potential for countertherapeutic identification may also result in the intensification of self-criticism in dependent patients who do not experience a positive therapeutic alliance and who perceive their therapists as unempathic or judgmental. Some of the deterioration observed among patients in therapy (Lambert, Shapiro, and Bergin

1986; Strupp, Hadley, and Gomes-Schwartz 1977) may well be attributable to this type of identification.

REPRESENTATIONS OF THE THERAPIST

We have seen that both phases of the proposed internalization formula have relevance for the study of patients' representations of their therapy and therapists. The concept of internalization as interiorization (phase 1) points to the process of forming an emotionally valent self-other schema in which the self component is based on the patient role and the other component is based on perceptions of and emotional responses to the therapist (self$_{pt}$-other$_{th}$). This links the study of patients' representations to the traditional domain of process research, and thus to such concepts as the therapeutic alliance (Bordin 1979; Luborsky 1976). In terms of our theoretical discussion, a plausible hypothesis is that the character and qualities of the patient's self$_{pt}$-other$_{th}$ schema, and the representations based on it, are determined at least in part by the actual character and qualities of interaction experienced in the patient-therapist relationship.

The concept of internalization as identification (phase 2) points to a variety of probable functions served by patients' representations of therapy and the therapist. Clinical theories of psychoanalytic therapy (e.g., Dorpat 1974; Kohut 1984; Loewald 1960; Sterba 1934; Strachey 1934) suggest that the patient's schematization of the therapist's actions becomes a model for constructive changes in the patient's self representation and ego functioning. This notion links the study of patients' representations to the traditional domain of outcome research. A plausible hypothesis in this regard is that positive outcomes, such as insightful self-analysis and realistic adaptation, will be determined in part by conditions which favor the patient's reflexive identification with the therapist.

The foregoing suggests that patients' representations of their therapy and therapists constitute an important bridge between the traditional domains of therapeutic process and outcome. Figure 22.1 places the patient's representation of both therapy and therapist in the context of successive sessions (the process domain) and in the context of earlier and later instances of the patient's personality and life situation (the outcome domain).

The patient's representations of therapy and therapist connect these contexts in several ways. First, the diagram depicts the patient's representation of therapy and the therapist as a joint product of actual in-session therapeutic interaction and of the patient's prior personality—in particular, of the patient's conscious and unconscious transference potentials. On one hand, the patient's representation reflects the real therapeutic relationship through the formation, by the patient, of a self-other schema in which the therapist is the significant other; on the other hand, the patient's representa-

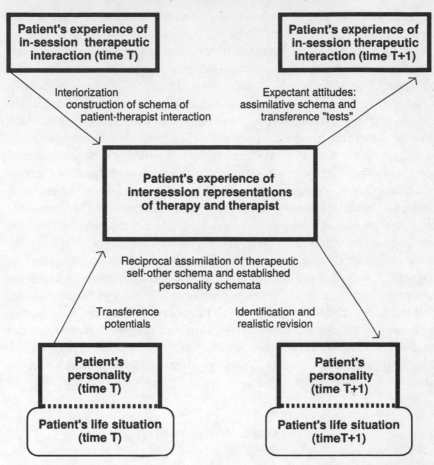

FIGURE 22.1
A functional analysis of patient representations.

tion of therapy and therapist also reflects a more or less distorting assimilation of perceptions to expectations rooted in previously formed emotionally significant schemas. The extent to which each influences the patient's representation no doubt varies from one individual to another—in terms of core conflicts, defense configurations, temperament variables, and personality style—and from one stage in therapy to another.

Second, the patient's representations of therapy and therapist comprise the psychological connective tissue between successive therapy sessions. By means of this link, patients are able to retain, rehearse, and accumulate the therapeutic impact of successive sessions. In this way, all that has gone before becomes the expectant context in which what happens in the next session is perceived and understood. The therapeutic alliance, for example, is probably best conceived as such a contextual phenomenon, built up bit by bit over time.

Third, the patient's representation of therapy and therapist connects the direct experience of in-session therapeutic process to the patient's subsequent personality and behavior in situations outside of therapy. Through this link, therapeutic process and outcome are joined; that is, the patient's representation of therapy and therapist functions as a conduit back into life situations for the insights and skills developed in treatment.

Fourth, the diagram is compatible with the further idea that patients' representations may have different functions at different stages of therapy. For example, the primary function of representations early in therapy with respect to treatment process is likely to be development of the therapeutic alliance over successive sessions; whereas, in relation to outcome variables, the primary function of representations early in therapy might be the reestablishment of morale in life situations (Frank 1974). Later in therapy, regarding process, representations of therapy and therapist probably serve as a primary vehicle for the transference "tests" (Weiss and Sampson 1986) that patients unconsciously arrange to occur during sessions. Also later in treatment, with regard to outcome variables, patients' representations might reflect a growing reflexive identification with the therapist's knowledge, attitude, and behavior, from which an autonomous self-analytic function might develop.

Research Instruments

These clinical and theoretical considerations define a conceptual framework in which patients' representations of their therapists and therapy constitute a meaningful focus for empirical research. The next question is how these representations ought to be studied. In our view, self and object representations reflect the activities of self-other schemas, insofar as those activities impinge on awareness. According to Freud ([1900] 1953, [1917a] 1957, [1925] 1961), whether such activities succeed in becoming conscious depends on dynamic and economic considerations. If highly cathected, the activated schemas may "force their way" into consciousness by attracting the mobile energy of attention; or, alternately, they may become activated as part of a sequence of free associations or a logical train of thought to which attention has been purposely directed. On the other hand, should an activated schema evoke anxiety, it is also likely to elicit a defensive reaction; and, if that reaction is sufficiently vigorous, the tendency to form a conscious representation may be effectively inhibited or otherwise distorted.

In our model, representations are essentially phenomena of consciousness. They may be direct or indirect, veridical or distorted reflections of dynamically activated schemas. Schemas may be activated without giving rise to representations, but if representations exist at all they exist in consciousness. Given this, a natural approach to their study would involve asking patients to report about what they consciously experience in regard to particular topics. Unless totally repressed, the patient's self$_{pt}$-other$_{th}$ schema should give rise to conscious representations on various occasions. Thus as a starting point it seems eminently reasonable to ask patients what they remember, think, fantasize, or dream about their therapists and therapy. How often? On what occasions? In what forms? With what feelings? And to what ends? Even these basic questions have yet to be asked in a systematic, quantitative fashion.

The two main ways of asking people questions about their experiences are the interview and the questionnaire, which are essentially parallel modes of inquiry. Both depend on language as a medium of communication, and both presuppose the linguistic competence of respondents. Open-ended or more highly structured questions may be formulated in both, according to whether one wants to know how respondents individually organize and express their experiences, or prefers instead to focus on a specific set of topics. The main difference between interviews and questionnaires is that interviews are conducted orally and in person, while questionnaires are presented and answered in writing (or, more recently, via interactive computer programs).

The strategy of studying the verbal productions of people to delineate their phenomenology—to infer what they experience from what they say—is a central and accepted part of the clinical method (Erikson 1958). Of course, no one knows better than the psychoanalytically informed researcher that there are limits to what can be learned by asking people to describe their experiences. There are some aspects of experience about which they will not tell, and some about which they cannot tell. The anonymity of the questionnaire helps to some extent overcome caution in self-disclosure, as does the rapport established by the interviewer.

To the psychoanalytically informed observer, people may say more than they intend or consciously "know" both in an interview and on a questionnaire. Early in the clinical studies that led to psychoanalysis, Freud likened consciousness to a "defile" or mountain gorge into which "only a single memory at a time can enter. . . . A patient who is occupied working through such a memory sees nothing of what is pushing after it and forgets what has already pushed its way through." Due to this, and to the effect of intermittent censorship, the whole "mass of psychogenic material is . . . drawn through a narrow cleft and thus arrives in consciousness cut up, as it were, into pieces or strips. It is the psychotherapist's business to put these together once more into the organization which he presumes to have existed" (Breuer and Freud [1895] 1955, p. 291). The psychoanalytic therapist does this in the interview by detecting and synthesizing recurrent themes or patterns in the patient's speech (Freud [1937] 1968). Using techniques such as cluster and factor analysis in an analogous fashion, the researcher discovers and interprets patterns in respondents' answers to questionnaires. Respondents to questionnaires, like patients in interviews, become conscious of their answers only one at a time, and cannot see how their answers fit into larger patterns of "psychogenic material." While such patterns are not necessarily dynamically unconscious or repressed, they go beyond what respondents can consciously formulate, and reveal something of the genuinely unconscious depths of the ego (Freud [1923] 1961). There is surface and depth, manifest content and latent content, in questionnaire as well as interview material.

In this section we shall describe two questionnaires developed to study the conscious and (in the sense defined above) the unconscious aspects of patients' representations of their therapists and therapy. The instruments differ in focus, and to some extent in their content. The first is the Therapist Representation Inventory, or TRI (Geller, Cooley, and Hartley 1981), which focuses on the patient's cumulative or aggregate image of the psychotherapist, rendered at a particular time. The emphasis is on the developmental complexity of the patient's representations, the sensory modalities evoked in forming them, and their functional value for the patient. The second is the Intersession Experience Questionnaire, or IEQ (Orlinsky and Tarragona 1986), which focuses on patients' experienced representations during the intervals between therapy sessions; it was designed specifically for repeated use over the course of treatment. Aside from examining the functional value of patient representations, the IEQ also emphasizes the states of mind in which they occur and the affective impact of their occurrence. These instruments are therefore complementary as well as partially overlapping and can be used jointly or separately according to the researcher's aims.

THERAPIST REPRESENTATION INVENTORY

The TRI is a set of self-administered measures designed to examine the contents, forms, and functions of patients' representations of their therapists and the therapeutic relationship.[9] In the TRI, current or former patients are asked to complete the following sequence of tasks: (1) to write a brief description of the therapist, in a form and words of their own devising; (2) to rate the relative contribution of words, pictures, sounds, bodily sensations, and other sense modalities to their conscious experiences of the therapist outside the therapeutic situation, as well as the

[9]Copies of the TRI may be obtained from J. D. Geller, Department of Psychology, Yale University, Box 11A Yale Station, New Haven, CT 06520.

frequency, vividness, and typical duration of these experiences and the circumstances in which they occur; (3) to rate the functional themes that characterize these representations; and (4) to rate the vividness and frequency of dreams in which the therapist appeared in the manifest content, to describe such a dream, and to indicate the point in therapy when the dream occurred.

Initial standardization of the TRI was based on data provided by 206 professional psychotherapists from the Yale University Department of Psychiatry, the Connecticut Society of Clinical Social Workers, and the Society for Psychotherapy Research who had experience as patients in psychoanalysis or psychotherapy. The sample consisted of 120 men and 86 women ranging in age from twenty-five to seventy-five years, and who had from one to forty-six years of clinical experience. Of these therapist/patients, 140 had terminated therapy and 66 were currently in treatment. A total of 128 reported being treated in psychoanalytically oriented therapy, with 46 in four to five times per week psychoanalysis. Although they hardly constitute a typical sample of patients, therapists were enlisted as subjects because of their presumed ability to access and describe representations of their therapists. Unless otherwise indicated, the psychometric properties ascribed to the TRI are those that emerged in the original study (Geller, Cooley, and Hartley 1981).

Levels of Cognitive Development. The first section of the TRI is designed to evaluate the thematic content and conceptual level of patients' representations of their therapists. At the top of an otherwise blank piece of paper, subjects are instructed as follows: "Please describe your (current/previous) therapist. Take no longer than five minutes to complete this task." This instructional set was adapted from a study by Blatt et al. (1979) in which individuals were asked to describe their parents, and it was chosen to elicit patients' representations of their therapists in the least structured way possible. The extraordinarily diverse descriptions by the subjects have been scored in two complementary ways: using Blatt et al.'s (1981) Conceptual Level of Object Representations Scale, based on Piaget's model, for rating overall developmental level; and using Hartley, Geller, and Behrends' (1986) Thematic Patterning Scale of Object Representation, which includes nine subscales focused on varied aspects of development.

The Conceptual Level of Object Representations Scale (CORS) is a 9-point rating scale with odd-numbered points defined as follows: (point 1) at the sensorimotor-preoperational level, therapists were described from a highly egocentric perspective that gave little sense of their having an independent existence, that is, primarily in terms of activity that gratified or frustrated the subject; (point 3) at the concrete-perceptual level, the description of therapists was literal, global, stereotypical, and/or concrete, so that it conveyed very little about them as unique individuals; (point 5) at the external-iconic level, therapists were described as separate beings in terms of observed activities and functions that were uniquely theirs; (point 7) at the internal-iconic level, therapists were, in addition, described in terms of internal attributes such as thoughts, feelings, values, and beliefs; (point 9) at the conceptual-representational level, therapists were described across a wide range of internal and external dimensions, with a sense of development over time and the resolution of apparent contradictions. The interrater reliability coefficients reported in the CORS manual are on the order of .85. Geller, Cooley, and Hartley (1981) found interrater reliability for the CORS with their own data to be .68 by Ebel's intraclass correlation and .71 by Finn's R. The median and modal score was 6, indicating a tendency of respondents to cluster around the internal-iconic level.

The nine subscales of the Thematic Patterning Scale of Object Representation (TPS) indicate the extent to which the subject's description: (1) embodies and physicalizes the therapist; (2) individualizes or conventionalizes the therapist; (3) acknowledges that the therapist gratifies and/or frustrates certain needs; (4) delineates internal attributes of the therapist; (5) conveys a sense of historicity or development over time; (6) constructively resolves apparent ambivalence; (7) differentiates self from other; (8) is complex; and (9) is structurally cohesive. Each dimension is rated on a 5-point scale, with definitions given at each of the five points.[10] Intraclass correlations for the nine scales were, respectively: .69, .68., .89, .77, .89, .83, .69, .83, and .91.

Comparable levels of interrater agreement regarding the nine scales have been reported by Barchat (1989), Honig (1989), Montgomery (1988), and Wzontek (1990). In Montgomery's and Honig's community-based samples, descriptions tended to fall between the concrete-perceptual and external-iconic levels; that is, they tended to focus on external attributes, conventional role characteristics, and the need-fulfilling functions of the therapist. On the basis of these studies, the TPS manual has been refined to include a representative sample of descriptions.

Formal Properties of Representations.

The concepts that guided construction of the TRI emphasized the fact that schemas must be given a particular form of representation in order to

[10]A manual for rating the emotional and conceptual maturity of self-descriptions has also recently been developed by Geller et al. (1990). It provides guidelines for scoring the extent to which a subject's self-description: (1) is complex; (2) acknowledges a discrepancy between public and private domains; (3) portrays the self in a positive light; (4) portrays the self in a negative light; (5) includes references to relations with others; (6) conveys a sense of loneliness or social isolation; (7) focuses on others as sources of frustration or gratification; (8) focuses on meeting the needs of others; (9) conveys a sense of self that is aspired to as "possible," or an ideal self against which the current sense of self is measured and criticized. Each dimension is rated on a 4-point scale, with each of the points defined.

become part of conscious experience. The items that comprise the second section of the TRI, the Therapist Embodiment Scale (TES), were written to provide information about the formal properties of patients' representations, as distinct from their particular thematic contents. This was accomplished by asking patients to describe the relative contribution of enactive, imagistic, and lexical modalities (Bruner 1964; Horowitz 1978) to conscious representations of their therapists, and then to rate the typical duration, frequency, intensity, and level of detail of these experiences.

Enactive representations correspond to patterns of muscular activation that move overtly or implicitly through and within the body. They find expression in facial expressions, the assumption of body attitudes (postures and gestures), the anticipatory tensing of various muscle groups, and the performance of motor skills. Freud ([1905] 1960, pp. 189–194) and others (e.g., Rorschach 1951) have recognized the role of kinesthetic "fantasies" or "ideational mimetics" in cognition, especially social cognition and empathy. Through enactive representations, the individual is able to sense what it would feel like to be in a certain position, take a given stance, or engage in a certain activity vis-à-vis an absent other, or to be in the role and position of another person. Enactive representations enter awareness in the form of lived bodily experience, as distinguished from images and thoughts that are experientially localized in one's head.

Imagistic representations typically involve sensory qualities of varying degrees of vividness. When consciously experienced, they can evoke concrete qualities of sound, sight, texture, temperature, taste, or odor. In the therapeutic context, patients who can "see a picture" of the therapist in their "mind's eye," or who can "hear" their therapists' "voices," are able to "evoke" the presence of their therapist when needed, to access affects associated with the perceived reality of the therapist and to hold imaginary conversations or have other forms of interaction with the therapist.

Lexical representations involve abstract ideas or concepts comprised by the semantic and syntactic patterns of natural (or other symbolic) languages. Lexical-conceptual representations make possible a variety of complex mental activities such as reasoning, generalizing, and decision making. By these means, patients can do more than hold imaginary dialogues with their therapists: they can apply the understanding they have acquired in therapy in their adaptive efforts by reasoning more soundly in difficult life situations outside of therapy.

Statistical analyses suggest that the Therapist Embodiment Scale can be scored as an overall index of representational vividness or in terms of its three factorial components. Item analysis indicated significant part-whole correlations for all twelve TES items. Principal components factor analysis with varimax rotation suggested that patients' formal representations varied along three dimensions. The first was defined primarily by visual images of the therapist in his or her office and may be called *visualization* (items include "My therapist is wearing a particular type of clothing" and "I imagine my therapist sitting in his/her office"). The second dimension involved a blend of imagery derived from more immediate kinesthetic, proprioceptive, and tactile senses and could be construed as reflecting a dimension of *proximal embodiment* (items include "I experience in myself certain characteristic bodily sensations" and "I am aware of a particular emotional atmosphere which gives me the sense that my therapist is with me"). The third factor did not emerge with as much salience, but included mainly auditory and lexical representations of real and imagined conversations with the therapist, and was tentatively identified as *conversational-conceptual representation* (items included "I imagine a particular quality to the sound of my therapist's voice" and "I think of my therapist as making specific statements to me"). Internal consistency coefficients for the three scales derived from these were .72, .69, and .49, respectively.[11]

Thematic Contents of Representations.

The third section of the Therapist Representation Inventory is the Therapist Involvement Scale (TIS), consisting of 38 items which rate the extent to which the therapeutic relationship is an active focus of consciously experienced thoughts, feelings, wishes, and fantasies. Item analyses indicated that a total score can be derived for the TIS, providing an overall index of how actively involved or preoccupied patients are with mental representations of their therapists. Factor analysis indicated that the TIS can also be used to assess the relative predominance of six distinguishable dimensions of patient interaction with mental representations of their therapists. These were called: (1) *sexual and aggressive involvement* ("I imagine having sex with my therapist" and "I imagine hurting my therapist in some way");[12] (2) *wish for reciprocity* ("I imagine our talking to each other outside of the therapy office" and "I imagine our sharing a meal"); (3) *continuing the therapeutic dialogue* ("When I am faced with a difficult situation

---

[11]The TES is one of several similar instruments constructed to assess the retrieval strategies used selectively by subjects to reconstruct and make contact with individuals who are not immediately present to their senses. A Supervisor Embodiment Scale (Geller and Schaffer 1988), a Parent Embodiment Scale (Geller, Smirnoff, and Bonanno 1988), and a Patient Embodiment Scale (Lehman 1990) have all yielded factor structures that replicate the findings based on the TES. Administration of the Parent Embodiment Scale and the TES to patients indicate that individuals, with varying degrees of skill, can identify and label the ways in which they rely in varying proportions on words, pictures, sounds, tastes, and bodily sensations to bring to awareness pleasurable and painful experiences involving absent others.

[12]Readers who are surprised by the explicitness of these items should recall that the original sample of patients studied by Geller, Cooley, and Hartley (1981) was comprised of experienced professional psychotherapists.

I sometimes ask myself, 'What would my therapist want me to do?' "); (4) *failure of benign internalization* ("In stressful situations, I don't seem able to use what I previously learned in therapy" and "I wish I had a different therapist"); (5) *effort to create a stable representation of the therapist* ("I rehearse what I will say to my therapist when we meet again" and "I daydream about my therapist"); and (6) *desiring contact (mourning)* ("I think about contacting my therapist" and "I miss my therapist"). Using more stringent criteria for item inclusion within a factor than were used in the original study, Farber and Geller (1988) found internal consistency coefficients for the six TIS factors to be, respectively, .86, .84, .81, .70, .67, and .76.

Alternative States of Consciousness.

In order to examine the consistency of patients' representations between waking and sleeping states, patients were asked in the fourth section of the TRI to rate the vividness and frequency of dreams in which their therapist appeared, and to report such a dream. About a third of the subjects in the original study reported a dream manifestly involving their therapists. Among patients in psychoanalysis, dreams portraying the therapist undisguised comprise as much as 10 percent of all dreams reported (Harris 1962; Rosenbaum 1965). Our evolving system of analysis currently includes ratings of the presence or absence of sexual, aggressive, and friendly interactions; ratings of the general mood of the dream (from "very unpleasant" to "very pleasant"), the therapist's behavior in the dream (from "very frustrating" to "very gratifying"), and the therapist's basic attitude toward the patient in the dream (from "malevolent" to "benevolent"), as well as ratings of the salient themes reflected in the dream. Sexual, aggressive, and friendly interactions were rated by the criteria of Hall and Van de Castle (1966). Alpha coefficients for these were .90, .72, and .70, respectively; interrater reliability coefficients for mood, therapist behavior, and therapist attitude were .89, .86, and .84, respectively.

The modal manifest dream was negative in mood and depicted a therapist who tended to be neutral or ambivalent, but seemed malevolent as often as benevolent and frustrating as often as gratifying. Four distinctive clusters of themes tended to be present in the dream narratives: separation/rejection, seduction/antagonism, protectiveness/responsiveness, and praise. Thus, whereas therapists in waking consciousness were represented primarily in terms of their supportive or gratifying functions, subjects' dreams tended to show them in a rather different light. A plausible interpretation of these findings is that under the regressive conditions of sleep, patients' representations of their therapists may be more readily influenced by the conflictual, typically infantile self-other schemas that constitute the dynamic unconscious.[13]

INTERSESSION EXPERIENCE QUESTIONNAIRE

The Intersession Experience Questionnaire (IEQ) is a 42-item structured response instrument that takes patients about five to ten minutes to complete.[14] Response alternatives for the items are "none," "some," and "a lot," and refer to the time "since your last session." The questions comprising the IEQ concern the frequency and incidence of experienced representations (four items); the psychological circumstances in which representations occurred (six items); the contexts and contents of the representations (eleven items, of which seven were adapted from the TRI Therapist Involvement Scale); the feelings evoked by the representations (seventeen items); and whether therapy or the therapist were talked about with others (four items).

The basic psychometric analyses were carried out on a sample of 279 male and female adult outpatients who were in individual, psychoanalytically oriented psychotherapy at Northwestern University's Institute of Psychiatry in Chicago. Two-thirds of this sample were women; four-fifths were between twenty and thirty-nine years old; approximately half were single, one-fourth married and one-fourth separated or divorced. Almost all patients in this sample were white; three-fifths had collegiate education, and one-third had graduate-level training. The therapists of these patients were advanced trainees, mainly psychology and psychiatry residents, with a substantial amount of prior experience (74 percent of the therapists had already seen at least twenty patients in individual psychotherapy). There were approximately equal numbers of male and female therapists, almost all of whom were between twenty and thirty-nine years of age. About one-half were married; four-fifths had or were having personal therapy or psychoanalysis. A special feature of this sample was that all the data were collected in the second through sixth sessions of treatment.[15]

[13]Also included in the TRI was a final section designed to assess the patient's sense of therapeutic change. Using a 9-point rating scale ranging from "worse" to "marked improvement," subjects were asked to rate the extent to which they feel therapy has made a difference for them in each of the following areas: subjective distress, interpersonal relations, self-esteem, work performance, and work satisfaction.

[14]Copies of the IEQ may be obtained from D. Orlinsky, Committee on Human Development, University of Chicago, Chicago, IL 60637.

[15]This selection reflects the constraints of institutional procedures at the time. No claim is made that these early sessions are representative of patients' representations at other points in treatment. However, it should be noted that, despite the psychoanalytic orientation of the clinic and its official commitment to the provision of long-term treatment, the median length of therapy was about thirteen sessions, and 24 percent of the patients who began treatment attended less than five sessions (as observed in a panel of 405 patients analyzed

Patterns of Intersession Experiences.

To determine the dimensionality of intersession experience, principal components factor analyses with varimax rotations were performed separately for each of the five sessions. Although the number of IEQs available varied from session to session, the same four dimensions of intersession experience could be identified in each of the analyses.

The most salient dimension was *recreating the therapeutic conversation,* defined by the tendency to think about therapy and therapist before and after sessions, between sessions overall, and on the day of taking the questionnaire. This dimension was particularly salient when patients were feeling distressed, and tended to take the form of an imagined conversation with the therapist. (This resembles the TIS dimension called *continuing the therapeutic dialogue.*)

The next most salient dimension was *evoking relief and remoralization,* defined primarily by positive feeling items checked by patients in response to a question concerning how they felt when thinking about their therapy or therapist. These feelings were interpreted as a reflection of morale heightened through the support of being in a "holding environment" (Winnicott 1965). Patients high on this dimension were able to experience an emotional uplift between sessions by evoking representations of their therapy.

The third factor was *evoking anxiety and frustration,* defined by negative feelings reported when patients were asked how thinking about therapy or the therapist made them feel. It is not clear whether patients' feelings were made worse by these thoughts, or if they were just remembering painful and disorganizing experiences with the therapist. In either case, patients high on this dimension clearly did not find thinking about their therapy and therapist between sessions an uplifting experience.

The dimension whose items were least frequently endorsed was *preconscious/unconscious processing of therapeutic experience,* defined by the tendency to daydream, fantasize, or actually remember having a dream about therapy or the therapist.

Analyses indicated highly satisfactory internal consistency for the first three dimensions from the very start of therapy (Cronbach's alpha = .78 to .92) and for the last dimension as early as the fifth or sixth session (.67 to .74). Correlations among factor scores for successive sessions at this point in treatment also indicated a fairly high level of stability (r = .57 to .81).

---

by Howard et al. 1989). Moreover, the median length of outpatient psychotherapy in general has been reported to be four or five sessions, and the mean to be between six and eight sessions (e.g., Phillips 1991).

To examine the overall patterning of intersession experience, factor scores were computed, and these were intercorrelated along with some additional items of clinical interest.[16] Two clusters emerged reflecting distinct patterns of intersession therapeutic experience.

The first was called *supportive-guiding representations,* and was defined by *recreating the therapeutic conversation* and *evoking relief and remoralization,* in association with items reflecting the patient's effort to evoke intersession experiences in problem-solving contexts. The second cluster was organized by *recreating the therapeutic conversation,* in association with *evoking anxiety and frustration* and *preconscious/unconscious processing of therapeutic experience.* This pattern was interpreted as reflecting patients' experiences of *conflict-containing representations*—"conflict-containing" in the descriptive sense of manifesting conflictual feelings about therapy and therapist, and also in the psychodynamic sense of struggling to limit and manage their emotional impact.

Replicability of Findings.

The generality of these findings has been checked through the study of a second sample of seventy patients at the Chicago Center for Family Studies, twenty-seven of whom were in individual therapy, twenty-five in couple therapy and eighteen in family therapy.[17] The Center for Family Studies, like the Institute of Psychiatry, is a unit of Northwestern University, also located at the medical campus in downtown Chicago. Demographically the two samples were similar, except that a higher proportion of the family therapy cases at the center were black or hispanic, and on average had briefer treatments. Other differences at the Center for Family Studies were: (1) treatment followed an "integrative problem-centered" approach, although most of the therapists had some psychodynamic background; (2) most of the patients were studied at later points in their treatment; (3) a slightly revised version of the IEQ was used; and (4) the sample was smaller, necessitating a different strategy in carrying out factor analyses. IEQs from patients in individual, couple, and family therapy were aggregated; then each section of the IEQ was factor analyzed separately, the factors were scored for salient items with unit weight, and the scores were intercorrelated and factor analyzed to obtain an overall structure.

[16]Only items that loaded significantly and uniquely on a factor were used in scores. Items that loaded significantly on more than one factor, or that failed to load significantly on any, were treated as separate scales in subsequent analyses.
[17]The data from these two samples were collected and analyzed in collaboration with Margarita Tarragona. We gratefully acknowledge the help provided by K. I. Howard, L. Bankoff, and B. Briscoe at the Institute of Psychiatry, and M. Lundy, W. Pinsof, and J. Lebow at the Center for Family Studies.

Despite the differences in samples and procedures, the results compared favorably with findings from the Institute of Psychiatry. The dimensions of *recreating the therapeutic conversation* and *evoking relief and remoralization* were clearly identified in both. The third and fourth factors were somewhat differently organized, but the two overall patterns of *supportive-guiding representation* and *conflict-containing representation* emerged in both samples. It remains to be seen how many of the specific differences in detail may prove to be attributable to differences in treatment modality, patient and therapist samples, time in treatment when intersession experiences were sampled, and so forth.

Thus far it seems plausible to suppose that there are two main types of intersession representation, each internally differentiated but corresponding to a major psychological function. In one, patients use the representation of therapy and therapist as a source of internally evoked emotional sustenance and orientation in coping with problems. In the other, patients use intersession representations as a means of managing and attempting to master conflictual feelings that are exposed in, or evoked by, therapy.

Forms and Functions of Patients' Representations: Some Initial Findings

The TRI and the IEQ are relatively new and as yet have been used in just a few studies. Nevertheless, accumulating results indicate that both instruments are capable of providing reliable and valid data regarding patients' representations of their therapists. These initial results begin to reveal the nature of therapist representations, their relation to patient characteristics, and their functions in relation to therapeutic process and outcome.

FREQUENCY AND OCCURRENCE OF THERAPIST REPRESENTATIONS

The most striking fact about patients' intersession representations is the sheer frequency of their occurrence. Over 90 percent of the patients given IEQs at the two clinics reported thinking about their therapists and therapy between sessions (Orlinsky and Tarragona 1989; Tarragona and Orlinsky 1987). The experience was very common both for those just starting therapy and for those further along in the process. Understandably, therapist representations were reported to occur most intensely just before sessions when patients were thinking about what they would say, and just after sessions, when they were remembering what had happened. Nevertheless, 25 percent of the patients said they thought "a lot" about their therapy and therapists at other times as well.

The fact that therapist representations also persist for considerable periods after the termination of treatment has been well documented by Geller, Cooley, and Hartley (1981) and by Wzontek (1990). Using a modified version of the IEQ to survey former patients between three and eighteen months after termination, Epstein (1989) found that about one-fourth of them said they thought about therapy at least once or twice a week, and as many as three-fifths thought about therapy once or twice a month. The tendency to experience representations of therapy was greatest soon after termination and diminished with the passage of time, but continued most strongly for those who had longer therapy and more positive relationships with their therapists.

In accord with these results, Farber and Geller (1988) found that current patients experienced the felt presence of their therapists between sessions significantly more often than former patients did in the post-treatment environment. However, no significant differences were found between these groups in duration or vividness of their representations. On average, these representations tended to last between thirty and sixty seconds and were reported to be "vivid." The correlation between number of years since termination and frequency of experiencing representations was statistically significant ($r = -.32$, $p < .001$), but the correlations of time since termination with the duration and vividness of representations were not.

FORMAL PROPERTIES OF THERAPIST REPRESENTATIONS

Auditory and visual imagery were the most characteristic forms of therapist representation in the original TRI study by Geller, Cooley, and Hartley (1981). According to frequencies of item endorsement on the Therapist Embodiment Scale, the most salient of these items were: "I imagine a particular quality to the sound of my therapist's voice," "I imagine my therapist sitting in his/her office," and "I think of my therapist as making specific statements to me." However, all the modes of representation studied were used to some extent, and there appeared to be wide stylistic variations in the forms of representation individuals used to evoke the experiences of listening, talking, and being with their therapists.

These stylistic variations were also detected by Barchat (1989) as part of the "August phenomenon," during the prolonged separation imposed by therapists' summer vacations. The subjects in her study were seventy-four graduate students in clinical psychology, in therapy from five to about 1,400 sessions. Those patients who felt more sadness in the therapist's absence were also more likely to experience representations in terms of proximal (kinesthetic, proprioceptive, and tactile) imagery. By contrast, a significant negative correlation was obtained between the salience of angry feelings toward the therapist and scores on the first (visualization) factor of the TES. Evidently the patients who experienced more intense resentment at their absence tended to be those who visualized their absent therapists less vividly, while those who visualized their therapists more vividly felt less resentment. Geller, Cooley, and Hartley (1981) also found that patients still in treatment who visualized therapist representations more vividly tended to feel more satisfied with their therapists, and to believe that they were being helped; while among patients who had terminated, ratings of self-perceived improvement were more strongly associated with access to proximal kinesthetic, proprioceptive, and tactile representations.

The meaning of these diverse findings involving specific formal modes of representation requires further clarification. However, it should be noted that patients who produced more vivid therapist representations tended to be more actively and intensely involved with those representations, as evidenced by consistent findings of a significant positive correlation between TES and TIS scales (Geller, Cooley, and Hartley 1981). Also, using Patient Embodiment and Patient Involvement scales modeled on the TRI, Lehman (1990) found that experienced therapists tended to construct multimodal, sensorially rich, and detailed representations of their clinical cases, while the case representations of inexperienced therapists tended to be relatively impoverished sensorially and dominated mainly by the verbal content of therapeutic dialogue. If we liken the formal modes of representation to psychological tools, it would seem that those participants in therapy who are more highly involved or more experienced make more and better use of the tools at their disposal. Just as physical tools can be used toward various material ends, perhaps the formal modes of representation can also serve diverse psychological functions.

FUNCTIONAL ASPECTS OF THERAPIST REPRESENTATIONS

Of the two functional types of representation revealed by the IEQ, *supportive-guiding representations* were most frequently evoked (> 75 percent) by patients at the beginning (Orlinsky and Tarragona 1989) and also further along in treatment (Tarragona 1989). Patients found themselves experiencing *supportive-guiding representations* most often when they were feeling distressed and when they were trying to think of how to deal with their problems. Doing so typically supported their morale by making them feel hopeful, determined, and accepted. (Yet patients often reported thinking of therapy and their therapists when they felt pleased about something, as if wanting to share the good times, too.)

Using the TRI, Geller, Cooley, and Hartley (1981) had also found that patients experienced therapist representations most vividly, and evoked them most often, under conditions of needfulness. Fifty-three percent of the patients still in treatment reported that they called on the image of their therapists in order to mitigate painful feelings such as sadness, anxiety, depression, and guilt (although only 28 percent of the patients who had already terminated did so). In addition, approximately 15 percent of current and former patients reported that they brought their therapist to awareness when experiencing a need for relatedness—e.g., when feeling lonely or alienated, or when dealing with a sense of loss. Convergent results were obtained in a study of the periods during therapists' vacations (Barchat 1989). Those patients who felt saddest experienced therapist representations most frequently and sustained the experiences for longer periods of time.

Besides support for morale at times of emotional distress, frequencies of item endorsement on the Therapist Involvement Scale showed that the most characteristic functions served by therapist representations were patients' desires to identify with the therapist and to gain the therapist's approval. The statements that patients endorsed as most characteristic were: "I would like my therapist to be proud of me," "I try to solve my problems in the way my therapist and I worked on them in psychotherapy," and "In a sense, I feel as though my therapist has become a part of me."

A parallel phenomenon was found by Geller and Schaffer (1988) in a study of the representations that therapists in training form of their supervisors and supervisory relationships. As with patients' representations of therapy, trainees' representations of supervision can be ordered quantitatively with respect to their frequency of evocation, duration, mode of entry into awareness, and complexity, as well as with regard to the psychological functions that they serve. In accord with the findings concerning patients' representations, therapists in training were most likely to evoke representations of their supervisors when attempting to regulate and cope with painful feelings evoked during therapy sessions, and when desiring confirmation of their therapeutic competence.

The use of therapist-representations as an aid in problem solving was characteristic both of patients just beginning treatment and of those who had already terminated. Two of the most frequent intersession experiences reported by the former were thinking about therapy and the therapist "When I was thinking about ways in which I could deal with a problem" (87 percent), and "Trying to solve my problems in the way my therapist and I had worked on them in therapy" (61 percent). The second statement was also found to be most salient in a sample of sixty former patients who had been in individual therapy for at least six months (Wzontek 1990). The extent of this "after work" was positively correlated with the patients' perceptions of their improvement.

THERAPIST REPRESENTATIONS AND THERAPEUTIC PROCESS

Clinically, it seems reasonable to suppose that patients' representations are related to their experiences during sessions with their therapists.

This hypothesis is supported by strong correlations (> .50) that have been found between measures of intersession representations and patients' descriptions of their in-session experiences on the Therapy Session Report questionnaire (Orlinsky and Tarragona 1989; Tarragona and Orlinsky 1988).[18] For example, the pattern of *supportive-guiding representations* was most likely to occur among patients who, during sessions, felt relief, acceptance, and determination; who gained encouragement and insight; who sensed that they were making progress; and who saw their therapists as feeling effective, expansive, and intimate. Patients' perceptions of a strong therapeutic alliance were also associated with this pattern (Orlinsky and Tarragona 1988; Tarragona 1989). Similarly strong correlations showed that the pattern of *conflict-containing representations* was most likely to occur among patients who, during their sessions, felt angry, depressed, inhibited, anxious, and confused; who saw their therapists as feeling uncertain and frustrated; and who sensed that they were deteriorating rather than improving (Orlinsky and Tarragona 1989).

Consistent with Tarragona's findings, Geller and Schaffer (1988) found that supervisors who were perceived by trainees as sincerely involved, competent, and actively participating in the establishment of a positive supervisory alliance were more likely to be brought to awareness as a means of dealing with the ambiguities and anxiety of doing therapy.

Attribution of causal influence at this stage of research, and on the basis of correlational findings, can be no more than conjecture. However, with this caveat in mind, we would conjecture that causal influence may well flow in both directions. The theoretical model depicted in figure 22.1 suggests that there may be potentially benign and vicious cycles of influence. In the benign cycle, interactions with the therapist during sessions which provide relief from emotional distress, and which enhance the patient's sense of mastery, constitute significant stimuli for the formation of a positively cathected $self_{pt}$-$other_{th}$ schema; and, in turn, the patient's resulting positive representations of therapist and therapy increase the patient's trust in the therapist and openness to influence in subsequent sessions. Conversely, in the vicious cycle, interactions with the therapist during sessions which involve disruptive emotional stress, and which undermine the patient's sense of mastery, constitute significant stimuli for the formation of a negatively cathected $self_{pt}$-$other_{th}$ schema; and reciprocally, the ensuing negative representations of the therapist and therapy increase the patient's sense of vulnerability and defensiveness in subsequent sessions. A qualitative mix of in-session experiences would give rise to a variably ambivalent schema, which in turn would

---

[18]Basic information about the Therapy Session Report questionnaires can be found in Orlinsky and Howard (1975, 1986a).

generate more complex and uncertain representations of the therapist and therapy.

Undoubtedly this model is oversimplified and requires the usual stipulation that "other things must be equal." One of the other things that most probably exerts a moderating effect on these cycles is the state of the therapeutic alliance. In the presence of a well-established positive alliance, for example, patients may be able to tolerate distressing emotional and regressive experiences during sessions without necessarily compromising the quality of their self$_{pt}$-other$_{th}$ schemas. Another factor that is likely to have an effect on these cycles is the type and severity of psychopathological disturbance; for instance, patients with narcissistic or borderline disorders may have positive experiences with their therapists during sessions without being able to form a reliably positive self$_{pt}$-other$_{th}$ schema. The activation of conflictual unconscious transference probably is another variable in the equation, and the skill with which the therapist manages the course of the treatment is yet another. Eventually, an empirically grounded model including the most important of these elements will certainly appear more complex and less linear than the diagram presented in figure 22.1. Figure 22.1 may give a fair approximation of only the beginning phase of therapy.

In fact, evidence suggests that typical changes in therapist representations occur over the course of treatment. Montgomery (1988) compared the developmental ratings of conceptual level for therapist representations of thirty-five patients after five weeks and after five months of treatment, and found consistently lower scores at the latter time, indicating that therapist-representations became less differentiated and less coherently organized as patients entered the middle phase of therapy. This could well reflect a process of therapeutic regression associated with the activation of core conflictual transference themes (Luborsky and Crits-Christoph 1990)—a psychodynamic hypothesis that remains to be tested by future research.

THERAPIST REPRESENTATIONS AND PATIENT CHARACTERISTICS

Preliminary findings indicate that therapist representations are influenced by certain patient characteristics. One study compared ratings of conceptual development for patients' therapist-representations on the TRI with their descriptions of their mothers and found a high correlation between the two (Honig 1989). Comparison of conceptual level with thematic pattern profiles also indicated that therapist representations were more clearly differentiated from mother representations by conceptually maturer patients.

Other patient characteristics also have been found to be correlated with types of intersession representations (Tarragona 1989). A particularly suggestive finding was that, for the one-fifth of the patients whose fathers had died, *supportive-guiding representations* were more often experienced by those who were younger at the time of their loss. A stronger disposition toward dependency among such patients might increase their readiness to form early positive transferences in treatment.

Tarragona (1989) also found that female patients in this sample were more likely than males to experience *supportive-guiding representations* and *conflict-containing representations,* indicating a more intense affective involvement or a greater propensity for internalization. Farber and Geller (1989) also found that gender pairing was related to dimensions of the TIS for patients still in treatment: female patients with male therapists experienced significantly higher scores than patients in other gender pairings on *wishing for reciprocity, desiring contact (mourning)* and *continuing the therapeutic dialogue.* However, neither patient gender nor gender pairing seemed to influence the modes of embodiment in which representations entered awareness, or the measured aspects of dreams about the therapist. These findings suggest a complex and selective relation between gender and representational processes.

THERAPIST REPRESENTATIONS AND THERAPEUTIC OUTCOME

Initial findings also imply that therapist-representations may play a significant role in relation to therapeutic outcome. At the level of micro-outcomes, for example, patients' sense of week-to-week improvement in functioning and their estimates of cumulative benefit from therapy were strongly correlated (> .50) with the concurrent intersession experience of *supportive-guiding representations* (Tarragona 1989). At a broader level, patients' self-perceived benefit was found to correlate significantly with *continuing the therapeutic dialogue,* as measured on the TIS (Geller, Cooley, and Hartley 1981).

In the period immediately following termination, a modified IEQ showed that evocation of positive feelings through therapist representations and recall of problem-solving aspects of therapy were strongly correlated with self-assessed benefit from treatment (Epstein 1989). Similarly, in another study, more than half the former patients who had terminated treatment between six months and five years earlier indicated that they continued to build on what they had accomplished in therapy (Wzontek 1990). Findings such as these suggest that the study of therapist representations may offer valuable insights into the psychological processes by which therapy becomes effective in patients' lives.

Questions for Future Research on Patients' Representations

Clearly, the work that has been done so far leaves many more questions than answers and does more to excite than to appease curiosity. Accordingly, we conclude with a list of research questions about patients' representations, and we invite readers and colleagues to join in the search for answers.[19]

1. Which aspects of therapy are most readily retained and reexperienced by patients, at various stages during therapy and at varying durations after termination?
2. What are the main types of representational experience at the intersession and at aggregate levels of analysis? How are they related to one another, and what are their distinctive functions?
3. How do sensory modalities enter into the construction of patients' representations? Do representations evoked in various sense modalities have differential determinants and different functions in therapy?
4. How much do patients' representations differ across treatment modalities and theoretical orientations?
5. How are patients' representational experiences influenced by aspects of therapeutic process—for example, by the state of the alliance, the frequency and types of interventions, the goals of treatment?
6. Do types and functions of representational experience vary with such patient characteristics as demographic group (age, gender, social class) or diagnostic group (neurotic, character-disordered, and borderline)?
7. Do types of patients' representational experiences vary with therapist characteristics or with specific patterns of patient-therapist pairing?
8. How do intersession representations and aggregate representations develop over the course of treatment?
9. What role do patients' intersession and aggregate representations have in determining the quality of therapeutic outcomes?
10. How do the characteristics of patients' representations of their therapy and therapist after termination affect the stability of therapeutic outcomes over time?

[19]Our emphasis on patients' representations ought not to deflect attention from the equally interesting possibilities that should emerge from the study of therapists' representations of their patients. Beginnings in this direction have been made by Lundy and Orlinsky (1987) and by Geller and Schaffer (1988). Two examples of the questions that might then be considered are: How does the therapist's representation of his or her patient relate to the patient's representations of the therapist? How does the therapist's representation of the patient relate to the process, course, and clinical outcome of therapy?

References

ANGYAL, A. (1941). *Foundations for a science of personality.* New York: The Commonwealth Fund.

ATWOOD, G., & STOLOROW, R. (1980). Psychoanalytic concepts and the representational world. *Psychoanalysis and Contemporary Thought, 3,* 267–290.

BANNISTER, D. (1975). Personal construct theory psychotherapy. In D. Bannister (Ed.), *Issues and approaches in the psychological therapies* (pp. 121–146). New York: Wiley.

BARCHAT, D. (1989, JUNE). *Representations and separations in therapy: The August phenomenon.* Paper presented to the annual meeting of the Society for Psychotherapy Research, Toronto.

BEHRENDS, R. S., & BLATT, S. J. (1985). Internalization and psychological development throughout the life cycle. *Psychoanalytic Study of the Child, 40,* 11–39.

BENEDICT, R. (1938). Continuities and discontinuities in cultural conditioning. *Psychiatry, 1,* 161–167.

BENJAMIN, L. S. (1974). Structural analysis of social behavior. *Psychological Review, 81,* 392–425.

BERGER, P., & LUCKMANN, T. (1966). *The social construction of reality.* New York: Doubleday.

BETTELHEIM, B. (1983). *Freud and man's soul.* New York: Knopf.

BLATT, S. J., CHEVRON, E., QUINLAN, D., & WEIN, S. (1981). *The assessment of qualitative and structural dimensions of object representations.* Department of Psychiatry, Yale University, New Haven, CT.

BLATT, S. J., WEIN, S., CHEVRON, E., & QUINLAN, D. (1979). Parental representations and depression in normal young adults. *Journal of Abnormal Psychology, 88,* 388–397.

BORDIN, E. S. (1979). The generalizability of the psychoanalytic concept of the working alliance. *Psychotherapy: Theory, Research, and Practice, 16,* 252–260.

BOWLBY, J. (1969). *Attachment and loss* (Vol. 1): *Attachment.* New York: Basic Books.

BOWLBY, J. (1980). *Attachment and loss* (Vol. 2): *Separation.* New York: Basic Books.

BREUER, J., & FREUD, S. (1895/1955). Studies on hysteria. In J. Strachey (Ed.), *The standard edition of the complete psychological works of Sigmund Freud* (Vol. 2). London: Hogarth Press.

BRUNER, J. S. (1964). The course of cognitive growth. *American Psychologist, 19,* 1–15.

CAMERON, N. (1961). Introjection, reprojection, and hallucination in the interaction between schizophrenic patient and therapist. *International Journal of Psycho-Analysis, 42,* 86–96.

DERBY, K. (1989). *Levels of internal therapist representations among heroin and cocaine addicts.* Doctoral dissertation, Department of Clinical Psychology, Teachers College, Columbia University.

DORPAT, T. L. (1974). Internalization of the patient-analyst relationship in patients with narcissistic disorders. *International Journal of Psycho-Analysis, 55,* 183–188.

DORPAT, T. L. (1979). Introjection and the idealizing transference. *International Journal of Psychoanalytic Psychotherapy, 7,* 26–51.

EPSTEIN, M. (1989). *Mental representations of the psychotherapeutic relationship during the post-termination period.* Doctoral dissertation, School of Social Service Administration, University of Chicago.

ERIKSON, E. H. (1958). On the nature of clinical evidence. In D. Lerner (Ed.), *Evidence and inference.* Cambridge, MA: M.I.T. Press.

ERIKSON, E. H. (1963). *Childhood and society* (2nd ed.). New York: Norton.

FAIRBAIRN, W. D. (1952). *An object-relations theory of the personality.* New York: Basic Books.

FARBER, B. A., & GELLER, J. D. (1988, JUNE). *Factors influencing the process of internalization during psychotherapy.* Paper presented to the annual meeting of the Society for Psychotherapy Research, Santa Fe, NM.

FARBER, B. A., & GELLER, J. D. (1989). *The relationship of therapist-patient gender pairings to representation and outcome in psychotherapy.* Paper presented to the annual meeting of the Society for Psychotherapy Research, Toronto.

FRANK, J. D. (1974). Psychotherapy: The restoration of morale. *American Journal of Psychiatry, 131,* 271–274.

FREUD, A. (1967). *The ego and the mechanisms of defense* (rev. ed.). New York: International Universities Press.

FREUD, S. (1900/1953). The interpretation of dreams. In J. Strachey (Ed.), *The standard edition of the complete psychological works of Sigmund Freud* (Vol. 5). London: Hogarth Press.

FREUD, S. (1903/1953). Three essays on the theory of sexuality. In J. Strachey (Ed.), *The standard edition of the complete psychological works of Sigmund Freud* (Vol. 7). London: Hogarth Press.

FREUD, S. (1905/1960). Jokes and their relation to the unconscious. In J. Strachey (Ed.), *The standard edition of the complete psychological works of Sigmund Freud* (Vol. 8). London: Hogarth Press.

FREUD, S. (1911/1958). Formulations on the two principles in mental functioning. In J. Strachey (Ed.), *The standard edition of the complete psychological works of Sigmund Freud* (Vol. 12). London: Hogarth Press.

FREUD, S. (1912/1958). The dynamics of the transference. In J. Strachey (Ed.), *The standard edition of the complete psychological works of Sigmund Freud* (Vol. 12). London: Hogarth Press.

FREUD, S. (1913/1958). On beginning the treatment (Further recommendations on the technique of psycho-analysis). In J. Strachey (Ed.), *The standard edition of the complete psychological works of Sigmund Freud* (Vol. 12). London: Hogarth Press.

FREUD, S. (1915/1957). Instincts and their vicissitudes. In J. Strachey (Ed.), *The standard edition of the complete psychological works of Sigmund Freud* (Vol. 14). London: Hogarth Press.

FREUD, S. (1917a/1957). A metapsychological supplement to the theory of dreams. In J. Strachey (Ed.), *The standard edition of the complete psychological works of Sigmund Freud* (Vol. 14). London: Hogarth Press.

FREUD, S. (1917b/1957). Mourning and melancholia. In J. Strachey (Ed.), *The standard edition of the complete psychological works of Sigmund Freud* (Vol. 14). London: Hogarth Press.

FREUD, S. (1920/1955). Beyond the pleasure principle. In J. Strachey (Ed.), *The standard edition of the complete psychological works of Sigmund Freud* (Vol. 18). London: Hogarth Press.

FREUD, S. (1921/1955). Group psychology and the analysis of the ego. In J. Strachey (Ed.), *The standard edition of the complete psychological works of Sigmund Freud* (Vol. 18). London: Hogarth Press.

FREUD, S. (1923/1961). The ego and the id. In J. Strachey (Ed.), *The standard edition of the complete psychological works of Sigmund Freud* (Vol. 19). London: Hogarth Press.

FREUD, S. (1925/1961). A note upon the "Mystic Writing Pad." In J. Strachey (Ed.), *The standard edition of the complete psychological works of Sigmund Freud* (Vol. 19). London: Hogarth Press.

FREUD, S. (1930/1961). Civilization and its discontents. In J. Strachey (Ed.), *The standard edition of the complete psychological works of Sigmund Freud* (Vol. 21). London: Hogarth Press.

FREUD, S. (1937/1968). Constructions in analysis. In J. Strachey (Ed.), *The standard edition of the complete psychological works of Sigmund Freud* (Vol. 23). London: Hogarth Press.

GELLER, J. D. (1984). Moods, feelings, and the process of affect formation. In C. Van Dyke, L, Temoshok, & L. S. Zegans (Eds.), *Emotions in health and illness: Applications to clinical practice.* Orlando, FL: Grune and Stratton.

GELLER, J. D. (1988). The process of psychotherapy: Separation and the complex interplay among empathy, insight and internalization. In J. Bloom-Feshbach & S. Bloom-Feshbach (Eds.), *The psychology of separation through the life span.* San Francisco: Jossey-Bass.

GELLER, J. D., COOLEY, R. S., & HARTLEY, D. (1981). Images of the psychotherapist: A theoretical and methodological perspective. *Imagination, Cognition and Personality, 1,* 123–146.

GELLER, J. D., GUISINGER, S., & SCHULBERG, D. (1989, JUNE). *The Freud of the psychotherapist's imagination.* Paper presented to the annual meeting of the Society for Psychotherapy Research, Toronto.

GELLER, J. D., LEHMAN, A., SILBERSTEIN, L., & STRIEGEL-MOORE, R. (1990). *A manual for scoring the emotional and conceptual maturity of self descriptions.* Department of Psychology, Yale University, New Haven, CT.

GELLER, J. D., & SCHAFFER, C. E. (1988, JUNE). *Internalization in the supervisory relationship.* Paper presented to the annual meeting of the Society for Psychotherapy Research, Santa Fe, NM.

GELLER, J. D., SMIRNOFF, D., & BONANNO, J. (1988). *Forms of remembering pleasurable and painful experiences with parents.* Unpublished manuscript.

GREENBERG, J. R., & MITCHELL, S. A. (1983). *Object relations in psychoanalytic theory.* Cambridge, MA: Harvard University Press.

GUNTRIP, H. (1969). *Schizoid phenomena, object relations and the self.* New York: International Universities Press.

HALL, C. S., & VAN DE CASTLE, R. L. (1966). *Content analysis of dreams.* New York: Appleton-Century-Crofts.

HARRIS, I. D. (1962). Dreams about the analyst. *International Journal of Psycho-Analysis, 43,* 151–158.

HARTLEY, D., GELLER, J. D., & BEHRENDS, R. S. (1986). *The thematic dimension scale of object representation.* Department of Psychiatry, University of California Medical School, San Francisco.

HASKELL, F. N., BLACKER, K. H., & OREMLAND, J. D. (1976). The fate of the transference neurosis after termination of a successful psychoanalysis. *Journal of the American Psychoanalytic Association, 24,* 471–498.

HOLT, R. R. (1973). On reading Freud. Introduction to C. L. Rothgeb (Ed.), *Abstracts of the standard edition of the complete psychological works of Sigmund Freud.* New York: Jason Aronson.

HONIG, J. (1989). *The effect of level of object representation on patients' internalized representations of their therapists during the beginning phase of treatment.* Doctoral dissertation, Department of Clinical Psychology, Teachers College, Columbia University.

HOROWITZ, M. J. (1978). *Image formation and cognition* (2nd ed.). New York: Appleton-Century-Crofts.

HOWARD, K. I., DAVIDSON, C. V., O'MAHONEY, M. T., ORLINSKY, D. E., & BROWN, K. P. (1989). Patterns of psychotherapy utilization. *American Journal of Psychiatry, 146,* 775–778.

KAKAR, S. (1978). *The inner world: A psychoanalytic study of childhood and society in India.* New York: Oxford University Press.

KEGAN, R. (1982). *The evolving self: Problem and process in human development.* Cambridge, MA: Harvard University Press.

KELLY, G. A. (1955). *The psychology of personal constructs* (2 volumes). New York: Norton.

KERNBERG, O. (1976). *Object relations theory and clinical psychoanalysis.* New York: Jason Aronson.

KLEIN, M. (1932). *Psychoanalysis of children.* London: Hogarth Press.

KOHUT, H. (1971). *The analysis of the self.* New York: International Universities Press.

KOHUT, H. (1977). *The restoration of the self.* New York: International Universities Press.

KOHUT, H. (1984). *How does psychoanalysis cure?* Chicago: University of Chicago Press.

LAKOFF, G., & JOHNSON, M. (1980). *Metaphors we live by.* Chicago: University of Chicago Press.

LAMBERT, M. J., SHAPIRO, D. A., & BERGIN, A. E. (1986). The effectiveness of psychotherapy. In S. L. Garfield, & A. E. Bergin (Eds.), *Handbook of psychotherapy and behavior change* (3rd ed.) New York: Wiley.

LAPLANCHE, J., & PONTALIS, J.-B. (1973). *The language of psychoanalysis.* New York: Norton.

LEHMAN, A. (1990). *The content and organization of therapists' mental representations of their patients and the psychotherapy process.* Doctoral dissertation, Department of Psychology, Yale University.

LOEWALD, H. W. (1960). On the therapeutic action of psychoanalysis. *International Journal of Psycho-Analysis, 41,* 16–33.

LOEWALD, H. W. (1962). Internalization, separation, mourning and the super-ego. *Psychoanalytic Quarterly, 31,* 483–504.

LOEWALD, H. W. (1976). *Psychoanalysis and the history of the individual.* New Haven: Yale University Press.

LOEWALD, H. W. (1988). Termination analyzable and unanalyzable. *Psychoanalytic Study of the Child, 43,* 155–166.

LUBORSKY, L. (1976). Helping alliances in psychotherapy: The groundwork for a study of their relationship to its outcome. In J. L. Claghorn (Ed.), *Successful psychotherapy.* New York: Brunner/Mazel.

LUBORSKY, L., & CRITS-CHRISTOPH, P. (1990). *Understanding transference: The CCRT method.* New York: Basic Books.

LUNDY, M. (1989). *The therapist's personal involvement in the psychotherapeutic process.* Doctoral dissertation, School of Social Service Administration, University of Chicago.

LUNDY, M., & ORLINSKY, D. E. (1987, JUNE). *Therapists' experiences of therapy between sessions.* Paper presented to the annual meeting of the Society for Psychotherapy Research, Ulm, Germany.

MACMURRAY, J. (1957). *The self as agent.* London: Faber and Faber.

MAHLER, M. S. (1979). *The selected papers of Margaret S. Mahler* (Vol. 2): *Separation-individuation.* New York: Jason Aronson.

McCALL, G. J., & SIMMONS, J. L. (1978). *Identities and interactions* (2nd ed.). New York: Free Press.

McDEVITT, J. B. (1979). The role of internalization in the development of object relations during the separation-individuation phase. *Journal of the American Psychoanalytic Association, 27,* 345–360.

McDOUGALL, J. (1985). *Theaters of the mind: Illusion and truth on the psychoanalytic stage.* New York: Basic Books.

MEAD, G. H. (1954). Self. In A. Strauss (Ed.), *The social psychology of George Herbert Mead.* Chicago: University of Chicago Press.

MEISSNER, W. W. (1979). Internalization and object relations. *Journal of the American Psychoanalytic Association, 27,* 345–360.

MEISSNER, W. W. (1981). *Internalization in psychoanalysis.* New York: International Universities Press.

Montgomery, S. H. (1988, June). *The unfolding of representations of the therapy relationship: Internalization in the supervisory relationship.* Paper presented to the annual meeting of the Society for Psychotherapy Research, Santa Fe, NM.

Orlinsky, D. E. (1989). Researchers' images of psychotherapy: Their origins and influence on research. *Clinical Psychology Review, 9,* 413–441.

Orlinsky, D. E., & Howard, K. I. (1975). *Varieties of psychotherapeutic experience: Multivariate analyses of patients' and therapists' reports.* New York: Teachers College Press.

Orlinsky, D. E., & Howard, K. I. (1986a). The psychological interior of psychotherapy: Explorations with the Therapy Session Report questionnaires. In L. S. Greenberg & W. Pinsof (Eds.), *The psychotherapeutic process: A research handbook.* New York: Guilford Press.

Orlinsky, D. E., & Howard, K. I. (1986b). In S. L. Garfield & A. E. Bergin (Eds.), *Handbook of psychotherapy and behavior change* (3rd ed.). New York: Wiley.

Orlinsky, D. E., & Lundy, M. (1986). *Intersession Experience Questionnaire* (Therapist Form). Chicago: University of Chicago Committee on Human Development.

Orlinsky, D. E., & Tarragona, M. (1986). *Intersession Experience Questionnaire* (Patient Form). Chicago: University of Chicago Committee on Human Development.

Orlinsky, D. E., & Tarragona, M. (1988, November). *"Chewing the cud" and "chewing the fat": Patients' ruminations about therapy sessions and the process of internalization.* Departmental colloquium, Department of Psychology, Yale University. Also presented April 1989 to the annual meeting of the U. K. Regional Chapter, Society for Psychotherapy Research, Ravenscar, England.

Orlinsky, D. E., & Tarragona, M. (1989). *Patients' representations of the therapist and experiences in therapy sessions: Further findings.* Paper presented to the annual meeting of the Society for Psychotherapy Research, Toronto.

Parsons, T. (1958). Social structure and the development of personality: Freud's contribution to the integration of psychology and sociology. *Psychiatry, 21,* 321–340. (Reprinted in T. Parsons, *Social structure and personality.* New York: Free Press, 1964.)

Pfeffer, A. Z. (1961). Follow-up study of a satisfactory analysis. *Journal of the American Psychoanalytic Association, 9,* 698–718.

Phillips, E. L. (1991). George Washington University's international data on psychotherapy delivery systems: Modeling new approaches to the study of therapy. In L. E. Beutler & M. Crago (Eds.), *Psychotherapy research: An international review of programmatic studies.* Washington, DC: American Psychological Association.

Piaget, J. (1950). *The psychology of intelligence.* London: Routledge & Kegan Paul.

PIAGET, J. (1981). *Intelligence and affectivity: Their relationship during child development.* Palo Alto, CA: Annual Reviews.

PINE, F. (1985). *Developmental theory and clinical process.* New Haven: Yale University Press.

QUINTANA, S. M., & MEARA, N. M. (1990). Internalization of therapeutic relationships in short-term psychotherapy. *Journal of Counseling Psychology, 37,* 123–130.

RHODES, R., ORLINSKY, D. E., FARBER, B. A., & DIOSO, J. (1987, JUNE). *Therapists' experience of patienthood as an influence upon their inter-session representations of their own patients.* Paper presented to the annual meeting of the Society for Psychotherapy Research, Ulm, Germany.

ROHDE, A., GELLER, J. D., & FARBER, B. A. (1989, JUNE). *Dreams about the therapist: A thematic analysis.* Paper presented to the annual meeting of the Society for Psychotherapy Research, Toronto.

RORSCHACH, H. (1951). *Psychodiagnostics.* Bern: Hans Huber.

ROSENBAUM, M. (1965). Dreams in which the analyst appears undisguised: A clinical and statistical study. *International Journal of Psycho-Analysis, 46,* 429–437.

RYLE, G. (1949). *The concept of mind.* New York: Barnes & Noble.

SCHAFER, R. (1968). *Aspects of internalization.* New York: International Universities Press.

SCHAFER, R. (1976). *A new language for psychoanalysis.* New Haven: Yale University Press.

SCHLESSINGER, N., & ROBBINS, F. (1983). *A developmental view of the psychoanalytic process.* New York: International Universities Press.

SEARLES, H. F. (1977). Dual and multiple-identity processes in borderline ego functioning. In P. Hartocollis (Ed.), *Borderline personality disorders: The concept, the patient, the syndrome.* New York: International Universities Press.

SINGER, J. L., & POPE, K. S. (1978). The use of imagery and fantasy techniques in psychotherapy. In J. L. Singer & K. S. Pope (Eds.), *The power of the human imagination.* New York: Plenum Press.

STERBA, R. (1934). The fate of the ego in analytic therapy. *International Journal of Psycho-Analysis, 38,* 140–157.

STRACHEY, J. (1934). The nature of the therapeutic action of psycho-analysis. *International Journal of Psycho-Analysis, 15,* 127–159.

STRUPP, H. H., HADLEY, S. W., & GOMES-SCHWARTZ, B. (1977). *Psychotherapy for better or worse: The problem of negative effects.* New York: Jason Aronson.

SULLIVAN, H. S. (1953). *The interpersonal theory of psychiatry.* New York: Norton.

TARRAGONA, M. (1989). *Patients' experiences of psychotherapy between sessions: Their relationship to some input, process and output variables of psychotherapy.* Doctoral dissertation, Department of Psychology, University of Chicago.

TARRAGONA, M., & ORLINSKY, D. E. (1987, JUNE). *Patients' experiences of therapy between sessions.* Paper presented to the annual meeting of the Society for Psychotherapy Research, Ulm, Germany.

TARRAGONA, M., & ORLINSKY, D. E. (1988, JUNE). *During and beyond the therapeutic hour: An exploration of the relationship between patients' experiences of therapy within and between sessions.* Paper presented to the annual meeting of the Society for Psychotherapy Research, Santa Fe, NM.

TOULMIN, S. (1990). *Cosmopolis: The hidden agenda of modernity.* New York: Free Press.

VYGOTSKY, L. S. (1962). *Thought and language.* New York: Wiley.

WACHTEL, P. (1977). *Psychoanalysis and behavior therapy.* New York: Basic Books.

WEISS, J., & SAMPSON, H. (1986). *The psychoanalytic process.* New York: Guilford Press.

WINNICOTT, D. W. (1965). *The maturational processes and the facilitating environment.* New York: International Universities Press.

WZONTEK, M. (1990). *Factors associated with patients' post-termination images of their psychotherapists.* Doctoral dissertation, Department of Clinical Psychology, Teachers College, Columbia University.

YALOM, I. D. (1975). *The theory and practice of group psychotherapy* (2nd ed.). New York: Basic Books.

PART V

MEASURING OUTCOMES

CHAPTER 23

Standard and Individualized Psychotherapy Outcome Measures: A Core Battery

---

LEIGH MCCULLOUGH

IN 1975, WASKOW AND PARLOFF recommended for the first time a set of assessment measures of the outcomes of psychotherapy. A common set of measures standardizes assessment procedures across research studies, which makes possible cross-study, cross-treatment, and meta-analytic comparisons. However, there have been many concerns about creating a standard set, including the limitations of applying the same battery to all patients, the values of and methodological difficulties with individualized measures, and the need to use as few measures as possible, to name a few (Lambert, Shapiro, and Bergin 1986). There have also been recommendations to develop several alternative batteries based on diagnostic criteria and varied sources of data, such as specific disorders or theoretical orientations (e.g., Lambert, Christensen, and DeJulio 1983; Ogles et al. 1990). The views of Lambert and his colleagues have influenced this review's recommendations for more idiographic domains within outcome assessment; refer to their excellent compilations for in-depth examinations of current issues in the assessment of psychotherapy.

There are a number of reasons to generate an updated core battery that can be individualized. The past fifteen years have seen many changes and improvements in outcome methodology and technology, and new instruments have been developed that have improved upon instruments in the original battery. Furthermore, the field has become more sophisticated in its understanding of how outcome assessment should be conducted, particularly for distinguishing between general and theory-specific or disorder-specific assessment. From a practical standpoint, at the Center for Psychotherapy Research at the University of Pennsylvania it was necessary to develop a state-of-the-art battery for clinical trials of specific diagnostic categories. The Waskow-Parloff core battery originally included Target Complaints (Battle et al. 1966), the Hopkins Symptom Checklist (Derogatis et al. 1974; Derogatis 1975a), the Psychiatric Status Schedule (Spitzer et al. 1970), the Global Assessment Scale (Endicott et al. 1976), and the MMPI (Ciarlo et al. 1989). Ciarlo's (1980) review suggested the inclusion of the Social Adjustment Scale (Weissman and Bothwell 1976) in a full battery.

To find out how often these recommended instruments had actually been used, the *Journal of Consulting and Clinical Psychology (JCCP)* and the *Archives of General Psychiatry (Archives)* were scanned for psychotherapy outcome studies from 1980 to 1990. At first pass, the wide variety in instruments supported the observation of Ogles et al. "that the diversity and lack of consensus is rampant" (1989, p. 322). As shown in Table 23.1, of 135 studies reviewed in *JCCP*, only nine used the SCL-90 or the Hopkins Checklist, three used the Social Adjustment Scale, two used Target Complaints, and four used the Global Assessment Scale. (Only four studies used two or more of these instruments in combination.) Upon closer inspection, however, there was more evidence of convergence toward cross-domain assessment in the behavioral and cognitive areas. Fifty-nine studies (44 percent) used one or more symptom scales (the SCL-90 or the Beck or Hamilton depression scales) and 56 studies counted frequencies of behaviors and cognitions. Seventy-six studies (56 percent) assessed two domains, such as behavior along with symptoms, attitudes, or cognitions. Since 1980, twenty-seven of these studies (20

TABLE 23.1 *Frequency of Outcome Studies from 1980 through 1990 Using Instruments Recommended in Waskow and Parloff's Core Battery*

	JCCP (N = 135)	Archives (N = 122)	Both Combined (N = 257)
Studies Using Instruments from the Core Battery:			
SCL-90	9 (7%)	22 (18%)	31 (11%)
Social Adjustment Scale (SAS)	3 (2%)	9 (7%)	12 (5%)
Target Complaints (TC)	2 (1%)	1 (1%)	3 (1%)
Global Assessment Scale (GAS)	4 (3%)	11 (9%)	15 (6%)
Studies Assessing Specific Domains (using core battery or other instruments):			
Symptom Assessment (SCL-90, Beck or Hamilton)	59 (44%)	64 (52%)	123 (48%)
Social Adjustment (SAS or others)	7 (5%)	9 (7%)	16 (6%)
Global Assessment (GAS or HSRS)	2 (1%)	17 (14%)	19 (7%)
Diagnostic Assessment	6 (6%)	53 (43%)	59 (23%)
Behavioral Frequencies	56 (41%)	2 (2%)	58 (23%)
Studies Assessing Multiple Domains:			
two domains	76 (56%)	29 (24%)	105 (41%)
three or more domains	27 (20%)	10 (8%)	37 (14%)

percent) assessed three or more domains, typically involving behavior, cognition, and affect or symptoms. Seven of these studies also assessed some form of social functioning, only six included diagnostic assessment, and only two included global assessments.

In *Archives*, which focuses more often on clinical trial research, 122 studies were reviewed from 1980 to 1990. These showed a fair amount of variability in instruments, but also a strong trend toward convergence across domains. Twenty-two of these studies (18 percent) used the SCL-90, nine studies used the Social Adjustment Scale, one used Target Complaints, and eleven used the Global Assessment Scale. An additional forty-two studies (for a total of sixty-four), used some symptom index, usually the Hamilton or Beck scale. Altogether, seventeen studies assessed global functioning using either the Global Assessment Scale or the Health-Sickness Rating Scale, and fifty-three studies (43 percent) included diagnostic assessment, twenty-nine of which also included a symptom scale for a second assessment domain (24%). Since 1983 there have been ten studies (8%) (one or two each year) that have incorporated three to five domains of assessment, generally including diagnostic and global assessment with symptoms, social adjustment, and individualized measures.

In both of the journals surveyed, many of the instruments used had been developed after Waskow and Parloff (1975). Unfortunately, these additional instruments were rarely used by articles in both journals, with the exception of the Beck Depression Inventory and the Hamilton indexes. The most common instruments used in the *JCCP* studies were often quite specific to cognitive therapy and theory (such as the Behavioral Avoidance Questionnaire, the Self Statement Questionnaire, the Dysfunctional Attitudes Scale). Studies in the *Archives* used instruments based on a psychiatric diagnostic orientation.

Although studies in both journals assess multiple domains of functioning, there are clear differences in the way the studies approach assessment. The *JCCP* studies emphasize behavior observation and status ratings, while the *Archives* studies use evaluative and descriptive methods. *JCCP* focused more on subject behavior and cognition and tended more often to use observational or status ratings of behavior or interpersonal interactions by therapists or relevant others such as teachers or family members. The *Archives* studies focused more exclusively on affect or symptoms. In the assessment of intrapersonal and interpersonal behavior, studies in the *Archives* used predominantly evaluative methods by trained observers (that is, diagnostic assessment). Both approaches are valuable, but it is unfortunate that so many of these studies did not also include more of the standardized instruments so that legitimate cross-comparisons could be made.

Recently, a few larger comparative studies and cross-theoretical studies have used instruments from multiple domains (e.g., Winston et al. 1991;

Piper 1990; Rounsaville et al. 1983; Thompson, Gallagher, and Brecken-ridge, 1987; Elkin et al. 1989) and have shown some convergence in the use of standardized instruments.

It is common in the evolution of a scientific field for there to be much diversity in the early stages; there is a move toward greater convergence and standardization as the field develops. The foregoing data suggest a convergence in the assessment of multiple domains of functioning and a beginning step toward standardized instruments within those domains. There is empirical support for standardization as well. Lambert, Christensen, and DeJulio (1983) have demonstrated that meta-analytic comparisons using different instruments are not valid. To address the need for both diversity and convergence, Kazdin (1986) offered a compromise: "Ideally [a few measures tailored to each particular study] could be superimposed upon a standard assessment battery that could be used generically to evaluate all therapeutic techniques (e.g., Waskow & Parloff, 1975)" (p. 100). Thus, adherence to a standardized battery may become more acceptable if flexibility is built into the structure so that the needs of each study are met.

This chapter examines the instruments available today and compares their relative merits so that an updated core battery might emerge. A secondary goal, in line with the focus of this book, will be to discuss instruments specific to the assessment of psychodynamic therapy. Thus outcome assessment can begin to develop a battery of instruments that tap both general and specific domains. Then each outcome study could incorporate a few standardized instruments for use in general outcome research along with standardized instruments relevant to the theoretical orientation, the disorder being evaluated, and each subject's presenting problem. The ideal battery would allow each study to reflect both nomothetic and idiographic aspects of outcome assessment. A third goal of this chapter is to encourage the use of these measures across a wider spectrum of studies. It seems increasingly important that the designers of clinical trials, as well as the judgments of journal editors and reviewers, take into consideration the need for standardization and convergence in the various domains of assessment across studies.

Domains of General Outcome Assessment

The assessment of outcome must incorporate many factors (see Lambert, Shapiro, and Bergin [1986] for a thorough discussion). Instruments will be presented according to (1) the type of problem domain being assessed (intrapersonal affect, behavior or cognition, interpersonal, social roles), (2) the technology in use (evaluation, description, observation, and status), and

(3) the source (patient, trained observer, significant other, therapist, or institution).

Some of the categories are not frequently represented, however. Behavioral observation is not typically included in psychodynamic studies. Status ratings (such as physiological measures) are rare, and ratings by others who know the patient are infrequent. This last category bears some discussion.

There has been some use of "ratings by others" to make behavioral observations, but, for the most part, data from significant others have not been widely incorporated into research designs (e.g., Ogles et al. 1990). It may be that there is considerable overlap between the patient's reports and those by others, but there may also be an additional slant that provides another valuable perspective. Beginning with Cattell (1946), who conducted many studies using ratings by others, there have been recommendations to use such information. For example, Cattell demonstrated that while data from ratings by others may overlap considerably with self-reports, they may also differ because of valid, though different, points of view. Recently a few studies have reported that improvement in one person may sometimes have beneficial effects but at other times adverse or deleterious effects on significant others (e.g., Brody and Farber 1989). Clinical interviews or more complex questionnaires may be needed to assess both the positive and potentially adverse impacts of the patient's changes, before data from significant others can be useful for psychotherapy research.

The focus of the assessment, or the type of problem areas tapped by an instrument, include the following: (1) presenting problems, (2) symptoms, (3) social adjustment, (4) global functioning, (5) structured diagnostic assessment, (6) theory-specific instruments, (7) disorder-specific instruments, (8) physiological measurement, and (9) longitudinal assessment. Waskow and Parloff (1975) included the first four of these categories in their core battery, but not the last five. Theory-specific and disorder-specific instruments were not in wide use in 1975, nor was longitudinal assessment, but these have become increasingly valued in recent years. Physiological measurement is not in the mainstream of outcome research even now, but it will be briefly discussed as a promising area to pursue. Computer-assisted data collection is increasing in usage, and this chapter will note when instruments are available on computer. The remainder of the chapter will discuss the existing outcome assessment instruments along the Lambert, Shapiro, and Bergin (1986) dimensions.

Overview of Instruments along
Problem-Area Dimensions

PRESENTING PROBLEMS: INDIVIDUALIZED MEASURES

The importance of tailoring change criteria to each individual (individualized measures) has been strongly encouraged. The problem has been to standardize the individualized measures enough for adequate psychometric properties to be achieved.

Target Complaint Ratings.

The Target Complaint measure elicits the problems the patient would like help with in treatment and rates their severity (Battle et al. 1966). It is a self-report measure tailored to each patient. The measure was recommended by Waskow and Parloff, but it has not been widely used. A review by Mintz and Kiesler (1982) did not show strong empirical support for the Target Complaint measure; those authors recommended standardization of the Target Complaint categories. A more standardized version of the Target Complaints was developed for computer (CASPER; McCullough, Farrell, and Longabaugh 1986), in an attempt to correct for some of Mintz's criticisms. Subsequent research has demonstrated the clinical utility and psychometric soundness of the CASPER interview (Farrell, Stiles, and McCullough 1987).

The other scale assessing individual improvement was the Goal Attainment Scale (Kiresuk and Sherman 1968). With this instrument the therapist measures the degree to which individualized patient/therapist goals are achieved. Three to five goals are selected and weights are assigned to reflect their relative importance. Individual goal scores as well as a summary goal attainment T-score can be calculated. Among the positive features of this technique is that the goals are tailored to each patient and the approach depends very little on theoretical orientation to therapy. Although this scale has gained wide attention and is conceptually appealing, it remains difficult to score reliably. Further work on standardization is needed.

SYMPTOMS: PATIENT SELF-REPORT

Symptom Checklists.

The Hopkins Symptom Checklist (Derogatis et al. 1974) and its derivative the Symptom Checklist-90 (SCL-90; Derogatis 1975a, 1975b) were recommended in the 1975 core battery. They are widely used. The SCL-90 consists of patient ratings of symptoms of distress for thirty-eight common complaints which cover the major dimensions of clinical psychopathology in predominantly neurotic outpatients (anxiety, depression, psychoticism, hostility, anxiety, and so on). Although there are numerous studies that demonstrate adequate reliability and validity for this instrument (e.g., Derogatis, Rickels, and Rock 1976), there has been criticism that the subscales are not well differentiated (Riskind et al. 1987). Therefore, its primary value may be as a measure of global symptomatology. The issue of importance for this scale is whether it should be replaced by the Beck Anxiety and Depression Scales. The Beck scales take less time (five minutes each), are easily scored, and have immediate clinical relevance. The SCL-90 takes fifteen to twenty minutes both to rate and to score. Because the additional subscales do not appear to offer much more than an overall sense of degree of pathology, there is a question whether the SCL-90 provides us with enough additional information to warrant its continued inclusion in a general battery which is already quite time consuming.

Beck Anxiety Inventory.

The Beck Anxiety Inventory (BAI; Beck et al. 1987) is a 21-item self-report symptom checklist designed to measure the severity of anxiety symptoms. The BAI is intended to complement the Beck Depression Inventory and to fill the need for an anxiety measure that overlaps only minimally with similar depression measures. Each BAI item consists of a short description of a common anxiety symptom that is rated by the respondent on a 0-3 Likert-type scale describing the severity of the symptom during the previous week (0 = "Not at all," 3 = "Very severe—I could barely stand it"). The individual items are summed to produce a total score (range 0–63). Good reliability has been demonstrated, and validity analyses compared favorably with other self-report anxiety measures (Beck et al. 1987).

Beck Depression Inventory.

The Beck Depression Inventory (BDI; Beck et al. 1979) consists of 21 items, each comprised of four statements that reflect gradations in the intensity of a particular depressive symptom. The respondent chooses the statement that best corresponds to the way that he or she has felt for the past week. The individual statements are scored from 0 to 3 and are summed to obtain a total score (range 0–63; 0–15 = low depression, 16–30 = moderate depression, and 30–63 = severe depression). The scale is intended for use within psychiatric populations as a measure of the symptom severity of depressed mood and as a screening instrument for use with nonpsychiatric populations. The mean coefficient alpha reported by Beck, Steer, and

Garbin (1988) in a meta-analysis of nine studies was .87 and test-retest reliability ranged from .69 to .86 over periods ranging from one week to one month.

The Beck Depression Inventory may be more widely used than the SCL-90. The BDI's advantage is that it is simple to score and the scores have immediate clinical relevance. However, it measures only one dimension of symptomatology. The Beck Anxiety Inventory adds the second important dimension in measurement of symptoms, but it is not yet as widely used. The other anxiety scale that is fairly widely recommended and used is the State-Trait Anxiety Inventory (STAI; Spielberger, Gorsuch, and Lushene 1970). Careful comparisons among the BDI, the BAI, the STAI, and the SCL-90 need to be made.

SYMPTOMS: RESEARCH INTERVIEWER-RATED

Psychiatric Status Schedule.

In the original core battery, the recommended interviewer-rated instrument was the Psychiatric Status Schedule Symptom Scales (PSS; Spitzer et al. 1970). The PSS covered a broad range of symptoms and role functioning but has not been often used in recent years. The more frequently used instruments for symptoms appear to be the Hamilton Anxiety and Depression Inventories. It is interesting that there is a trend toward assessment of only anxiety and depression in both the self-report and interviewer versions of symptom scales.

Hamilton Anxiety Rating Scale.

The Hamilton Anxiety Rating Scale, or HARS (Hamilton 1959), contains 14 items that are designed to assess the severity of various signs and symptoms of anxiety. The HARS is a standard, widely used clinician-rated anxiety assessment instrument of accepted reliability and validity (Hedlund and Viewig 1978). A revised version of HARS has also been derived that has been shown to discriminate depression and anxiety more effectively than the original HARS (Riskind et al., 1987).

Hamilton Rating Scale for Depression.

The Hamilton Rating Scale for Depression (HRSD; Hamilton 1960) is a clinician-administered measure of severity of depression and represents the standard for clinician-rated measures of depression. Various overlapping versions of the scale exist and have been used extensively in a variety of research settings. The expanded 28-item version was used in the NIMH Collaborative Treatment Study of Depression since it provided coverage of more of the signs and symptoms that may be part of a depressive episode. There is also a structured version (Williams 1988). The revision, HRSD-R, demonstrates greater discriminant validity than the standard scale (Riskind et al. 1987).

SOCIAL ADJUSTMENT: PATIENT SELF-REPORT

Social Adjustment Scale.

The 1975 core battery did not recommend an instrument for patient self-report of social adjustment. However the Social Adjustment Scale (SAS; Weissman and Bothwell 1976) was published in the same year and has been fairly widely used since. The SAS-SR is a 42-item self-report measure of social adjustment. Items are rated on a 5-point scale, with higher scores indicating greater impairment. Mean scores are calculated for seven role areas (work, family, and so on), and an overall adjustment score is derived. Research by Weissmann has demonstrated the measure's sound psychometric properties (Weissman and Bothwell 1976). Comparison of the SAS with its predecessor, the Structured and Scaled Interview to Assess Maladjustment (SSIAM), has shown that the self-report format may be used to replace the former interviewer-administered test.

The Social Adjustment Scale was an important contribution and presented a challenge to the field of outcome research. While it is common to demonstrate significant changes on symptom indexes from pre- to posttreatment, it has appeared to be more difficult to achieve significant improvement in social behavior. When improvement is demonstrated in social behavior, effect sizes have tended to be much lower than the comparable changes in symptoms. For example, Smith, Glass, and Miller (1980) demonstrated that for verbal treatments the change in fear/anxiety had an effect size of 1.21 (for 117 of these effect sizes) while social behavior had an effect size of .65 (about half as much) for 37 effect sizes (p. 100). Similarly, Winston et al. (1990) demonstrated that in a forty-week time-limited psychotherapy for Cluster C personality disorders, the effect size for reduction in symptoms averaged .96 while the effect size for improvement in social adjustment was .32 (about one-third the effect size of symptoms). Thus, it appears that psychotherapies have more effect on symptoms than on social adjustment.

Inventory of Interpersonal Problems.

The evolution in the assessment of social behavior has been toward greater probing of interpersonal intimacy (an even more challenging task for research in psychotherapy to accomplish). One scale which reflects a greater sophistication in assessment of interpersonal relatedness is the Inventory of Interpersonal Problems (IIP; Horowitz et al. 1988). The IIP was originally a 127-item inventory reflecting a wide range of interpersonal problems rated on a 5-point Likert scale ranging from not at all (0) to extremely (4). More recently, a 64-item version was developed by Alden and her colleagues (Alden, Wiggins, and Pincus 1990). Items fall into two categories: (1) interpersonal behaviors that are "hard for you to do" (join in groups, express admiration, open up to others, and so on) and (2) interpersonal behaviors that "you do too much" (argue, be affected by others' misery, let others take advantage, and so on). In contrast to the Social Adjustment Scale, which asks about "number of friends visited each week" or "level of satisfaction with relationships," the IIP items probe the emotional expression within relationships.

SOCIAL ADJUSTMENT: OBSERVER RATINGS

The 1975 battery recommended that the Psychiatric Status Schedule (Role Scales) (PSS; Spitzer et al. 1970) be used for the assessment of patient social adjustment. It is noteworthy that this instrument is no longer in wide use, nor has it been replaced. It is possible that the need for an objective rating of this sort has been addressed by the Global Assessment Form (Axis V of the DSM-IIIR), which includes an assessment of social and occupational functioning as well as symptoms.

ASSESSMENT OF GLOBAL FUNCTIONING

Health-Sickness Rating Scale.

The Health-Sickness Rating Scale (HSRS), the original measure of global functioning, was developed by Luborsky (1962), and further described in Luborsky and Bachrach (1974), and Luborsky (1975). It consists of a global scale and seven criterion scales, which range from 0 to 100. The seven scales include: ability to function autonomously, seriousness of symptoms, degree of discomfort, effect on environment, utilization of abilities, quality of interpersonal relationships, and breadth and depth of interests. The global single-item scale is most often used, but the mean of the seven subscales is more reliable than the single-item global scale. The scales assess degree of dysfunction, irrespective of diagnosis. The HSRS has been used worldwide for many years (Luborsky et al., in press) and has been shown to be applicable interculturally (Armelius et al. 1991). It has been shown to more reliably predict treatment outcome than DSM-III/IIIR diagnosis.

Global Assessment Scale.

The Global Assessment Scale (GAS; Endicott et al. 1976) is a simplified version of the HSRS and therefore correlates .9 or higher with it. It dispenses with the seven criterion scales and the thirty case examples and relies on the global scale of the HSRS, slightly altered. The GAS, like the HSRS, is a clinician-rated single-item scale which ranges from 0 to 100. The GAS is anchored at each 10-point interval with a clinical description which includes the level of occupational and social functioning, as well as level of subjective distress, and like the HSRS is independent of diagnosis. The GAS has proved useful in a variety of studies. As is true for the HSRS, the interrater reliability has been found to be quite high (.76 to .91; see Clark and Friedman 1983; Endicott et al. 1976). In addition, the GAS has been shown to exhibit construct validity in several studies (e.g., Vogel et al. 1977), and is the most sensitive of a group of change measures (Endicott et al. 1976).

Global Assessment Form.

The Global Assessment Form (GAF) is intended to replace the GAS and has been incorporated into the DSM-IIIR as Axis V. It is identical to the GAS except that its ratings range from 0 to 90, dropping the 91–100 category of superb and symptom-free social and occupational functioning. Although this 91–100 high level of functioning may be rare, it seems important to retain the category (if not statistically, then at least theoretically) as a challenge to ourselves and to the field.

Diagnostic Assessment

The advent of the DSM-III (American Psychiatric Association 1980) changed diagnostic assessment practice dramatically because specific criteria were established for each diagnostic category. The following discussion provides an overview of those instruments that have incorporated the DSM-IIIR criteria (American Psychiatric Association 1987). For more of the history of the evolution of diagnostic instruments the reader is directed to Spitzer et al. (1992a).

AXIS I: LIVE INTERVIEWS

Structured Clinical Interview for the DSM-IIIR: Axis I.

The most widely used instrument for Axis I assessment is the SCID-I, (Spitzer et al. 1992b) a semistructured interview designed to facilitate the determination of DSM-IIIR diagnoses. Diagnostic criteria are embedded directly in the SCID, and the sequence of questions approximates the decision trees used to make differential diagnostic decisions. Research on the SCID indicates that diagnosticians achieve satisfactory levels of inter-rater agreement, comparable to that obtained by other instruments (e.g., Riskind et al. 1987). The Axis I component of the SCID takes approximately seventy-five to ninety minutes to administer by a trained interviewer and yields diagnoses for the major psychiatric disorders in Axis I.

Schedule for Affective Disorders and Schizophrenia.

The SADS (Endicott and Spitzer 1978), based on the Research Diagnostic Criteria, was one of the most widely used diagnostic instruments before DSM-III came out in 1980. The SADS has recently been updated to conform more closely, though not entirely, to DSM-IIIR criteria.

Anxiety Disorders Interview Schedule, Revised.

The ADIS-R (DiNardo, O'Brien, and Barlow 1983) is designed for studies focusing on anxiety and related mood disorders, where other DSM-III diagnoses such as psychotic symptoms and substance abuse need only be evaluated and ruled out. It is psychometrically sound and suitable for disorder-specific research; the instrument also streamlines the diagnostic process.

AXIS I: COMPUTER-ASSISTED INTERVIEWS

Diagnostic Interview Schedule.

The DIS (Robins et al. 1983) is a fully structured interview designed to be used by laypersons so that clinical judgment is minimized in determining diagnoses. Using a computer program, CATEGO, to input the patient data, it is less costly because less training is required. The validity of this approach to diagnostic assessment has been questioned; however, due to the inflexibility in its structure: it does not allow for open-ended or spontaneous questioning by the interviewer (Spitzer 1983).

D-TREE.

The D-TREE (First, Gibbon, Williams, and Spitzer 1989) is an "easy to use, menu-driven" computer version of the DSM-IIIR criteria. D-TREE is to the DSM-IIIR what the DIAGNO computer program (Spitzer et al. 1968) was for DSM-II. It begins with a twenty-question screen, followed by six diagnostic trees (including psychoses, mood disorders, psychoactive substance abuse, organicity, and somatoform and anxiety disorders). The interviewer follows an electronic program and enters answers as they are obtained from the patient. It is commercially available from Mental Health Systems, Toronto, Canada, for under $300. Preliminary research comparing D-TREE diagnoses to "gold standard" diagnoses generated by experienced clinicians has shown very good agreement in a psychiatric population (First et al., in press, 1993).

Present State Examination.

The PSE is only partially assisted by computer. Interviews are conducted by clinicians who follow a structure that has been updated to conform more closely to DSM-IIIR and ICD-10 diagnoses. The clinical data are entered into a computer which is programmed to generate a diagnosis. This instrument is used predominantly in international research.

AXIS I: PATIENT SELF-REPORTS

The only self-report versions for Axis I diagnoses are recently developed computer versions, the SHORTI (Greist 1990) and the Mini-SCID (First et al. 1990).

SHORTI.

The SHORTI is a computer-presented, brief version of the Diagnostic Interview Schedule. This instrument provides Axis I diagnoses which have been demonstrated in preliminary studies to correlate with clinician diagnoses ($r = .74$; Greist, personal communication).

Mini-SCID.

The Mini-SCID is an automated screening version of the Structured Clinical Interview for the DSM-IIIR. Both of these instruments provide a quick (twenty- to twenty-five-minute) method of screening for many of the Axis I disorders. They can be obtained for under $300. The advantage of the Mini-SCID is that its items follow the DSM-IIIR criteria more closely than do those of the SHORTI. The SHORTI has the advantage of having preliminary reliability data. Both appear to be promising instruments, and they should be compared to each other as well as to longer interview methods. Because problems with diagnostic reliability continue to plague the field, abbreviated, self-report versions can be expected only to approach the soundness of the much longer clinical diagnostic interviews. However, to the extent that self-report formats can begin to approximate the time-consuming and costly interview procedures now in use, they will contribute in a substantial way to the advancement of research.

AXIS II: INTERVIEWER-PRESENTED INSTRUMENTS

Three interviewer-presented instruments for Axis II diagnoses are widely used: the SCID-II, the PDE, and the SID-P. While levels of reliability are adequate, diagnoses yielded by these instruments often disagree. Concurrent validity for interview-administered and for self-report measures is poor (Skodol et al. 1988, 1991).

Structured Clinical Interview for the DSM-IIIR: Axis II.

The SCID-II is a two-part assessment procedure which uses a self-report form as the initial screening device and follows up by having an interviewer inquire about all *yes* responses (Spitzer et al. 1992c). Each item follows directly from the DSM-IIIR criteria, and each disorder is rated in its entirety before the next is begun, a process that simplifies scoring but does not resemble the usual exploratory flows in a clinical interview. The self-report form takes the patient about twenty minutes to complete, and the subsequent review of the *yes* responses averages from thirty to ninety minutes, depending on the prevalence of positive responses. Thus the SCID requires less interviewer time than the two instruments discussed next, which require the review of every item. Initial research on this and the PDE demonstrates the adequate capability of these instruments to identify the presence of a personality disorder, but neither instrument adequately distinguishes among the specific disorders. Note that the SCID-II questionnaire is optional for the core battery. There is an automated version of the SCID-II which is given to patients by computer (AUTOS-CID-II) (First et al. 1991) and then guides the clinician in the evaluation of the positive items to determine the diagnosis.

Personality Disorder Examination.

The PDE (Loranger 1988) is a semistructured interview consisting of 126 items designed to systematically review the criteria necessary to arrive at all the personality disorders contained in the DSM-IIIR. Its items follow the

DSM-IIIR criteria, which means that its items are often very similar to those of the SCID. The main difference between the PDE and the SCID-II is that the PDE's items are presented according to function (work, self, interpersonal relationships, affects, reliability testing and impulse control) rather than diagnosis, which makes scoring more difficult. Each section is introduced by an open-ended inquiry. The PDE takes longer to administer because all items must be assessed; the SCID assesses only the items to which the patient responded *yes* on the screening form. Interrater reliability of the PDE for the number of criteria met was good on each disorder (range .72 to .95, median .87). Test-retest reliability of number of criteria met was adequate to very good (range .54 to .93, median .78). Interrater agreement in assigning diagnosis ranged from .54 to .93 with a median of .78 (kappa). Test-retest categorical diagnostic agreement ranged from .37 to .56 with a median of .49 (kappa) (Loranger et al. 1987). The PDE was selected for use in an ADAMHA/WHO Study of Personality Disorder.

Structured Interview for Diagnosis: Personality Disorders.

The SID-P (Stangl et al. 1985) is a 160-item interview which is divided into sections relevant to personality styles. It takes about forty-five to ninety minutes to administer. There is a question or set of questions to tap each DSM-IIIR criterion; these are thoughtfully but not directly derived from the wording of the DSM criteria items. Questions are not in diagnostic order so that the SID-P is somewhat time consuming to score but unfolds more like a clinical interview, having criteria organized by context rather than diagnosis. It has been shown to be reliable for several personality disorders and has been validated against the MMPI and the Mark-Nyman scales for an inpatient sample (Stangl et al. 1985).

AXIS II: PATIENT SELF-REPORTS

Three instruments have been under development during the past decade: the PDQ, the MCMI-II, and the WISPI. While such self-report instruments for Axis II are less costly in terms of clinician or researcher time and training, the major shortcoming of self-reports for personality diagnosis is unreliability in patients' responses. Patients generally overreport symptoms, so that responses must be reviewed by a trained observer to eliminate false positives which preliminary research suggests occurs on average about 17 percent (McCullough and Cohen 1992).

Personality Diagnostic Questionnaire.

The PDQ (Hyler et al. 1985) is a 152-item true/false instrument which assesses the eleven DSM-III personality disorders. Its items often follow the DSM criteria, but in some cases DSM criteria are not tapped. It takes about thirty minutes to complete and about twenty minutes to score. Reliabilities have not been adequate, and as with all self-report Axis II instruments, clinical experience has indicated that there are many false positive responses; as a result, some categories can be overdiagnosed.

Millon Clinical Multiaxial Inventory-II.

The MCMI-II (Millon 1987) is a 175-item true/false test based on Millon's (1969) theory of normal personality and psychopathology. The inventory consists of twenty-two clinical subscales. Thirteen scales assess enduring personality characteristics which parallel the personality disorders (Axis II) of DSM-IIIR, but the items often do not follow DSM criteria (McCullough and Cohen 1988). The nine other scales assess more acute symptom syndromes parallel to a subset of DSM-IIIR Axis I disorders. Piersma (1986) reports evidence indicating that the MCMI (the earlier version of the MCMI-II) is a reliable measure of personality style and clinical symptomatology. Using the MCMI-II, Millon (1987) reports stability coefficients for a heterogeneous outpatient sample to range from .59 to .81 for the personality scales and .43 to .66 for the symptom scales. The overall diagnostic power of the MCMI-II as reported in the MCMI-II manual ranged from 89 percent to 98 percent for the personality disorders.

Wisconsin Personality Disorders Inventory.

A newly developed instrument, the WISPI (Klein et al. 1993, in press), is derived from an interpersonal view of DSM-IIIR personality disorders. One study so far has shown internal consistency and two-week test-retest reliability to be very high, and content validity to be good. Interscale correlations were higher than desirable, and the authors plan to include additional diagnostic criteria to improve upon this. Patients scored higher than nonpatients on most scales, and patients with current clinical diagnoses of any personality disorder scored higher than those with no Axis II disorders. There were high to moderate correlations with the PDQ and the MCMI as well as with clinician ratings on the Personality Assessment Form. Marjorie Klein (personal communication, 1990) reports that the WISPI helps to control for patient overreport of symptoms because of the dimensional rather than true/false response format and the thresholds for diagnoses obtained from normative samples. The WISPI is available on computer software which automatically scores responses and provides cross-referencing of dimensions of Benjamin's "Structural Analysis of Social Behavior" (1974). Thus initial research on the WISPI suggests that this is a very promising instrument, and the ease of the self-report format makes this scale potentially an important contribution.

Theory-Specific Change Measures

The theory-specific change measures can be especially relevant for dynamic psychotherapy. Many of them tap the central relationship pattern, which includes the transference pattern. Since the first of these operational measures of central relationship patterns was developed (Luborsky 1976), fourteen others have been constructed (Luborsky and Crits-Christoph 1990).

Luborsky, Barber, and Crits-Christoph (1990) have reviewed the theory-specific change measures for dynamic psychotherapy. Measures which assess changes in the therapeutic alliance (in this volume, see chapter 14), in the transference pattern (chapter 17) and in the internalization of the gains (chapter 22). Alliance measures have had the greatest attention thus far, and a number of popular instruments have emerged. Two widely accepted theory-specific change measures that assess internalization of gains will be described here. Refer to the comprehensive review by Luborsky, Barber, and Crits-Christoph (1990) for a more thorough discussion of research specific to dynamic psychotherapy. It is important to note that many of these instruments are thought of as process measures, but they can also be used as methods of assessing intermediate outcomes or shifts in responding throughout therapy. These are described in chapter 17 as transference-related measures, so they will be merely listed here.

CORE CONFLICTUAL RELATIONSHIP THEME

The Core Conflictual Relationship Theme (CCRT; Luborsky 1977, Luborsky and Crits-Christoph 1990; chapter 17) uses patients' spontaneous narratives during psychotherapy about interactions with other people, including the therapist. This method has been shown to be reliably judged, and changes in the pattern are associated with the benefits of psychotherapy (Crits-Christoph and Luborsky 1990). The wide acceptance of the CCRT reflects both its conceptual appeal and its simple, straightforward method of categorization, which makes it relatively easy to learn and to use.

STRUCTURAL ANALYSIS OF SOCIAL BEHAVIOR

The Structural Analysis of Social Behavior (SASB; Benjamin 1974) is a method of coding a therapy session in terms of thought units—the focus of the message, the friendliness versus hostility of the message, and the degree of independence. These judgments form a three-pronged circumplex classification which has been shown to be reliable and can offer a method of assessing psychodynamic change. The popularity of this coding method reflects its clinical soundness and relevance; many find the SASB classification representative of important dimensions of human interaction. Its one drawback is that it is a somewhat difficult system to learn to code. Nevertheless, it has been increasingly used in recent research studies.

PLAN DIAGNOSIS AND OTHER METHODS

The Plan Diagnosis method (Curtis and Silberschatz 1986; Silberschatz, Curtis, and Nathans 1989) has enabled clinicians to develop reliable case formulations that include the patients' goals, obstructions, tests of pathogenic beliefs, and needed insights.

As this domain of assessment develops, it will be important to identify categories of theory-specific change that might span different orientations. One conceptual schema that might be useful is Weinburger's Common Factors Model (1993), which suggests that therapeutic change is attributable to four factors regardless of theoretical orientation: alliance, exposure (to internal or external conflictual stimuli), mastery (maintenance of gains), and attribution. The identification or development of instruments that evaluate these components might provide valuable cross-theoretical comparisons. For example, shifts in the CCRT might provide evidence of mastery. Patient response to therapist interventions can be seen as degree of exposure. Thus research could begin to study the relative merits of exposure to intrapsychic stimuli (such as, psychodynamic confrontation or interpretation of feeling) in contrast to exposure in the behavioral sense to external stimuli (approach strategies for phobic behavior) in the acquisition of mastery over, for example, phobic avoidance (see McCullough 1991, for a discussion of such hypotheses).

Other Assessments

DISORDER-SPECIFIC ASSESSMENT

Space does not permit an in-depth discussion of the complexities of disorder-specific assessment. The reader is referred to Lambert and his colleagues (Ogles and Lambert 1989; Lambert, Christensen, and DeJulio 1983) for a well-developed approach to disorder-specific research. In brief, this is an assessment domain in the midst of discovery. Recommendations include the following: (1) instruments need to be compared to find the best methods of measuring change, (2) new methods of measurement are needed in frequently neglected categories (such as institutional sources and social role measures), and (3) researchers need to work toward consensually agreed upon measures to facilitate cross-study comparisons (Ogles et al. 1990).

Instruments that are representative of this thrust include the Fear Survey Schedule (Wolpe and Lang 1964) for agoraphobia and the Worry Questionnaire for generalized anxiety disorder (Meyer et al. 1990). This domain should, as much as possible, remain theory-free so that disorder-specific changes can be assessed across theoretical orientations.

PHYSIOLOGICAL MEASURES

We are standing on the brink of the development of this aspect of psychotherapy research. No core battery would be complete without the recognition of the growing importance and potential of the assessment of mind—body relationships, their interaction in psychotherapy, and their effects on outcome. However, much more work is needed to obtain data about relationship to outcome. The measures to be examined are measures of temperament, measures of frustration tolerance, and measures of rigidity versus flexibility.

The two main problems with physiological assessment appear to be the tremendous variability of the measures and the difficulty in linking specific measures (heart rate, GSR) with specific limbic, hormonal, or immune system responses so that an accurate theory of responding can be provided (Luborsky et al. 1992). Andreassi (1989), reviewing concepts in psychophysiology, reports that there is not yet an all-inclusive conceptual framework within which most of the collected data may be tested, integrated, and interpreted. In addition, many of the experimental findings contradict one another, so that few conclusions can be reached. Thus, this domain of assessment awaits progress in the field of psychophysiology. The reader is referred to Andreassi's excellent overview (1989) for a clear discussion of current psychophysiological concepts and related research.

LONGITUDINAL ASSESSMENT

The need to do longitudinal follow-up of psychiatric disorders has become increasingly acknowledged, and a few researchers have begun to incorporate repeated measurement to assess the course of disorders present at intake. At present one scale developed specifically for longitudinal analysis has received wide attention: the Longitudinal Internal Follow-up Evaluation (LIFE). The LIFE (Keller et al. 1987) procedures assesses the longitudinal course of the psychiatric disorders through a semistructured interview and rating system. Data are elicited on the course and outcome of psychopathology, psychosocial functions, treatment, and medical illness. Reliability coefficients for the course of psychopathology, psychosocial functions, and treatment generally ranged from .70 to .90 (Keller, Lavori, and McDonald-Scott 1983; Keller et al. 1987).

Summary and Recommendations

Based on the empirical and practical examination of the instruments presented here Table 23.2 lists the choices for the assessment battery of the Center for Psychotherapy Research at the University of Pennsylvania. For individualized outcome measurement, the Target Complaint measure was chosen because the time required is so brief (three to five minutes), and it gives a record of the patient's chief complaints. However, the CASPER standardized ratings of target complaints is used as a backup and will allow further research on the utility and degree of representativeness of the briefer method.

Standardized across-subjects measures for symptoms should include the Beck scales. The SCL-90 is recommended as optional for those who wish further comparisons among the symptom scales and cross-comparisons to other studies. For assessment of social adjustment, we have

TABLE 23.2 *Revised Core Battery*

Assessment Focus	Patient Self-Report	Clinician or Researcher Interview
Presenting Problem	Target Complaints CASPER-Pt	Target Complaints CASPER-Therapist [a]
Symptoms	BDI and BAI SCL-90	HDI and HAI
Social Adjustment	IIP	GAF
Diagnostic Assessment		
Axis I	Mini-SCID/SHORTI [a]	SCID-I
Axis II	WISPI	SCID-II
Axis III and IV		(on DSM-IIIR)
Axis V (global functioning)		GAF
Theory-Specific		CCRT, SASB
Disorder-Specific	Worry Questionnaire Fear Survey Schedule (Many others)	
Physiological Assessment	None	
Longitudinal Assessment	None	LIFE

[a] Optional

chosen the Inventory of Interpersonal Process (IIP) because of the sophistication of its items, but we are using the 64-item version developed by Alden because it is psychometrically sounder than the original 128-item version and it takes less time (fifteen minutes).

For diagnostic assessment, the SCID-I is the most widely used Axis I instrument corresponding most closely to the DSM-IIIR. The SHORTI and the Mini-SCID are listed as optional to encourage comparisons among the interviewer and self-report versions. The SCID-II was chosen for Axis II assessment because the interviewer-presented Axis II instruments demonstrated similar psychometric properties and the SCID-II was the most efficient to administer.

Theory-specific assessment is well under way, and some measures are fairly well developed (CCRT, SASB). Exploration and development are in process. More work needs to be done to establish standard domains that would allow cross-theoretical comparisons.

Disorder-specific assessment is just being recognized. At present, this domain reflects a state of divergence in methods of assessment. Recommendations are to examine areas of convergence within and across disorders as this assessment domain continues to grow. Again, the Ogles et al. (1990) paper can serve as a model.

In a similar vein, no recommendations for instruments can be made in the area of physiological assessment at this time. This domain is in a period of discovery, and the review by Andreassi (1989) can be helpful in guiding exploration. Longitudinal assessment is important to consider, and Keller and his colleagues have made an important contribution (1983, 1987). At the Center for Psychotherapy Research, it was decided to present all instruments in their entirety rather than use Keller's more abbreviated format. Further research is needed to assess whether a shortened form of an instrument is a sound way of testing over time, or whether entire measures should be repeatedly presented.

In conclusion, during the past decade the field of psychotherapy assessment has developed considerably in terms of better instruments and methods. In addition, there appears to be movement toward the standardization of instruments and the use of multiple domains of assessment. Of the total studies reviewed in table 23.1, 41 percent assessed two domains and 14 percent assessed three or more domains. If a similar review is conducted in ten or fifteen years, perhaps it will reflect a continually increasing trend toward flexible standardization as well as toward the measurement of multiple domains in the assessment of psychotherapy outcomes.

References

ALDEN, L. E., WIGGINS, J. S., & PINCUS, A. L. (1990). Construction of circumplex scales for interpersonal problems. *Journal of Personality Assessment, 55,* 521–536.

ANDREASSI, J. (1989). Concepts in psychophysiology. In J. Andreassi (Ed.), *Psychophysiology: Human behavior and physiological response* (2nd ed.). Hillsdale, NJ: Erlbaum.

AMERICAN PSYCHIATRIC ASSOCIATION. (1980). *Diagnostic and statistical manual of mental disorders* (3rd ed.). Washington, DC: American Psychiatric Association.

AMERICAN PSYCHIATRIC ASSOCIATION. (1987). *Diagnostic and statistical manual of mental disorders* (3rd ed., rev.). Washington, DC: American Psychiatric Association.

ARMELIUS, B., GERIN, P., LUBORSKY, L., & ALEXANDER, L. (1991). Clinicians' judgment of mental health: An international validation of HSRS. *Psychotherapy Research, 1,* 31–38.

BATTLE, C., IMBER, S., HOEHN-SARIC, R., STONE, A., NASH, E., & FRANK, J. (1966). Target complaints as criteria of improvement. *American Journal of Psychotherapy, 20,* 184–192.

BECK, A. T., EPSTEIN, N., BROWN, G., & STEER, R. A. (1987). *An inventory for measuring clinical anxiety: The Beck Anxiety Inventory.* Paper submitted for publication.

BECK, A. T., RUSH, A. J., SHAW, B. F., & EMERY, G. (1979). *Cognitive therapy of depression.* New York: Guilford Press.

BECK, A. T., STEER, R. A., & GARBIN, M. G. (1988). Psychometric properties of the Beck Depression Inventory: Twenty-five years later. *Clinical Psychology Review, 8,* 77–100.

BENJAMIN, L. S. (1974). Structural Analysis of Social Behavior. *Psychological Review, 81,* 392–425.

BRODY, E. M., & FARBER, B. A. (1989). The effect of psychotherapy on significant others. *Professional Psychology: Research and Practice, 20*(2), 116–122.

CATTELL, R. B. (1946). *Description and measurement of personality.* New York: World.

CIARLO, J. A., EDWARDS, D. W., KIRESUK, T. J., NEWMAN, F. L., & BROWN, T. R. (1980). The assessment of client/patient outcomes techniques for use in mental health programs. Rockville, MD: NIMH Division of Biometry & Epidemiology. Mental Health Services Research Series.

CLARK, A., & FRIEDMAN, M. J. (1983). Nine standardized scales for evaluating therapy outcome in a mental health clinic. *Journal of Clinical Psychology, 39,* 939–950.

CRITS-CHRISTOPH, P., & LUBORSKY, L. (1990). Changes in CCRT pervasiveness during psychotherapy. In L. Luborsky & P. Crits-Christoph, *Understanding* transference: *The Core Conflictual Relationship Theme method* (pp. 133–146). New York: Basic Books.

CURTIS, T. J., & SILBERSCHATZ, G. (1986). Clinical implications of research on brief dynamic psychotherapy: I. Formulating the patient's problems and goals. *Psychoanalytic Psychology, 3,* 13–25.

DEROGATIS, L. R. (1975a). *SCL-90-R: Administration, scoring and procedure manual.* Baltimore: Clinical Psychometric Research.

DEROGATIS, L. R. (1975b). *The SCL-90-R.* Baltimore: Clinical Psychometric Research.

DEROGATIS, L. R., LIPMAN, R. S., RICKELS, K., UHLENHUTH, E. A., & COVI, L. (1974). The Hopkins Symptom Checklist (HSCL): A self-report symptom inventory. *Behavioral Science, 19*(1), 1–15.

DEROGATIS, L. R., RICKELS, K., & ROCK, A. F. (1976). The SCL-90 and the MMPI: A step in the validation of a new self-report scale. *British Journal of Psychiatry, 128,* 208–289.

DiNARDO, P. A., O'BRIEN, G. T., & BARLOW, D. H. (1983). Reliability of DSM-III anxiety disorder categories using a new structured interview. *Archives of General Psychiatry, 40*(10), 1070–1074.

ELKIN, I., SHEA, T., WATKINS, J., IMBER, S., SOTSKY, S., COLLINS, J., GLASS, D., LEBER, W., DOCHERTY, J., FIESTER, S., & PARLOFF, M. (1989). National Institute of Mental Health treatment of depression collaborative research program: General effectiveness of treatments. *Archives of General Psychiatry, 46,* 971–982.

ENDICOTT, J., & SPITZER, R. L. (1978). A diagnostic interview: The Schedule for Affective Disorders and Schizophrenia. *Archives of General Psychiatry, 35,* 837–844.

ENDICOTT, J., SPITZER, R., FLEISS, J. L., & COHEN, J. (1976). The Global Assessment Scale: A procedure for measuring the overall severity of psychiatric disturbance. *Archives of General Psychiatry, 33,* 766–771.

FARRELL, A. D., STILES, P. A., & McCULLOUGH, L. (1987). Identification of target complaints by computer interview: Evaluation of computerized assessment system for psychotherapy evaluation and research. *Journal of Consulting and Clinical Psychology, 55*(5), 691–700.

FIRST, M. D., GIBBON, M., WILLIAMS, J. B., & SPITZER, R. L. (1989). D-TREE: The Electronic DSM-IIIR (computer software, user's guide, casework book). Washington, DC: American Psychiatric Press, Fall Catalog, 1992, p. 120. Distributed by Multi-Health Systems, Toronto, Canada.

FIRST, M. D., GIBBON, M., WILLIAMS, J. B., & SPITZER, R. L. (1990). Mini-SCID: Computer Administered DSM-IIIR Screener based on the Structured-Clinical Interview for DSM-IIIR Axis I (computer software, user's guide, casework book). Washington, DC: American Psychiatric Press, Fall Catalog, 1992, p. 120. Distributed by Multi-Health Systems, Toronto, Canada.

FIRST, M. D., GIBBON, M., WILLIAMS, J. B., & SPITZER, R. L. (1991). AUTO SCID-II: Computer Administered Version of the SCID-II for DSM-IIIR

Personality Disorders (computer software, user's guide, casework book). Washington, DC: American Psychiatric Press, Fall Catalog, 1992, p. 120. Distributed by Multi-Health Systems, Toronto, Canada.

FIRST, M. D., OPLER, L. A., HAMILTON, R. M., LINDA, J., LYNNFIELD, C. S., SILVER, J. M., TOSHAV, N. L., KAHN, D., WILLIAMS, J. B., & SPITZER, R. L. (IN PRESS) Utility of computer assisted DSM-III-R diagnosis. *Comprehensive Review of Psychiatry.*

GREIST, J. (1991). *The SHORTI Computerized Interview for DSM III.* Unpublished software, Department of Psychiatry, University of Wisconsin, 600 Highland Ave., Madison, WI 53792.

HAMILTON, M. (1959). The assessment of anxiety states by rating. *British Journal of Medical Psychology, 32,* 50–55.

HAMILTON, M. (1960). A rating scale for depression. *Journal of Neurology, Neurosurgery and Psychiatry, 23,* 56–61.

HEDLUND, J. L., & VIEWIG, B. W. (1978). The Hamilton Rating Scale for Depression: A comprehensive review. *Journal of Operational Psychiatry, 2,* 149–164.

HOROWITZ, L. M., ROSENBERG, S. E., BAUER, B. A., URENO, G., & VILLASENOR, V. S. (1988). Inventory of Interpersonal Problems: Psychometric properties and clinical applications. *Journal of Consulting and Clinical Psychology, 56,* 885–892.

HYLER, S. E., REIDER, R. O., SPITZER, R. L., & WILLIAMS, J. B. W. (1985). *Personality Diagnostic Questionnaire (PDQ).* New York: New York State Psychiatric Institute.

KAZDIN, A. (1986). The evaluation of psychotherapy: Research design and methodology. In S. Garfield & A. Bergin (Eds.), *Handbook of psychotherapy and behavior change* (pp. 23–68). New York: Wiley.

KELLER, M. B., LAVORI, P. W., FRIEDMAN, B., NEILSEN, E., ENDICOTT, J., McDONALD-SCOTT, P., & ANDREASEN, N. C. (1987). The Longitudinal Interval Follow-up Evaluation. *Archives of General Psychiatry, 44,* 540–548.

KELLER, M. B., LAVORI, P. W., & McDONALD-SCOTT, P. (1983). The reliability of retrospective treatment reports. *Psychiatry Research, 9,* 81–88.

KIRESUK, T. J., & SHERMAN, R. E. (1968). Goal attainment scaling: A general method for evaluating comprehensive community health programs. *Community Mental Health Journal, 4*(6), 443–453.

KLEIN, M., BENJAMIN, L., ROSENFELD, R., TREECE, C., HUSTED, J., & GRIEST, J. H. (IN PRESS). The Wisconsin Personality Disorder Inventory I: Development, Reliability and Validity. *Journal of Personality Disorders.*

LAMBERT, M. J., CHRISTENSEN, E. R., & DEJULIO S. S. (EDS.). (1983). *The assessment of psychotherapy outcome.* New York: Wiley.

LAMBERT, M. J., SHAPIRO, D., & BERGIN, A. E. (1986). The effectiveness of psychotherapy. In S. L. Garfield & A. E. Bergin (Eds.), *Handbook of psychotherapy and behavior change* (3rd ed., pp. 157–212). New York: Wiley.

LORANGER, A. W. (1988). *A personality disorder examination (PDE) manual.* D V Communications: Yonkers, NY.

LORANGER, A. W., SUSMAN, V. L., OLDHAM, J. M., & RUSSAKOFF, M. (1987). The

Personality Disorder Examination: A preliminary report. *Journal of Personality Disorders, 1,* 1–13.

LUBORSKY, L. (1962). Clinicians' judgments of mental health: A proposed scale. *Archives of General Psychiatry, 7,* 407–417.

LUBORSKY, L. (1975). Clinicians' judgments of mental health: Specimen case descriptions and forms for the Health-Sickness Rating Scale. *Bulletin of the Menninger Clinic, 35,* 448–480.

LUBORSKY, L. (1976). Helping alliances in psychotherapy: The groundwork for a study of their relationship to its outcome. In J. L. Claghorn (Ed.), *Successful psychotherapy* (pp. 92–116). New York: Brunner/Mazel.

LUBORSKY, L. (1977). Measuring a pervasive psychic structure in psychotherapy: The Core Conflictual Relationship Theme. In N. Freedman & S. Grand (Eds.), *Communicative structure and psychic structures* (pp. 367–395). New York: Plenum Press.

LUBORSKY, L., & BACHRACH, H. (1974). Factors influencing clinicians' judgments of mental health: Experiences with the Health-Sickness Rating Scale. *Archives of General Psychiatry, 31,* 292–299.

LUBORSKY, L., BARBER, J., & CRITS-CHRISTOPH, P. (1990). Theory relevant research on dynamic psychotherapy. *Journal of Consulting and Clinical Psychology, 58,* 281–287.

LUBORSKY, L., BARBER, J., SCHMIDT, K., REDEI, E., PRYSTOWSKI, M., LEVINSON, A., CACCIOLA, J., CRIVARO, A., & SCHRETZENMAIR, R. (1992, JUNE). *Depression and immunocompetence: Do they inversely interact during psychotherapy?* Paper presented to the meeting of the Society for Psychotherapy Research, Berkeley, CA.

LUBORSKY, L., & CRITS-CHRISTOPH, P. (1990). *Understanding transference: The Core Conflictual Relationship Theme method.* New York: Basic Books.

LUBORSKY, L., DIGUER, L., LUBORSKY, E., McLELLAN, T., & WOODY, G. (IN PRESS). Psychological health as a predictor of outcomes of psychotherapy. *Journal of Consulting and Clinical Psychiatry.*

McCULLOUGH, L. (1991). Davanloo's short-term dynamic psychotherapy: A cross-theoretical analysis of change mechanism. In R. Curtis & G. Stricker, (Eds.). *How people change: Inside and outside therapy.* New York: Plenum Press.

McCULLOUGH, L., & COHEN, L. (1988). *A comparative analysis of items across six personality disorders inventories: Clusters A, B, & C.* San Rafael, CA: Social Sciences Documents.

McCULLOUGH, L., & COHEN, L. (1992). Frequency of negative responding on axis II questionnaires: A preliminary study. Unpublished manuscript. Study for Adult Development. Brookline, MA: Brigham & Women's Hospital, Harvard Medical School.

McCULLOUGH, L., FARRELL, A., & LONGABAUGH, R. (1986). A microcomputer-based mental health information system: A potential tool for bridging the scientist-practitioner gap. *American Psychologist, Special Issue: Psychotherapy Research, 14*(2), 207–214.

Meyer, T. J., Miller, M. L., Metzger, R. L., & Borkovec, T. O. (1990). Development and validation of the Penn State Worry Questionnaire. *Behavior Research and Therapy, 28,* 487–495.

Millon, T. (1969). *Modern psychopathology.* Philadelphia: Saunders.

Millon, T. (1987). *Millon Clinical Multiaxial Inventory Manual* (3rd ed.). Minneapolis: National Computer Systems.

Mintz, J., & Kiesler, D. J. (1982). Individualized measures of psychotherapy outcome. In P. C. Kendall & J. N. Butcher (Eds.), *Handbook of research methods in clinical psychology* (pp. 491–534). New York: Wiley.

Ogles, B. M., & Lambert, M. J. (1989). Meta-analytic comparisons of twelve agoraphobic outcome measures. *Phobia Practice and Research Journal, 16,* 25–33.

Ogles, B. M., Lambert, M. J., Weight, D. G., & Payne, I. R. (1990). Agoraphobia outcome measurement: A review and meta-analysis. *Psychological Assessment: A Journal of Consulting & Clinical Psychology, 2,* 317–325.

Peterson, C., Semmel; A., Von Baeyer, C., Abramson, L. Y., Metalsky, G. I., & Seligman, M. E. P. (1982). The attributional style questionnaire. *Cognitive Therapy and Research, 6,* 287–300.

Piersma, H. L. (1986). The stability of the Millon Clinical Multiaxial Inventory for psychiatric inpatients. *Journal of Personality Assessments, 50,* 193–197.

Pilkonis, P. A., & Frank, E. (1988). Personality pathology in recurrent depression: Nature prevalence, and relationship to treatment response. *American Journal of Psychiatry, 145,* 435–500.

Piper, W. E., Azim, H. F., McCallum, M., & Joyce, A. S. (1990). Patient suitability and outcome in short-term dynamic psychotherapy. *Journal of Consulting and Clinical Psychology.*

Reich, J. (1887). Sex distribution of DSM-III personality disorders in psychiatric outpatients. *American Journal of Psychiatry, 144,* 485–488.

Riskind, J. H., Beck, A. T., Brown, G., & Steer, R. A. (1987). Taking the measure of anxiety and depression: Validity of the reconstructed Hamilton Rating Scale. *Journal of Nervous and Mental Disease, 175(8),* 474–479.

Robins, L., Helzer, J. E., Croughan, J., & Ratcliff, K. S. (1983). National Institute of Mental Health Diagnostic Interview Schedule: Its history, characteristics, and validity. *Archives of General Psychiatry, 35,* 837–844.

Rounsaville, B. J., Glazer, W., Wilbur, C. H., Weissman, M. M., & Kleber, H. D. (1983). Short-term interpersonal psychotherapy in methadone-maintained opiate addicts. *Archives of General Psychiatry, 40,* 629–636.

Silberschatz, G., Curtis, J. T., & Nathans, S. (1989). Using the patient plan to assess progress in psychotherapy. *Psychotherapy, 26,* 40–46.

Skodol, A. E., Oldham, J. M., Rosnick, L., Kellerman, D. H., & Hyler, S. E. (1991). Diagnosis of DSM-III-R personality disorders: A comparison of two structured interviews. *International Journal of Methods in Psychiatric Research, 1,* 13–26.

Skodol, A. E., Rosnick, L., Kellman, D., Oldham, J. M., & Hyler, S. E. (1988).

Validating structured DSM-III personality disorder assessments with longitudinal data. *American Journal of Psychiatry, 145,* 1297–1299.

SMITH, M. L., GLASS, G. V., & MILLER, T. (1980). *The benefits of psychotheraphy.* Baltimore: Johns Hopkins University Press.

SPIELBERGER, C. D., GORSUCH, R. L., & LUSHENE, R. (1970). *STAI manual.* Palo Alto, CA: Consulting Psychologists Press.

SPITZER, R. L. (1983). Psychiatric diagnosis: Are clinicians still necessary? *Comprehensive Psychiatry, 24,* 399–411.

SPITZER, R. L., & ENDICOTT, J. (1968). DIAGNO: A computer program for psychiatric diagnosis utilizing the differential diagnostic procedure. *Archives of General Psychiatry, 18,* 746–756.

SPITZER, R. L., ENDICOTT, J., FLEISS, J., & COHEN, J. (1970). The Psychiatric Status Schedule. *Archives of General Psychiatry, 23,* 41–55.

SPITZER, R. L., WILLIAMS, J. B., GIBBON, M., & FIRST, M. P. (1992a). The Structured Clinical Interview for DSM-III-R (SCID) I: History, rationale and description. *Archives of General Psychiatry, 49,* 624–629.

SPITZER, R. L., WILLIAMS, J. B. W., GIBBON, M., & FIRST, M. B. (1992b). *Structured Clinical Interview for DSM-III-R (SCID-P).* Fall Catalog, Washington, DC: American Psychiatric Press, p. 43.

SPITZER, R. L., WILLIAMS, J. B. W., GIBBON, M., & FIRST, M. B. (1992c). *Structured Clinical Interview for DSM-III-R personality disorders (SCID-II).* Washington, DC: American Psychiatric Press, p. 43.

STANGL, D., PFOHL, B., ZIMMERMAN, M., BOWERS, W., & CORENTHAL, C. (1985). A structured interview for DSM-III personality disorders. *Archives of General Psychiatry, 44,* 557–563.

STECKETEE, G., & DOPPELT, H. (1986). Measurement of obsessive-compulsive symptomatology utility of the Hopkins Symptom Checklist. *Psychiatry Research, 19,* 135–145.

THOMPSON, L. W., GALLAGHER, D., & BRECKENRIDGE, J. S. (1987). Comparative effectiveness of psychotherapies for depressed elders. *Journal of Consulting and Clinical Psychology, 55,* 385–390.

VOGEL, G. W., MCABEE, R., BARKER, K., & THURMOND, A. (1977). Endogenous depression improvement and REM pressure. *Archives of General Psychiatry, 34,* 96–97.

WASKOW, I., & PARLOFF, M. (EDS.). (1975). *Psychotherapy change measures* (DHEW Publications No. 74–120), Washington, DC: U.S. Government Printing Office.

WEINBURGER, J. (in press, 1993). The common factors model of psychotherapy. In G. Stricker & J. Gold (Eds.) *Comprehensive handbook of integrative psychotherapy.* New York: Plenum.

WEISSMAN, M. M., & BOTHWELL, S. (1976). Assessment of social adjustment by patient self-report. *Archives of General Psychiatry, 33,* 1111–1115.

WILLIAMS, J. B. (1988). Structured interview guides for the Hamilton Rating Scales. *Archives of General Psychiatry, 45,* 742–747.

Williams, J. B., Gibbon, M., First, M. B., Spitzer, R. L., Davies, M., Borus, J., Howes, M. J., Kane, J., Pope, H. G., Jr., Rounsaville, B., et al. (1992). The Structured Clinical Interview for DSM-III-R (SCID) II: Multi-site test-retest reliability. *Archives of General Psychiatry, 49,* 630–636.

Winston, A., Pollack, J., McCullough, L., Flegenheimer, N., Kestenbaum, R., & Trujillo, M. (1991). Brief psychotherapy of personality disorders. *Journal of Nervous and Mental Disease, 179*(4), 188–193.

Wolpe, J., & Lang, P. (1964). A fear survey schedule for use in behavior therapy. *Behavior Research and Therapy, 2,* 27–30.

CHAPTER 24

The Efficacy of Dynamic Psychotherapies: Is It True That "Everyone Has Won and All Must Have Prizes"?

LESTER LUBORSKY, LOUIS DIGUER, ELLEN LUBORSKY,
BARTON SINGER, DAVID DICKTER, AND
KELLY A. SCHMIDT

IT IS THE FOND WISH OF THE PRACTITIONERS of each form of psychotherapy that theirs be the most effective in treating patients; that wish even tends to become a conviction. Our wish here is to guard against any such tendency, by surveying the evidence for efficacy of each of the main forms of psychotherapy. We will focus on the dynamic therapies versus other therapies, a comparison that was omitted from the earlier version of this review (Luborsky, Singer, and Luborsky 1975).

Ideally, an impeccable definitive study would settle the question of comparative worth once and for all. But that is not possible: every study has distinctive sample characteristics and measuring instruments, among other less easily defined qualities. Even that unique monumental comparative treatment study, the collaborative study of depression (Elkin et al. 1989), must be viewed as "human" in this sense. In fact, we must always rely on the verdict of a series of comparative treatment studies.

Our review includes only studies in which attention was paid to the main requisites of controlled comparative treatment research. These requisites were judged according to the twelve criteria listed here (given in more detail in Luborsky, Singer, and Luborsky 1975, the first review to evaluate each study according to detailed quality criteria). Each criterion contributed $+1$ or $+1/2$ or 0. The primary purpose of our grading system was not to provide highly reliable subdivisions of grading as much as to weed out the worst studies. Nevertheless, it was reassuring to find in the first agreement study that the independent grading judgments on the scale by two of us (L.L. and B.S.) on sixteen randomly selected studies yielded a reliable correlation of .84 ($p < .001$). In the present study the level of agreement of the two judges (L.L. and L.D.) on twelve dynamic versus other studies was again satisfactory ($r = .90$, $p = .0001$).

These were the main criteria for judging a study's adequacy of design:

1. Random assignment of patients (or stratified assignment on prognostic variables) were made to each group.
2. Real patients were used, not actors or student volunteers.
3. Therapists for each group were equally competent.
4. Therapists were not inexperienced; they were knowledgeable about the form of therapy they were to do.
5. Treatments were equally valued by the patients and therapists in each group.
6. The outcome measures took into account the target goals of the treatment (weight ½).
7. Treatment outcome was evaluated by independent measures.
8. Information was obtained about the patients' concurrent use of treatments other than that intended, both formal and informal (weight ½).
9. Samples of each of the compared treatments were independently evaluated for extent to which the therapists adhered to the manual-designated form of the treatment (weight ½).
10. Each of the compared treatments was given in equal amounts in terms of length or frequency.
11. Each treatment was given in an amount that was reasonable and appropriate to the form of treatment.
12. Sample size was adequate.

The studies in this review had to meet several other criteria as well. (1) The studies had to be of young adults or adults. (2) Most patients were nonpsychotic, but a few were borderline or psychotic, most of them schizophrenic. (3) The treatments had to be bona fide treatments, so we excluded role-playing studies; that makes our results more relevant to practitioners. (4) We did not include the many studies of patients who had only specific "habit" disturbances such as smoking or overeating. (5) We included mainly individual psychotherapy (except in the comparisons with other forms of psychotherapy, such as group psychotherapy). This meant, for example, that we could not include studies of marital therapy or family therapy. The various forms of individual psychotherapy were all included even though some were merely designated "verbal psychotherapy." (6) The two main types of outcome measures were included, that is, general adjustment outcome measures and specific symptom outcome measures. When results differed on these two types, we noted the trend of the difference. (7) Outcome measures were also included from both the termination of treatment and follow-up. Our solution for the review was to count each outcome measure's results at both termination of treatment and follow-up. Finally, to prevent the review from overweighing the results of a few studies containing many outcome measures, an upper limit was set of four outcome comparisons at termination and four at follow-up. (This limit affected just a few studies: for example, Pierloot and Vinck 1978; and Cross, Sheehan, and Khan 1982.)

Our review builds on studies collected in other reviews: Smith, Glass, and Miller (1980); Shapiro and Shapiro (1982); Lambert, Shapiro, and Bergin (1986); Meltzoff and Kornreich (1970); Svartberg and Stiles (1991); Crits-Christoph (1992); and Elliott, Stiles, and Shapiro (in press). Despite the many reviews, the difficulties in locating and evaluating the studies are impressive. Thus, it is not surprising that some previous reviewers (such as Eysenck 1952) have come to biased conclusions on the relative value of some types of psychotherapy.

Our results are expressed as box scores and effect sizes. Box scores give results in only three categories: "significantly better," significantly worse," and "not significantly different." The box score method is not as precise as the effect-size methods that are in vogue. But experience has shown that when the sample of studies is large, box scores adequately convey the general trend; for example, the box scores in the 1975 version of this paper were in line with the effect-size-based results described in Smith, Glass, and Miller (1980).

Comparisons among Psychotherapies

We will first briefly report on the main trend in the results of five categories of comparisons among psychotherapies: group versus individual psychotherapy; time-limited versus time-unlimited psychotherapy; client-centered versus other psychotherapy; behavior therapy versus other therapies; and dynamic therapy versus other therapies. The main trend within these five treatment comparisons is obvious: the nonsignificant difference effect is the most impressive result (Luborsky, Singer, and Luborsky 1975). This main trend shows about equally in all five comparisons.

Even with updated results this main trend has not changed since 1975. As an example, the comparison for behavior therapies versus other therapies was completely updated for the present review, with a box score of forty-five comparisons of outcome measures from sixteen studies. That preparatory box score, not given here, shows that behavior therapy was better for nine comparisons, a nonsignificant difference in thirty-five comparisons; behavior therapy was worse in one comparison. For those studies where effect-size translations could be done, the results show the main nonsignificant difference trend strongly; then with a correction for the "reactivity" (the responsivity) of the outcome measures, as done by Smith, Glass, and Miller (1980), the main trend was even stronger.

By contrast, the other types of comparisons—such as comparisons of psychotherapies with other (nonpsychological) forms of therapy (Luborsky, Singer, and Luborsky 1975)—do *not* show such a heavy preponderance of nonsignificant difference effects: the combinations of psychotherapy with medications tend to produce more benefit than the therapies alone. The combination of psychotherapy with a medical regimen for psychosomatic conditions shows superiority for the combination versus medication regimen alone. Finally, the comparison of psychotherapy alone with control (nonpsychotherapy) treatments shows an overwhelming superiority for psychotherapy.

Dynamic Psychotherapies versus Other Therapies

Dynamic psychotherapy versus other psychotherapies is the only category of comparison that we will review in detail. Dynamic psychotherapy is an early derivative of psychoanalytic treatment; it copies the parent in its principles but is shorter (Luborsky 1984). Dynamic psychotherapy itself has evolved into two forms: the time-limited (for example, Luborsky and Mark 1991) and the time-unlimited (Luborsky 1984). The earliest short versions were those of Ferenczi (1920), Rank (1936), and Grinker and Spiegel (1944). The trend toward shortening was continued by Alexander and French (1946), with the aim of making treatment with psychoanalytic techniques more affordable than classical psychoanalysis.

Just when we had almost completed our review of dynamic psychotherapies versus other psychotherapies, the review by Svartberg and Stiles (1991) appeared. In their meta-analysis of studies, effect sizes were smaller for dynamic therapy. But shortly afterward, an even more controlled review was done by Crits-Christoph (1992), including eleven studies. These studies were all manual-guided, used therapists who were trained to do the therapies, and fulfilled other criteria as well. The four studies in the Crits-Christoph review that compared dynamic therapy with other therapies had shown effect sizes that were about equal for dynamic and other therapies and dynamic therapy was better than minimal or no therapy.

Comparisons of our sample of studies with the meta-analyses by Svartberg and Stiles (1991) were illuminating. Our sample of thirteen studies overlapped with only seven of Svartberg and Stiles's sample of studies. They included comparisons of dynamic versus controls, whereas we focused only on dynamic versus other therapies. When there were multiple measures in a study, we calculated a mean Cohen's r by averaging the Fisher's Z transformation of these measures' r. (Statistics were calculated following Rosenthal (1984, pp. 19–39, 88–92), and Rosenthal and Rubin (1986).) For combining results from different studies, we averaged Z and Z(r). Averaged corrected (that is, weighted by quality ratings) Z and r across studies were computed. When researchers said only that a result was nonsignificant, we assumed that Z equals 0.

For outcome measures we used the well-known measures in three areas: (a) general mental-health and symptom indexes—HRSR, GAS, BPRS, SCL-90; (b) depression scales—BDI, Hamilton; (c) social adjustment—SAS. (We considered original measures that had been devised for a specific study only in the cases where well-known measures were not available.)

Our effect sizes sometimes differed from those in Svartberg and Stiles (1991) when dynamic therapy was compared with more than one other type of therapy in a study—they averaged their results; we did not. A few of the other bases for differences are in errors we found. It was an error for Svartberg and Stiles to take Strupp and Hadley (1979) as wholly dynamic because some experiential therapists were included. It also was an error to include Brockman et al. (1987) because the treatment in that study was not dynamic but something else, perhaps "spontaneous and interactive." Another error is that Woody et al. (1983) are listed as having no termination evaluation; their seven-month evaluation is a termination assessment—it comes within the month following termination.

Our quality controls required that a study be designed to pass muster on the set of twelve criteria listed earlier (6.5 or higher on our quality scale). One of these criteria was the presence of evidence that the treatment was dynamic. Actually for some studies we accepted less than the current high standard for adherence measures. With a few studies we relied on experienced therapists' intention to do insight-oriented psychotherapy. But the most fitting studies followed the example of Woody et al. (1983) with careful guidance by a treatment manual for psychoanalytic psychotherapy.

We report the results of the meta-analysis of the thirteen studies by the easy to understand box score method and then by the more complex effect size method (an evaluation of box score versus effect size methods is in an American Psychiatric Association Commission on Psychotherapies 1982, pp. 117–126). The box score for our thirteen studies is shown below both in a box and in table 24.1. At termination fourteen of the seventeen comparisons in the studies had nonsignificant differences, with one where dynamic therapy was better and two where the other treatment was better (two comparisons are given for one study). For the seven studies with a one-year follow-up, eight comparisons showed nonsignificant differences, with one dynamic was better and two where the other treatment was significantly better.

TABLE 24.1 Significance of Differences in Effect Sizes, Dynamic versus Other Psychotherapies

Study	Dynamic Versus:	Quality Ratings	Termination			One-year Follow-Up			Box Score	
			Cohen's			Cohen's				
			r	Z	N	r	Z	N	T	FU
Beutler & Mitchell 1981	Experiential	10.5	−.41	−2.59*	40				−	
Brodaty & Andrews 1983	Family doctor	6	.03	.18	24	−.20	−1.13	32	0	0
Brom et al. 1989	Desensitization	9.5	.12	.93	60				0	
	Hypnotherapy		.19	1.45	58				0	
Cross et al. 1982	Behavior	7	.08	.44	30	−.40	−1.65	17	0	0
Elkin et al. 1989	Cognitive[b]	11	.08	.73	84				0	
Gallagher & Thompson 1982	Cognitive-Behavior	8	−.33	−1.92	20	−1.57	−1.44	18	0	−
	Behavior		−.18	−.80	20	−.46	−1.95*	18	0	−
Marmar et al. 1988	Group	7	.20	1.56	61	.17	1.33	61	0	0
Patterson et al. 1971	Behavior	6.5	−.25	−1.82*	53	0	0	20	−a	0
									0	
Pierloot & Vinck 1978	Desensitization	8	.12	.56	60				0	
Sloane et al. 1975	Behavior	10	.07	.54	60	0	0	60	0	0
Thompson et al. 1987	Cognitive-Behavior	10	−.01	−.08	61				0	
	Behavior		−.07	−.54	60				0	
Woody et al. 1983	Cognitive-Behavior	10	.24	2.02*	71				0	+
	Drug counseling		.26	2.19*	71				+	
Zitrin et al. 1978	Behavior	9.5	.13	1.37	111				0	

Overall results				
Termination	uncorrected	Z = .80	r = .008	p = .40
	corrected	Z = 1.17	r = .01	p = .24
Follow-up	uncorrected	Z = −1.43	r = −.14	p = .15
	corrected	Z = −1.85	r = −.19	p = .06

Box Score: Dynamic better = +; Non-sig. diff. = 0; Dynamic worse = −; a = worse in 1st period; same in the 2nd period

* = Z was significant at p < .05
b = IPT was the therapy instead of dynamic

	Termination	Follow-up
Dynamic theraples were better	1	1
Nonsignificant difference	14	5
Other psychotherapies were better	2	2

The overall effect sizes (table 24.1) are based on this measure: the mean difference in the outcome measures between the treated and control groups divided by the standard deviation of the control groups (Cohen 1969). They reveal that there is no significant difference in terms of efficacy at the end of treatment between dynamic therapy and other forms of psychotherapy (corrected by the studies' quality). At one year- follow-up, there is also no significant difference. This is consistent with our hypothesis of non-significant difference.

Our original review (Luborsky, Singer, and Luborsky 1975) included about 100 studies. Smith, Glass, and Miller's (1980) review of 475 studies accepted all studies, regardless of the quality of their research methods. They even included analogue studies—with simulated treatments and simulated patients. Their decision to be all inclusive reflected their desire to avoid any selection bias and was also an extrapolation from the observation of Luborsky, Singer, and Luborsky (1975) that trends in the results were similar for studies with different ratings of quality. As it turned out, Smith, Glass, and Miller (1980, 126) found a slight advantage in effect size for more rigorous studies.

Their main conclusion was that there is a nonsignificant difference among the outcomes of different psychotherapies, a conclusion that is the same as our own. In addition, their use of an effect size measure enabled them to provide estimates of the amount of benefits from psychotherapy, for example, "A typical therapy client is better off than 75% of untreated individuals" (p. 60).

Conclusions and Implications

Conclusion 1. The main trend of the comparative studies among all forms of psychotherapy is nonsignificant differences in the patient's benefits.

Because of this trend and because these psychotherapies produce a high percentage of benefit (see conclusion 2), we can reach a "dodo bird" verdict—"Everyone has won and all must have prizes," meaning that nonsignificant differences predominate when different forms of psychotherapy are compared. (The Dodo bird in *Alice in Wonderland* handed down this happy verdict after judging the race.) The phrase was also the subtitle of the classic and prescient article by Rosenzweig (1936), "Some Implicit Common Factors in Diverse Methods of Psychotherapy," which inspired our first paper.

Our examination of the comparisons clearly shows that dynamic psychotherapy is in general no better or worse in its benefits than other therapies. Conclusion 1 applies to all five types of comparisons between psychotherapies: group versus individual psychotherapy, time-limited versus time-unlimited psychotherapy, client-centered versus other traditional psychotherapies, behavior therapy versus other psychotherapies, and dynamic psychotherapies versus other psychotherapies.

In addition, the few studies we reviewed that also reported results at follow-up are consistent with the main trend in the studies: patients who show improvement at termination are generally able to maintain their gains (Garfield and Bergin 1986, pp. 164–165).

The finding of nonsignificant differences among treatments should gain in impressiveness when one considers that (1) researchers as well as editors of journals probably have tended to hesitate about publishing results of studies with nonsignificant differences; (2) many of these comparisons are studied by partisans of one treatment or the other; and (3) this same conclusion also emerged from the much larger sample of comparative studies in Smith, Glass, and Miller (1980).

Conclusion 2. A high percentage of patients who go through each of these different psychotherapies gain from them.

One early review, Meltzoff and Kornreich (1970), estimated that for both individual and group therapy about 80 percent of patients show mainly positive results. Similarly high levels of treatment benefits were found for the other treatments in this review—for example, the Penn Psychotherapy sample (Luborsky et al. 1988) and the studies reviewed in Lambert, Shapiro, and Bergin (1986) and Smith, Glass, and Miller (1980, p. 183). This generally reported high level of benefits may contribute to the nonsignificant differences: the higher the percentage of patients receiving benefits from therapy, the harder it is to find significant differences between different forms of psychotherapy.

The effectiveness of psychotherapy in terms of effect sizes has been estimated by several meta-analyses. Smith, Glass, and Miller (1980) report an effect size of .32, which accounts for only 10 percent of the variance. However, it is important to point out, as Rosenthal (1990) notes, that the benefits of psychotherapy versus control are even more dramatic when shown in a binomial effect size display. Thus it is incorrect to label the .32 effect as modest: an effect size is impressive that reflects increases in the success rate from 34 percent to 66 percent.

The practice of using minimal treatments as controls has a limiting effect on estimates of the benefits of psychotherapy. Even within minimal "treatments," such as their "wait-list control," a moderate percentage of patients seem to make gains, as pointed out by Sloane et al. (1975). Many control groups are actually minimal treatment groups; this fact may have contributed to a slight reduction in the true effect sizes and may also have contributed to our otherwise surprising finding that approximately one-third of the comparisons of psychotherapy with control groups did not show significant differences (Luborsky, Singer, and Luborsky 1975).

A fleeting furor was set off by Prioleau, Murdock, and Brody's (1983) selection of thirty-two studies from the Smith, Glass, and Miller (1980) comparisons of treated groups with "placebo control groups," where the differences in outcome between them were nonsignificant. The most cogent explanations for this apparently paradoxical finding are consistent with the existence of treatment benefits from minimal treatment groups: some of these "placebo" treatments are not justifiably considered as placebos, as pointed out by Garfield and Bergin (1986, p. 292) and by Rosenthal (1984, pp. 298–299). Rosenthal demonstrates from his reanalysis of subgroups within these thirty-two studies that much depends on the particular kind of placebo control group. For the subgroup of college students and patients who were given *psychological* placebo controls, differences were significant at $p < .001$.

Another major limitation in the studies of effectiveness is that almost all of the studies reviewed so far have been about brief therapy—they do not include long-term therapy. The improvement might be greater for long-term therapy such as psychoanalysis. A review by Bachrach et al. (1991) summarized the results from six clinical-quantitative studies of psychoanalysis with a total of more than five hundred patients. Improvement rates within these studies were in the 60 to 90 percent range, which suggests some comparability of results for psychoanalysis and the other treatments. It should be noted, however, that the studies are not comparative treatment studies but large single-sample studies.

Conclusion 3. The nonsignificant difference effect does not apply as clearly to comparisons of psychotherapy with drug treatments or control "treatments."

1. The nonsignificant difference effect does not hold when psychotherapy and different types of therapy, such as pharmacotherapy, are compared. While Smith, Glass, and Miller (1980) found that the effect sizes for psychotherapy versus pharmacotherapy were fairly similar for patients with severe psychological disorders, both Smith, Glass, and Miller (1980) and Steinbrueck et al. (1983) showed psychotherapy to have larger effect sizes for depressed patients.

2. The Dodo bird verdict does not apply to combined treatments versus single treatments. The advantage for combined treatment is striking: it appears for psychotherapy plus pharmacotherapy versus psychotherapy alone; for psychotherapy plus pharmacotherapy versus pharmacotherapy

alone; and for psychotherapy plus a medical regimen versus a medical regimen alone (for psychosomatic illnesses). Thus, combinations of treatments offer even more benefit than a single treatment provides. Smith, Glass, and Miller (1980, p. 180) confirm that combined treatments produce an effect which is larger (0.60) than either separate treatment effect; the sum of the effects of the two treatments applied separately is slightly less than the added treatment effect size. A similar result is reported for treatment of ambulatory, nonpsychotic, nonbipolar, moderately ill depressed patients (Weissman 1979): four studies of medication (tricyclic antidepressants) combined with psychotherapy found the combination to be largely additive.

3. The verdict does not apply to comparisons of psychotherapy with control groups (absence of or minimal psychotherapy)—about two-thirds of these comparisons favor psychotherapy.

Conclusion 4. Only a few special matches of type of treatment with type of patient show special efficacy.

The difficulty of finding special matches is a logical consequence of the trend stated in conclusion 1. Even in the huge data base in Smith, Glass, and Miller (1980), little convincing evidence for special matches appeared, although a few special matches may be identified.

Good Match 1. Psychotherapy and other psychological treatments added to appropriate medical treatment versus a medical regimen alone is a good match for the alleviation of a variety of psychosomatic symptoms (Luborsky, Singer, and Luborsky 1975). Two main factors may contribute to this patient-treatment match: (a) a combined treatment is being compared with a single treatment; (b) the reassurance and support provided by psychotherapy may be especially beneficial for patients with psychosomatic symptoms. The latter factor may also be the reason for findings of a decrease in medical utilization for patients in psychotherapy. The evidence for this is impressive. Schlesinger, Mumford, and Glass (1980) found that in fourteen of fifteen studies patients in psychotherapy were found to reduce their physician visits and medical hospitalizations from the year prior to psychotherapy. In the Penn study (Luborsky et al. 1988), we noted a reduction in physical as well as psychological symptoms during psychotherapy, as measured by the Hopkins Symptom Checklist and an independent physician's checklist.

Good Match 2. Panic attacks may be most effectively treated with psychotherapies that focus on the patient's faulty catastrophic interpretations of physical symptoms. There is accumulating evidence that cognitive therapies for these patients is highly effective as well (Clark and Salkovskis 1989; Barlow and Craske 1989).

Good Match 3. Mild phobias may be more advantageously treated by behavior therapy than by the other therapies. However, only one of the studies cited in our 1975 review supports this match (Gelder, Marks, and

Wolff 1967). Smith, Glass, and Miller (1980) report that the behavior therapies (including systematic desensitization, implosive therapy, and behavior modifications) achieved outcomes similar to those of the dynamic therapies for simple phobics. They also found that for simple phobics, the cognitive and cognitive-behavioral therapies produced positive results, reliably higher than those of other therapies.

Good Match 4. Schizophrenic patients may derive special benefit from forms of family therapy and social skills training. The studies by Hogarty et al. (1991) on psychoeducational management and by Falloon (1987, 1988) on behavioral family treatment support this conclusion.

Good Match 5. Suicidal patients appear to be especially helped by additional treatments that are designed to remedy the problems of these patients, such as assertiveness training and training in problem solving (Linehan et al. 1991).

In conclusion, in our review of the many attempts to find matches between patient and treatment (e.g., Bergin and Lambert 1978) it is surprising that we have come upon so few matches. McLellan et al. (1983) uncovered one explanation. They demonstrated in a group of about eight hundred drug abuse patients in six different treatment programs that few patient-treatment matches were evident until the patients who were extreme on psychological health-sickness were excluded. The rationale for this stratification was that the patients with the highest psychiatric severity tended to derive few benefits from any of the programs, while those with the lowest psychiatric severity tended to derive many benefits from all of the programs. When these extremes were excluded, more patient-treatment matches emerged. For example, alcohol- or drug-addicted patients with moderate psychiatric severity at admission and serious family or employment problems showed significantly better outcomes in the inpatient treatment programs.

Reasons for the Dodo Bird Verdict

We will finish this chapter by bringing together the reasons for the verdict. They are ordered from most to least important. Some of these have been noted at various places in the chapter and elsewhere (Stiles, Shapiro, and Elliott 1986).

COMMON COMPONENTS IN DIFFERENT PSYCHOTHEREAPIES

The different forms of psychotherapy have major components in common. This factor may be the most influential: the common components may be so large and so much more effective than the specific ingredients of the therapies that they obscure differences between them. Therefore, it must be wrong to lump the horse-sized common components and the canary-sized specific ones together in the sense of giving them equal weight.

These common components include the support of the helping relationship with the therapist, the opportunity to express one's thoughts (sometimes called abreaction), and the opportunity to gain better self-understanding. This explanation of common components was put forward by Rosenzweig (1936), Frank and Frank (1991), and Strupp and Hadley (1979). Research has been done on the differing helping relationships provided by trained versus untrained therapists (Strupp and Hadley 1979). Another common component, supportiveness, was found to be virtually the same in amount in three differently designed treatments as judged by two independent judges (Luborsky et al. 1982). One other generally applicable aspect of treatments that deserves further research was suggested by Rosenzweig (1936), that is, the inclusion in all psychotherapies of a plausible system of explanation of the patient's problems. Such an organized explanatory and guidance system may facilitate achieving the benefits from all forms of psychotherapy.

EXTRATHERAPEUTIC CONDITIONS VARY

The extratherapeutic conditions vary for each study; these conditions may differ between treatment groups despite the attempts of the researcher to equate the groups. This reason may be crucial in explaining the Dodo bird verdict. Such conditions reflect likely-to-be influential prognostic factors that include: psychiatric severity, as measured by the Health-Sickness Rating Scale; differences between patients in their capacity to form an alliance; differences in the adherence of therapists to treatment manuals; differences in patients' capacity to internalize the gains of treatment; and differences in therapists' capacities to effect change in their patients. These main prognostic factors are separate from the intrinsic quality of the treatment itself. And, to complete this argument, these differences in prognostic factors may almost randomly favor one group or the other in different studies; therefore a large set of studies will show a preponderance of nonsignificant difference effects.

RESEARCHER BIAS FOR OR AGAINST EACH THERAPY

Subtle researcher bias can have some effect on the amount of benefit from each treatment, as first tallied in Luborsky, Singer, and Luborsky 1975 (p. 1003) and extensively demonstrated in Smith, Glass, and Miller (1980);

because the bias can vary for each treatment compared, the net effect in a set of studies might be nonsignificant differences among treatments.

In recent reviews the theoretical orientation of the researcher has been shown to have a considerable association with the outcome of a comparative treatment study (Berman 1989). In comparisons of cognitive and behavioral interventions (Berman, Miller, and Massman 1985), adjustments of the findings for theoretical orientation show that superiorities of one particular treatment evaporate when the researcher's theoretical orientation is taken into account.

The therapeutic allegiance of the researchers might influence the results in ways they are not aware of, since the comparisons are often not double-blind and are flawed in other ways. In our first review (Luborsky et al. 1975), we sorted the list of authors by therapeutic allegiance. The majority of the researchers had an allegiance with one of the treatments and in consequence may have had a relatively negative view of the treatment with which it was compared. Most of the studies comparing behavior therapy with psychotherapy, for example, were done by partisans of behavior therapy.

The researcher's allegiance may have played a small part in the results of the thirteen comparative studies. The evidence is not conclusive but may be worth noting: the only two studies where the other treatment was significantly better than dynamic psychotherapy happened to have been carried out by nondynamic researchers.

Smith, Glass, and Miller (1980, p. 118–120) reported a more systematic examination of researchers' orientations. They found that the effect sizes of treatments conducted by experimenters who had allegiance to the therapy was .95, versus only .66 for treatments conducted by experimenters who were inclined against the therapy. Apparently, allegiance to the therapy on the part of the experimenter produces a higher than usual effect size, while a predisposition against the therapy produces a positive but smaller effect size. Little is known about how such influences on effect sizes are mediated. Conceivably, the experimenters' attitude affects the way they design the studies; the attitude may get transmitted to the therapists and through them may filter through to the patients.

The ideal of nonpartisan researchers may sometimes be achieved, but this occurs less often than expected. Yet it should not be surprising that proponents and opponents do such research. Who else would spend the time and energy on such a taxing and time-consuming task?

THERAPISTS' COMPETENCE

The variation in therapists' competence may make more difference than we know. This may be another extratherapy factor, because therapists are assigned in treatment comparisons on the basis of the luck of the draw or meeting minimal standards of past experience. Since therapists' previous success rates are not considered and those appear to differ considerably (Luborsky et al. 1985) the usual mode of distributing therapists may make for nonsignificant differences among treatments.

INSENSITIVITY OF OUTCOME MEASURES

Some curative components in therapies may not be strong enough to influence the outcome measures because of the insensitivity of these measures. One example may serve here: Auerbach and Johnson's (1977) review of the impact of the therapist's capacity to generate the patient's level of experiencing found twelve studies in which experienced therapists had established better relationships with their patients than had inexperienced therapists. Nevertheless, the outcome measures did not show a significant difference between the two groups.

UNSUITABLE OUTCOME MEASURES

The outcome measures may not be representative of the treatment's intended outcomes. The most typical example is dynamic psychotherapy: the therapy emphasizes the development of insight, yet its outcomes are typically measured by global ratings of improvement—which may neglect changes in insight. The usual outcome measures also do not make an adequate distinction between short-term and long-lasting improvement, nor do they make a distinction between the parallel related changes referred to as nonstructural and structural change. A structural change is one that makes a long-lasting change in a central component of the transference.

HIGH PERCENTAGES OF BENEFITS

Since all forms of psychotherapy tend to achieve high percentages of improved patients (as in our conclusion 2), it is difficult for any form of psychotherapy to show a statistically significant advantage over any other form; the higher the percentages of benefit in the compared treatments, the less room at the top for significant differences among treatments.

SMALL SAMPLES AND SMALL EFFECTS

The nonsignificant differences between the treatments may often come about because the studies are not sufficiently powerful to register meaningful differences. As explained by Kazdin and Bass (1989), in most of the comparisons of psychotherapies, statistical power may be weak because in small sample sizes it is difficult to detect the small effect sizes that may appear. Statistical power reflects the probability that a test will find differences when the treatments are truly different in their outcomes.

The Hope for the Future

The Dodo bird verdict may not be upheld forever. First, the large number of comparative treatment studies that are devoted to finding specific matches of types of psychotherapy with types of patients is beginning to come up with more promising matches than those listed earlier. The efforts at the University of Pennsylvania's Center for Psychotherapy Research and other centers may reveal special matches. Second, the discoveries of the curative factors in dynamic psychotherapy (chapters 14, 19, 21, and 22) have set the stage for a new kind of psychotherapy training: attempts to teach therapists to maximize the patient's benefits from psychotherapy by knowledge of the curative factors (chapter 25). For example, dynamic psychotherapists can be taught to identify the Core Conflictual Relationship Theme and to address it consistently in their interpretations. Third, certain designs might improve the chances of dealing with the numerous variables in psychotherapy studies. Beutler (1991), for example, suggests selecting contrasting patient groups about which there are differential efficacy hypotheses.

We can best point to the hoped-for direction of future research by an imaginary dialogue, paraphrasing the responses of many psychotherapy researchers and practitioners to these findings.

QUESTION: I hadn't realized that the Dodo bird trends you found emerge so clearly within studies in which the quality of the research is considered. I was especially surprised about behavior therapy, which I thought had more comparative treatment studies with results that showed its superiority. And I hadn't realized the advantages for combined treatments. Wouldn't we learn more in future studies if we constructed studies to investigate specific treatments for specific types of patients?

ANSWER: Yes. Not enough of these studies have been done, yet the outlook is good. Persistence aided by our design recommendations will, bit by bit, add more specific matches.

QUESTION: Don't you feel, despite all the evidence for the nonsignificant difference effect, that dynamic therapies have some special virtues to offer that are still not well enough recognized?

ANSWER: I'm glad you asked that. The answer is definitely yes. The studies have not yet dealt with possible long-term benefits. Nor have they dealt well enough with the distinction between changes in symptoms and changes in general adjustment. The benefits of a treatment tend to reflect the focus of the treatment; dynamic treatment tends to be focused less on the symptom improvement and more on the general adjustment changes, which are harder to accomplish. And, of course, the concept of insight has not yet been adequately operationalized and therefore has not been used as an outcome measure in any form of psychotherapy. All of such mediators and moderators may not yet be well enough reflected in the results of meta-analyses, as Shadish and Sweeney (1991) point out.

References

ALEXANDER, F., & FRENCH, T. (1946). *Psychoanalytic therapy: Principles and applications.* New York: Ronald Press.

AMERICAN PSYCHIATRIC ASSOCIATION, COMMISSION ON PSYCHIATRIC THERAPIES (T. KARASU, CHAIR). (1982). *Manual for psychiatric treatments.* Washington, DC: American Psychiatric Association.

AUERBACH, A., & JOHNSON, M. (1977). Research on the therapist's level of experience. In A. Gurman & A. Razin (Eds.), *Effective psychotherapy* (pp. 84–102). New York: Pergamon Press.

BACHRACH, H., GALATZER-LEVY, R., SKOLNIKOFF, A., & WALDRON, S. (1991). On the efficacy of psychoanalysis. *Journal of the American Psychoanalytic Association, 39,* 871–916.

BARLOW, D., & CRASKE, M. (1989). *Mastery of your anxiety and panic.* Center for Stress and Anxiety Disorders, Albany: State University of New York.

BERGIN, A., & LAMBERT, M. (1978). The evaluation of therapeutic outcomes. In S. L. Garfield & A. Bergin (Eds.), *Handbook of psychotherapy and behavior change: An empirical analysis* (2nd ed., pp. 139–190). New York: Wiley.

BERMAN, J. (1989, June). Investigator allegiance and the findings from comparative outcome researchers. Paper presented at the meeting of the Society for Psychotherapy Research, Toronto.

BERMAN, J., MILLER, R., & MASSMAN, P. (1985). Cognitive therapy vs. systematic desensitization: Is one treatment superior? *Psychological Bulletin, 97,* 451–461.

BEUTLER, L. (1991). Have all won and must all have prizes? Revisiting Luborsky et al.'s verdict. *Journal of Consulting and Clinical Psychology, 59,* 226–232.

BEUTLER, L., & MITCHELL, R. (1981). Differential psychotherapy outcome among depressed and impulsive patients as a function of analytic and experiential treatment procedures. *Psychiatry, 44,* 297–306.

BROCKMAN, B., POYNTON, A., RYLE, A., & WATSON, J. (1987). Effectiveness of time-limited therapy carried out by trainees: Comparison of two methods. *British Journal of Psychiatry, 151,* 602–610.

BRODATY, H., & ANDREWS, G. (1983). Brief psychotherapy in family practice: A controlled prospective intervention trial. *British Journal of Psychiatry, 143,* 11–19.

BROM, D., KLEBER, R., & DEFARES, P. (1989). Brief psychotherapy for post-traumatic stress disorders. *Journal of Consulting and Clinical Psychology, 57,* 607–612.

CLARK, D. M., & SALKOVSKIS, P. (1989). *Cognitive treatment of panic and hypochondrias.* New York: Pergamon Press.

COHEN, J. (1969). *Statistical power analysis in the behavioral sciences.* New York: Academic Press.

CRITS-CHRISTOPH, P. (1992). The efficacy of brief dynamic psychotherapy: A meta-analysis. *American Journal of Psychiatry, 149,* 151–158.

CROSS, D., SHEEHAN, P., & KHAN, J. (1982). Short- and long-term follow-up of clients receiving insight-oriented therapy and behavior therapy. *Journal of Consulting and Clinical Psychology, 30,* 103–112.

ELKIN, I., SHEA, T., WATKINS, J., IMBER, S., SOTSKY, S., COLLINS, J., GLASS, D., LEBER, W., DOCHERTY, J., FIESTER, S., & PARLOFF, M. (1989). National Institute of Mental Health treatment of depression collaborative research program: General effectiveness of treatments. *Archives of General Psychiatry, 46,* 971–982.

ELLIOTT, R., STILES, W., & SHAPIRO, D. (IN PRESS). Are some psychotherapies more equivalent than others? In *Handbook of effective psychotherapy.* New York: Plenum Press.

EYSENCK, H. (1952). The effects of psychotherapy: An evaluation. *Journal of Consulting Psychology, 16,* 319–324.

FALLOON, I. R. (1988). Behavioral family management in coping with functional psychosis: Principles, practice, and recent developments. Special Issue: Preventing disability and relapse in schizophrenia: II. Psychosocial techniques and working with families. *International Journal of Mental Health, 17,* 35–47.

FALLOON, I. R., MCGILL, C. W., BOYD, J. L., & PEDERSON, J. (1987). Family management in the prevention of morbidity of schizophrenia: Social outcome of a two-year longitudinal study. *Psychological Medicine, 17,* 59–66.

FERENCZI, S. (1920). *Further contributions to the theory and technique of psychoanalysis.* London: Hogarth Press.

FRANK, J. D., & FRANK, J. (1991). *Persuasion and healing: A comparative study of psychotherapy* (3rd ed.). Baltimore, MD: Johns Hopkins University Press.

GALLAGHER, D. E., & THOMPSON, L. W. (1982). Treatment of major depressive disorder in older adult outpatients with brief psychotherapies. *Psychotherapy: Theory, Research and Practice, 19,* 482–490.

GARFIELD, S., & BERGIN, A. (EDS.). (1986). *Handbook of psychotherapy and behavior change: An empirical analysis* (3rd ed.). New York: Wiley.

GELDER, M. G., MARKS, I. M., & WOLFF, H. H. (1967). Desensitization and psychotherapy in the treatment of phobic states: A controlled inquiry. *British Journal of Psychiatry, 113,* 53–73.

Grinker, R., & Spiegel, J. (1944). Brief psychotherapy in war neuroses. *Psychosomatic Medicine, 6,* 123–131.

Hogarty, G., Anderson, C., Reiss, D., Kornblith, S., Greenwald, D., Ulrich, R., & Carter, M. (1991). Family psychoeducation, social skills training, and maintenance chemotherapy in the aftercare treatments of schizophrenia: II. Two-year effects of a controlled study on relapse and adjustment. *Archives of General Psychiatry, 48,* 340–347.

Kazdin, A., & Bass, D. (1989). Power to detect differences between alternate treatments in comparative psychotherapy outcome research. *Journal of Consulting and Clinical Psychology, 57,* 138–147.

Lambert, M., Shapiro, D., & Bergin, A. (1986). The effectiveness of psychotherapy. In S. Garfield & A. Bergin (Eds.), *Handbook of psychotherapy and behavior change: An empirical analysis* (pp. 157–212). New York: Wiley.

Linehan, M., Armstrong, H., Suarez, A., Allmon, D., & Heard, H. (1991). Cognitive-behavioral treatment of chronically parasuicidal borderline patients. *Archives of General Psychiatry, 48,* 1060–1064.

Luborsky, L. (1984). *Principles of psychoanalytic psychotherapy: A manual for supportive-expressive treatment.* New York: Basic Books.

Luborsky, L., Crits-Christoph, P., Mintz, J., & Auerbach, A., (1988). *Who will benefit from psychotherapy? Predicting therapeutic outcomes.* New York: Basic Books.

Luborsky, L., McLellan, A. T., Woody, G. E., O'Brien, C. P., & Auerbach, A. (1985). Therapist success and its determinants. *Archives of General Psychiatry, 42,* 602–611.

Luborsky, L., & Mark, D. (1991). Short-term supportive-expressive psychoanalytic psychotherapy. In P. Crits-Christoph & J. Barber (Eds.), *Handbook of brief dynamic therapies.* New York: Basic Books.

Luborsky, L., Singer, B., & Luborsky, L. (1975). Comparative studies of psychotherapies: Is it true that "Everybody has won and all must have prizes"? *Archives of General Psychiatry, 32,* 995–1008.

Luborsky, L., Woody, G. E., McLellan, A. T., O'Brien, C. P., & Rosenzweig, J. (1982). Can independent judges recognize different psychotherapies? An experience with manual-guided therapies. *Journal of Consulting and Clinical Psychology, 50,* 49–62.

Marmar, C., Gaston, L., Gallagher, D., & Thompson, L. (1989). Alliance and outcome in late-life depression. *Journal of Nervous and Mental Disease, 177,* 464–472.

Marmar, C., Horowitz, M. J., Weiss, D. S., Wilner, N. R., & Kaltreider, N. B. (1988). A controlled trial of brief psychotherapy and mutual-help group treatment of conjugal bereavement. *American Journal of Psychiatry, 145,* 203–209.

McLellan, A. T., Woody, G., Luborsky, L., O'Brien, C., & Druley, K. (1983). Increased effectiveness of substance abuse treatment: A prospective study of patient-treatment "matching." *Journal of Nervous and Mental Disease, 171,* 597–603.

MELTZOFF, J., & KORNREICH, M. (1970). *Research in psychotherapy*. New York: Atherton.

PATTERSON, V., LEVENE, H., & BERGER, L. (1971). Treatment and training outcomes with two time limited therapies. *Archives of General Psychiatry, 25,* 161–167.

PIERLOOT, R., & VINCK, J. (1978). Differential outcome of short-term dynamic psychotherapy and systematic desensitization in the treatment of anxious out-patients: A preliminary report. *Psychology Belgium, 18,* 87–98.

PRIOLEAU, L., MURDOCK, M., & BRODY, N. (1983). An analysis of psychotherapy versus placebo studies. *Behavioral and Brain Sciences, 6,* 275–310.

RANK, O. (1936). *Will therapy*. New York: Knopf.

ROSENTHAL, R. (1984). *Meta-analytic procedures for social research*. Beverly Hills, CA: Sage.

ROSENTHAL, R. (1990). How are we doing in soft psychology? *American Psychologist, 58,* 775–777.

ROSENTHAL, R., & RUBIN, D. B. (1986). Meta-analytic procedures for combining studies with multiple effect sizes. *Psychological Bulletin, 99,* 400–406.

ROSENZWEIG, S. (1936). Some implicit common factors in diverse methods of psychotherapy. *American Journal of Orthopsychiatry, 6,* 412–415.

SCHLESINGER, H., MUMFORD, E., & GLASS, G. (1980). Mental health services and medical utilization. In G. VandenBos (Ed.), *Psychotherapy: From practice to research to policy*. Beverly Hills, CA: Sage.

SHADISH, W., & SWEENEY, R. (1991). Medicators and moderators and meta-analysis: There's a reason we don't let Dodo birds tell us which psychotherapies should have prizes. *Journal of Consulting and Clinical Psychology, 59,* 883–893.

SHAPIRO, D. A., & SHAPIRO, D. (1982). Meta-analysis of comparative therapy outcome studies: A replication and refinement. *Psychological Bulletin, 92,* 581–604.

SLOANE, R., STAPLES, F., CRISTOL, A., YORKSTON, N., & WHIPPLE, K. (1975). *Psychotherapy versus behavior therapy*. Cambridge, MA: Harvard University Press.

SMITH, M., GLASS, G., & MILLER, T. (1980). *The benefits of psychotherapy*. Baltimore: Johns Hopkins University Press.

STEINBRUEK, S., MAXWELL, S., & HOWARD, G. (1983). A meta-analysis of psychotherapy and drug therapy in the treatment of unipolar depression with adults. *Journal of Consulting and Clinical Psychology, 51,* 856–863.

STILES, W., SHAPIRO, D., & ELLIOTT, R. (1986). Are all psychotherapies equivalent? *American Psychologist, 41,* 165–180.

STRUPP, H., & HADLEY, S. (1979). Specific vs. non-specific factors in psychotherapy. *Archives of General Psychiatry, 36,* 1125–1136.

SVARTBERG, M., & STILES, T. (1991). Comparative effects of short-term psychodynamic psychotherapy: A meta-analysis. *Journal of Consulting and Clinical Psychology, 59,* 704–714.

THOMPSON, L., GALLAGHER, D., & BRECKENRIDGE, J. (1987). Comparative effectiveness of psychotherapies for depressed elders. *Journal of Consulting and Clinical Psychology, 55,* 385–390.

WEISSMAN, M. (1979). The psychological treatment of depression: Evidence for the efficacy of psychotherapy alone in comparison with, and in combination with pharmacotherapy. *Archives of General Psychiatry, 36,* 1261–1269.

WOODY, G., LUBORSKY, L., McLELLAN, A. T., O'BRIEN, C., BECK, A. T., BLAINE, J., HERMAN, I., & HOLE, A. V. (1983). Psychotherapy for opiate addicts: Does it help? *Archives of General Psychiatry, 40,* 639–645.

ZITRIN, C., KLEIN, D., & WOENER, M. (1978). Behavior therapy, supportive psychotherapy, imipramine and phobias. *Archives of General Psychiatry, 35,* 307–316.

PART VI

WHAT'S NEW AND
WHAT'S NEXT

CHAPTER 25

How to Maximize the Curative Factors in Dynamic Psychotherapy

LESTER LUBORSKY

R ECENT RESEARCH HAS TAUGHT US ABOUT the curative factors in dynamic psychotherapy, as this handbook has demonstrated. But we need now to examine how, and to what degree, therapists can be trained to maximize the patient's gains by applying our new knowledge about these curative factors.[1]

Two important questions in dynamic psychotherapy are not often addressed: (1) What does quantitative research have to teach us about curative factors? (2) What is known about the degree to which therapists can be trained to maximize these curative factors?

The main curative factors in dynamic psychotherapy come about through working toward three changes: achieving a helping relationship, achieving understanding, and incorporating the gains of treatment (Luborsky 1984). Each of these changes is fostered by a corresponding technical ability of the therapist.

The curative factors that have been confirmed by research results will be described, and ways to maximize them will be illustrated through two case examples. Each case is profiled at the start and end of dynamic psychotherapy.

[1]This chapter is an enlarged version of Luborsky (1990b).

The Case Examples

MR. NORRIS

Initial Evaluation.

Mr. Norris, a third-year college student, had as his main complaints a fear of impotence and difficulty in speaking in front of groups. He was guarded and suspicious with other people. He also felt he was floundering in finding his vocational direction; he was dissatisfied with his performance; he felt he was not working at his level of ability; and he had great difficulty standing up against opposition.

Six months earlier he had completed eight months of psychotherapy aimed at similar symptoms, including the impotence and feelings of inadequacy. He benefited somewhat, but after termination he lost his gains and spent several months in drug-taking, especially LSD. He then limited his social contacts, and consumed much time reading.

Termination Evaluation.

After twenty months of therapy Mr. Norris no longer had the problem of impotence, but the improvement may have been situational. His general pattern was to be impotent when he started a new relationship with a woman. Later he would become potent, although the impotence would sometimes return. At termination he had been living with a woman for about eight months and had experienced only the initial impotence with her. He felt that she was nonthreatening and that he was the stronger one in the relationship. He expected to be impotent again at the start of any new relationship.

Through the treatment he seemed to have become better able to tolerate anxiety. In talking to people, he noticed that he was usually anxious at first but that when he exerted himself to carry on, the anxiety usually subsided. He believed that the anxiety about speaking had become better, but he was not sure. After his graduation from college (which occurred during therapy) he had not often been in front of groups, so it was difficult to test his adequacy. He sometimes still used marijuana and LSD, which may have been in part anxiety related. The last LSD use was three months before termination, and he continued to use marijuana about once every three weeks. His feeling of not accomplishing as much intellectually as he should remained a problem. He received a fellowship to study sociology and he hoped to do better in an academic environment. He was not sure whether he would pursue further education after his master's degree.

The termination interviewer felt that the patient had improved somewhat. Mr. Norris obviously felt that he had improved, and he gave the impression of a young man who had done some growing up over the two years of therapy. The interviewer thought there was something lacking in the patient's level of insight. The decision to terminate was a mutual one based on the fact that the patient had become more comfortable and had achieved some of his goals.

MR. HOWARD

Initial Evaluation.

Mr. Howard, an eighteen-year-old who had completed his first year of college, came to psychotherapy with complaints of these problems: resentment of his parents, sporadic pain in the penis, anxiety, and guilt. While growing up he had never felt close to his father, but he was very close to his mother. He felt she needed him to comfort and take care of her. However, he recurrently felt he could not achieve the closeness and responsiveness from others that he needed.

On the one hand, the interviewer expected him to have a good prognosis with the help of psychotherapy. He seemed to relate well to doctors, he was warm and open. He appeared to be well motivated and able to learn. Also, his conflicts were seen as perhaps no more than an exacerbation of normal adolescent conflicts, chiefly intense guilt over sex.

On the other hand, his thoughts about wanting to be like an exalted spiritual leader were somewhat confused: "I'd like to have what he had, without the preliminary steps." By "what he had," perhaps he meant the leader's spiritual power. This may simply be an expression of the patient's desire to be a great person, or it may reflect schizoid trends. It was not clear whether there was prognostic significance in the fact that his guilt over sex took the form of a conversion symptom—pain in his penis—rather than just experience of guilt. The initial evaluation could predict only that failure to improve would indicate either that he had schizoid tendencies or that his underlying guilt was too strong, particularly his guilty attachment to his mother.

Termination Evaluation.

The initial evaluation had revealed his difficulties in knowing how to be assertive, establish an identity, become separate from his family, become less passive, and relate better to his peers, especially women. Although there was no evidence of an active thought disorder, before therapy the patient described "panicky feelings" about not being able to keep himself "in control" and the sense that he was so weak that he would need to be a spiritual leader in order to obtain any of his desires. There was concern about the possibility of psychotic deterioration.

After his return from a holiday visit with his parents, the patient appeared to be remarkably more stable. He had not used the medication that had been offered because he felt that it was not necessary. During the spring he examined his fear of closeness in relationships; he also continued a relationship with another freshman and experienced his first sexual intercourse with her. Through his relationship with his new girlfriend and with his therapist, he began to reexperience many of his oedipal conflicts.

During the summer he began more actively to examine his ambivalence in relationships. He experienced increased periods of anxiety, during which he described events that suggested what appeared to be ideas of reference. However, when he visited his parents during the summer he found himself able to respond in a much more satisfactory and assertive fashion and felt encouraged by that.

In the fall the patient returned to school; he and his girlfriend made arrangements to live together. As the anticipated problems developed, the patient became aware of the transference relationship in the triangle created between him, his girlfriend, and his therapist; he saw more clearly the mechanism of his "need to be better" and found himself able to maintain and form relationships.

He responded to the therapist's departure and the impending separation with a reawakening of his feelings of needing to be all-powerful in order to survive. But by the time of the final appointment the patient was able to understand much of his current difficulty not only in terms of transference but also in light of the way he had learned to respond to his situation at home during his earlier years. He entertained (ambivalently) the idea of marriage to his current girlfriend and made plans involving education and training.

Research Measures and Curative Factors

Psychotherapy research has contributed to our knowledge of theoretically important curative factors and each of these will be briefly described here: the therapeutic alliance, the formulation of the central relationship pattern, the accuracy of the therapist's interpretations, self-understanding, internalization leading to the maintenance of gains, and psychological health or ego strength.

THERAPEUTIC ALLIANCE

The association of the therapeutic alliance with the outcome of treatment is consistent with the finding that the patient for whom the alliance is largely positive early in treatment tends to be improved by the end of treatment (chapter 14). In contrast, an initially negative alliance is not correlated with outcome, meaning that the patient who starts with a largely negative alliance may or may not be improved at the end of treatment. Since the first application of these measures to transcripts of psychotherapy sessions (Luborsky 1976), studies have proven that the quality of the therapeutic alliance can predict the outcome of psychotherapy (Luborsky and Auerbach 1985; Luborsky et al. 1988).

Both Mr. Norris and Mr. Howard showed signs of a developing therapeutic alliance by the time of their sessions 3 and 5. Both patients made beneficial changes in the course of the treatment and ended therapy as improved. But Mr. Howard's alliance appeared to be more solidly and internally based than Mr. Norris's, which may have explained Mr. Howard's better outcome.

FORMULATION OF THE CENTRAL RELATIONSHIP PATTERN

Beyond working toward a positive alliance, the therapist must make a formulation of the transference, which is the usual version of the central relationship pattern. Guided measures for formulations are a major development in the past fifteen years. Fifteen measures have been developed (chapter 17). The first of these was the Core Conflictual Relationship Theme method (Luborsky 1977), based on the consistencies across the narratives in psychotherapy or psychoanalytic sessions. The method is used during sessions (or scored from transcripts) by the therapist to help formulate the central relationship pattern, which in turn helps to guide the interpretations. Because the method is a formalization of what most dynamic therapists already do, therapists find they can comfortably use the method in the course of therapy.

An example of the method is provided from the sessions of Mr. Howard. In the course of session 3 he told a series of narratives ("relationship episodes," or REs); brief summaries of the first six of these are given in table 25.1. In scoring the CCRT the judge reads the actual episodes in the session and locates three components: the wishes, needs, or intentions; the patient's responses or expected responses from other people; and the responses of the self to these responses from other people. The CCRT is based on the most frequent of each of the types of these components. For example, for Mr. Howard these are listed in the central circle in figure 25.1 (the outer circles are condensed REs). The CCRT is the most central

TABLE 25.1 *First Six Relationship Episodes, Mr. Howard, Session 3*

1. *Mother*

   This might have been a dream. Mother says it didn't happen. Up until we moved, whenever I had questions about sex, mother would explain. One day I asked and she said, sorry we can't talk about that anymore. You're getting to that age. Bothered me 'cause my young sister, age 9 or 10, went into fits of laughter.

2. *Mother*

   Another incident Mother said never happened. We, brother and I—before sister was born—when it was really cold, would sleep with parents. Parents took my brother in bed with them and they wouldn't take me.

3. *Therapist*

   [What's happening now?]

   I feel generally unresponsive. I'm getting a headache, tense, been thinking about relating all this stuff to what I was 10 years ago (sigh) and not getting any . . . like groups of guys who have embarrassing moments of silence. It proves no perfect rapport exists. They weren't ready to jump out of the window because they couldn't communicate. I feel blank.

4. *Mother*

   Before I went to school I always used to kiss mother. I'm not sure it was a big thing, but it was a big thing when it stopped. She made a big thing about how I didn't want to kiss her anymore. I was suddenly out in the cold again.

5. *E (girlfriend)*

   I'm beginning to feel a lot of resentment to E [girlfriend]. I went with her for a couple of years. It's just been severed. I'm fearful of seeing her and feeling something for her. She just doesn't give a damn. Bothers me I used to be so screwed up about her.

6. *Mother*

   One thing that started my resentment against my parents. I told her about E that everything was cut off. I said, it upsets me. She said, "Well, I'm sure about you and you aren't sure about her." That really cut me up because of the rel—relationship she, she, a—assumes between *us* is like between E and me.

relationship pattern in the senses that its components have the highest frequency and that versions of it are reported early and late in the psychotherapy and probably throughout life.

ACCURACY OF INTERPRETATION

Although there have been clinical studies on accuracy of interpretation, there have been few quantitative studies in this area. The problem has been to find a measure of accuracy that makes sense clinically. One of these, reported in chapter 19, requires two separate sets of judges. One set identifies the essence of the patient's message in terms of the CCRT; then the other set establishes the degree of accuracy of the therapist's main interpretations, one at a time, in terms of their congruence with the patient's CCRT. For forty-three patients in psychoanalytic psychotherapy the significant correlation of this measure with outcome was .44 ($p < .01$). Similarly, in Weiss and Sampson's (1986) procedure, accuracy is defined as the convergence of the interpretations with their measure of the central

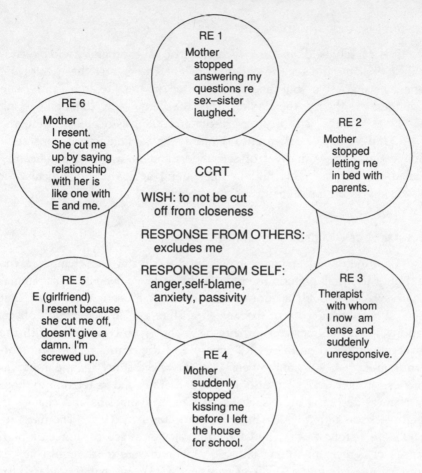

FIGURE 25.1

Relationship episodes in clockwise sequence and relationship pattern (transference) by the CCRT method (for Mr. Howard, session 3).

relationship pattern, the Plan Diagnosis (Silberschatz, Fretter, and Curtis 1986).

The way in which accuracy of interpretation is used in clinical practice is readily illustrated by an example from Mr. Howard (table 25.1). In relationship episode 3, about the therapist, the patient stops, becomes silent, and is obviously upset and anxious (anxiety was one of his main initial symptoms). The therapist had already formulated the patient's central relationship pattern (as it is presented in the center of figure 25.1) because the therapist chose an interpretation which converged with the patient's response of self and response from others; that is, the therapist said, "Naturally you feel upset and anxious now. You see me as unresponsive to you".

SELF-UNDERSTANDING AND INSIGHT

It is a firmly held tenet in psychoanalytic psychotherapy and psycho-analysis that the greater the patient's insight, the greater the therapeutic benefits. Yet of the four findings reported in the literature, only one confirmed the theory: the finding from the Penn study (Luborsky et al. 1988) was that the early *level* of self-understanding is related to outcome ($r = .31$; $p < .05$). The theoretically more relevant finding was nonsignificant, that is, *change* in level of self-understanding was not significantly related to outcome. This finding does point again to the difficulty of developing good measures of insight (chapter 21).

CHANGE IN CENTRAL RELATIONSHIP PATTERNS

Our theoretical assumption is that the greater the change in the central relationship pattern, the greater the patient's benefits. This familiar curative factor would be more recognizable if it were worded so that "central relationship pattern" became "transference." In fact, Freud's observations about the transference have been shown to correspond with the observations based on the CCRT measure of the central relationship pattern (Luborsky 1990a). In the Penn project we did study change in pervasiveness of the CCRT from early to late in therapy and its relation to more usual measures of change, such as change in symptoms and change in health-sickness rating (Crits-Christoph and Luborsky 1990). The main results were as follows: (1) The CCRT pervasiveness scores showed a high degree of agreement among judges. (2) There were meaningful changes from early to late in the CCRT pervasiveness. (3) The changes differed for different parts of the CCRT; for example, wishes did not change significantly while responses did change. The biggest changes were a decrease in negative responses of self, a decrease in degree of negative responses from other, and an increase in positive responses from other. (4) Change in CCRT pervasiveness was significantly correlated with change in symptoms for three of the five CCRT measures, and change in health-sickness correlated significantly with change in the negative responses of self.

These data have implications for psychoanalytic theories of change. They lend support to clinical theories that hold that some aspects of the central relationship pattern, such as the wishes, will remain the same even after successful treatment.

MAINTENANCE OF GAINS OR INTERNALIZATION

It is not enough to improve during psychotherapy: the patient must be able to hold on to the gains after treatment. Only very recently have measures of lasting gains been developed; chapter 22 describes these as "representations of therapists and therapy." If we had these measures for Mr. Norris, they would show a precarious sense of being able to hold on to the memory of the relationship and to its benefits—for example, "Only when I imagine talking with you can I figure out what to do." Mr. Howard's sense of contact with the therapist and therapy is much more secure. In fact, Mr. Norris's level of functioning declined almost immediately when the end of therapy came; Mr. Howard continued to function well.

PSYCHOLOGICAL HEALTH-SICKNESS

Psychological health-sickness (PHS) is a major pretreatment factor. Studies of PHS confirm the old observation in Freud's ([1937] 1964) review of the factors influencing outcomes of psychoanalytic treatment in which he listed three factors: "The influence of traumas, constitutional strength of the instincts and alterations of the ego" (p. 224). Of the three, alterations of the ego most closely corresponds to psychological health-sickness. Patients with greater alterations of the ego are sicker and not as likely to benefit as much from psychotherapy.

The main trend in studies of PHS is that greater psychological health at the start of treatment is associated with greater benefits (chapter 10; Luborsky, Diguer, et al., in press). For all studies in which a correlation is given the mean correlation is .27. Note that the mean correlation is for global PHS measures, but some of the other types of PHS measures are higher—for example, the Barron Ego Strength Scale and the Rorschach. (More research on the other types of measures, especially chronicity, is needed.) Also note that Axis V of the DSM-IIIR refers to the Global Assessment Scale for psychiatric severity, a scale which is essentially a renamed Health-Sickness Rating Scale (HSRS); the HSRS was devised by a group of psychoanalysts at the Menninger Foundation (Luborsky 1961, 1975).

The clinical applications of psychological health-sickness can be illustrated by the evaluation interviews for Mr. Norris and Mr. Howard. On the 100-point Health-Sickness Rating Scale Mr. Norris started at about 50 and Mr. Howard somewhat higher, at 55. Both of them made considerable improvement by termination. However, the follow-up showed that Mr. Norris had lost the gains within some months after terminating while Mr. Howard had retained them. Mr. Norris had been the sicker of the two patients initially. Their relative position is consistent with the principle that the sicker the patient, the more limited the gains at termination and after treatment.

Training Therapists to Maximize the
Curative Factors

Having discovered which factors are associated with the patient's benefits in dynamic psychotherapy, we have been experimenting with different systems for training the therapist to maximize the patient's benefits. The following is a summary for each of the components of the training systems that have been devised so far.

PSYCHIATRIC SEVERITY

It can be useful to the tharapist to know about the general relation between psychiatric severity and outcome. The knowledge should not be used to diminish the therapist's efforts with severely ill patients. Instead, it is the therapist's job to tailor the psychotherapy to the needs and capacities of each patient. The principle to be followed (Luborsky 1984) is that, in general, the sicker the patient the more supportiveness is required and the less expressiveness is permissible (more research is needed on the degree to which the principle is followed and its effects on outcome). This principle is illustrated in the two case examples: Mr. Norris is clearly the sicker of the two patients, and he received a more supportive and less expressive therapy than Mr. Howard.

TRAINING IN EVALUATION AND DEVELOPING A THERAPEUTIC ALLIANCE

Freud ([1912] 1958) assumed the importance of establishing rapport and of continuing to monitor it. Freud's ([1913] 1958) tried-and-tested advice was to take a sympathetic listening attitude toward the patient and do nothing to interfere with the alliance and it will develop. That basic time-tested advice should certainly be given to therapists as part of their training in dynamic psychotherapy.

We also have research evidence that therapists who perform more successfully with their patients are better able to establish a helping relationship, according to the patients' ratings of the Helping Alliance Questionnaire at the end of the third session (Luborsky et al. 1985). We have also discovered that there is a moderately high correlation (about .7) between the level of the alliance and the Therapist's Facilitating Behaviors. But that is correlational evidence—we do not yet have research evidence about the degree to which the therapist's capacity to establish an alliance is trainable.

TRAINING IN FORMULATING THE CENTRAL RELATIONSHIP PATTERN

Therapists must be able to formulate the central relationship pattern and the problems within it. A more familiar way to say this is that therapists need a way to recognize and to conceptualize the main transference issues. Some of the following methods are part of the usual training in dynamic psychotherapy (Luborsky 1984).

Supervision with the CCRT.

One method is to give clinical supervision that includes explanations and practice in the CCRT. As described in the case example for Mr. Howard, the CCRT provides a convenient help for the therapist.

Practice Cases with the CCRT.

A further question is whether specific training in the recognition of CCRTs can help the therapist. Such procedures have never been evaluated systematically. One design for a study would be to assemble a set of relationship episodes and allow therapists to review them and identify the CCRT within each one. Presumably their skill would increase with practice. This procedure is not essentially different from what happens in supervision, but the focus is more specific.

TRAINING IN ACCURACY OF INTERPRETATION

Therapists should be trained to improve linkage between the CCRT and the content of interpretations (as was illustrated for Mr. Howard; see also Crits-Christoph, Cooper, and Luborsky 1988). The concept is easy; yet to put it into practice appears to be hard. To be accurate in this sense requires that the therapist first construct a transference-related formulation guided by the CCRT system, and then make interpretations that focus around the part of the CCRT that is clinically indicated. In time-limited therapies this focus needs to be maintained more consistently than in open-ended therapies.

Researchers are now examining this principle further. There is evidence in one correlational study (Piper et al. 1991) that the frequency of transference interpretations should remain moderate. There is an association between high concentration of transference interpretations and *poor* alliance and treatment outcomes; but this association was evident only for patients with high quality of object relations.

TRAINING IN HELPING PATIENTS TO INTERNALIZE THE GAINS OF PSYCHOTHERAPY

The manual for supportive-expressive psychotherapy (Luborsky 1984) offers ways of carrying out the termination that should enable the patient to hold on better to the gains of treatment. These are based on working through the meaning of termination; the working through restores and improves the relationship to the therapist and provides for long-term internalization of the gains of the treatment. However, it must be acknowledged that some patients have so severe a problem in internalization capacity that retention of gains may not improve much, even with special ministrations by the therapist (as in the example of Mr. Norris).

A SPECIAL FORMAT FOR TRAINING

A new training format improves the therapist's skills in maximizing the curative factors in dynamic psychotherapy (Luborsky 1990b). It relies on the unusual vehicle for training of repeated experiences as a supervisor of one's peers. In contrast, the overwhelming majority of therapists and counselors reported on a questionnaire that they never had been trained by any method in how to supervise (Matarazzo and Patterson 1986).

The training format for learning to practice and to supervise psychodynamic psychotherapy has several distinctive aspects: (1) the inclusion in the learning group of four psychotherapists who are peers in their level of training; (2) a seasoned supervisor as leader, to be called here a group orchestrator; (3) an experience for each member as supervisor; and (4) an experience as the therapist being supervised. Such a learning group is probably most suited to psychotherapists with at least several years of experience, for example, fourth-year psychiatric residents and postdoctoral clinical psychologists.

For an entire year the group meets once a week for seventy-five minutes. During the first thirty minutes Therapist A presents and the presentation is discussed by the other three peer apprentice therapists. During the second thirty minutes Therapist B presents and the presentation is discussed by the other three people. At the end of six months the two who were only discussants (Therapists C and D) become presenters within the same format.

The first fifteen minutes of each half-hour is for the presentation of an account of the latest session (along with a bit of the audio or video); the remaining fifteen minutes is for discussion. After the discussion there is occasional illustrative role-playing; at the very end there is some discussion of general principles of technique.

The patients chosen to be presented are selected by the therapist from those the therapist is treating, or about to start in treatment, on no other basis than the therapist's interest in presenting the patient. The patient should be one who is likely to stay in treatment for the period of the supervision. The usual participants in the groups have been fourth-year psychiatric residents, pre- or postdoctoral psychologists and staff members of the Department of Psychiatry.

Each year the participants have provided evaluations of the supervision training. For the sixteen groups conducted during the last eight years, several trends emerged.

Supervision by Peers Has a Special Value.

From the therapist-as-presenter's point of view, much can be learned from one's peers in a supervisory role as well as from the response of a seasoned supervisor. The role of peers as supervisors in the four-person group was tried at first with uncertainty. The concern was about the degree of comfort with openness the presenters would feel in the presence of their peers. Actually, they experienced much less inhibition and anxiety in this respect than had been expected, because the group was supportive and helpful. Although in individual supervision the supervisor had more often discussed countertransference issues, the slight advantage in this respect was more than compensated for by the beneficial effects of hearing the supervisory responses of peers.

The Orchestrator's Role Differs from that in Individual Supervision.

As the group gains in experience the orchestrator's role becomes shared by the group. The orchestrator can even be absent from some of the meetings, yet the group will persist and continue to function on its own. In fact, these groups tend to be maintained on their own after the initial year is over. The extension provides group members with an opportunity for continued supervision.

The orchestrator's functions are (1) to sum up the comments of the therapist and the supervisors by a review of the main transactions of the patient and the therapist as presented; (2) to relate the nature of these transactions to the central relationship pattern and the conflicts within it, including in the relationship with the therapist; and (3) to review everyone's technical suggestions.

Role Playing Can Speed the Learning.

From time to time role playing can be helpful to the therapist. Someone in the group plays the patient and someone, often the therapist involved, plays the therapist. The "patient" says what the patient might say, and the therapist responds as suggested by the group. The role playing illustrates more concretely what is meant by the group's suggestions, allows the therapist to become comfortable with trying out the group's suggestions, and gets the therapist to rehearse ideas that will bring countertransference into awareness, as in this example:

Example: Dr. Harry Norman.

On several occasions the group members became aware that Dr. Norman was refraining from directly discussing the patient's pervasive main wish: that he be able to be accepting of and not put off by the patient's wish that the therapist be supportive and protective. The therapist's main response was to say nothing about this wish. (The patient, Ms. J, had also revealed that her father had been put off and was nonresponsive to her wish). After a role-playing experience, Dr. Norman was asked about how he felt about Ms. J's wish. The therapist replied that it was hard for him to discuss it with her because he was afraid of being oversupportive and overprotective toward her if he began to discuss this wish. It was as if the therapist experienced *discussing* the patient's wish as requiring that he actually *respond* in the way she wished. After the role playing and the discussion, in subsequent sessions Dr. Norman was able to discuss with Ms. J. her wish.

Small Samples of Audio or Video Recordings Can Be Helpful.

The mainstay of the group's understanding of the patient and the patient's interaction with the therapist is the therapist's process notes. Long experience shows that process notes are often sufficient documentation to support learning of the process of psychodynamic psychotherapy. They provide an adequate, condensed overview of the patient–therapist interaction.

But relying on the process notes alone can at times be a liability, because the patient is not heard or seen. To overcome this liability it helps to occasionally use a brief sample of audio or video recording. Afterwards the listener to the process notes can more easily "hear" or "see" the patient's presentation through the memory of the samples. Selections of audio or video must be made with time constraints in mind.

In the groups where we have used short samples of video in addition to the process notes, we have found that our estimate of the basic relationship pattern and the problems within it have often been confirmed. Occasionally, however, our understanding has been markedly broadened from that based on the process notes alone.

An important use of recordings is to allow more precise monitoring of the therapist's degree of adherence to the treatment manual. Such information can reveal to the therapist and to the supervisor information about the therapist's capacity to follow the recommended type of treatment.

Discussion of General Principles of Dynamic Psychotherapy Is Done Routinely but Briefly.

In each supervisory session the focus of most discussion tends to be on understanding the session presented. Only a little time is spent on the general principles of psychodynamic treatment. But it is valuable to routinely discuss the general principles and to relate these to the case material just presented. The manual which contains the general principles about curative factors (Luborsky 1984) is to be read before the group begins, and it is to be reread bit by bit as relevant to the stage of the treatment.

Comparison with Other Supervision Systems.

This system for supervision training appears to work well. The participants find it an exciting experience for learning. But it is still worth comparing the system with other successful systems. In the system used by the University of Pennsylvania Center for Cognitive Therapy, the supervisor first spends time alone listening to the tape or viewing the video of the psychotherapy sessions submitted by the therapist in training. After that the supervisor talks with the therapist, often by phone, about aspects of the therapist's style or behavior, and including the therapist's adherence to the manual for the treatment. The system's reliance on the telephone is most convenient for therapists who are in private practice and find it difficult to come to a training session. The system as a whole is also effective, and participants express considerable satisfaction with it.

Summary and Discussion

The theory of curative factors in dynamic psychotherapy was reexamined in order to select the parts that could be translated into operational measures. The functions of operational measures are to facilitate the making of reliable estimates of these curative factors and to be able to examine each factor for its predictive validity in relation to the outcomes of psychotherapy. Operational measures were examined for the therapeutic alliance, the central relationship pattern (transference), the accuracy of interpretation, the quality of self-understanding, and the change in the pervasiveness of the central relationship conflicts. An important pretreatment factor was also examined, that is, a measure of psychological health-sickness.

Other curative factors need to be spelled out and attempts made to operationalize them. A few of the most promising of them are: the patient's increased tolerance for his or her own thoughts and feelings, the patient's motivation to change, and the therapist's ability to offer a consistent set of techniques that comes across to the patient as clear, reasonable, and likely to be of help.

The second topic of the chapter was the question of which of the curative factors are most susceptible to the influence of training. Of all of the factors examined, the ones that appeared most promising in terms of improving the therapist's performance were the capacity of the therapist to recognize the central relationship pattern and the capacity of the therapist to use the information about the main relationship pattern in guiding interpretations. The remainder of the chapter presented a special supervision training format that has been effective in enhancing the therapist's performance as a dynamic psychotherapist.

References

CRITS-CHRISTOPH, P., COOPER, A., & LUBORSKY, L. (1988). The accuracy of therapist's interpretations and the outcome of dynamic psychotherapy. *Journal of Consulting and Clinical Psychology*, 56, 490–495.

CRITS-CHRISTOPH, P., & LUBORSKY, L. (1990). Changes in CCRT pervasiveness during psychotherapy. In L. Luborsky & P. Crits-Christoph, *Understanding transference: The Core Conflictual Relationship Theme method.* New York: Basic Books.

FREUD, S. (1912/1958). The dynamics of the transference. In J. Strachey (Ed.), *The standard edition of the complete psychological works of Sigmund Freud* (Vol. 12, pp. 99–108). London: Hogarth Press.

FREUD, S. (1913/1958). On beginning the treatment. In J. Strachey (Ed.), *The standard edition of the complete psychological works of Sigmund Freud* (Vol. 12, pp. 147–156). London: Hogarth Press.

FREUD, S. (1937/1964). Analysis terminable and interminable. In J. Strachey (Ed.), *The Standard Edition of the complete psychological work of Sigmund Freud* (Vol. 23, pp. 216–253). London: Hogarth Press.

LUBORSKY, L. (1976). Helping alliances in psychotherapy: The groundwork for a study of their relationship to its outcome. In J. L. Claghorn (Ed.), *Successful psychotherapy* (pp. 92–116). New York: Brunner/Mazel.

LUBORSKY, L. (1977). Measuring a pervasive psychic structure in psychotherapy: The Core Conflictual Relationship Theme. In N. Freedman & S. Grand (Eds.), *Communicative structures and psychic structures* (pp. 367–395). New York: Plenum.

LUBORSKY, L. (1984). *Principles of psychoanalytic psychotherapy: A manual for supportive-expressive treatment.* New York: Basic Books.

LUBORSKY, L. (1987). Research can now affect clinical practice—a happy turnaround. *Clinical Psychologist, 40,* 56–60.

LUBORSKY, L. (1990a). The convergence of Freud's observations about transference with CCRT evidence. In L. Luborsky & P. Crits-Christoph, *Understanding transference: The Core Conflictual Relationship Theme method.* New York: Basic Books.

LUBORSKY, L. (1990b). Theory and technique in dynamic psychotherapy: Curative factors and training therapists to maximize them. *Psychotherapy and Psychosomatics, 53,* 50–57.

LUBORSKY, L., & AUERBACH, A. (1985). The therapeutic relationship in psychodynamic psychotherapy: The research evidence and its meaning for practice. In R. Hales & A. Frances (Eds.), *Psychiatry update: The American Psychiatric Association annual review* (Vol. 4, pp. 550–561). Washington, DC: American Psychiatric Press.

LUBORSKY, L., & CRITS-CHRISTOPH, P. (1988). Measures of psychoanalytic concepts: The last decade of research from "The Penn Studies." *International Journal of Psycho-analysis, 69,* 75–86.

LUBORSKY, L., & CRITS-CHRISTOPH, P. (1990). *Understanding transference: The Core Conflictual Relationship Theme method.* New York: Basic Books.

LUBORSKY, L., CRITS-CHRISTOPH, P., MINTZ, J., & AUERBACH, A., (1988). *Who will benefit from psychotherapy? Predicting therapeutic outcomes.* New York: Basic Books.

LUBORSKY, L., DIGUER, L., LUBORSKY, E., MCLELLAN, A.T., & WOODY, G. (IN PRESS). Psychological health as a predictor of the outcomes of psychotherapy. *Journal of Consulting and Clinical Psychology.* (Special Section).

LUBORSKY, L., MELLON, J., ALEXANDER, K., VAN RAVENSWAAY, P., CHILDRESS, A., LEVINE, F., COHEN, K. D., HOLE, A. V., & MING, S. (1985). A verification of Freud's grandest clinical hypothesis: The transference. *Clinical Psychology Review, 5,* 231–246.

MATARAZZO, R., & PATTERSON, D. (1986). Methods of teaching therapeutic skill. In S. Garfield & A. Bergin (Eds.), *Handbook of psychotherapy and behavior change.* New York: Wiley.

PIPER, W., AZIM, H., JOYCE, A., & MCCALLUM, M. (1991). Transference interpretations, therapeutic alliance and outcome in short-term individual psychotherapy. *Archives of General Psychiatry, 48,* 946–953.

SILBERSCHATZ, G., FRETTER, P., & CURTIS, J. (1986). How do interpretations influence the process of psychotherapy? *Journal of Consulting and Clinical Psychology, 54,* 646–652.

WEISS, J., SAMPSON, H., & THE MOUNT ZION PSYCHOTHERAPY RESEARCH GROUP (1986). *The psychoanalytic process: Theory, clinical observations, and empirical research.* New York: Guilford Press.

CHAPTER 26

What's Here and What's Ahead in Dynamic Therapy Research and Practice?

LESTER LUBORSKY, JOHN P. DOCHERTY, NANCY E. MILLER, AND JACQUES P. BARBER

T HIS FINAL CHAPTER FULFILLS THE AGENDA for the two aims of our handbook: (1) to point out the field's current areas of progress and (2) to forecast where we are going and where we should go from here in clinically relevant research and research-informed practice.

The Main Areas of Progress

We decided at the beginning of the handbook that the rate of progress should get a mixed review: the field has been slow in assembling a research base; yet in the last two decades, the field, like the economy, has shown signs of revitalization. Now there are more occasions for celebration about research progress on topics that should become familiar to all practitioners and even to some researchers.

The following accomplishments of the field will be explained:

1. The efficacy of dynamic psychotherapy has been well established.
2. The new treatment manuals have helped to establish the efficacy of psychotherapy.
3. Solid research has discovered many of the factors that influence the outcomes of psychotherapy.
4. Psychological health-sickness has become a major predictive factor.
5. The alliance has become a major predictive factor.
6. Operational measures of the transference have been constructed.

7. Therapists' level of success with their patients has begun to be studied systematically.
8. A new era has arrived in widely used reliable systems of diagnosis.

INCREASED EVIDENCE FOR THE EFFICACY OF DYNAMIC PSYCHOTHERAPY

In the past decade the field of psychotherapy research has arrived at an amazing achievement: the nearly general acceptance of the research support for the substantial benefits of psychotherapy (Luborsky, Singer, and Luborsky 1975; Smith, Glass, and Miller 1980; Lambert, Shapiro, and Bergin 1986; Rosenthal 1990). The most common form of psychotherapy, dynamic psychotherapy, is now clearly included in the main trend that shows the benefits of the psychotherapies (chapter 24 and Crits-Christoph 1992). Research on our closest relative, psychoanalysis, is just beginning in its accumulation of evidence of benefits as well (Bachrach et al. 1991); controlled comparisons of these benefits with those of other therapies are still needed.

But a major mystery remains even after our attempts in chapter 24 to demystify it: despite the field's success in establishing the benefits of psychotherapy, comparisons of different forms of psychotherapy tend to show nonsignificant differences from each other in amount of benefits. But at this stage much effort must be dedicated to an understanding of the trend. Therefore, the agenda for research on the efficacy of psychotherapy calls for better comparative studies of psychotherapies, including dynamic psychotherapy, to allow a better understanding of the usual nonsignificant-difference findings. Significant clinical differences may be found when duration of the benefits, patient types, and the possible mechanisms of change are taken into account.

THE NEW ERA OF TREATMENT MANUALS AND ADHERENCE MEASURES

In the last decade psychotherapy research has been the scene of a small revolution in research and practice: treatment manuals have appeared for many of the main forms of psychotherapy. These treatment manuals are essential for defining each form of psychotherapy so that proper comparative treatment studies can be done. The general manuals for dynamic psychotherapies are by Luborsky (1984) and by Strupp and Binder (1984); a specific manual for borderline patients was produced by Kernberg and his associates (chapter 12). An adaptation of the general manual for supportive-expressive psychotherapy has been written for depression (Luborsky, Mark, et al. 1992), for opiate addiction (Luborsky et al. 1977), and for cocaine addiction (Mark and Luborsky in press). To help the field keep up with these productions, a collection of such manuals is forthcoming

(Barber and Crits-Christoph, in press). Advances have already resulted for techniques for constructing manuals, for knowledge of effects of training in the use of manuals, and for scales of the therapist's adherence to manuals (chapters 7 through 12), although manuals may not eliminate all therapist differences or improve treatment outcomes.

INCREASED KNOWLEDGE OF CURATIVE FACTORS

After gathering evidence for the benefits of dynamic psychotherapy, researchers have concentrated on testing its main theory-based propositions about the factors responsible for the benefits. A special section of the *Journal of Consulting and Clinical Psychology* will be devoted to this topic (Luborsky, Barber, and Beutler, in press). A good part of this book is devoted to reporting representative studies that test these factors (chapters 14, 17, 19, 21, 22, and 25). Six of these main curative factors are: level of psychological health (or its opposite pole, psychiatric severity), quality of the therapeutic alliance, formulation of transference, focus on transference in the therapist's interpretations, gains in insight and self-understanding, and internalization of benefits.

Much of the evidence for these curative factors was derived from several large research centers: the University of Pennsylvania Center for Psychotherapy Research (Luborsky, Crits-Christoph, and Barber 1991), the Mount Zion Psychotherapy Research Group (Weiss and Sampson 1986), the Vanderbilt Psychotherapy Project (Henry and Strupp 1991), the University of Alberta Psychotherapy Research Center (Piper et al. 1991), and the Northwestern University–University of Chicago Psychotherapy Research Project (Howard et al. 1991). The bulk of their evidence is positive for almost all of the six factors, but it is weaker for the factor on increased self-understanding as a precursor, or concomitant, of the benefits of psychotherapy. The agenda from here on must be to continue with more studies of these propositions.

The field must go on to learn how much is predicted by different constellations of the curative factors, not just by each of the factors separately. Each factor separately predicts only a small percentage of the variance in the outcome measures, but their interactions may predict much more.

RECOGNITION OF THE ROLE OF PSYCHOLOGICAL HEALTH IN PREDICTION OF OUTCOME

In 1949 a psychotherapy research group at the Menninger Foundation began work on an operational measure of the concept of health-sickness, expecting that it would predict the outcomes of psychotherapy.

It took several decades of accumulated research studies there and elsewhere before a clearly confirming trend emerged (chapters 10, 23). Only now a dedicated review has assembled all the evidence for this trend (Luborsky, Diguer, et al., in press).

By 1988, seventy-one psychological health-sickness studies of all types had appeared (Luborsky et al. 1988). Of these, forty-seven (67 percent) yielded significant levels of prediction of outcomes from different types of therapy. These correlations tended to fall within the range of .2 to .6. The mean correlation for eleven studies of observer-rated global psychological health-sickness ratings was .27.

Because it is at least as predictive in dynamic therapies as in other therapies, including psychopharmacological ones, psychological health has been recommended to be a routine accompaniment of the diagnosis (Luborsky and Bachrach 1974). In fact, it has happened—a renamed version of the Health-Sickness Rating Scale, the Global Assessment Scale, has been incorporated in the DSM-IIIR and DSM-IV. Thus, a simple measure of a clinical idea that started within the dynamic terrain has produced widespread benefits to research across different types of psychotherapy and psychopharmacotherapy.

DEVELOPMENT OF RELIABLE OPERATIONAL MEASURES OF THE THERAPEUTIC ALLIANCE

The therapeutic alliance has been a clinically important concept for close to a century (Freud [1912] 1958). Beginning with the questionnaire by Barrett-Lennard (1962) and the session-based rating method by Luborsky (1976), a series of therapeutic alliance measures have been developed. These typically show that the alliance measures achieve significant prediction of the outcomes of psychotherapy (chapter 14).

THE CREATION OF RELIABLE TRANSFERENCE-RELATED MEASURES

A whole new cottage industry has grown up around the crafting of operational measures for guided clinical judgment of transference-related concepts based on psychotherapy sessions. There are now fifteen such measures, beginning with the Core Conflictual Relationship Theme (CCRT) method (Luborsky 1976). We had planned to assign a large separate section to such measures in this handbook. But that section became too long; it will become part of a special issue of *Psychotherapy Research* (Luborsky, Popp, et al., in press). A short overview of the topic was retained as chapter 17.

The developers of each new transference-related measure work to advance its psychometric usefulness through better reliability, validity, and clinical applications. In the short time since the first book on the CCRT appeared (Luborsky and Crits-Christoph 1990), sixty-eight ongoing studies worldwide have been listed in the *CCRT Interest Group Newsletter* (Luborsky, Kächele, et al. 1992). Other ambitious programs of research on transference-related measures have continued their agenda for long-term development. These include the Plan Diagnosis method (Weiss and Sampson 1986), the Structural Analysis of Social Behavior (SASB) method (Benjamin 1974), the Frame method (Teller and Dahl 1986), and the Consensual Response Formulation method (Horowitz et al. 1989).

THE CONFIRMATION OF DIFFERENCES IN THERAPISTS' SUCCESS

Recent studies have demonstrated significant differences among therapists in their level of success with their patients (Luborsky et al. 1985, 1986; McLellan et al. 1988). This knowledge promises considerable contributions to the field. With the greater evidence of the size of such differences, the field will inevitably continue to explore the correlates of measures of therapists' success with their patients. It has already been shown (Crits-Christoph et al. 1991) that there is one condition under which differences among therapists in their success are only modest: when therapists have been trained to guide their therapy by the use of manuals. This finding is relevant to clinical practice and potentially even to the regulation of practice.

THE TREND TOWARD IMPROVED DIAGNOSIS

Although some clinicians have objections, the increased reliance on the DSMs and on assessment instruments—such as the Structured Clinical Interview for DSM-IIIR (SCID)—reflects the revolution in diagnosis that evolved from Spitzer, Endicott, and Robins (1978). As a result of this sharpening of diagnosis, patients in comparative studies are now better defined, as in the personality disorders (chapter 8). And, there has been better research on the most suitable treatments for each type of DSM-defined patient. Yet studies of single diagnosis groups tend to exclude those with co-morbid disorders; much more needs to be known about treatment effectiveness with such disorders.

What's Next?

Our progress report on the current research scene can be viewed as prologue. A thoughtful reinspection of the scene reveals our best forecasts for the rest of the nineties and perhaps for the first decade of the twenty-first century.

FORECAST: MORE THERAPIES TAILORED TO SPECIFIC TYPES OF PATIENTS

All of the forms of psychotherapy benefit all types of patients, yet not one of the psychotherapies, even dynamic, offers much evidence of special benefits for specific types of patients. What has been coming and will soon arrive, therefore, are more specific therapies for specific types of patients. As an example, Blatt and Ford (1993) show that the division of patients into anaclitic and introjective reveals different outcomes and differential responses to supportive versus expressive treatments.

This forecast is easy because there have been a few spectacular successes for psychosocial treatments. A 1991 workshop attended by experts on the development of psychosocial treatments demonstrated this so vividly that a brief account will be given here: The workshop was sponsored by the Psychotherapy and Rehabilitation Research Consortium (PARRC). The moderators were H. Alice Lowery, Chair of the PARRC Treatment Development Committee, and Barry Wolfe, Chair of the Psychotherapy and Rehabilitation Research Consortium.

At the meeting, I thought it would interest the group to see whether we agreed about which were the most promising treatments of the last fifteen years.[1] I was struck by a historical contrast: the spirit in this current group versus the to-be-expected spirit of a comparable group that might have met fifteen years earlier. The tone of the earlier one would have been more sober, with enthusiasm dampened by an expectation of only re-finding a "NSDE" ("nonsignificant difference effect") which was suggested by Rosenzweig (1936) and demonstrated by Luborsky et al. (1975). From both papers the most likely expected fate of any new psychosocial treatment would be the Dodo bird's verdict that all the treatments compared were likely to show positive results, but no one psychosocial treatment would show much better results than any other. In my 1975 review there were only a few tentatively established exceptions to this main trend (chapter 23).

I came to the workshop prepared to report my own rankings of the most promising psychosocial treatment advances of the last fifteen years, treatments that had paid off in a treatment match with special efficacy. I expected that my ranked list would help the group to focus on the essential phases of the development of promising treatments. There was in fact much interest in hearing the contents of my list, but before I shared my list I asked the conference participants to make out their own ranked list of the most promising treatments of the last fifteen years. Of the nineteen participants I got rankings from fourteen. With my own rankings added the

---

[1]In these paragraphs, the "I" is Lester Luborsky, and the rest of this section is based on Luborsky (1993).

sample size was fifteen (listed in table 26.1). Several outstanding findings appear from this poll of the assembled experts:

1. There was high agreement on the top choices (panic disorder, schizophrenia, and parasuicide).
2. A very wide array of choices was made, with many having only one vote.
3. The choices mainly included treatments designed for specific diagnostic groups, but a few also were problematic behaviors (suicidal patients). A few of the choices were of promising new therapies (e.g., Cognitive-Behavioral, Supportive-Expressive Dynamic, Interpersonal Therapy).
4. Psychotherapies as well as other psychosocial treatments have played a major part in the new treatment developments.
5. Each new psychosocial treatment went through its own special developmental phases, except that they all started with a clinical hypothesis and each was gradually refined by experience in practice.
6. The successful development of a *new* psychosocial treatment depends on the capacity of the treatment developer to find and then to fashion techniques that cope with the essence of the patient's problems, for example, for panic attacks the essence of the problem was determined to be the patient's misinterpretation of physical sensations as life threatening. The treatment procedure for panic disorder instructs the patient in that concept. For suicidal patients the essence of their problem was determined to be the patient's hopelessness about their capacity to cope, therefore, assertiveness training and other techniques are given to increase the patient's power to cope.

It was the encouraging experience of meeting with the experts in treatment development that bolstered our forecast that the field will beat the odds of the non-significant difference effect and succeed with other specific treatments for specific disorders. Yet, it is still likely that the odds will not so easily be beaten for the treatment of general adjustment problems and mixed symptom disorders.

The field is already launched on a period of higher expectation of progress in the development of new psychosocial treatments and a task force report of the American Psychiatric Association offers recommendations and strong endorsement for its expansion and continuation (American Psychiatric Association, Task Force Report, in press).

FORECAST: INCREASED USE OF SHORT-TERM PSYCHOTHERAPIES

Not only are more manuals for short-term treatments being fashioned, but more and more races will be run comparing results among

TABLE 26.1 *Rankings of the Most Effective Psychosocial Treatments of the Past Fifteen Years*

No. of Mentions	Rank	Treatment
11	1	Psychosocial treatments for panic disorder—very high levels of success are reported, perhaps about 80 percent, as compared with psychopharmacological treatments at about 70 percent (Clark 1989; Beck 1989; Barlow et al. 1989).
10	2	Psychotherapies for patients with schizophrenia, including family therapy and social skills training (Hogarty et al. 1991; Falloon 1988).
8	3	Psychosocial treatments for suicidal patients (Linehan et al. 1991).
6	4	Psychosocial treatments for phobias, including exposure treatment, social skills treatment, and other treatments (Chambless & Goldstein 1980).
6	5	Cognitive-behavioral psychotherapy (Beck et al. 1979).
6	6	Interpersonal psychotherapy (Klerman et al. 1984).
5	7	Dynamic supportive-expressive psychotherapy, with CCRT (Luborsky 1984).
3	8	Psychosocial treatments for eating disorders including bulimia (Agras et al. 1989).
3	9	The discovery of the curative factors in psychotherapy—psychological health-sickness, alliance, etc. (Luborsky et al. 1988).
2	10	Dynamic supportive-expressive and cognitive-behavioral psychotherapy added to treatment as usual for opiate addiction disorders (Woody et al. 1983).
2	11	Psychosocial treatments for depression (Elkin et al. 1989) and the Collaborative Study of Depression.
1	12	Interpersonal therapy as a maintenance treatment for depression (Frank et al. 1991).
1	13	New technology for time-limited psychotherapy (especially manuals and adherence measures).
1	14	Brief psychotherapies.
1	15	Psychosocial treatments added to medical regimens for psychosomatic illness (Luborsky et al. 1975).
1	16	Psychotherapies in the treatment of depression of the elderly.
1	17	Therapies for depression among caregivers.
1	18	Behavioral treatment of obsessive-compulsive disorder.
1	19	Group treatment for bipolar disorder.

Note: *Psychosocial* here refers to psychotherapies as well as other psychological (nonpharmacological) treatments.

short-term treatments. The use of short-term treatments does not mean that longer treatments will not continue to be widely used. Both short- and long-term treatments will continue side by side, perhaps with greater foresight about the appropriateness of which mode is best for which patient, and with greater realization that the major psychiatric disorders are more chronic than had been thought and require more than short-term treatment.

Dynamic short-term treatments will be better specified along with evidence for their effectiveness, as supplied in Crits-Christoph and Barber (1991); the therapies include some of the earliest to be manualized, starting with supportive-expressive dynamic psychotherapy (Luborsky and Mark 1991) and time-limited dynamic psychotherapy (Binder and Strupp 1991). But there will continue to be questions about the long-term benefits of short-term treatment. As just one impressive example (Shea et al., 1992), the follow-up for patients with major depressive disorder treated for 16 weeks in the National Institute of Mental Health Treatment of Depression Collaborative Research Program: the percentage of recovered patients who remained well during follow-up did not significantly differ among the four treatments: 30 percent for those in cognitive-behavioral therapy, 26 percent for those in interpersonal therapy, 19 percent in imipramine plus clinical management, and 20 percent for those in placebo plus clinical management. For these recovered patients, major depressive disorder relapse was high: 36 percent for cognitive behavior therapy, 33 percent for interpersonal therapy, 50 percent for imipramine plus clinical management, and 33 percent for placebo plus clinical management. The major question that was raised by this follow-up study was whether the 16-week length of treatment had been sufficient for treating major depressive disorder.

FORECAST: MORE COMPARISONS OF SHORT-TERM WITH LONG-TERM PSYCHOTHERAPY

It is natural to expect that treatments specified in advance as long-term would produce more benefits than treatments specified in advance as short-term. But despite the importance of the topic and its having been on the research agenda for a long time, such comparisons have hardly been studied systematically.

There is a review of a few comparisons of time-limited versus time unlimited psychotherapy (Luborsky et al. 1975). You can easily guess its main finding: the non-significant-difference-effect wins. Of the eight studies summarized, five were non-significantly different, in two time-limited was better, in one time-unlimited was better. The verdict is clear, yet it is not fully believable for at least two reasons: (1) the comparison is mainly between brief and somewhat longer psychotherapy but not with really long psychotherapy (2) the result is based on outcome measures that may not locate the kinds of expected advantages of long-term psychotherapy.

Our forecast is that the field will do more research on this topic. The research will be of two kinds, controlled studies and naturalistic studies. It is certain that the controlled studies will be a long time in coming because long-term psychotherapy takes a long time and because of the difficulty of arranging random assignment of patients to short-term and to long-term. Imagine the protests of the patients and the clinicians!

The naturalistic studies are already on their way through a study in progress by Kenneth Howard and associates (personal communication, January 1993). The practical gain from naturalistic studies is that the field need not suffer a long wait for their results. The psychotherapy data banks (chapter 4) contain samples of long-term psychotherapy that can, should, and are already being tapped for studies of long-term psychotherapy.

FORECAST: MORE STUDIES OF COMBINED THERAPIES (PSYCHOTHERAPY WITH PHARMOCOTHERAPY)

It is certainly the intent of the NIMH, with its new combined psycho-social-psychopharmacological research review committee to foster studies of combined therapies. In fact, the intent is widely shared—Karasu (1992), for example, predicted that the future psychotherapist will be a "pharmacopsychotherapist."

There is some evidence that combined treatments made up of psychotherapies and medication treatments tend to produce more benefits than single treatments (Rounsaville, Klerman, and Weissman 1981; Klerman 1986). This trend was even true for the Collaborative Study of Depression, where the one treatment that could be called combined treatment, clinical management plus imipramine, did the best with the more severely depressed of these severely depressed patients (Elkin et al. 1989). The most likely basis for the increased benefit from combined treatments is that some patients will benefit from one of the compared treatments and some from the other, so their combined benefit will be greater than that of the single treatments.

One variant of such combination treatment is the advantageous use of psychotherapy as a maintenance treatment after psychopharmaco-therapy, as illustrated by Frank et al. (1991) for the aftercare of depressed patients. But some combinations are not always advantageous. In the study by Agras et al. (1989), for example, the combination of antidepressive medication and cognitive-behavioral psychotherapy interacted negatively, perhaps because the two therapies work on antithetical principles. Inevitably, future research will have to distinguish *which* therapies will do well in combination.

It is easy to forecast that there will continue to be misconceptions about the relative value of psychotherapeutic versus medication treatments. The polarization has already begun. Yet in one sense it is strange that it is happening now; there is now much more evidence than ever before for the effectiveness of psychotherapy (chapter 24). But in another sense it is not surprising. There are always some practitioners and some researchers whose allegiance to a form of therapy distorts their judgment and their knowledge about its relative value (Luborsky and Diguer 1993). Such distortion can even harm training programs. For example, some residency programs in psychiatry have curtailed or cut out training in psychotherapy! There is actually a strong record for both the psychotherapeutic and the medication treatments, both separately and in combination.

FORECAST: MORE KNOWLEDGE ABOUT THE FACTORS INFLUENCING OUTCOMES.

The research on predictive factors in dynamic psychotherapies has already produced much knowledge of significant predictors (Luborsky et al. 1988; chapter 9). The applications to clinical practice described in chapter 25 already illustrate ways to maximize treatment benefits by paying attention to the predictive factors.

We have some clues about the areas in which new measures of factors that influence outcomes will be developed. Several of them have already been launched: referential activity (chapter 20); psychological-mindedness (Piper et al. 1991); patterns of interpersonal relationships (Hartley 1987; chapter 9; L. Horowitz et al., in press); and qualities of the representation of the therapist and therapy (chapter 22).

We should look for a moment beyond our narrow focus on the predictive factors in the process of treatment to the broader context of the psychotherapy delivery system because that system must impact on the outcomes of treatments. A new system is being developed to help in tracking patients through the treatment delivery process (Howard, Vessy, Lueger, and Schank 1992; Howard, Brill, Lueger, and O'Mahoney 1992). This new system will help us to understand the practice patterns of different types of providers, the types of therapists who treat patients of different types, and the process by which patients get into different forms of psychotherapy, such as dynamic versus behavioral.

This larger context of treatment delivery should be broad enough to include both psychological and medical treatments so that more might be found out about the basis for the well-researched, recurrent finding that psychotherapy is associated with cost savings because the usage of medical treatments declines (Mumford and Schlesinger 1987).

FORECAST: GREATER INTEGRATION OF CONCEPTS AMONG PSYCHOTHERAPIES

Not only is the field of psychotherapy research becoming more empirical, but it is becoming more integrative, as reflected in the agenda of the growing Society for Exploration of Psychotherapy Integration. *Integrative* means that the concepts that were unique to one form of psychotherapy have become part of other forms of psychotherapy as well. Two examples follow: cognitive-behavioral psychotherapy involves a marriage of dynamic and behavioral concepts; interpersonal psychotherapy appears to involve an integration of several forms of dynamic psychotherapy. Almost all of the forms of short-term psychotherapy, including supportive-expressive dynamic psychotherapy, emphasize the importance of the therapist's focus on a few central relationship themes. The same trend toward integration of theory and technique is shown in the many variants of psychoanalysis, as is thoroughly traced in the review by Kernberg (in press) on convergences and divergences among contemporary psychoanalytic techniques.

This trend is likely to continue. It probably reflects progress, but we need evidence that greater integration of concepts is related to greater effectiveness of psychotherapy.

FORECAST: MORE BRIDGES TO THE MORE ESTABLISHED SCIENCES

There have been signs of the rapprochement between psychotherapy and other sciences, and there will be even more. Outstanding successes include the work of Kandel (1979) on the alteration of neurons during learning in snails, which must somehow also apply in principle to the learning of people during psychotherapy; developmental studies in very young children (Stern 1985); changes in immunocompetence in relation to changes in depression during psychotherapy (Luborsky, Barber, et al. 1992); and cognitive style matches in patient–therapist interactions during psychotherapy (Witkin, Lewis, and Weil 1968). A huge advance in research on the registration of unconscious meanings has been achieved by Shevrin's method (chapter 16) based on the use of evoked cortical potentials in relation to different subliminal meanings of stimuli. Finally, a broad program for examining the intercorrelations of cognitive and dynamic psychology has been sponsored by Horowitz (1988). These methods and their findings are only a small sampling of a promising harvest. This research genre can be generous and ingenious and, therefore, fits with the recommendation by Holzman and Aronson (1992) that psychoanalysis should "look to neighboring sciences for revivifying perspectives."

FORECAST: GREATER ATTENTION TO COST/BENEFIT RATIOS

Until recently, the predominant focus of treatment assessment research has been on the efficacy of a treatment; now fiscal pressures impinge on evaluation research to require the inclusion of cost/benefit of a treatment as a component of its usefulness.

FORECAST: GREATER ATTENTION TO APPLYING RESEARCH TO PRACTICE

Until at least 1970, few researchers thought the field was ready for the applications of research to practice. Luborsky titled an article in 1969 "Research can *not* influence practice." But beginning about ten years ago researchers and clinicians began to examine more seriously how research in psychotherapy could be applied to practice. In 1987 Luborsky wrote a new article: "Research can *now* influence practice." This change in verdict came because the evidence suggested useful clinical applications (see chapter 25). For example, because accuracy of interpretation has been shown to be related to the benefits patients receive (chapter 19), training methods are being developed for increasing therapists' accuracy. Likewise, because the therapeutic alliance is an important curative factor (chapter 14), training therapists to evaluate it and, when necessary, to foster it, is a promising research application.

Yet there are still very different views about the place of psychotherapy research in everyday practice. Edelson (1992) observes that psychotherapy researchers are interested in general principles while psychotherapists are interested in the particular patient and the events that have shaped that patient. Our view is that there is a joint agenda for resolving the different interests of researchers and psychotherapists. It is this: although the psychotherapists must build formulations from the data of the individual patient, some general principles from psychotherapy research may still help with building the individual formulations. After all, that has been exactly the same use of general principles from clinical wisdom: some of such wisdom may help with formulations for the individual case. In short, *both* clinical wisdom and research findings offer general principles that may be of interest to the clinician from time to time in understanding the individual patient. It is to that balanced joint agenda that our handbook has been dedicated.

References

AGRAS, W. S., SCHNEIDER, J., ARNOW, B., RAEBURN, S. (1989). Cognitive-behavioral and response-prevention treatments for bulimia nervosa. *Journal of Consulting and Clinical Psychology, 57,* 215–221.

AMERICAN PSYCHIATRIC ASSOCIATION TASK FORCE FOR PSYCHOSOCIAL TREATMENT RESEARCH IN PSYCHIATRY, J. DOCHERTY (CHAIR). (IN PRESS). *Psychosocial treatment research in psychiatry.*

BACHRACH, H., GALATZER-LEVY, R., SKOLNIKOFF, A., & WALDRON, S. (1991). On the efficacy of psychoanalysis. *Journal of the American Psychoanalytic Association, 39,* 871–916.

BARBER, J. P., & CRITS-CHRISTOPH, P. (IN PRESS). *Psychodynamic psychotherapies for Axis-I disorders.* New York: Basic Books.

BARLOW, D., CRASKE, M., CERNY, J., & KLOSKO, J. (1989). Behavioral treatment of panic disorder. *Behavior Therapy, 20,* 261–282.

BARRETT-LENNARD, G. (1962). Dimensions of the client's experience of his therapist associated with personality change. *Genetic Psychology Monographs* (Monograph 43).

BECK, A. (1989). Cognitive therapy for depression and panic disorder. *Western Journal of Medicine, 151,* 9–89.

BECK, A., RUSH, A., SHAW, B., & EMERY, G. (1979). *Cognitive therapy of depression.* New York: Guilford Press.

BENJAMIN, L. S. (1974). Structural Analysis of Social Behavior. *Psychological Review, 81,* 392–425.

BEUTLER, L., & CRAGO, M. (EDS.). (1991). *Psychotherapy research: An international review of programmatic studies.* Washington, DC: American Psychological Association.

BINDER, J., & STRUPP, H. (1991). The Vanderbilt approach to time-limited dynamic psychotherapy. In P. Crits-Christoph & J. P. Barber (Eds.), *Handbook of short-term dynamic psychotherapy* (pp. 137–165). New York: Basic Books.

BLATT, S., & FORD, R. (1993). *Therapeutic change: An object relations perspective.* New York: Plenum.

CHAMBLESS, D., & GOLDSTEIN, A. (1980). The treatment of agorophobia. In A. Goldstein & E. B. Foa (Eds.) *Handbook of behavioral interventions.* New York: Wiley.

CLARK, D. (1989). Anxiety states: Panic and generalized anxiety. In K. Hawton, P. Salkovskis, Kirk, & D. Clark (Eds.). *Cognitive behavior therapy for psychiatric problems: A practical guide.* Oxford: Oxford University Press.

CRITS-CHRISTOPH, P., & BARBER, J. P. (EDS.). (1991). *Handbook of short-term dynamic psychotherapy.* New York: Basic Books.

CRITS-CHRISTOPH, P., BARNACKIE, K., KURCIAS, J., BECK, A. T., CARROLL, K., PERRY, K., LUBORSKY, L., MCLELLAN, A. T., WOODY, G., THOMPSON, L., GALLAGHER, D., & ZITRIN, C. (1991). Meta-analysis of therapist effects in psychotherapy outcome studies. *Psychotherapy Research, 1,* 81–91.

EDELSON, M. (1992). Can psychotherapy research answer this psychotherapist's questions? *Contemporary Psychoanalysis, 28,* 118–151.

ELKIN, I., SHEA, T., WATKINS, J., IMBER, S., SOTSKY, S., COLLINS, J., GLASS, D., PILKONIS, P., LEBER, W., DOCHERTY, J., FIESTER, S., & PARLOFF, M. (1989). National Institute of Mental Health Treatment of Depression Collaborative

Research Program: General effectiveness of treatments. *Archives of General Psychiatry, 46,* 971–982.

FALLOON, I. (1988). Behavioral family management in coping with functional psychosis: Principles, practice, and recent developments. *International Journal of Mental Health, 17,* 35–47.

FRANK, E., KUPFER, D., WAGNER, E., MCEACHRAN, A., & CORNES, C. (1991). Efficacy of interpersonal psychotherapy as a maintenance treatment of recurrent depression. *Archives of General Psychiatry, 48,* 1053–1059.

FREUD, S. (1912/1958). The dynamics of the transference. In J. Strachey (Ed.), *The standard edition of the complete psychological works of Sigmund Freud* (Vol. 12, pp. 99–108). London: Hogarth Press.

HARTLEY, D. (1987, JUNE). *Developmental level of object representations and psychotherapy outcome.* Paper presented at the Annual Meeting of the Society for Psychotherapy Research, Ulm, Germany.

HENRY, W., & STRUPP, H. (1991). Vanderbilt University: Vanderbilt Center for Psychotherapy Research. In L. Beutler & M. Crago (Eds.), *Psychotherapy research: An international review of programmatic studies* (pp. 166–174). Washington, DC: American Psychological Association.

HOGARTY, G., ANDERSON, C., REISS, D., KORNBLITH, S., GREENWALD, D., ULRICH, R., & CARTER, M. (1991). Family psychoeducation, social skills training and maintenance chemotherapy in the aftercare treatments of schizophrenia: 2. Two-year effects of a controlled study on relapse and adjustment. *Archives of General Psychiatry, 48,* 340–347.

HOLZMAN, P., & ARONSON, G. (1992). Psychoanalysis and its neighboring sciences: Paradigms and opportunities. *Journal of the American Psychoanalytic Association, 40,* 63–88.

HOLZMAN, P., SOLOMON, C., LEVIN, S., & WATERNAUX, C. (1984) Pursuit eye movement dysfunctions in schizophrenia: Family evidence for specificity. *Archives of General Psychiatry, 41,* 136–139.

HOROWITZ, L. M., ROSENBERG, S., URENO, G., KALEHZAN, B., & O'HALLORAN, P. (1989). Psychodynamic formulation, consensual response method, and interpersonal problems. Journal of *Consulting and Clinical Psychology, 57,* 599–606.

HOROWITZ, M. (ED.). (1988). *Psychodynamics and cognition.* Chicago: University of Chicago Press.

HOWARD, K., BRILL, P., LUEGER, R., & O'MAHONEY, M. (1992). *Integra outpatient tracking assessment.* Philadelphia: Integra Inc.

HOWARD, K., ORLINSKY, D., SAUNDERS, S., BANKOFF, E., DAVIDSON, C., & O'MAHONEY, M. (1991). Northwestern University–University of Chicago Psychotherapy Research Program. In L. Beutler & M. Crago (Eds.), *Psychotherapy research: An international review of programmatic studies* (pp. 65–73). Washington, DC: American Psychological Association.

HOWARD, K., VESSY, J., LUEGER, R., & SCHANK, D. (1992). The psychotherapeutic service delivery system. *Psychotherapy Research, 2,* 164–180.

KANDEL, E. (1979). *Behavioral biology of aplasia.* San Francisco: Freeman.

KARASU, T. (1992). The worst of times, the best of times: Psychotherapy in the 90's. *Journal of Psychotherapy Practice and Research, 1,* 2–15.

KERNBERG, O. (IN PRESS). Convergence and divergences in contemporary psychoanalytic techniques. In E. Nace et al. (Eds.), *Future directions in psychotherapy.*

KLERMAN, E., WEISSMAN, M., ROUNSAVILLE, B., & CHEVRON, E. (1984). *Interpersonal psychotherapy of depression.* New York: Basic Books.

KLERMAN, J. (1986). Drugs and psychotherapy. In S. Garfield & A. Bergin. (Eds.), *Handbook of psychotherapy and behavior change.* New York: Wiley.

LAMBERT, M., SHAPIRO, D., & BERGIN, A. (1986). The effectiveness of psychotherapy. In S. Garfield & A. Bergin (Eds.), *Handbook of psychotherapy and behavior change: An empirical analysis* (pp. 157–212). New York: Wiley.

LINEHAN, M., ARMSTRONG, H., SUAREZ, A., ALLMON, D., & HEARD, H. (1991). Cognitive-behavioral treatment of chronically parasuicidal borderline patients. *Archives of General Psychiatry, 48,* 1060–1064.

LUBORSKY, L. (1969). Research can not influence clinical practice. *International Joural of Psychiatry, 7,* 135–140.

LUBORSKY, L. (1976). Helping alliances in psychotherapy: The groundwork for a study of their relationship to its outcome. In J. L. Claghorn (Ed.), *Successful psychotherapy* (pp. 92–116). New York: Brunner/Mazel.

LUBORSKY, L. (1984). *Principles of psychoanalytic psychotherapy: A manual for supportive-expressive treatment.* New York: Basic Books.

LUBORSKY, L. (1987). Research can now affect clinical practice: A happy turn-around. *Clinical Psychologist, 40,* 56–60.

LUBORSKY, L. (1993). The promise of new psychosocial treatments. Report for a workshop of the Psychotherapy and Rehabilitation Research Consortium of the NIMH, Bethesda, MD.

LUBORSKY, L., & BACHRACH, H. (1974). Factors influencing clinician's judgments of mental health: Eighteen experiences with the Health-Sickness Rating Scale. *Archives of General Psychiatry, 31,* 292–299.

LUBORSKY, L., BARBER, J. P., & BEUTLER, L. E. (IN PRESS). A briefing for the JCCP's special section on curative factors in dynamic psychotherapy. *Journal of Consulting and Clinical Psychology.*

LUBORSKY, L., BARBER, J. P., SCHMIDT, K., REDEI, E., PRYSTOWSKY, M., LEVINSON, A., CACCIOLA, J., CRIVARO, A., & SCHRETZENMAIR, R. (1992, JUNE). *Depression and immunocompetence: Do they inversely interact during psychotherapy?* Paper presented at the Annual Meeting of the Society for Psychotherapy Research, Berkeley, CA.

LUBORSKY, L., CRITS-CHRISTOPH, P., & BARBER, J. P. (1991). The Penn Psychotherapy Research Project. In L. Beutler & M. Crago (Eds.), *Psychotherapy research: An international review of programmatic studies* (pp. 134–141). Washington, DC: American Psychological Association.

LUBORSKY, L., CRITS-CHRISTOPH, P., McLELLAN, T., WOODY, G., PIPER, W.,

IMBER, S., & LIBERMAN, B. (1986). Do therapists vary much in their success: Findings from four outcome studies. *American Journal of Orthopsychiatry, 56,* 501–512.

LUBORSKY, L., CRITS-CHRISTOPH, P., MINTZ, J., & AUERBACH, A. (1988). *Who will benefit from psychotherapy? Predicting therapeutic outcomes.* New York: Basic Books.

LUBORSKY, L., & DIGUER, L. (1993, JUNE). *The "wild card" in comparative treatment studies: The researcher's therapeutic allegiance.* Paper presented to the Annual Meeting of the Society for Psychotherapy Research, Pittsburgh.

LUBORSKY, L., DIGUER, L., LUBORSKY, L., MCLELLAN, A. T., & WOODY, G. (IN PRESS). Psychological health as a predictor of the outcomes of psychotherapy. *Journal of Consulting and Clinical Psychology.*

LUBORSKY, L., KÄCHELE, H., DAHLBENDER, R., & CIERPKA, M. (EDS.). (1992). *CCRT Newsletter* (annual publication, University of Pennsylvania).

LUBORSKY, L., & MARK, D. (1991). Short-term supportive expressive psychoanalytic psychotherapy. In P. Crits-Christoph & J. P. Barber (Eds.), *Short-term dynamic psychotherapies* (pp. 110–136). New York: Guilford Press.

LUBORSKY, L., MARK, D., HOLE, A. V., POPP, C., & CACCIOLA, J. (1992). *A manual for supportive-expressive dynamic psychotherapy of depression.* Unpublished manuscript, University of Pennsylvania.

LUBORSKY, L., MCLELLAN, A. T., WOODY, G. E., O'BRIEN, C. P., & AUERBACH, A. (1985). Therapist success and its determinants. *Archives of General Psychiatry, 42,* 602–611.

LUBORSKY, L., POPP, C., BARBER, J. P., SHAPIRO, D., & MILLLER, N. (EDS.). (IN PRESS). Seven transference-related measures, each applied to an interview with Ms. Smithfield. *Psychotherapy Research.*

LUBORSKY, L., SINGER, B., & LUBORSKY, L. (1975). Comparative studies of psychotherapies: Is it true that "Everyone has won and all must have prizes"? *Archives of General Psychiatry, 32,* 995–1008.

LUBORSKY, L., WOODY, G., HOLE, A. V., & VELLECO, A. (1977). *A manual for supportive-expressive dynamic psychotherapy of opiate addiction.* Unpublished manuscript. University of Pennsylvania.

MARK, D., & LUBORSKY, L. (IN PRESS). A manual for supportive-expressive (SE) dynamic psychotherapy of cocaine abuse. In J. P. Barber & P. Crits-Christoph (Eds.), *Psychodynamic psychotherapies for Axis-I disorders.* New York: Basic Books.

MCLELLAN, A. T., WOODY, G., LUBORSKY, L., & GOEHL, L. (1988). Is the counsellor an "active ingredient" in methadone treatment? An examination of treatment success among four counsellors. *Journal of Nervous and Mental Disease, 176,* 423–430.

MUMFORD, E., & SCHLESINGER, H. (1987). Assessing consumer benefit: Cost offset as an incidental effect of psychotherapy. *General Hospital Psychiatry, 9,* 360–363.

PIPER, W., AZIM, H., MCCALLUM, M., & JOYCE, A. (1991). The University of

Alberta Psychotherapy Research Center. In L. Beutler & M. Crago (Eds.), *Psychotherapy research: An international review of programmatic studies* (pp. 82–89). Washington, DC: American Psychological Association.

ROSENTHAL, R. (1990). How are we doing in soft psychology? *American Psychologist, 58,* 775–777.

ROSENZWEIG, S. (1936). Some implicit common factors in diverse methods of psychotherapy. *American Journal of Orthopsychiatry, 6,* 412–415.

ROUNSAVILLE, R., KLERMAN, G., & WEISSMAN, M. (1981). Do psychotherapy and pharmacotherapy for depression conflict? *Archives of General Psychiatry, 38,* 24–29.

SHEA, M. T., ELKIN, I., IMBER, S., SOTSKY, S. M., WATKINS, J. T., COLLINS, J. F., PILKONIS, P. A., BECKHAM, E., GLASS, D. R., DOLAN, R. T., & PARLOFF, M. B. (1992). Course of depressive symptoms over follow-up. *Archives of General Psychiatry, 49,* 782–787.

SMITH, M., GLASS, G., & MILLER, T. (1980). *The benefits of psychotherapy.* Baltimore: Johns Hopkins University Press.

SPITZER, R., ENDICOTT, J., & ROBINS, E. (1978). Research Diagnostic Criteria: Rationale and reliability. *Archives of General Psychiatry, 35,* 777–782.

STERN, D. (1985). *The interpersonal world of the infant.* New York: Basic Books.

STRUPP, H. H., & BINDER, J. L. (1984). *Psychotherapy in a new key: A guide to time-limited dynamic psychotherapy.* New York: Basic Books.

TELLER, V., & DAHL, H. (1986). The microstructure of free association. *Journal of the American Psychoanalytic Association, 34,* 763–798.

WALLERSTEIN, R. (1990). Psychoanalysis: The common ground. *International Journal of Psycho-analysis, 71,* 3–20.

WEISS, J., SAMPSON, H., & THE MOUNT ZION PSYCHOTHERAPY RESEARCH GROUP. (1986). *The psychoanalytic process: Theory, clinical observations, and empirical research.* New York: Guilford Press.

WITKIN, H., LEWIS, H., & WEIL, E. (1968). Affective reactions and patient–therapist interactions among more differentiated and less differentiated patients early in therapy. *Journal of Nervous and Mental Disorders, 146,* 193–208.

WOODY, G., LUBORSKY, L., MCLELLAN, A. T., O'BRIEN, C., BECK, A. T., BLAINE, J., HERMAN, I., & HOLE, A. V. (1983). Psychotherapy for opiate addicts: Does it help? *Archives of General Psychiatry, 40,* 639–645.

Index